HARLEY'S LITTLE BLACK BOOK

WRITERS | AMANDA CONNER • JIMMY PALMIOTTI

ARTISTS | JOSEPH MICHAEL LINSNER • NEAL ADAMS • SIMON BISLEY • BILLY TUCCI • AMANDA CONNER • DAVE JOHNSON
JOHN TIMMS • MAURICET • FLAVIANO

Harley's Bla

LETTERERS | DAVE SHARPE • MARILYN PATRIZIO

COLORISTS | PAUL MOUNTS • HI-FI

COLLECTION COVER ARTISTS | AMANDA CONNER AND PAUL MOUNTS

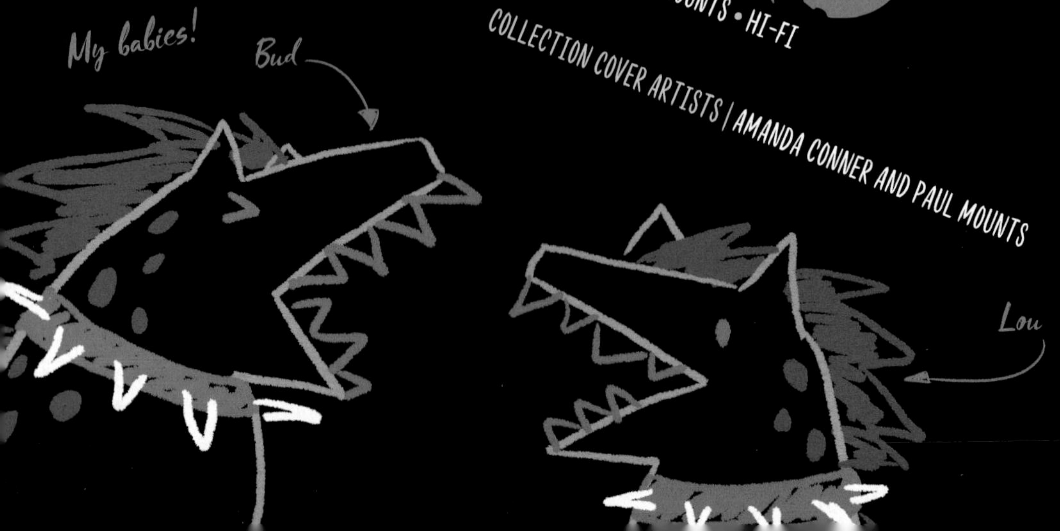
My babies!
Bud
Lou

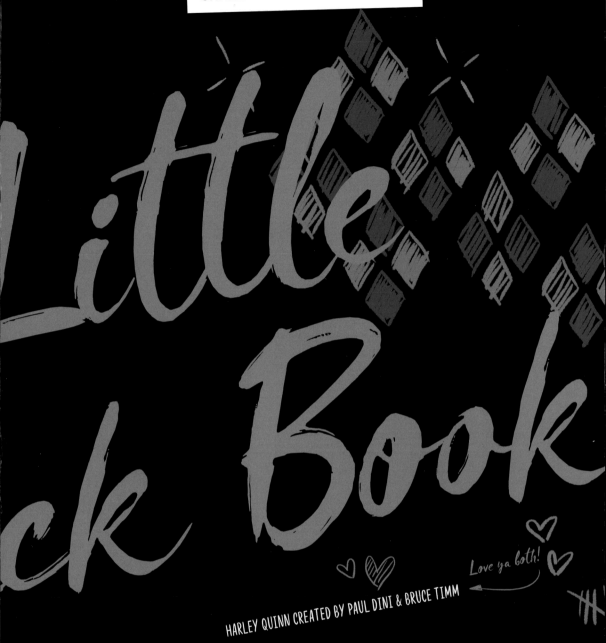

Little ck Book

Love ya both!

HARLEY QUINN CREATED BY PAUL DINI & BRUCE TIMM

WONDER WOMAN CREATED BY WILLIAM MOULTON MARSTON

ZATANNA CREATED BY GARDNER FOX AND MURPHY ANDERSON

LOBO CREATED BY KEITH GIFFEN AND ROGER SLIFER

SUPERMAN CREATED BY JERRY SIEGEL AND JOE SHUSTER
BY SPECIAL ARRANGEMENT WITH THE JERRY SIEGEL FAMILY

CHRIS CONROY Editor – Original Series
DAVE WIELGOSZ Assistant Editor – Original Series
JEB WOODARD Group Editor – Collected Editions
ROBIN WILDMAN Editor – Collected Edition
STEVE COOK Design Director – Books
MONIQUE NARBONETA Publication Design

BOB HARRAS Senior VP – Editor-in-Chief, DC Comics
PAT McCALLUM Executive Editor, DC Comics

DAN DiDIO Publisher
JIM LEE Publisher & Chief Creative Officer
AMIT DESAI Executive VP – Business & Marketing Strategy,
          Direct to Consumer & Global Franchise Management
BOBBIE CHASE VP & Executive Editor, Young Reader & Talent Development
MARK CHIARELLO Senior VP – Art, Design & Collected Editions
JOHN CUNNINGHAM Senior VP – Sales & Trade Marketing
BRIAR DARDEN VP – Business Affairs
ANNE DePIES Senior VP – Business Strategy, Finance & Administration
DON FALLETTI VP – Manufacturing Operations
LAWRENCE GANEM VP – Editorial Administration & Talent Relations
ALISON GILL Senior VP – Manufacturing & Operations
JASON GREENBERG VP – Business Strategy & Finance
HANK KANALZ Senior VP – Editorial Strategy & Administration
JAY KOGAN Senior VP – Legal Affairs
NICK J. NAPOLITANO VP – Manufacturing Administration
LISETTE OSTERLOH VP – Digital Marketing & Events
EDDIE SCANNELL VP – Consumer Marketing
COURTNEY SIMMONS Senior VP – Publicity & Communications
JIM (SKI) SOKOLOWSKI VP – Comic Book Specialty Sales & Trade Marketing
NANCY SPEARS VP – Mass, Book, Digital Sales & Trade Marketing
MICHELE R. WELLS VP – Content Strategy

HARLEY'S LITTLE BLACK BOOK

DC Comics, 2900 West Alameda Ave., Burbank, CA 91505
Printed by LSC Communications, Kendallville, IN, USA. 10/19/18. First Printing.
ISBN: 978-1-4012-7360-6

Library of Congress Cataloging-in-Publication Data is available.

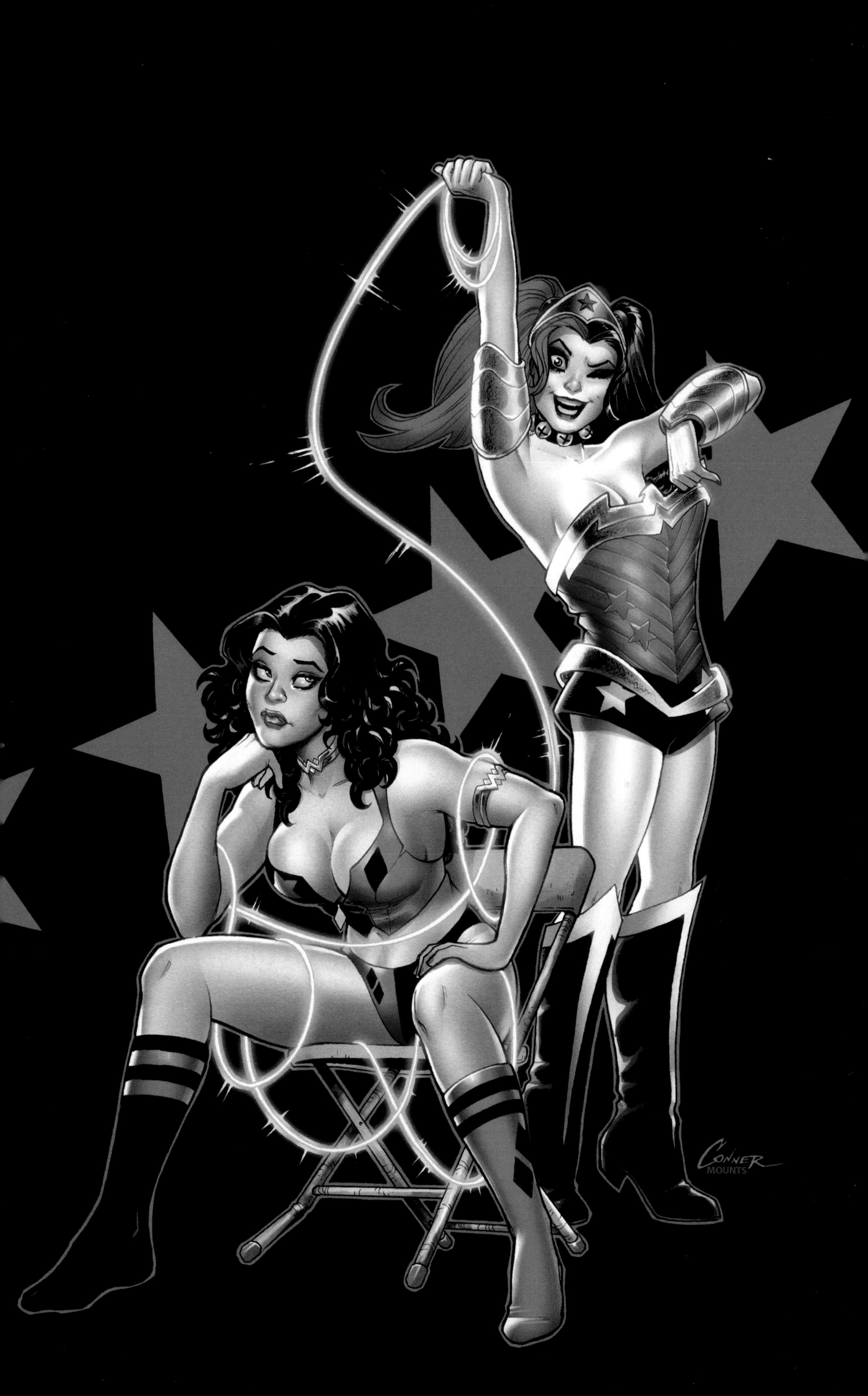
CONNER
MOUNTS

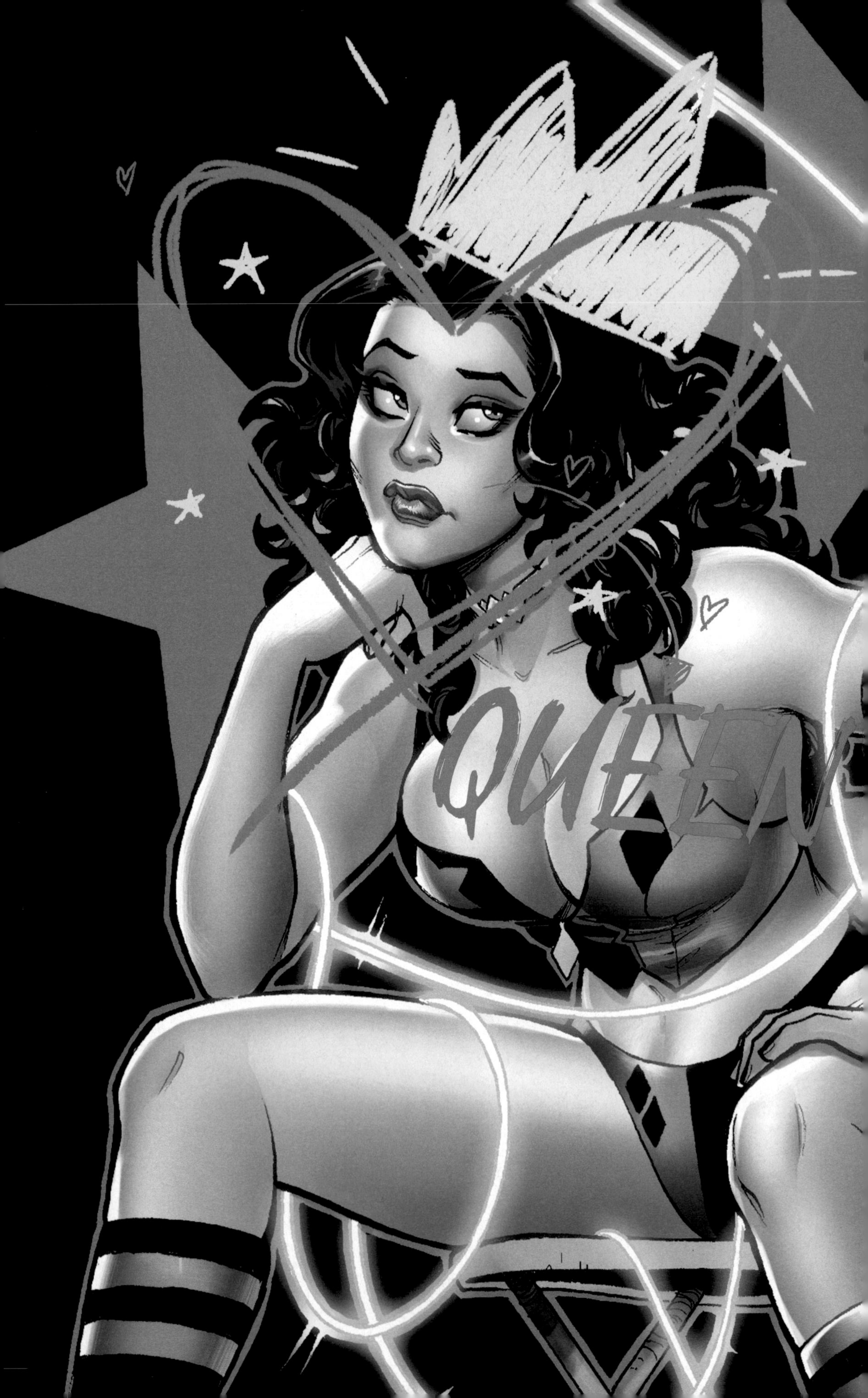
QUEEN

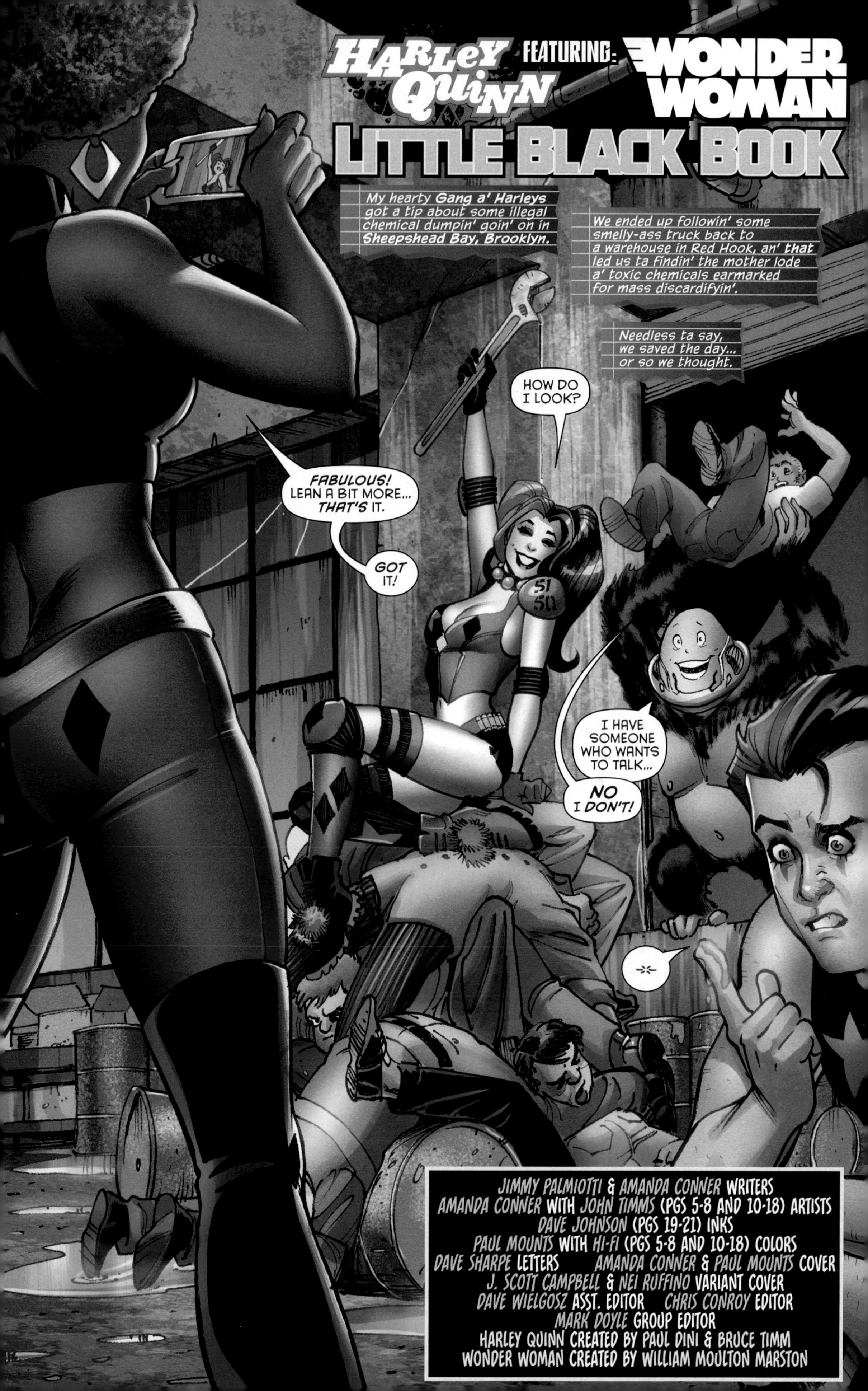
HARLEY QUINN FEATURING: WONDER WOMAN
LITTLE BLACK BOOK
My hearty Gang a' Harleys got a tip about some illegal chemical dumpin' goin' on in Sheepshead Bay, Brooklyn.
We ended up followin' some smelly-ass truck back to a warehouse in Red Hook, an' that led us ta findin' the mother lode a' toxic chemicals earmarked for mass discardifyin'.
Needless ta say, we saved the day... or so we thought.
HOW DO I LOOK?
FABULOUS! LEAN A BIT MORE... THAT'S IT.
GOT IT!
I HAVE SOMEONE WHO WANTS TO TALK...
NO I DON'T!
JIMMY PALMIOTTI & AMANDA CONNER WRITERS
AMANDA CONNER WITH JOHN TIMMS (PGS 5-8 AND 10-18) ARTISTS
DAVE JOHNSON (PGS 19-21) INKS
PAUL MOUNTS WITH HI-FI (PGS 5-8 AND 10-18) COLORS
DAVE SHARPE LETTERS AMANDA CONNER & PAUL MOUNTS COVER
J. SCOTT CAMPBELL & NEI RUFFINO VARIANT COVER
DAVE WIELGOSZ ASST. EDITOR CHRIS CONROY EDITOR
MARK DOYLE GROUP EDITOR
HARLEY QUINN CREATED BY PAUL DINI & BRUCE TIMM
WONDER WOMAN CREATED BY WILLIAM MOULTON MARSTON

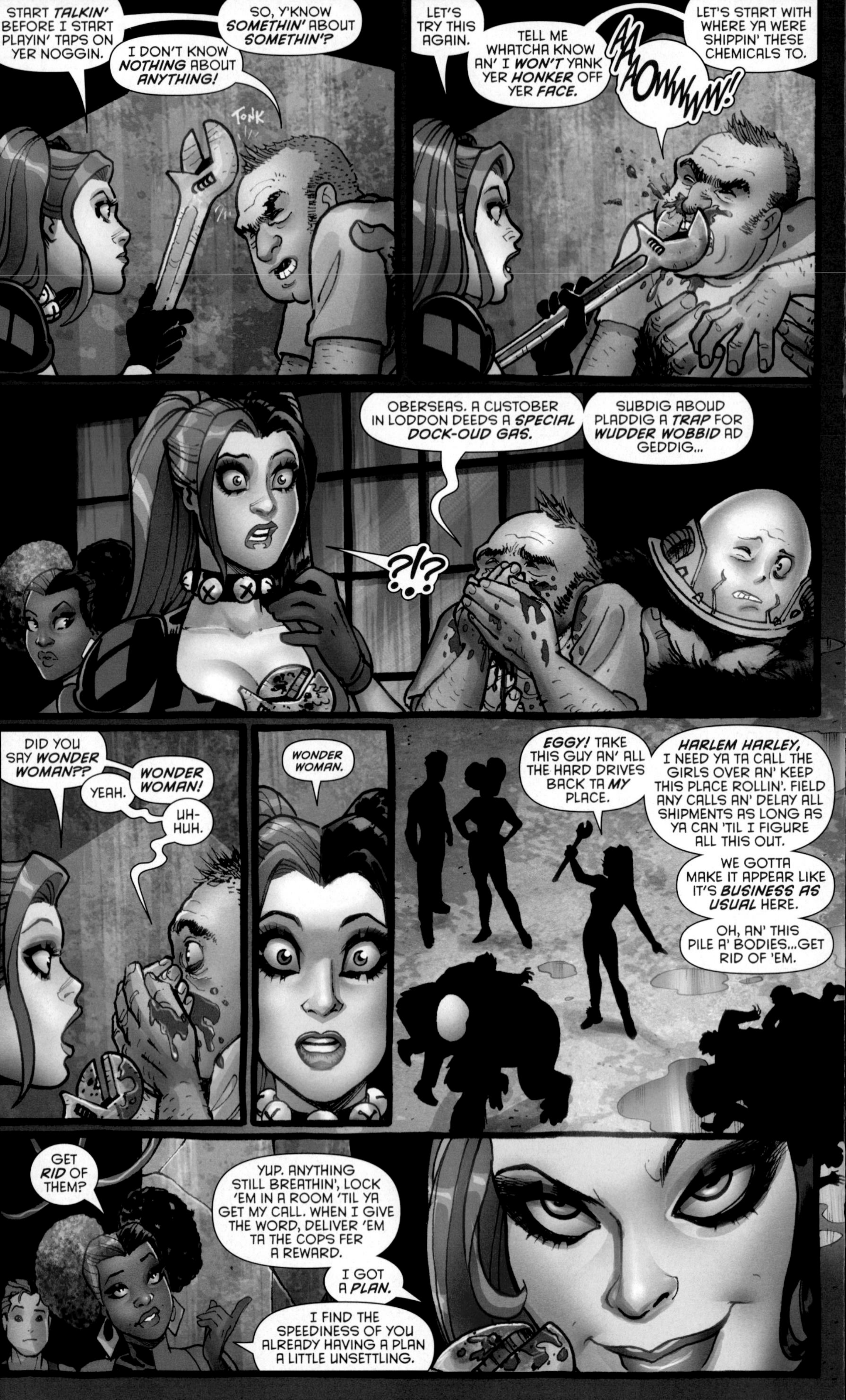

START *TALKIN'* BEFORE I START PLAYIN' TAPS ON YER NOGGIN.
SO, Y'KNOW *SOMETHIN'* ABOUT *SOMETHIN'?*
I DON'T KNOW *NOTHING* ABOUT *ANYTHING!*
TONK
LET'S TRY THIS AGAIN.
TELL ME WHATCHA KNOW AN' I *WON'T* YANK YER *HONKER* OFF YER *FACE.*
AAAOWWWW!
LET'S START WITH WHERE YA WERE SHIPPIN' THESE CHEMICALS TO.
OBERSEAS. A CUSTOBER IN LODDON DEEDS A *SPECIAL DOCK-OUD GAS.*
SUBDIG ABOUD PLADDIG A *TRAP* FOR *WUDDER WOBBID* AD GEDDIG...
?!?
DID YOU SAY *WONDER WOMAN??*
YEAH.
WONDER WOMAN!
UH-HUH.
WONDER WOMAN.
EGGY! TAKE THIS GUY AN' ALL THE HARD DRIVES BACK TA *MY* PLACE.
HARLEM HARLEY, I NEED YA TA CALL THE GIRLS OVER AN' KEEP THIS PLACE ROLLIN'. FIELD ANY CALLS AN' DELAY ALL SHIPMENTS AS LONG AS YA CAN 'TIL I FIGURE ALL THIS OUT.
WE GOTTA MAKE IT APPEAR LIKE IT'S *BUSINESS AS USUAL* HERE.
OH, AN' THIS PILE A' BODIES...GET RID OF 'EM.
GET *RID* OF THEM?
YUP. ANYTHING STILL BREATHIN', LOCK 'EM IN A ROOM 'TIL YA GET MY CALL. WHEN I GIVE THE WORD, DELIVER 'EM TA THE COPS FER A REWARD.
I GOT A *PLAN.*
I FIND THE SPEEDINESS OF YOU ALREADY HAVING A PLAN A LITTLE UNSETTLING.

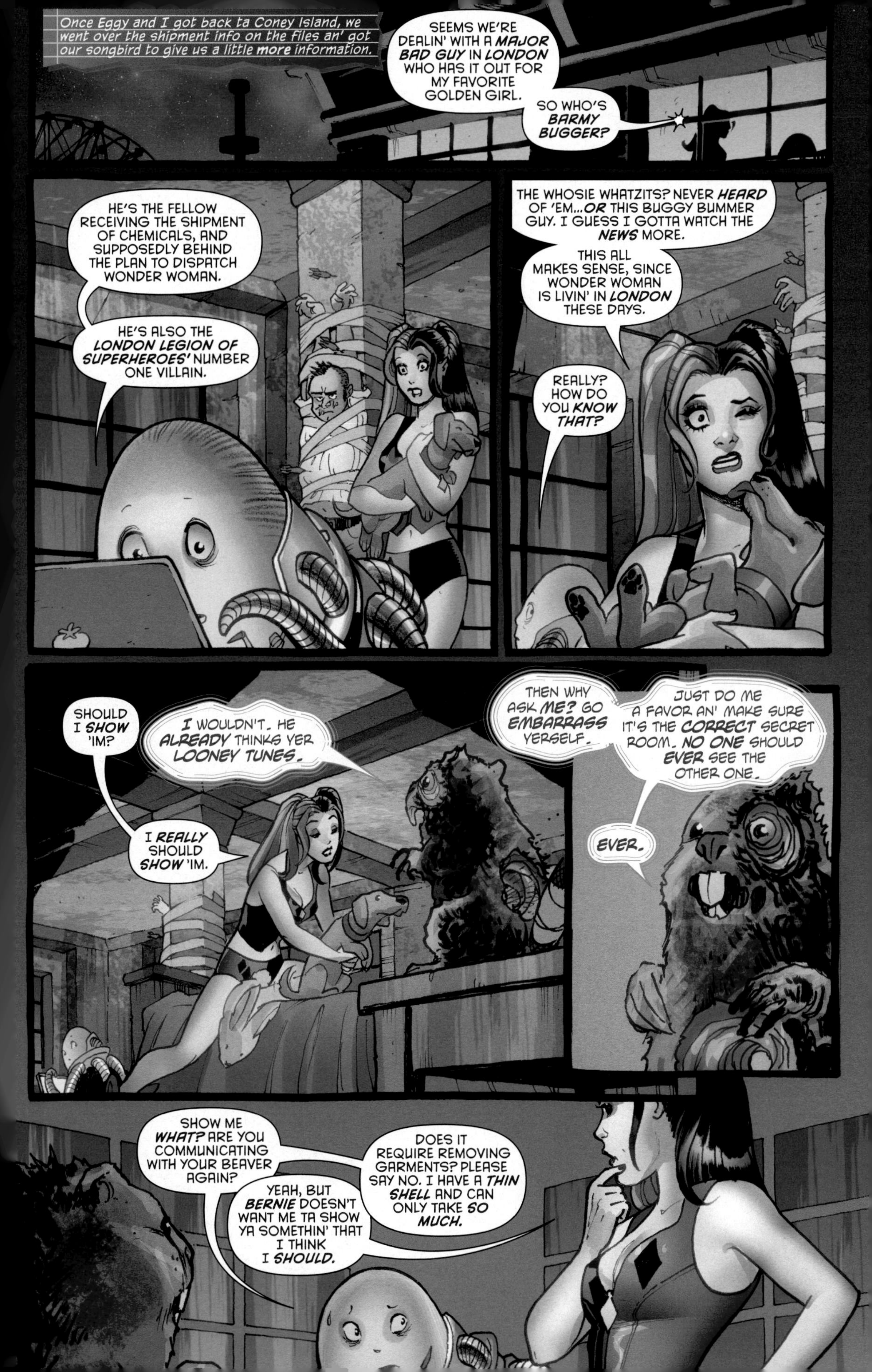
Once Eggy and I got back ta Coney Island, we went over the shipment info on the files an' got our songbird to give us a little more information.
SEEMS WE'RE DEALIN' WITH A MAJOR BAD GUY IN LONDON WHO HAS IT OUT FOR MY FAVORITE GOLDEN GIRL.
SO WHO'S BARMY BUGGER?
HE'S THE FELLOW RECEIVING THE SHIPMENT OF CHEMICALS, AND SUPPOSEDLY BEHIND THE PLAN TO DISPATCH WONDER WOMAN.
HE'S ALSO THE LONDON LEGION OF SUPERHEROES' NUMBER ONE VILLAIN.
THE WHOSIE WHATZITS? NEVER HEARD OF 'EM...OR THIS BUGGY BUMMER GUY. I GUESS I GOTTA WATCH THE NEWS MORE.
THIS ALL MAKES SENSE, SINCE WONDER WOMAN IS LIVIN' IN LONDON THESE DAYS.
REALLY? HOW DO YOU KNOW THAT?
SHOULD I SHOW 'IM?
I WOULDN'T. HE ALREADY THINKS YER LOONEY TUNES.
I REALLY SHOULD SHOW 'IM.
THEN WHY ASK ME? GO EMBARRASS YERSELF.
JUST DO ME A FAVOR AN' MAKE SURE IT'S THE CORRECT SECRET ROOM. NO ONE SHOULD EVER SEE THE OTHER ONE.
EVER.
SHOW ME WHAT? ARE YOU COMMUNICATING WITH YOUR BEAVER AGAIN?
YEAH, BUT BERNIE DOESN'T WANT ME TA SHOW YA SOMETHIN' THAT I THINK I SHOULD.
DOES IT REQUIRE REMOVING GARMENTS? PLEASE SAY NO. I HAVE A THIN SHELL AND CAN ONLY TAKE SO MUCH.

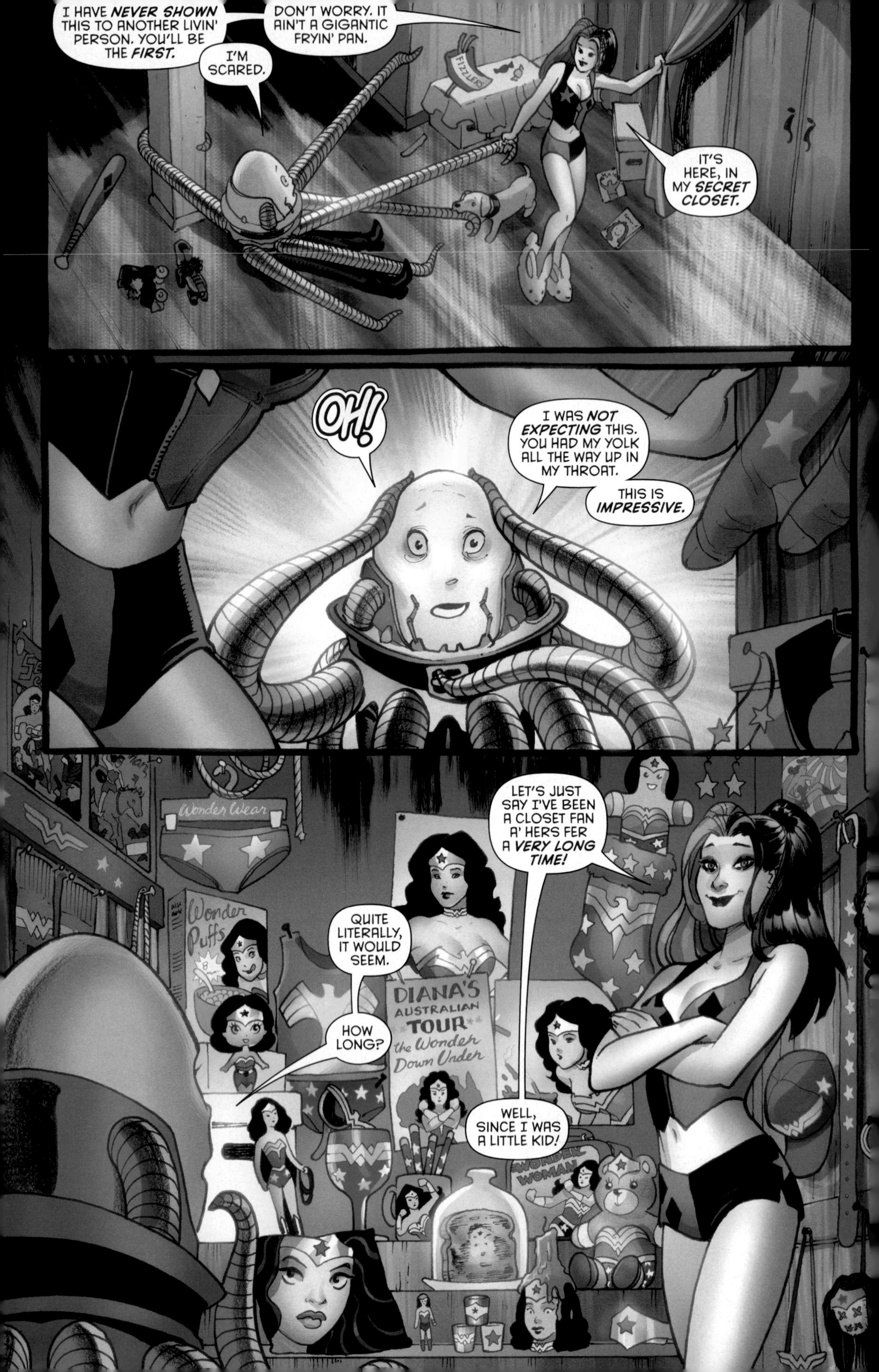
I HAVE NEVER SHOWN THIS TO ANOTHER LIVIN' PERSON. YOU'LL BE THE FIRST.
I'M SCARED.
DON'T WORRY. IT AIN'T A GIGANTIC FRYIN' PAN.
FIZZLERS
IT'S HERE, IN MY SECRET CLOSET.
OH!
I WAS NOT EXPECTING THIS. YOU HAD MY YOLK ALL THE WAY UP IN MY THROAT.
THIS IS IMPRESSIVE.
Wonder Wear
Wonder Puffs
LET'S JUST SAY I'VE BEEN A CLOSET FAN A' HERS FER A VERY LONG TIME!
QUITE LITERALLY, IT WOULD SEEM.
DIANA'S AUSTRALIAN TOUR the Wonder Down Under
HOW LONG?
WELL, SINCE I WAS A LITTLE KID!
WONDER WOMAN

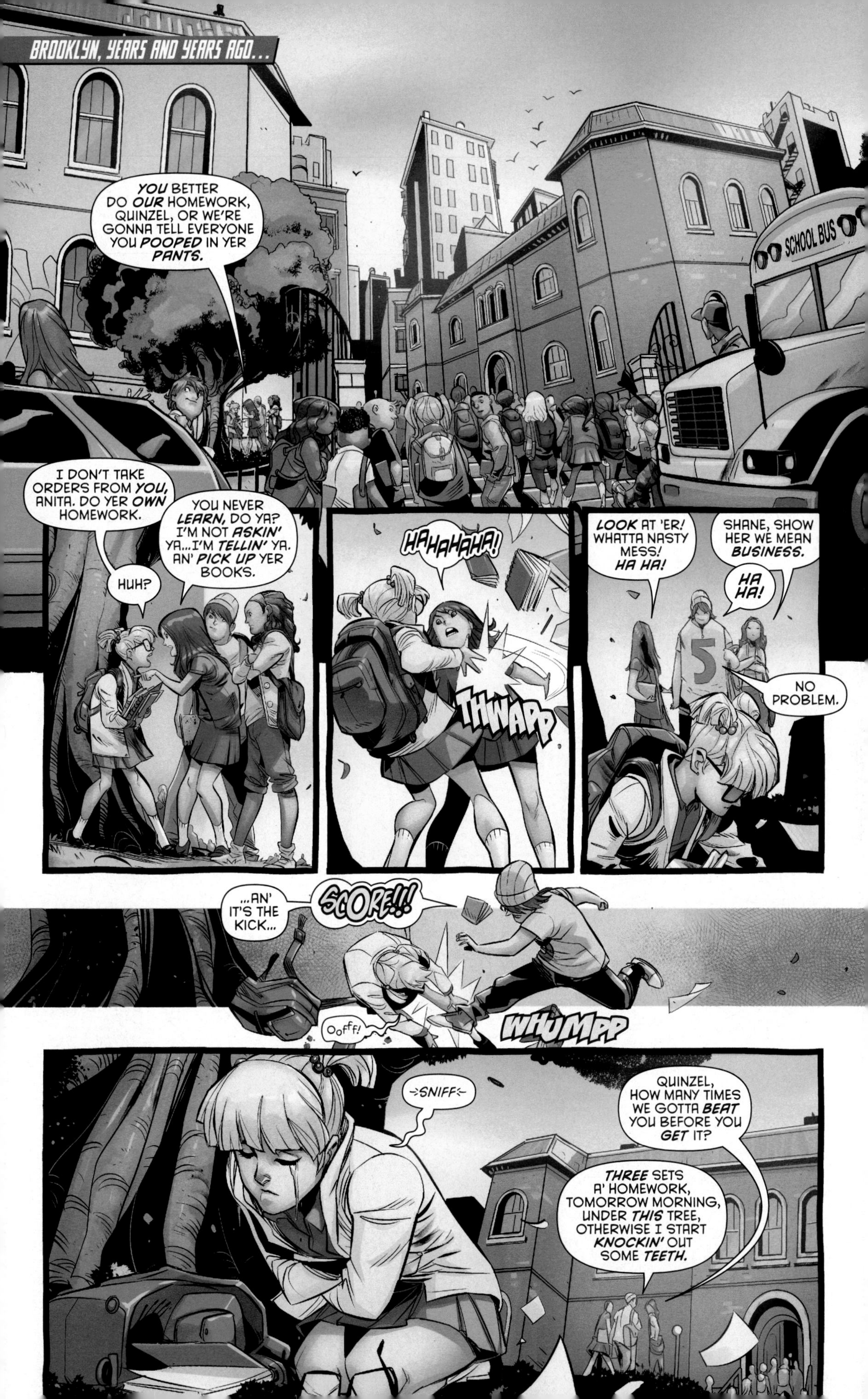
BROOKLYN, YEARS AND YEARS AGO...
SCHOOL BUS
YOU BETTER DO OUR HOMEWORK, QUINZEL, OR WE'RE GONNA TELL EVERYONE YOU POOPED IN YER PANTS.
I DON'T TAKE ORDERS FROM YOU, ANITA. DO YER OWN HOMEWORK.
HUH?
YOU NEVER LEARN, DO YA? I'M NOT ASKIN' YA...I'M TELLIN' YA. AN' PICK UP YER BOOKS.
HAHAHAHA!
THWAPP
LOOK AT 'ER! WHATTA NASTY MESS! HA HA!
SHANE, SHOW HER WE MEAN BUSINESS.
HA HA!
NO PROBLEM.
...AN' IT'S THE KICK...
SCORE!!!
Oofff!
WHUMPP
-SNIFF-
QUINZEL, HOW MANY TIMES WE GOTTA BEAT YOU BEFORE YOU GET IT?
THREE SETS A' HOMEWORK, TOMORROW MORNING, UNDER THIS TREE, OTHERWISE I START KNOCKIN' OUT SOME TEETH.

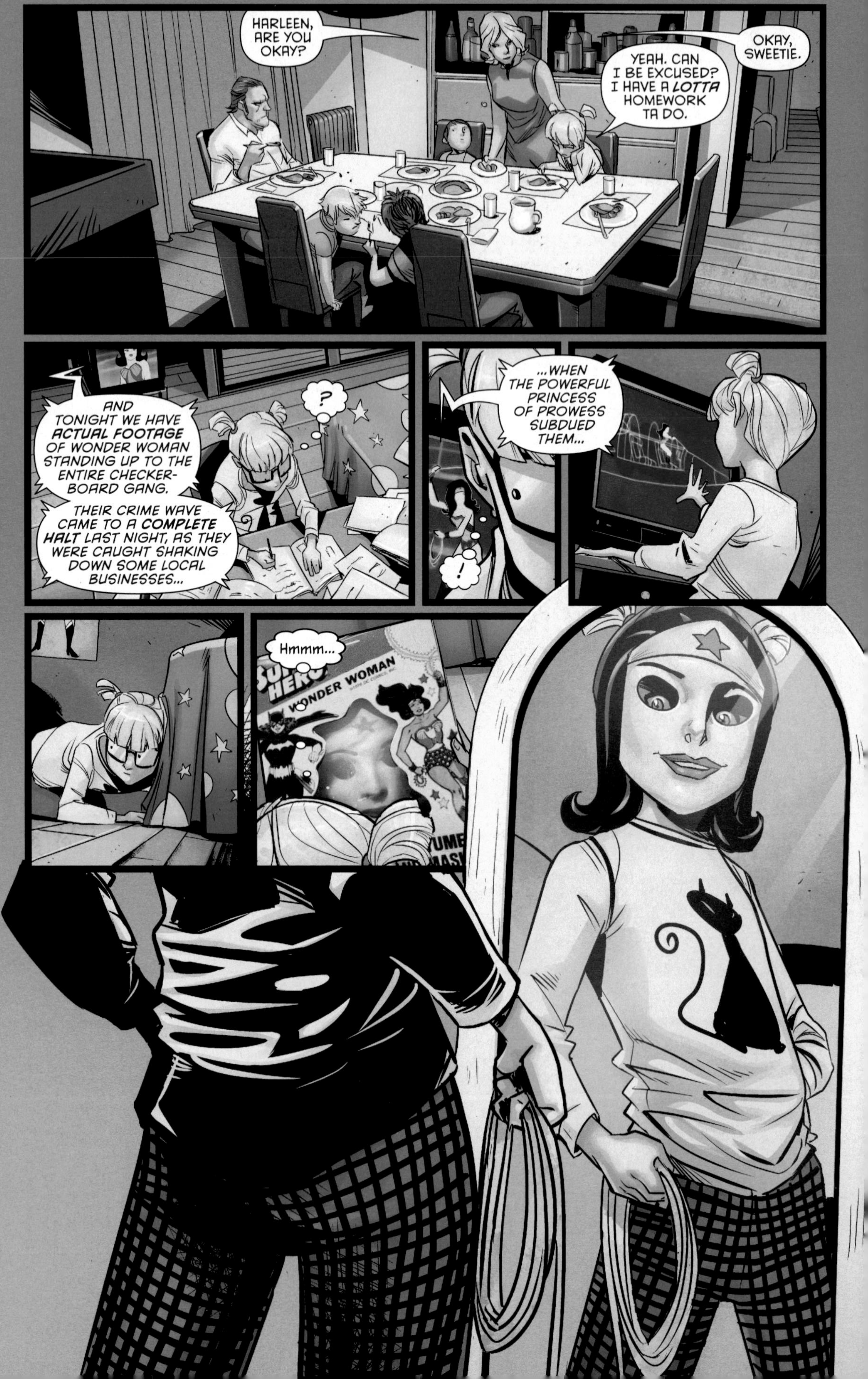
HARLEEN, ARE YOU OKAY?
YEAH. CAN I BE EXCUSED? I HAVE A *LOTTA* HOMEWORK TA DO.
OKAY, SWEETIE.
AND TONIGHT WE HAVE **ACTUAL FOOTAGE** OF WONDER WOMAN STANDING UP TO THE ENTIRE CHECKER-BOARD GANG.
THEIR CRIME WAVE CAME TO A **COMPLETE HALT** LAST NIGHT, AS THEY WERE CAUGHT SHAKING DOWN SOME LOCAL BUSINESSES...
?
...WHEN THE POWERFUL PRINCESS OF PROWESS SUBDUED THEM...
!
Hmmm...
WONDER WOMAN

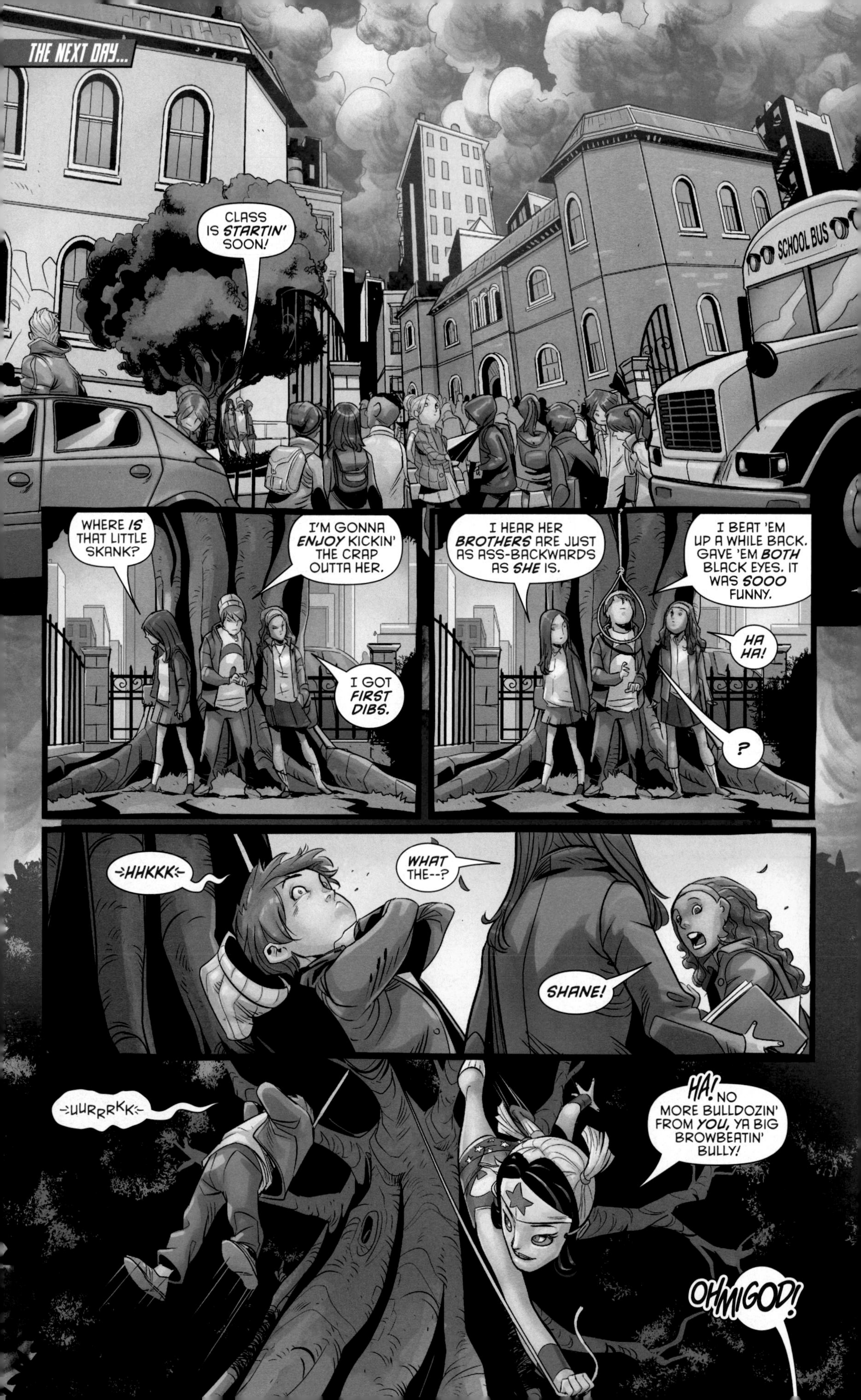

THE NEXT DAY...
CLASS IS STARTIN' SOON!
SCHOOL BUS
WHERE IS THAT LITTLE SKANK?
I'M GONNA ENJOY KICKIN' THE CRAP OUTTA HER.
I GOT FIRST DIBS.
I HEAR HER BROTHERS ARE JUST AS ASS-BACKWARDS AS SHE IS.
I BEAT 'EM UP A WHILE BACK. GAVE 'EM BOTH BLACK EYES. IT WAS SOOO FUNNY.
HA HA!
?
HHKKK
WHAT THE--?
SHANE!
UURRRKK
HA! NO MORE BULLDOZIN' FROM YOU, YA BIG BROWBEATIN' BULLY!
OHMIGOD!

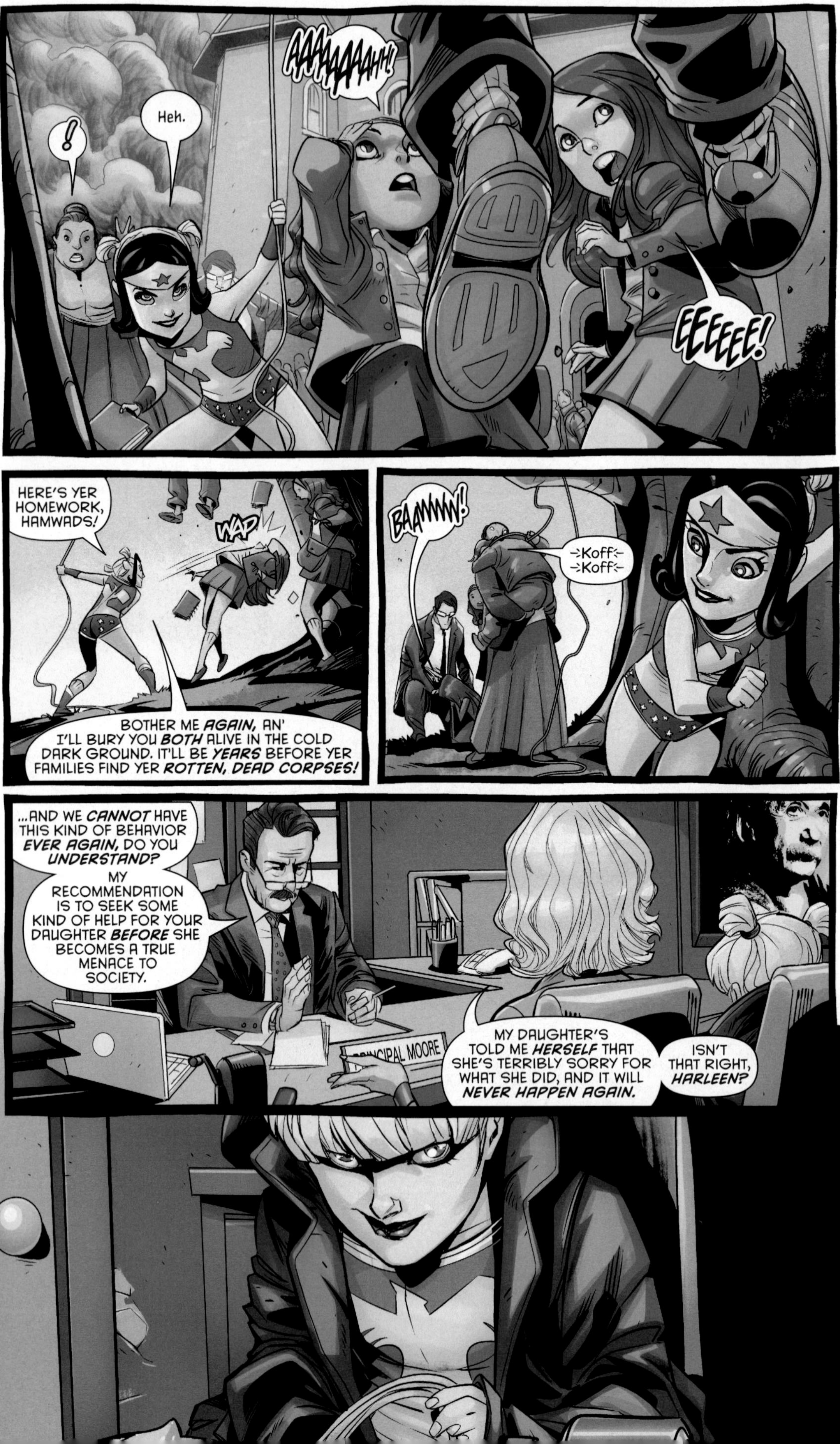

Heh.
!
AAAAAAAAHH!
EEEEEE!
HERE'S YER HOMEWORK, HAMWADS!
WAP
BOTHER ME AGAIN, AN' I'LL BURY YOU BOTH ALIVE IN THE COLD DARK GROUND. IT'LL BE YEARS BEFORE YER FAMILIES FIND YER ROTTEN, DEAD CORPSES!
BAAWWW!
Koff Koff
...AND WE CANNOT HAVE THIS KIND OF BEHAVIOR EVER AGAIN, DO YOU UNDERSTAND?
MY RECOMMENDATION IS TO SEEK SOME KIND OF HELP FOR YOUR DAUGHTER BEFORE SHE BECOMES A TRUE MENACE TO SOCIETY.
PRINCIPAL MOORE
MY DAUGHTER'S TOLD ME HERSELF THAT SHE'S TERRIBLY SORRY FOR WHAT SHE DID, AND IT WILL NEVER HAPPEN AGAIN.
ISN'T THAT RIGHT, HARLEEN?

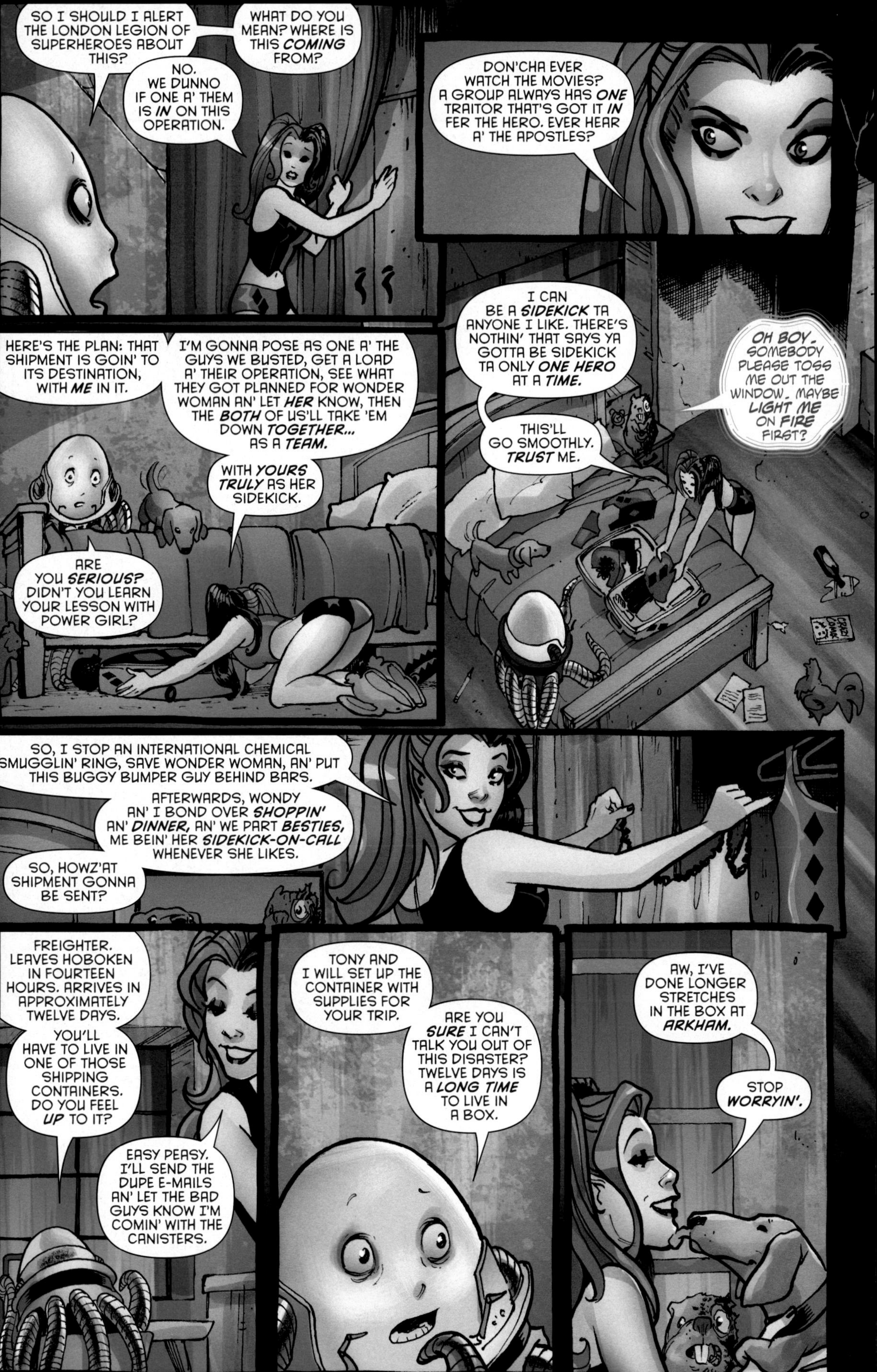
SO I SHOULD I ALERT THE LONDON LEGION OF SUPERHEROES ABOUT THIS?
WHAT DO YOU MEAN? WHERE IS THIS COMING FROM?
NO. WE DUNNO IF ONE A' THEM IS IN ON THIS OPERATION.
DON'CHA EVER WATCH THE MOVIES? A GROUP ALWAYS HAS ONE TRAITOR THAT'S GOT IT IN FER THE HERO. EVER HEAR A' THE APOSTLES?
HERE'S THE PLAN: THAT SHIPMENT IS GOIN' TO ITS DESTINATION, WITH ME IN IT.
I'M GONNA POSE AS ONE A' THE GUYS WE BUSTED, GET A LOAD A' THEIR OPERATION, SEE WHAT THEY GOT PLANNED FOR WONDER WOMAN AN' LET HER KNOW, THEN THE BOTH OF US'LL TAKE 'EM DOWN TOGETHER... AS A TEAM.
WITH YOURS TRULY AS HER SIDEKICK.
ARE YOU SERIOUS? DIDN'T YOU LEARN YOUR LESSON WITH POWER GIRL?
I CAN BE A SIDEKICK TA ANYONE I LIKE. THERE'S NOTHIN' THAT SAYS YA GOTTA BE SIDEKICK TA ONLY ONE HERO AT A TIME.
THIS'LL GO SMOOTHLY. TRUST ME.
OH BOY. SOMEBODY PLEASE TOSS ME OUT THE WINDOW. MAYBE LIGHT ME ON FIRE FIRST?
SO, I STOP AN INTERNATIONAL CHEMICAL SMUGGLIN' RING, SAVE WONDER WOMAN, AN' PUT THIS BUGGY BUMPER GUY BEHIND BARS.
AFTERWARDS, WONDY AN' I BOND OVER SHOPPIN' AN' DINNER, AN' WE PART BESTIES, ME BEIN' HER SIDEKICK-ON-CALL WHENEVER SHE LIKES.
SO, HOWZ'AT SHIPMENT GONNA BE SENT?
FREIGHTER. LEAVES HOBOKEN IN FOURTEEN HOURS. ARRIVES IN APPROXIMATELY TWELVE DAYS.
YOU'LL HAVE TO LIVE IN ONE OF THOSE SHIPPING CONTAINERS. DO YOU FEEL UP TO IT?
EASY PEASY. I'LL SEND THE DUPE E-MAILS AN' LET THE BAD GUYS KNOW I'M COMIN' WITH THE CANISTERS.
TONY AND I WILL SET UP THE CONTAINER WITH SUPPLIES FOR YOUR TRIP.
ARE YOU SURE I CAN'T TALK YOU OUT OF THIS DISASTER? TWELVE DAYS IS A LONG TIME TO LIVE IN A BOX.
AW, I'VE DONE LONGER STRETCHES IN THE BOX AT ARKHAM.
STOP WORRYIN'.

LONDON'S NOT CALLING

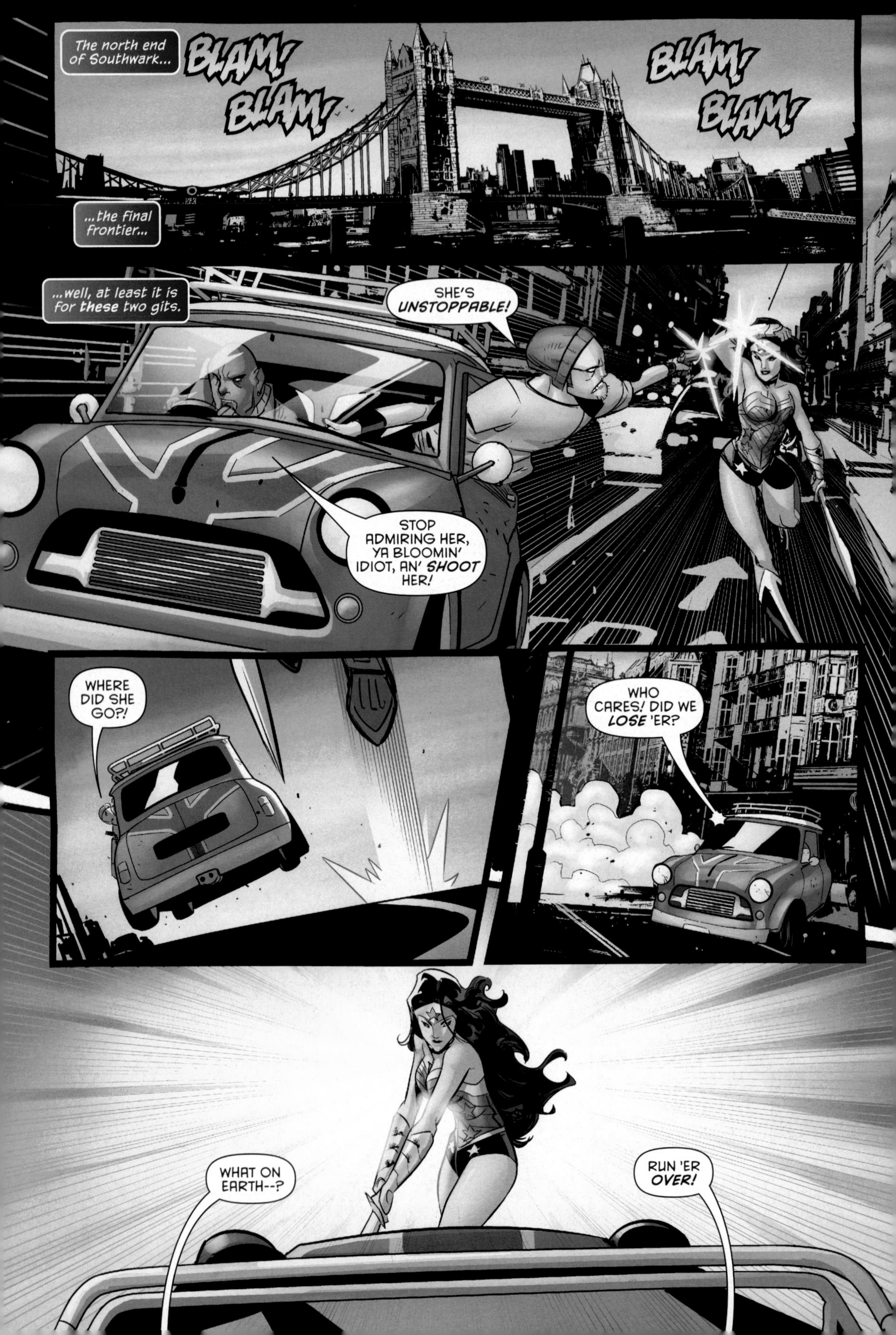
The north end of Southwark...
BLAM! BLAM!
BLAM! BLAM!
...the final frontier...
...well, at least it is for these two gits.
SHE'S UNSTOPPABLE!
STOP ADMIRING HER, YA BLOOMIN' IDIOT, AN' SHOOT HER!
WHERE DID SHE GO?!
WHO CARES! DID WE LOSE 'ER?
WHAT ON EARTH--?
RUN 'ER OVER!

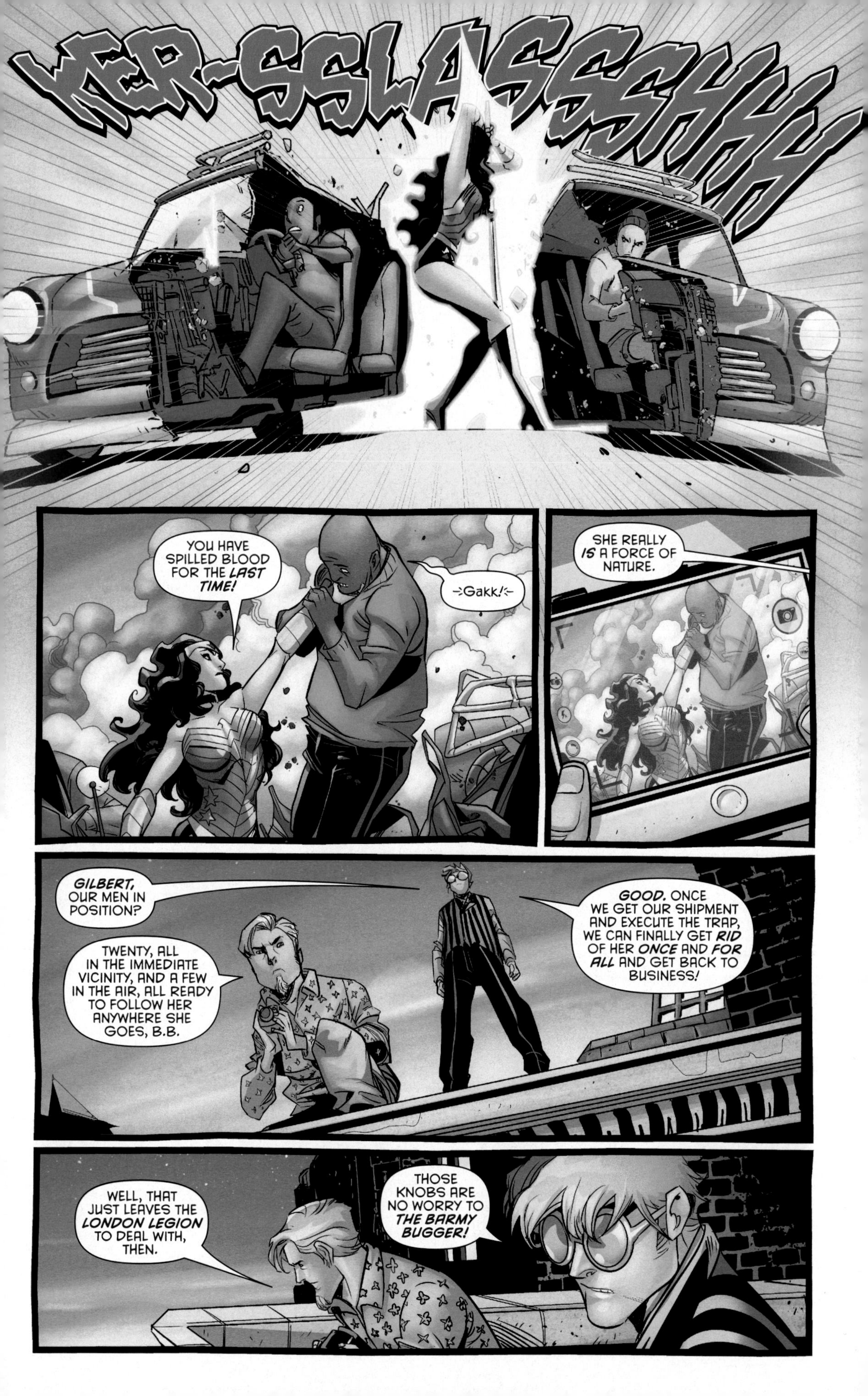
KER-SSLASSSHHH
YOU HAVE SPILLED BLOOD FOR THE *LAST TIME!*
-Gakk!-
SHE REALLY *IS* A FORCE OF NATURE.
GILBERT, OUR MEN IN POSITION?
TWENTY, ALL IN THE IMMEDIATE VICINITY, AND A FEW IN THE AIR, ALL READY TO FOLLOW HER ANYWHERE SHE GOES, B.B.
GOOD. ONCE WE GET OUR SHIPMENT AND EXECUTE THE TRAP, WE CAN FINALLY GET *RID* OF HER *ONCE* AND *FOR ALL* AND GET BACK TO BUSINESS!
WELL, THAT JUST LEAVES THE *LONDON LEGION* TO DEAL WITH, THEN.
THOSE KNOBS ARE NO WORRY TO *THE BARMY BUGGER!*

KNOBS OF WORRY

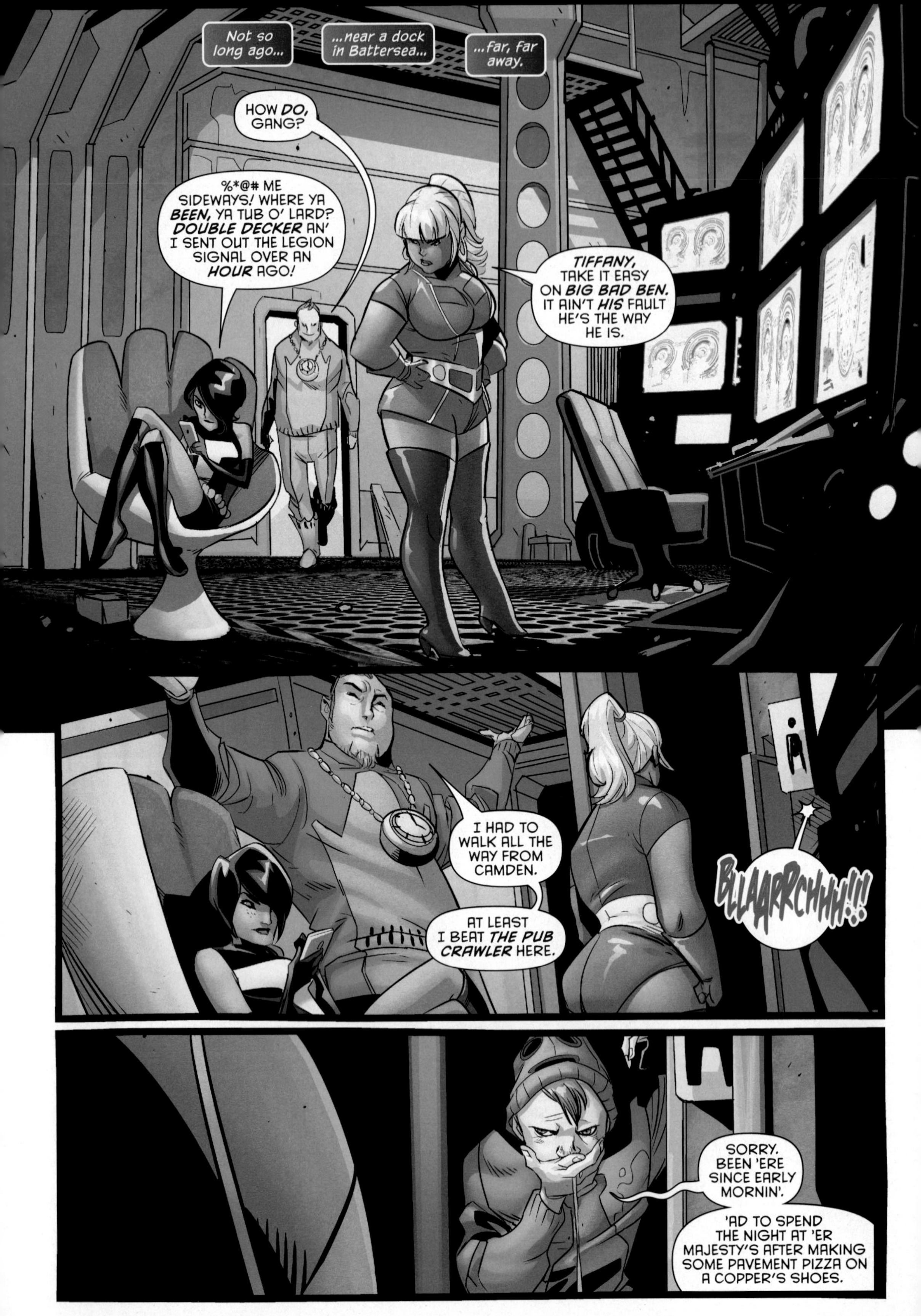
Not so long ago...
...near a dock in Battersea...
...far, far away.
HOW DO, GANG?
%*@# ME SIDEWAYS! WHERE YA BEEN, YA TUB O' LARD? DOUBLE DECKER AN' I SENT OUT THE LEGION SIGNAL OVER AN HOUR AGO!
TIFFANY, TAKE IT EASY ON BIG BAD BEN. IT AIN'T HIS FAULT HE'S THE WAY HE IS.
I HAD TO WALK ALL THE WAY FROM CAMDEN.
AT LEAST I BEAT THE PUB CRAWLER HERE.
BLLAARRCHHH!!!
SORRY. BEEN 'ERE SINCE EARLY MORNIN'.
'AD TO SPEND THE NIGHT AT 'ER MAJESTY'S AFTER MAKING SOME PAVEMENT PIZZA ON A COPPER'S SHOES.

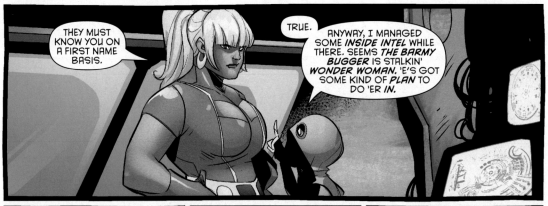

THEY MUST KNOW YOU ON A FIRST NAME BASIS.

TRUE.

ANYWAY, I MANAGED SOME *INSIDE INTEL* WHILE THERE. SEEMS *THE BARMY BUGGER* IS STALKIN' *WONDER WOMAN.* 'E'S GOT SOME KIND OF *PLAN* TO DO 'ER *IN.*

BLOODY 'ELL! LIKE WE AIN'T GOT ENOUGH CRAP TO WORRY ABOUT WITH ALL THESE BLOOMIN' TERRORISTS AN' EVERYTHIN'...

I SAY WE JUST %#@* KILL THAT KNOB *ONCE* AND *FOR ALL!*

TIFFANY TERROR, YOU KNOW BETTER THAN ANYONE ELSE THE LONDON LEGION OF SUPERHEROES' DECREE OF *NEVER KILLING!* IF IT WORKS FOR THE *BATMAN,* IT CAN WORK FOR *US.*

GORBLIMY!

IF YA #@$% LOVE THE BATMAN SO MUCH, WHY DON'T YA MOVE TO GOTHAM AN' MARRY 'IM?

YOU *KNOW* I WOULD IF HE WOULD *HAVE* ME. WHY MUST YOU BE SO *CRUEL?*

MY NAME IS *TIFFANY TERROR,* NOT *DEBBIE DUMPLING!* WHAT THE @3$* DO YOU *EXPECT* FROM ME?

ENOUGH, YOU TWO. WHAT *ELSE* DID YOU FIND OUT?

BARMY IS GETTIN' A DELIVERY O' SOMETHIN' *TOMORROW NIGHT,* COMIN' IN FROM NEW JERSEY. IT'S SUPPOSED TO BE *KEY* TO 'IS *PLAN.*

IF WE CAN *INTERCEPT* THIS, WE CAN PUT 'IM OUT OF BUSINESS *PERMANENTLY!*

BINGO!

ONLY *ONE SHIP* FROM THERE, LANDIN' AT THE PORT O' TILBURY TOMORROW NIGHT. THAT *HAS* TO BE IT. THEY'RE NEVER GOING TO KNOW WHAT *HIT* 'EM!

BOX LUNCH

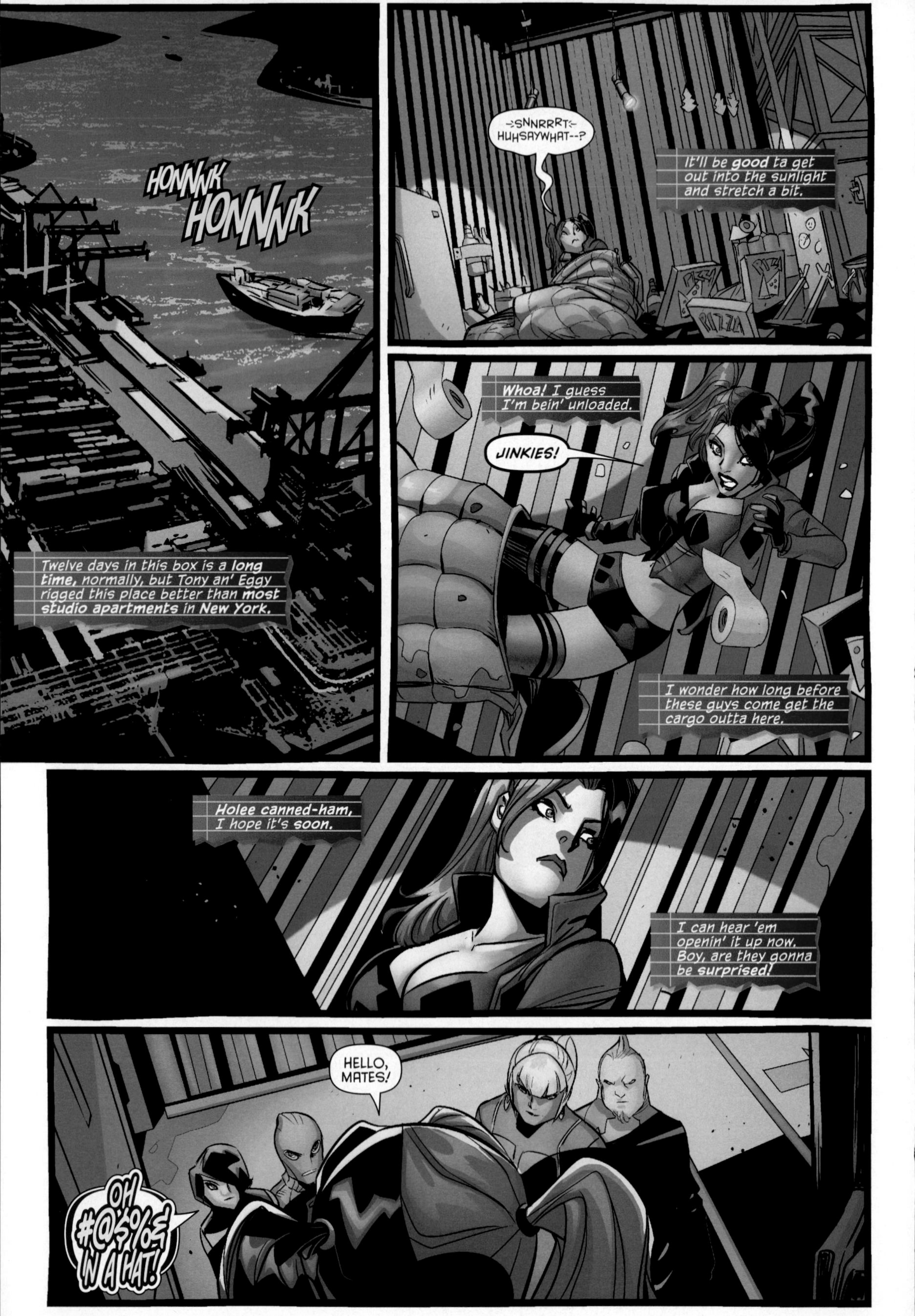
HONNNK HONNNK
Twelve days in this box is a **long time,** normally, but Tony an' Eggy rigged this place better than **most studio apartments** in **New York.**
SNNRRRT HUHSAYWHAT--?
It'll be **good** ta get out into the sunlight and stretch a bit.
Whoa! I guess I'm bein' unloaded.
JINKIES!
I wonder how long before these guys come get the cargo outta here.
Holee canned-ham, I hope it's **soon.**
I can hear 'em openin' it up now. Boy, are they gonna be **surprised!**
HELLO, MATES!
OH #@$%& IN A HAT!

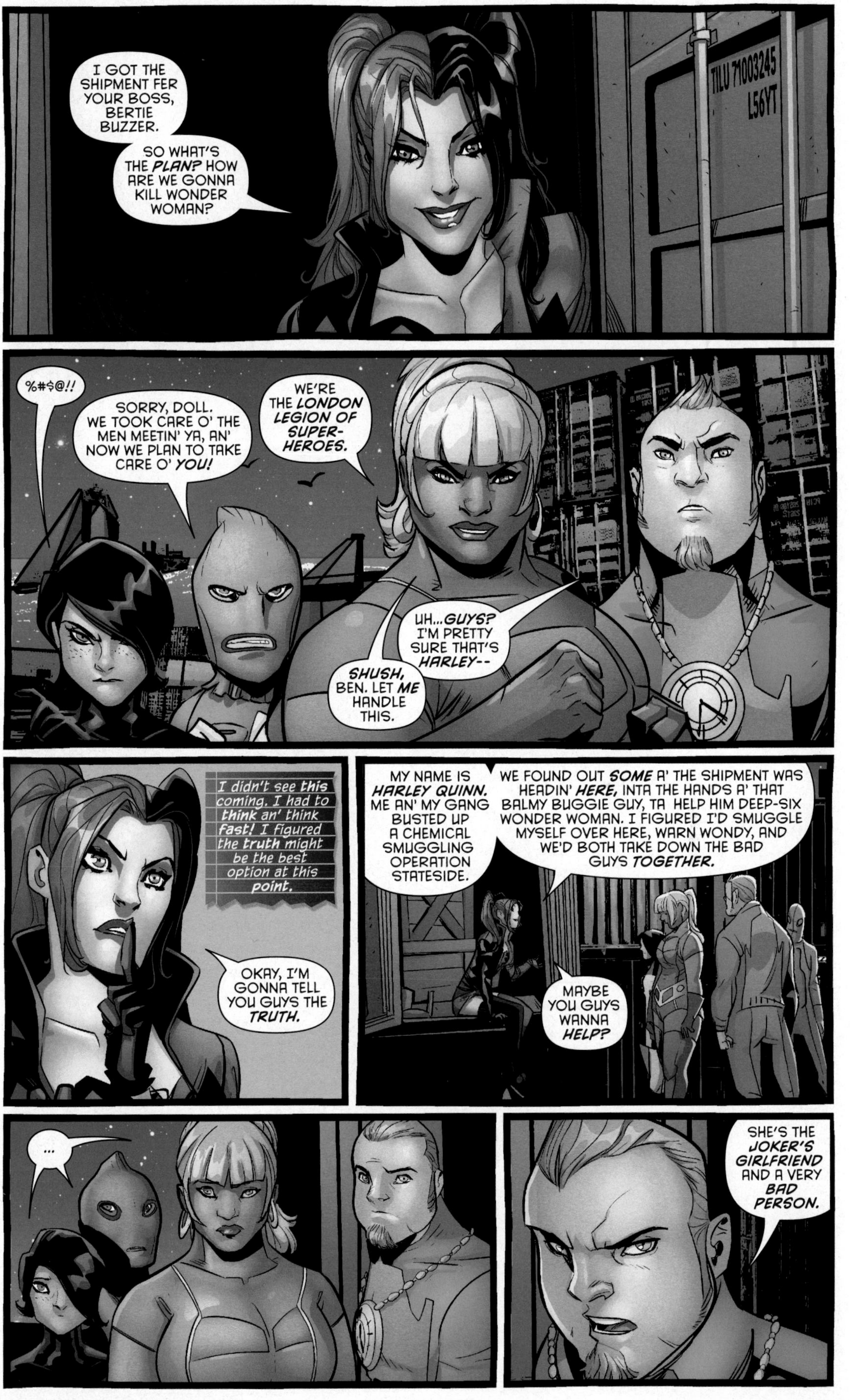
I GOT THE SHIPMENT FER YOUR BOSS, BERTIE BUZZER.
SO WHAT'S THE *PLAN?* HOW ARE WE GONNA KILL WONDER WOMAN?
TILU 71003245
L56YT
%#$@!!
SORRY, DOLL. WE TOOK CARE O' THE MEN MEETIN' YA, AN' NOW WE PLAN TO TAKE CARE O' *YOU!*
WE'RE THE *LONDON LEGION OF SUPER-HEROES.*
UH...*GUYS?* I'M PRETTY SURE THAT'S *HARLEY--*
SHUSH, BEN. LET *ME* HANDLE THIS.
I didn't see **this** coming. I had to **think** an' think **fast!** I figured the **truth** might be the best option at this **point.**
OKAY, I'M GONNA TELL YOU GUYS THE *TRUTH.*
MY NAME IS *HARLEY QUINN.* ME AN' MY GANG BUSTED UP A CHEMICAL SMUGGLING OPERATION STATESIDE.
WE FOUND OUT *SOME* A' THE SHIPMENT WAS HEADIN' *HERE,* INTA THE HANDS A' THAT BALMY BUGGIE GUY, TA HELP HIM DEEP-SIX WONDER WOMAN. I FIGURED I'D SMUGGLE MYSELF OVER HERE, WARN WONDY, AND WE'D BOTH TAKE DOWN THE BAD GUYS *TOGETHER.*
MAYBE YOU GUYS WANNA *HELP?*
...
SHE'S THE *JOKER'S GIRLFRIEND* AND A VERY *BAD PERSON.*

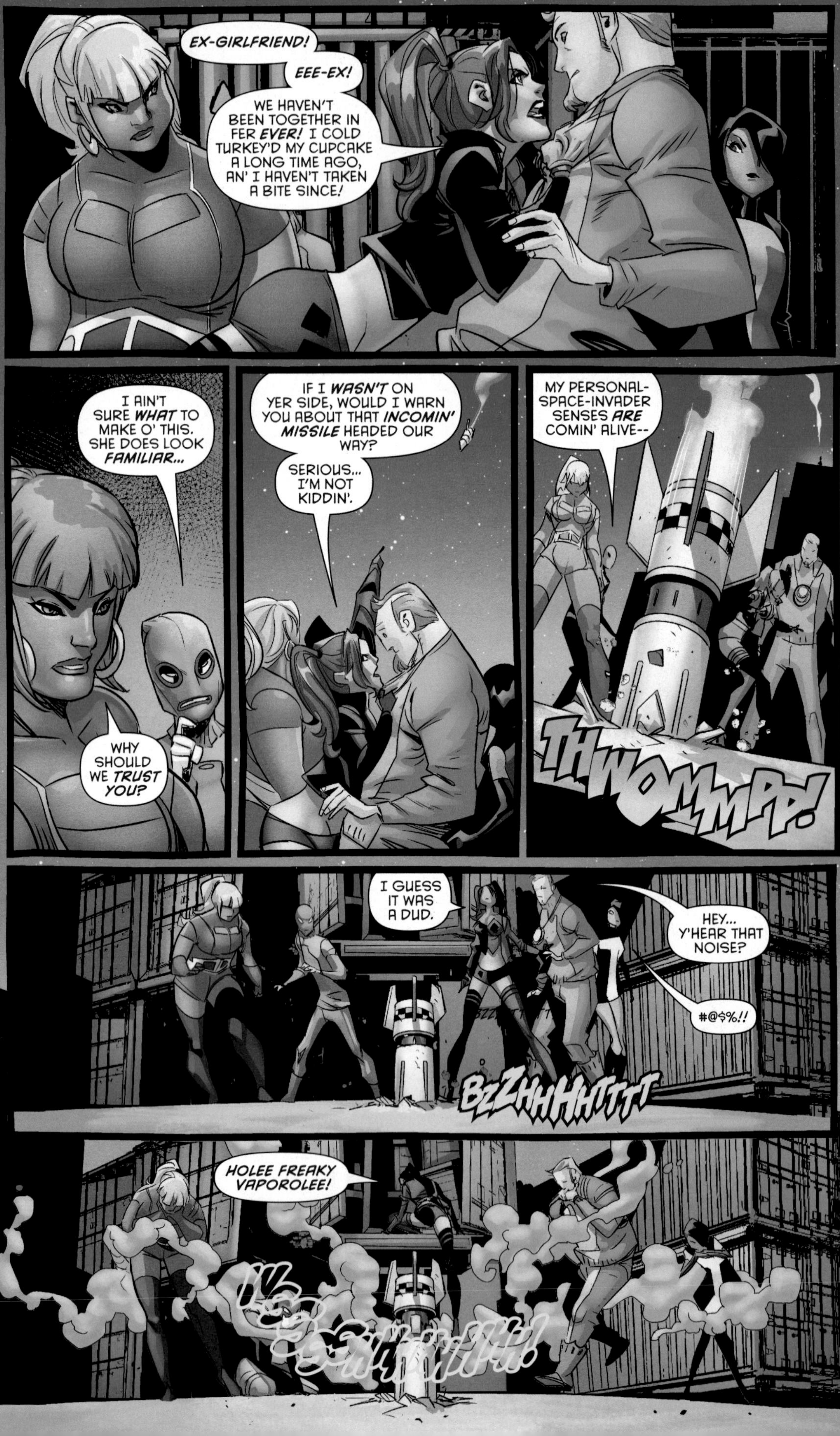
EX-GIRLFRIEND!
EEE-EX!
WE HAVEN'T BEEN TOGETHER IN FER EVER! I COLD TURKEY'D MY CUPCAKE A LONG TIME AGO, AN' I HAVEN'T TAKEN A BITE SINCE!
I AIN'T SURE WHAT TO MAKE O' THIS. SHE DOES LOOK FAMILIAR...
WHY SHOULD WE TRUST YOU?
IF I WASN'T ON YER SIDE, WOULD I WARN YOU ABOUT THAT INCOMIN' MISSILE HEADED OUR WAY?
SERIOUS... I'M NOT KIDDIN'.
MY PERSONAL-SPACE-INVADER SENSES ARE COMIN' ALIVE--
THWOMMPP!
I GUESS IT WAS A DUD.
HEY... Y'HEAR THAT NOISE?
#@$%!!
BZZHHHHHTTTT
HOLEE FREAKY VAPOROLEE!

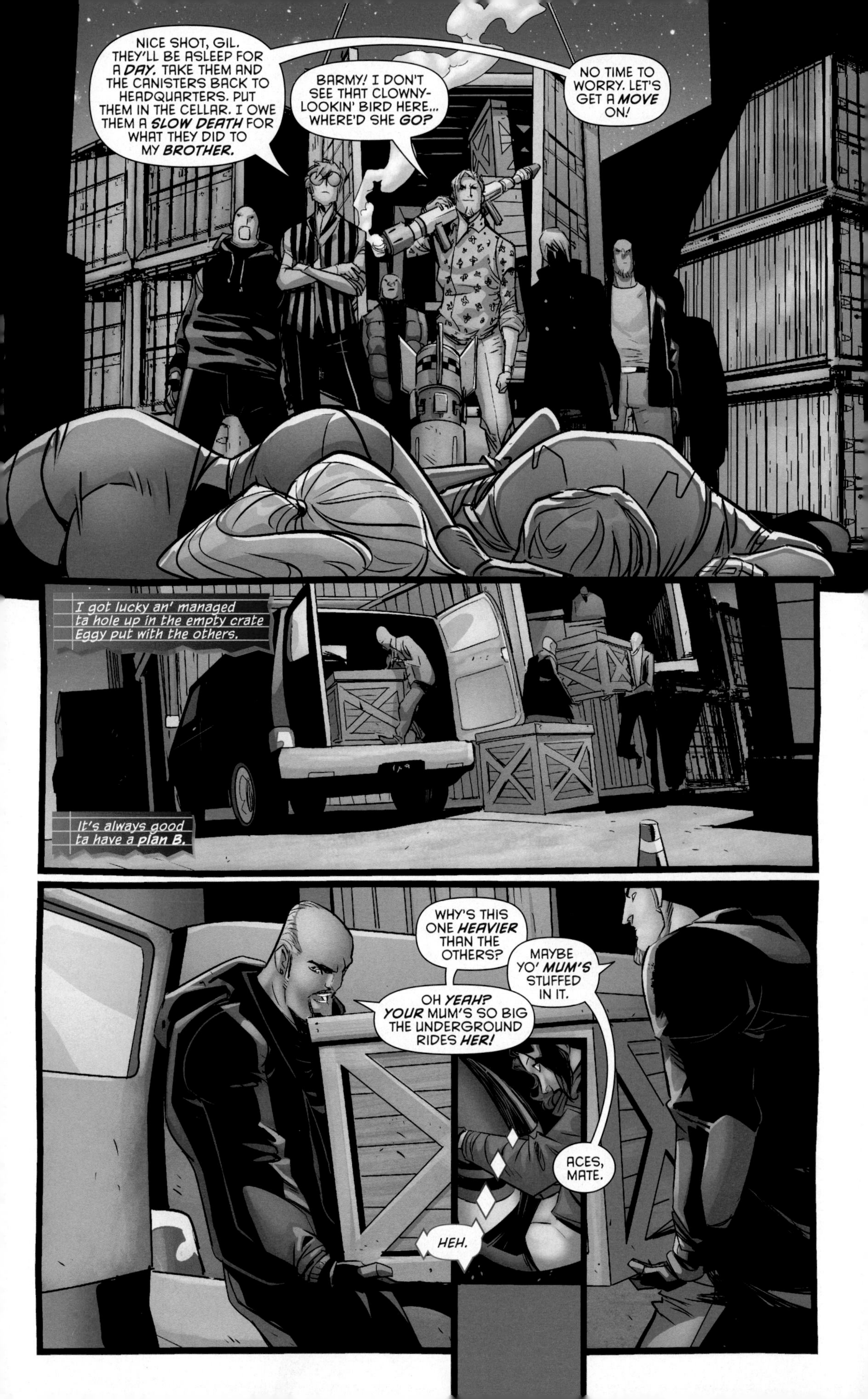

NICE SHOT, GIL. THEY'LL BE ASLEEP FOR A DAY. TAKE THEM AND THE CANISTERS BACK TO HEADQUARTERS. PUT THEM IN THE CELLAR. I OWE THEM A SLOW DEATH FOR WHAT THEY DID TO MY BROTHER.
BARMY! I DON'T SEE THAT CLOWNY-LOOKIN' BIRD HERE... WHERE'D SHE GO?
NO TIME TO WORRY. LET'S GET A MOVE ON!
I got lucky an' managed ta hole up in the empty crate Eggy put with the others.
It's always good ta have a plan B.
WHY'S THIS ONE HEAVIER THAN THE OTHERS?
MAYBE YO' MUM'S STUFFED IN IT.
OH YEAH? YOUR MUM'S SO BIG THE UNDERGROUND RIDES HER!
ACES, MATE.
HEH.

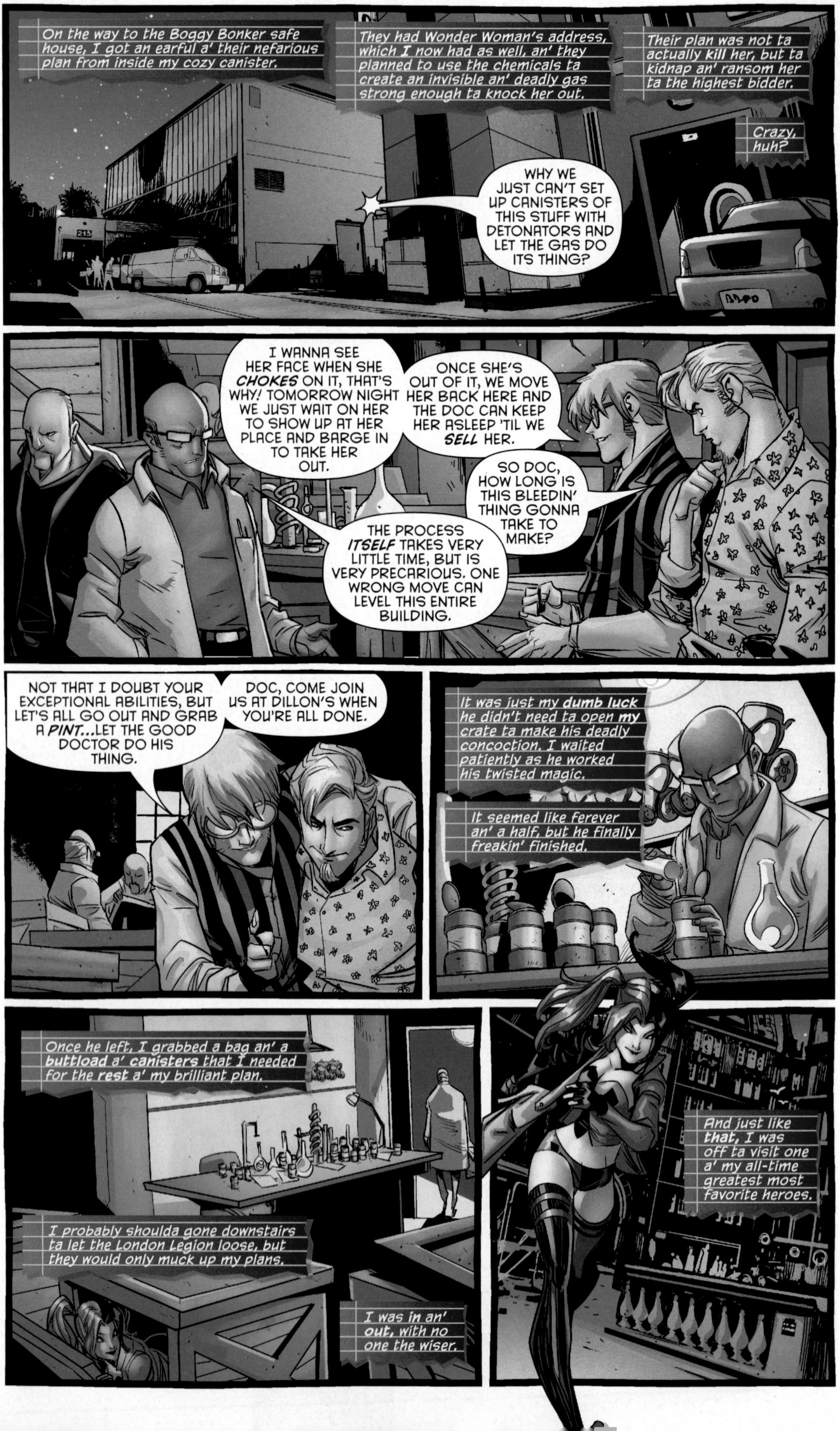

On the way to the Boggy Bonker safe house, I got an earful a' their nefarious plan from inside my cozy canister.
They had Wonder Woman's address, which I now had as well, an' they planned to use the chemicals ta create an invisible an' deadly gas strong enough ta knock her out.
Their plan was not ta actually kill her, but ta kidnap an' ransom her ta the highest bidder.
Crazy, huh?
WHY WE JUST CAN'T SET UP CANISTERS OF THIS STUFF WITH DETONATORS AND LET THE GAS DO ITS THING?
I WANNA SEE HER FACE WHEN SHE CHOKES ON IT, THAT'S WHY! TOMORROW NIGHT WE JUST WAIT ON HER TO SHOW UP AT HER PLACE AND BARGE IN TO TAKE HER OUT.
ONCE SHE'S OUT OF IT, WE MOVE HER BACK HERE AND THE DOC CAN KEEP HER ASLEEP 'TIL WE SELL HER.
SO DOC, HOW LONG IS THIS BLEEDIN' THING GONNA TAKE TO MAKE?
THE PROCESS ITSELF TAKES VERY LITTLE TIME, BUT IS VERY PRECARIOUS. ONE WRONG MOVE CAN LEVEL THIS ENTIRE BUILDING.
NOT THAT I DOUBT YOUR EXCEPTIONAL ABILITIES, BUT LET'S ALL GO OUT AND GRAB A PINT...LET THE GOOD DOCTOR DO HIS THING.
DOC, COME JOIN US AT DILLON'S WHEN YOU'RE ALL DONE.
It was just my dumb luck he didn't need ta open my crate ta make his deadly concoction. I waited patiently as he worked his twisted magic.
It seemed like ferever an' a half, but he finally freakin' finished.
Once he left, I grabbed a bag an' a buttload a' canisters that I needed for the rest a' my brilliant plan.
I probably shoulda gone downstairs ta let the London Legion loose, but they would only muck up my plans.
I was in an' out, with no one the wiser.
And just like that, I was off ta visit one a' my all-time greatest most favorite heroes.

HOME INVASION

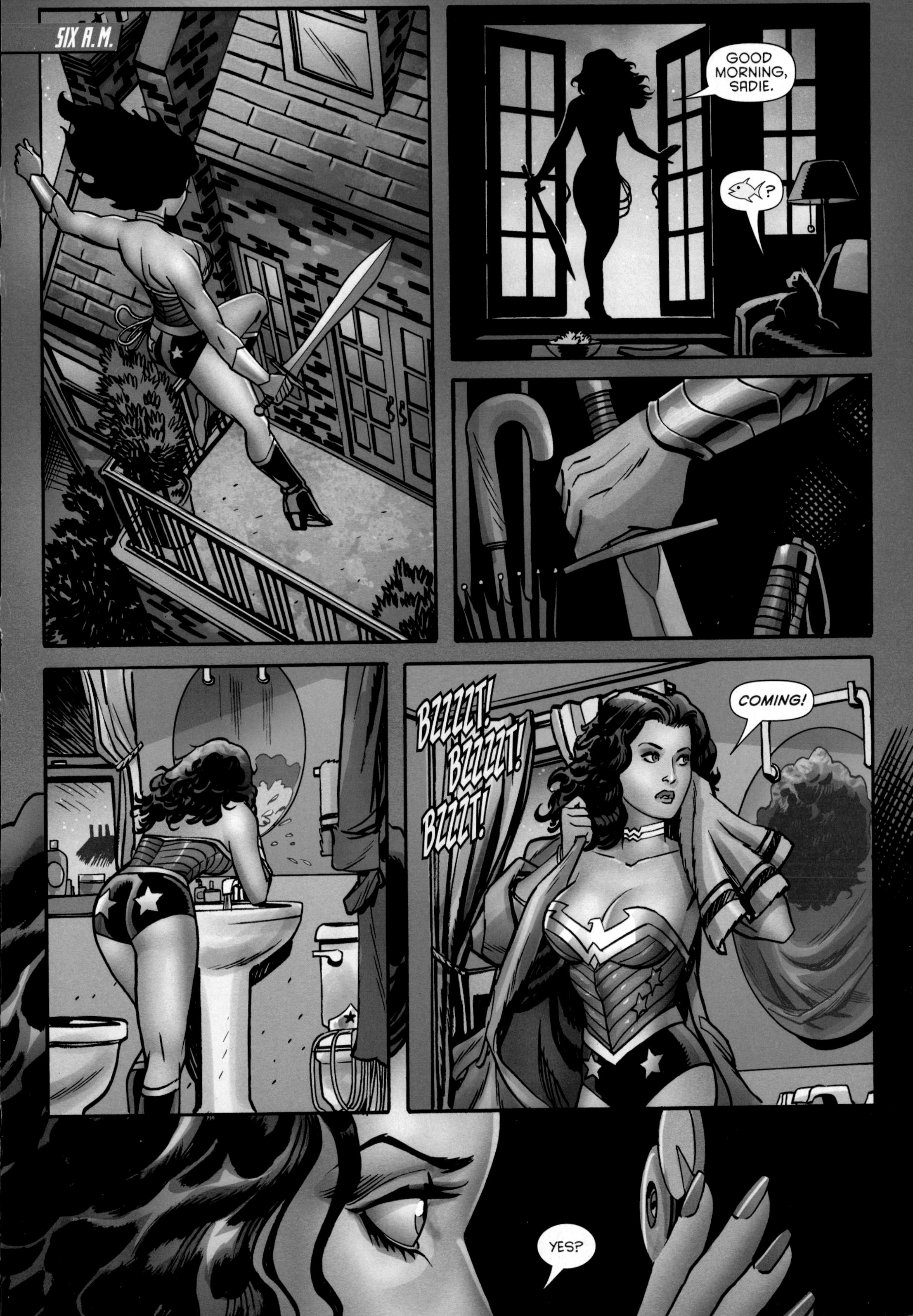
SIX A.M.
GOOD MORNING, SADIE.
?
BZZZZT! BZZZZT! BZZZT!
COMING!
YES?

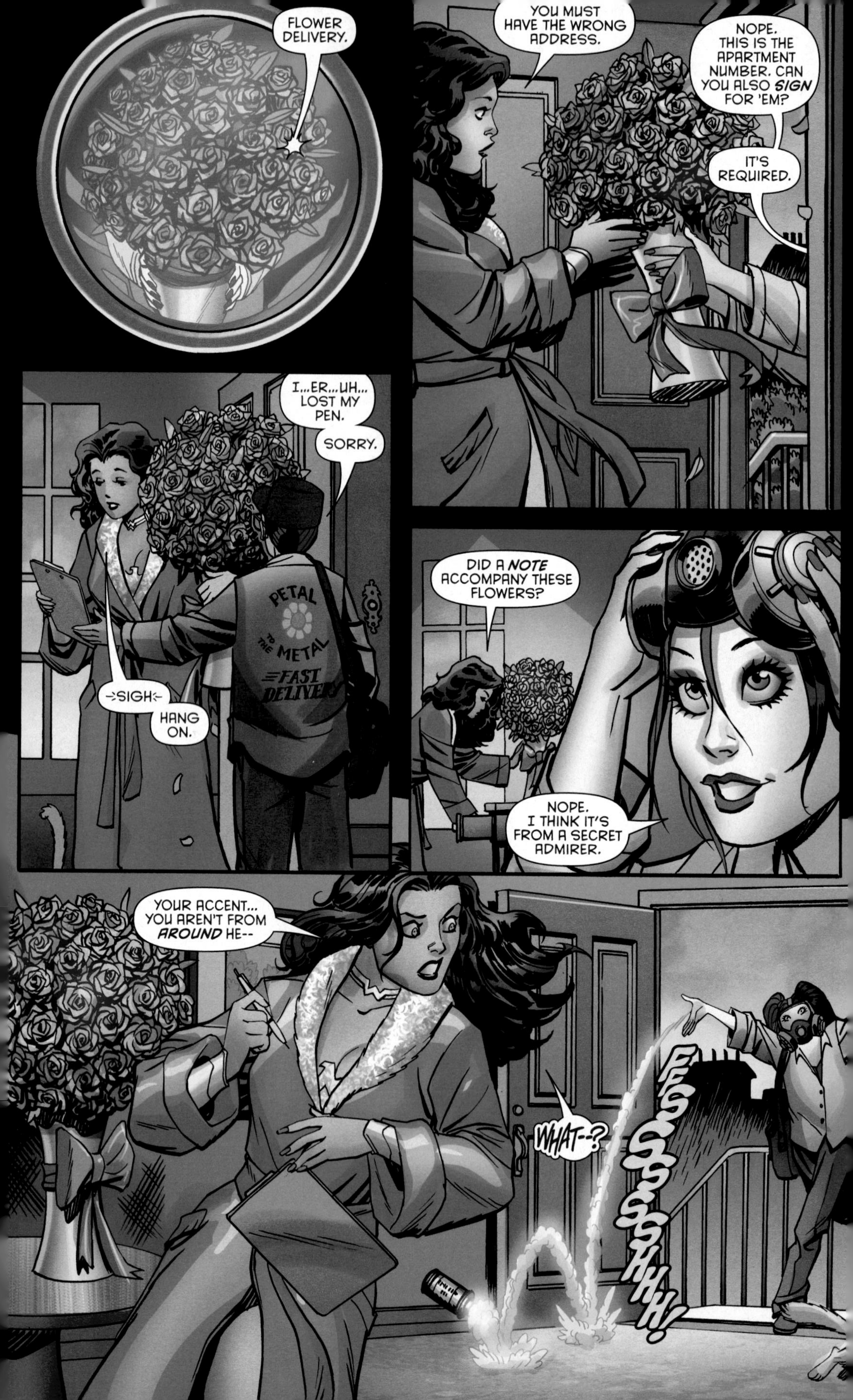
FLOWER DELIVERY.
YOU MUST HAVE THE WRONG ADDRESS.
NOPE. THIS IS THE APARTMENT NUMBER. CAN YOU ALSO SIGN FOR 'EM?
IT'S REQUIRED.
I...ER...UH... LOST MY PEN.
SORRY.
PETAL TO THE METAL
FAST DELIVERY
SIGH
HANG ON.
DID A NOTE ACCOMPANY THESE FLOWERS?
NOPE. I THINK IT'S FROM A SECRET ADMIRER.
YOUR ACCENT... YOU AREN'T FROM AROUND HE--
WHAT--?
FFSSSSSHHH!

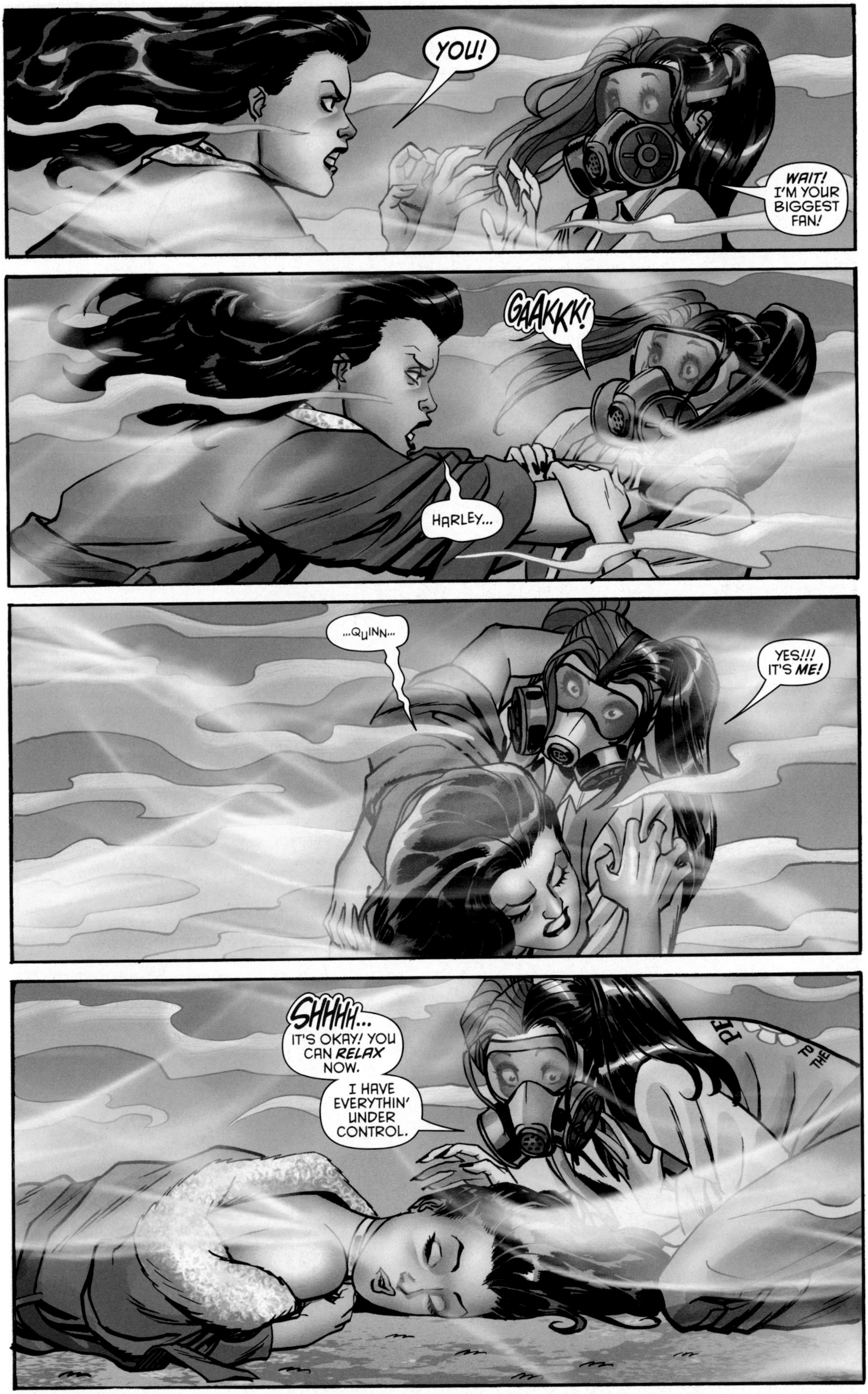
YOU!
WAIT! I'M YOUR BIGGEST FAN!
GAAKKK!
HARLEY...
...QUINN...
YES!!! IT'S ME!
SHHHH... IT'S OKAY! YOU CAN RELAX NOW.
I HAVE EVERYTHIN' UNDER CONTROL.

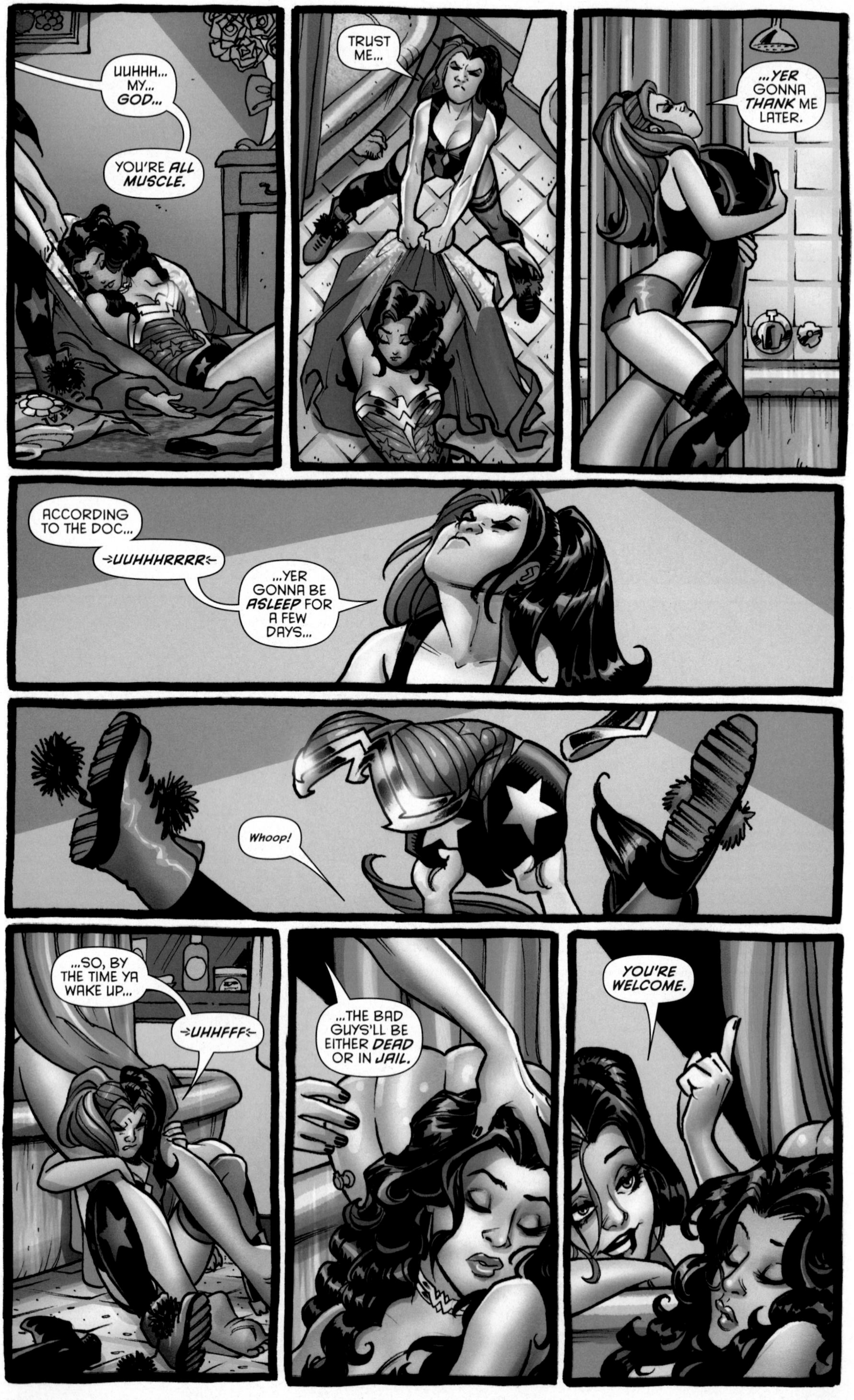
UUHHH... MY... GOD...
YOU'RE ALL MUSCLE.
TRUST ME...
...YER GONNA THANK ME LATER.
ACCORDING TO THE DOC...
UUHHHRRRR
...YER GONNA BE ASLEEP FOR A FEW DAYS...
Whoop!
...SO, BY THE TIME YA WAKE UP...
UHHFFF
...THE BAD GUYS'LL BE EITHER DEAD OR IN JAIL.
YOU'RE WELCOME.

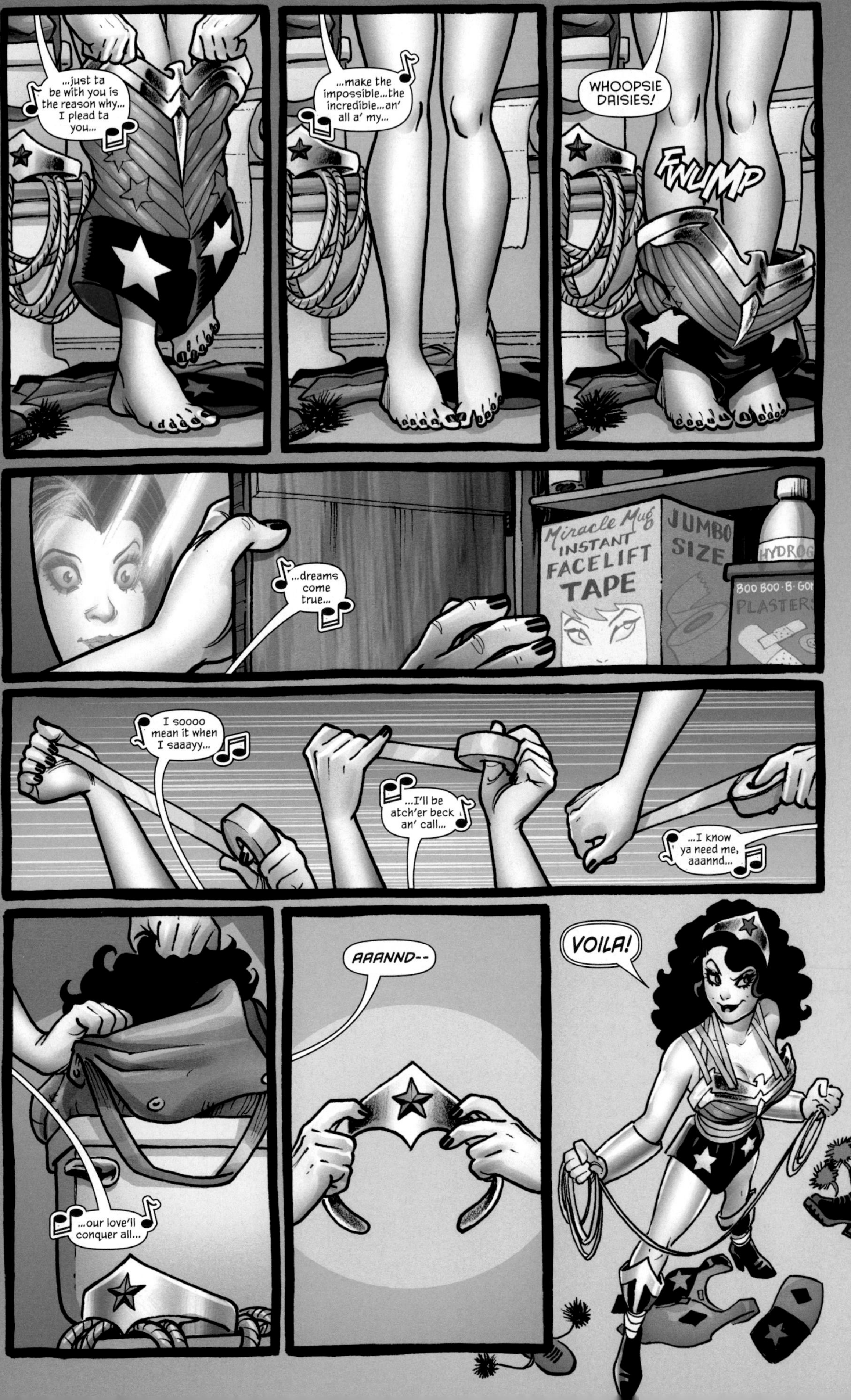
...just ta be with you is the reason why... I plead ta you...
...make the impossible...the incredible...an' all a' my...
WHOOPSIE DAISIES!
FWUMP
...dreams come true...
Miracle Mug INSTANT FACELIFT TAPE
JUMBO SIZE
HYDROG
BOO BOO-B-GO
PLASTERS
I soooo mean it when I saaayy...
...I'll be atch'er beck an' call...
...I know ya need me, aaannd...
...our love'll conquer all...
AAANND--
VOILA!

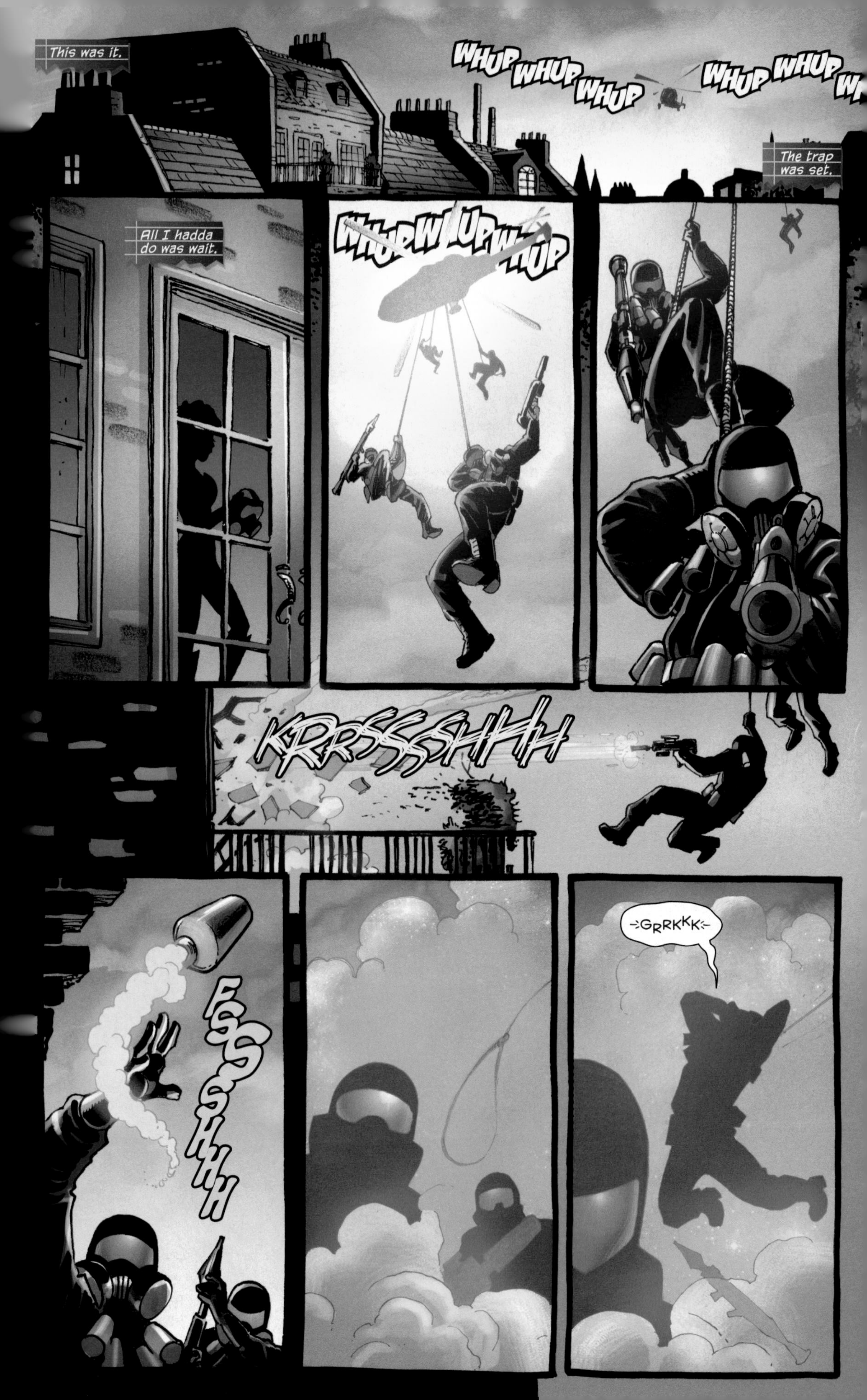
This was it.
WHUP WHUP WHUP
WHUP WHUP WH
The trap was set.
All I hadda do was wait.
WHUP WHUP WHUP
KRRSSSSHHH
FSSSHHHH
GRRKKK

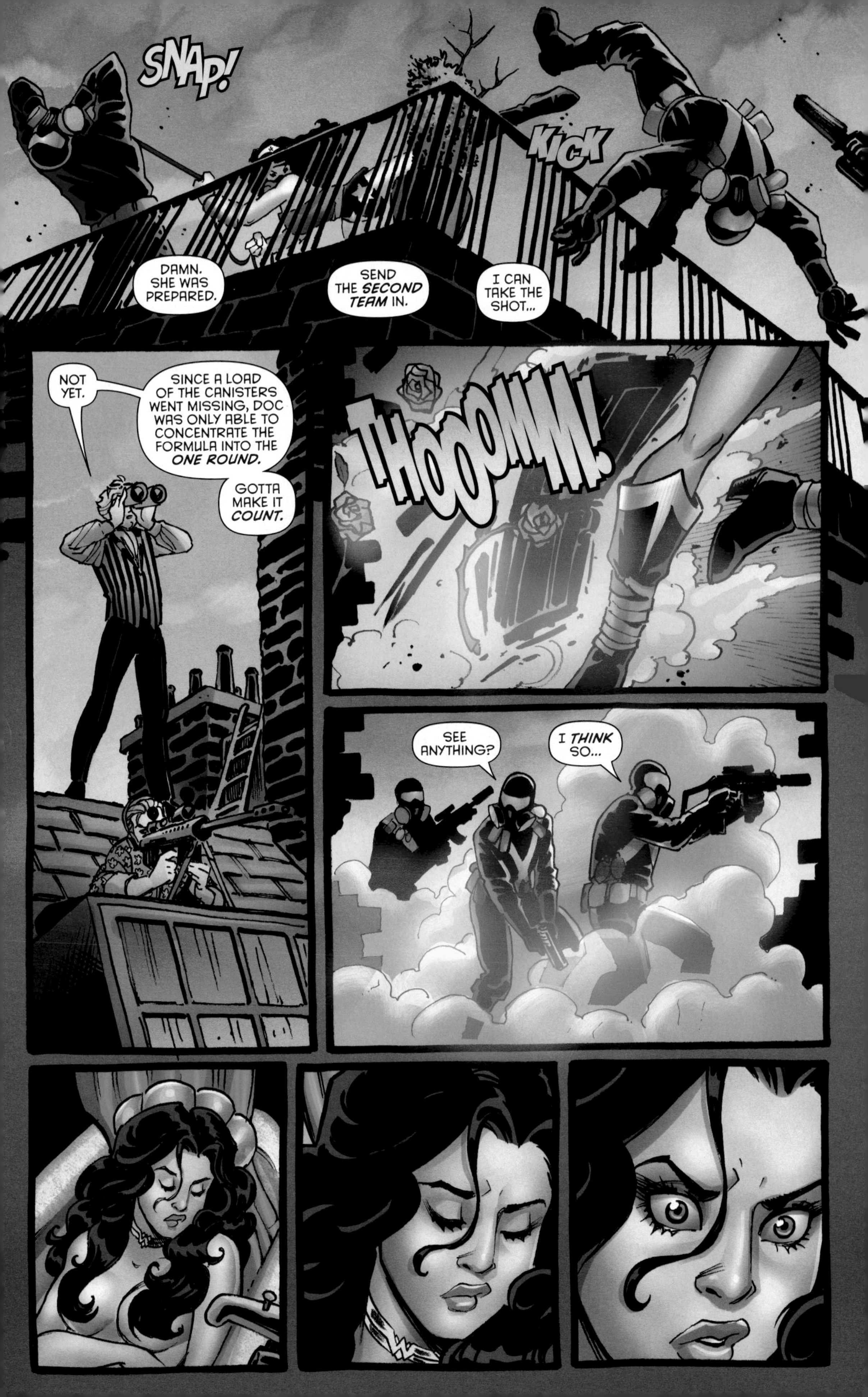
SNAP!
KICK
DAMN. SHE WAS PREPARED.
SEND THE *SECOND TEAM* IN.
I CAN TAKE THE SHOT...
NOT YET.
SINCE A LOAD OF THE CANISTERS WENT MISSING, DOC WAS ONLY ABLE TO CONCENTRATE THE FORMULA INTO THE *ONE ROUND.*
GOTTA MAKE IT *COUNT.*
THOOOMMM!
SEE ANYTHING?
I *THINK* SO...

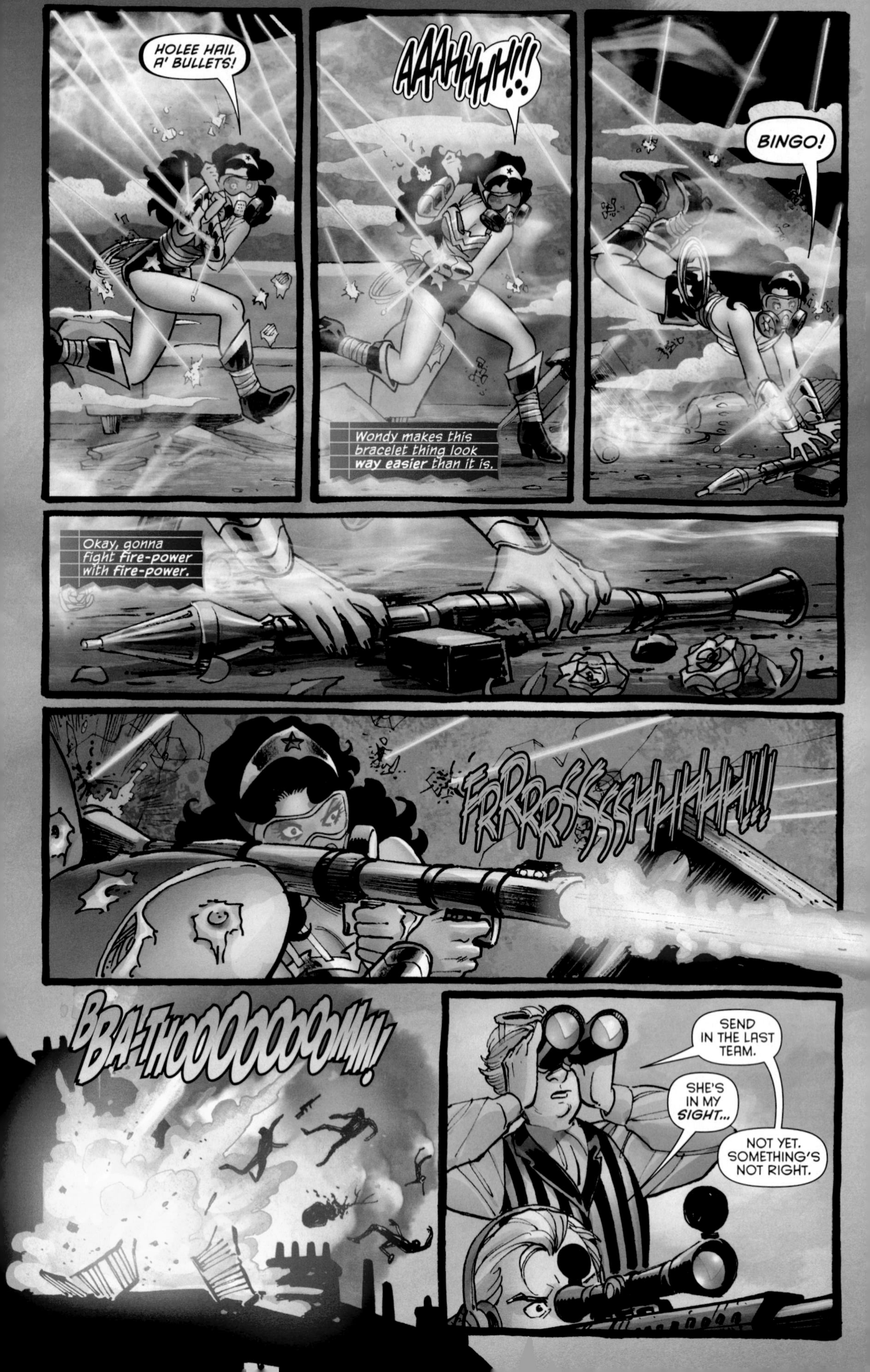
HOLEE HAIL A' BULLETS!
AAAHHHH!!!
Wondy makes this bracelet thing look way easier than it is.
BINGO!
Okay, gonna fight fire-power with fire-power.
FRRRRSSSSSHHHHHH!!
BBA-THOOOOOOOOMM!
SEND IN THE LAST TEAM.
SHE'S IN MY SIGHT...
NOT YET. SOMETHING'S NOT RIGHT.

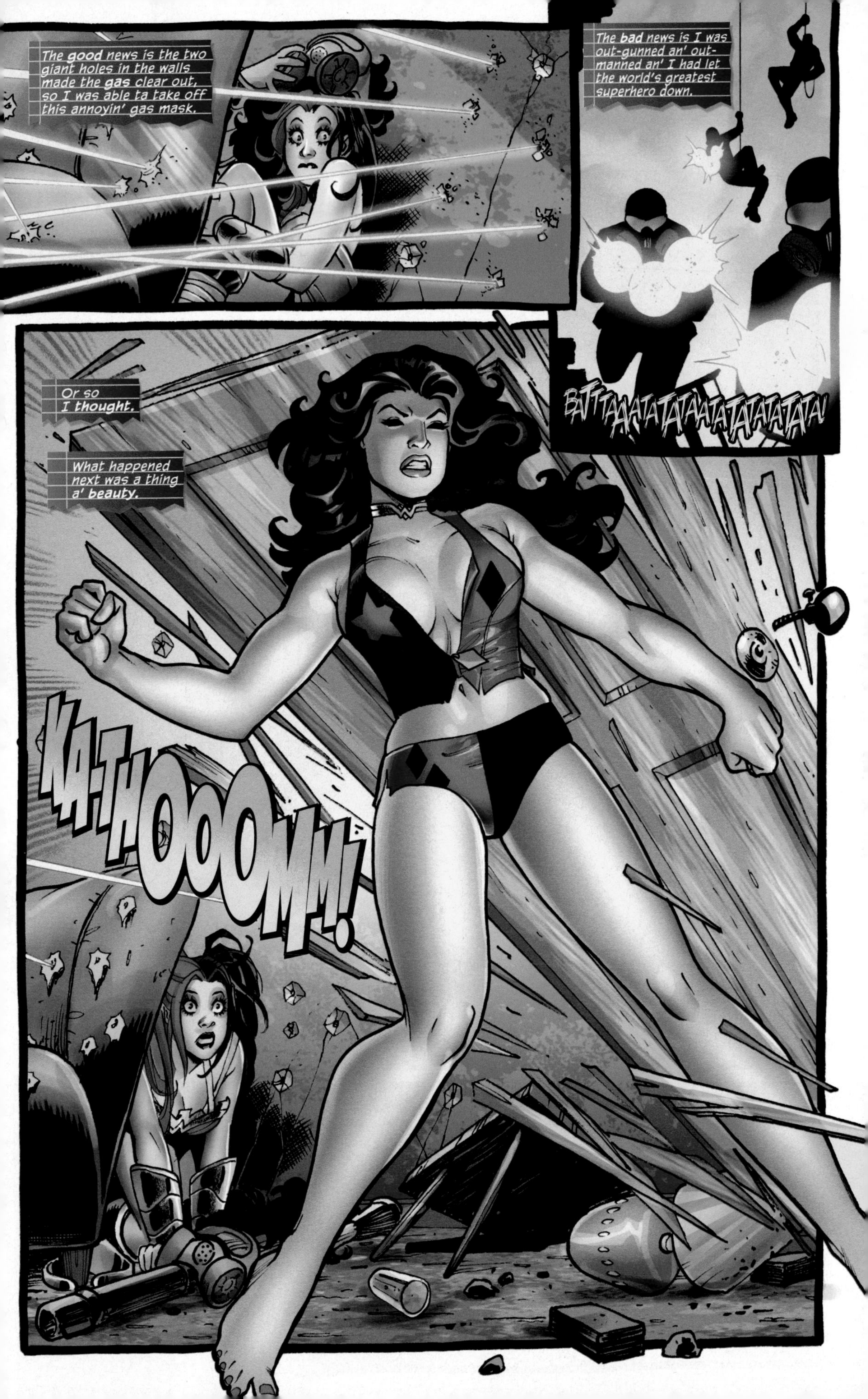
The good news is the two giant holes in the walls made the gas clear out, so I was able ta take off this annoyin' gas mask.
The bad news is I was out-gunned an' out-manned an' I had let the world's greatest superhero down.
BATTTAAATATATAATATATATATATA!
Or so I thought.
What happened next was a thing a' beauty.
KA-THOOOMM!

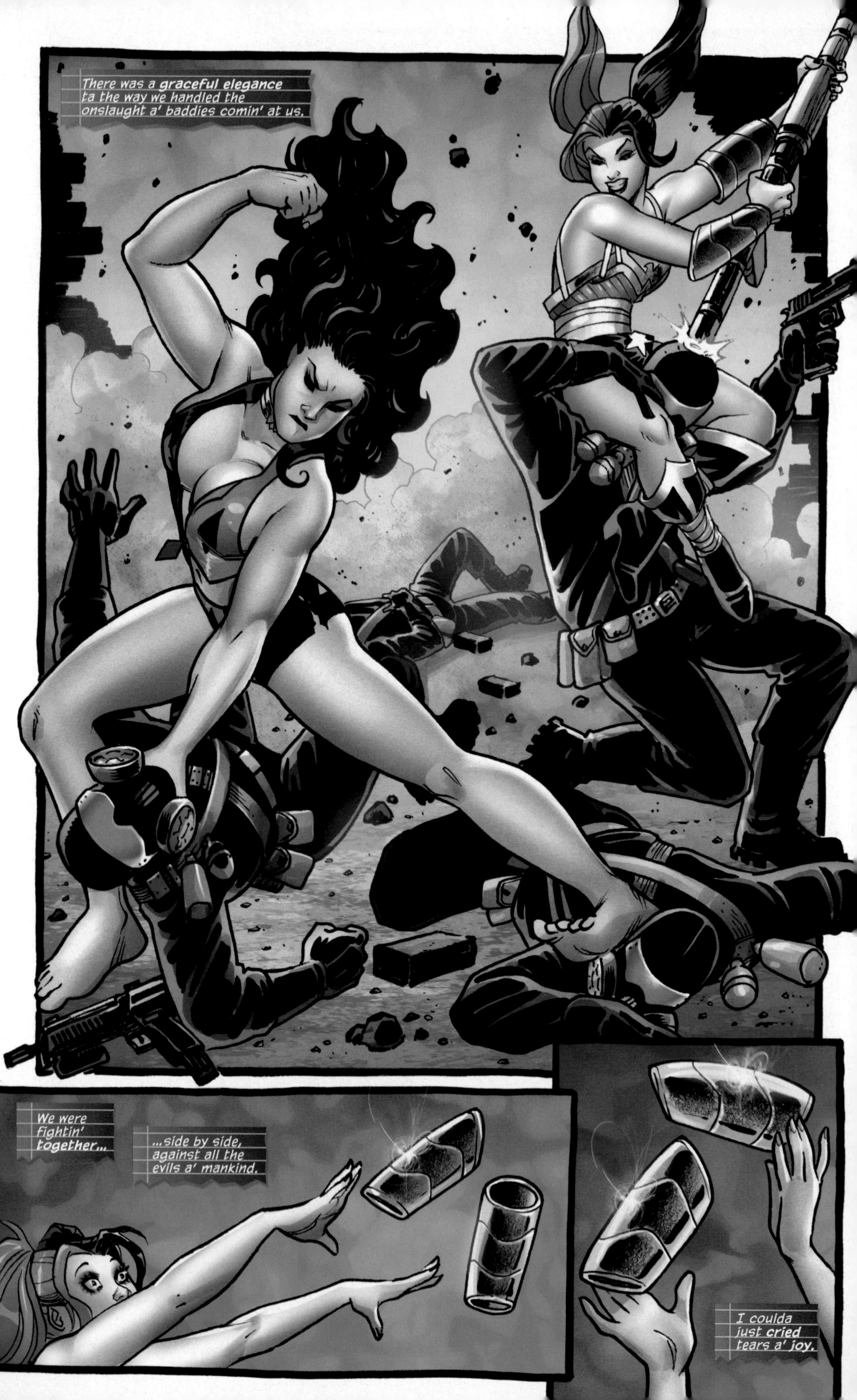
There was a graceful elegance ta the way we handled the onslaught a' baddies comin' at us.
We were fightin' together...
...side by side, against all the evils a' mankind.
I coulda just cried tears a' joy.

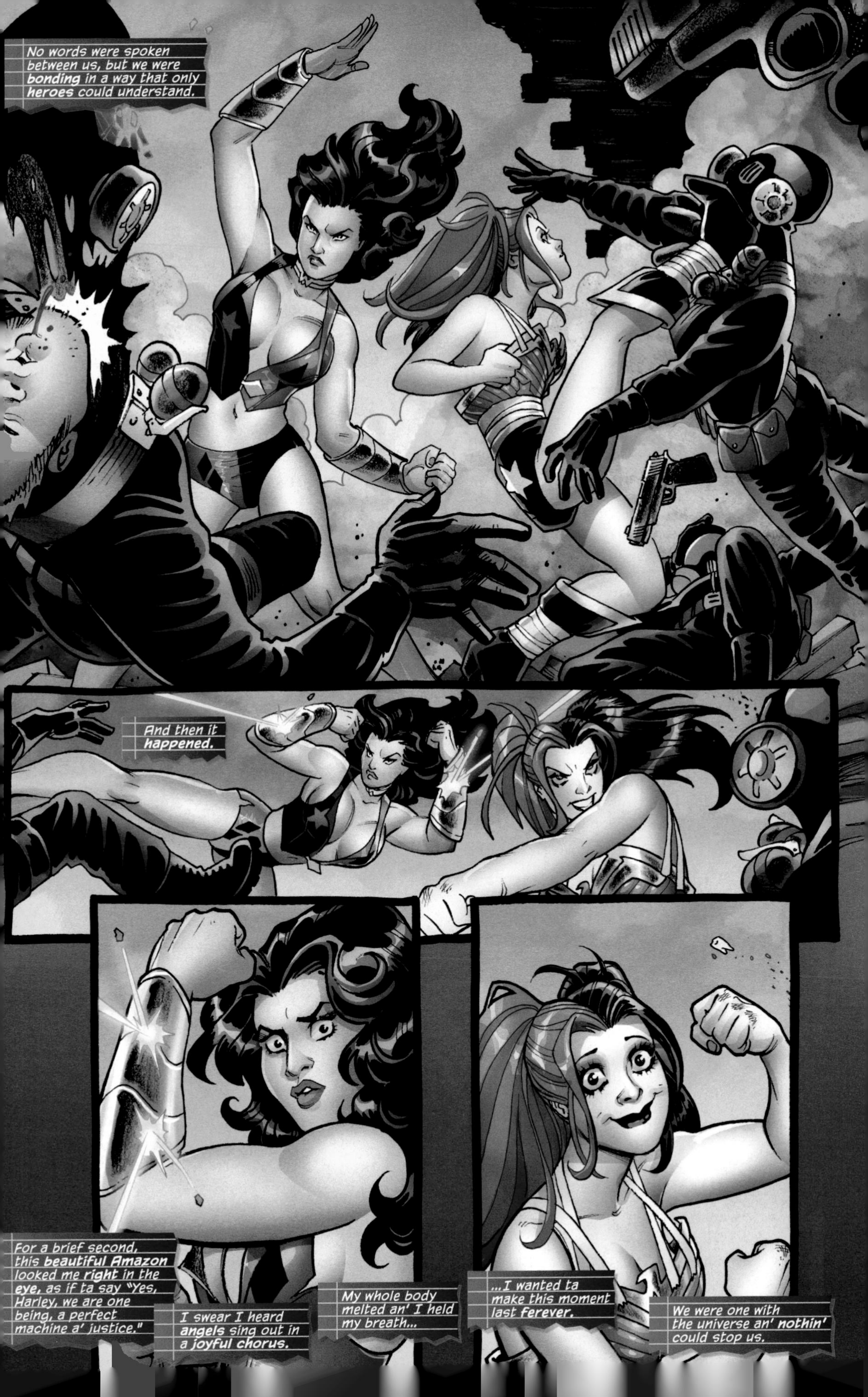
No words were spoken between us, but we were bonding in a way that only heroes could understand.
And then it happened.
For a brief second, this beautiful Amazon looked me right in the eye, as if ta say "Yes, Harley, we are one being, a perfect machine a' justice."
I swear I heard angels sing out in a joyful chorus.
My whole body melted an' I held my breath...
...I wanted ta make this moment last ferever.
We were one with the universe an' nothin' could stop us.

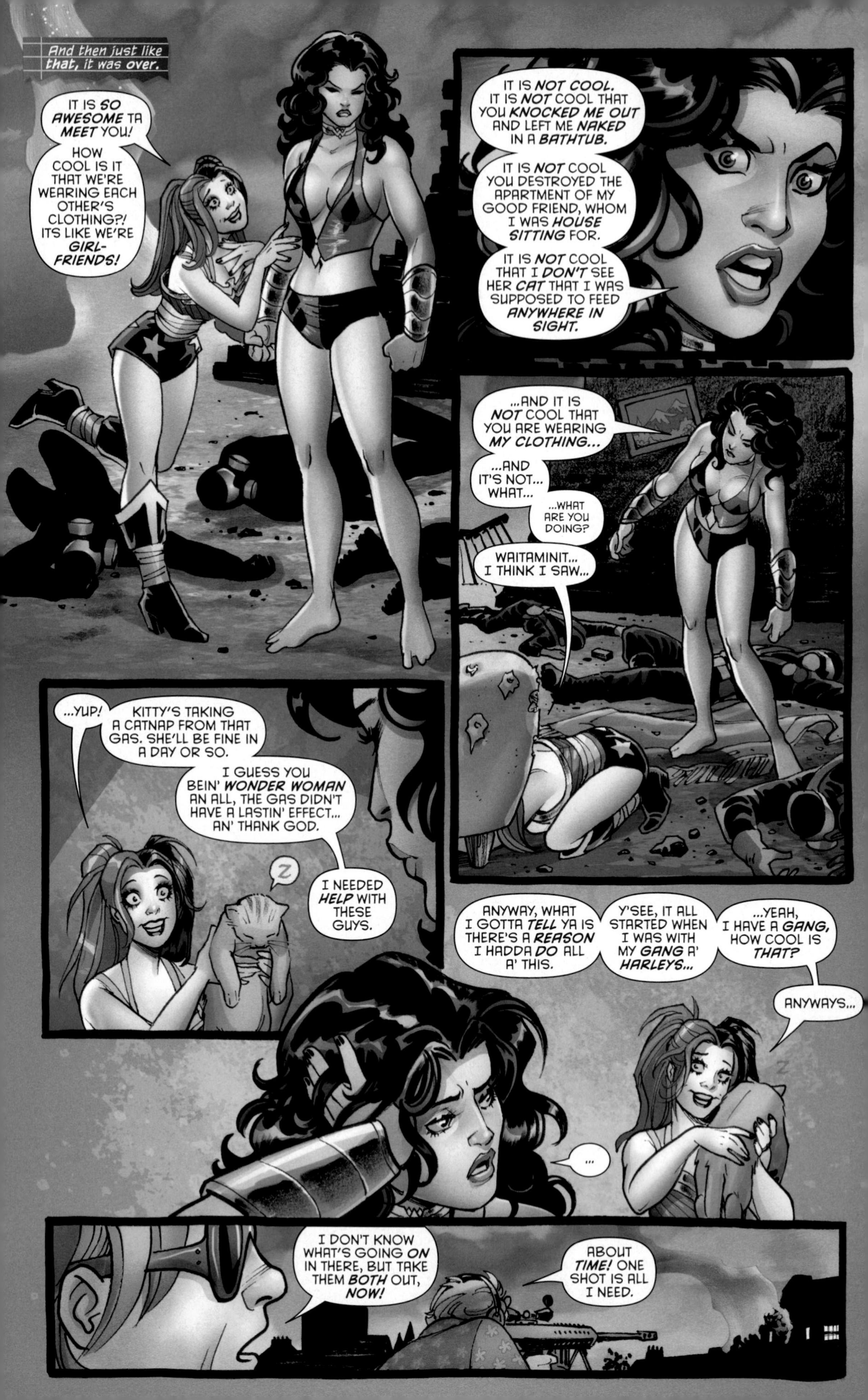
And then just like that, it was over.
IT IS SO AWESOME TA MEET YOU!
HOW COOL IS IT THAT WE'RE WEARING EACH OTHER'S CLOTHING?! ITS LIKE WE'RE GIRL-FRIENDS!
IT IS NOT COOL. IT IS NOT COOL THAT YOU KNOCKED ME OUT AND LEFT ME NAKED IN A BATHTUB.
IT IS NOT COOL YOU DESTROYED THE APARTMENT OF MY GOOD FRIEND, WHOM I WAS HOUSE SITTING FOR.
IT IS NOT COOL THAT I DON'T SEE HER CAT THAT I WAS SUPPOSED TO FEED ANYWHERE IN SIGHT.
...AND IT IS NOT COOL THAT YOU ARE WEARING MY CLOTHING...
...AND IT'S NOT... WHAT...
...WHAT ARE YOU DOING?
WAITAMINIT... I THINK I SAW...
...YUP!
KITTY'S TAKING A CATNAP FROM THAT GAS. SHE'LL BE FINE IN A DAY OR SO.
I GUESS YOU BEIN' WONDER WOMAN AN ALL, THE GAS DIDN'T HAVE A LASTIN' EFFECT... AN' THANK GOD.
I NEEDED HELP WITH THESE GUYS.
Z
ANYWAY, WHAT I GOTTA TELL YA IS THERE'S A REASON I HADDA DO ALL A' THIS.
Y'SEE, IT ALL STARTED WHEN I WAS WITH MY GANG A' HARLEYS...
...YEAH, I HAVE A GANG, HOW COOL IS THAT?
ANYWAYS...
...
I DON'T KNOW WHAT'S GOING ON IN THERE, BUT TAKE THEM BOTH OUT, NOW!
ABOUT TIME! ONE SHOT IS ALL I NEED.

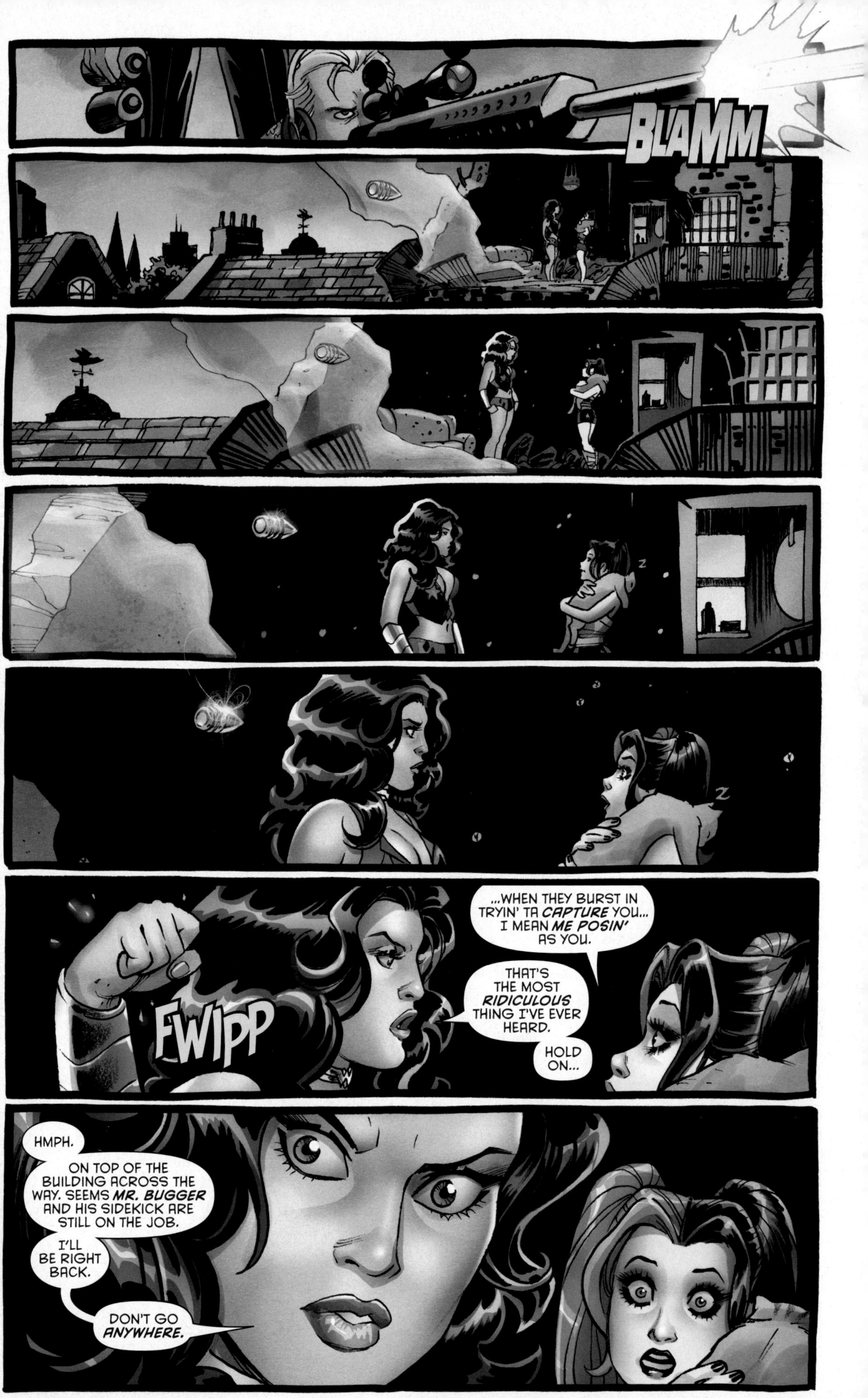
BLAMM
FWIPP
...WHEN THEY BURST IN TRYIN' TA CAPTURE YOU... I MEAN ME POSIN' AS YOU.
THAT'S THE MOST RIDICULOUS THING I'VE EVER HEARD.
HOLD ON...
HMPH.
ON TOP OF THE BUILDING ACROSS THE WAY. SEEMS MR. BUGGER AND HIS SIDEKICK ARE STILL ON THE JOB.
I'LL BE RIGHT BACK.
DON'T GO ANYWHERE.

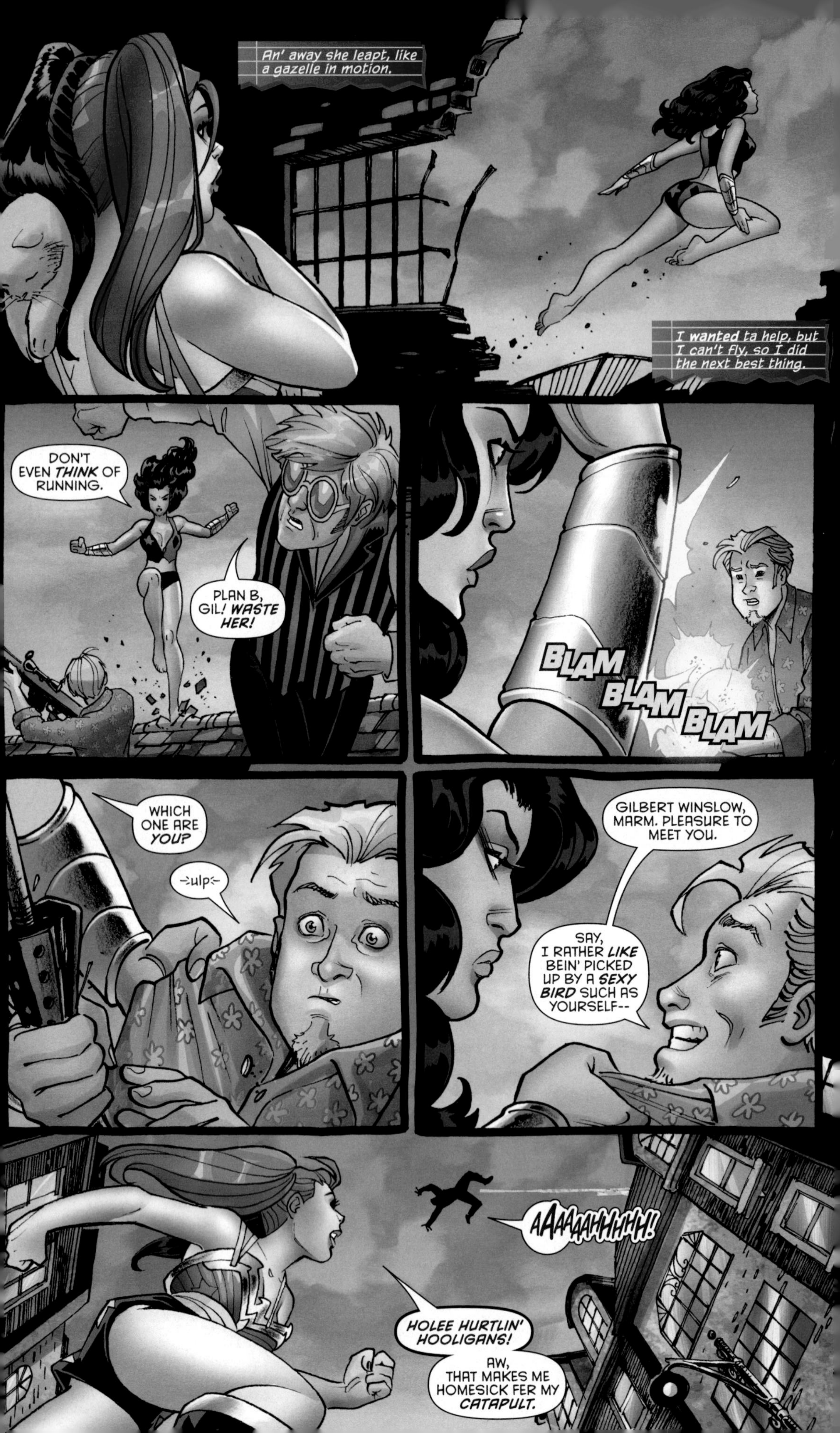
An' away she leapt, like a gazelle in motion.
I wanted ta help, but I can't fly, so I did the next best thing.
DON'T EVEN THINK OF RUNNING.
PLAN B, GIL! WASTE HER!
BLAM
BLAM
BLAM
WHICH ONE ARE YOU?
-ulp-
GILBERT WINSLOW, MARM. PLEASURE TO MEET YOU.
SAY, I RATHER LIKE BEIN' PICKED UP BY A SEXY BIRD SUCH AS YOURSELF--
AAAAAAHHHHHH!
HOLEE HURTLIN' HOOLIGANS!
AW, THAT MAKES ME HOMESICK FER MY CATAPULT.

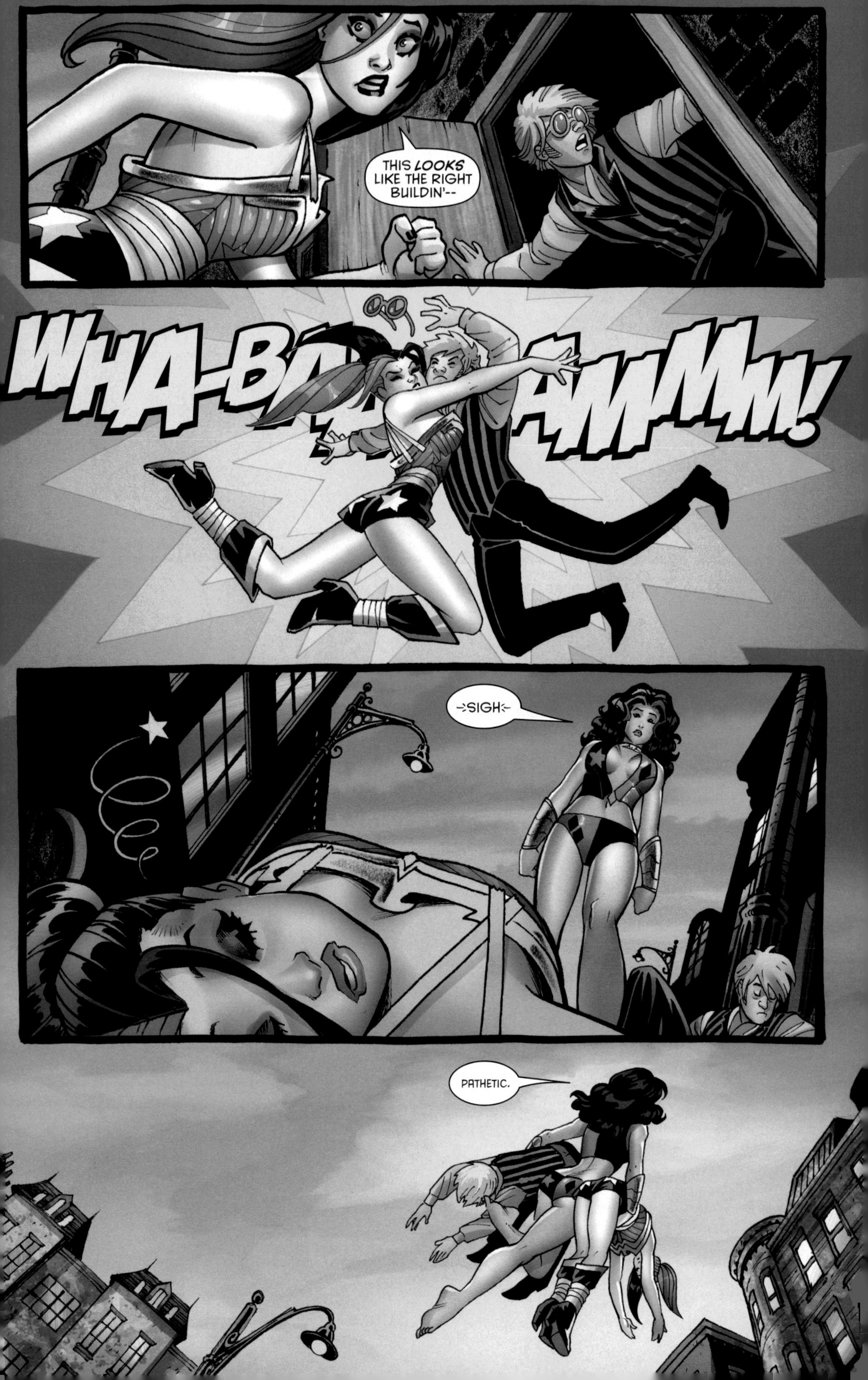
THIS LOOKS LIKE THE RIGHT BUILDIN'--
WHA-BAMMMM!
-SIGH-
PATHETIC.

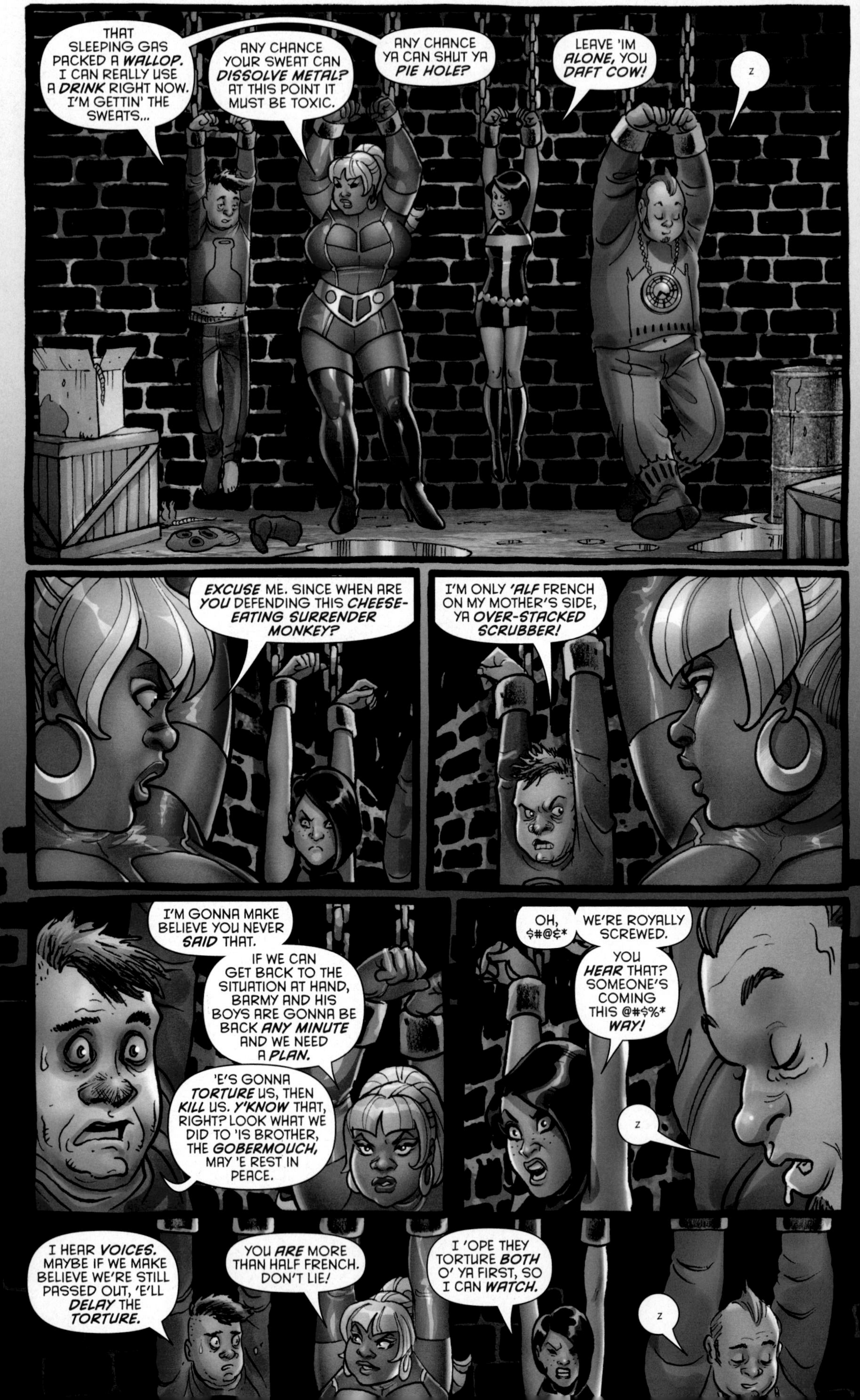
THAT SLEEPING GAS PACKED A WALLOP. I CAN REALLY USE A DRINK RIGHT NOW. I'M GETTIN' THE SWEATS...
ANY CHANCE YOUR SWEAT CAN DISSOLVE METAL? AT THIS POINT IT MUST BE TOXIC.
ANY CHANCE YA CAN SHUT YA PIE HOLE?
LEAVE 'IM ALONE, YOU DAFT COW!
Z
EXCUSE ME. SINCE WHEN ARE YOU DEFENDING THIS CHEESE-EATING SURRENDER MONKEY?
I'M ONLY 'ALF FRENCH ON MY MOTHER'S SIDE, YA OVER-STACKED SCRUBBER!
I'M GONNA MAKE BELIEVE YOU NEVER SAID THAT.
IF WE CAN GET BACK TO THE SITUATION AT HAND, BARMY AND HIS BOYS ARE GONNA BE BACK ANY MINUTE AND WE NEED A PLAN.
'E'S GONNA TORTURE US, THEN KILL US. Y'KNOW THAT, RIGHT? LOOK WHAT WE DID TO 'IS BROTHER, THE GOBERMOUCH, MAY 'E REST IN PEACE.
OH, $#@&*
WE'RE ROYALLY SCREWED.
YOU HEAR THAT? SOMEONE'S COMING THIS @#$%* WAY!
Z
I HEAR VOICES. MAYBE IF WE MAKE BELIEVE WE'RE STILL PASSED OUT, 'E'LL DELAY THE TORTURE.
YOU ARE MORE THAN HALF FRENCH. DON'T LIE!
I 'OPE THEY TORTURE BOTH O' YA FIRST, SO I CAN WATCH.
Z

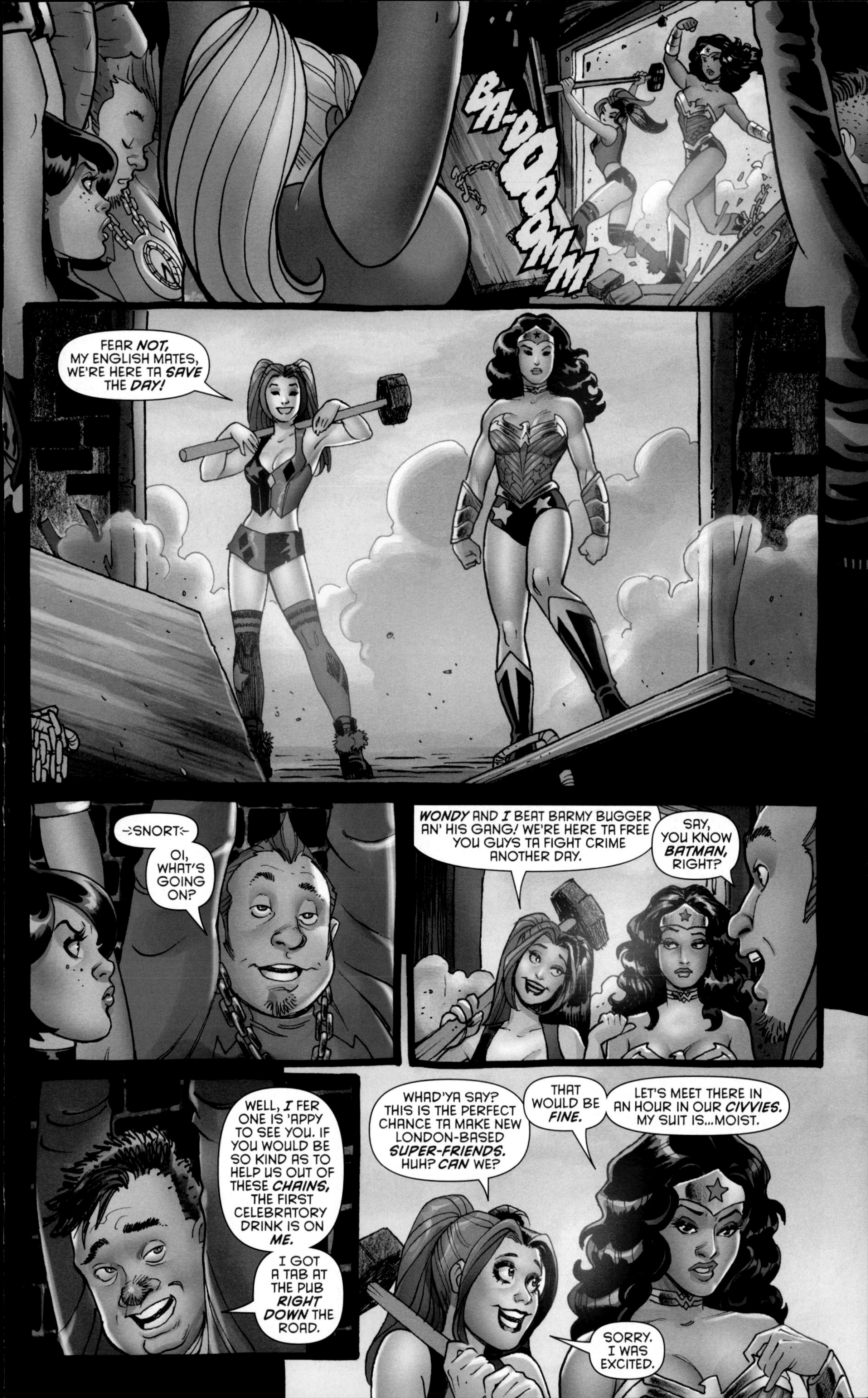

BA-DOOOOMM
FEAR NOT, MY ENGLISH MATES, WE'RE HERE TA SAVE THE DAY!
-SNORT-
OI, WHAT'S GOING ON?
WONDY AND I BEAT BARMY BUGGER AN' HIS GANG! WE'RE HERE TA FREE YOU GUYS TA FIGHT CRIME ANOTHER DAY.
SAY, YOU KNOW BATMAN, RIGHT?
WELL, I FER ONE IS 'APPY TO SEE YOU. IF YOU WOULD BE SO KIND AS TO HELP US OUT OF THESE CHAINS, THE FIRST CELEBRATORY DRINK IS ON ME.
I GOT A TAB AT THE PUB RIGHT DOWN THE ROAD.
WHAD'YA SAY? THIS IS THE PERFECT CHANCE TA MAKE NEW LONDON-BASED SUPER-FRIENDS. HUH? CAN WE?
THAT WOULD BE FINE.
LET'S MEET THERE IN AN HOUR IN OUR CIVVIES. MY SUIT IS...MOIST.
SORRY. I WAS EXCITED.

THE BRITISH INQUISITION

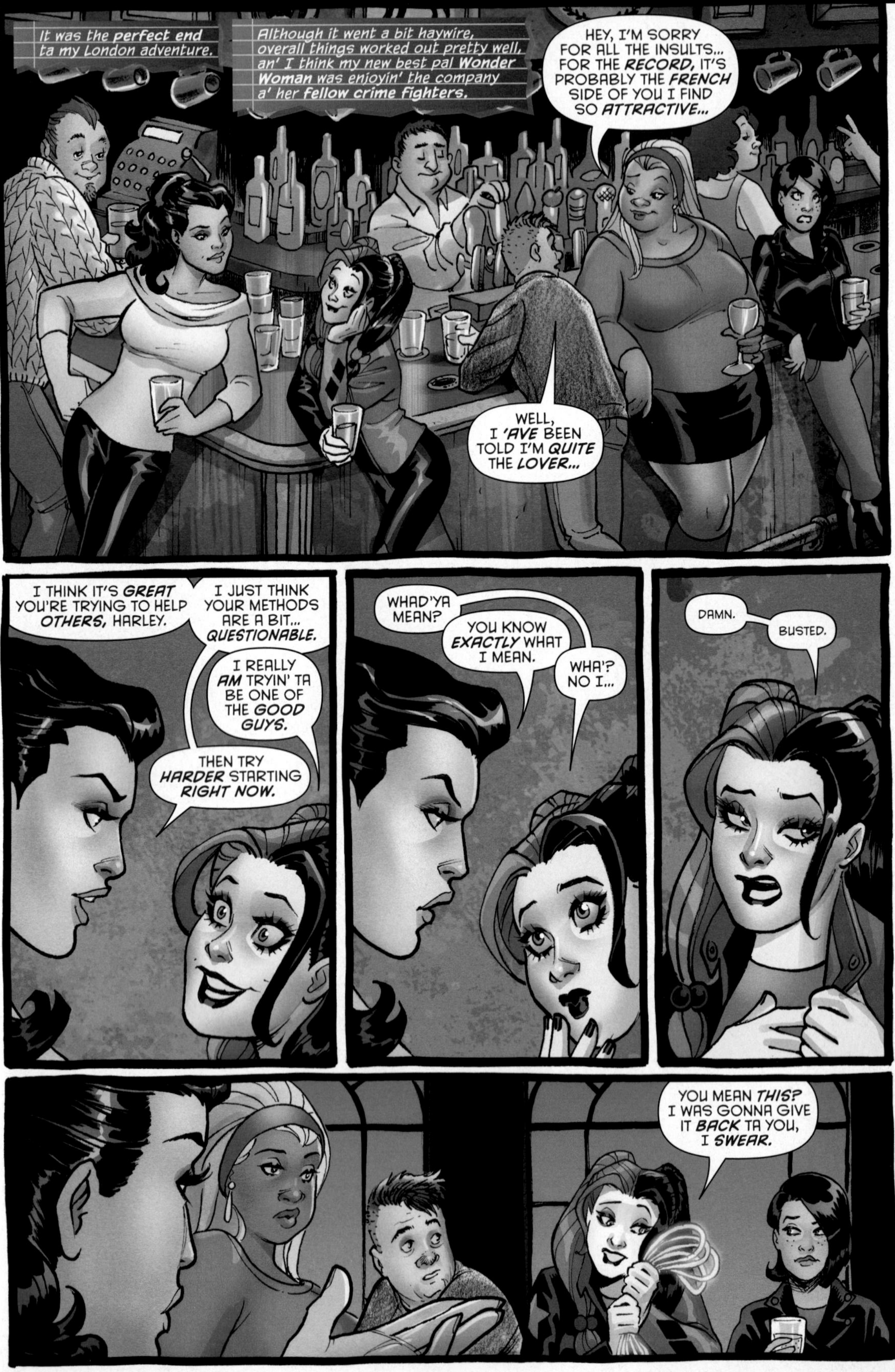

It was the perfect end ta my London adventure.
Although it went a bit haywire, overall things worked out pretty well, an' I think my new best pal Wonder Woman was enjoyin' the company a' her fellow crime fighters.
HEY, I'M SORRY FOR ALL THE INSULTS... FOR THE RECORD, IT'S PROBABLY THE FRENCH SIDE OF YOU I FIND SO ATTRACTIVE...
WELL, I 'AVE BEEN TOLD I'M QUITE THE LOVER...
I THINK IT'S GREAT YOU'RE TRYING TO HELP OTHERS, HARLEY.
I JUST THINK YOUR METHODS ARE A BIT... QUESTIONABLE.
I REALLY AM TRYIN' TA BE ONE OF THE GOOD GUYS.
THEN TRY HARDER STARTING RIGHT NOW.
WHAD'YA MEAN?
YOU KNOW EXACTLY WHAT I MEAN.
WHA'? NO I...
DAMN.
BUSTED.
YOU MEAN THIS? I WAS GONNA GIVE IT BACK TA YOU, I SWEAR.

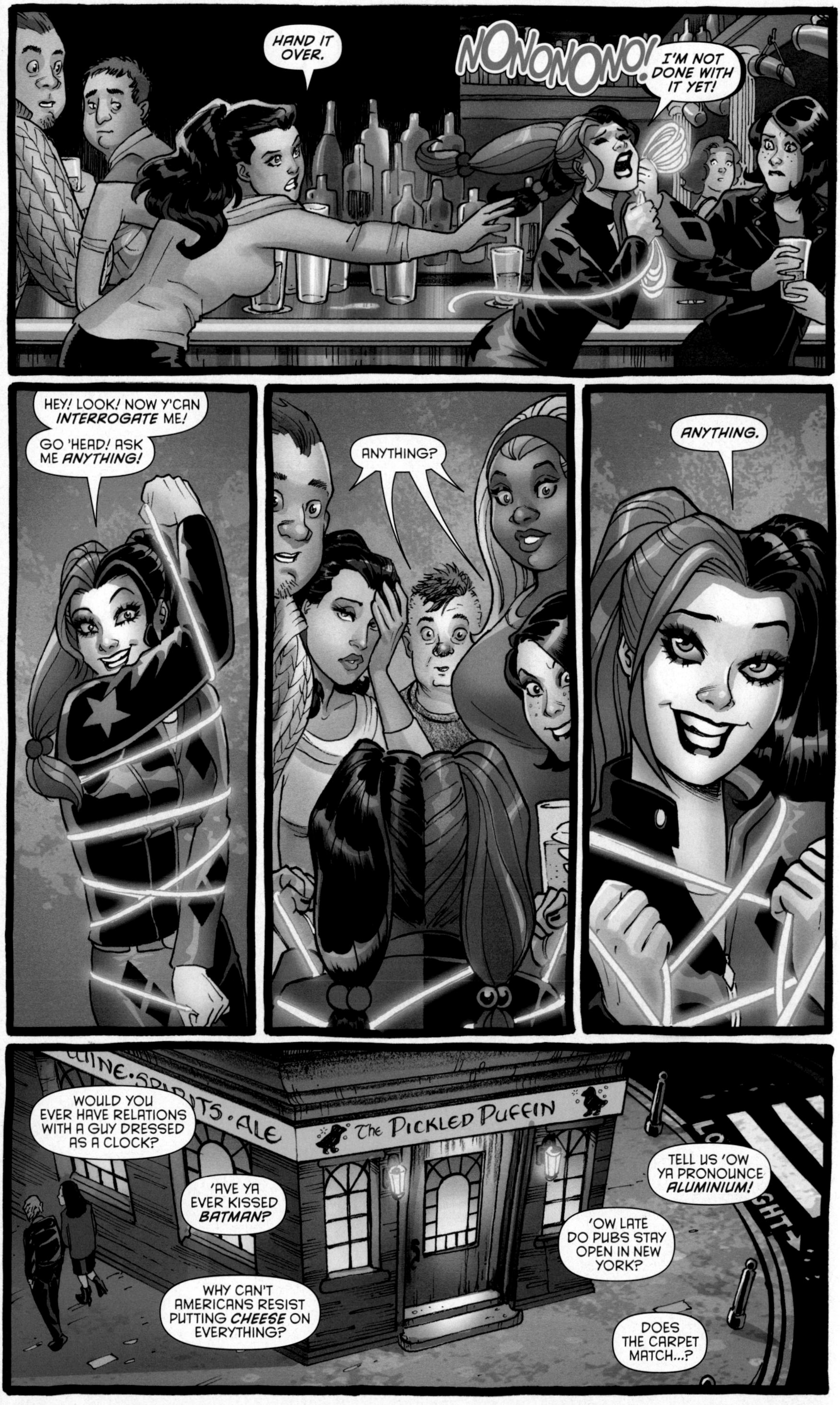

HAND IT OVER.
NONONONONO!
I'M NOT DONE WITH IT YET!
HEY! LOOK! NOW Y'CAN INTERROGATE ME!
GO 'HEAD! ASK ME ANYTHING!
ANYTHING?
ANYTHING.
WINE • SPIRITS • ALE
The PICKLED PUFFIN
WOULD YOU EVER HAVE RELATIONS WITH A GUY DRESSED AS A CLOCK?
'AVE YA EVER KISSED BATMAN?
WHY CAN'T AMERICANS RESIST PUTTING CHEESE ON EVERYTHING?
TELL US 'OW YA PRONOUNCE ALUMINIUM!
'OW LATE DO PUBS STAY OPEN IN NEW YORK?
DOES THE CARPET MATCH...?

AND BOB'S YOUR UNCLE

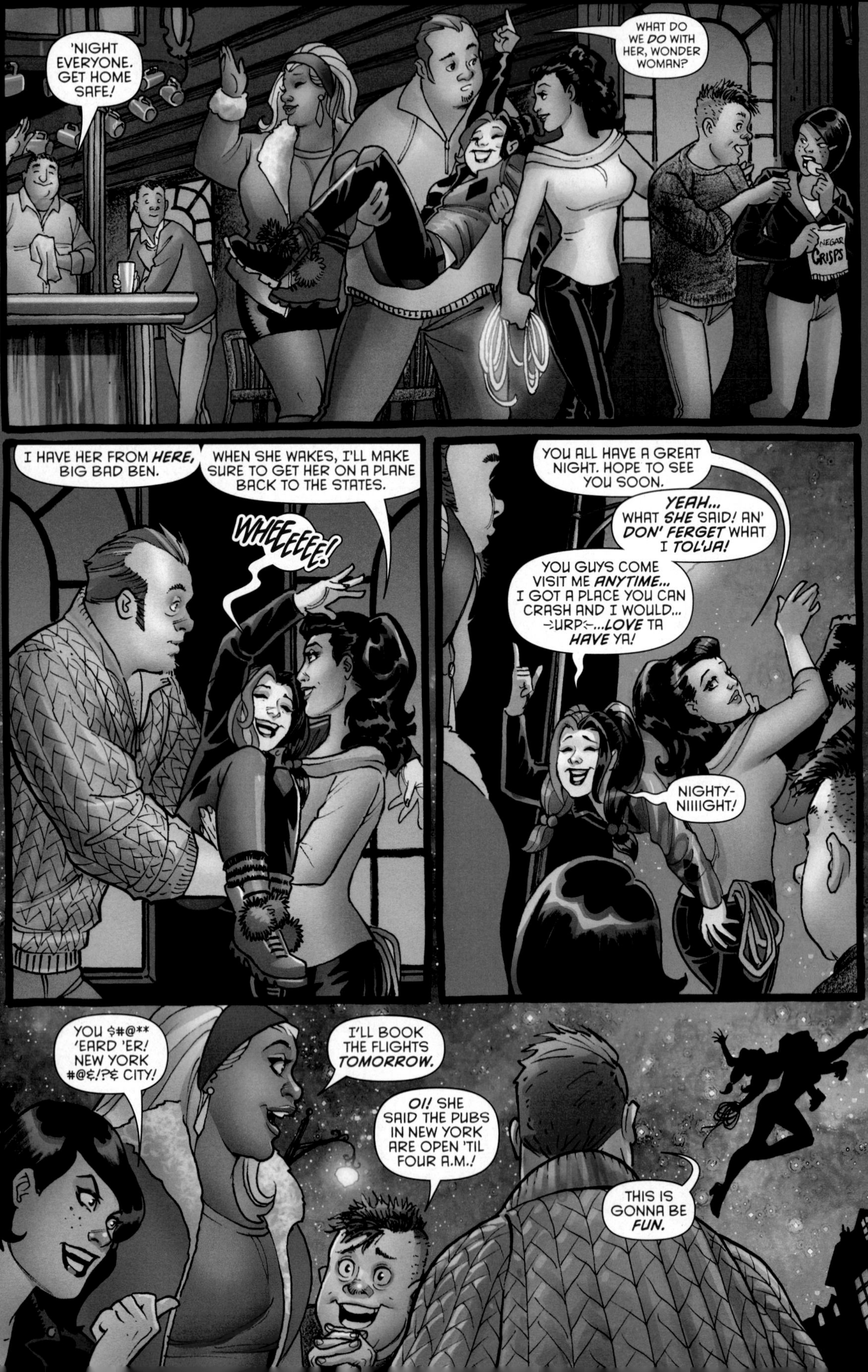

'NIGHT EVERYONE. GET HOME SAFE!
WHAT DO WE *DO* WITH HER, WONDER WOMAN?
NEGAR CRISPS
I HAVE HER FROM *HERE,* BIG BAD BEN.
WHEN SHE WAKES, I'LL MAKE SURE TO GET HER ON A PLANE BACK TO THE STATES.
WHEEEEEE!
YOU ALL HAVE A GREAT NIGHT. HOPE TO SEE YOU SOON.
YEAH... WHAT *SHE* SAID! AN' *DON' FERGET* WHAT I *TOL'JA!*
YOU GUYS COME VISIT ME *ANYTIME...* I GOT A PLACE YOU CAN CRASH AND I WOULD... ⇒URP⇐...*LOVE* TA *HAVE* YA!
NIGHTY-NIIIIGHT!
YOU $#@** 'EARD 'ER! NEW YORK #@&!?& CITY!
I'LL BOOK THE FLIGHTS *TOMORROW.*
OI! SHE SAID THE PUBS IN NEW YORK ARE OPEN 'TIL FOUR A.M.!
THIS IS GONNA BE *FUN.*

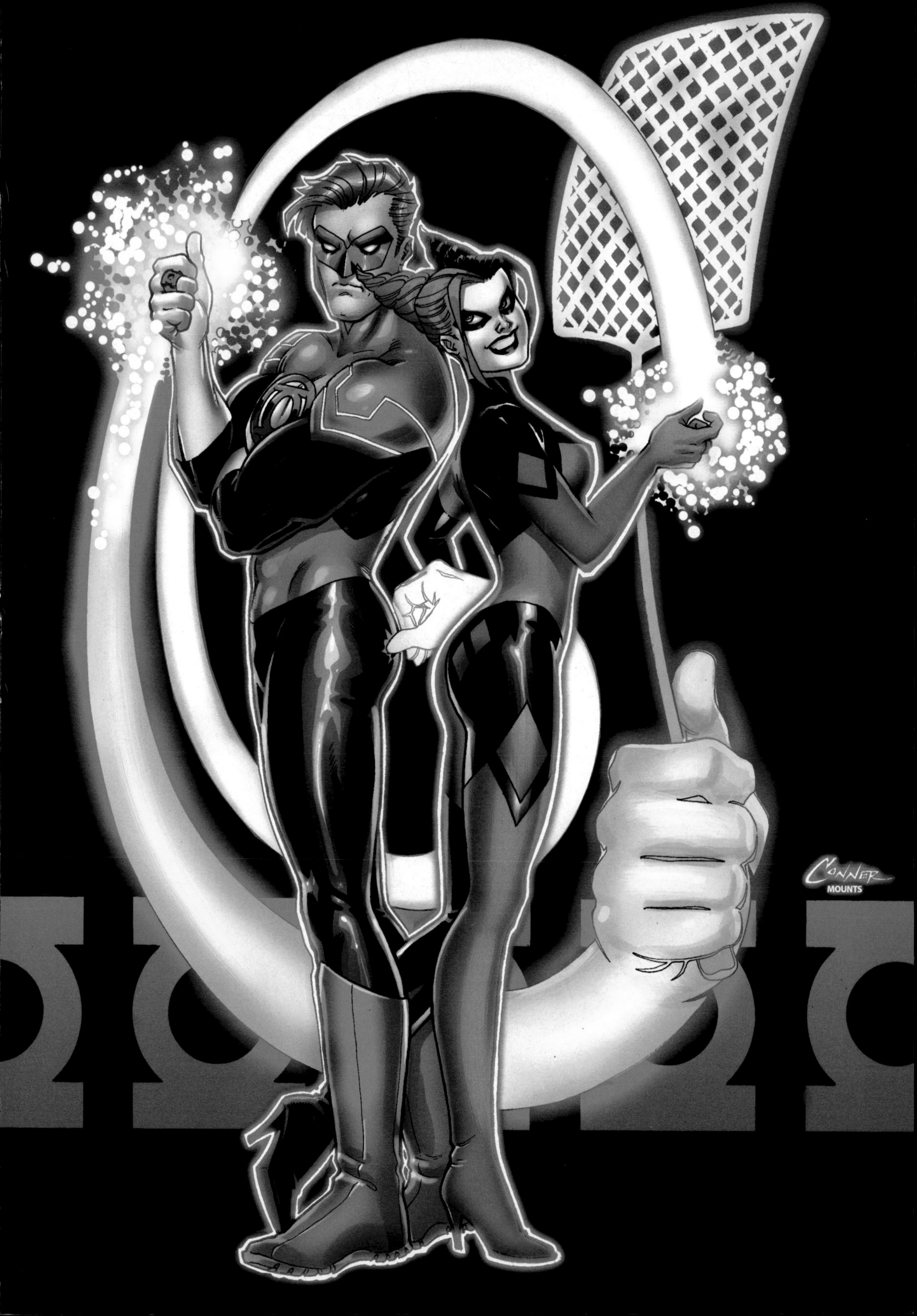
CONNER
MOUNTS

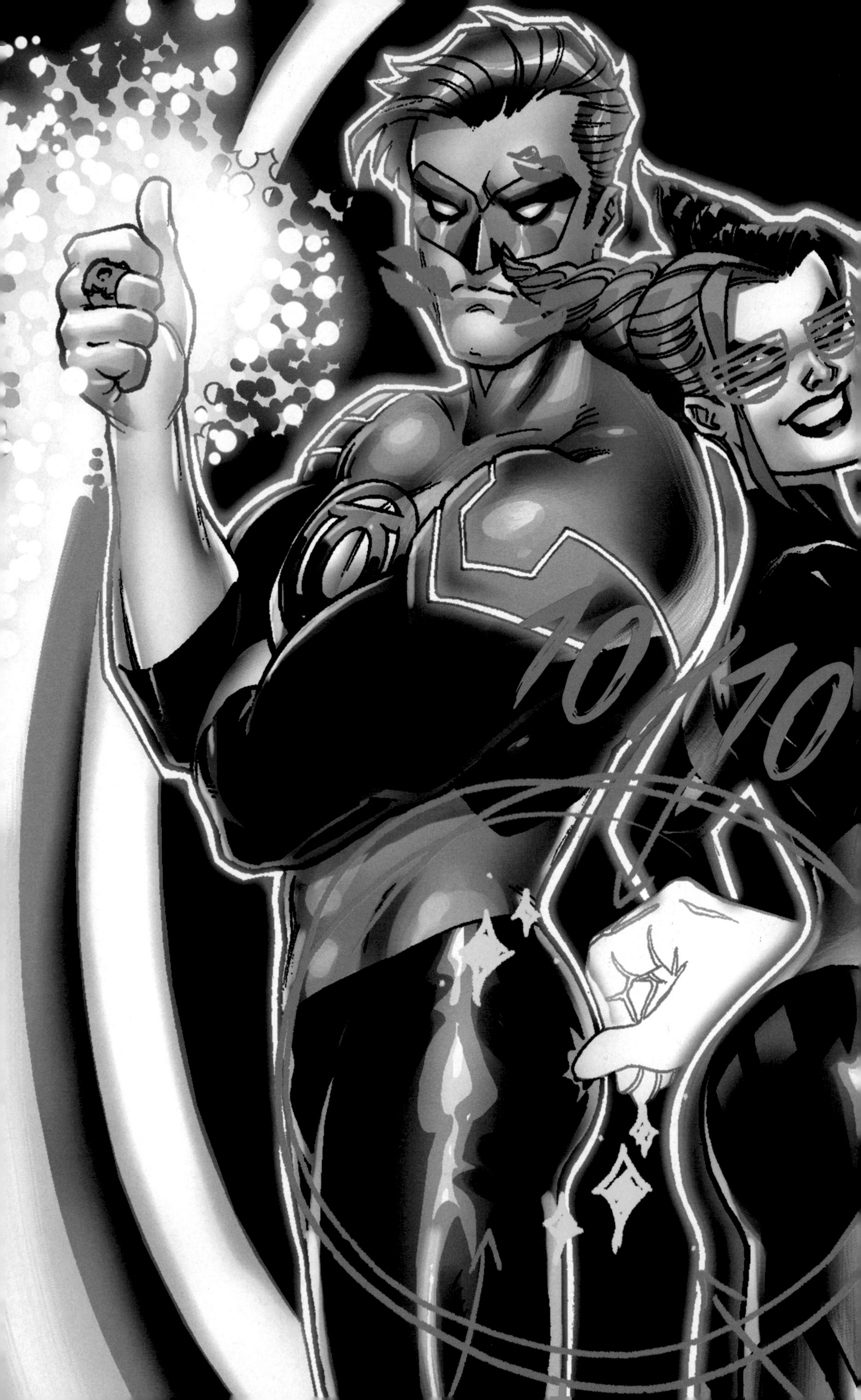
10/10

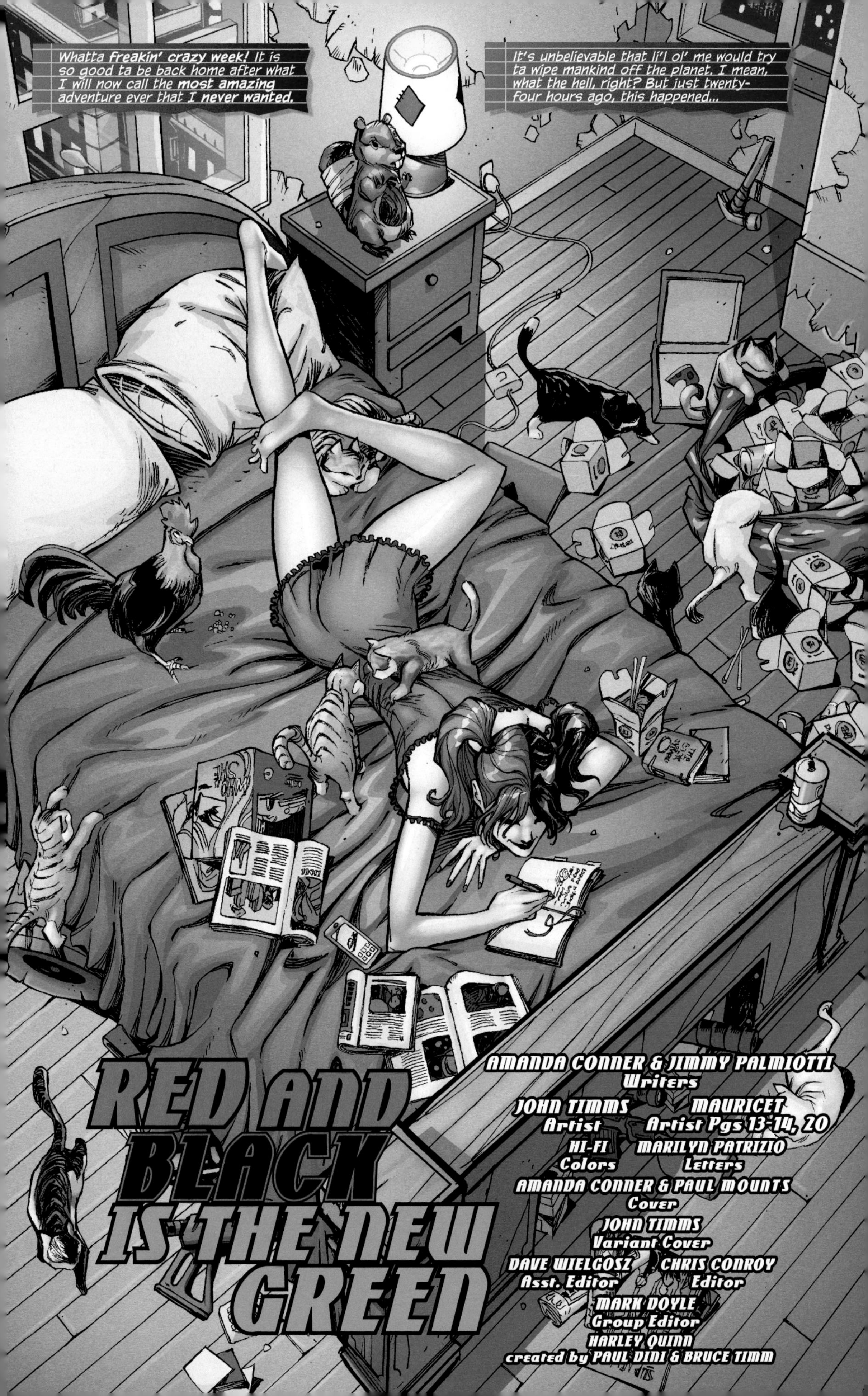
Whatta freakin' crazy week! It is so good ta be back home after what I will now call the most amazing adventure ever that I never wanted.
It's unbelievable that li'l ol' me would try ta wipe mankind off the planet. I mean, what the hell, right? But just twenty-four hours ago, this happened...
RED AND BLACK IS THE NEW GREEN
AMANDA CONNER & JIMMY PALMIOTTI Writers
JOHN TIMMS Artist
MAURICET Artist Pgs 13-14, 20
HI-FI Colors
MARILYN PATRIZIO Letters
AMANDA CONNER & PAUL MOUNTS Cover
JOHN TIMMS Variant Cover
DAVE WIELGOSZ Asst. Editor
CHRIS CONROY Editor
MARK DOYLE Group Editor
HARLEY QUINN created by PAUL DINI & BRUCE TIMM

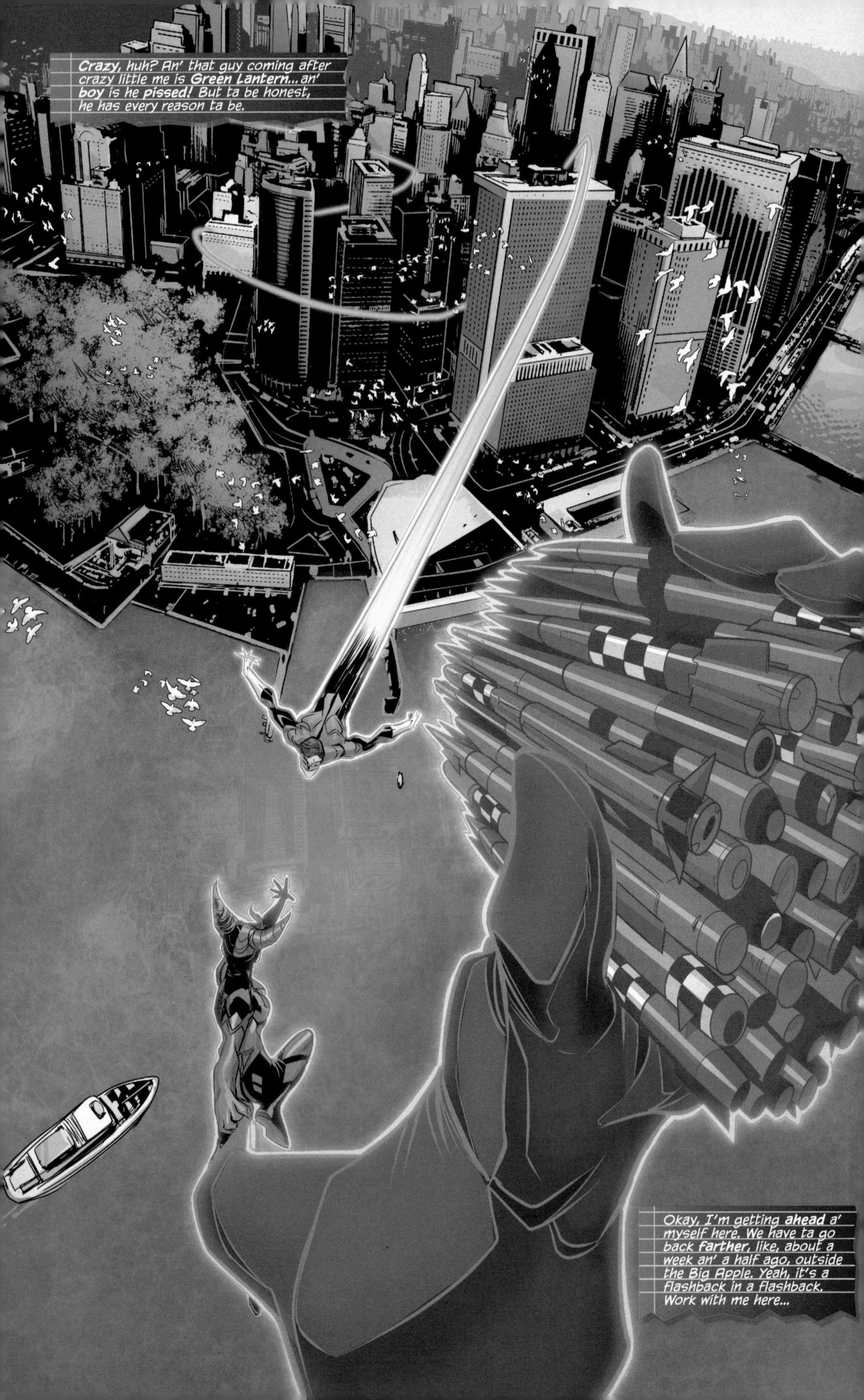
Crazy, huh? An' that guy coming after crazy little me is Green Lantern...an' boy is he pissed! But ta be honest, he has every reason ta be.
Okay, I'm getting ahead a' myself here. We have ta go back farther, like, about a week an' a half ago, outside the Big Apple. Yeah, it's a flashback in a flashback. Work with me here...

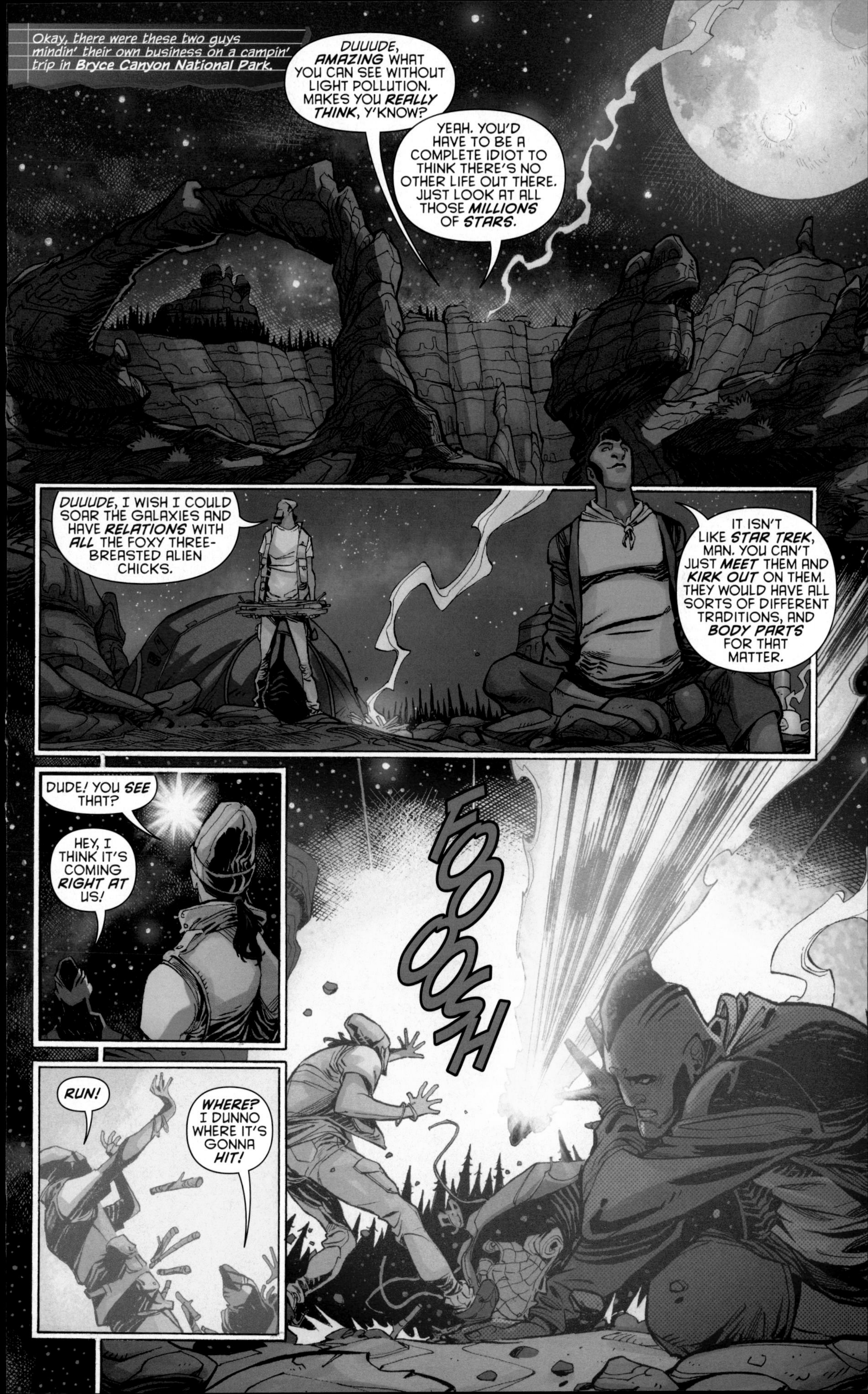

Okay, there were these two guys mindin' their own business on a campin' trip in Bryce Canyon National Park.
DUUUDE, AMAZING WHAT YOU CAN SEE WITHOUT LIGHT POLLUTION. MAKES YOU REALLY THINK, Y'KNOW?
YEAH. YOU'D HAVE TO BE A COMPLETE IDIOT TO THINK THERE'S NO OTHER LIFE OUT THERE. JUST LOOK AT ALL THOSE MILLIONS OF STARS.
DUUUDE, I WISH I COULD SOAR THE GALAXIES AND HAVE RELATIONS WITH ALL THE FOXY THREE-BREASTED ALIEN CHICKS.
IT ISN'T LIKE STAR TREK, MAN. YOU CAN'T JUST MEET THEM AND KIRK OUT ON THEM. THEY WOULD HAVE ALL SORTS OF DIFFERENT TRADITIONS, AND BODY PARTS FOR THAT MATTER.
DUDE! YOU SEE THAT?
HEY, I THINK IT'S COMING RIGHT AT US!
RUN!
WHERE? I DUNNO WHERE IT'S GONNA HIT!
FOOOOOSH

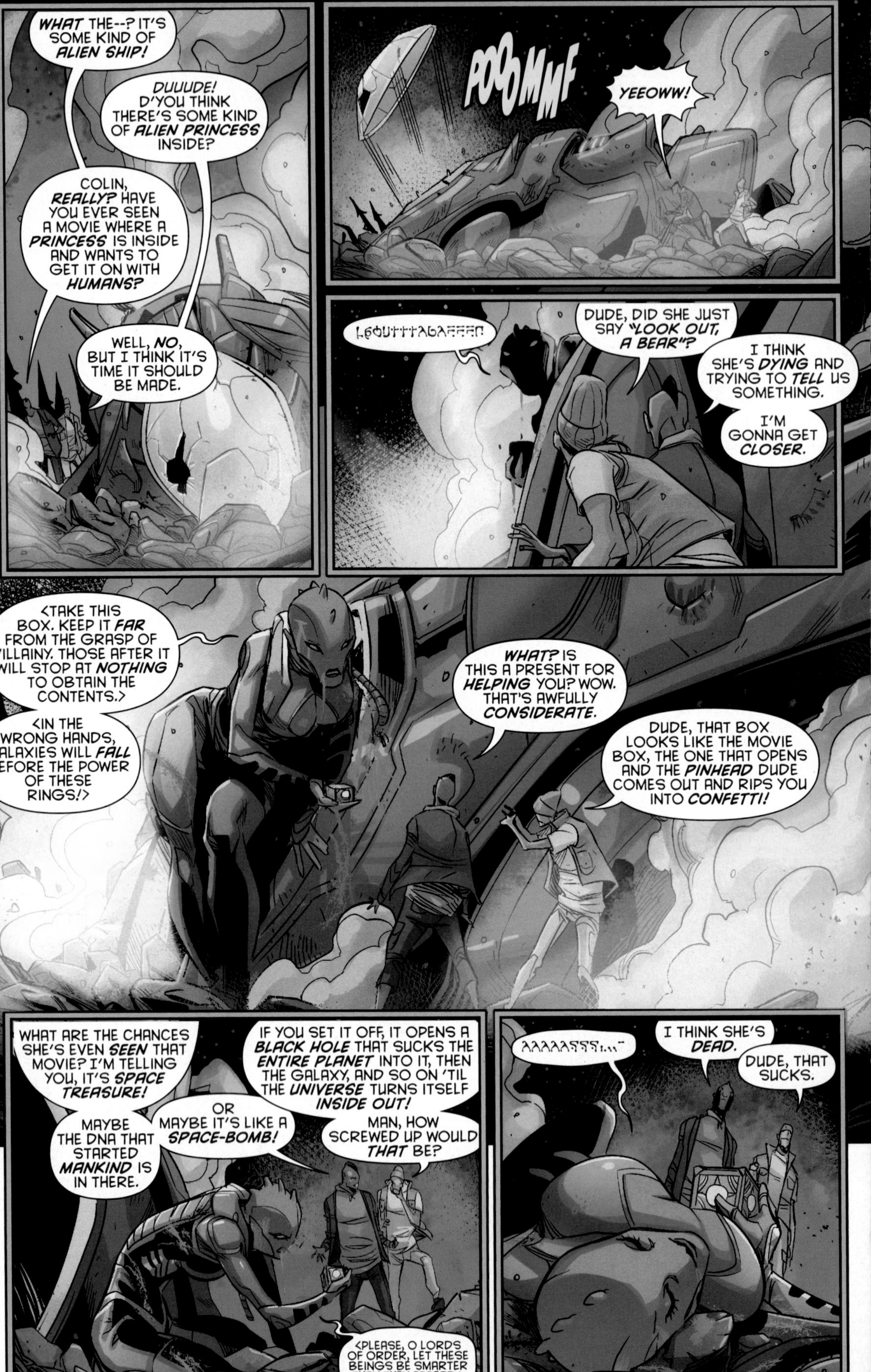

WHAT THE--? IT'S SOME KIND OF ALIEN SHIP!
DUUUDE! D'YOU THINK THERE'S SOME KIND OF ALIEN PRINCESS INSIDE?
COLIN, REALLY? HAVE YOU EVER SEEN A MOVIE WHERE A PRINCESS IS INSIDE AND WANTS TO GET IT ON WITH HUMANS?
WELL, NO, BUT I THINK IT'S TIME IT SHOULD BE MADE.
POOOMMF
YEEOWW!
DUDE, DID SHE JUST SAY "LOOK OUT, A BEAR"?
I THINK SHE'S DYING AND TRYING TO TELL US SOMETHING.
I'M GONNA GET CLOSER.
<TAKE THIS BOX. KEEP IT FAR FROM THE GRASP OF VILLAINY. THOSE AFTER IT WILL STOP AT NOTHING TO OBTAIN THE CONTENTS.>
<IN THE WRONG HANDS, GALAXIES WILL FALL BEFORE THE POWER OF THESE RINGS!>
WHAT? IS THIS A PRESENT FOR HELPING YOU? WOW. THAT'S AWFULLY CONSIDERATE.
DUDE, THAT BOX LOOKS LIKE THE MOVIE BOX, THE ONE THAT OPENS AND THE PINHEAD DUDE COMES OUT AND RIPS YOU INTO CONFETTI!
WHAT ARE THE CHANCES SHE'S EVEN SEEN THAT MOVIE? I'M TELLING YOU, IT'S SPACE TREASURE!
IF YOU SET IT OFF, IT OPENS A BLACK HOLE THAT SUCKS THE ENTIRE PLANET INTO IT, THEN THE GALAXY, AND SO ON 'TIL THE UNIVERSE TURNS ITSELF INSIDE OUT!
MAYBE THE DNA THAT STARTED MANKIND IS IN THERE.
OR MAYBE IT'S LIKE A SPACE-BOMB!
MAN, HOW SCREWED UP WOULD THAT BE?
<PLEASE, O LORDS OF ORDER, LET THESE BEINGS BE SMARTER THAN THEY APPEAR.>
I THINK SHE'S DEAD.
DUDE, THAT SUCKS.

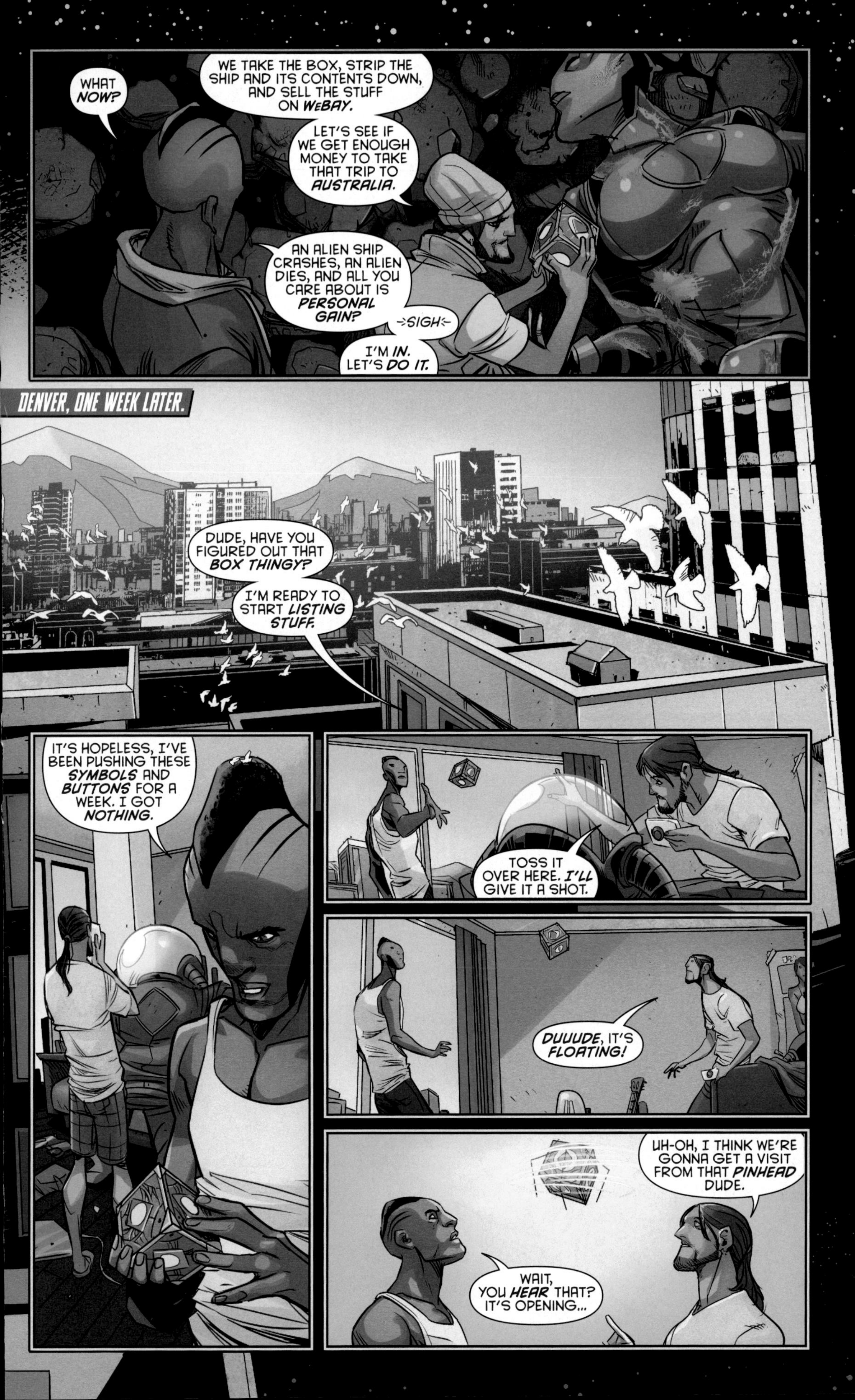
WHAT NOW?
WE TAKE THE BOX, STRIP THE SHIP AND ITS CONTENTS DOWN, AND SELL THE STUFF ON WEBAY.
LET'S SEE IF WE GET ENOUGH MONEY TO TAKE THAT TRIP TO AUSTRALIA.
AN ALIEN SHIP CRASHES, AN ALIEN DIES, AND ALL YOU CARE ABOUT IS PERSONAL GAIN?
SIGH
I'M IN. LET'S DO IT.
DENVER, ONE WEEK LATER.
DUDE, HAVE YOU FIGURED OUT THAT BOX THINGY?
I'M READY TO START LISTING STUFF.
IT'S HOPELESS, I'VE BEEN PUSHING THESE SYMBOLS AND BUTTONS FOR A WEEK. I GOT NOTHING.
TOSS IT OVER HERE. I'LL GIVE IT A SHOT.
DUUUDE, IT'S FLOATING!
WAIT, YOU HEAR THAT? IT'S OPENING...
UH-OH, I THINK WE'RE GONNA GET A VISIT FROM THAT PINHEAD DUDE.

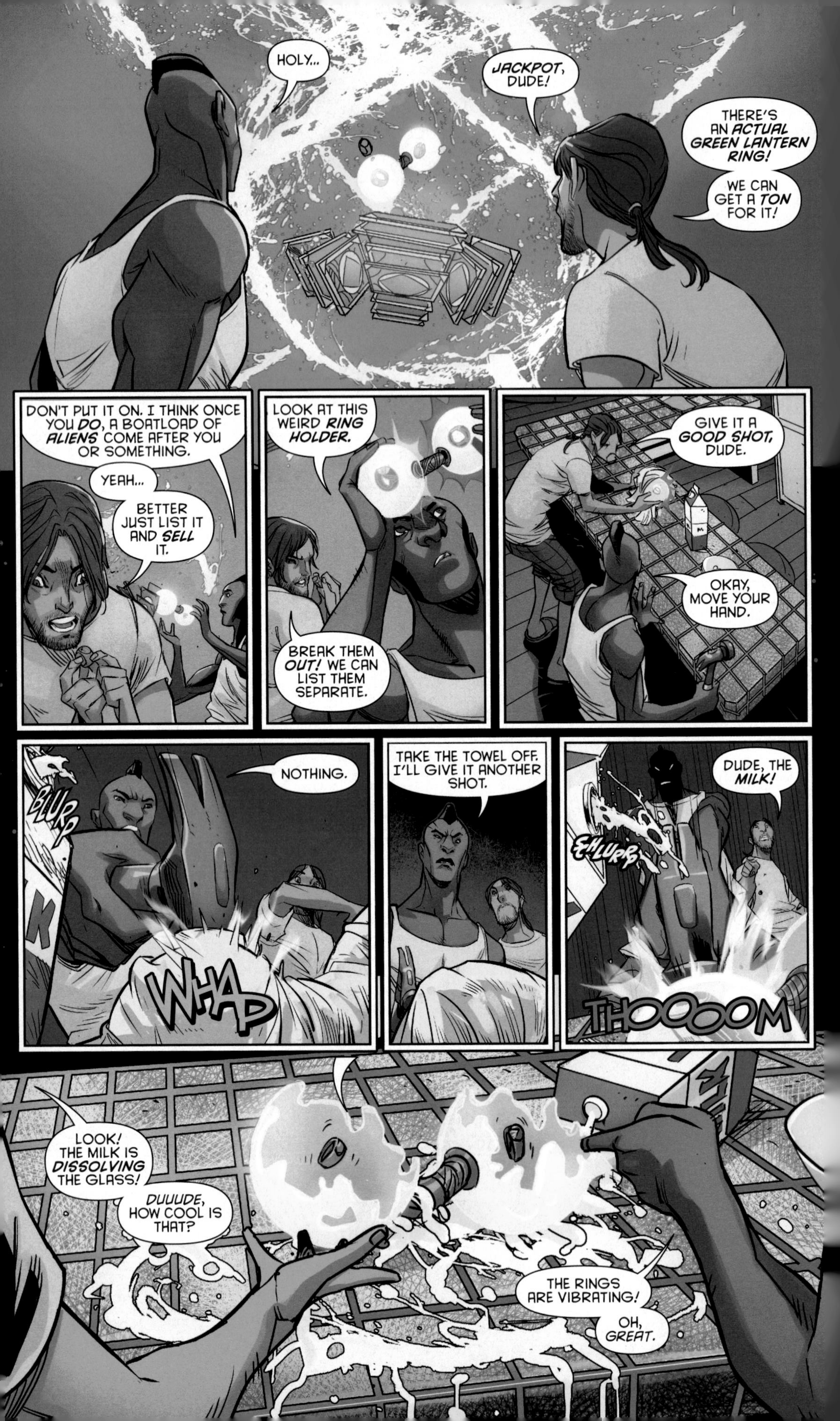
HOLY...
JACKPOT, DUDE!
THERE'S AN ACTUAL GREEN LANTERN RING!
WE CAN GET A TON FOR IT!
DON'T PUT IT ON. I THINK ONCE YOU DO, A BOATLOAD OF ALIENS COME AFTER YOU OR SOMETHING.
YEAH...
BETTER JUST LIST IT AND SELL IT.
LOOK AT THIS WEIRD RING HOLDER.
BREAK THEM OUT! WE CAN LIST THEM SEPARATE.
GIVE IT A GOOD SHOT, DUDE.
OKAY, MOVE YOUR HAND.
BLURP
NOTHING.
WHAP
TAKE THE TOWEL OFF. I'LL GIVE IT ANOTHER SHOT.
DUDE, THE MILK!
SHLURP
THOOOOOM
LOOK! THE MILK IS DISSOLVING THE GLASS!
DUUUDE, HOW COOL IS THAT?
THE RINGS ARE VIBRATING!
OH, GREAT.

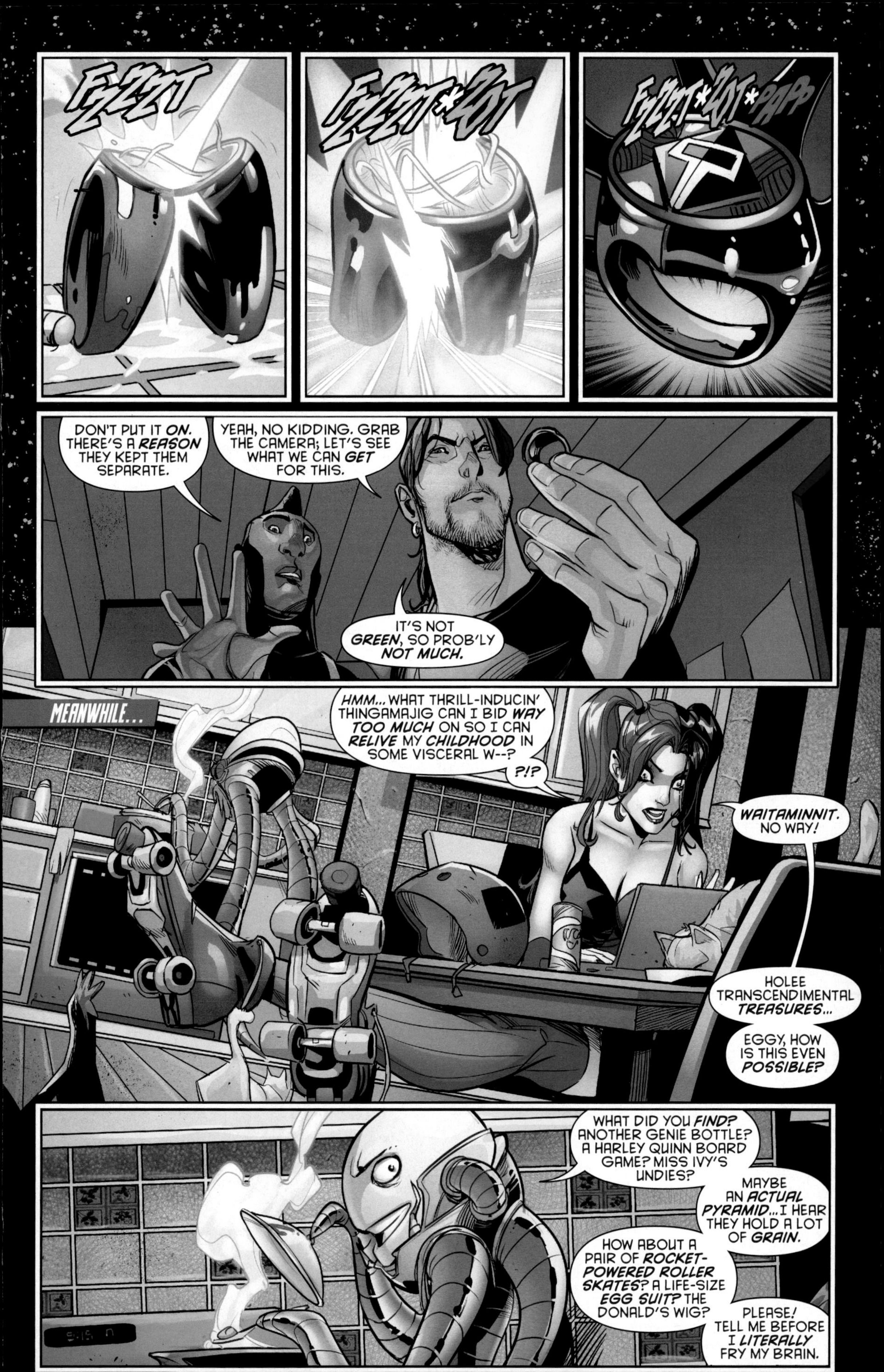

FZZZT
FZZZT*ZOT
FZZZT*ZOT*PAPP
DON'T PUT IT ON. THERE'S A REASON THEY KEPT THEM SEPARATE.
YEAH, NO KIDDING. GRAB THE CAMERA; LET'S SEE WHAT WE CAN GET FOR THIS.
IT'S NOT GREEN, SO PROB'LY NOT MUCH.
MEANWHILE...
HMM... WHAT THRILL-INDUCIN' THINGAMAJIG CAN I BID WAY TOO MUCH ON SO I CAN RELIVE MY CHILDHOOD IN SOME VISCERAL W--?
?!?
WAITAMINNIT. NO WAY!
HOLEE TRANSCENDIMENTAL TREASURES...
EGGY, HOW IS THIS EVEN POSSIBLE?
WHAT DID YOU FIND? ANOTHER GENIE BOTTLE? A HARLEY QUINN BOARD GAME? MISS IVY'S UNDIES?
MAYBE AN ACTUAL PYRAMID... I HEAR THEY HOLD A LOT OF GRAIN.
HOW ABOUT A PAIR OF ROCKET-POWERED ROLLER SKATES? A LIFE-SIZE EGG SUIT? THE DONALD'S WIG?
PLEASE! TELL ME BEFORE I LITERALLY FRY MY BRAIN.

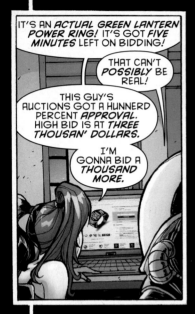

IT'S AN *ACTUAL GREEN LANTERN POWER RING!* IT'S GOT *FIVE MINUTES* LEFT ON BIDDING!

THAT CAN'T *POSSIBLY* BE REAL!

THIS GUY'S AUCTIONS GOT A HUNNERD PERCENT APPROVAL. HIGH BID IS AT *THREE THOUSAN' DOLLARS.*

I'M GONNA BID A *THOUSAND* MORE.

FOUR MORE MINUTES AND YOU'RE *MINE,* MY SWEET EMERALD BEAUTY!

DING — GEOFF JOHNS

WHAT?! I'M BEING OUTBID BY *"SHOPAHARLIC"?*

NO WAY. NOT HAPPENING.

OUTBID? *OUTBID?!* OH, *YEAH?* HOW DOES *TEN GRAND* SOUND?

OH *NO.*

TEN GRAND? HOW ABOUT *THIRTY GRAND,* BUDDY?

DC RULES

TAKE THIS *FIFTY GRAND AN' SHOVE IT!*

OH MY GOODNESS. THIS IS A MISTAKE.

MISS *HARLEY, PLEASE!*

I *NEVER* LOSE WHEN I WEAR MY *LUCKY LANTERN* SHIRT...

...OKAY...

A *HUNDRED GRAND.* LET'S SEE YOU BEAT *THAT* BID, BOZO!

DC RULES

OOOOO! *FINE!* A *HUNNERT AN' FIFTY GRAND!* SUCK ON *THAT,* PAL!

UGGHH...

HE ONLY HAS *TWENNY* SECONDS LEFT! HA! I GOT *THIS!*

TWO HUNDRED GRAND... AND *THREE...*

TWO...

ONE...

IT'S MINE!

MINE!

ALL...

...MINE...

OH BOY. WHAT DID I JUST DO?

MY WIFE IS GONNA KILL ME.

NOoOoOo!

I LOST THE BID.

HOW COULD THIS *HAPPEN*...?

DING

HUH?

I JUST GOT AN E-MAIL FROM THE SELLER SAYIN' HE HAS *ANOTHER* LANTERN RING FER SALE!

IT'S ONLY *FIVE GRAND* IF I WANT IT.

HE SAYS IT'S DIFFERENT COLORS, BUT IT *SEEMS* TO BE CHARGED.

IS IT CHARGED?

I DON'T CARE. I *WANT* IT!

SOLD.

enter

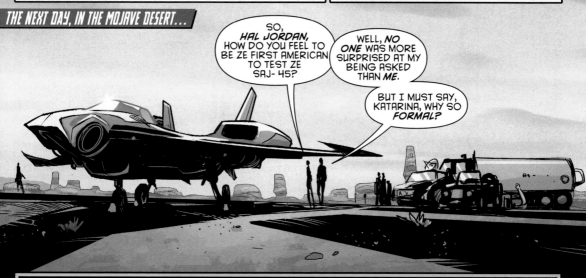

THE NEXT DAY, IN THE MOJAVE DESERT...

SO, *HAL JORDAN,* HOW DO YOU FEEL TO BE ZE FIRST AMERICAN TO TEST ZE SAJ- 45?

WELL, *NO ONE* WAS MORE SURPRISED AT MY BEING ASKED THAN *ME.*

BUT I MUST SAY, KATARINA, WHY SO *FORMAL?*

VHAT HAPPENED LAST NIGHT EES BUSINESS BETWEEN *US.* ZE TEST RUN TODAY EES BUSINESS BETWEEN OUR *COUNTRIES.*

IF THINGS GO AS *SMOOTHLY* AS LAST NIGHT, I SEE OUR NATIONS HAVING A *VERY* LONG-LASTING, FAVORABLE RELATIONSHIP.

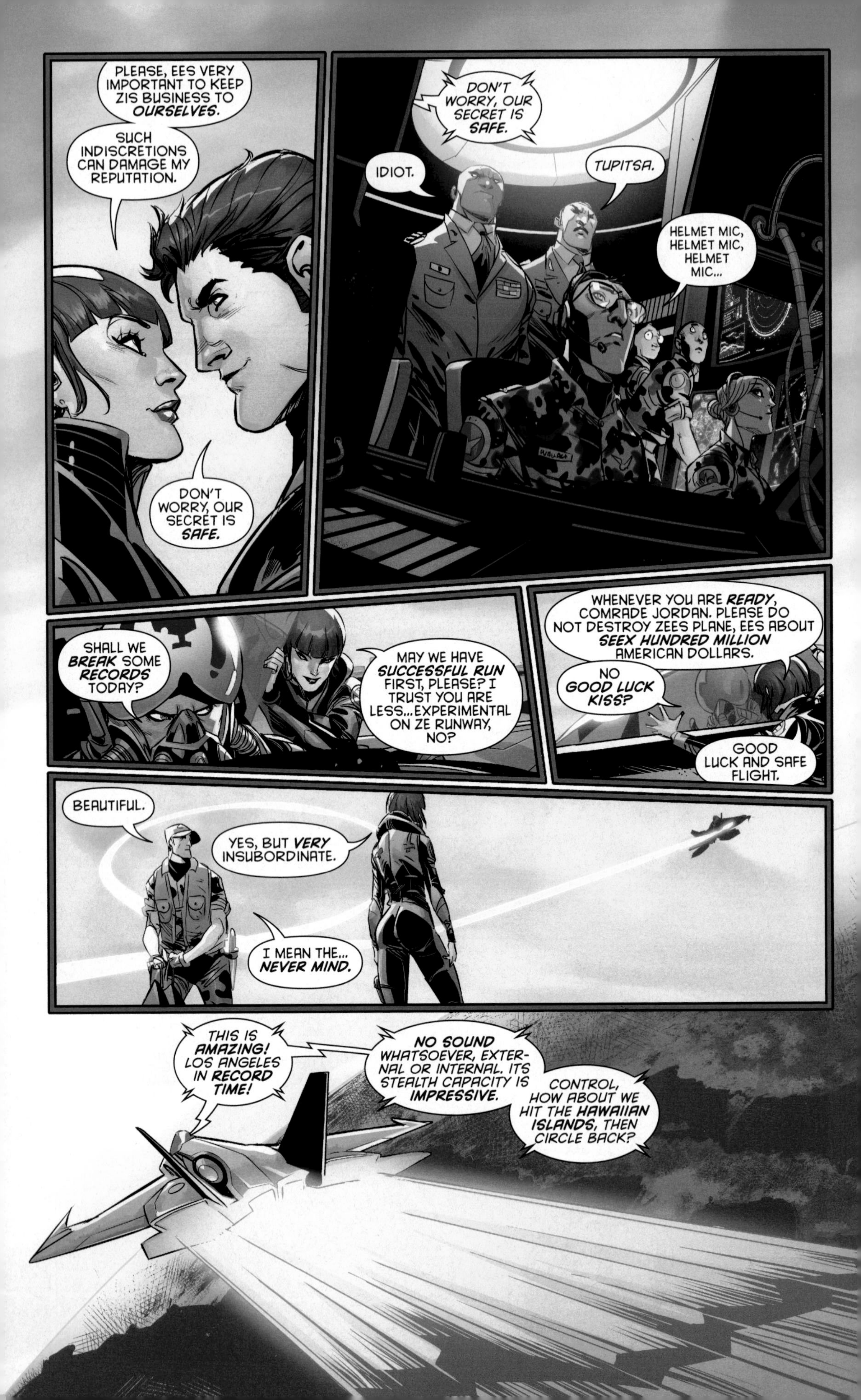
PLEASE, EES VERY IMPORTANT TO KEEP ZIS BUSINESS TO OURSELVES.
SUCH INDISCRETIONS CAN DAMAGE MY REPUTATION.
DON'T WORRY, OUR SECRET IS SAFE.
DON'T WORRY, OUR SECRET IS SAFE.
IDIOT.
TUPITSA.
HELMET MIC, HELMET MIC, HELMET MIC...
SHALL WE BREAK SOME RECORDS TODAY?
MAY WE HAVE SUCCESSFUL RUN FIRST, PLEASE? I TRUST YOU ARE LESS...EXPERIMENTAL ON ZE RUNWAY, NO?
WHENEVER YOU ARE READY, COMRADE JORDAN. PLEASE DO NOT DESTROY ZEES PLANE, EES ABOUT SEEX HUNDRED MILLION AMERICAN DOLLARS.
NO GOOD LUCK KISS?
GOOD LUCK AND SAFE FLIGHT.
BEAUTIFUL.
YES, BUT VERY INSUBORDINATE.
I MEAN THE... NEVER MIND.
THIS IS AMAZING! LOS ANGELES IN RECORD TIME!
NO SOUND WHATSOEVER, EXTERNAL OR INTERNAL. ITS STEALTH CAPACITY IS IMPRESSIVE.
CONTROL, HOW ABOUT WE HIT THE HAWAIIAN ISLANDS, THEN CIRCLE BACK?

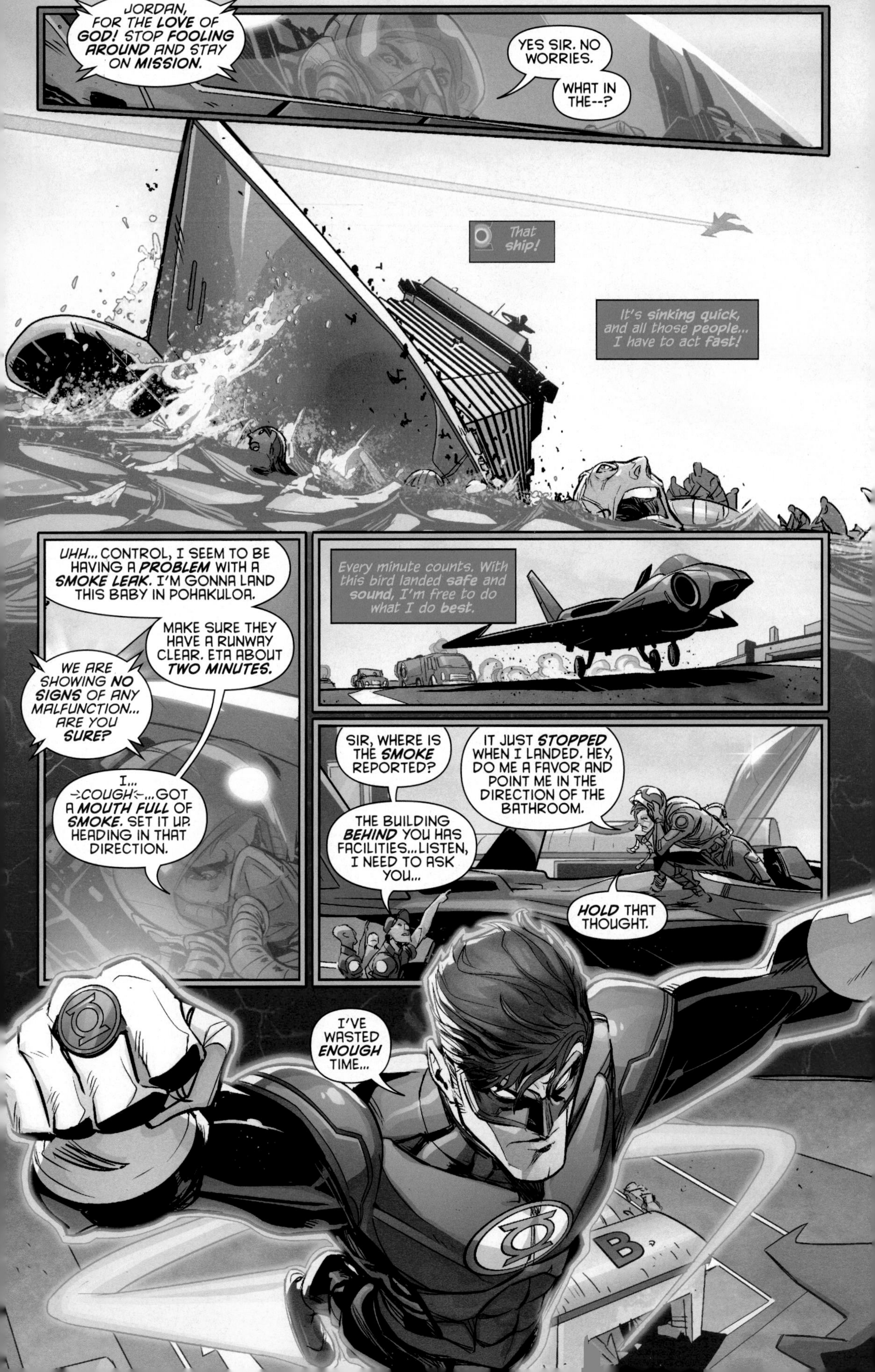

JORDAN, FOR THE LOVE OF GOD! STOP FOOLING AROUND AND STAY ON MISSION.
YES SIR. NO WORRIES.
WHAT IN THE--?
That ship!
It's sinking quick, and all those people... I have to act fast!
UHH... CONTROL, I SEEM TO BE HAVING A PROBLEM WITH A SMOKE LEAK. I'M GONNA LAND THIS BABY IN POHAKULOA.
WE ARE SHOWING NO SIGNS OF ANY MALFUNCTION... ARE YOU SURE?
MAKE SURE THEY HAVE A RUNWAY CLEAR. ETA ABOUT TWO MINUTES.
I... >COUGH<...GOT A MOUTH FULL OF SMOKE. SET IT UP. HEADING IN THAT DIRECTION.
Every minute counts. With this bird landed safe and sound, I'm free to do what I do best.
SIR, WHERE IS THE SMOKE REPORTED?
IT JUST STOPPED WHEN I LANDED. HEY, DO ME A FAVOR AND POINT ME IN THE DIRECTION OF THE BATHROOM.
THE BUILDING BEHIND YOU HAS FACILITIES...LISTEN, I NEED TO ASK YOU...
HOLD THAT THOUGHT.
I'VE WASTED ENOUGH TIME...
B

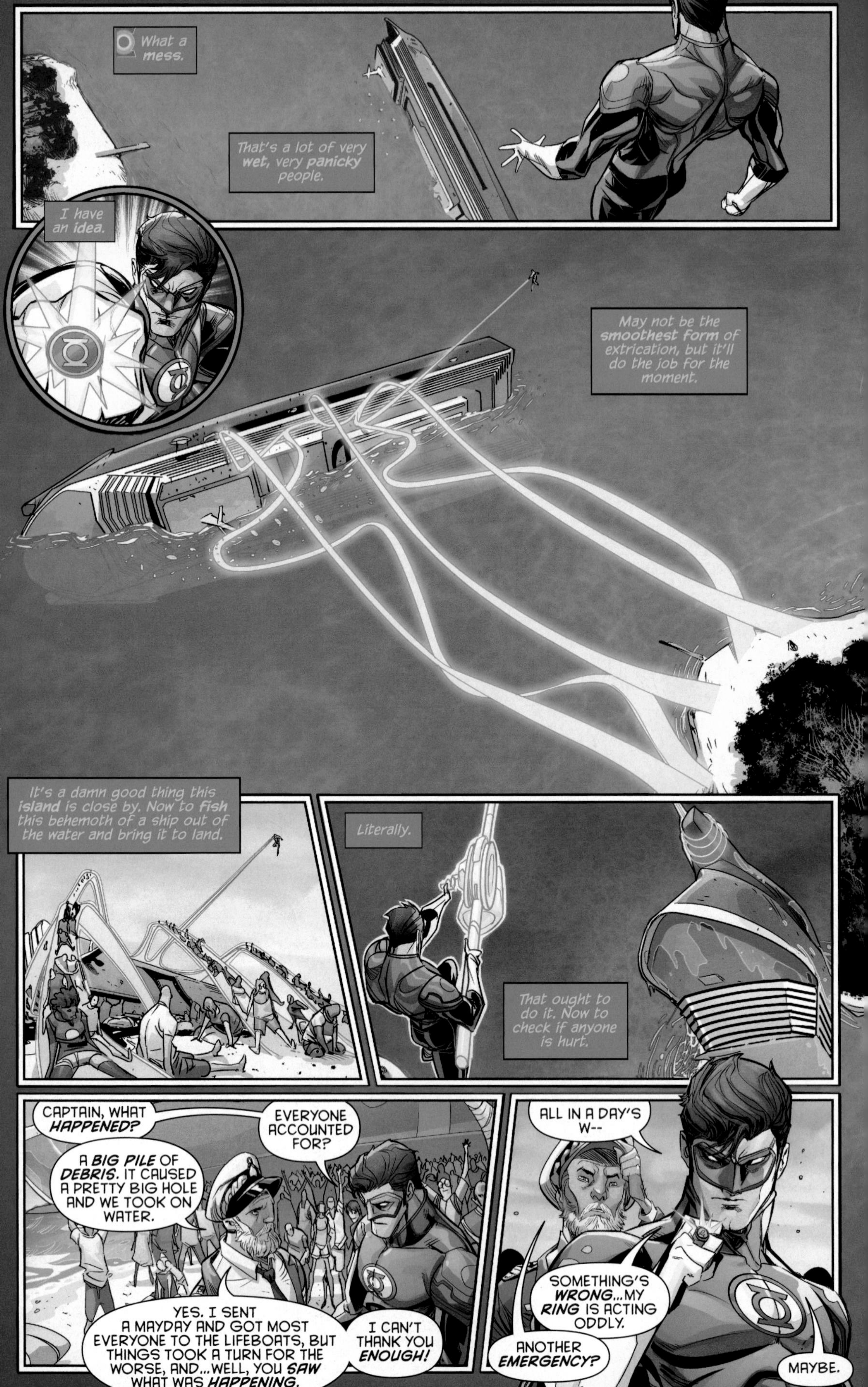
What a mess.
That's a lot of very wet, very panicky people.
I have an idea.
May not be the smoothest form of extrication, but it'll do the job for the moment.
It's a damn good thing this island is close by. Now to fish this behemoth of a ship out of the water and bring it to land.
Literally.
That ought to do it. Now to check if anyone is hurt.
CAPTAIN, WHAT HAPPENED?
EVERYONE ACCOUNTED FOR?
A BIG PILE OF DEBRIS. IT CAUSED A PRETTY BIG HOLE AND WE TOOK ON WATER.
YES. I SENT A MAYDAY AND GOT MOST EVERYONE TO THE LIFEBOATS, BUT THINGS TOOK A TURN FOR THE WORSE, AND...WELL, YOU SAW WHAT WAS HAPPENING.
I CAN'T THANK YOU ENOUGH!
ALL IN A DAY'S W--
SOMETHING'S WRONG...MY RING IS ACTING ODDLY.
ANOTHER EMERGENCY?
MAYBE.

NEW YORK #$%&!' CITY

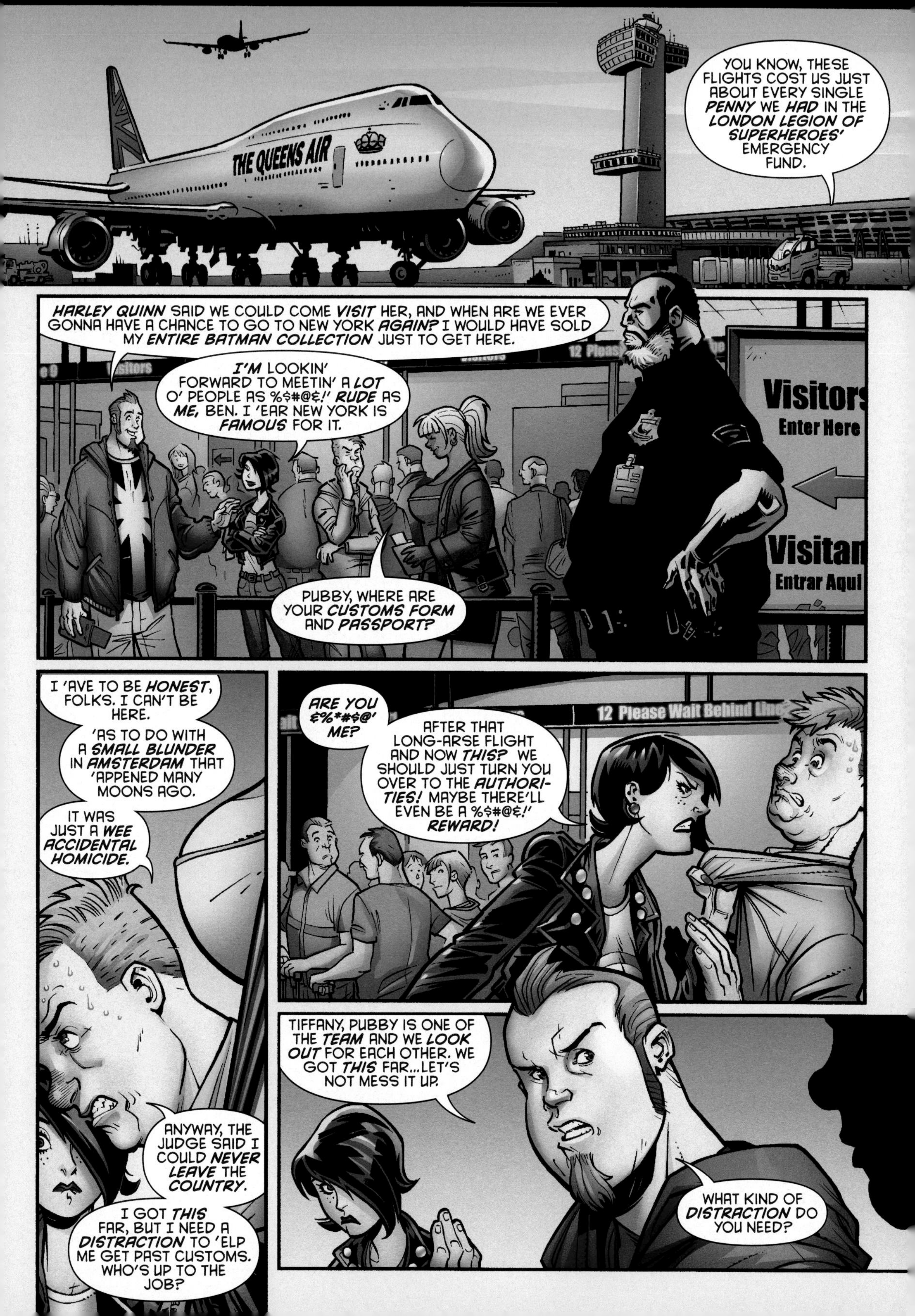
THE QUEENS AIR
YOU KNOW, THESE FLIGHTS COST US JUST ABOUT EVERY SINGLE PENNY WE HAD IN THE LONDON LEGION OF SUPERHEROES' EMERGENCY FUND.
HARLEY QUINN SAID WE COULD COME VISIT HER, AND WHEN ARE WE EVER GONNA HAVE A CHANCE TO GO TO NEW YORK AGAIN? I WOULD HAVE SOLD MY ENTIRE BATMAN COLLECTION JUST TO GET HERE.
I'M LOOKIN' FORWARD TO MEETIN' A LOT O' PEOPLE AS %$#@&!' RUDE AS ME, BEN. I 'EAR NEW YORK IS FAMOUS FOR IT.
PUBBY, WHERE ARE YOUR CUSTOMS FORM AND PASSPORT?
Visitors
Visitors
Enter Here
Visitan
Entrar Aqui
I 'AVE TO BE HONEST, FOLKS. I CAN'T BE HERE.
'AS TO DO WITH A SMALL BLUNDER IN AMSTERDAM THAT 'APPENED MANY MOONS AGO.
IT WAS JUST A WEE ACCIDENTAL HOMICIDE.
ARE YOU &%*#$@' ME?
AFTER THAT LONG-ARSE FLIGHT AND NOW THIS? WE SHOULD JUST TURN YOU OVER TO THE AUTHORI-TIES! MAYBE THERE'LL EVEN BE A %$#@&!' REWARD!
12 Please Wait Behind Line
ANYWAY, THE JUDGE SAID I COULD NEVER LEAVE THE COUNTRY.
I GOT THIS FAR, BUT I NEED A DISTRACTION TO 'ELP ME GET PAST CUSTOMS. WHO'S UP TO THE JOB?
TIFFANY, PUBBY IS ONE OF THE TEAM AND WE LOOK OUT FOR EACH OTHER. WE GOT THIS FAR...LET'S NOT MESS IT UP.
WHAT KIND OF DISTRACTION DO YOU NEED?

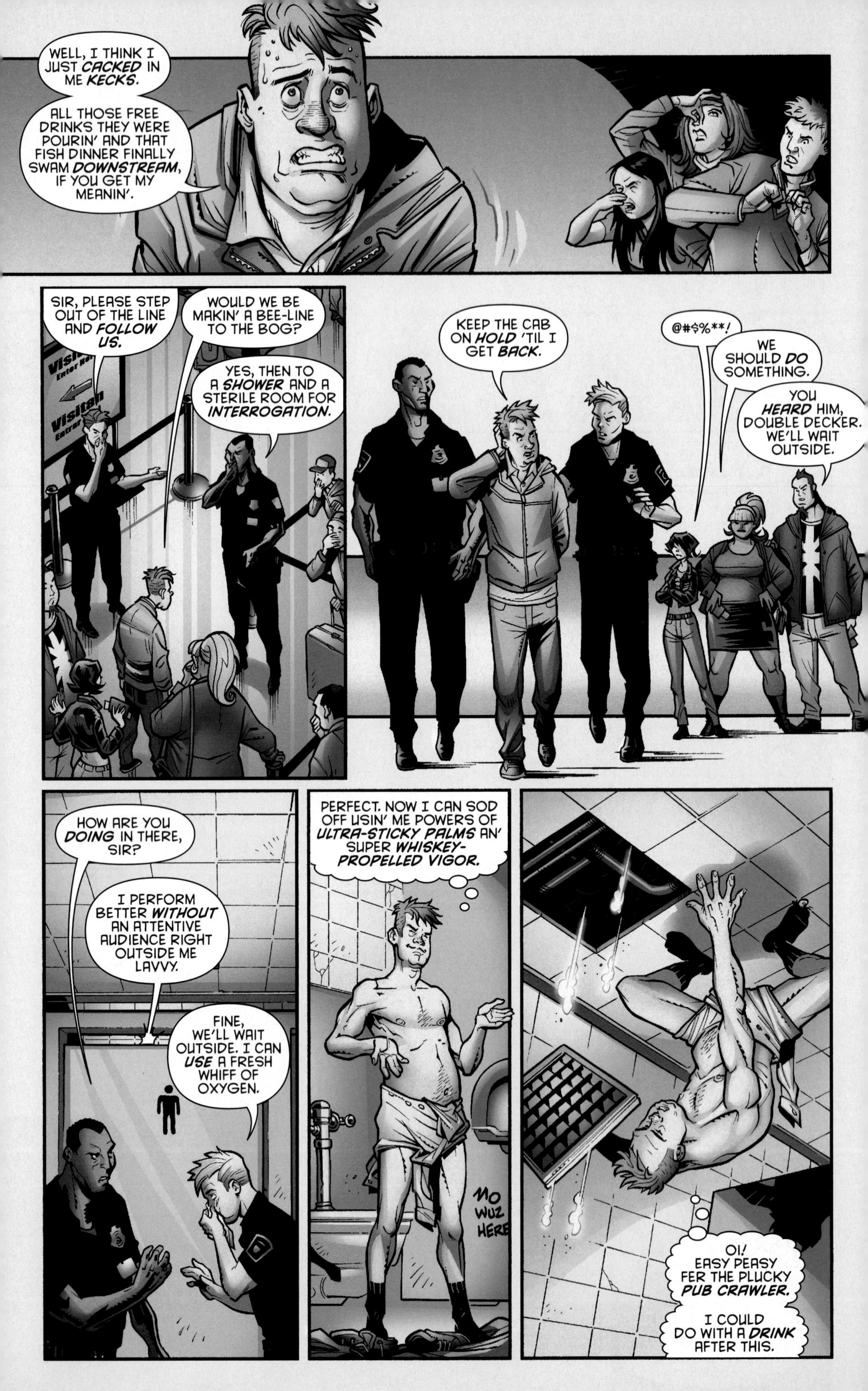
WELL, I THINK I JUST CACKED IN ME KECKS.
ALL THOSE FREE DRINKS THEY WERE POURIN' AND THAT FISH DINNER FINALLY SWAM DOWNSTREAM, IF YOU GET MY MEANIN'.
SIR, PLEASE STEP OUT OF THE LINE AND FOLLOW US.
WOULD WE BE MAKIN' A BEE-LINE TO THE BOG?
YES, THEN TO A SHOWER AND A STERILE ROOM FOR INTERROGATION.
KEEP THE CAB ON HOLD 'TIL I GET BACK.
@#$%**!
WE SHOULD DO SOMETHING.
YOU HEARD HIM, DOUBLE DECKER. WE'LL WAIT OUTSIDE.
HOW ARE YOU DOING IN THERE, SIR?
I PERFORM BETTER WITHOUT AN ATTENTIVE AUDIENCE RIGHT OUTSIDE ME LAVVY.
FINE, WE'LL WAIT OUTSIDE. I CAN USE A FRESH WHIFF OF OXYGEN.
PERFECT. NOW I CAN SOD OFF USIN' ME POWERS OF ULTRA-STICKY PALMS AN' SUPER WHISKEY-PROPELLED VIGOR.
MO WUZ HERE
OI! EASY PEASY FER THE PLUCKY PUB CRAWLER.
I COULD DO WITH A DRINK AFTER THIS.

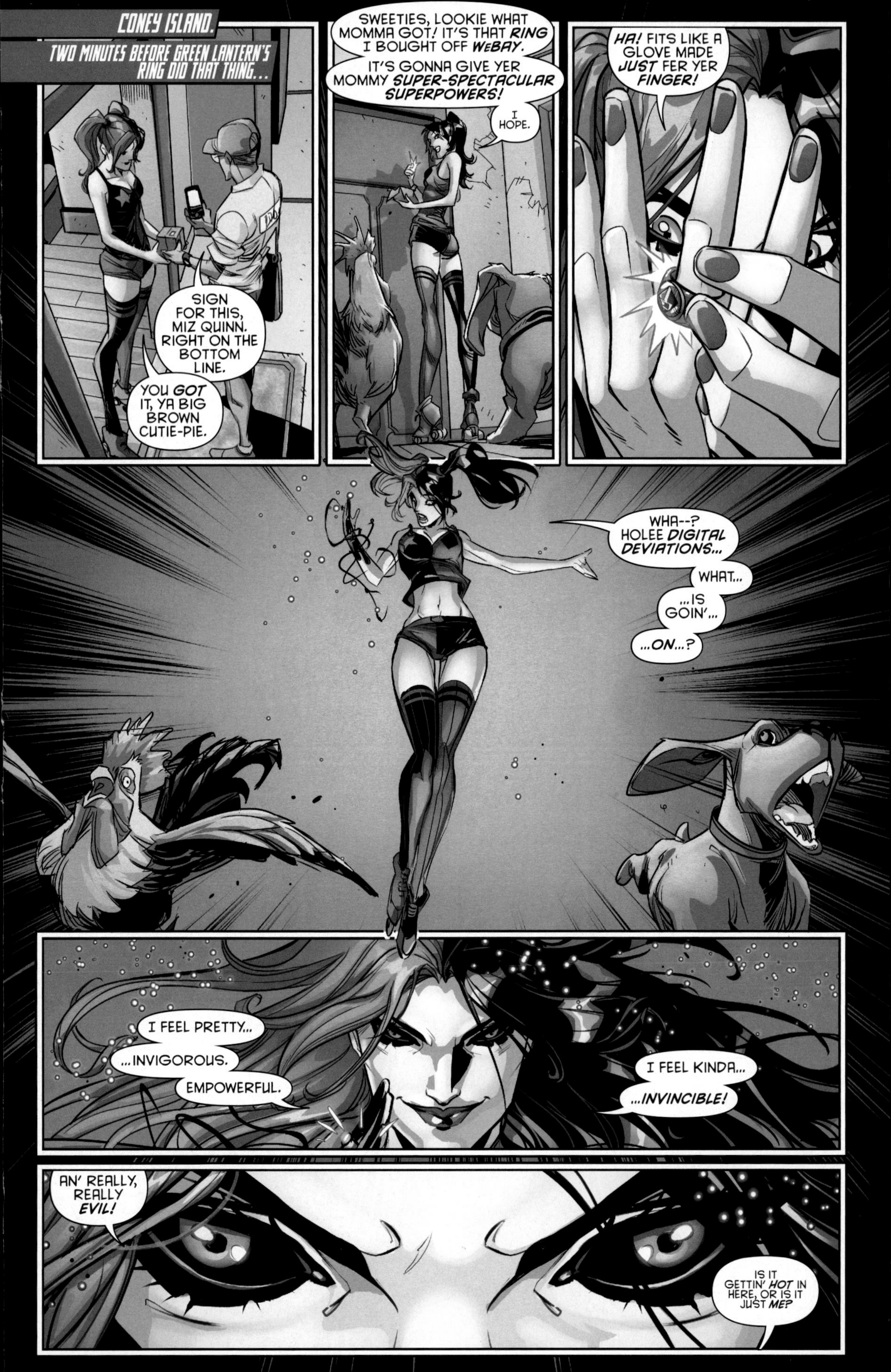
CONEY ISLAND.
TWO MINUTES BEFORE GREEN LANTERN'S RING DID THAT THING...
SIGN FOR THIS, MIZ QUINN. RIGHT ON THE BOTTOM LINE.
YOU GOT IT, YA BIG BROWN CUTIE-PIE.
SWEETIES, LOOKIE WHAT MOMMA GOT! IT'S THAT RING I BOUGHT OFF WEBAY.
IT'S GONNA GIVE YER MOMMY SUPER-SPECTACULAR SUPERPOWERS!
I HOPE.
HA! FITS LIKE A GLOVE MADE JUST FER YER FINGER!
WHA--? HOLEE DIGITAL DEVIATIONS...
WHAT...
...IS GOIN'...
...ON...?
I FEEL PRETTY...
...INVIGOROUS.
EMPOWERFUL.
I FEEL KINDA...
...INVINCIBLE!
AN' REALLY, REALLY EVIL!
IS IT GETTIN' HOT IN HERE, OR IS IT JUST ME?

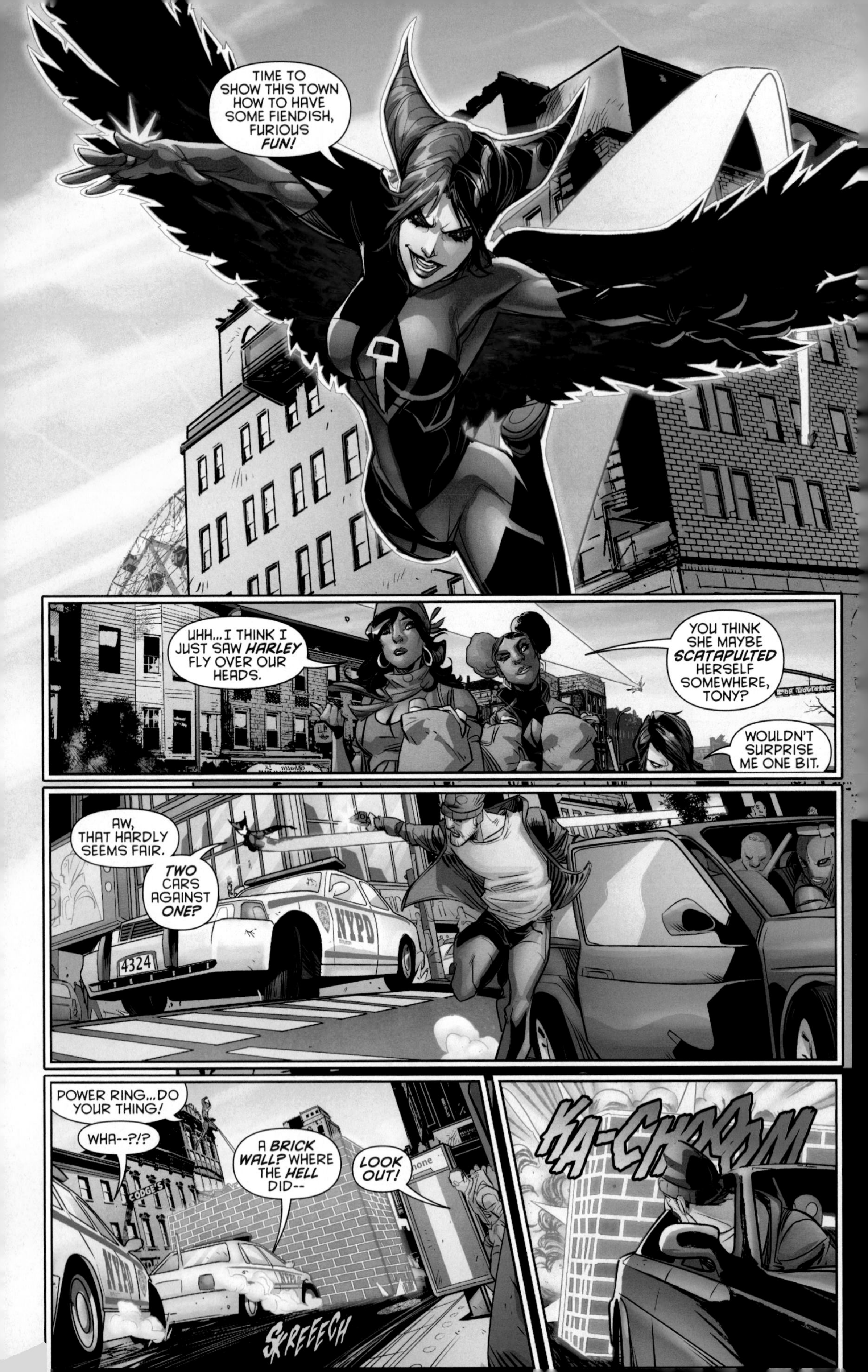
TIME TO SHOW THIS TOWN HOW TO HAVE SOME FIENDISH, FURIOUS *FUN!*
UHH...I THINK I JUST SAW *HARLEY* FLY OVER OUR HEADS.
YOU THINK SHE MAYBE *SCATAPULTED* HERSELF SOMEWHERE, TONY?
WOULDN'T SURPRISE ME ONE BIT.
AW, THAT HARDLY SEEMS FAIR.
TWO CARS AGAINST *ONE?*
NYPD
4324
POWER RING...DO YOUR THING!
WHA--?!?
A *BRICK WALL?* WHERE THE *HELL* DID--
LOOK OUT!
SKREEEECH
KA-CHOOOM

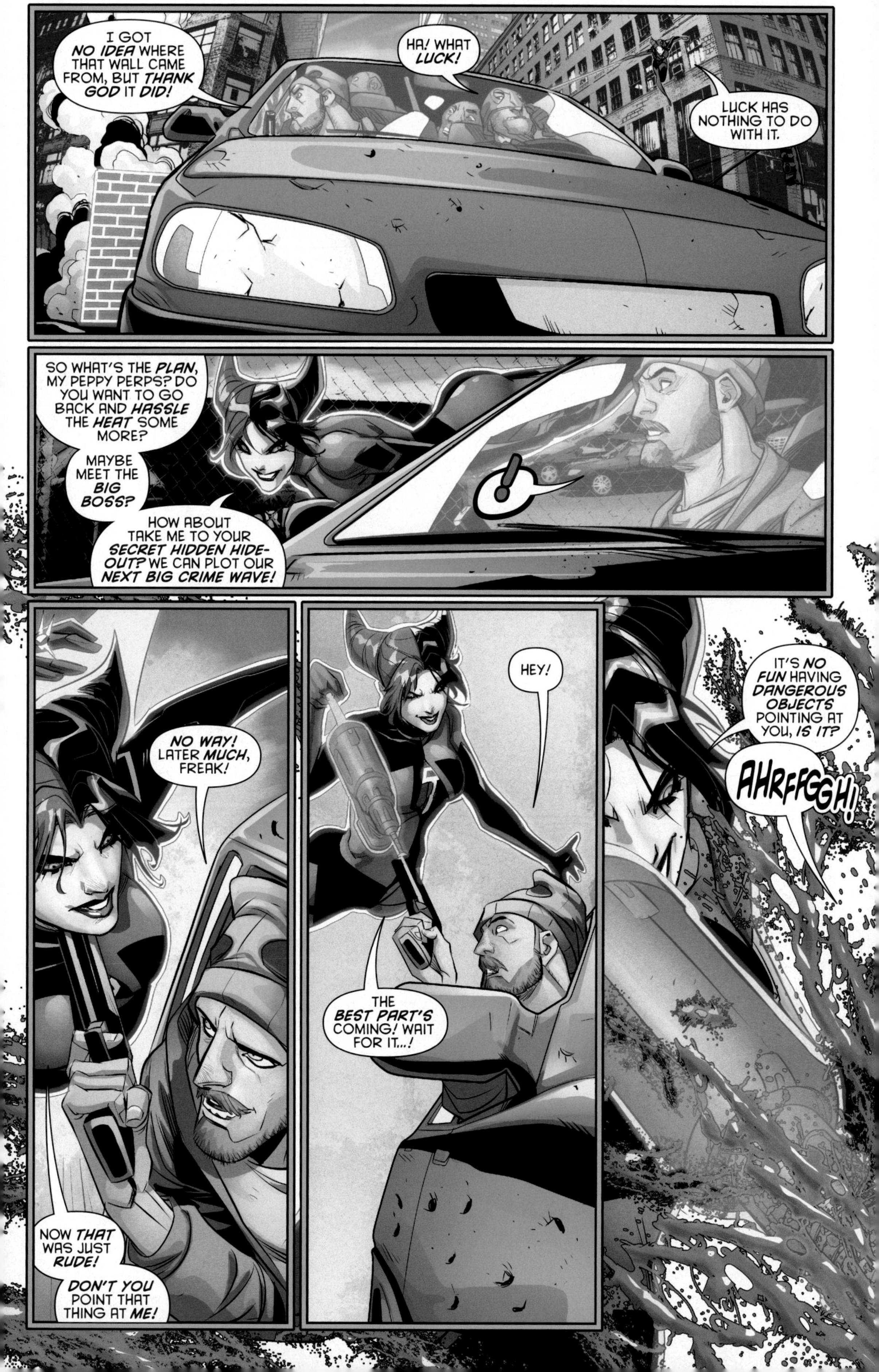
I GOT NO IDEA WHERE THAT WALL CAME FROM, BUT THANK GOD IT DID!
HA! WHAT LUCK!
LUCK HAS NOTHING TO DO WITH IT.
SO WHAT'S THE PLAN, MY PEPPY PERPS? DO YOU WANT TO GO BACK AND HASSLE THE HEAT SOME MORE?
MAYBE MEET THE BIG BOSS?
HOW ABOUT TAKE ME TO YOUR SECRET HIDDEN HIDE-OUT? WE CAN PLOT OUR NEXT BIG CRIME WAVE!
!
NO WAY! LATER MUCH, FREAK!
NOW THAT WAS JUST RUDE!
DON'T YOU POINT THAT THING AT ME!
HEY!
THE BEST PART'S COMING! WAIT FOR IT...!
IT'S NO FUN HAVING DANGEROUS OBJECTS POINTING AT YOU, IS IT?
AHRFFGGH!

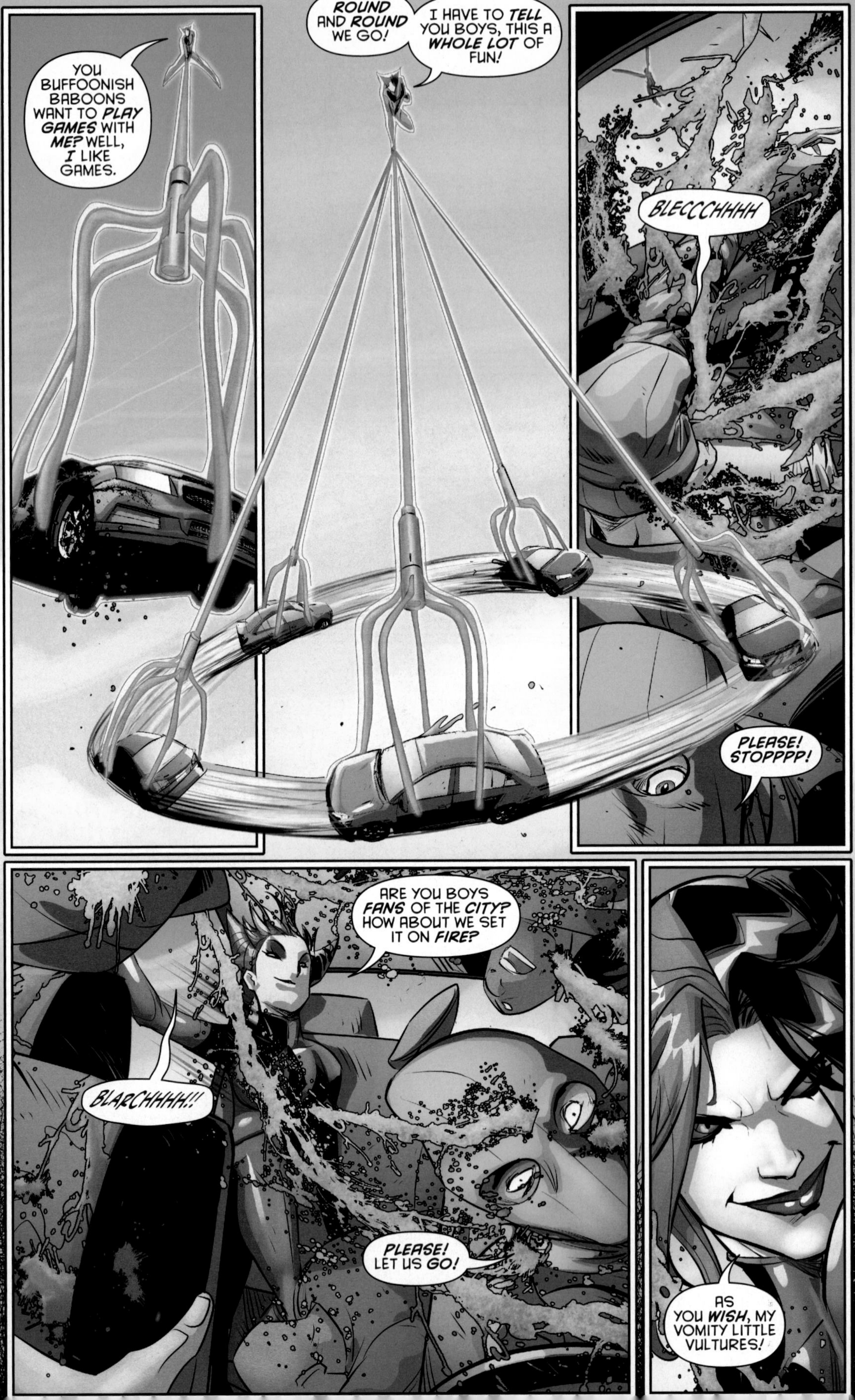

YOU BUFFOONISH BABOONS WANT TO PLAY GAMES WITH ME? WELL, I LIKE GAMES.
ROUND AND ROUND WE GO!
I HAVE TO TELL YOU BOYS, THIS A WHOLE LOT OF FUN!
BLECCCHHHH
PLEASE! STOPPPP!
ARE YOU BOYS FANS OF THE CITY? HOW ABOUT WE SET IT ON FIRE?
BLARCHHHH!!
PLEASE! LET US GO!
AS YOU WISH, MY VOMITY LITTLE VULTURES!

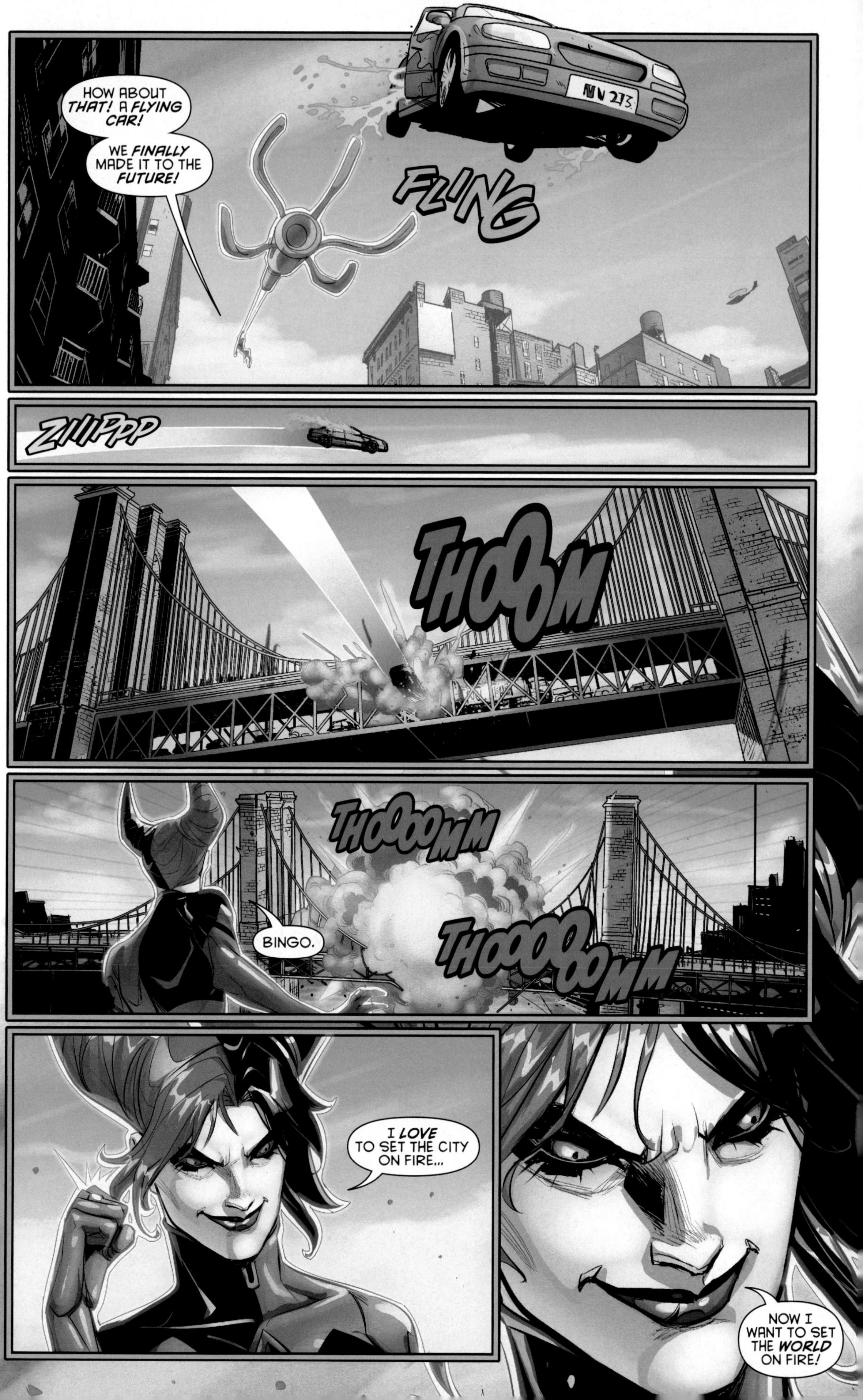
HOW ABOUT THAT! A FLYING CAR!
WE FINALLY MADE IT TO THE FUTURE!
FLING
ZIIIPPP
THOOOM
THOOOOMM
BINGO.
THOOOOOOMM
I LOVE TO SET THE CITY ON FIRE...
NOW I WANT TO SET THE WORLD ON FIRE!

BIG LITTLE TOWN.

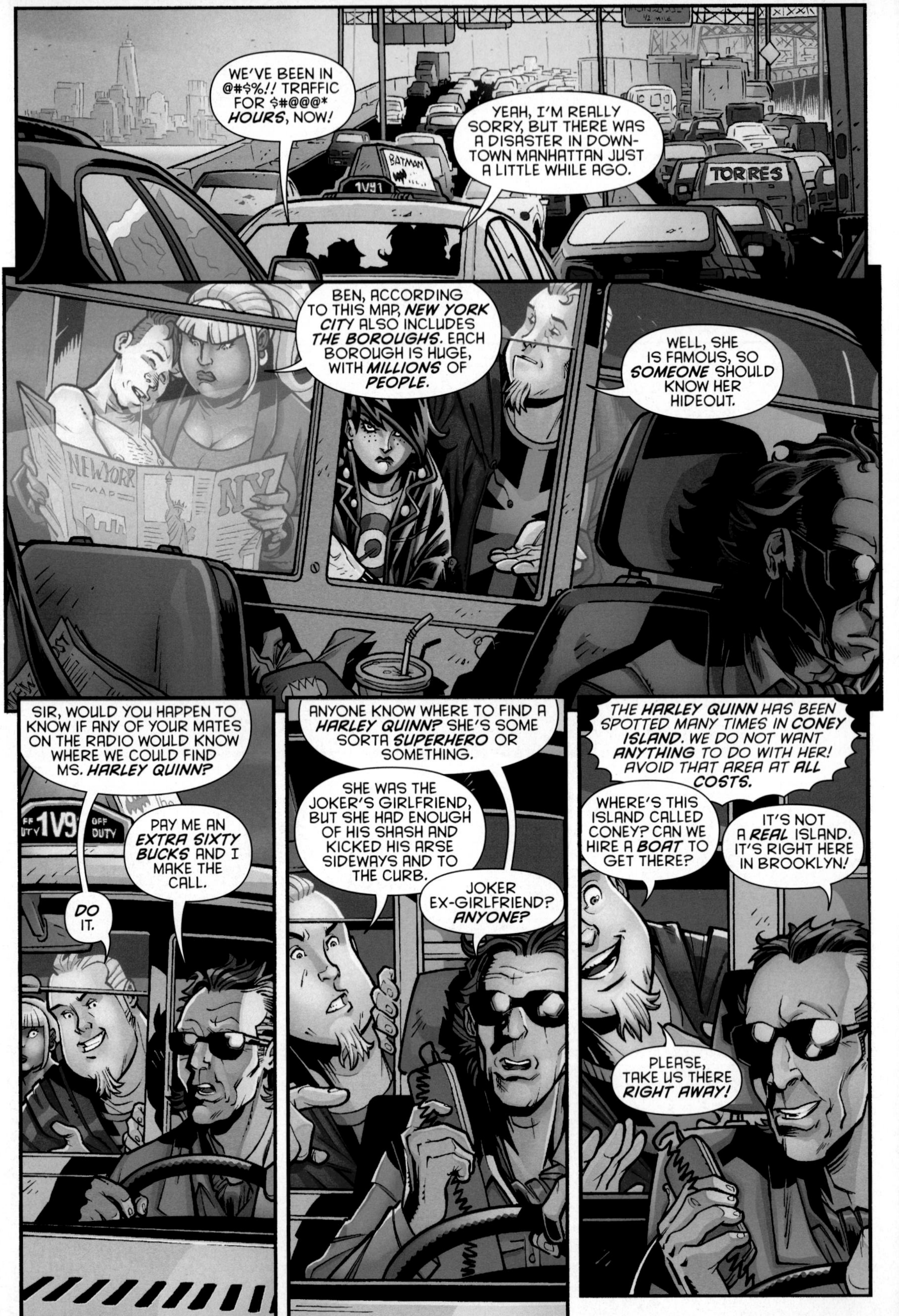

WE'VE BEEN IN @#$%!! TRAFFIC FOR $#@@@* HOURS, NOW!
YEAH, I'M REALLY SORRY, BUT THERE WAS A DISASTER IN DOWN-TOWN MANHATTAN JUST A LITTLE WHILE AGO.
BATMAN
1V91
TORRES
BEN, ACCORDING TO THIS MAP, NEW YORK CITY ALSO INCLUDES THE BOROUGHS. EACH BOROUGH IS HUGE, WITH MILLIONS OF PEOPLE.
WELL, SHE IS FAMOUS, SO SOMEONE SHOULD KNOW HER HIDEOUT.
NEW YORK MAP
NY
SIR, WOULD YOU HAPPEN TO KNOW IF ANY OF YOUR MATES ON THE RADIO WOULD KNOW WHERE WE COULD FIND MS. HARLEY QUINN?
1V91 OFF DUTY
PAY ME AN EXTRA SIXTY BUCKS AND I MAKE THE CALL.
DO IT.
ANYONE KNOW WHERE TO FIND A HARLEY QUINN? SHE'S SOME SORTA SUPERHERO OR SOMETHING.
SHE WAS THE JOKER'S GIRLFRIEND, BUT SHE HAD ENOUGH OF HIS SHASH AND KICKED HIS ARSE SIDEWAYS AND TO THE CURB.
JOKER EX-GIRLFRIEND? ANYONE?
THE HARLEY QUINN HAS BEEN SPOTTED MANY TIMES IN CONEY ISLAND. WE DO NOT WANT ANYTHING TO DO WITH HER! AVOID THAT AREA AT ALL COSTS.
WHERE'S THIS ISLAND CALLED CONEY? CAN WE HIRE A BOAT TO GET THERE?
IT'S NOT A REAL ISLAND. IT'S RIGHT HERE IN BROOKLYN!
PLEASE, TAKE US THERE RIGHT AWAY!

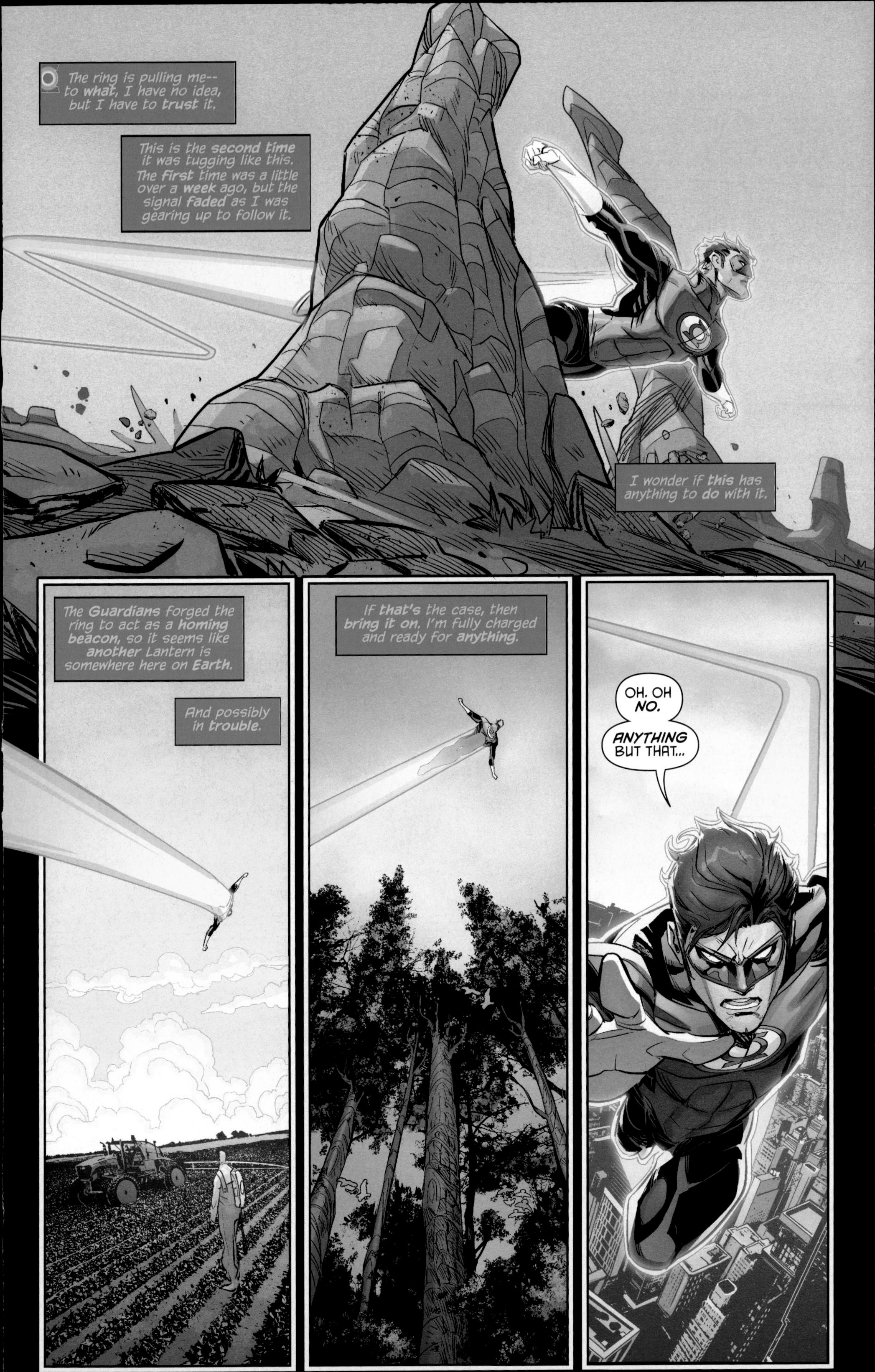

The ring is pulling me-- to what, I have no idea, but I have to trust it.
This is the second time it was tugging like this. The first time was a little over a week ago, but the signal faded as I was gearing up to follow it.
I wonder if this has anything to do with it.
The Guardians forged the ring to act as a homing beacon, so it seems like another Lantern is somewhere here on Earth.
And possibly in trouble.
If that's the case, then bring it on. I'm fully charged and ready for anything.
OH. OH NO. ANYTHING BUT THAT...

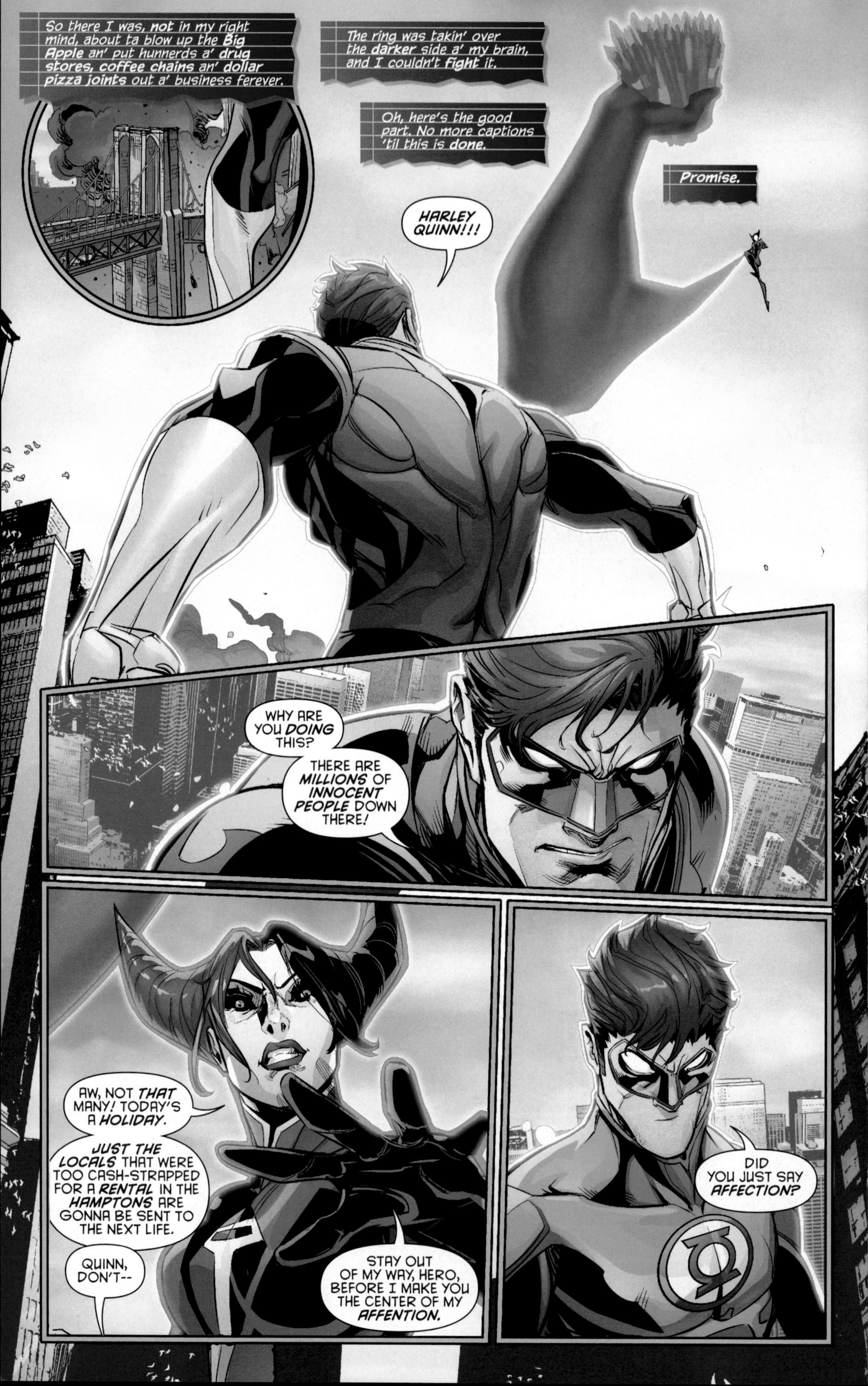
So there I was, not in my right mind, about ta blow up the Big Apple an' put hunnerds a' drug stores, coffee chains an' dollar pizza joints out a' business forever.
The ring was takin' over the darker side a' my brain, and I couldn't fight it.
Oh, here's the good part. No more captions 'til this is done.
Promise.
HARLEY QUINN!!!
WHY ARE YOU DOING THIS?
THERE ARE MILLIONS OF INNOCENT PEOPLE DOWN THERE!
AW, NOT THAT MANY! TODAY'S A HOLIDAY.
JUST THE LOCALS THAT WERE TOO CASH-STRAPPED FOR A RENTAL IN THE HAMPTONS ARE GONNA BE SENT TO THE NEXT LIFE.
QUINN, DON'T--
STAY OUT OF MY WAY, HERO, BEFORE I MAKE YOU THE CENTER OF MY AFFENTION.
DID YOU JUST SAY AFFECTION?

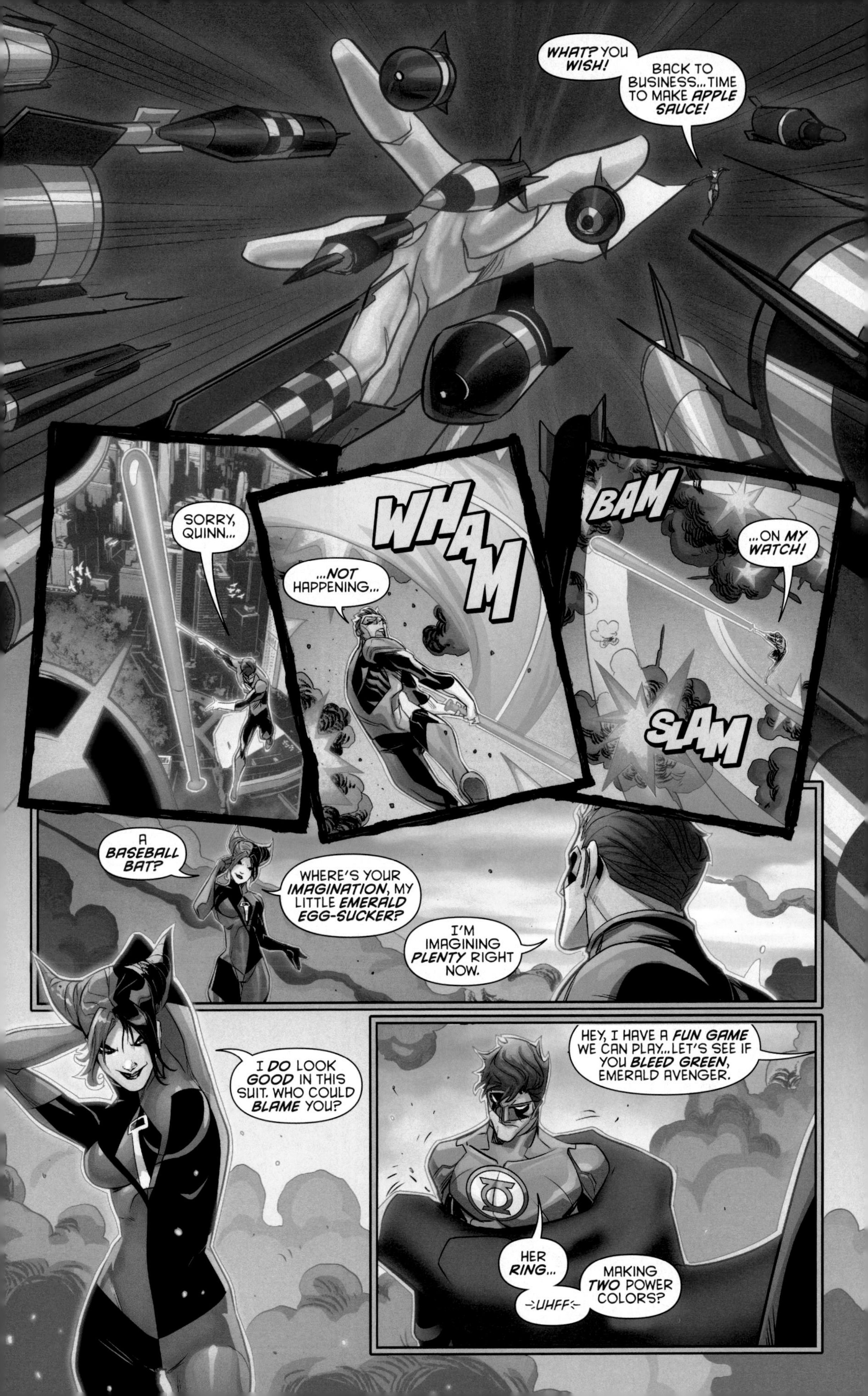
WHAT? YOU WISH!
BACK TO BUSINESS... TIME TO MAKE APPLE SAUCE!
SORRY, QUINN...
WHAM
...NOT HAPPENING...
BAM
...ON MY WATCH!
SLAM
A BASEBALL BAT?
WHERE'S YOUR IMAGINATION, MY LITTLE EMERALD EGG-SUCKER?
I'M IMAGINING PLENTY RIGHT NOW.
I DO LOOK GOOD IN THIS SUIT. WHO COULD BLAME YOU?
HEY, I HAVE A FUN GAME WE CAN PLAY... LET'S SEE IF YOU BLEED GREEN, EMERALD AVENGER.
HER RING...
-UHFF-
MAKING TWO POWER COLORS?

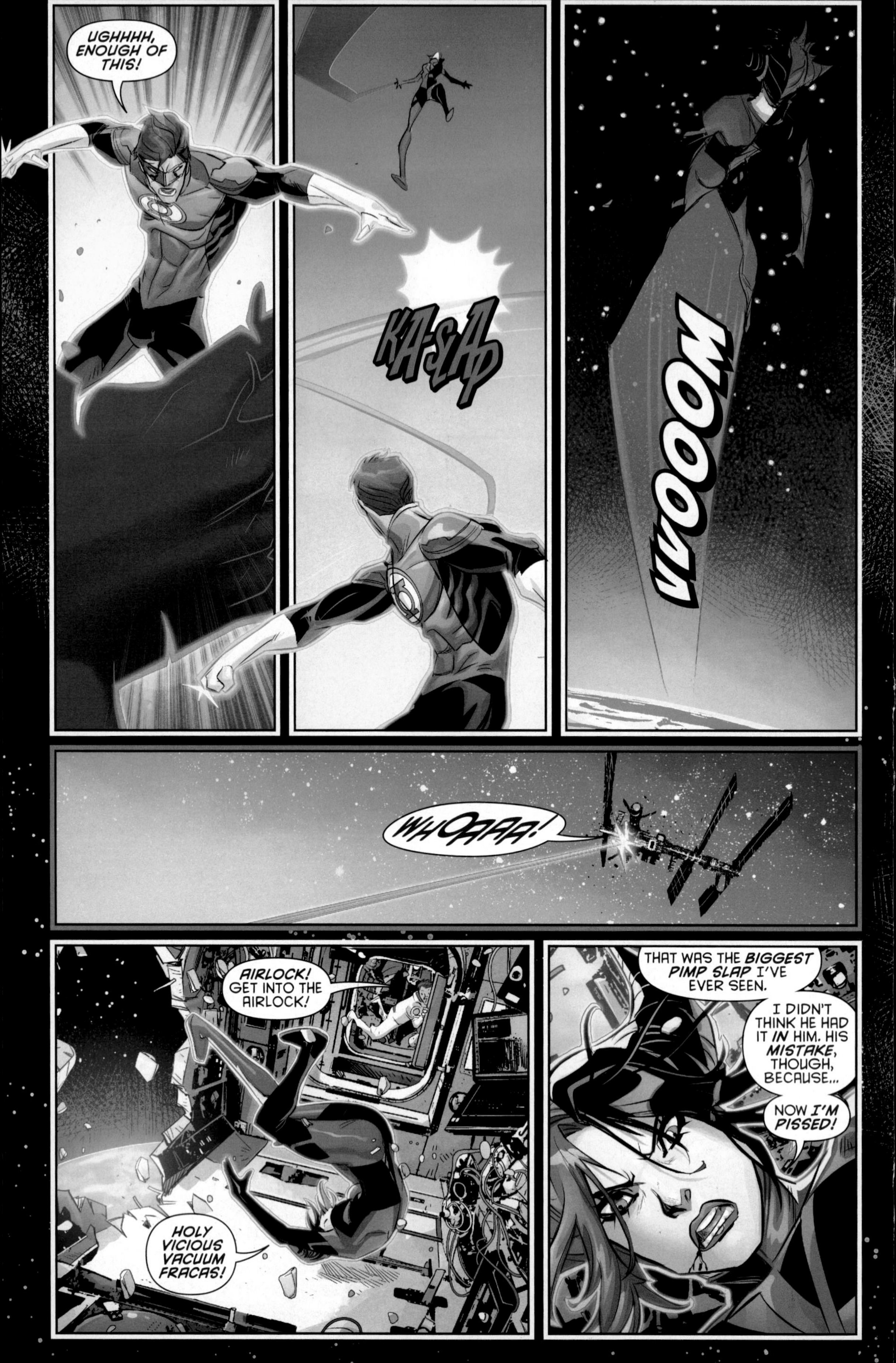
UGHHHH, ENOUGH OF THIS!
KA-SLAP
VWOOOM
WHOAAAA!
AIRLOCK! GET INTO THE AIRLOCK!
HOLY VICIOUS VACUUM FRACAS!
THAT WAS THE BIGGEST PIMP SLAP I'VE EVER SEEN.
I DIDN'T THINK HE HAD IT IN HIM. HIS MISTAKE, THOUGH, BECAUSE...
NOW I'M PISSED!

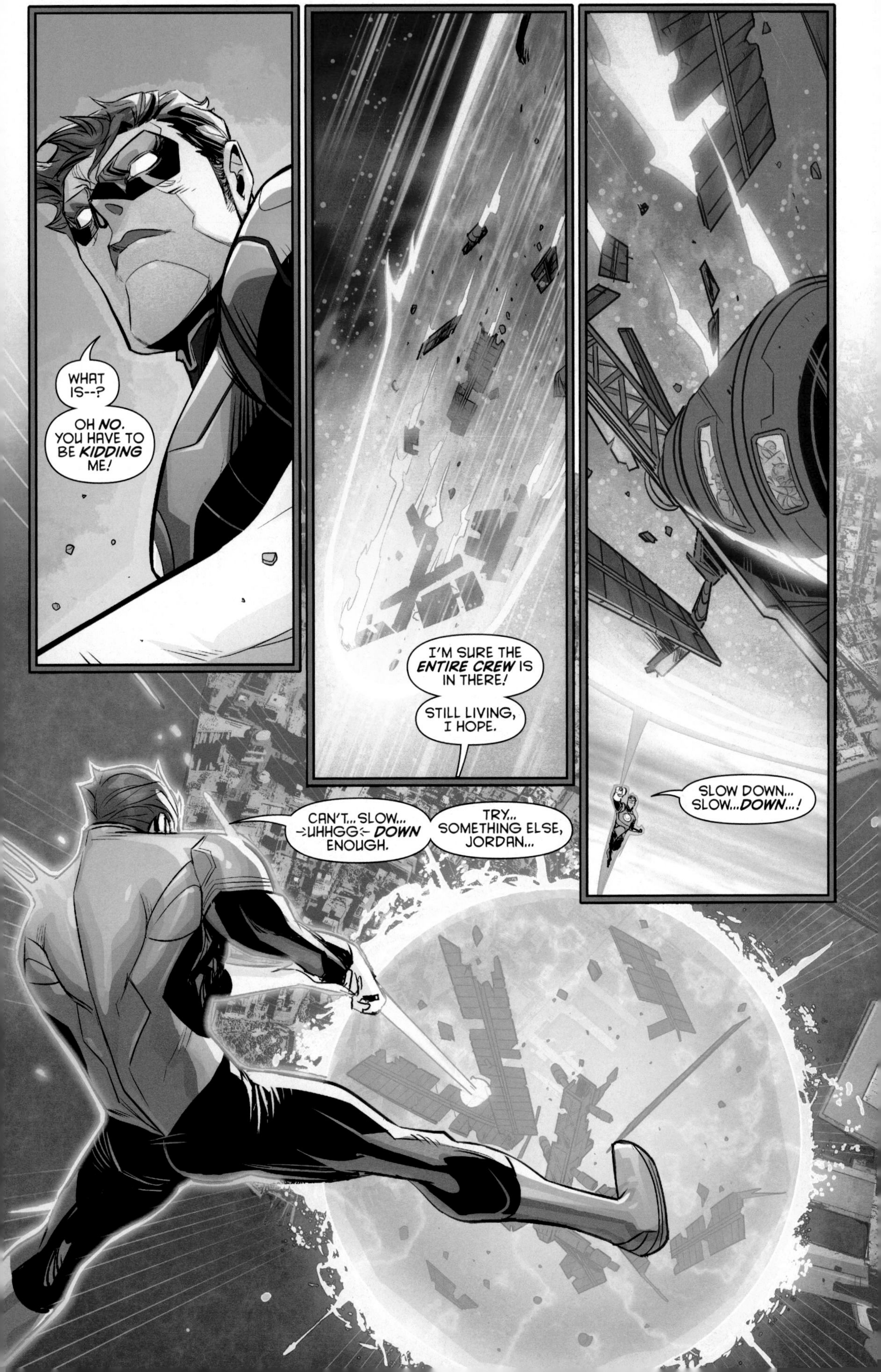
WHAT IS--?
OH NO. YOU HAVE TO BE KIDDING ME!
I'M SURE THE ENTIRE CREW IS IN THERE!
STILL LIVING, I HOPE.
SLOW DOWN... SLOW...DOWN...!
CAN'T...SLOW... ->UHHGG<- DOWN ENOUGH.
TRY... SOMETHING ELSE, JORDAN...

FOOOMMP

THAT SHOULD DO IT.

ASTRONAUTS ACCOUNTED FOR...

...COAST GUARD'S IN...

...GOOD.

WHOA!

WHAT NOW?

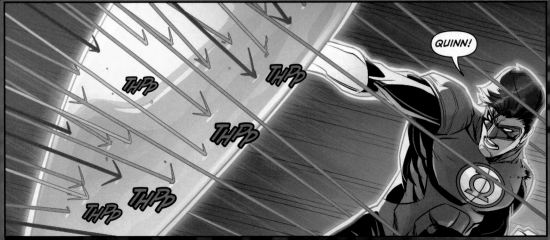

THPP

THPP

THPP

THPP

THPP

QUINN!

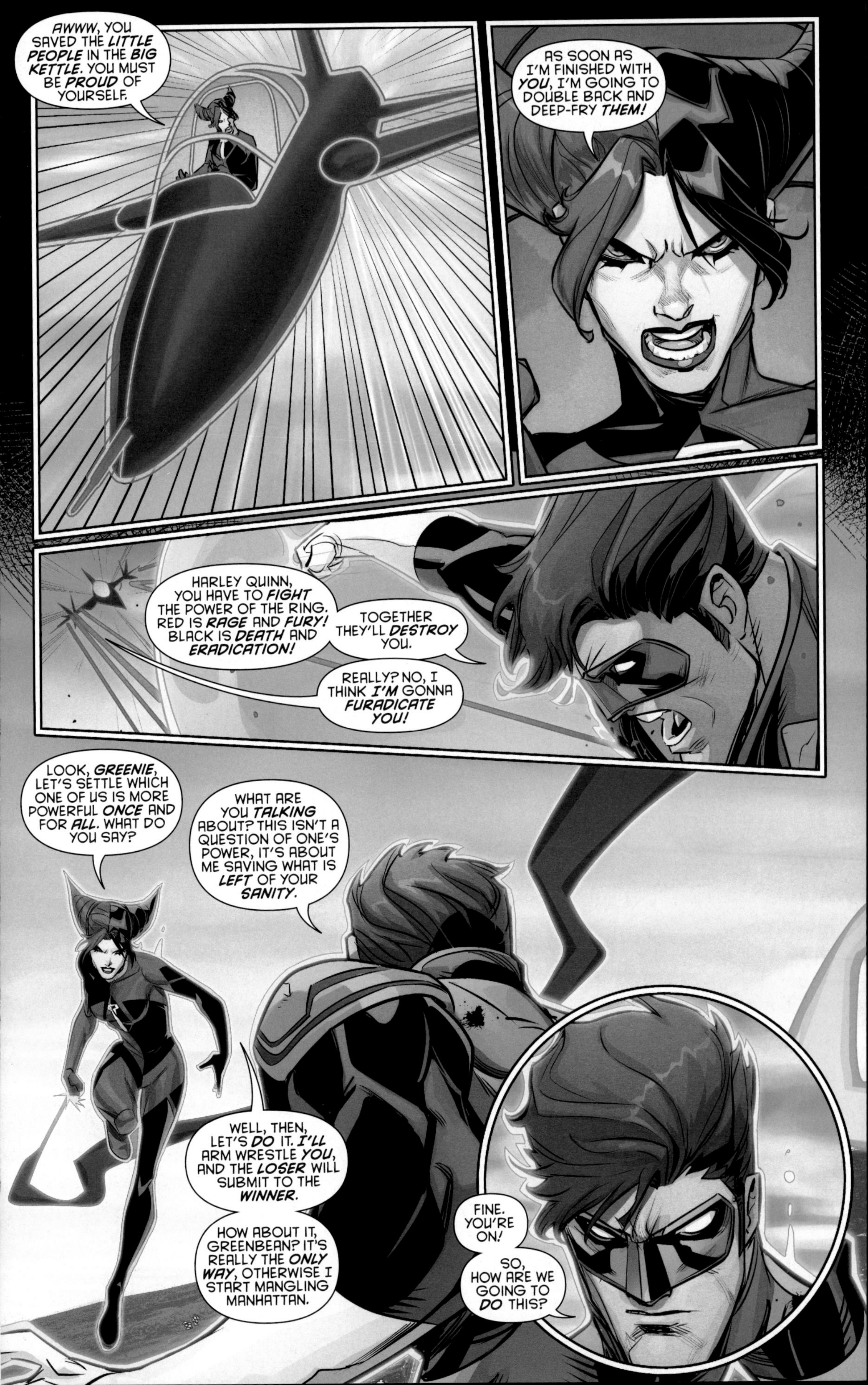
AWWW, YOU SAVED THE LITTLE PEOPLE IN THE BIG KETTLE. YOU MUST BE PROUD OF YOURSELF.
AS SOON AS I'M FINISHED WITH YOU, I'M GOING TO DOUBLE BACK AND DEEP-FRY THEM!
HARLEY QUINN, YOU HAVE TO FIGHT THE POWER OF THE RING. RED IS RAGE AND FURY! BLACK IS DEATH AND ERADICATION!
TOGETHER THEY'LL DESTROY YOU.
REALLY? NO, I THINK I'M GONNA FURADICATE YOU!
LOOK, GREENIE, LET'S SETTLE WHICH ONE OF US IS MORE POWERFUL ONCE AND FOR ALL. WHAT DO YOU SAY?
WHAT ARE YOU TALKING ABOUT? THIS ISN'T A QUESTION OF ONE'S POWER, IT'S ABOUT ME SAVING WHAT IS LEFT OF YOUR SANITY.
WELL, THEN, LET'S DO IT. I'LL ARM WRESTLE YOU, AND THE LOSER WILL SUBMIT TO THE WINNER.
HOW ABOUT IT, GREENBEAN? IT'S REALLY THE ONLY WAY, OTHERWISE I START MANGLING MANHATTAN.
FINE. YOU'RE ON!
SO, HOW ARE WE GOING TO DO THIS?

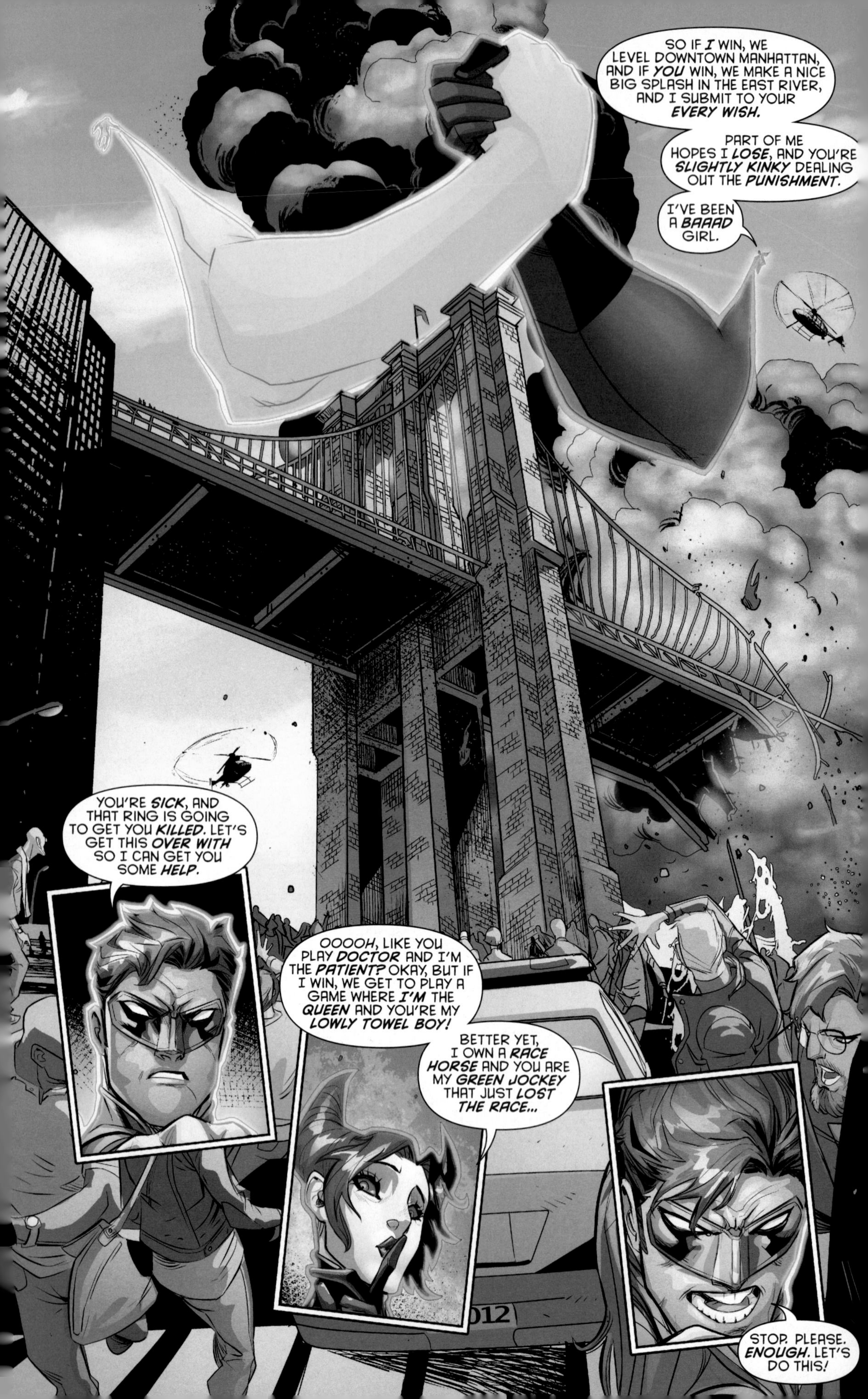
SO IF *I* WIN, WE LEVEL DOWNTOWN MANHATTAN, AND IF *YOU* WIN, WE MAKE A NICE BIG SPLASH IN THE EAST RIVER, AND I SUBMIT TO YOUR *EVERY WISH.*
PART OF ME HOPES I *LOSE*, AND YOU'RE *SLIGHTLY KINKY* DEALING OUT THE *PUNISHMENT*.
I'VE BEEN A *BAAAD* GIRL.
YOU'RE *SICK*, AND THAT RING IS GOING TO GET YOU *KILLED*. LET'S GET THIS *OVER WITH* SO I CAN GET YOU SOME *HELP*.
OOOOH, LIKE YOU PLAY *DOCTOR* AND I'M THE *PATIENT?* OKAY, BUT IF I WIN, WE GET TO PLAY A GAME WHERE *I'M* THE *QUEEN* AND YOU'RE MY *LOWLY TOWEL BOY!*
BETTER YET, I OWN A *RACE HORSE* AND YOU ARE MY *GREEN JOCKEY* THAT JUST *LOST THE RACE...*
STOP. PLEASE. *ENOUGH*. LET'S DO THIS!

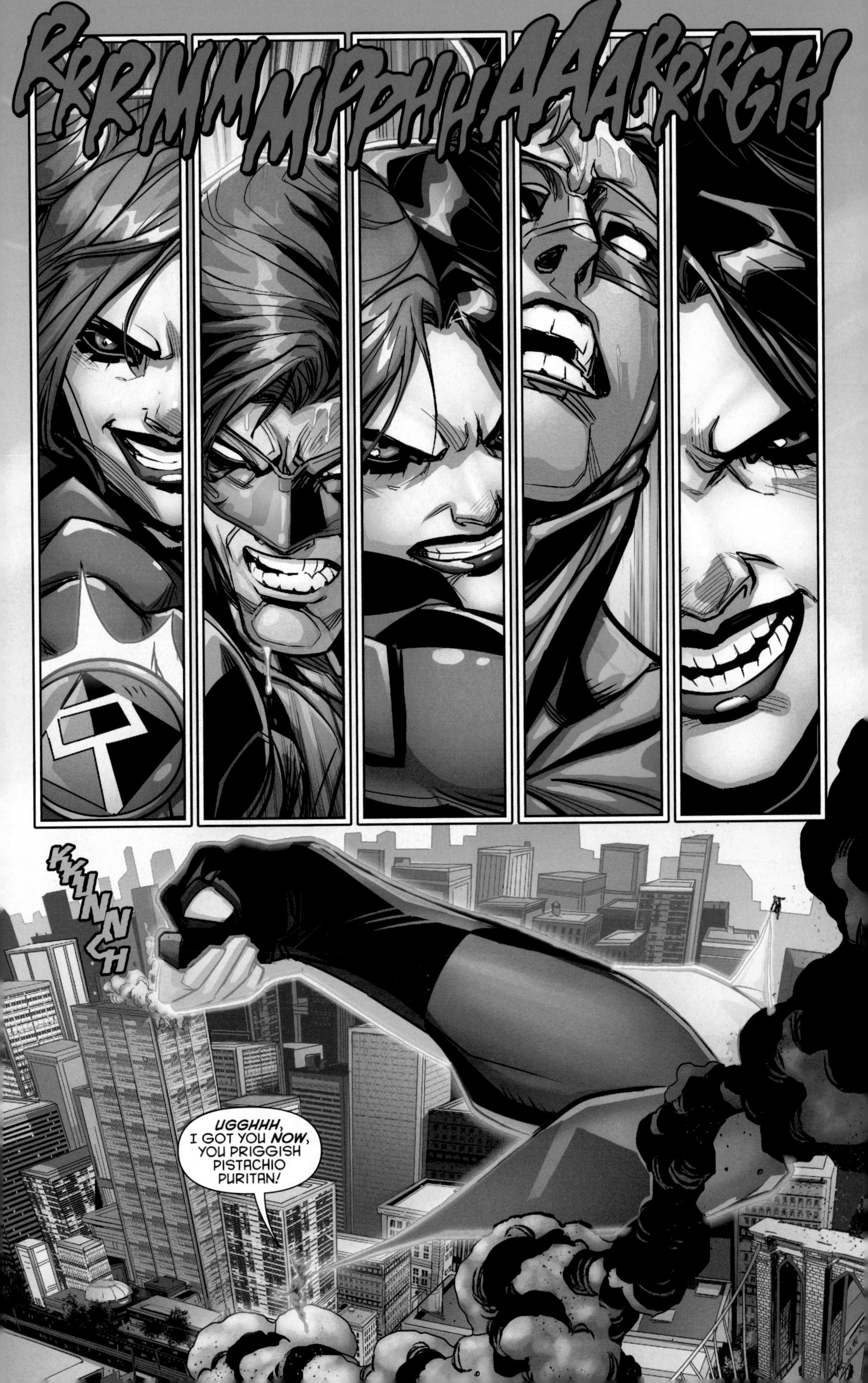
RRRMMMMPPHHAAAARRRGH
KKUNNCH
UGGHHH, I GOT YOU NOW, YOU PRIGGISH PISTACHIO PURITAN!

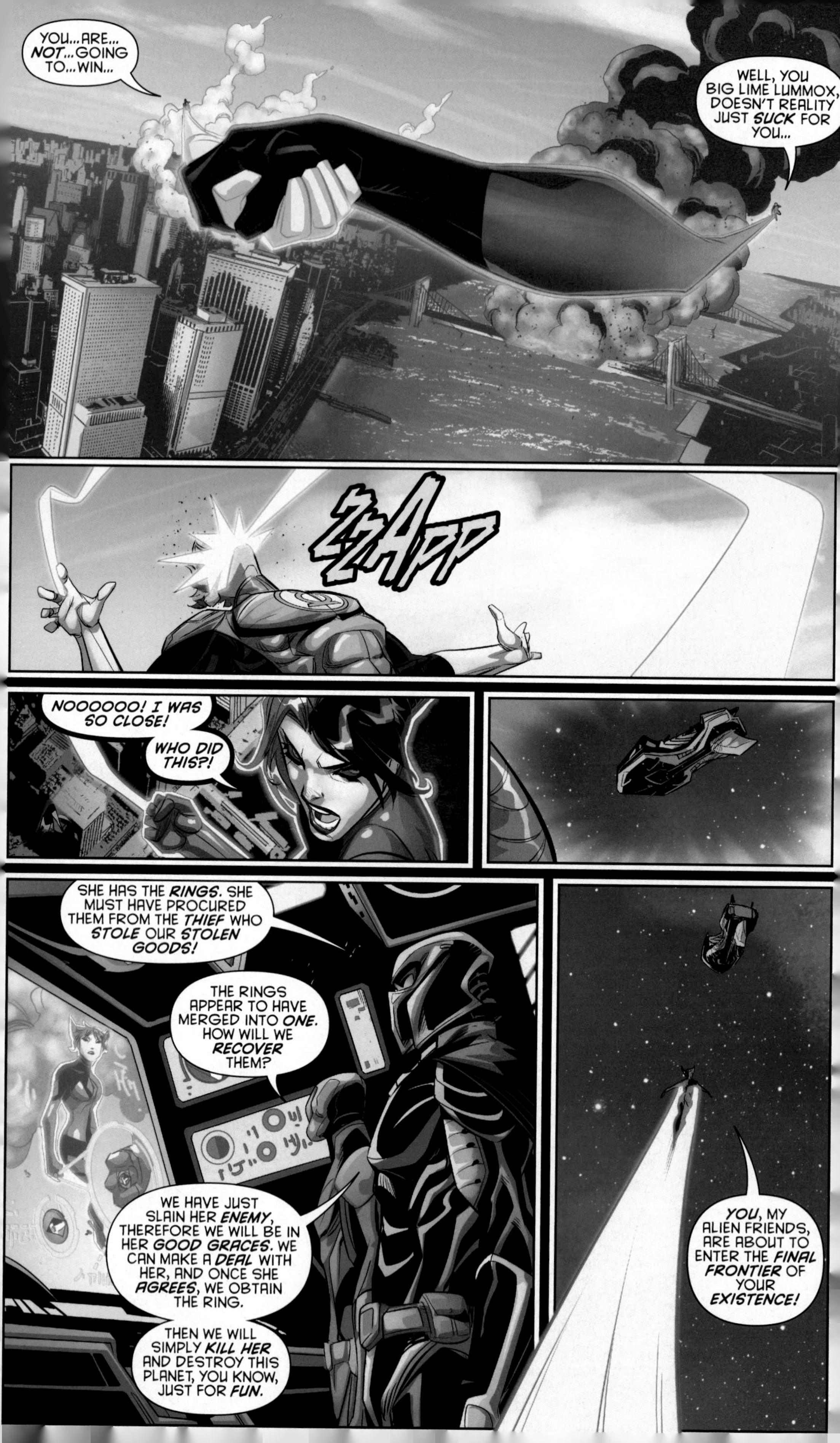
YOU...ARE... NOT...GOING TO...WIN...
WELL, YOU BIG LIME LUMMOX, DOESN'T REALITY JUST SUCK FOR YOU...
ZZAPP
NOOOOOO! I WAS SO CLOSE!
WHO DID THIS?!
SHE HAS THE RINGS. SHE MUST HAVE PROCURED THEM FROM THE THIEF WHO STOLE OUR STOLEN GOODS!
THE RINGS APPEAR TO HAVE MERGED INTO ONE. HOW WILL WE RECOVER THEM?
WE HAVE JUST SLAIN HER ENEMY, THEREFORE WE WILL BE IN HER GOOD GRACES. WE CAN MAKE A DEAL WITH HER, AND ONCE SHE AGREES, WE OBTAIN THE RING.
THEN WE WILL SIMPLY KILL HER AND DESTROY THIS PLANET, YOU KNOW, JUST FOR FUN.
YOU, MY ALIEN FRIENDS, ARE ABOUT TO ENTER THE FINAL FRONTIER OF YOUR EXISTENCE!

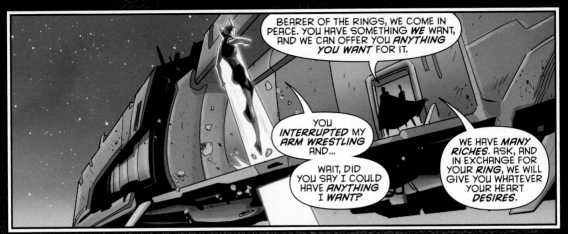

BEARER OF THE RINGS, WE COME IN PEACE. YOU HAVE SOMETHING *WE* WANT, AND WE CAN OFFER YOU *ANYTHING YOU WANT* FOR IT.

YOU *INTERRUPTED* MY *ARM WRESTLING* AND...

WAIT, DID YOU SAY I COULD HAVE *ANYTHING* I *WANT*?

WE HAVE *MANY RICHES*. ASK, AND IN EXCHANGE FOR YOUR *RING*, WE WILL GIVE YOU WHATEVER YOUR HEART *DESIRES*.

SO, I GIVE YOU THIS RING AND YOU CAN GIVE ME, LET'S SAY, AN *ARMY* OF FIRE-BREATHING *DRAGONS*, OR PERHAPS A MILLION *PEPPERONI PIZZA PIES*?

I AM SURE IF YOU TELL US WHAT A *PEPPERONI PIZZA PIE* IS, WE CAN ACCOMMODATE YOU.

HOW ABOUT A PLANET'S WORTH OF KITTENS AND PUPPIES THAT DON'T *POO*?

AGAIN, IF YOU LET US KNOW WHAT *KITTENS, PUPPIES, AND POO* ARE, WE SHALL MAKE IT HAPPEN.

I...I... ~*UGGHH*~ WHY AM I SO *TIRED* ALL OF A SUDDEN?

THE RING TAKES A TOLL ON THOSE WHO WIELD ITS POWER. SIMPLY *REMOVE* IT AND GIVE IT TO *ME*. NOT ONLY SHALL YOU FEEL *IMPROVED*, BUT ALL YOUR WISHES WILL BE INDULGED.

WAIT, THE *RING*...IT'S *TALKING* TO ME...

THAT'S...AN *AZAKARIAN WAR SHIP*... SHE HAS NO IDEA...

WE *GOT* YOU BUDDY.

SEEMS THIS RING CAN ALSO READ *MINDS*, AND IT'S TELLING ME YOU ARE *FULL OF IT.* IT MEANING *"POO".*

I DON'T LIKE *LIARS*, ANAKIN.

YOU HAVE *ANY IDEA* WHAT HAPPENS TO *LIARS*?

ENOUGH OF THIS.

ARRGGGHH!

WEAK HUMAN.

THE RING IS **MINE.** NOW NOTHING STANDS IN MY **WAY!**

*

HUH? WHA'S **HAPPENIN'**? WHERE **AM** I?

WHAT'S BROOKLYN DOIN' WAY DOWN **THERE,** AN' WHY AM I WAY UP **HERE?**

I CAN HELP ANSWER THAT.

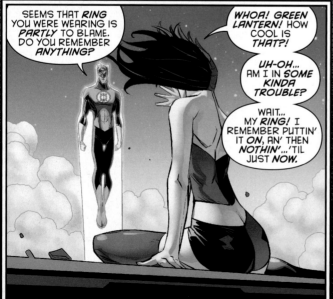

SEEMS THAT **RING** YOU WERE WEARING IS **PARTLY** TO BLAME. DO YOU REMEMBER **ANYTHING?**

WHOA! **GREEN LANTERN!** HOW COOL IS **THAT?!**

UH-OH... AM I IN **SOME KINDA** TROUBLE?

WAIT... MY **RING!** I REMEMBER PUTTIN' IT **ON,** AN' THEN **NOTHIN'**...'TIL JUST **NOW.**

EEYAAHHH!

SOMEONE STOLE MY **RING!**

THIS SHIP IS AZAKARIAN, AN ALIEN RACE OF **THIEVES** AND **KILLERS.** I AM AFRAID WITH THAT **RING** IN THEIR POSSESSION, **NOTHING GOOD** WILL HAPPEN.

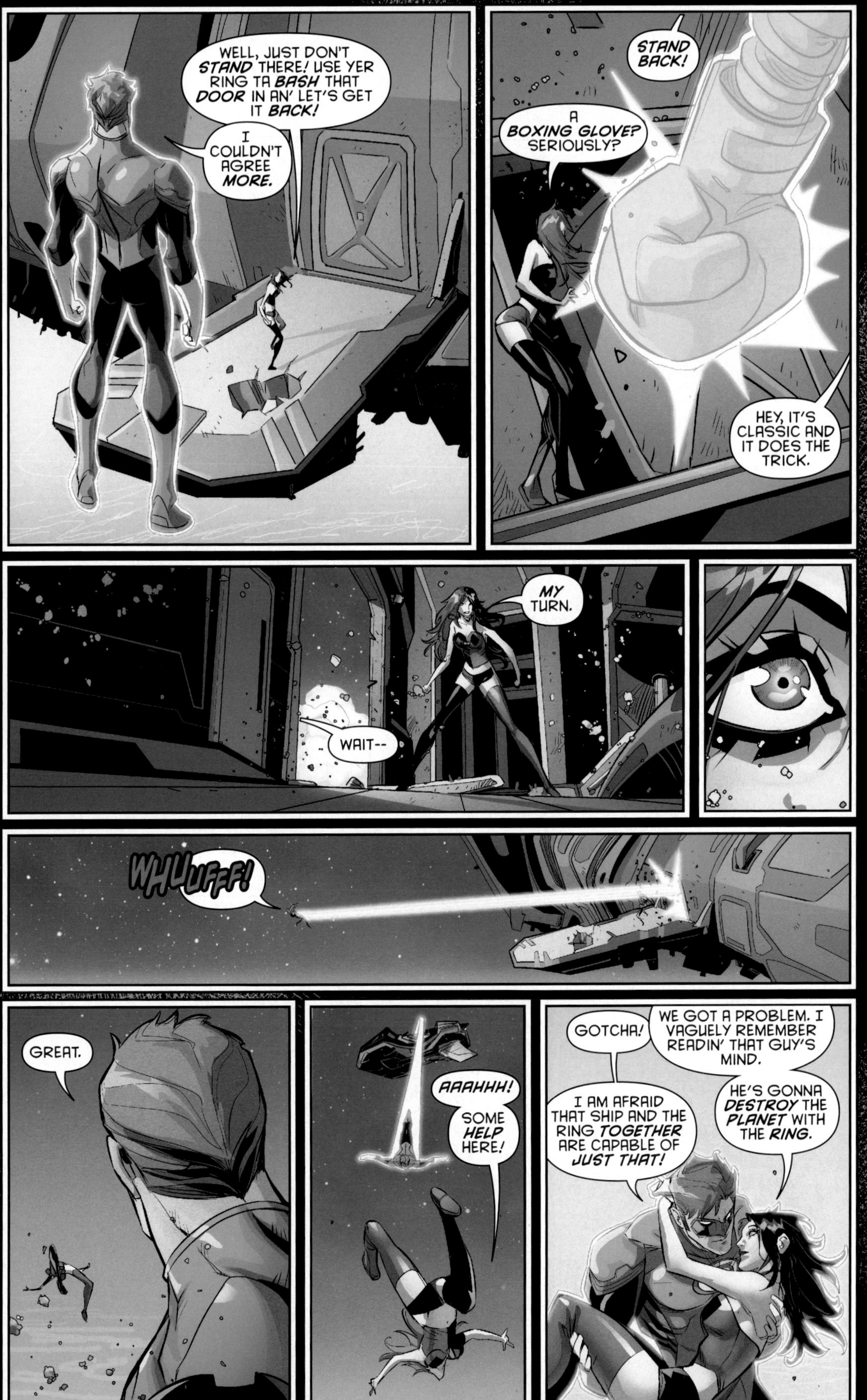

WELL, JUST DON'T STAND THERE! USE YER RING TA BASH THAT DOOR IN AN' LET'S GET IT BACK!
I COULDN'T AGREE MORE.
STAND BACK!
A BOXING GLOVE? SERIOUSLY?
HEY, IT'S CLASSIC AND IT DOES THE TRICK.
MY TURN.
WAIT--
WHUUFFF!
GREAT.
AAAHHH!
SOME HELP HERE!
GOTCHA!
WE GOT A PROBLEM. I VAGUELY REMEMBER READIN' THAT GUY'S MIND.
HE'S GONNA DESTROY THE PLANET WITH THE RING.
I AM AFRAID THAT SHIP AND THE RING TOGETHER ARE CAPABLE OF JUST THAT!

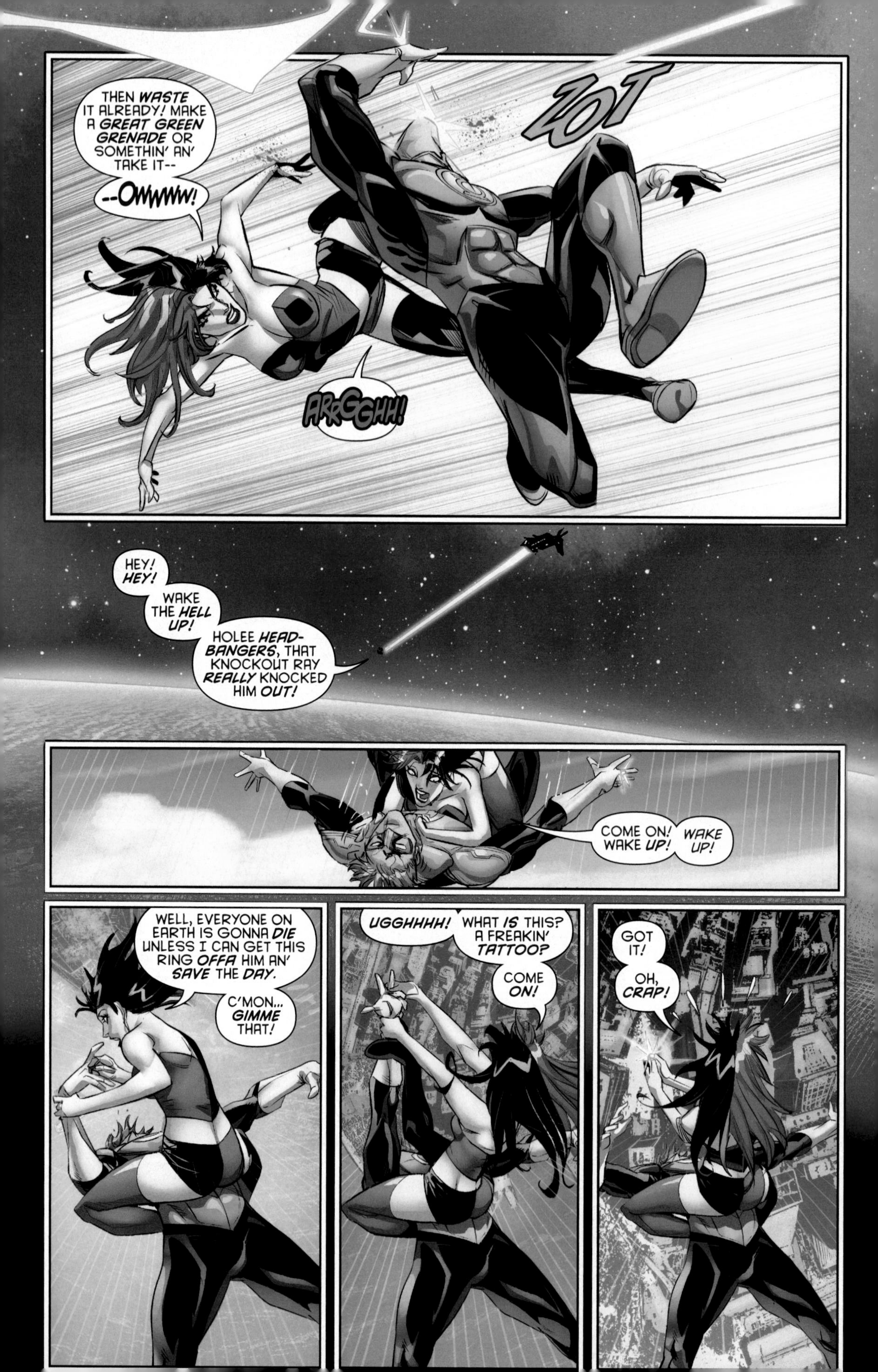

THEN WASTE IT ALREADY! MAKE A GREAT GREEN GRENADE OR SOMETHIN' AN' TAKE IT--
--OWWWW!
ZOT
ARRGGHH!
HEY! HEY!
WAKE THE HELL UP!
HOLEE HEAD-BANGERS, THAT KNOCKOUT RAY REALLY KNOCKED HIM OUT!
COME ON! WAKE UP!
WAKE UP!
WELL, EVERYONE ON EARTH IS GONNA DIE UNLESS I CAN GET THIS RING OFFA HIM AN' SAVE THE DAY.
C'MON... GIMME THAT!
UGGHHHH!
WHAT IS THIS? A FREAKIN' TATTOO?
COME ON!
GOT IT!
OH, CRAP!

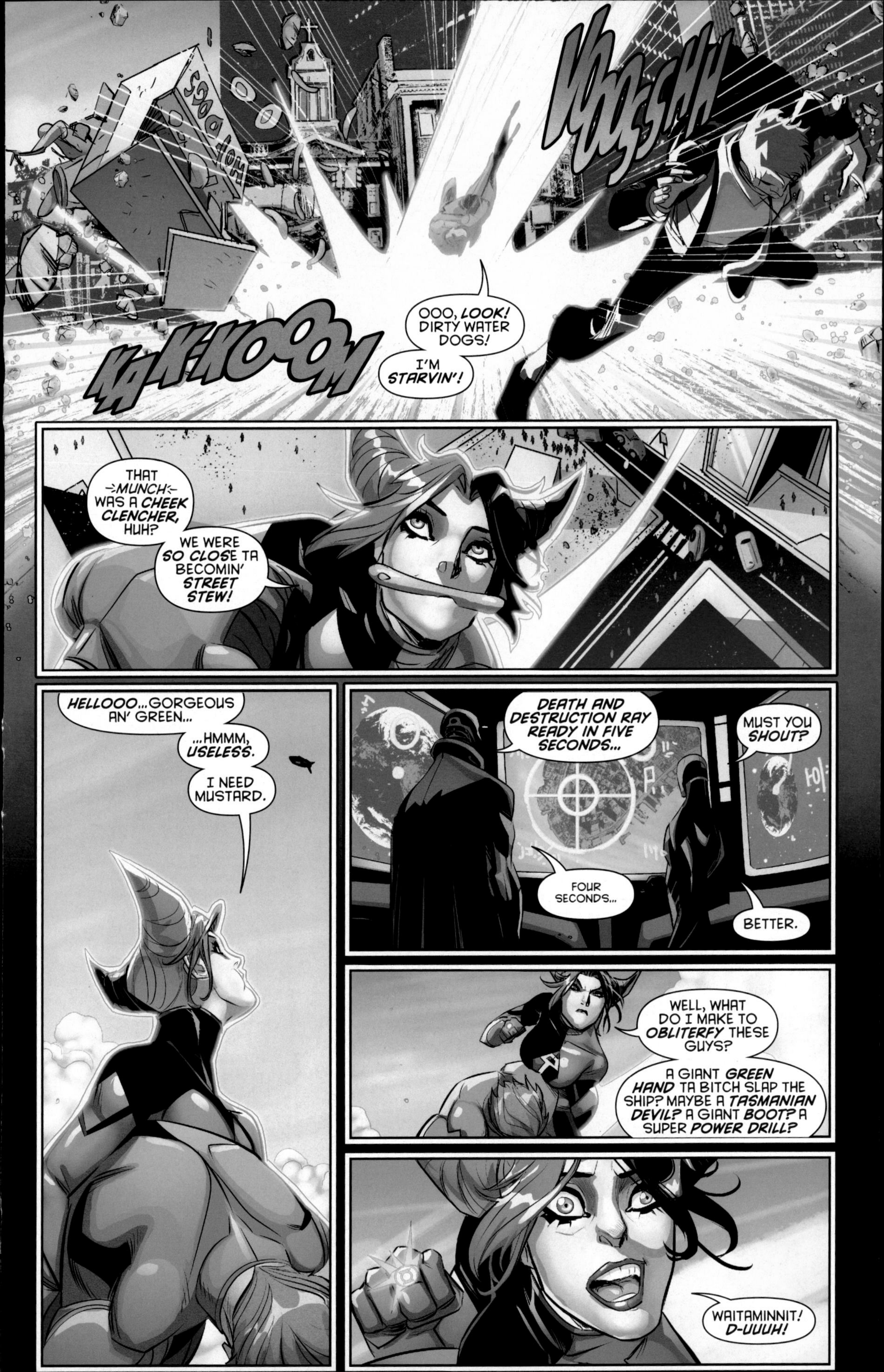
VOOSSHH
KA-K-KOOOOM
OOO, LOOK! DIRTY WATER DOGS!
I'M STARVIN'!
THAT *MUNCH* WAS A CHEEK CLENCHER, HUH?
WE WERE SO CLOSE TA BECOMIN' STREET STEW!
HELLOOO... GORGEOUS AN' GREEN...
...HMMM, USELESS.
I NEED MUSTARD.
DEATH AND DESTRUCTION RAY READY IN FIVE SECONDS...
MUST YOU SHOUT?
FOUR SECONDS...
BETTER.
WELL, WHAT DO I MAKE TO OBLITERFY THESE GUYS?
A GIANT GREEN HAND TA BITCH SLAP THE SHIP? MAYBE A TASMANIAN DEVIL? A GIANT BOOT? A SUPER POWER DRILL?
WAITAMINNIT! D-UUUH!

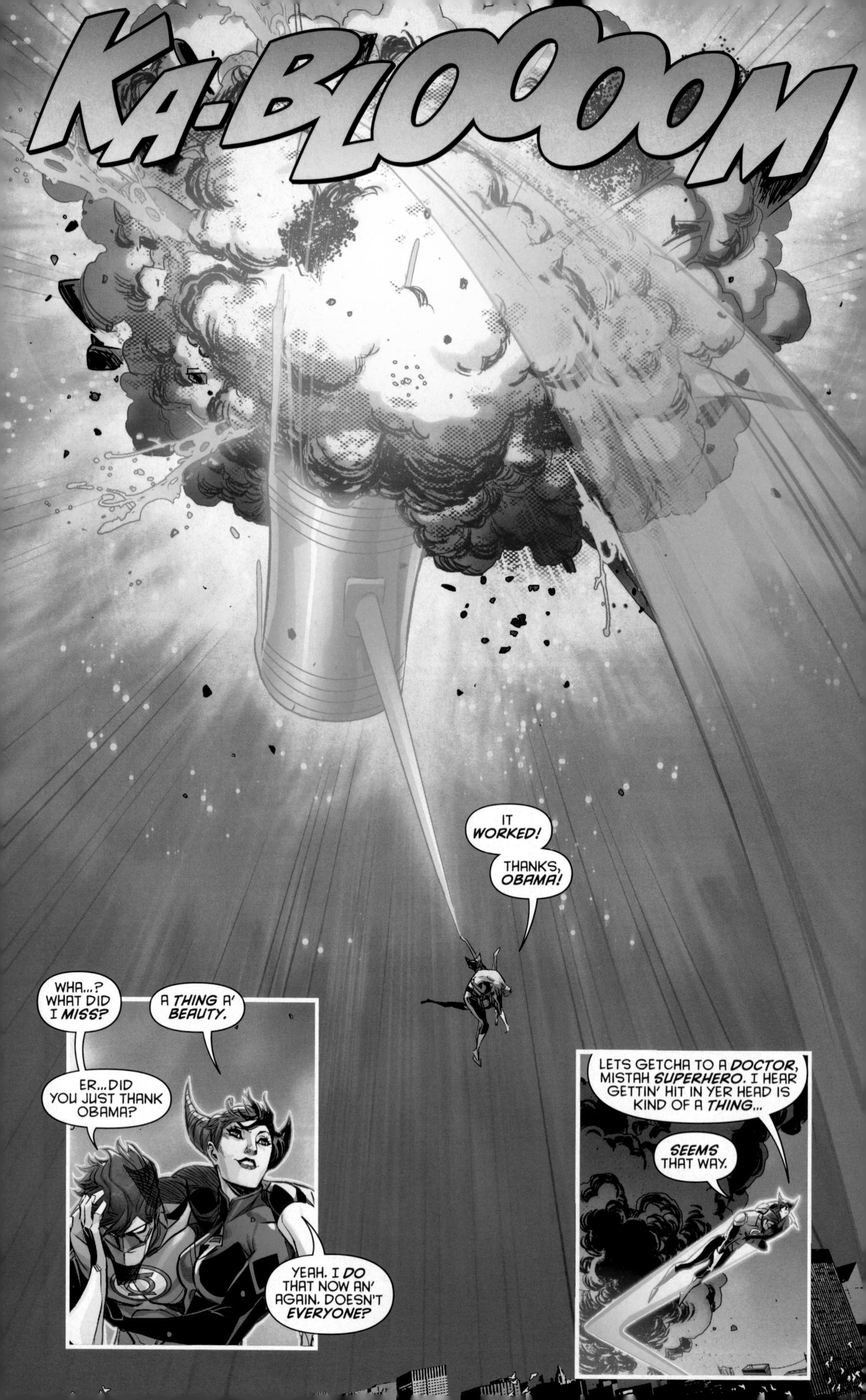
KA-BLOOOOM
IT WORKED!
THANKS, OBAMA!
WHA...? WHAT DID I MISS?
A THING A' BEAUTY.
ER...DID YOU JUST THANK OBAMA?
YEAH. I DO THAT NOW AN' AGAIN. DOESN'T EVERYONE?
LETS GETCHA TO A DOCTOR, MISTAH SUPERHERO. I HEAR GETTIN' HIT IN YER HEAD IS KIND OF A THING...
SEEMS THAT WAY.

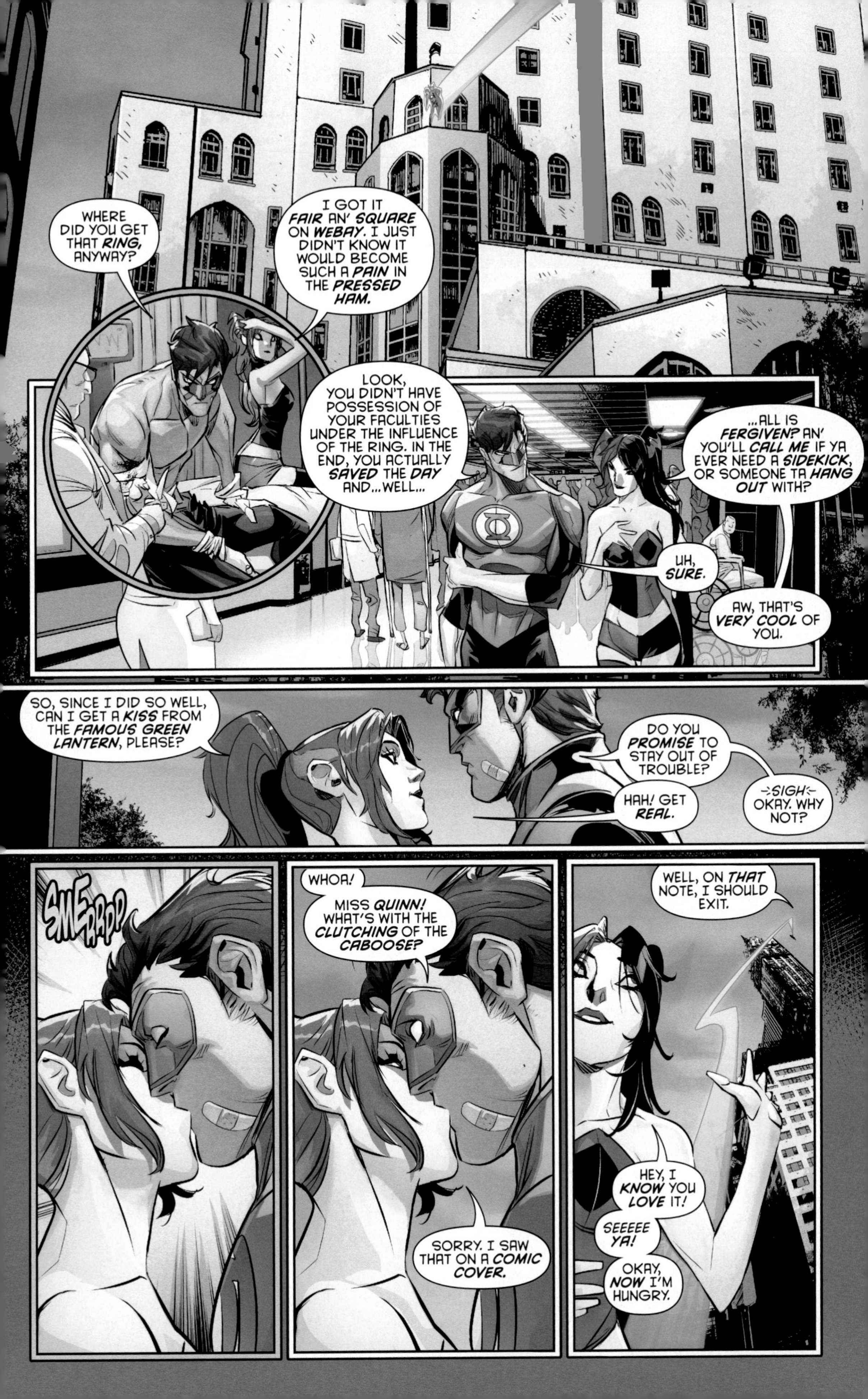
WHERE DID YOU GET THAT RING, ANYWAY?
I GOT IT FAIR AN' SQUARE ON WEBAY. I JUST DIDN'T KNOW IT WOULD BECOME SUCH A PAIN IN THE PRESSED HAM.
LOOK, YOU DIDN'T HAVE POSSESSION OF YOUR FACULTIES UNDER THE INFLUENCE OF THE RING. IN THE END, YOU ACTUALLY SAVED THE DAY AND...WELL...
...ALL IS FERGIVEN? AN' YOU'LL CALL ME IF YA EVER NEED A SIDEKICK, OR SOMEONE TA HANG OUT WITH?
UH, SURE.
AW, THAT'S VERY COOL OF YOU.
SO, SINCE I DID SO WELL, CAN I GET A KISS FROM THE FAMOUS GREEN LANTERN, PLEASE?
DO YOU PROMISE TO STAY OUT OF TROUBLE?
HAH! GET REAL.
-SIGH- OKAY. WHY NOT?
SMERRPP
WHOA!
MISS QUINN! WHAT'S WITH THE CLUTCHING OF THE CABOOSE?
SORRY. I SAW THAT ON A COMIC COVER.
WELL, ON THAT NOTE, I SHOULD EXIT.
HEY, I KNOW YOU LOVE IT!
SEEEEE YA!
OKAY, NOW I'M HUNGRY.

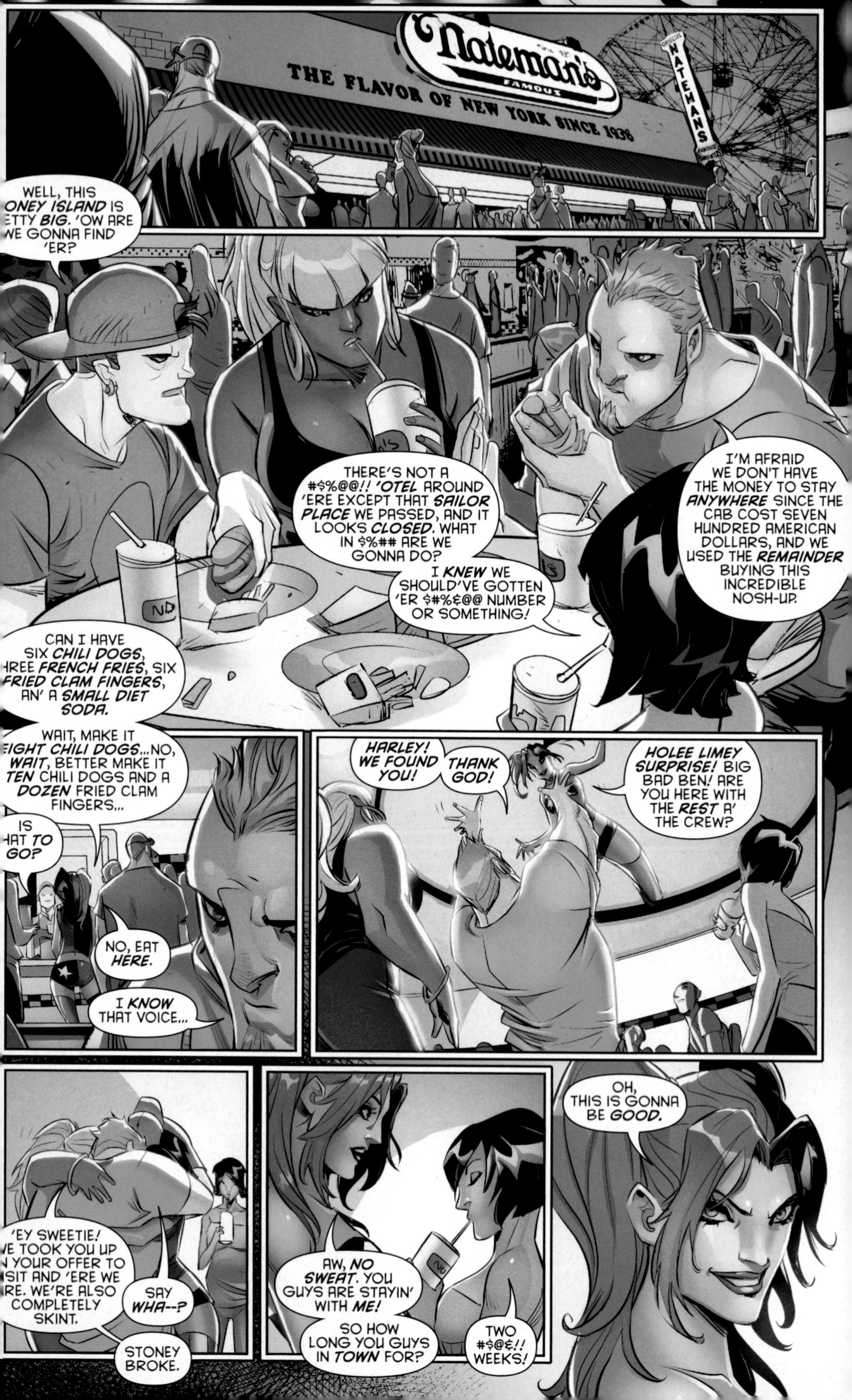
NATEMAN'S FAMOUS EST. 1936
THE FLAVOR OF NEW YORK SINCE 1936
ORIGINAL NATEMANS FAMOUS
WELL, THIS ONEY ISLAND IS ETTY BIG. 'OW ARE WE GONNA FIND 'ER?
THERE'S NOT A #$%@@!! 'OTEL AROUND 'ERE EXCEPT THAT SAILOR PLACE WE PASSED, AND IT LOOKS CLOSED. WHAT IN $%## ARE WE GONNA DO?
I'M AFRAID WE DON'T HAVE THE MONEY TO STAY ANYWHERE SINCE THE CAB COST SEVEN HUNDRED AMERICAN DOLLARS, AND WE USED THE REMAINDER BUYING THIS INCREDIBLE NOSH-UP.
I KNEW WE SHOULD'VE GOTTEN 'ER $#%&@@ NUMBER OR SOMETHING!
CAN I HAVE SIX CHILI DOGS, HREE FRENCH FRIES, SIX FRIED CLAM FINGERS, AN' A SMALL DIET SODA.
WAIT, MAKE IT EIGHT CHILI DOGS...NO, WAIT, BETTER MAKE IT TEN CHILI DOGS AND A DOZEN FRIED CLAM FINGERS...
IS HAT TO GO?
NO, EAT HERE.
I KNOW THAT VOICE...
HARLEY! WE FOUND YOU!
THANK GOD!
HOLEE LIMEY SURPRISE! BIG BAD BEN! ARE YOU HERE WITH THE REST A' THE CREW?
'EY SWEETIE! E TOOK YOU UP N YOUR OFFER TO SIT AND 'ERE WE RE. WE'RE ALSO COMPLETELY SKINT.
SAY WHA--?
STONEY BROKE.
AW, NO SWEAT. YOU GUYS ARE STAYIN' WITH ME!
SO HOW LONG YOU GUYS IN TOWN FOR?
TWO #$@&!! WEEKS!
OH, THIS IS GONNA BE GOOD.

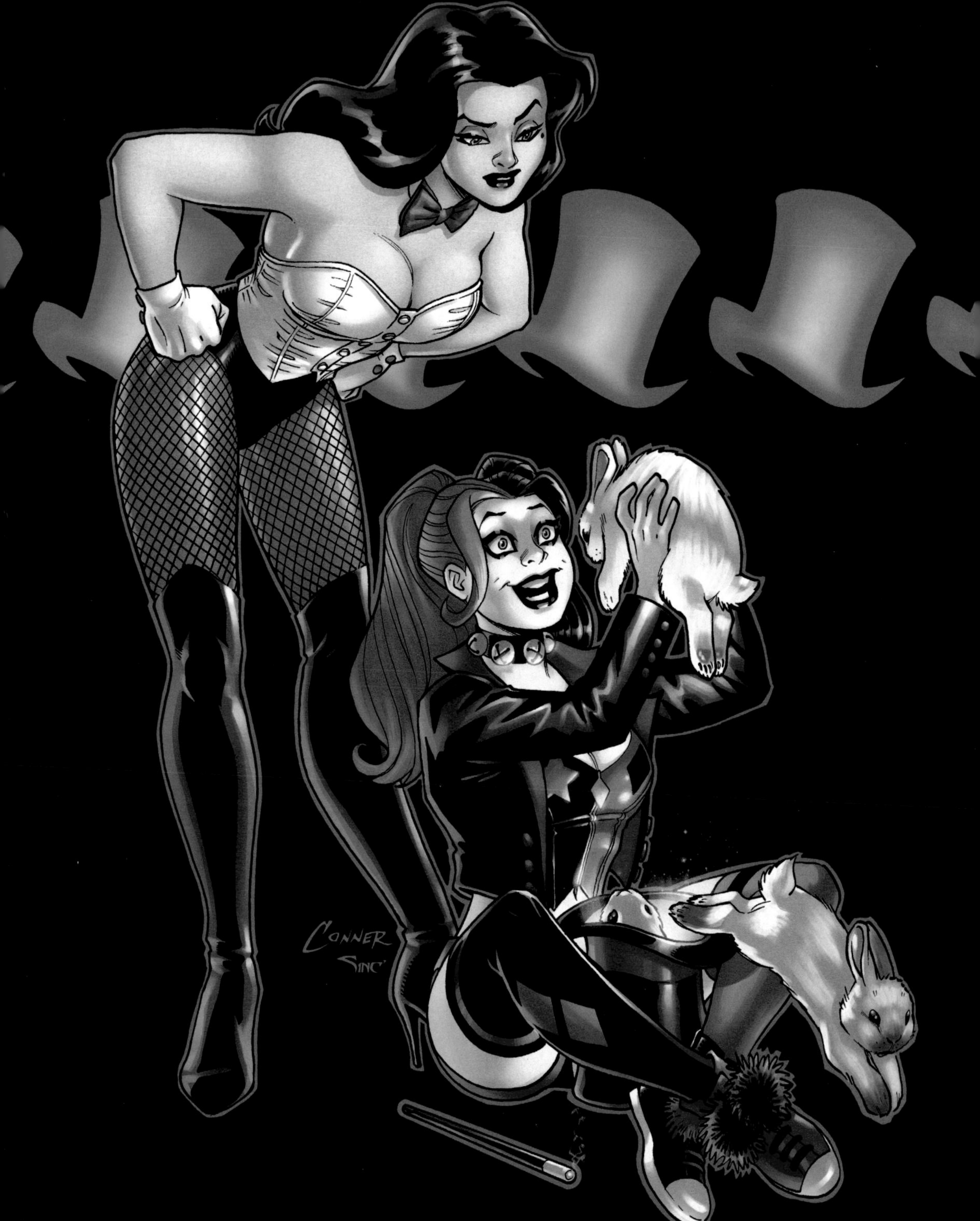
CONNER
SINC'

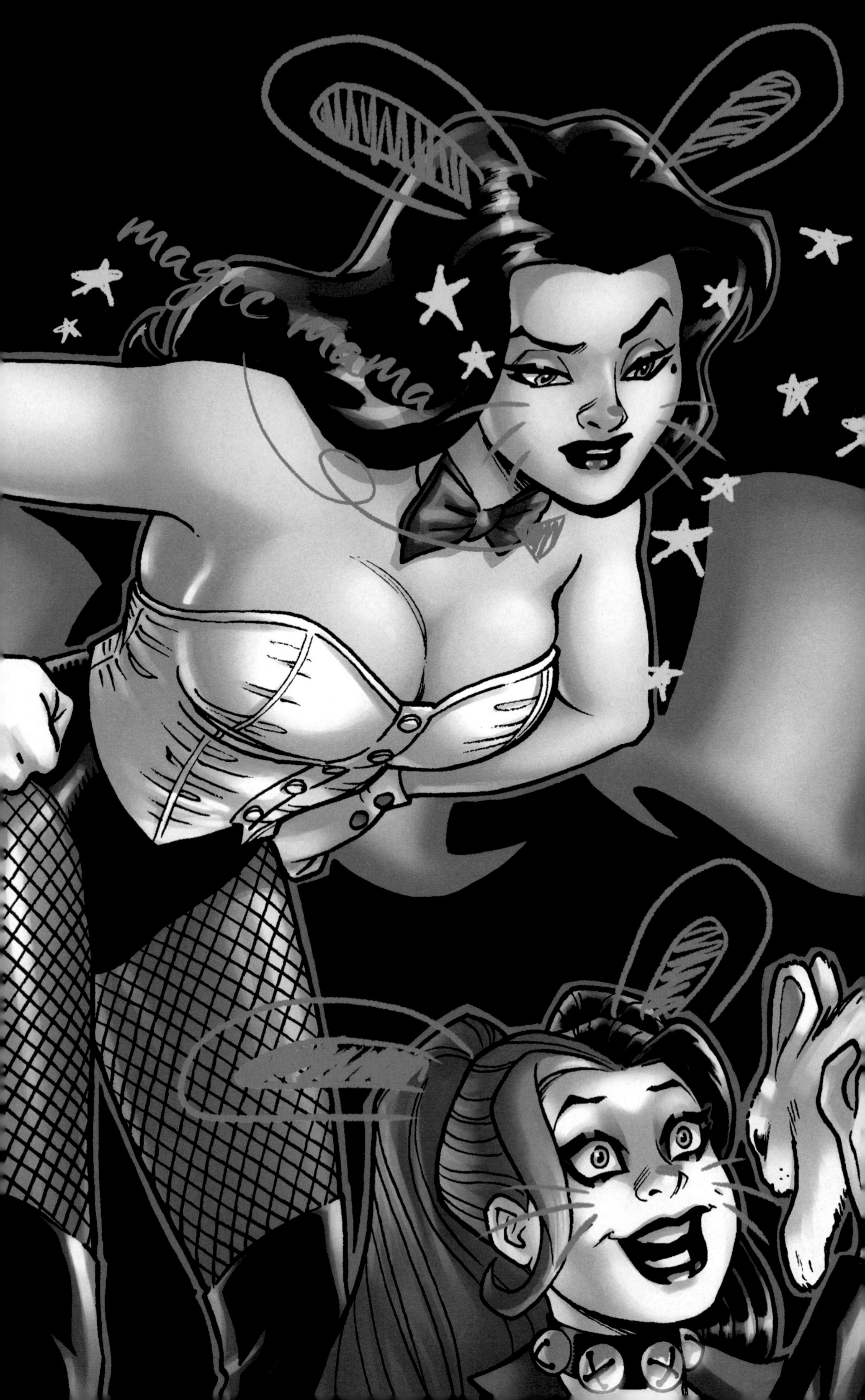
magic mama

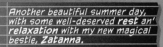

HARLEY QUINN IN DISPIRITED SPIRITS

Another beautiful summer day, with some well-deserved *rest an' relaxation* with my new magical bestie, Zatanna.

After the crazy few days we just had, we damn well *deserve* it.

How crazy, you ask? Lemme explain.

A long time ago, when I was in medical school, I was *workin' late* one night. I had just finished a double shift, when I *swear*, I kid you *not*, I saw a *ghost* walk out a' the morgue a' the hospital.

I put it off ta *exhaustion*, but this once non-believer is no more.

It was just a few days ago...

AMANDA CONNER & JIMMY PALMIOTTI **WRITERS**
JOSEPH MICHAEL LINSNER **ARTIST**   HI-FI **COLORS**   DAVE SHARPE **LETTERS**
AMANDA CONNER & ALEX SINCLAIR **COVER**   JOSEPH MICHAEL LINSNER **VARIANT COVER**
DAVE WIELGOSZ **ASST. EDITOR**   CHRIS CONROY **EDITOR**   MARK DOYLE **GROUP EDITOR**
HARLEY QUINN **CREATED BY** PAUL DINI & BRUCE TIMM

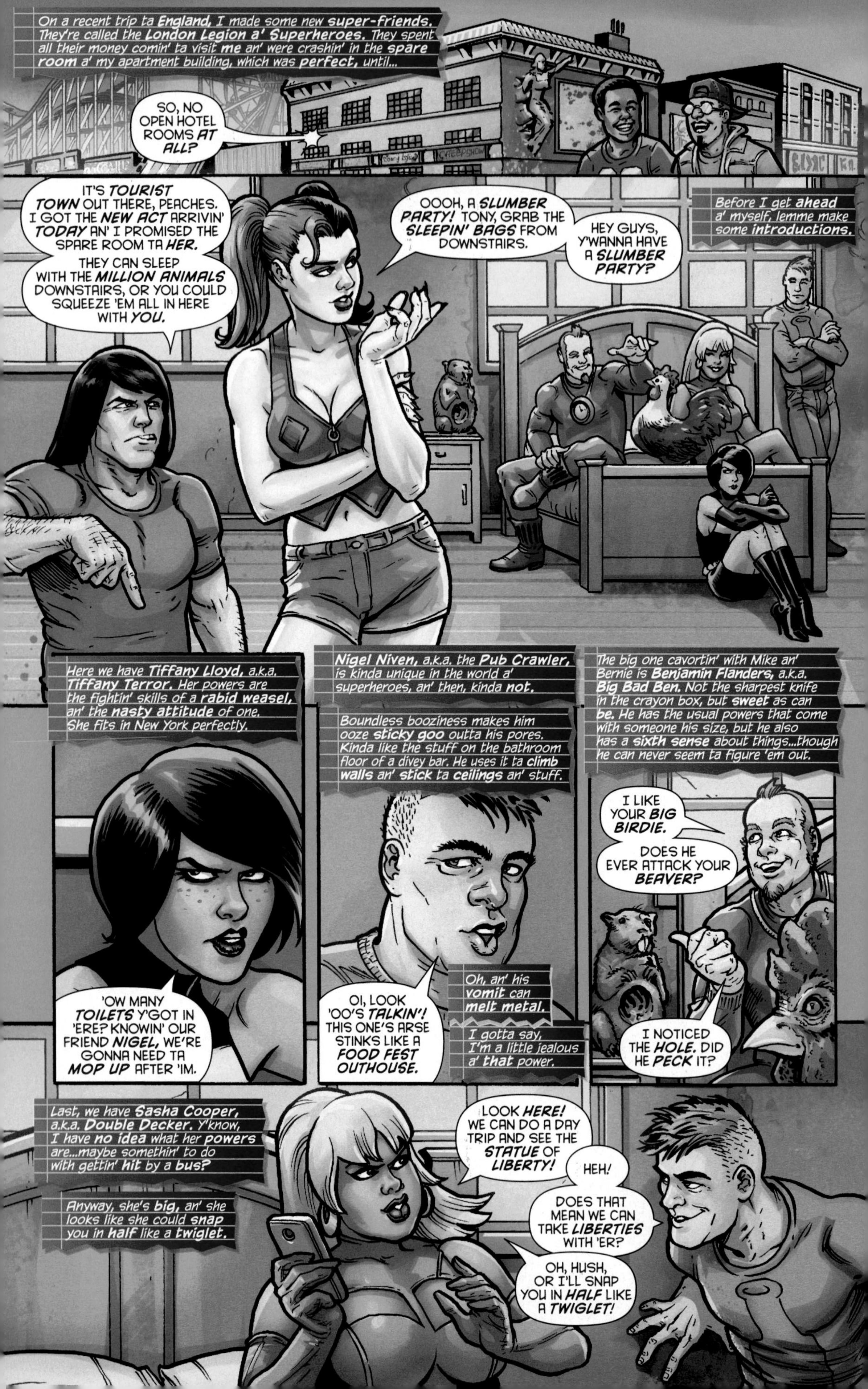
On a recent trip ta England, I made some new super-friends. They're called the London Legion a' Superheroes. They spent all their money comin' ta visit me an' were crashin' in the spare room a' my apartment building, which was perfect, until...
SO, NO OPEN HOTEL ROOMS AT ALL?
IT'S TOURIST TOWN OUT THERE, PEACHES. I GOT THE NEW ACT ARRIVIN' TODAY AN' I PROMISED THE SPARE ROOM TA HER.
THEY CAN SLEEP WITH THE MILLION ANIMALS DOWNSTAIRS, OR YOU COULD SQUEEZE 'EM ALL IN HERE WITH YOU.
OOOH, A SLUMBER PARTY! TONY, GRAB THE SLEEPIN' BAGS FROM DOWNSTAIRS.
HEY GUYS, Y'WANNA HAVE A SLUMBER PARTY?
Before I get ahead a' myself, lemme make some introductions.
Here we have Tiffany Lloyd, a.k.a. Tiffany Terror. Her powers are the fightin' skills of a rabid weasel, an' the nasty attitude of one. She fits in New York perfectly.
'OW MANY TOILETS Y'GOT IN 'ERE? KNOWIN' OUR FRIEND NIGEL, WE'RE GONNA NEED TA MOP UP AFTER 'IM.
Nigel Niven, a.k.a. the Pub Crawler, is kinda unique in the world a' superheroes, an' then, kinda not.
Boundless booziness makes him ooze sticky goo outta his pores. Kinda like the stuff on the bathroom floor of a divey bar. He uses it ta climb walls an' stick ta ceilings an' stuff.
OI, LOOK 'OO'S TALKIN'! THIS ONE'S ARSE STINKS LIKE A FOOD FEST OUTHOUSE.
Oh, an' his vomit can melt metal.
I gotta say, I'm a little jealous a' that power.
The big one cavortin' with Mike an' Bernie is Benjamin Flanders, a.k.a. Big Bad Ben. Not the sharpest knife in the crayon box, but sweet as can be. He has the usual powers that come with someone his size, but he also has a sixth sense about things...though he can never seem ta figure 'em out.
I LIKE YOUR BIG BIRDIE.
DOES HE EVER ATTACK YOUR BEAVER?
I NOTICED THE HOLE. DID HE PECK IT?
Last, we have Sasha Cooper, a.k.a. Double Decker. Y'know, I have no idea what her powers are...maybe somethin' to do with gettin' hit by a bus?
Anyway, she's big, an' she looks like she could snap you in half like a twiglet.
LOOK HERE! WE CAN DO A DAY TRIP AND SEE THE STATUE OF LIBERTY!
HEH!
DOES THAT MEAN WE CAN TAKE LIBERTIES WITH 'ER?
OH, HUSH, OR I'LL SNAP YOU IN HALF LIKE A TWIGLET!

TRICK AND TREAT

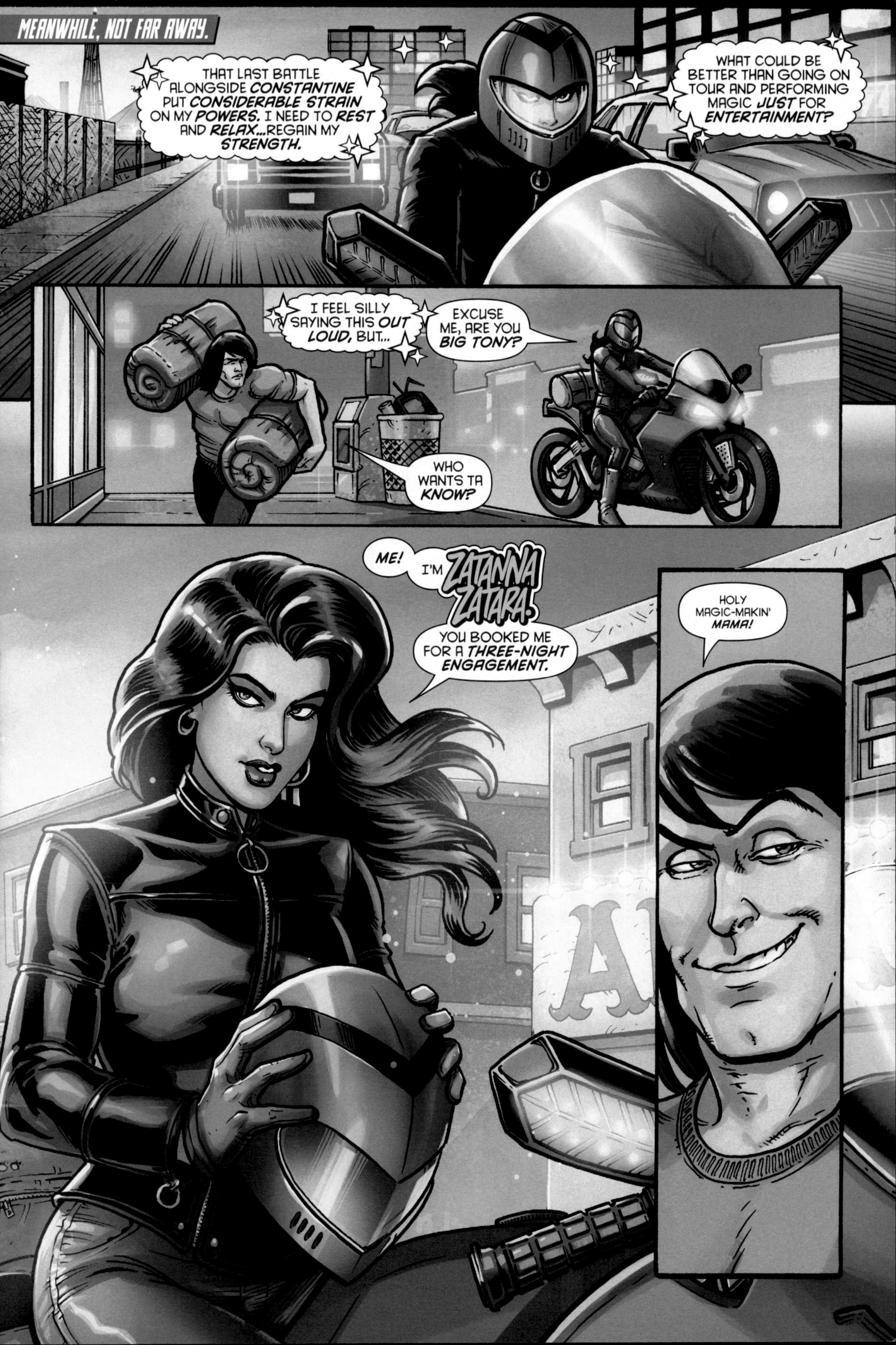
MEANWHILE, NOT FAR AWAY.
THAT LAST BATTLE ALONGSIDE CONSTANTINE PUT CONSIDERABLE STRAIN ON MY POWERS. I NEED TO REST AND RELAX...REGAIN MY STRENGTH.
WHAT COULD BE BETTER THAN GOING ON TOUR AND PERFORMING MAGIC JUST FOR ENTERTAINMENT?
I FEEL SILLY SAYING THIS OUT LOUD, BUT...
EXCUSE ME, ARE YOU BIG TONY?
WHO WANTS TA KNOW?
ME!
I'M ZATANNA ZATARA.
YOU BOOKED ME FOR A THREE-NIGHT ENGAGEMENT.
HOLY MAGIC-MAKIN' MAMA!

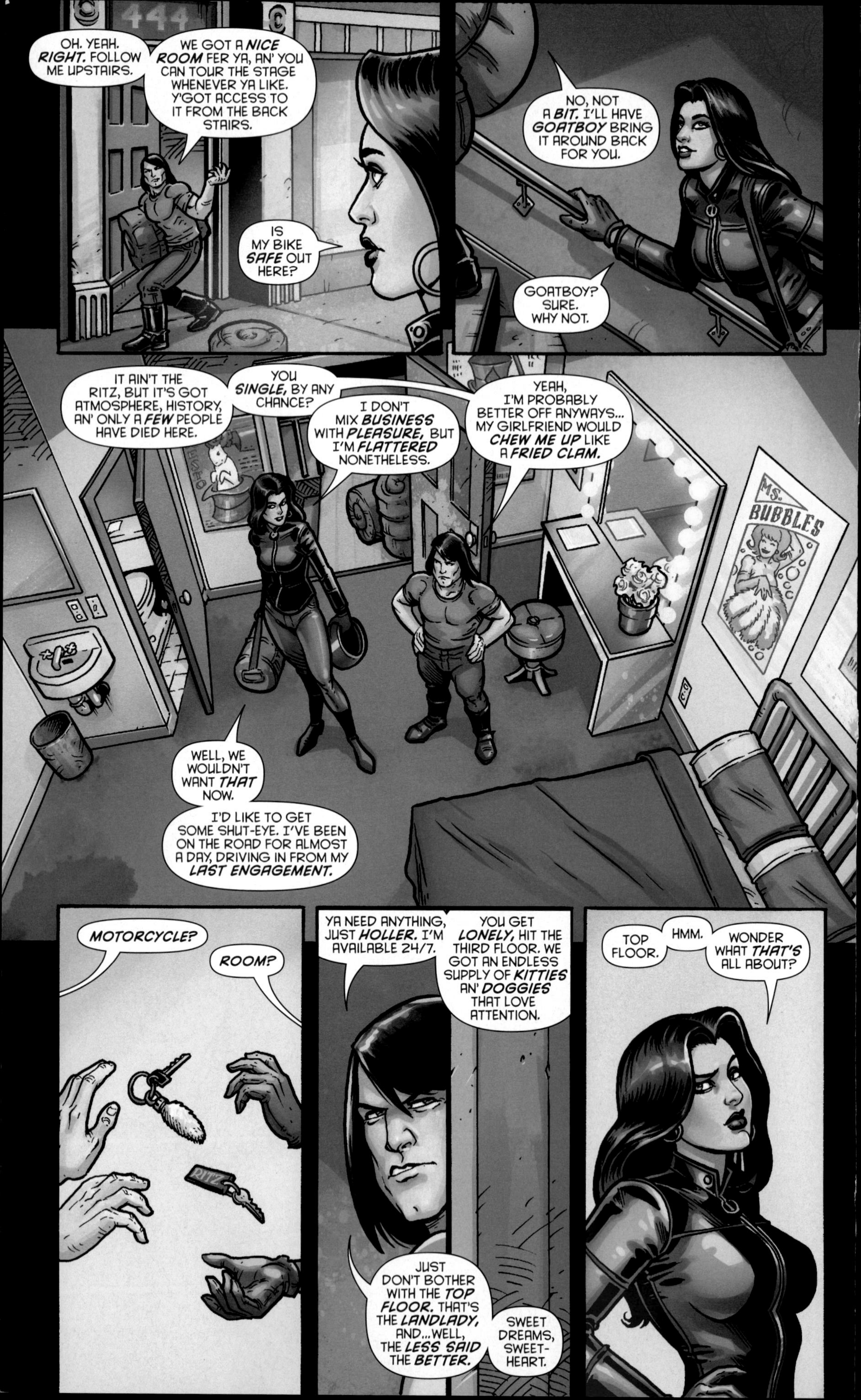
OH. YEAH. RIGHT. FOLLOW ME UPSTAIRS.
WE GOT A NICE ROOM FER YA, AN' YOU CAN TOUR THE STAGE WHENEVER YA LIKE. Y'GOT ACCESS TO IT FROM THE BACK STAIRS.
IS MY BIKE SAFE OUT HERE?
NO, NOT A BIT. I'LL HAVE GOATBOY BRING IT AROUND BACK FOR YOU.
GOATBOY? SURE. WHY NOT.
IT AIN'T THE RITZ, BUT IT'S GOT ATMOSPHERE, HISTORY, AN' ONLY A FEW PEOPLE HAVE DIED HERE.
YOU SINGLE, BY ANY CHANCE?
I DON'T MIX BUSINESS WITH PLEASURE, BUT I'M FLATTERED NONETHELESS.
YEAH, I'M PROBABLY BETTER OFF ANYWAYS... MY GIRLFRIEND WOULD CHEW ME UP LIKE A FRIED CLAM.
MS. BUBBLES
WELL, WE WOULDN'T WANT THAT NOW.
I'D LIKE TO GET SOME SHUT-EYE. I'VE BEEN ON THE ROAD FOR ALMOST A DAY, DRIVING IN FROM MY LAST ENGAGEMENT.
MOTORCYCLE?
ROOM?
RITZ
YA NEED ANYTHING, JUST HOLLER. I'M AVAILABLE 24/7.
YOU GET LONELY, HIT THE THIRD FLOOR. WE GOT AN ENDLESS SUPPLY OF KITTIES AN' DOGGIES THAT LOVE ATTENTION.
JUST DON'T BOTHER WITH THE TOP FLOOR. THAT'S THE LANDLADY, AND...WELL, THE LESS SAID THE BETTER.
SWEET DREAMS, SWEET-HEART.
TOP FLOOR.
HMM.
WONDER WHAT THAT'S ALL ABOUT?

BE AFRAID OF THE DARK

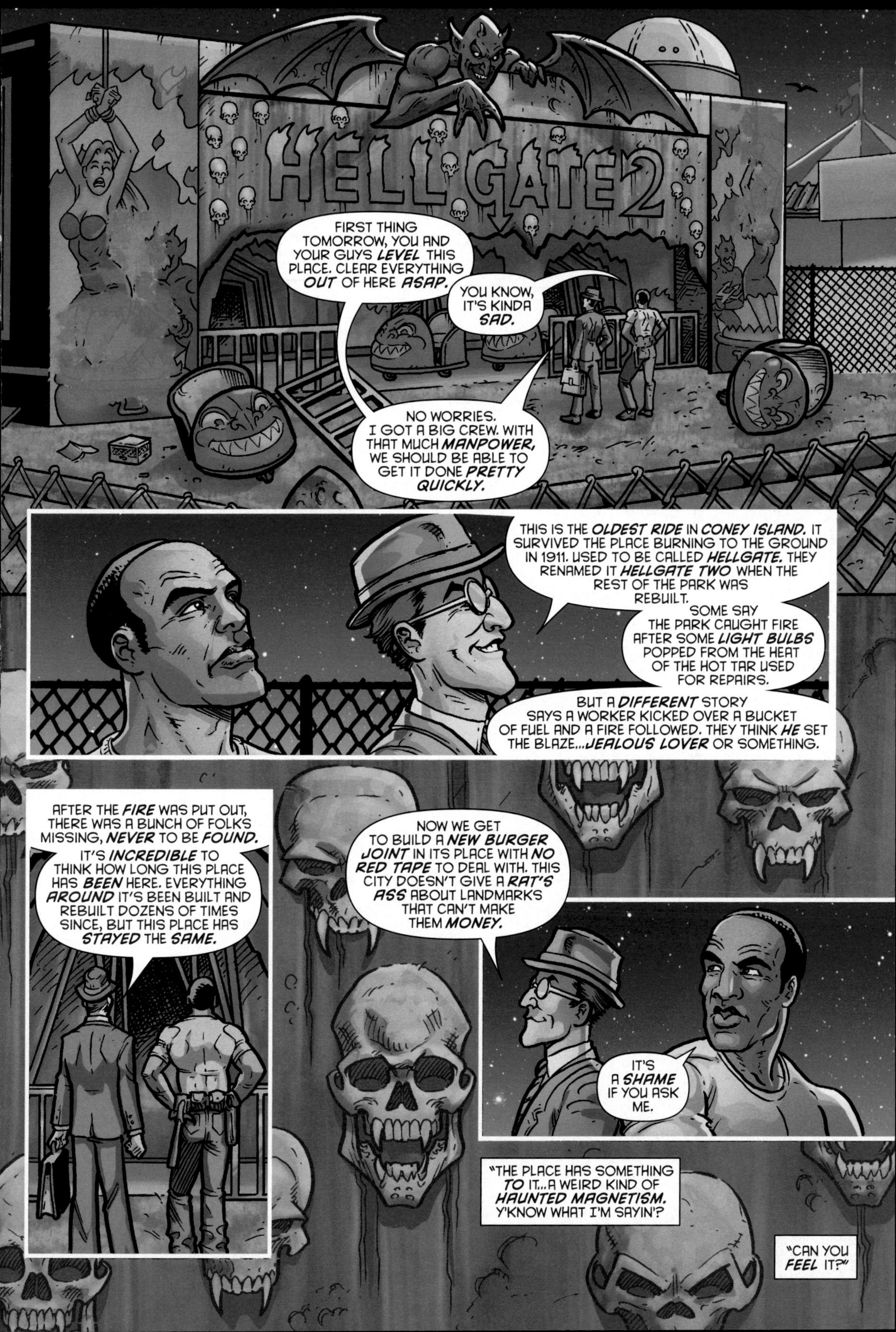
HELL GATE 2
FIRST THING TOMORROW, YOU AND YOUR GUYS LEVEL THIS PLACE. CLEAR EVERYTHING OUT OF HERE ASAP.
YOU KNOW, IT'S KINDA SAD.
NO WORRIES. I GOT A BIG CREW. WITH THAT MUCH MANPOWER, WE SHOULD BE ABLE TO GET IT DONE PRETTY QUICKLY.
THIS IS THE OLDEST RIDE IN CONEY ISLAND. IT SURVIVED THE PLACE BURNING TO THE GROUND IN 1911. USED TO BE CALLED HELLGATE. THEY RENAMED IT HELLGATE TWO WHEN THE REST OF THE PARK WAS REBUILT.
SOME SAY THE PARK CAUGHT FIRE AFTER SOME LIGHT BULBS POPPED FROM THE HEAT OF THE HOT TAR USED FOR REPAIRS.
BUT A DIFFERENT STORY SAYS A WORKER KICKED OVER A BUCKET OF FUEL AND A FIRE FOLLOWED. THEY THINK HE SET THE BLAZE...JEALOUS LOVER OR SOMETHING.
AFTER THE FIRE WAS PUT OUT, THERE WAS A BUNCH OF FOLKS MISSING, NEVER TO BE FOUND.
IT'S INCREDIBLE TO THINK HOW LONG THIS PLACE HAS BEEN HERE. EVERYTHING AROUND IT'S BEEN BUILT AND REBUILT DOZENS OF TIMES SINCE, BUT THIS PLACE HAS STAYED THE SAME.
NOW WE GET TO BUILD A NEW BURGER JOINT IN ITS PLACE WITH NO RED TAPE TO DEAL WITH. THIS CITY DOESN'T GIVE A RAT'S ASS ABOUT LANDMARKS THAT CAN'T MAKE THEM MONEY.
IT'S A SHAME IF YOU ASK ME.
"THE PLACE HAS SOMETHING TO IT...A WEIRD KIND OF HAUNTED MAGNETISM. Y'KNOW WHAT I'M SAYIN'?
"CAN YOU FEEL IT?"

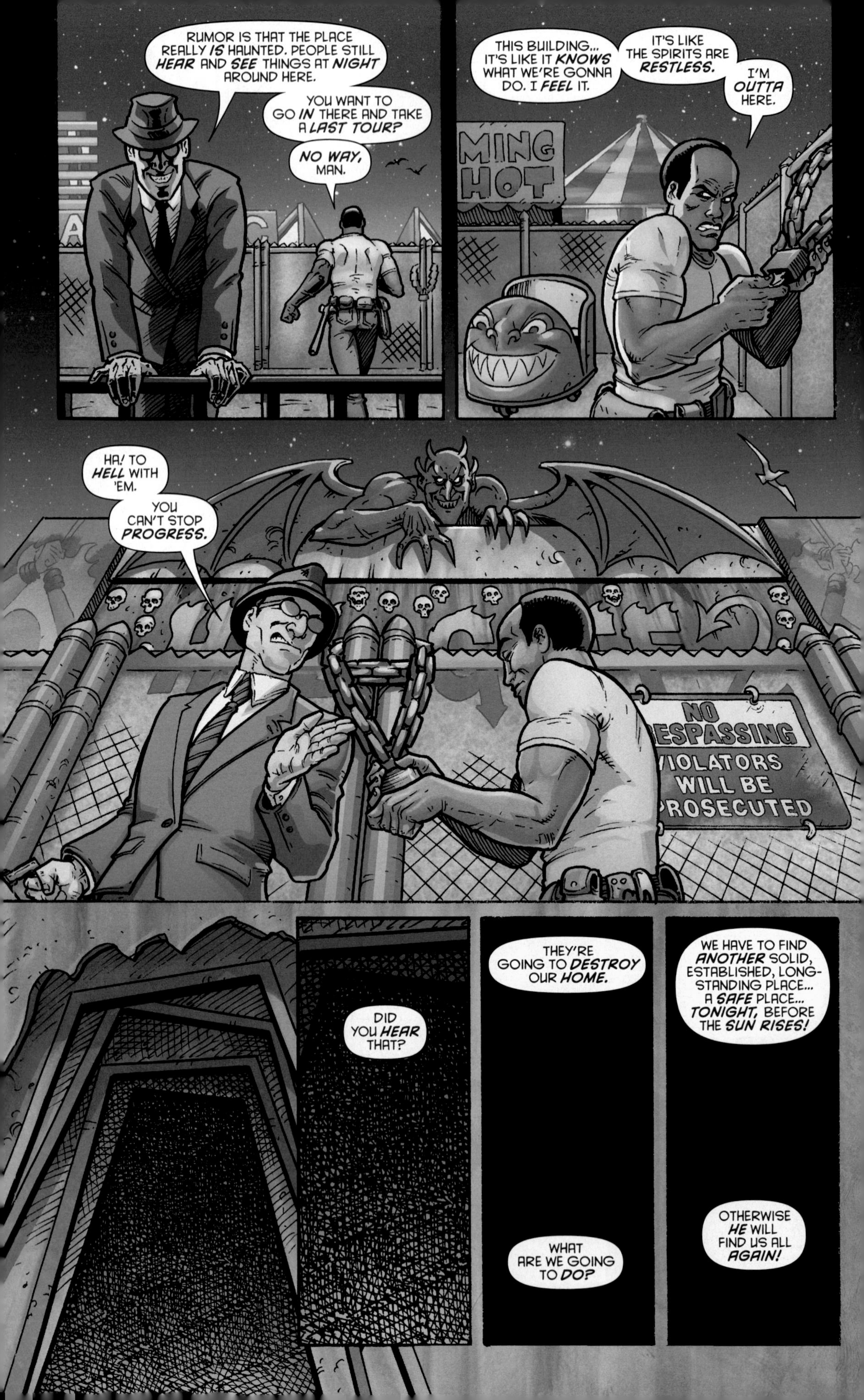
RUMOR IS THAT THE PLACE REALLY *IS* HAUNTED. PEOPLE STILL *HEAR* AND *SEE* THINGS AT *NIGHT* AROUND HERE.
YOU WANT TO GO *IN* THERE AND TAKE A *LAST TOUR?*
NO WAY, MAN.
THIS BUILDING... IT'S LIKE IT *KNOWS* WHAT WE'RE GONNA DO. I *FEEL* IT.
IT'S LIKE THE SPIRITS ARE *RESTLESS.*
I'M *OUTTA* HERE.
MING
HOT
HA! TO *HELL* WITH 'EM.
YOU CAN'T STOP *PROGRESS.*
NO
ESPASSING
IOLATORS
WILL BE
ROSECUTED
DID YOU *HEAR* THAT?
THEY'RE GOING TO *DESTROY* OUR *HOME.*
WHAT ARE WE GOING TO *DO?*
WE HAVE TO FIND *ANOTHER* SOLID, ESTABLISHED, LONG-STANDING PLACE... A *SAFE* PLACE... *TONIGHT,* BEFORE THE *SUN RISES!*
OTHERWISE *HE* WILL FIND US ALL *AGAIN!*

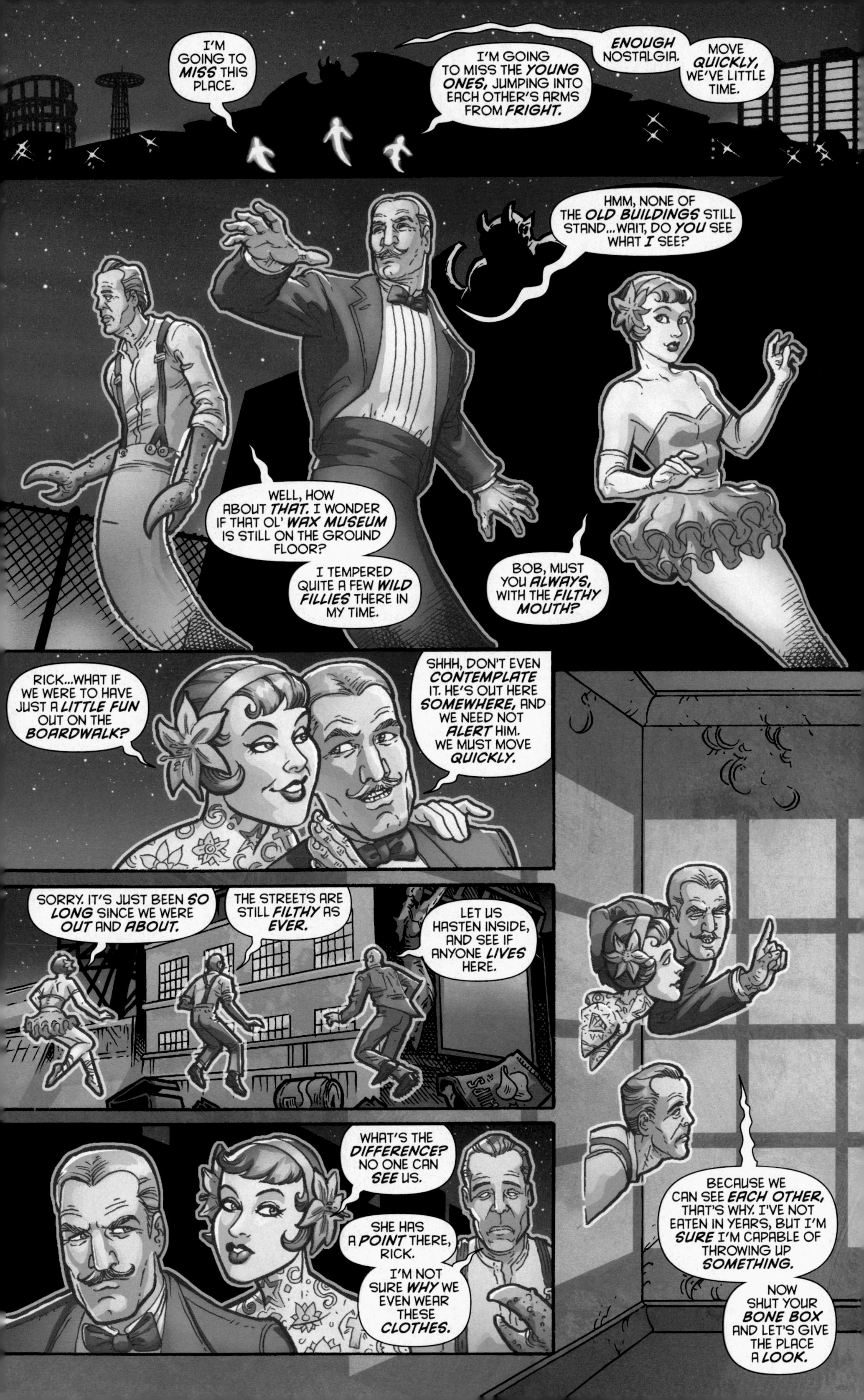

I'M GOING TO MISS THIS PLACE.
I'M GOING TO MISS THE YOUNG ONES, JUMPING INTO EACH OTHER'S ARMS FROM FRIGHT.
ENOUGH NOSTALGIA.
MOVE QUICKLY, WE'VE LITTLE TIME.
HMM, NONE OF THE OLD BUILDINGS STILL STAND...WAIT, DO YOU SEE WHAT I SEE?
WELL, HOW ABOUT THAT. I WONDER IF THAT OL' WAX MUSEUM IS STILL ON THE GROUND FLOOR?
I TEMPERED QUITE A FEW WILD FILLIES THERE IN MY TIME.
BOB, MUST YOU ALWAYS, WITH THE FILTHY MOUTH?
RICK...WHAT IF WE WERE TO HAVE JUST A LITTLE FUN OUT ON THE BOARDWALK?
SHHH, DON'T EVEN CONTEMPLATE IT. HE'S OUT HERE SOMEWHERE, AND WE NEED NOT ALERT HIM. WE MUST MOVE QUICKLY.
SORRY. IT'S JUST BEEN SO LONG SINCE WE WERE OUT AND ABOUT.
THE STREETS ARE STILL FILTHY AS EVER.
LET US HASTEN INSIDE, AND SEE IF ANYONE LIVES HERE.
CHIPS
WHAT'S THE DIFFERENCE? NO ONE CAN SEE US.
SHE HAS A POINT THERE, RICK.
I'M NOT SURE WHY WE EVEN WEAR THESE CLOTHES.
BECAUSE WE CAN SEE EACH OTHER, THAT'S WHY. I'VE NOT EATEN IN YEARS, BUT I'M SURE I'M CAPABLE OF THROWING UP SOMETHING.
NOW SHUT YOUR BONE BOX AND LET'S GIVE THE PLACE A LOOK.

BEAUTY SLEEP

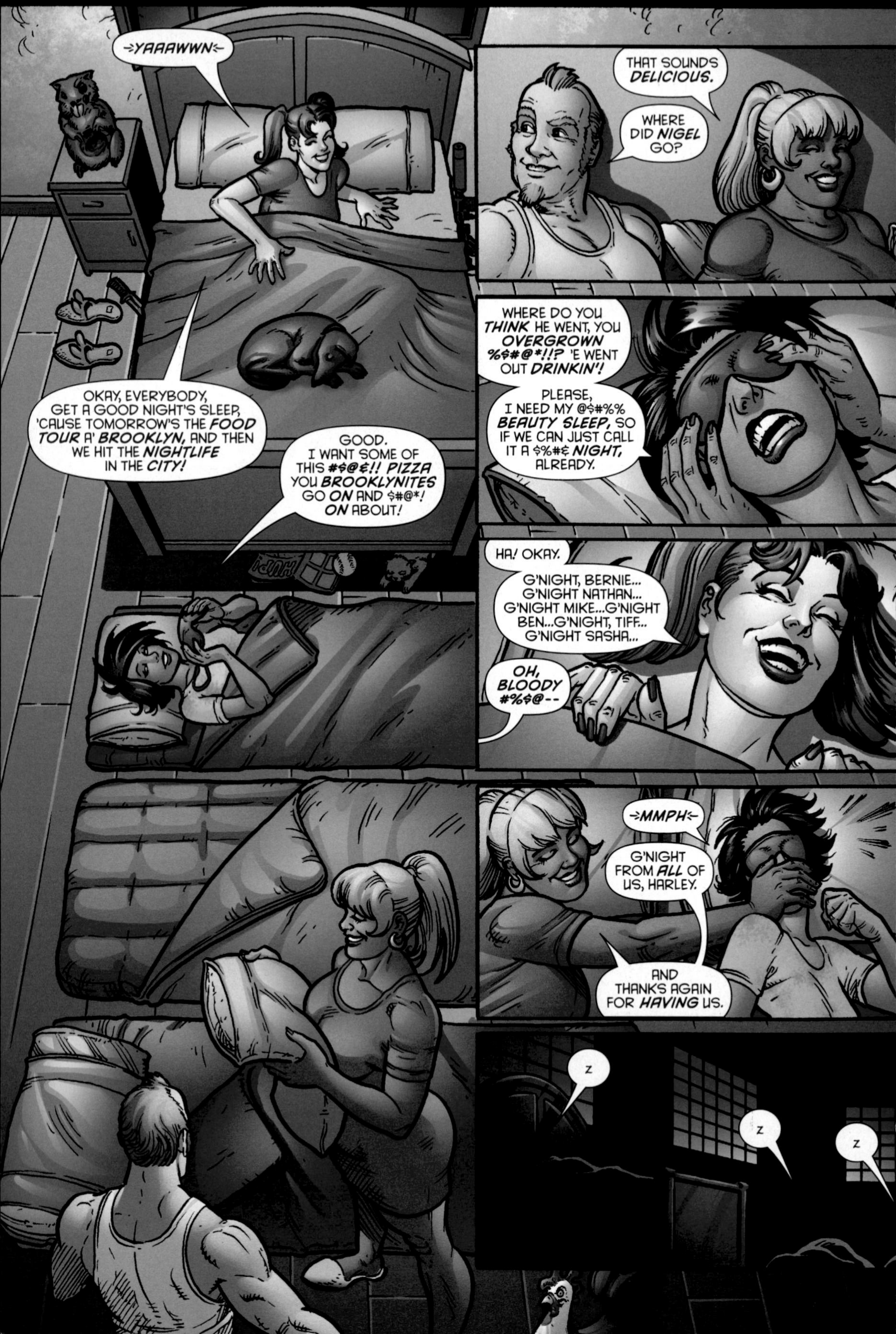

~YAAAWWN~
OKAY, EVERYBODY, GET A GOOD NIGHT'S SLEEP, 'CAUSE TOMORROW'S THE FOOD TOUR A' BROOKLYN, AND THEN WE HIT THE NIGHTLIFE IN THE CITY!
GOOD. I WANT SOME OF THIS #$@&!! PIZZA YOU BROOKLYNITES GO ON AND $#@*! ON ABOUT!
THAT SOUNDS DELICIOUS.
WHERE DID NIGEL GO?
WHERE DO YOU THINK HE WENT, YOU OVERGROWN %$#@*!!? 'E WENT OUT DRINKIN'!
PLEASE, I NEED MY @$#%% BEAUTY SLEEP, SO IF WE CAN JUST CALL IT A $%#& NIGHT, ALREADY.
HA! OKAY.
G'NIGHT, BERNIE... G'NIGHT NATHAN... G'NIGHT MIKE...G'NIGHT BEN...G'NIGHT, TIFF... G'NIGHT SASHA...
OH, BLOODY #%$@--
~MMPH~
G'NIGHT FROM ALL OF US, HARLEY.
AND THANKS AGAIN FOR HAVING US.
Z
Z
Z

DRINK AND DROP

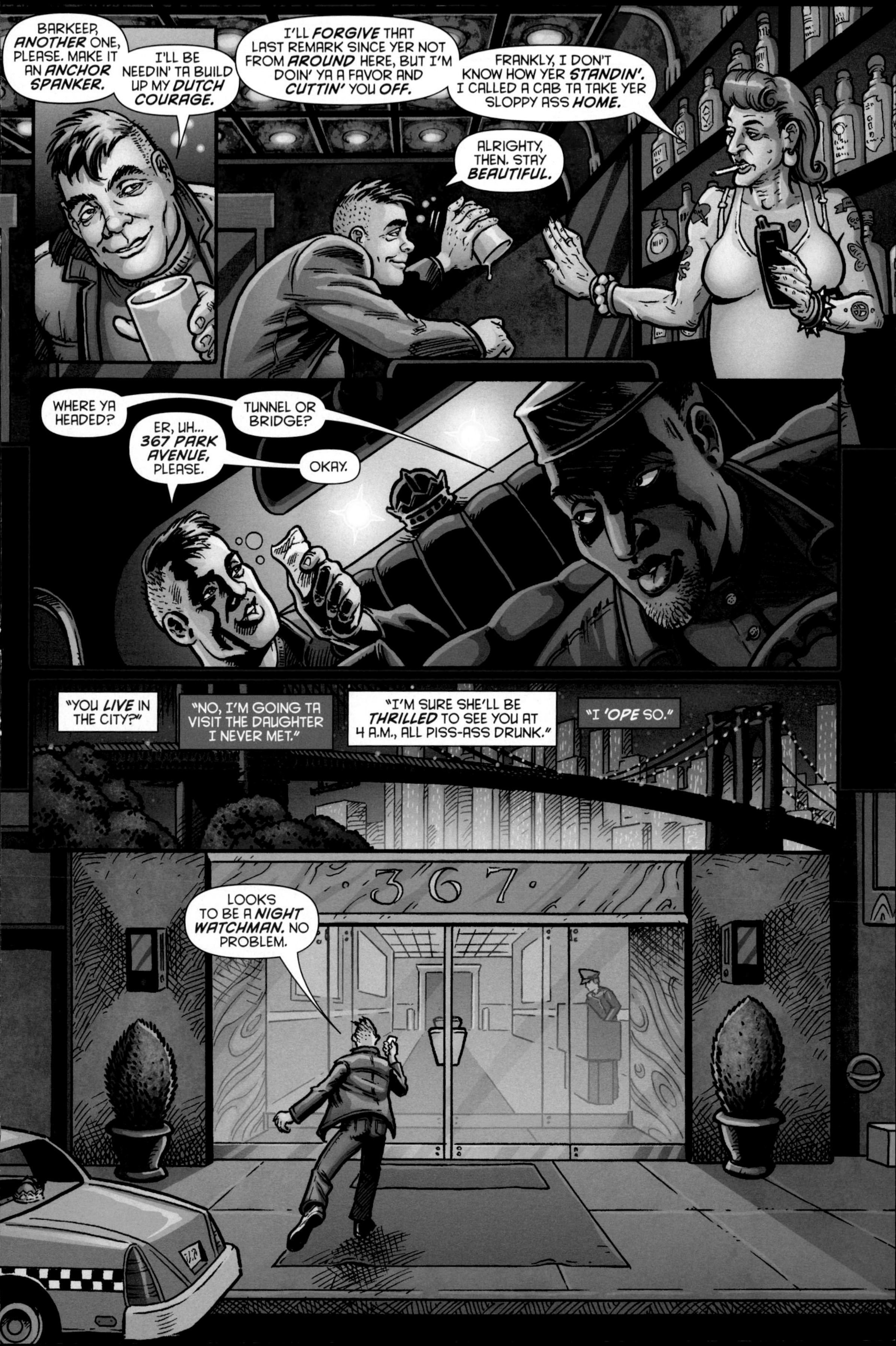

BARKEEP, ANOTHER ONE, PLEASE. MAKE IT AN ANCHOR SPANKER.
I'LL BE NEEDIN' TA BUILD UP MY DUTCH COURAGE.
I'LL FORGIVE THAT LAST REMARK SINCE YER NOT FROM AROUND HERE, BUT I'M DOIN' YA A FAVOR AND CUTTIN' YOU OFF.
FRANKLY, I DON'T KNOW HOW YER STANDIN'. I CALLED A CAB TA TAKE YER SLOPPY ASS HOME.
ALRIGHTY, THEN. STAY BEAUTIFUL.
WHERE YA HEADED?
TUNNEL OR BRIDGE?
ER, UH... 367 PARK AVENUE, PLEASE.
OKAY.
"YOU LIVE IN THE CITY?"
"NO, I'M GOING TA VISIT THE DAUGHTER I NEVER MET."
"I'M SURE SHE'LL BE THRILLED TO SEE YOU AT 4 A.M., ALL PISS-ASS DRUNK."
"I 'OPE SO."
367
LOOKS TO BE A NIGHT WATCHMAN. NO PROBLEM.

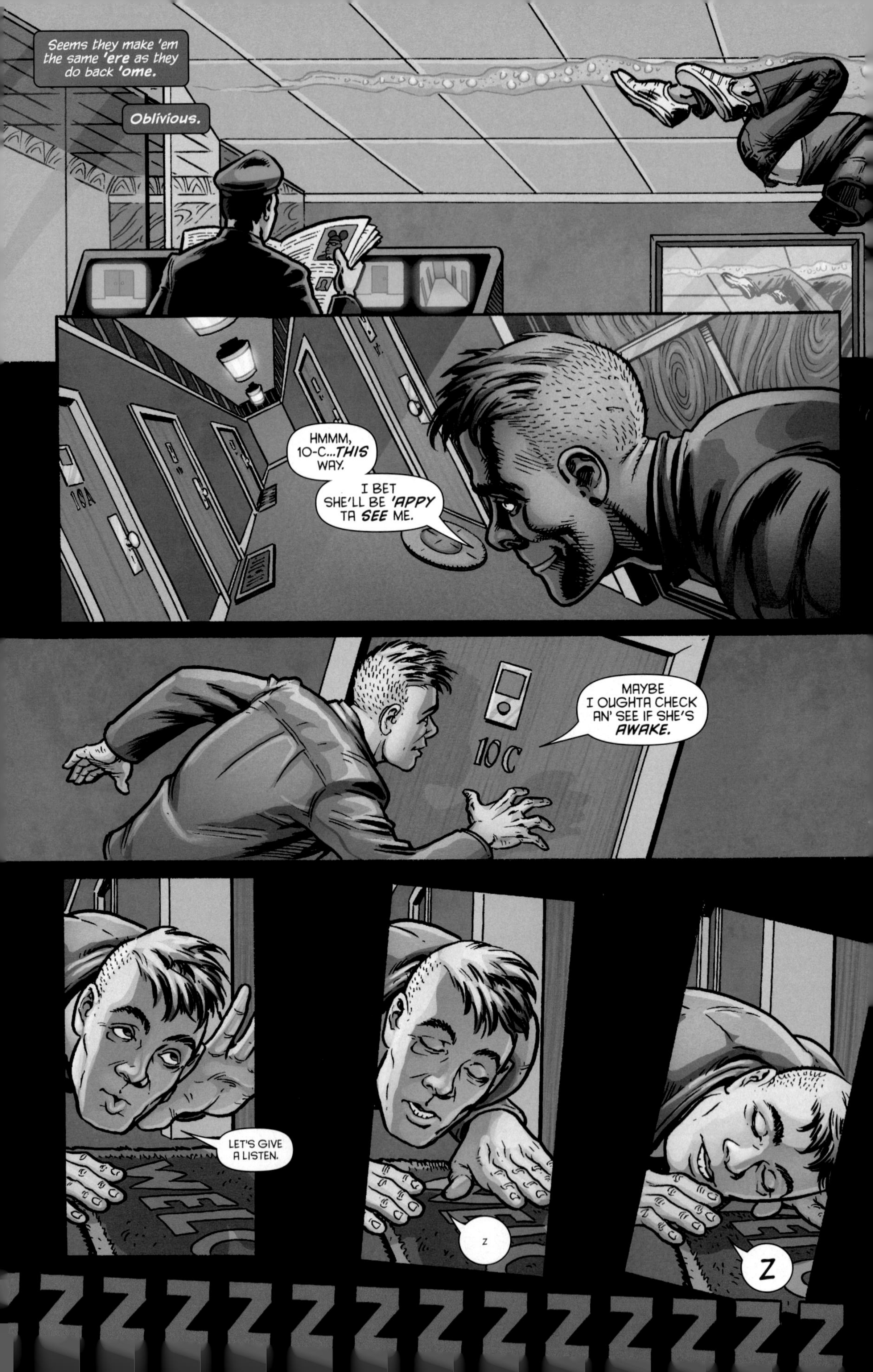
Seems they make 'em the same 'ere as they do back 'ome.
Oblivious.
HMMM, 10-C...THIS WAY.
I BET SHE'LL BE 'APPY TA SEE ME.
10A
MAYBE I OUGHTA CHECK AN' SEE IF SHE'S AWAKE.
10C
LET'S GIVE A LISTEN.
Z
Z
ZZZZZZZZZZZZZ

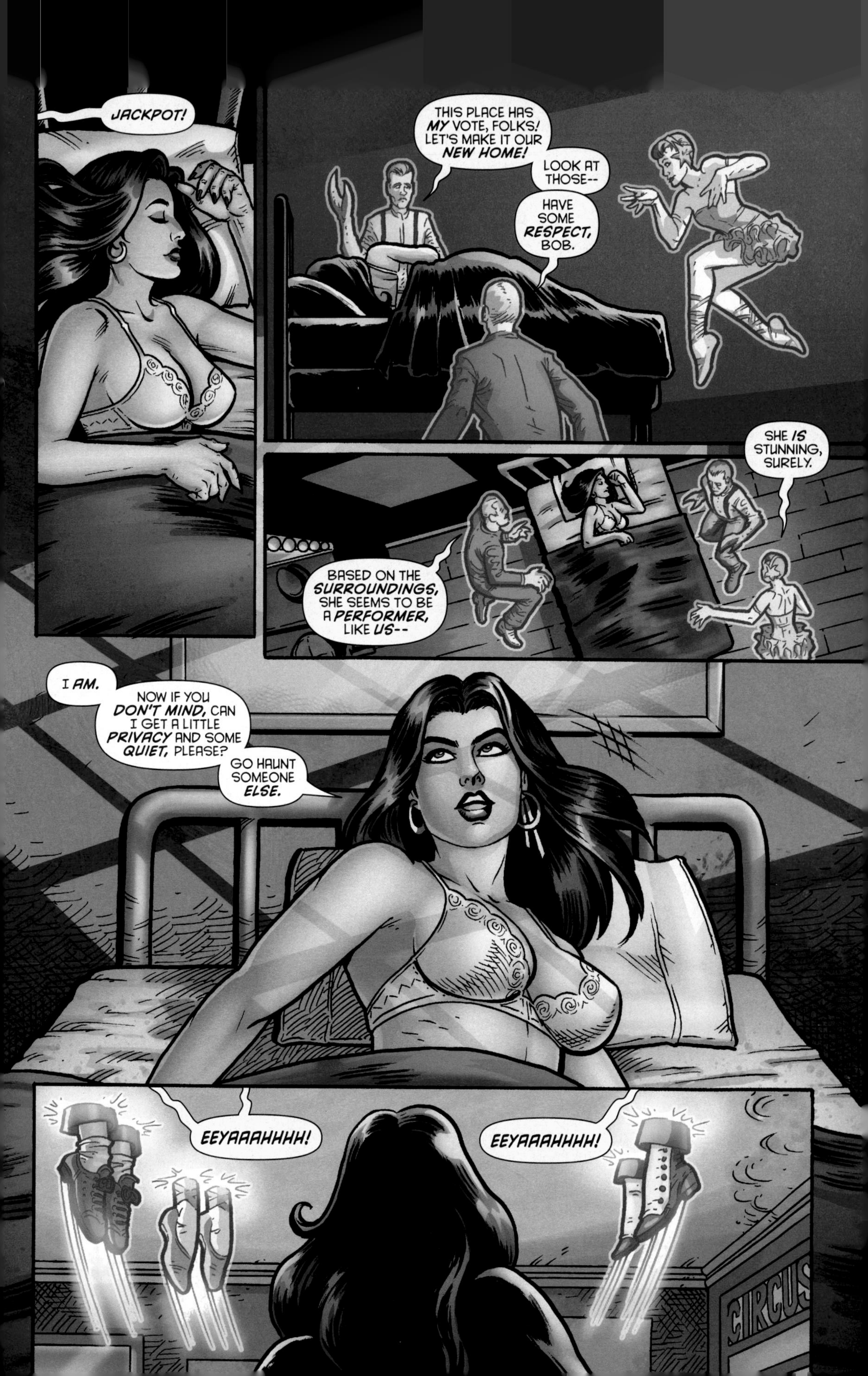
JACKPOT!
THIS PLACE HAS MY VOTE, FOLKS! LET'S MAKE IT OUR NEW HOME!
LOOK AT THOSE--
HAVE SOME RESPECT, BOB.
SHE IS STUNNING, SURELY.
BASED ON THE SURROUNDINGS, SHE SEEMS TO BE A PERFORMER, LIKE US--
I AM.
NOW IF YOU DON'T MIND, CAN I GET A LITTLE PRIVACY AND SOME QUIET, PLEASE?
GO HAUNT SOMEONE ELSE.
EEYAAAHHHH!
EEYAAAHHHH!
CIRCUS

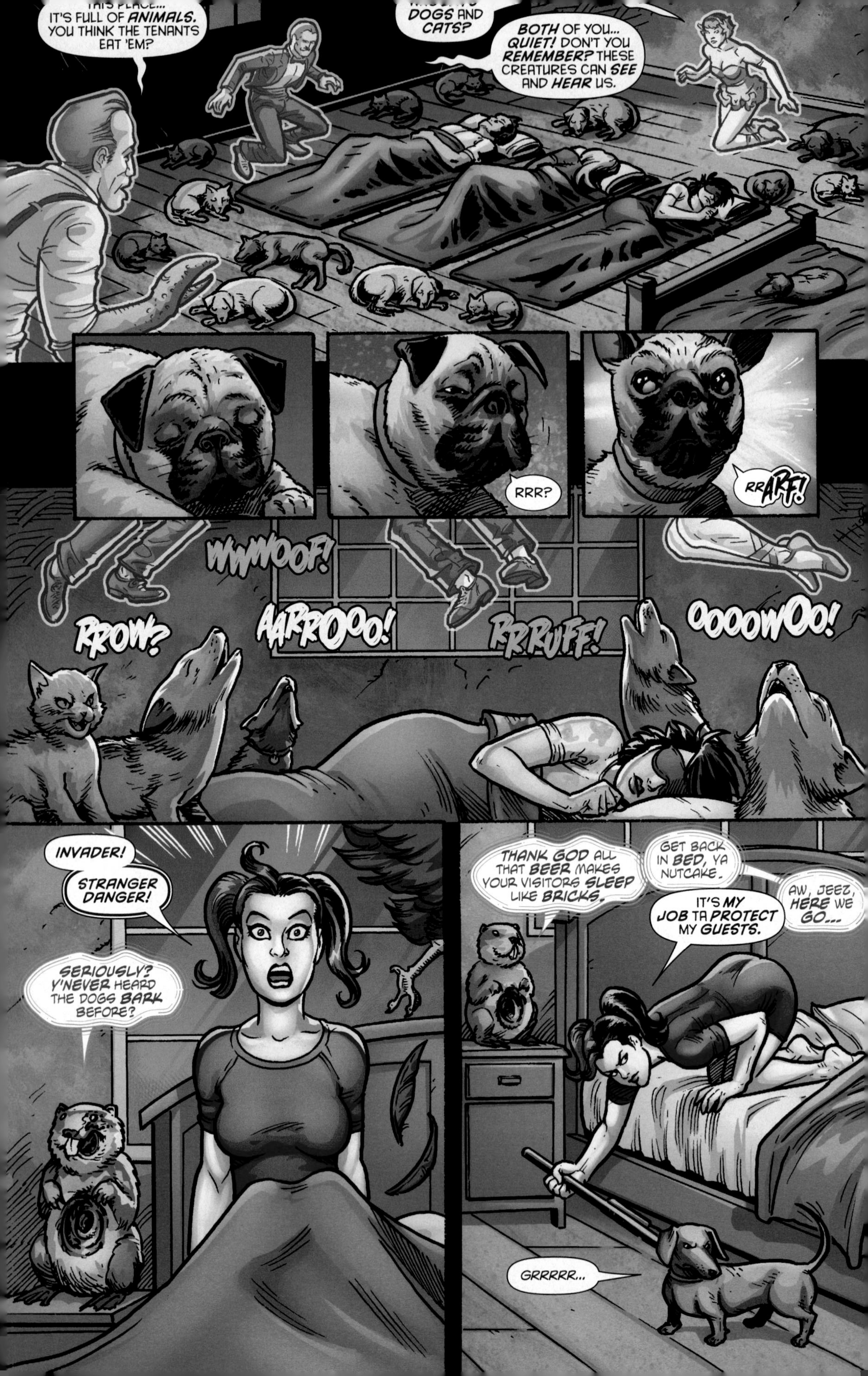
IT'S FULL OF ANIMALS. YOU THINK THE TENANTS EAT 'EM?
DOGS AND CATS?
BOTH OF YOU... QUIET! DON'T YOU REMEMBER? THESE CREATURES CAN SEE AND HEAR US.
RRR?
RRARF!
WWWOOF!
RROW?
AARROOoo!
RRRUFF!
OOOOWOO!
INVADER!
STRANGER DANGER!
SERIOUSLY? Y'NEVER HEARD THE DOGS BARK BEFORE?
THANK GOD ALL THAT BEER MAKES YOUR VISITORS SLEEP LIKE BRICKS.
GET BACK IN BED, YA NUTCAKE.
AW, JEEZ, HERE WE GO...
IT'S MY JOB TA PROTECT MY GUESTS.
GRRRRR...

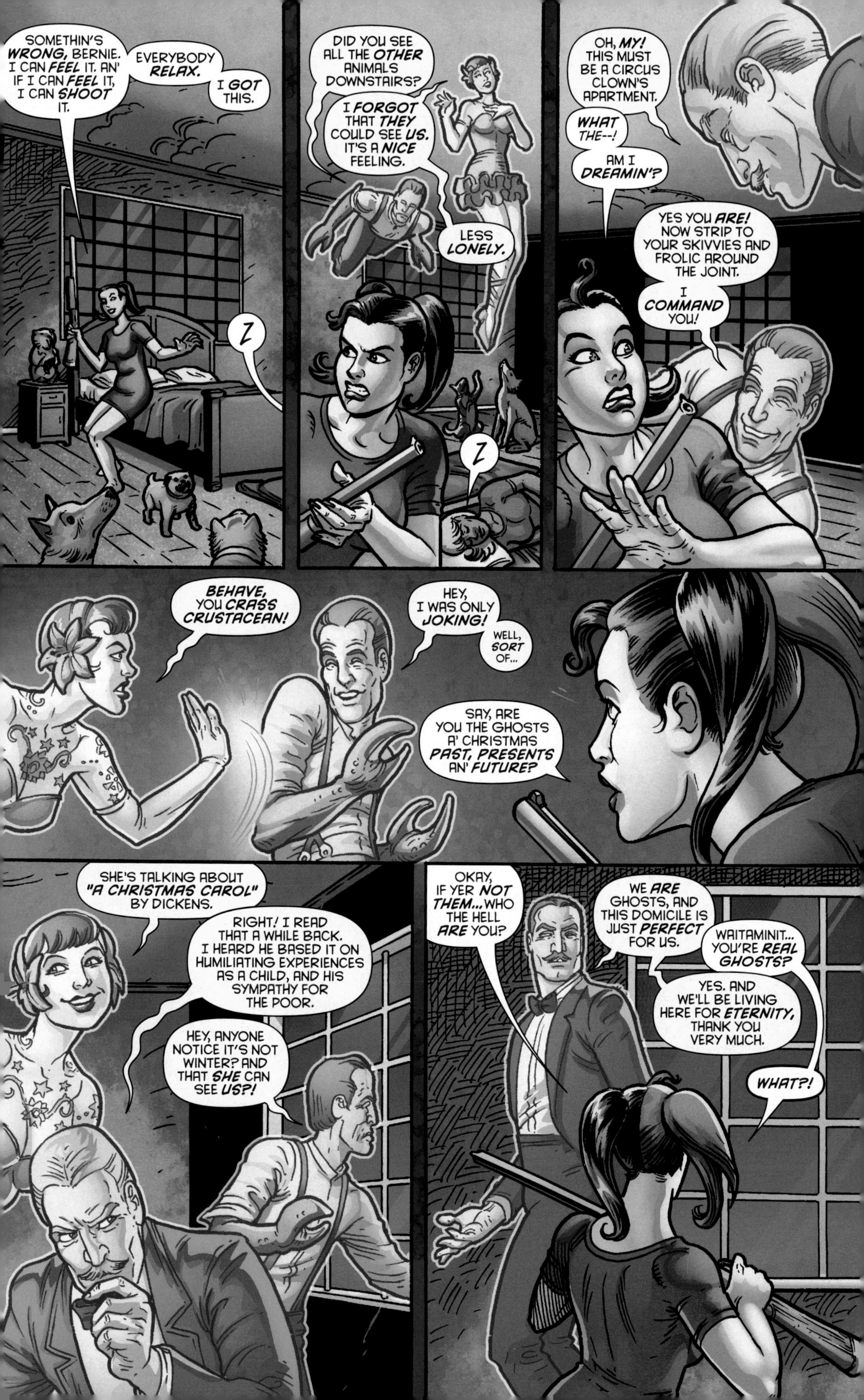
SOMETHIN'S WRONG, BERNIE. I CAN FEEL IT. AN' IF I CAN FEEL IT, I CAN SHOOT IT.
EVERYBODY RELAX.
I GOT THIS.
Z
DID YOU SEE ALL THE OTHER ANIMALS DOWNSTAIRS?
I FORGOT THAT THEY COULD SEE US. IT'S A NICE FEELING.
LESS LONELY.
Z
OH, MY! THIS MUST BE A CIRCUS CLOWN'S APARTMENT.
WHAT THE--!
AM I DREAMIN'?
YES YOU ARE! NOW STRIP TO YOUR SKIVVIES AND FROLIC AROUND THE JOINT.
I COMMAND YOU!
BEHAVE, YOU CRASS CRUSTACEAN!
HEY, I WAS ONLY JOKING!
WELL, SORT OF...
SAY, ARE YOU THE GHOSTS A' CHRISTMAS PAST, PRESENTS AN' FUTURE?
SHE'S TALKING ABOUT "A CHRISTMAS CAROL" BY DICKENS.
RIGHT! I READ THAT A WHILE BACK. I HEARD HE BASED IT ON HUMILIATING EXPERIENCES AS A CHILD, AND HIS SYMPATHY FOR THE POOR.
HEY, ANYONE NOTICE IT'S NOT WINTER? AND THAT SHE CAN SEE US?!
OKAY, IF YER NOT THEM... WHO THE HELL ARE YOU?
WE ARE GHOSTS, AND THIS DOMICILE IS JUST PERFECT FOR US.
WAITAMINIT... YOU'RE REAL GHOSTS?
YES. AND WE'LL BE LIVING HERE FOR ETERNITY, THANK YOU VERY MUCH.
WHAT?!

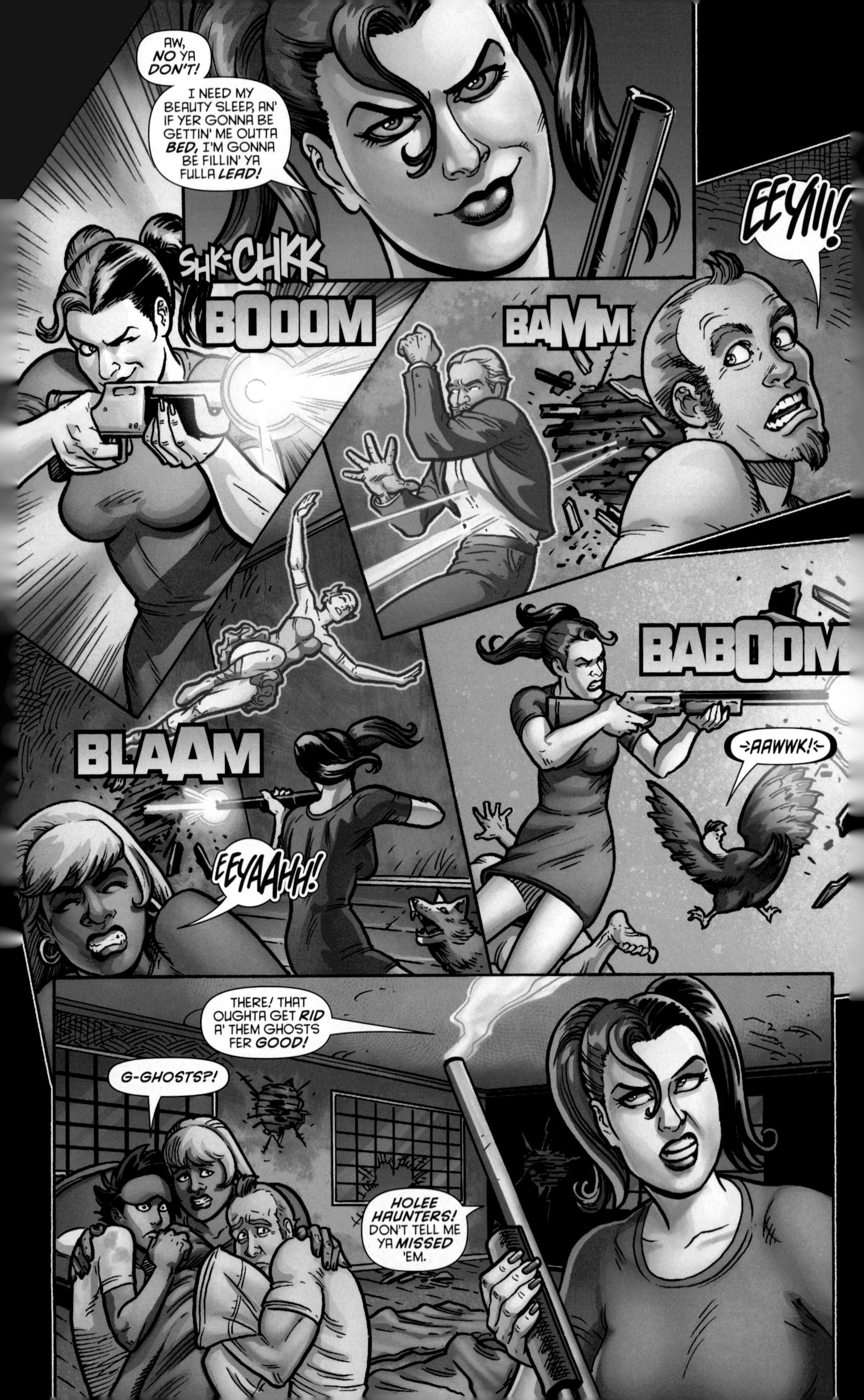
AW, NO YA DON'T!
I NEED MY BEAUTY SLEEP, AN' IF YER GONNA BE GETTIN' ME OUTTA BED, I'M GONNA BE FILLIN' YA FULLA LEAD!
SHK-CHKK
EEYII!!
BOOOM
BAMM
BABOOM
BLAAM
-AAWWK!-
EEYAAHH!
THERE! THAT OUGHTA GET RID A' THEM GHOSTS FER GOOD!
G-GHOSTS?!
HOLEE HAUNTERS! DON'T TELL ME YA MISSED 'EM.

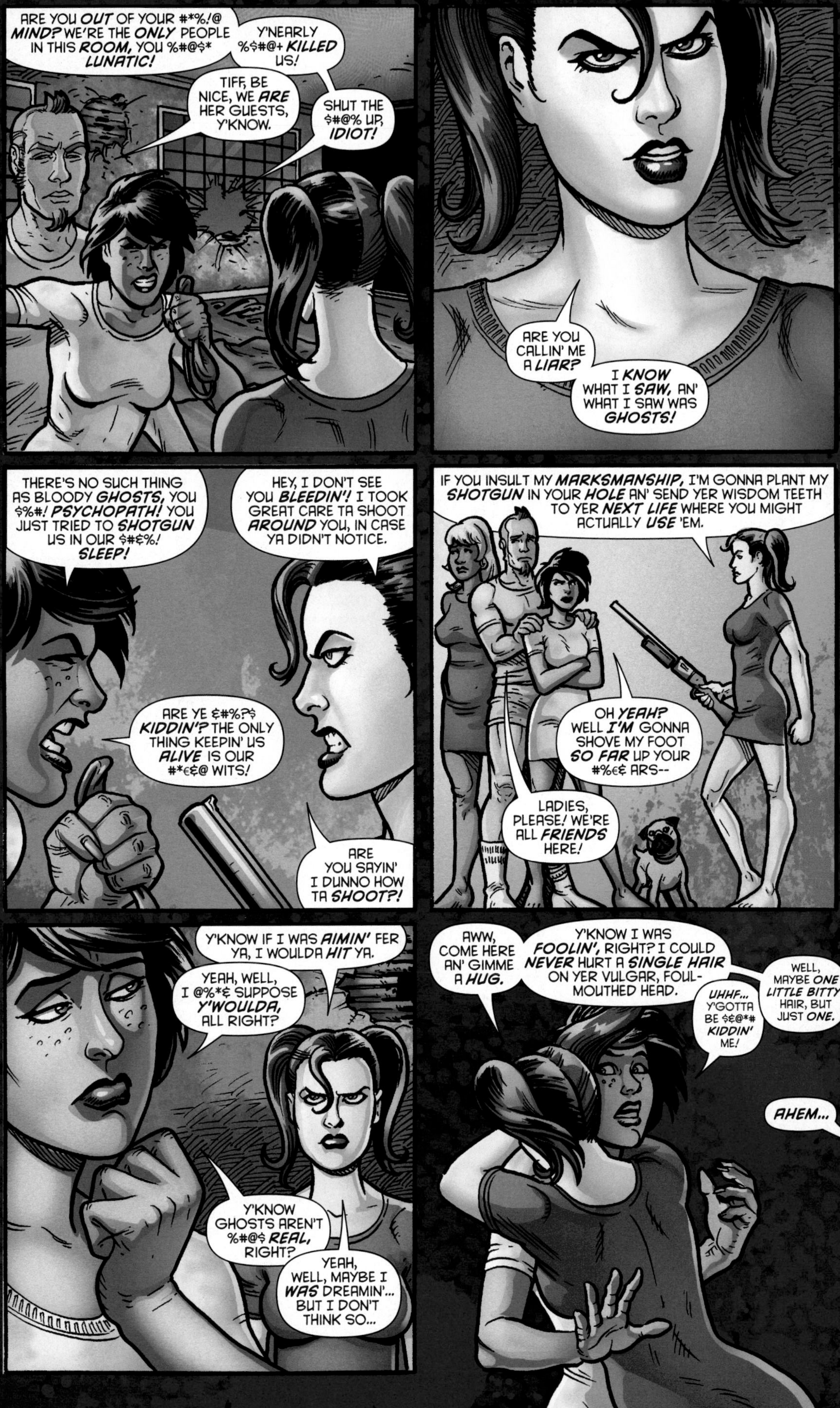
ARE YOU OUT OF YOUR #*%.!@ MIND? WE'RE THE ONLY PEOPLE IN THIS ROOM, YOU %#@$* LUNATIC!
Y'NEARLY %$#@+ KILLED US!
TIFF, BE NICE, WE ARE HER GUESTS, Y'KNOW.
SHUT THE $#@% UP, IDIOT!
ARE YOU CALLIN' ME A LIAR?
I KNOW WHAT I SAW, AN' WHAT I SAW WAS GHOSTS!
THERE'S NO SUCH THING AS BLOODY GHOSTS, YOU $%#! PSYCHOPATH! YOU JUST TRIED TO SHOTGUN US IN OUR $#€%! SLEEP!
HEY, I DON'T SEE YOU BLEEDIN'! I TOOK GREAT CARE TA SHOOT AROUND YOU, IN CASE YA DIDN'T NOTICE.
ARE YE €#%?$ KIDDIN'? THE ONLY THING KEEPIN' US ALIVE IS OUR #*€€@ WITS!
ARE YOU SAYIN' I DUNNO HOW TA SHOOT?!
IF YOU INSULT MY MARKSMANSHIP, I'M GONNA PLANT MY SHOTGUN IN YOUR HOLE AN' SEND YER WISDOM TEETH TO YER NEXT LIFE WHERE YOU MIGHT ACTUALLY USE 'EM.
OH YEAH? WELL I'M GONNA SHOVE MY FOOT SO FAR UP YOUR #%€€ ARS--
LADIES, PLEASE! WE'RE ALL FRIENDS HERE!
Y'KNOW IF I WAS AIMIN' FER YA, I WOULDA HIT YA.
YEAH, WELL, I @%*€ SUPPOSE Y'WOULDA, ALL RIGHT?
Y'KNOW GHOSTS AREN'T %#@$ REAL, RIGHT?
YEAH, WELL, MAYBE I WAS DREAMIN'... BUT I DON'T THINK SO...
AWW, COME HERE AN' GIMME A HUG.
Y'KNOW I WAS FOOLIN', RIGHT? I COULD NEVER HURT A SINGLE HAIR ON YER VULGAR, FOUL-MOUTHED HEAD.
WELL, MAYBE ONE LITTLE BITTY HAIR, BUT JUST ONE.
UHHF... Y'GOTTA BE $€@*# KIDDIN' ME!
AHEM...

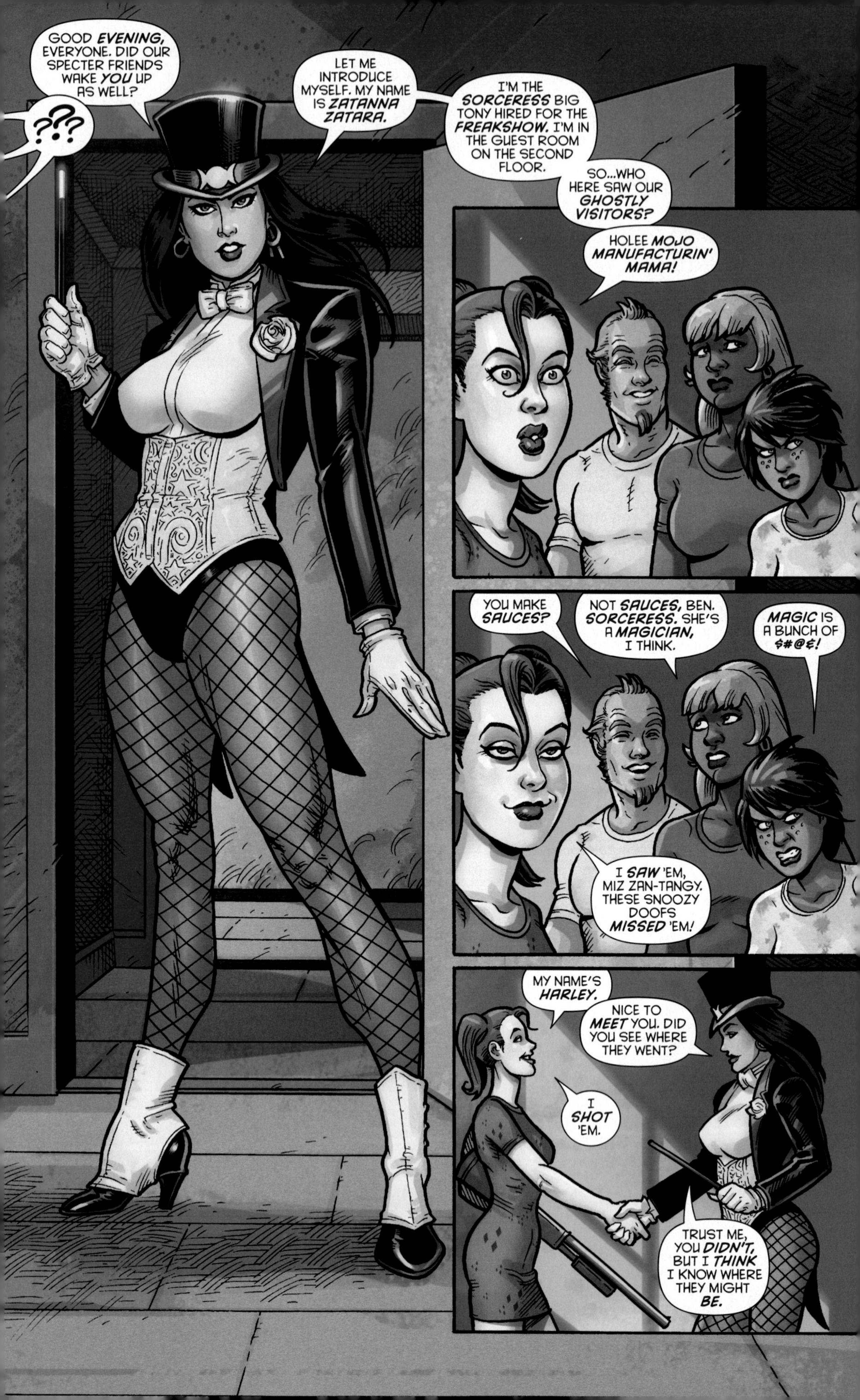
GOOD EVENING, EVERYONE. DID OUR SPECTER FRIENDS WAKE YOU UP AS WELL?
???
LET ME INTRODUCE MYSELF. MY NAME IS ZATANNA ZATARA.
I'M THE SORCERESS BIG TONY HIRED FOR THE FREAKSHOW. I'M IN THE GUEST ROOM ON THE SECOND FLOOR.
SO...WHO HERE SAW OUR GHOSTLY VISITORS?
HOLEE MOJO MANUFACTURIN' MAMA!
YOU MAKE SAUCES?
NOT SAUCES, BEN. SORCERESS. SHE'S A MAGICIAN, I THINK.
MAGIC IS A BUNCH OF $#@&!
I SAW 'EM, MIZ ZAN-TANGY. THESE SNOOZY DOOFS MISSED 'EM!
MY NAME'S HARLEY.
NICE TO MEET YOU. DID YOU SEE WHERE THEY WENT?
I SHOT 'EM.
TRUST ME, YOU DIDN'T, BUT I THINK I KNOW WHERE THEY MIGHT BE.

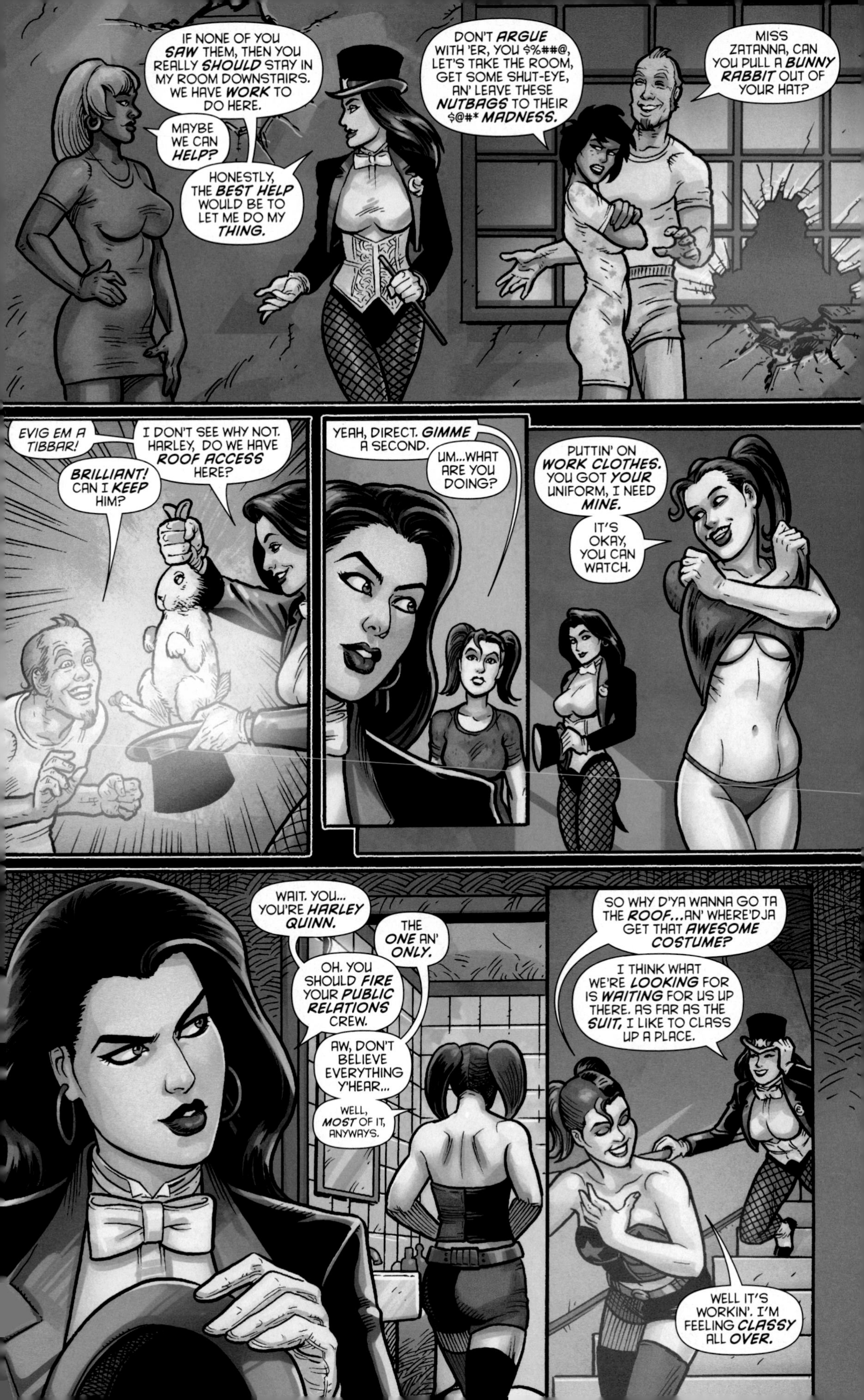
IF NONE OF YOU SAW THEM, THEN YOU REALLY SHOULD STAY IN MY ROOM DOWNSTAIRS. WE HAVE WORK TO DO HERE.
MAYBE WE CAN HELP?
HONESTLY, THE BEST HELP WOULD BE TO LET ME DO MY THING.
DON'T ARGUE WITH 'ER, YOU $%##@, LET'S TAKE THE ROOM, GET SOME SHUT-EYE, AN' LEAVE THESE NUTBAGS TO THEIR $@#* MADNESS.
MISS ZATANNA, CAN YOU PULL A BUNNY RABBIT OUT OF YOUR HAT?
EVIG EM A TIBBAR!
I DON'T SEE WHY NOT. HARLEY, DO WE HAVE ROOF ACCESS HERE?
BRILLIANT! CAN I KEEP HIM?
YEAH, DIRECT. GIMME A SECOND.
UM...WHAT ARE YOU DOING?
PUTTIN' ON WORK CLOTHES. YOU GOT YOUR UNIFORM, I NEED MINE.
IT'S OKAY, YOU CAN WATCH.
WAIT. YOU... YOU'RE HARLEY QUINN.
THE ONE AN' ONLY.
OH. YOU SHOULD FIRE YOUR PUBLIC RELATIONS CREW.
AW, DON'T BELIEVE EVERYTHING Y'HEAR...
WELL, MOST OF IT, ANYWAYS.
SO WHY D'YA WANNA GO TA THE ROOF...AN' WHERE'DJA GET THAT AWESOME COSTUME?
I THINK WHAT WE'RE LOOKING FOR IS WAITING FOR US UP THERE. AS FAR AS THE SUIT, I LIKE TO CLASS UP A PLACE.
WELL IT'S WORKIN'. I'M FEELING CLASSY ALL OVER.

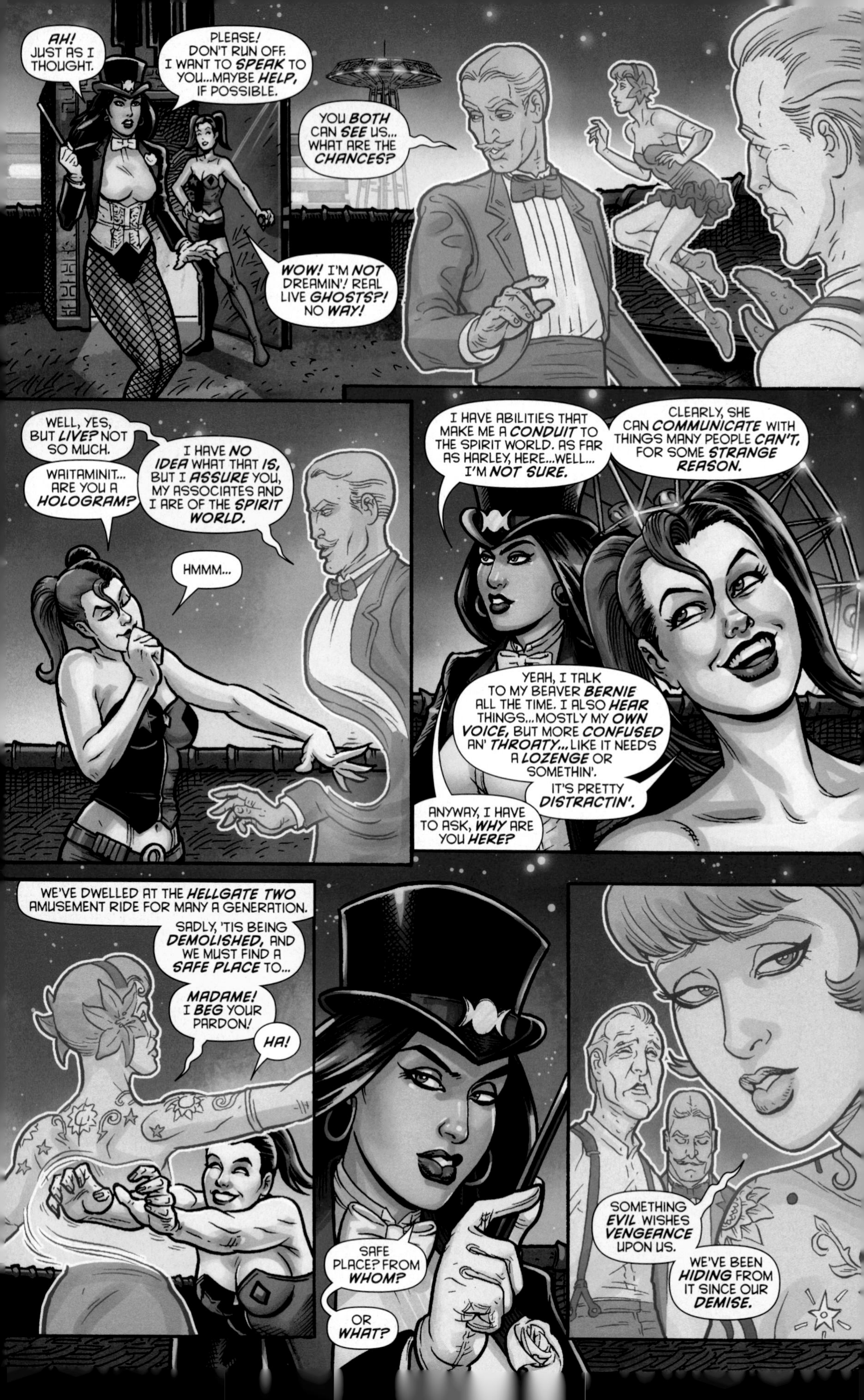
AH! JUST AS I THOUGHT.
PLEASE! DON'T RUN OFF. I WANT TO SPEAK TO YOU...MAYBE HELP, IF POSSIBLE.
YOU BOTH CAN SEE US... WHAT ARE THE CHANCES?
WOW! I'M NOT DREAMIN'! REAL LIVE GHOSTS?! NO WAY!
WELL, YES, BUT LIVE? NOT SO MUCH.
WAITAMINIT... ARE YOU A HOLOGRAM?
I HAVE NO IDEA WHAT THAT IS, BUT I ASSURE YOU, MY ASSOCIATES AND I ARE OF THE SPIRIT WORLD.
HMMM...
I HAVE ABILITIES THAT MAKE ME A CONDUIT TO THE SPIRIT WORLD. AS FAR AS HARLEY, HERE...WELL... I'M NOT SURE.
CLEARLY, SHE CAN COMMUNICATE WITH THINGS MANY PEOPLE CAN'T, FOR SOME STRANGE REASON.
YEAH, I TALK TO MY BEAVER BERNIE ALL THE TIME. I ALSO HEAR THINGS...MOSTLY MY OWN VOICE, BUT MORE CONFUSED AN' THROATY...LIKE IT NEEDS A LOZENGE OR SOMETHIN'.
IT'S PRETTY DISTRACTIN'.
ANYWAY, I HAVE TO ASK, WHY ARE YOU HERE?
WE'VE DWELLED AT THE HELLGATE TWO AMUSEMENT RIDE FOR MANY A GENERATION.
SADLY, 'TIS BEING DEMOLISHED, AND WE MUST FIND A SAFE PLACE TO...
MADAME! I BEG YOUR PARDON!
HA!
SAFE PLACE? FROM WHOM?
OR WHAT?
SOMETHING EVIL WISHES VENGEANCE UPON US.
WE'VE BEEN HIDING FROM IT SINCE OUR DEMISE.

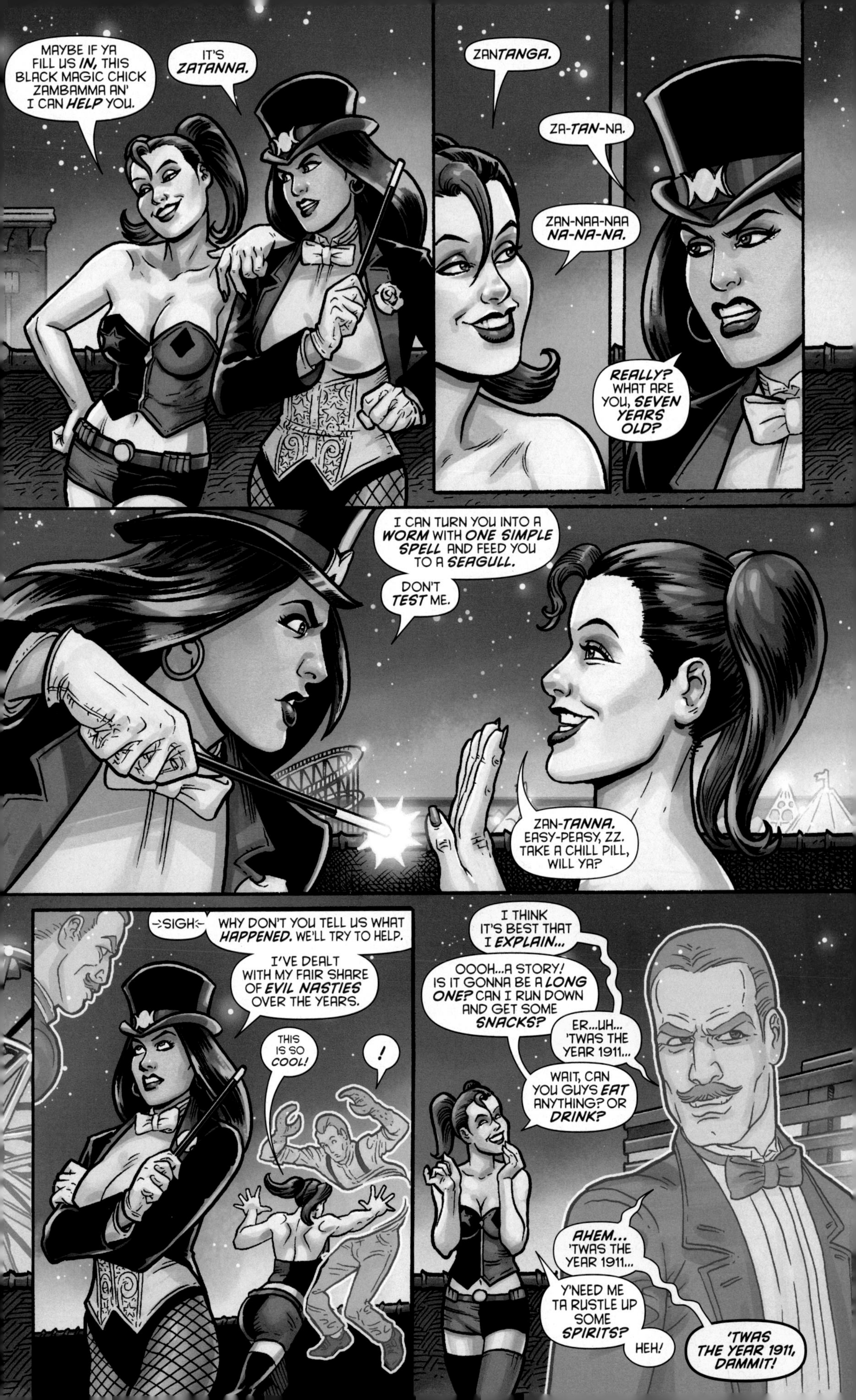
MAYBE IF YA FILL US IN, THIS BLACK MAGIC CHICK ZAMBAMMA AN' I CAN HELP YOU.
IT'S ZATANNA.
ZANTANGA.
ZA-TAN-NA.
ZAN-NAA-NAA NA-NA-NA.
REALLY? WHAT ARE YOU, SEVEN YEARS OLD?
I CAN TURN YOU INTO A WORM WITH ONE SIMPLE SPELL AND FEED YOU TO A SEAGULL.
DON'T TEST ME.
ZAN-TANNA. EASY-PEASY, ZZ. TAKE A CHILL PILL, WILL YA?
-SIGH-
WHY DON'T YOU TELL US WHAT HAPPENED. WE'LL TRY TO HELP.
I'VE DEALT WITH MY FAIR SHARE OF EVIL NASTIES OVER THE YEARS.
THIS IS SO COOL!
!
I THINK IT'S BEST THAT I EXPLAIN...
OOOH...A STORY! IS IT GONNA BE A LONG ONE? CAN I RUN DOWN AND GET SOME SNACKS?
ER...UH... 'TWAS THE YEAR 1911...
WAIT, CAN YOU GUYS EAT ANYTHING? OR DRINK?
AHEM... 'TWAS THE YEAR 1911...
Y'NEED ME TA RUSTLE UP SOME SPIRITS?
HEH!
'TWAS THE YEAR 1911, DAMMIT!

THE BAD DEAL

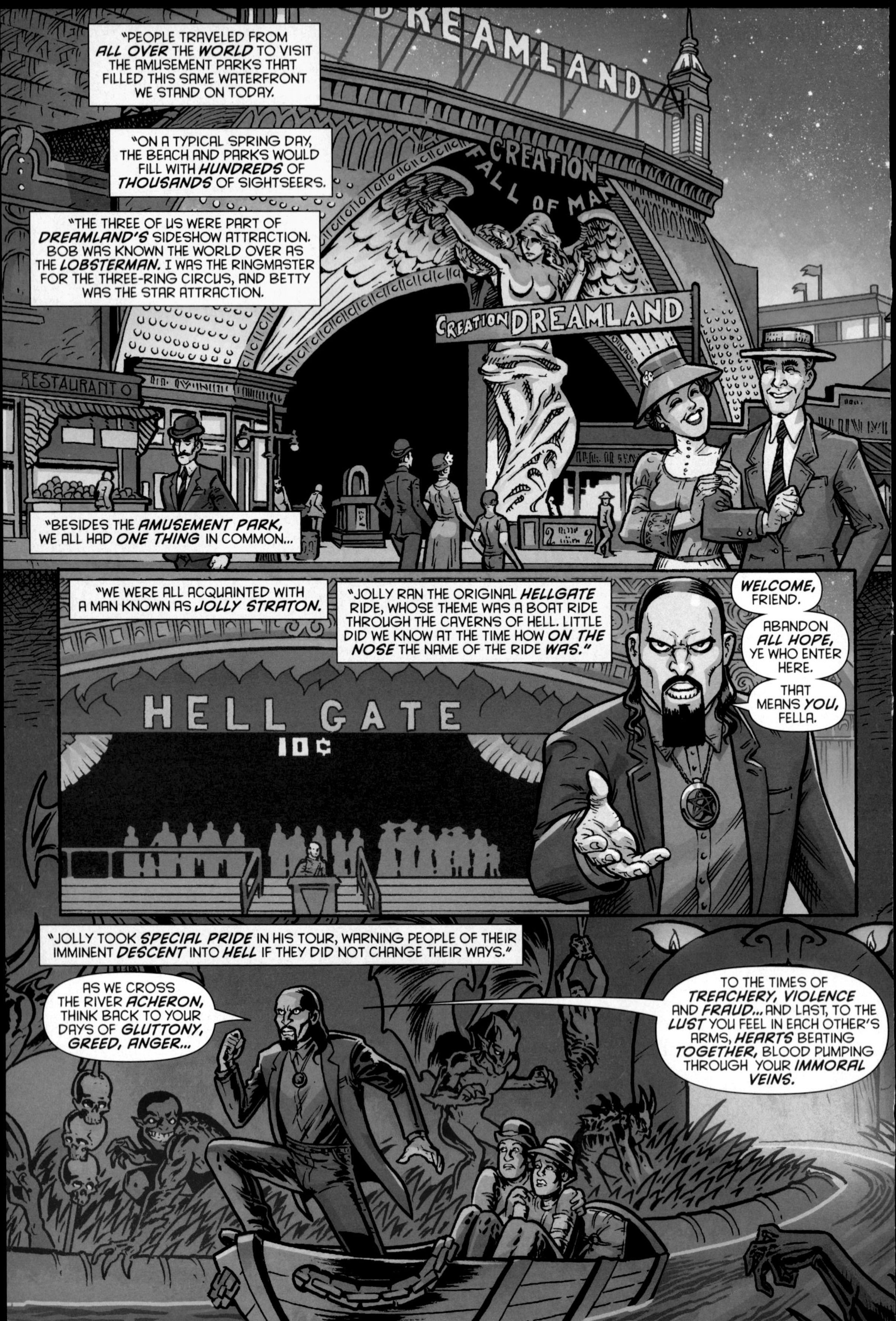

DREAMLAND
"PEOPLE TRAVELED FROM ALL OVER THE WORLD TO VISIT THE AMUSEMENT PARKS THAT FILLED THIS SAME WATERFRONT WE STAND ON TODAY.
"ON A TYPICAL SPRING DAY, THE BEACH AND PARKS WOULD FILL WITH HUNDREDS OF THOUSANDS OF SIGHTSEERS.
CREATION
FALL OF MAN
"THE THREE OF US WERE PART OF DREAMLAND'S SIDESHOW ATTRACTION. BOB WAS KNOWN THE WORLD OVER AS THE LOBSTERMAN. I WAS THE RINGMASTER FOR THE THREE-RING CIRCUS, AND BETTY WAS THE STAR ATTRACTION.
CREATION DREAMLAND
RESTAURANT
"BESIDES THE AMUSEMENT PARK, WE ALL HAD ONE THING IN COMMON...
"WE WERE ALL ACQUAINTED WITH A MAN KNOWN AS JOLLY STRATON.
"JOLLY RAN THE ORIGINAL HELLGATE RIDE, WHOSE THEME WAS A BOAT RIDE THROUGH THE CAVERNS OF HELL. LITTLE DID WE KNOW AT THE TIME HOW ON THE NOSE THE NAME OF THE RIDE WAS."
WELCOME, FRIEND.
ABANDON ALL HOPE, YE WHO ENTER HERE.
THAT MEANS YOU, FELLA.
HELL GATE
10¢
"JOLLY TOOK SPECIAL PRIDE IN HIS TOUR, WARNING PEOPLE OF THEIR IMMINENT DESCENT INTO HELL IF THEY DID NOT CHANGE THEIR WAYS."
AS WE CROSS THE RIVER ACHERON, THINK BACK TO YOUR DAYS OF GLUTTONY, GREED, ANGER...
TO THE TIMES OF TREACHERY, VIOLENCE AND FRAUD... AND LAST, TO THE LUST YOU FEEL IN EACH OTHER'S ARMS, HEARTS BEATING TOGETHER, BLOOD PUMPING THROUGH YOUR IMMORAL VEINS.

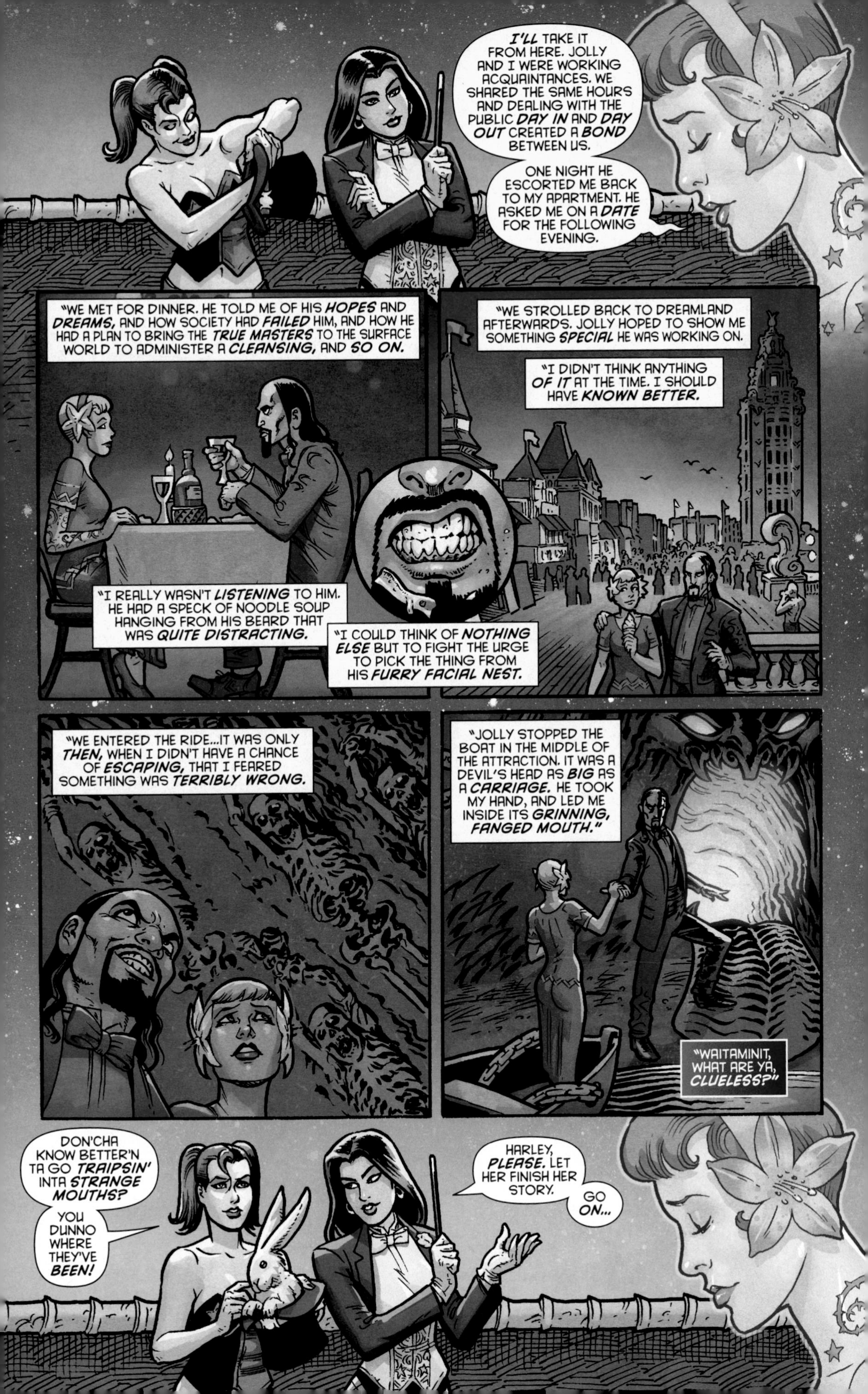

I'LL TAKE IT FROM HERE. JOLLY AND I WERE WORKING ACQUAINTANCES. WE SHARED THE SAME HOURS AND DEALING WITH THE PUBLIC DAY IN AND DAY OUT CREATED A BOND BETWEEN US.
ONE NIGHT HE ESCORTED ME BACK TO MY APARTMENT. HE ASKED ME ON A DATE FOR THE FOLLOWING EVENING.
"WE MET FOR DINNER. HE TOLD ME OF HIS HOPES AND DREAMS, AND HOW SOCIETY HAD FAILED HIM, AND HOW HE HAD A PLAN TO BRING THE TRUE MASTERS TO THE SURFACE WORLD TO ADMINISTER A CLEANSING, AND SO ON.
"I REALLY WASN'T LISTENING TO HIM. HE HAD A SPECK OF NOODLE SOUP HANGING FROM HIS BEARD THAT WAS QUITE DISTRACTING.
"I COULD THINK OF NOTHING ELSE BUT TO FIGHT THE URGE TO PICK THE THING FROM HIS FURRY FACIAL NEST.
"WE STROLLED BACK TO DREAMLAND AFTERWARDS. JOLLY HOPED TO SHOW ME SOMETHING SPECIAL HE WAS WORKING ON.
"I DIDN'T THINK ANYTHING OF IT AT THE TIME. I SHOULD HAVE KNOWN BETTER.
"WE ENTERED THE RIDE...IT WAS ONLY THEN, WHEN I DIDN'T HAVE A CHANCE OF ESCAPING, THAT I FEARED SOMETHING WAS TERRIBLY WRONG.
"JOLLY STOPPED THE BOAT IN THE MIDDLE OF THE ATTRACTION. IT WAS A DEVIL'S HEAD AS BIG AS A CARRIAGE. HE TOOK MY HAND, AND LED ME INSIDE ITS GRINNING, FANGED MOUTH."
"WAITAMINIT, WHAT ARE YA, CLUELESS?"
DON'CHA KNOW BETTER'N TA GO TRAIPSIN' INTA STRANGE MOUTHS?
YOU DUNNO WHERE THEY'VE BEEN!
HARLEY, PLEASE. LET HER FINISH HER STORY.
GO ON...

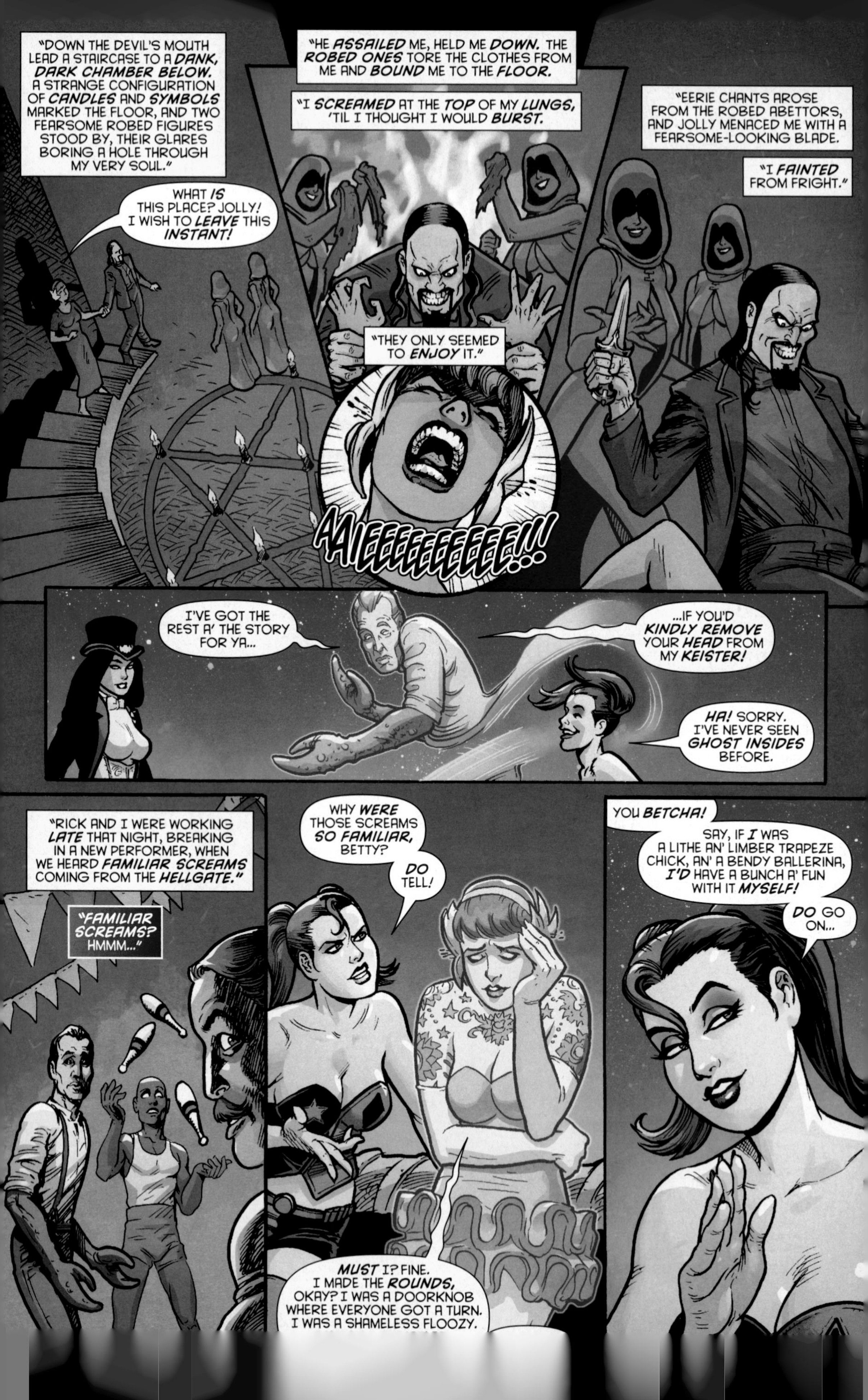
"DOWN THE DEVIL'S MOUTH LEAD A STAIRCASE TO A DANK, DARK CHAMBER BELOW. A STRANGE CONFIGURATION OF CANDLES AND SYMBOLS MARKED THE FLOOR, AND TWO FEARSOME ROBED FIGURES STOOD BY, THEIR GLARES BORING A HOLE THROUGH MY VERY SOUL."
WHAT IS THIS PLACE? JOLLY! I WISH TO LEAVE THIS INSTANT!
"HE ASSAILED ME, HELD ME DOWN. THE ROBED ONES TORE THE CLOTHES FROM ME AND BOUND ME TO THE FLOOR.
"I SCREAMED AT THE TOP OF MY LUNGS, 'TIL I THOUGHT I WOULD BURST.
"THEY ONLY SEEMED TO ENJOY IT."
AAIEEEEEEEEEEE!!!
"EERIE CHANTS AROSE FROM THE ROBED ABETTORS, AND JOLLY MENACED ME WITH A FEARSOME-LOOKING BLADE.
"I FAINTED FROM FRIGHT."
I'VE GOT THE REST A' THE STORY FOR YA...
...IF YOU'D KINDLY REMOVE YOUR HEAD FROM MY KEISTER!
HA! SORRY. I'VE NEVER SEEN GHOST INSIDES BEFORE.
"RICK AND I WERE WORKING LATE THAT NIGHT, BREAKING IN A NEW PERFORMER, WHEN WE HEARD FAMILIAR SCREAMS COMING FROM THE HELLGATE."
"FAMILIAR SCREAMS? HMMM..."
WHY WERE THOSE SCREAMS SO FAMILIAR, BETTY?
DO TELL!
MUST I? FINE. I MADE THE ROUNDS, OKAY? I WAS A DOORKNOB WHERE EVERYONE GOT A TURN. I WAS A SHAMELESS FLOOZY.
YOU BETCHA!
SAY, IF I WAS A LITHE AN' LIMBER TRAPEZE CHICK, AN' A BENDY BALLERINA, I'D HAVE A BUNCH A' FUN WITH IT MYSELF!
DO GO ON...

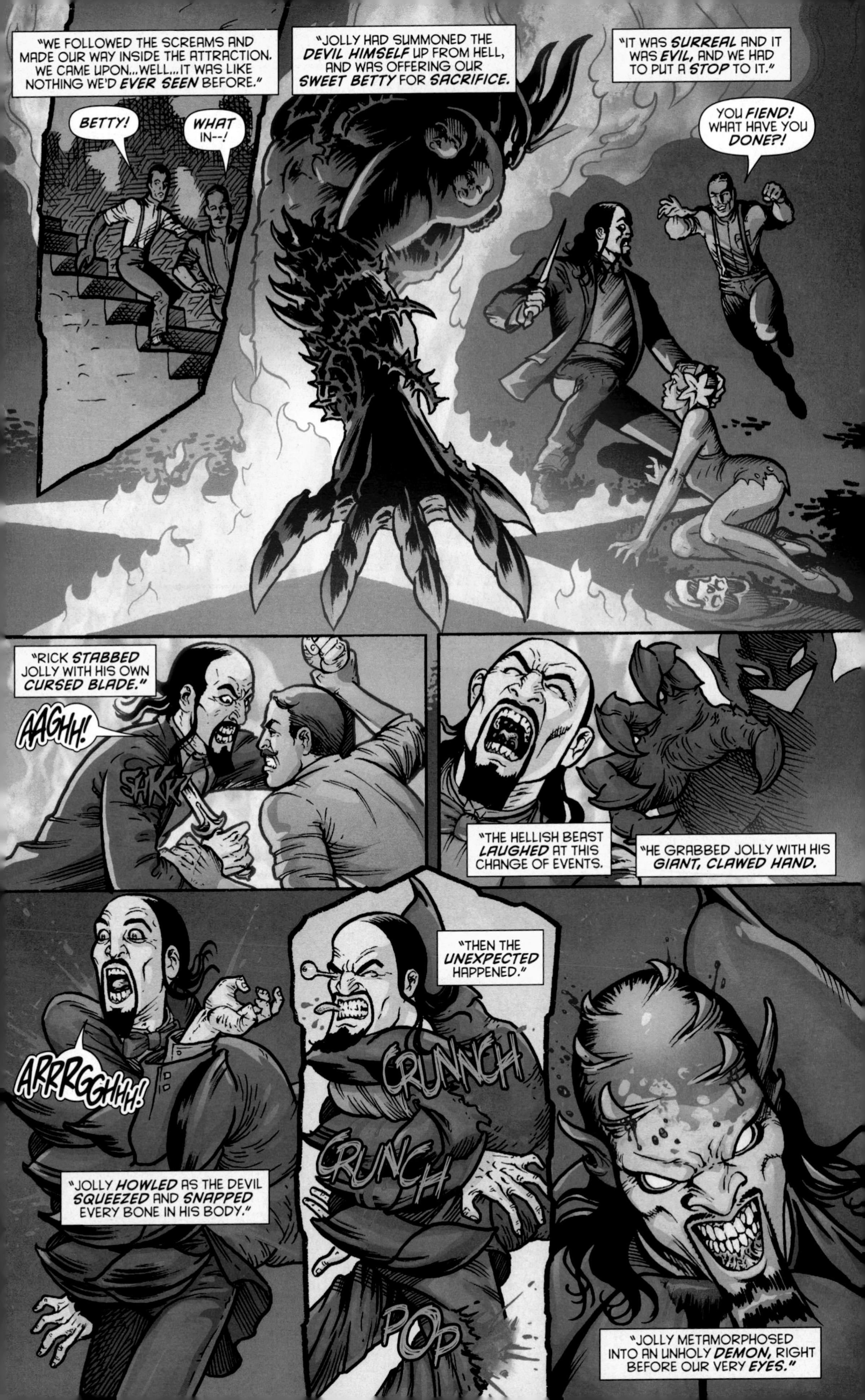
"WE FOLLOWED THE SCREAMS AND MADE OUR WAY INSIDE THE ATTRACTION. WE CAME UPON...WELL...IT WAS LIKE NOTHING WE'D EVER SEEN BEFORE."
BETTY!
WHAT IN--!
"JOLLY HAD SUMMONED THE DEVIL HIMSELF UP FROM HELL, AND WAS OFFERING OUR SWEET BETTY FOR SACRIFICE.
"IT WAS SURREAL AND IT WAS EVIL, AND WE HAD TO PUT A STOP TO IT."
YOU FIEND! WHAT HAVE YOU DONE?!
"RICK STABBED JOLLY WITH HIS OWN CURSED BLADE."
AAGHH!
SHKK
"THE HELLISH BEAST LAUGHED AT THIS CHANGE OF EVENTS.
"HE GRABBED JOLLY WITH HIS GIANT, CLAWED HAND.
ARRRGGHHH!
"JOLLY HOWLED AS THE DEVIL SQUEEZED AND SNAPPED EVERY BONE IN HIS BODY."
"THEN THE UNEXPECTED HAPPENED."
CRUNNCH
CRUNCH
POP
"JOLLY METAMORPHOSED INTO AN UNHOLY DEMON, RIGHT BEFORE OUR VERY EYES."

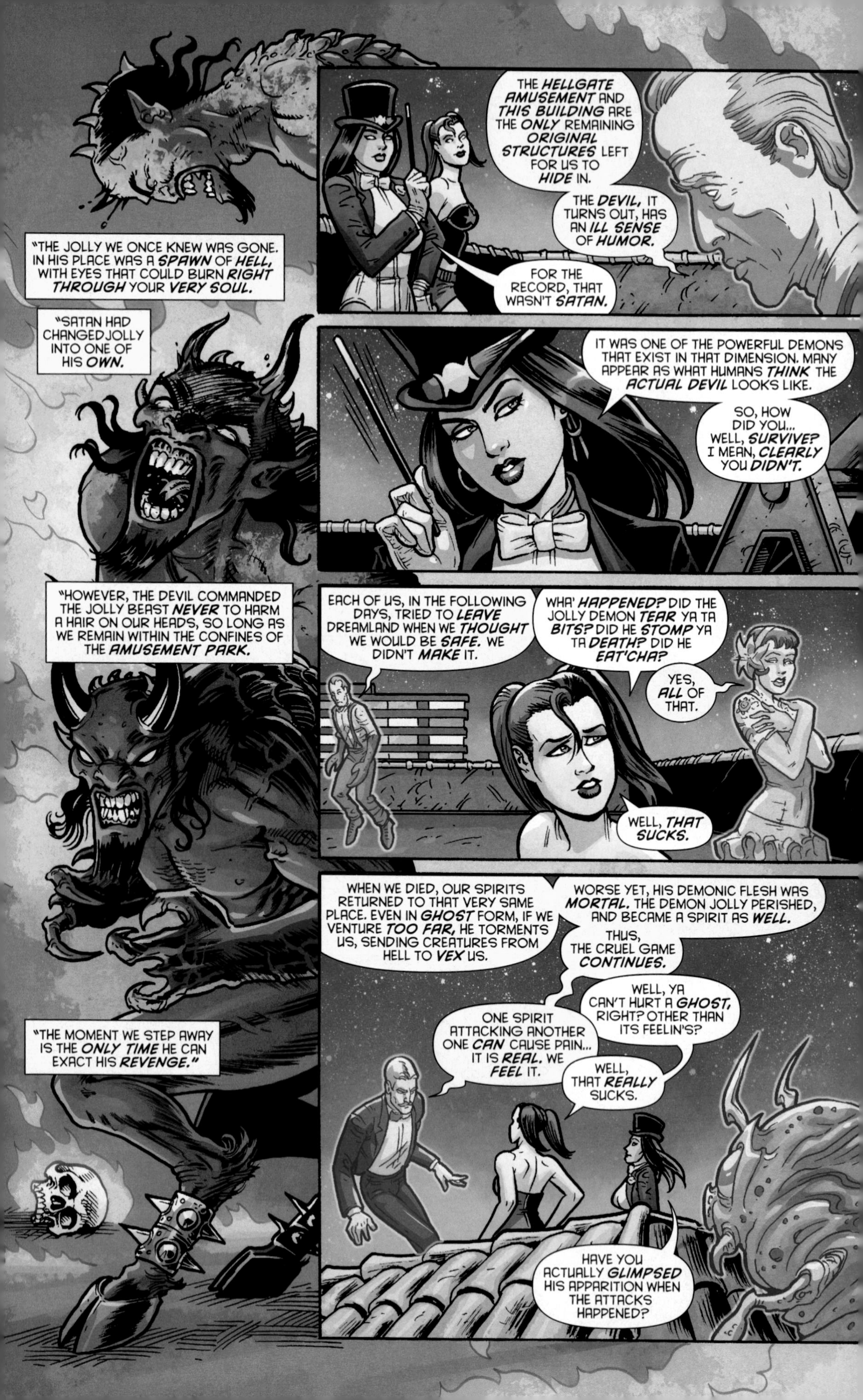
"THE JOLLY WE ONCE KNEW WAS GONE. IN HIS PLACE WAS A SPAWN OF HELL, WITH EYES THAT COULD BURN RIGHT THROUGH YOUR VERY SOUL.
"SATAN HAD CHANGED JOLLY INTO ONE OF HIS OWN.
THE HELLGATE AMUSEMENT AND THIS BUILDING ARE THE ONLY REMAINING ORIGINAL STRUCTURES LEFT FOR US TO HIDE IN.
THE DEVIL, IT TURNS OUT, HAS AN ILL SENSE OF HUMOR.
FOR THE RECORD, THAT WASN'T SATAN.
IT WAS ONE OF THE POWERFUL DEMONS THAT EXIST IN THAT DIMENSION. MANY APPEAR AS WHAT HUMANS THINK THE ACTUAL DEVIL LOOKS LIKE.
SO, HOW DID YOU... WELL, SURVIVE? I MEAN, CLEARLY YOU DIDN'T.
"HOWEVER, THE DEVIL COMMANDED THE JOLLY BEAST NEVER TO HARM A HAIR ON OUR HEADS, SO LONG AS WE REMAIN WITHIN THE CONFINES OF THE AMUSEMENT PARK.
EACH OF US, IN THE FOLLOWING DAYS, TRIED TO LEAVE DREAMLAND WHEN WE THOUGHT WE WOULD BE SAFE. WE DIDN'T MAKE IT.
WHA' HAPPENED? DID THE JOLLY DEMON TEAR YA TA BITS? DID HE STOMP YA TA DEATH? DID HE EAT'CHA?
YES, ALL OF THAT.
WELL, THAT SUCKS.
WHEN WE DIED, OUR SPIRITS RETURNED TO THAT VERY SAME PLACE. EVEN IN GHOST FORM, IF WE VENTURE TOO FAR, HE TORMENTS US, SENDING CREATURES FROM HELL TO VEX US.
WORSE YET, HIS DEMONIC FLESH WAS MORTAL. THE DEMON JOLLY PERISHED, AND BECAME A SPIRIT AS WELL.
THUS, THE CRUEL GAME CONTINUES.
WELL, YA CAN'T HURT A GHOST, RIGHT? OTHER THAN ITS FEELIN'S?
ONE SPIRIT ATTACKING ANOTHER ONE CAN CAUSE PAIN... IT IS REAL. WE FEEL IT.
WELL, THAT REALLY SUCKS.
"THE MOMENT WE STEP AWAY IS THE ONLY TIME HE CAN EXACT HIS REVENGE."
HAVE YOU ACTUALLY GLIMPSED HIS APPARITION WHEN THE ATTACKS HAPPENED?

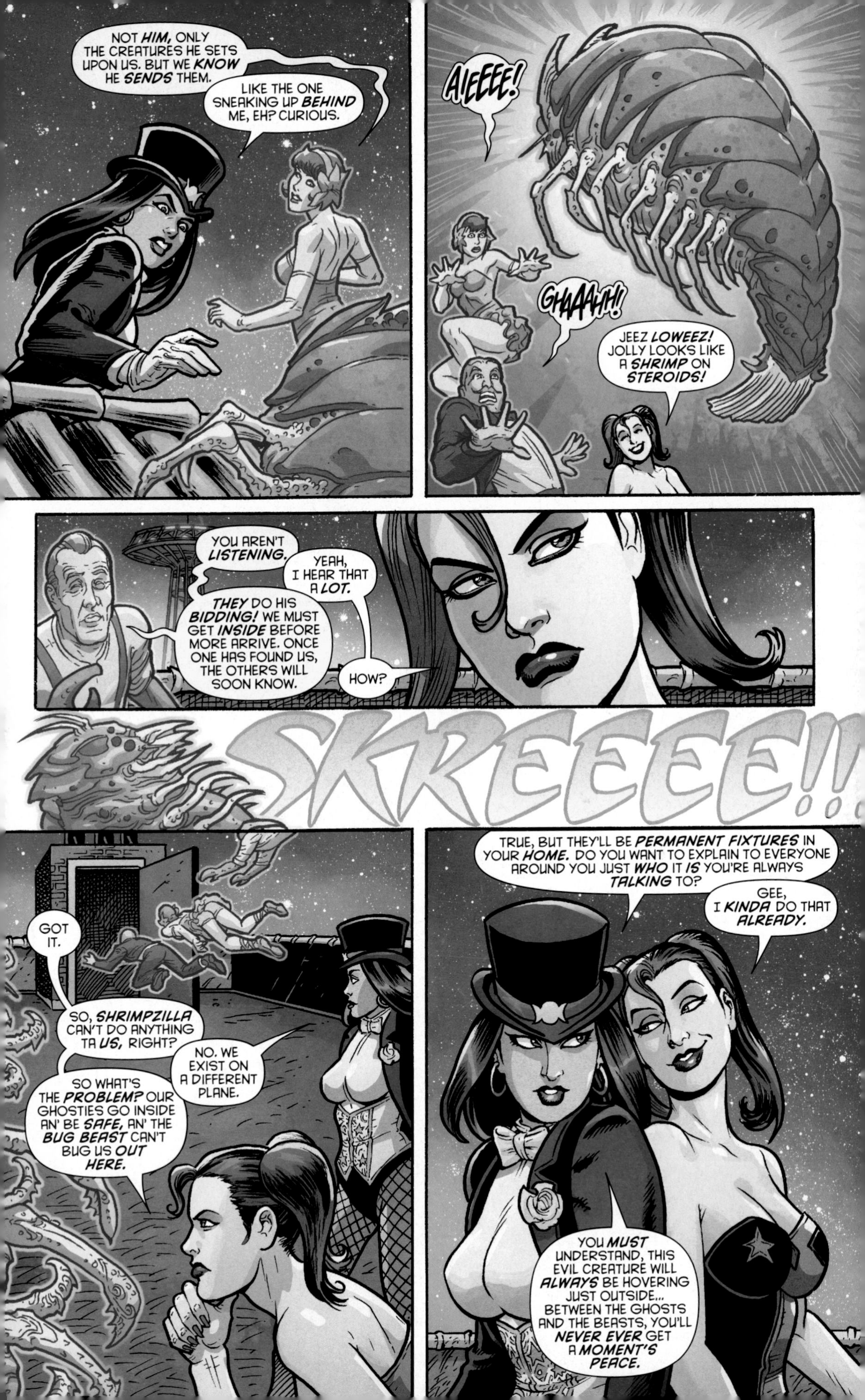
NOT HIM, ONLY THE CREATURES HE SETS UPON US. BUT WE KNOW HE SENDS THEM.
LIKE THE ONE SNEAKING UP BEHIND ME, EH? CURIOUS.
AIEEEE!
GHAAAHH!
JEEZ LOWEEZ! JOLLY LOOKS LIKE A SHRIMP ON STEROIDS!
YOU AREN'T LISTENING.
YEAH, I HEAR THAT A LOT.
THEY DO HIS BIDDING! WE MUST GET INSIDE BEFORE MORE ARRIVE. ONCE ONE HAS FOUND US, THE OTHERS WILL SOON KNOW.
HOW?
SKREEEE!!
GOT IT.
SO, SHRIMPZILLA CAN'T DO ANYTHING TA US, RIGHT?
NO. WE EXIST ON A DIFFERENT PLANE.
SO WHAT'S THE PROBLEM? OUR GHOSTIES GO INSIDE AN' BE SAFE, AN' THE BUG BEAST CAN'T BUG US OUT HERE.
TRUE, BUT THEY'LL BE PERMANENT FIXTURES IN YOUR HOME. DO YOU WANT TO EXPLAIN TO EVERYONE AROUND YOU JUST WHO IT IS YOU'RE ALWAYS TALKING TO?
GEE, I KINDA DO THAT ALREADY.
YOU MUST UNDERSTAND, THIS EVIL CREATURE WILL ALWAYS BE HOVERING JUST OUTSIDE... BETWEEN THE GHOSTS AND THE BEASTS, YOU'LL NEVER EVER GET A MOMENT'S PEACE.

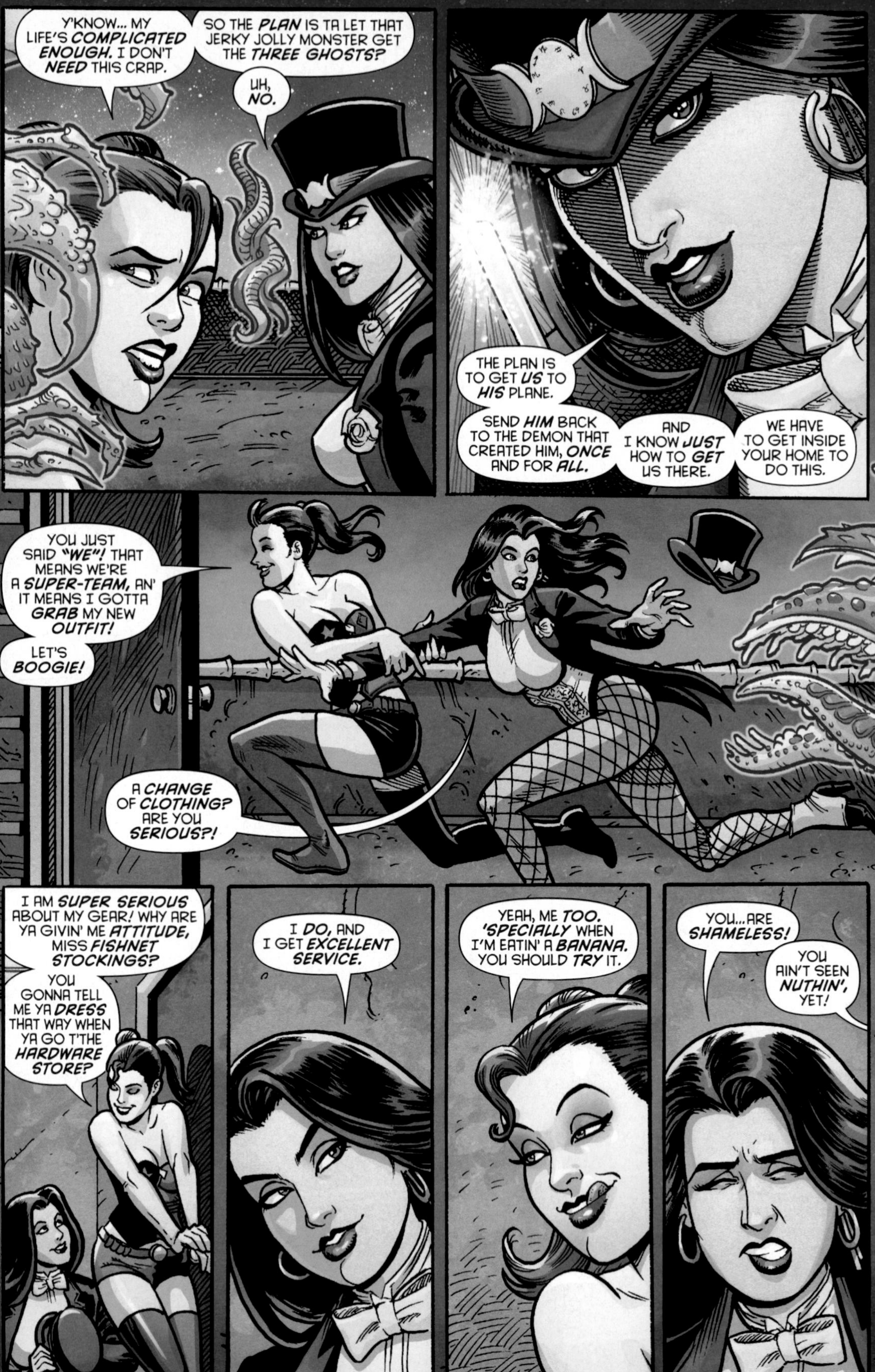
Y'KNOW... MY LIFE'S COMPLICATED ENOUGH. I DON'T NEED THIS CRAP.
SO THE PLAN IS TA LET THAT JERKY JOLLY MONSTER GET THE THREE GHOSTS?
UH, NO.
THE PLAN IS TO GET US TO HIS PLANE.
SEND HIM BACK TO THE DEMON THAT CREATED HIM, ONCE AND FOR ALL.
AND I KNOW JUST HOW TO GET US THERE.
WE HAVE TO GET INSIDE YOUR HOME TO DO THIS.
YOU JUST SAID "WE"! THAT MEANS WE'RE A SUPER-TEAM, AN' IT MEANS I GOTTA GRAB MY NEW OUTFIT!
LET'S BOOGIE!
A CHANGE OF CLOTHING? ARE YOU SERIOUS?!
I AM SUPER SERIOUS ABOUT MY GEAR! WHY ARE YA GIVIN' ME ATTITUDE, MISS FISHNET STOCKINGS?
YOU GONNA TELL ME YA DRESS THAT WAY WHEN YA GO T'THE HARDWARE STORE?
I DO, AND I GET EXCELLENT SERVICE.
YEAH, ME TOO. 'SPECIALLY WHEN I'M EATIN' A BANANA. YOU SHOULD TRY IT.
YOU...ARE SHAMELESS!
YOU AIN'T SEEN NUTHIN', YET!

GHOST BUSTED

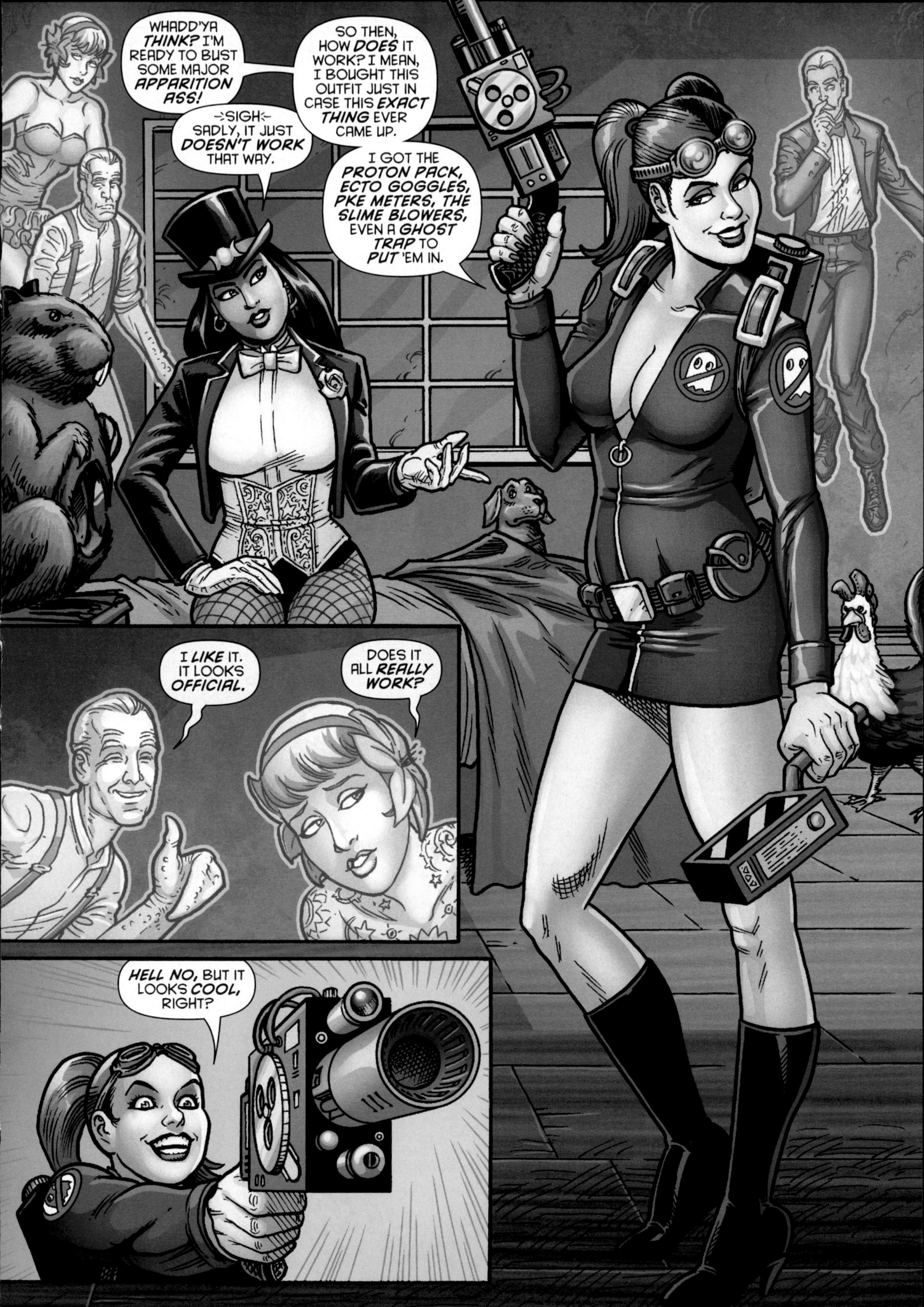

WHADD'YA THINK? I'M READY TO BUST SOME MAJOR APPARITION ASS!
⇒SIGH⇐ SADLY, IT JUST DOESN'T WORK THAT WAY.
SO THEN, HOW DOES IT WORK? I MEAN, I BOUGHT THIS OUTFIT JUST IN CASE THIS EXACT THING EVER CAME UP.
I GOT THE PROTON PACK, ECTO GOGGLES, PKE METERS, THE SLIME BLOWERS, EVEN A GHOST TRAP TO PUT 'EM IN.
I LIKE IT. IT LOOKS OFFICIAL.
DOES IT ALL REALLY WORK?
HELL NO, BUT IT LOOKS COOL, RIGHT?

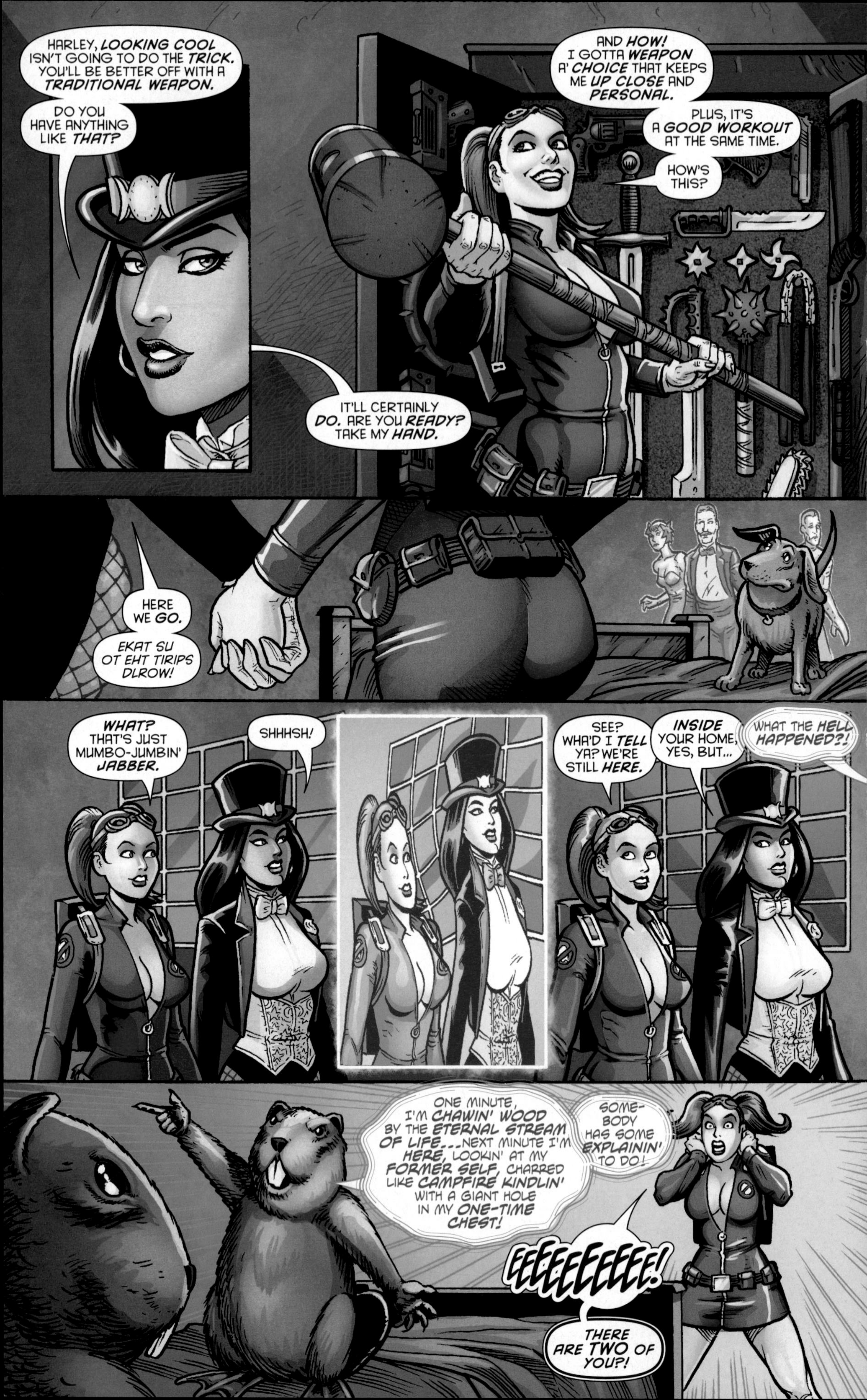
HARLEY, LOOKING COOL ISN'T GOING TO DO THE TRICK. YOU'LL BE BETTER OFF WITH A TRADITIONAL WEAPON.
DO YOU HAVE ANYTHING LIKE THAT?
AND HOW! I GOTTA WEAPON A' CHOICE THAT KEEPS ME UP CLOSE AND PERSONAL.
PLUS, IT'S A GOOD WORKOUT AT THE SAME TIME.
HOW'S THIS?
IT'LL CERTAINLY DO. ARE YOU READY? TAKE MY HAND.
HERE WE GO.
EKAT SU OT EHT TIRIPS DLROW!
WHAT? THAT'S JUST MUMBO-JUMBIN' JABBER.
SHHHSH!
SEE? WHA'D I TELL YA? WE'RE STILL HERE.
INSIDE YOUR HOME, YES, BUT...
WHAT THE HELL HAPPENED?!
ONE MINUTE, I'M CHAWIN' WOOD BY THE ETERNAL STREAM OF LIFE...NEXT MINUTE I'M HERE, LOOKIN' AT MY FORMER SELF, CHARRED LIKE CAMPFIRE KINDLIN' WITH A GIANT HOLE IN MY ONE-TIME CHEST!
SOME-BODY HAS SOME EXPLAININ' TO DO!
EEEEEEEEEE!
THERE ARE TWO OF YOU?!

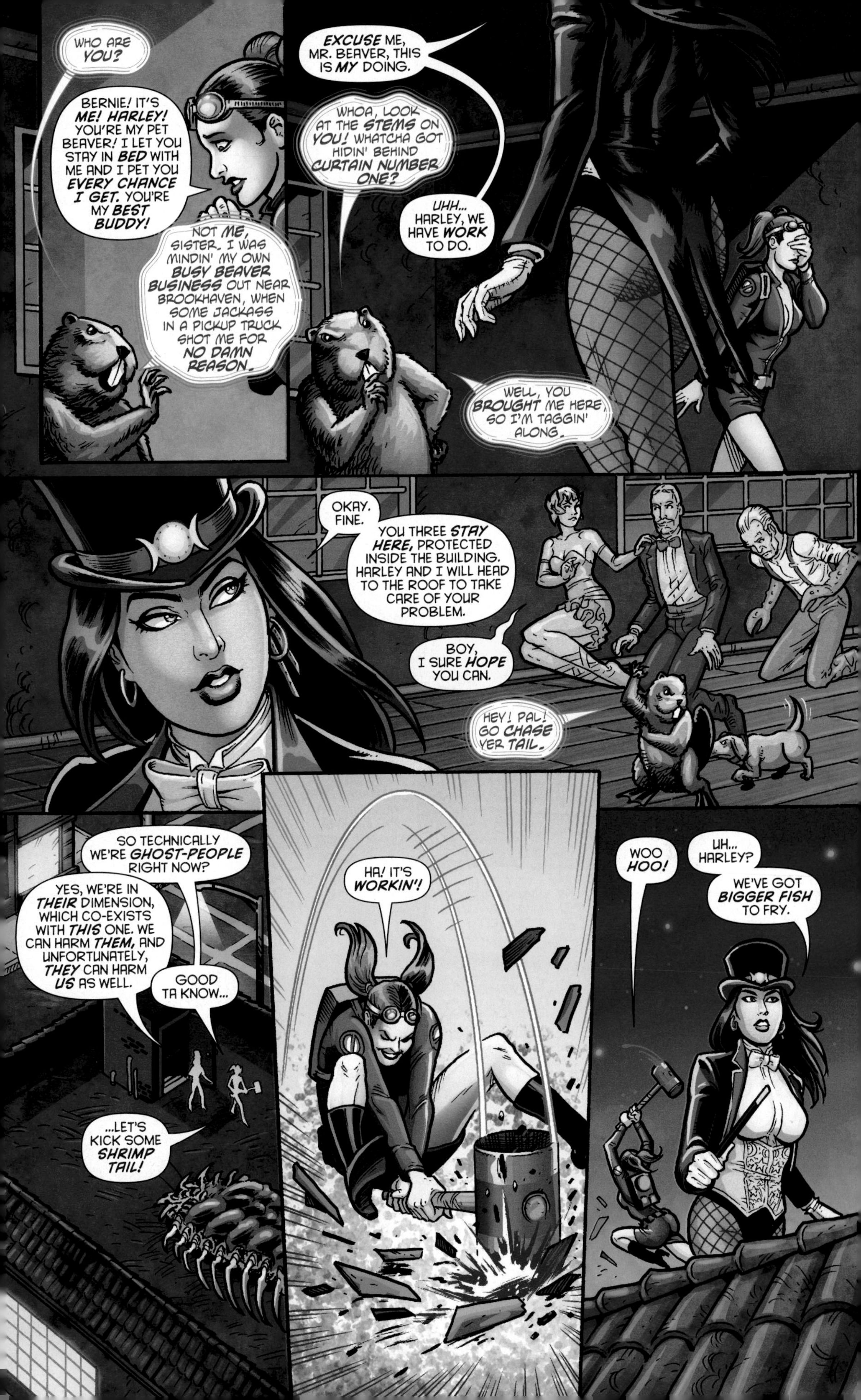
WHO ARE YOU?
BERNIE! IT'S ME! HARLEY! YOU'RE MY PET BEAVER! I LET YOU STAY IN BED WITH ME AND I PET YOU EVERY CHANCE I GET. YOU'RE MY BEST BUDDY!
NOT ME, SISTER. I WAS MINDIN' MY OWN BUSY BEAVER BUSINESS OUT NEAR BROOKHAVEN, WHEN SOME JACKASS IN A PICKUP TRUCK SHOT ME FOR NO DAMN REASON.
EXCUSE ME, MR. BEAVER, THIS IS MY DOING.
WHOA, LOOK AT THE STEMS ON YOU! WHATCHA GOT HIDIN' BEHIND CURTAIN NUMBER ONE?
UHH... HARLEY, WE HAVE WORK TO DO.
WELL, YOU BROUGHT ME HERE, SO I'M TAGGIN' ALONG.
OKAY. FINE.
YOU THREE STAY HERE, PROTECTED INSIDE THE BUILDING. HARLEY AND I WILL HEAD TO THE ROOF TO TAKE CARE OF YOUR PROBLEM.
BOY, I SURE HOPE YOU CAN.
HEY! PAL! GO CHASE YER TAIL.
SO TECHNICALLY WE'RE GHOST-PEOPLE RIGHT NOW?
YES, WE'RE IN THEIR DIMENSION, WHICH CO-EXISTS WITH THIS ONE. WE CAN HARM THEM, AND UNFORTUNATELY, THEY CAN HARM US AS WELL.
GOOD TA KNOW...
...LET'S KICK SOME SHRIMP TAIL!
HA! IT'S WORKIN'!
WOO HOO!
UH... HARLEY?
WE'VE GOT BIGGER FISH TO FRY.

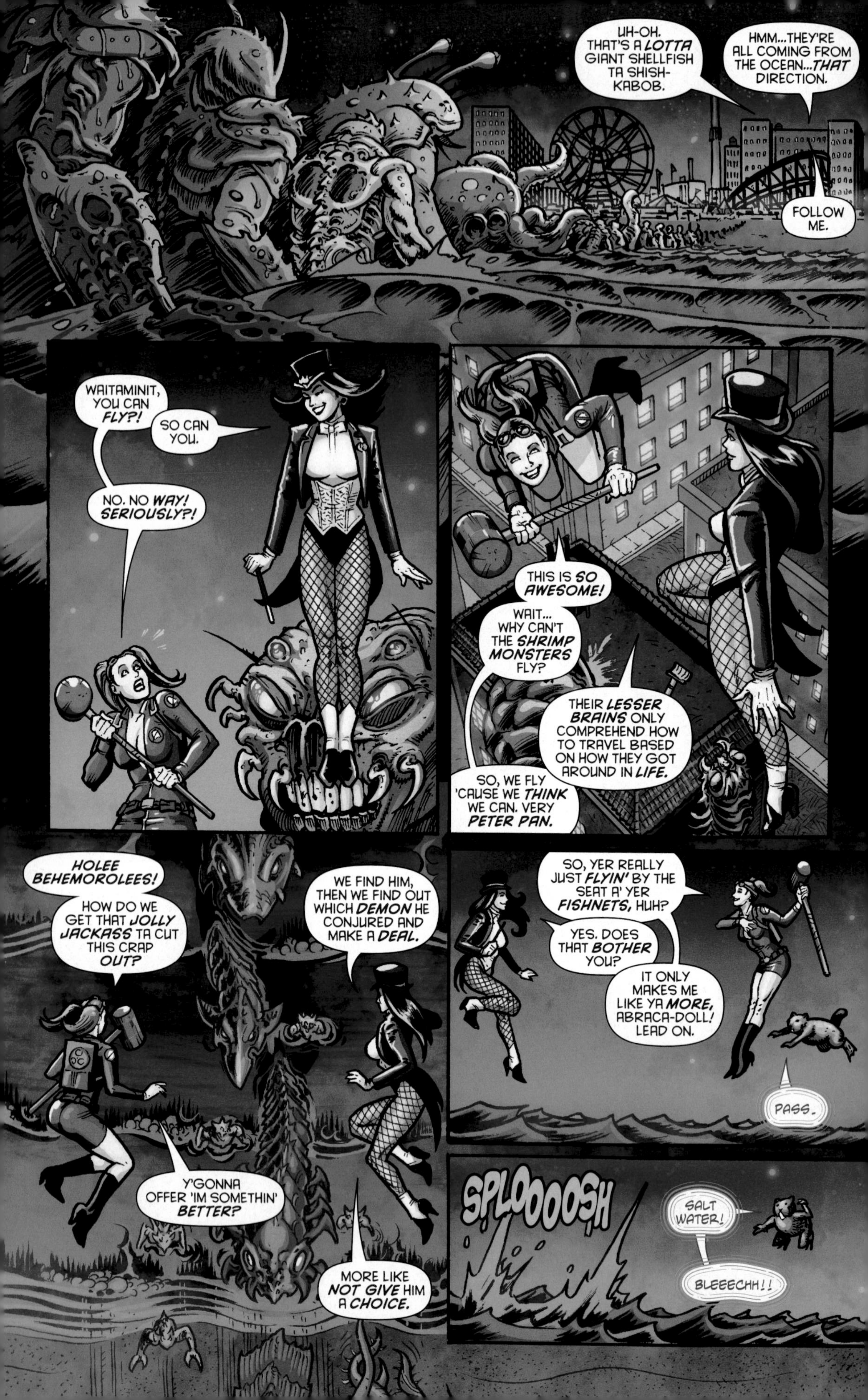
UH-OH. THAT'S A LOTTA GIANT SHELLFISH TA SHISH-KABOB.
HMM...THEY'RE ALL COMING FROM THE OCEAN...THAT DIRECTION.
FOLLOW ME.
WAITAMINIT, YOU CAN FLY?!
SO CAN YOU.
NO. NO WAY! SERIOUSLY?!
THIS IS SO AWESOME!
WAIT... WHY CAN'T THE SHRIMP MONSTERS FLY?
THEIR LESSER BRAINS ONLY COMPREHEND HOW TO TRAVEL BASED ON HOW THEY GOT AROUND IN LIFE.
SO, WE FLY 'CAUSE WE THINK WE CAN. VERY PETER PAN.
HOLEE BEHEMOROLEES!
HOW DO WE GET THAT JOLLY JACKASS TA CUT THIS CRAP OUT?
WE FIND HIM, THEN WE FIND OUT WHICH DEMON HE CONJURED AND MAKE A DEAL.
Y'GONNA OFFER 'IM SOMETHIN' BETTER?
MORE LIKE NOT GIVE HIM A CHOICE.
SO, YER REALLY JUST FLYIN' BY THE SEAT A' YER FISHNETS, HUH?
YES. DOES THAT BOTHER YOU?
IT ONLY MAKES ME LIKE YA MORE, ABRACA-DOLL! LEAD ON.
PASS.
SPLOOOOSH
SALT WATER!
BLEEECHH!!

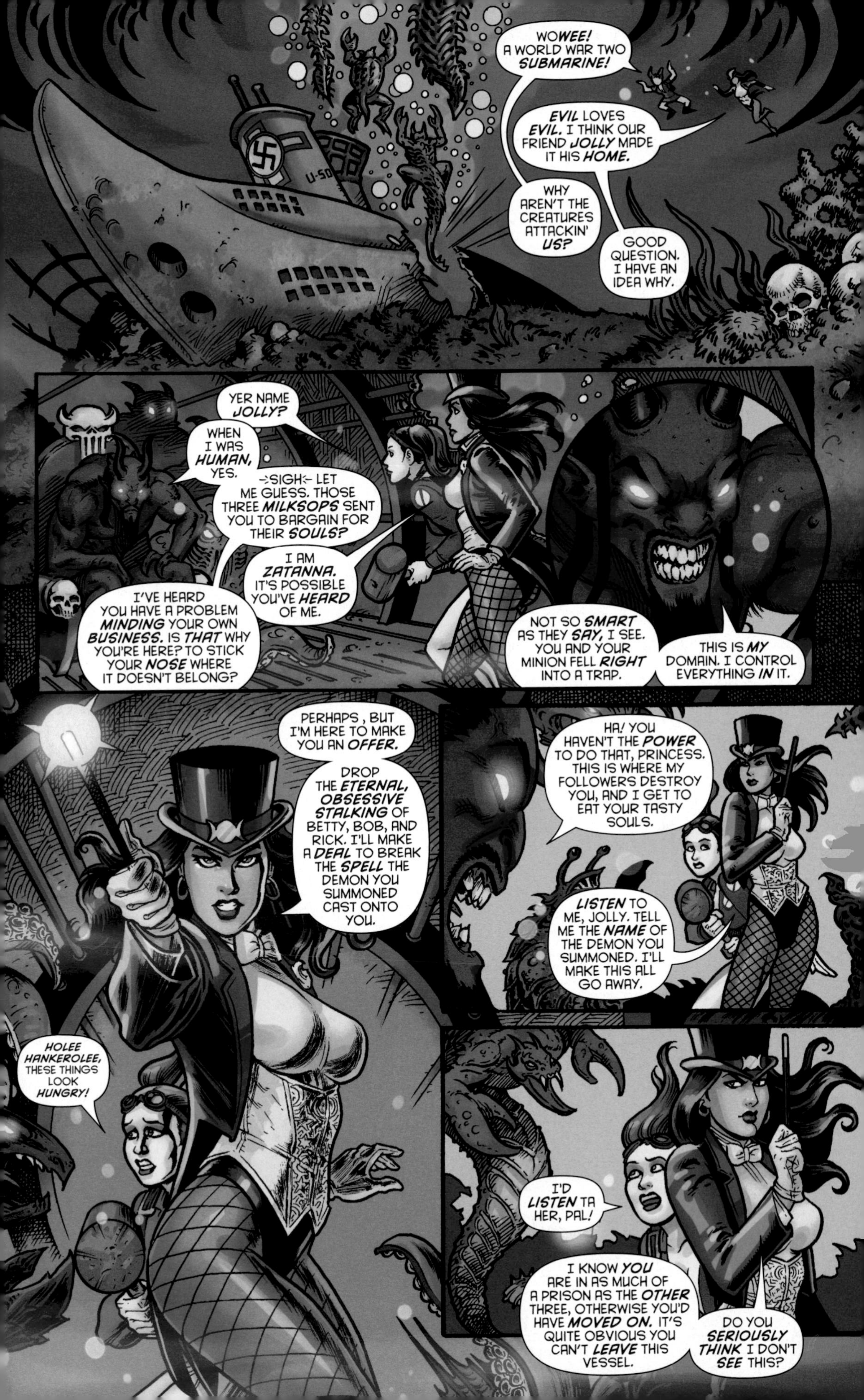

WOWEE! A WORLD WAR TWO SUBMARINE!
EVIL LOVES EVIL. I THINK OUR FRIEND JOLLY MADE IT HIS HOME.
WHY AREN'T THE CREATURES ATTACKIN' US?
GOOD QUESTION. I HAVE AN IDEA WHY.
U-50
YER NAME JOLLY?
WHEN I WAS HUMAN, YES.
⇒SIGH⇐ LET ME GUESS. THOSE THREE MILKSOPS SENT YOU TO BARGAIN FOR THEIR SOULS?
I AM ZATANNA. IT'S POSSIBLE YOU'VE HEARD OF ME.
I'VE HEARD YOU HAVE A PROBLEM MINDING YOUR OWN BUSINESS. IS THAT WHY YOU'RE HERE? TO STICK YOUR NOSE WHERE IT DOESN'T BELONG?
NOT SO SMART AS THEY SAY, I SEE. YOU AND YOUR MINION FELL RIGHT INTO A TRAP.
THIS IS MY DOMAIN. I CONTROL EVERYTHING IN IT.
PERHAPS, BUT I'M HERE TO MAKE YOU AN OFFER.
DROP THE ETERNAL, OBSESSIVE STALKING OF BETTY, BOB, AND RICK. I'LL MAKE A DEAL TO BREAK THE SPELL THE DEMON YOU SUMMONED CAST ONTO YOU.
HOLEE HANKEROLEE, THESE THINGS LOOK HUNGRY!
HA! YOU HAVEN'T THE POWER TO DO THAT, PRINCESS. THIS IS WHERE MY FOLLOWERS DESTROY YOU, AND I GET TO EAT YOUR TASTY SOULS.
LISTEN TO ME, JOLLY. TELL ME THE NAME OF THE DEMON YOU SUMMONED. I'LL MAKE THIS ALL GO AWAY.
I'D LISTEN TA HER, PAL!
I KNOW YOU ARE IN AS MUCH OF A PRISON AS THE OTHER THREE, OTHERWISE YOU'D HAVE MOVED ON. IT'S QUITE OBVIOUS YOU CAN'T LEAVE THIS VESSEL.
DO YOU SERIOUSLY THINK I DON'T SEE THIS?

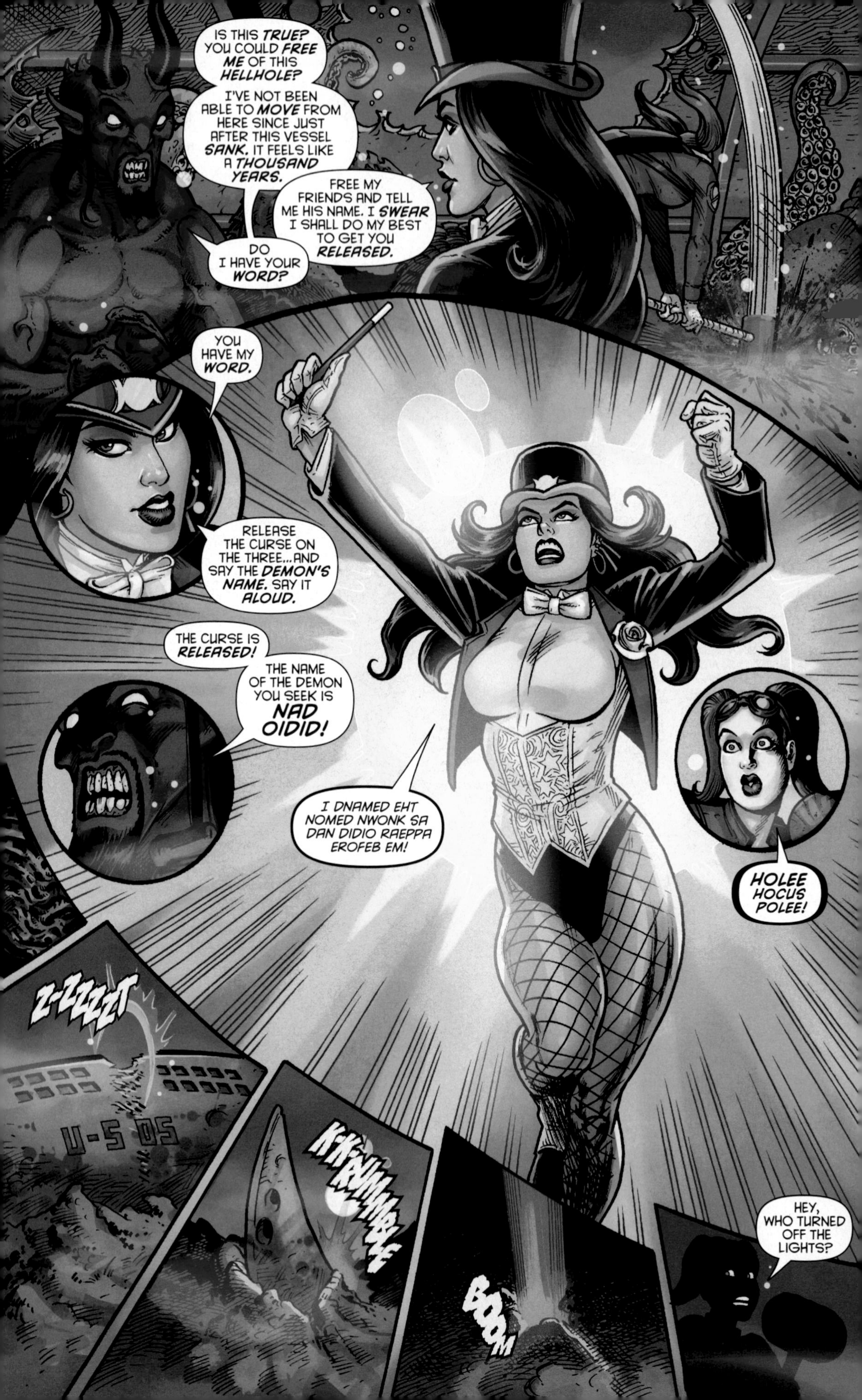
IS THIS TRUE? YOU COULD FREE ME OF THIS HELLHOLE?
I'VE NOT BEEN ABLE TO MOVE FROM HERE SINCE JUST AFTER THIS VESSEL SANK. IT FEELS LIKE A THOUSAND YEARS.
DO I HAVE YOUR WORD?
FREE MY FRIENDS AND TELL ME HIS NAME. I SWEAR I SHALL DO MY BEST TO GET YOU RELEASED.
YOU HAVE MY WORD.
RELEASE THE CURSE ON THE THREE...AND SAY THE DEMON'S NAME. SAY IT ALOUD.
THE CURSE IS RELEASED!
THE NAME OF THE DEMON YOU SEEK IS NAD OIDID!
I DNAMED EHT NOMED NWONK SA DAN DIDIO RAEPPA EROFEB EM!
HOLEE HOCUS POLEE!
Z-ZZZZZT
U-S 05
K-K-RUMMBLE
BOOM
HEY, WHO TURNED OFF THE LIGHTS?

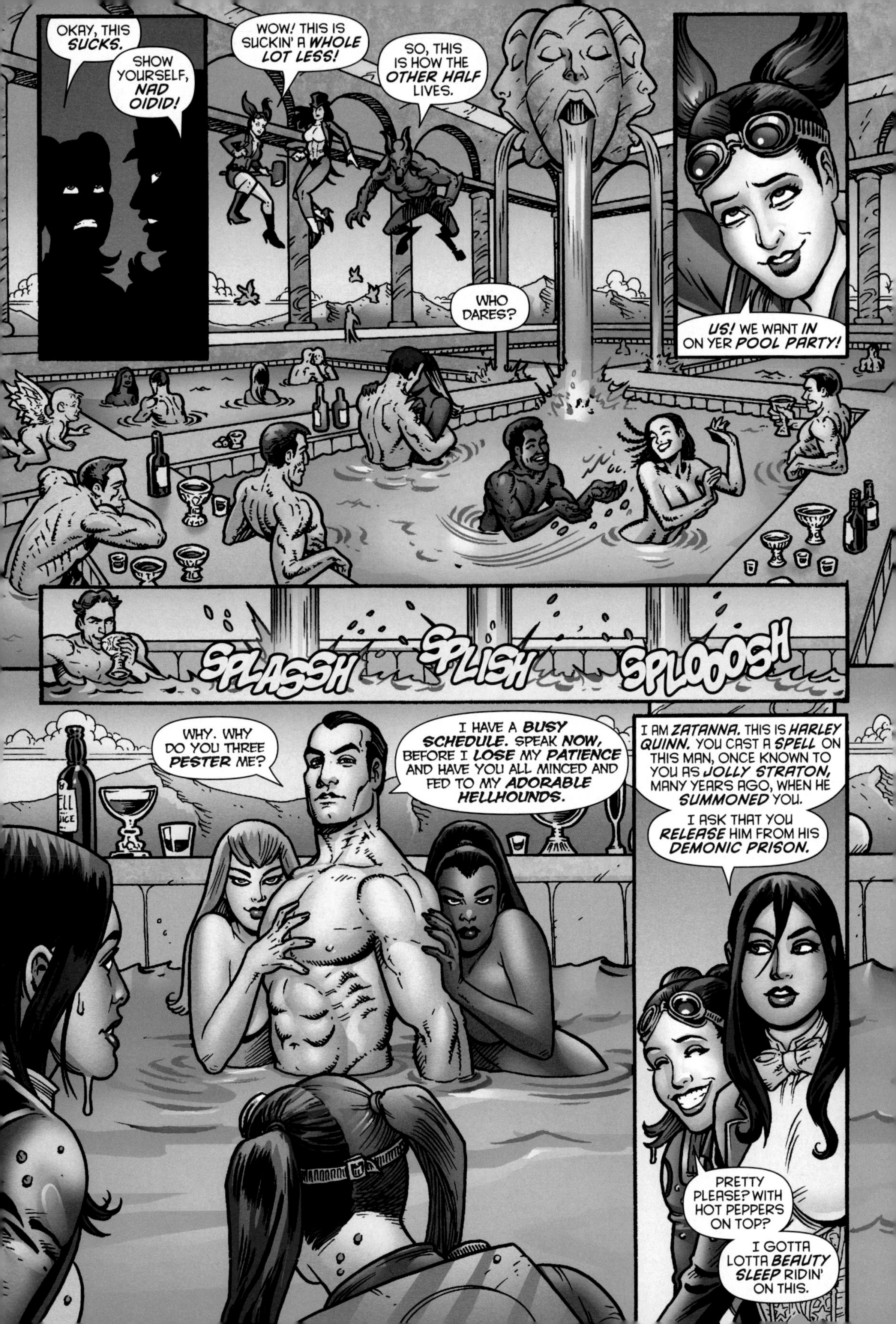

OKAY, THIS SUCKS.
SHOW YOURSELF, NAD OIDID!
WOW! THIS IS SUCKIN' A WHOLE LOT LESS!
SO, THIS IS HOW THE OTHER HALF LIVES.
WHO DARES?
US! WE WANT IN ON YER POOL PARTY!
SPLASSH
SPLISH
SPLOOOSH
WHY. WHY DO YOU THREE PESTER ME?
I HAVE A BUSY SCHEDULE. SPEAK NOW, BEFORE I LOSE MY PATIENCE AND HAVE YOU ALL MINCED AND FED TO MY ADORABLE HELLHOUNDS.
I AM ZATANNA. THIS IS HARLEY QUINN. YOU CAST A SPELL ON THIS MAN, ONCE KNOWN TO YOU AS JOLLY STRATON, MANY YEARS AGO, WHEN HE SUMMONED YOU.
I ASK THAT YOU RELEASE HIM FROM HIS DEMONIC PRISON.
PRETTY PLEASE? WITH HOT PEPPERS ON TOP?
I GOTTA LOTTA BEAUTY SLEEP RIDIN' ON THIS.

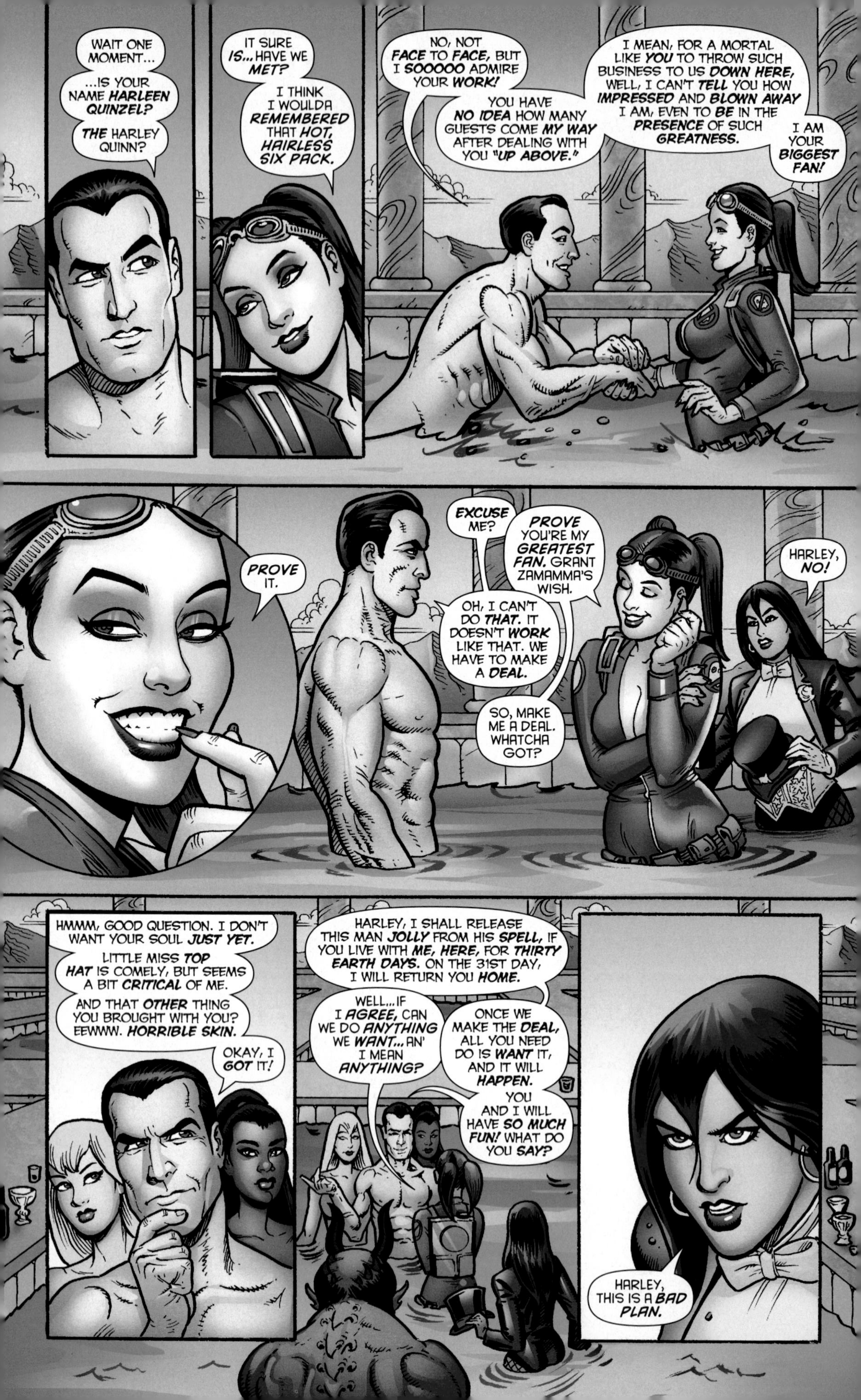

WAIT ONE MOMENT...
...IS YOUR NAME HARLEEN QUINZEL?
THE HARLEY QUINN?
IT SURE IS... HAVE WE MET?
I THINK I WOULDA REMEMBERED THAT HOT, HAIRLESS SIX PACK.
NO, NOT FACE TO FACE, BUT I SOOOOO ADMIRE YOUR WORK!
YOU HAVE NO IDEA HOW MANY GUESTS COME MY WAY AFTER DEALING WITH YOU "UP ABOVE."
I MEAN, FOR A MORTAL LIKE YOU TO THROW SUCH BUSINESS TO US DOWN HERE, WELL, I CAN'T TELL YOU HOW IMPRESSED AND BLOWN AWAY I AM, EVEN TO BE IN THE PRESENCE OF SUCH GREATNESS.
I AM YOUR BIGGEST FAN!
PROVE IT.
EXCUSE ME?
PROVE YOU'RE MY GREATEST FAN. GRANT ZAMAMMA'S WISH.
HARLEY, NO!
OH, I CAN'T DO THAT. IT DOESN'T WORK LIKE THAT. WE HAVE TO MAKE A DEAL.
SO, MAKE ME A DEAL. WHATCHA GOT?
HMMM, GOOD QUESTION. I DON'T WANT YOUR SOUL JUST YET.
LITTLE MISS TOP HAT IS COMELY, BUT SEEMS A BIT CRITICAL OF ME.
AND THAT OTHER THING YOU BROUGHT WITH YOU? EEWWW. HORRIBLE SKIN.
OKAY, I GOT IT!
HARLEY, I SHALL RELEASE THIS MAN JOLLY FROM HIS SPELL, IF YOU LIVE WITH ME, HERE, FOR THIRTY EARTH DAYS. ON THE 31ST DAY, I WILL RETURN YOU HOME.
WELL... IF I AGREE, CAN WE DO ANYTHING WE WANT... AN' I MEAN ANYTHING?
ONCE WE MAKE THE DEAL, ALL YOU NEED DO IS WANT IT, AND IT WILL HAPPEN.
YOU AND I WILL HAVE SO MUCH FUN! WHAT DO YOU SAY?
HARLEY, THIS IS A BAD PLAN.

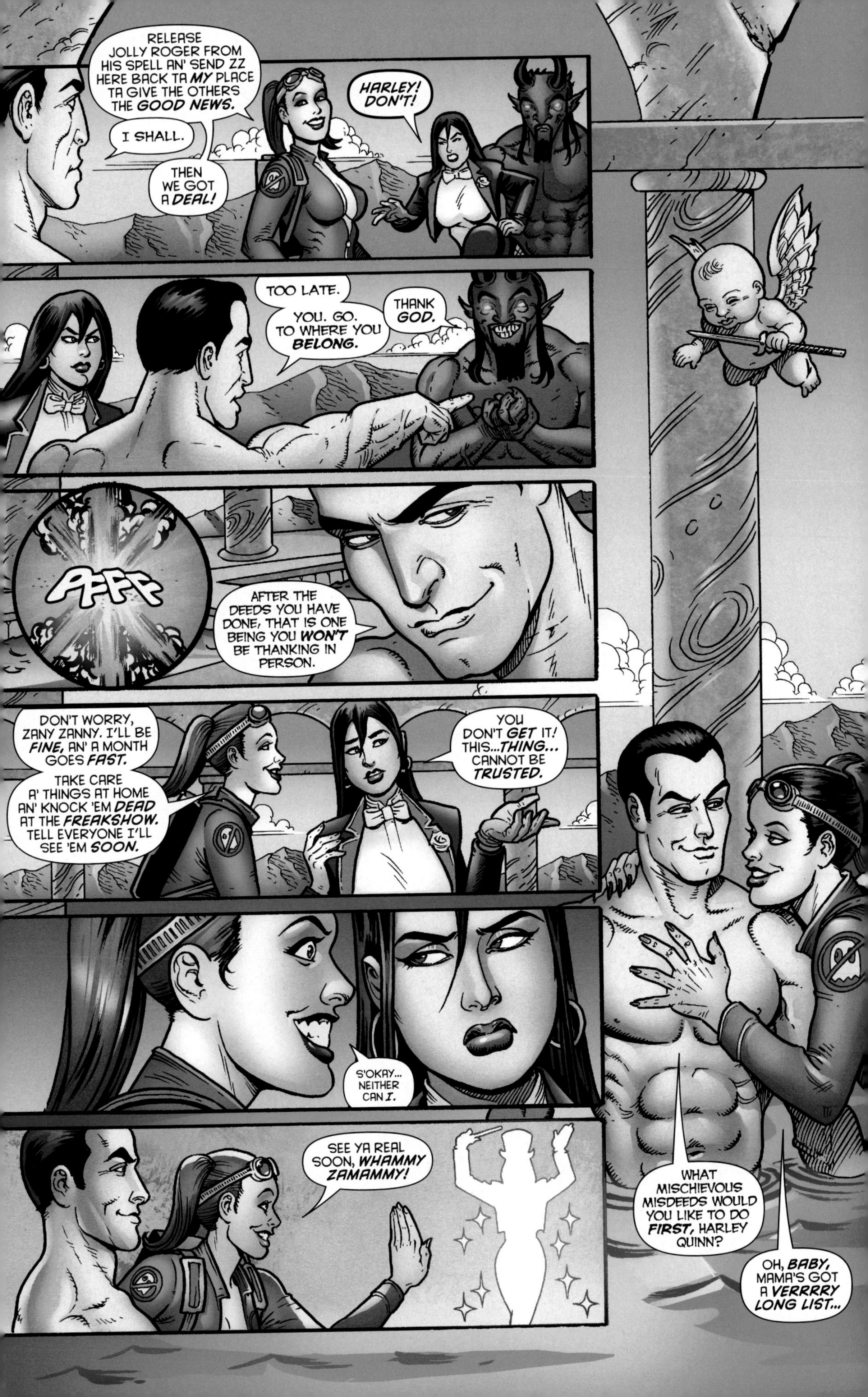

RELEASE JOLLY ROGER FROM HIS SPELL AN' SEND ZZ HERE BACK TA MY PLACE TA GIVE THE OTHERS THE GOOD NEWS.
HARLEY! DON'T!
I SHALL.
THEN WE GOT A DEAL!
TOO LATE.
YOU. GO. TO WHERE YOU BELONG.
THANK GOD.
PFFF
AFTER THE DEEDS YOU HAVE DONE, THAT IS ONE BEING YOU WON'T BE THANKING IN PERSON.
DON'T WORRY, ZANY ZANNY. I'LL BE FINE, AN' A MONTH GOES FAST.
TAKE CARE A' THINGS AT HOME AN' KNOCK 'EM DEAD AT THE FREAKSHOW. TELL EVERYONE I'LL SEE 'EM SOON.
YOU DON'T GET IT! THIS...THING... CANNOT BE TRUSTED.
S'OKAY... NEITHER CAN I.
SEE YA REAL SOON, WHAMMY ZAMAMMY!
WHAT MISCHIEVOUS MISDEEDS WOULD YOU LIKE TO DO FIRST, HARLEY QUINN?
OH, BABY, MAMA'S GOT A VERRRRY LONG LIST...

QUICK TURNAROUND

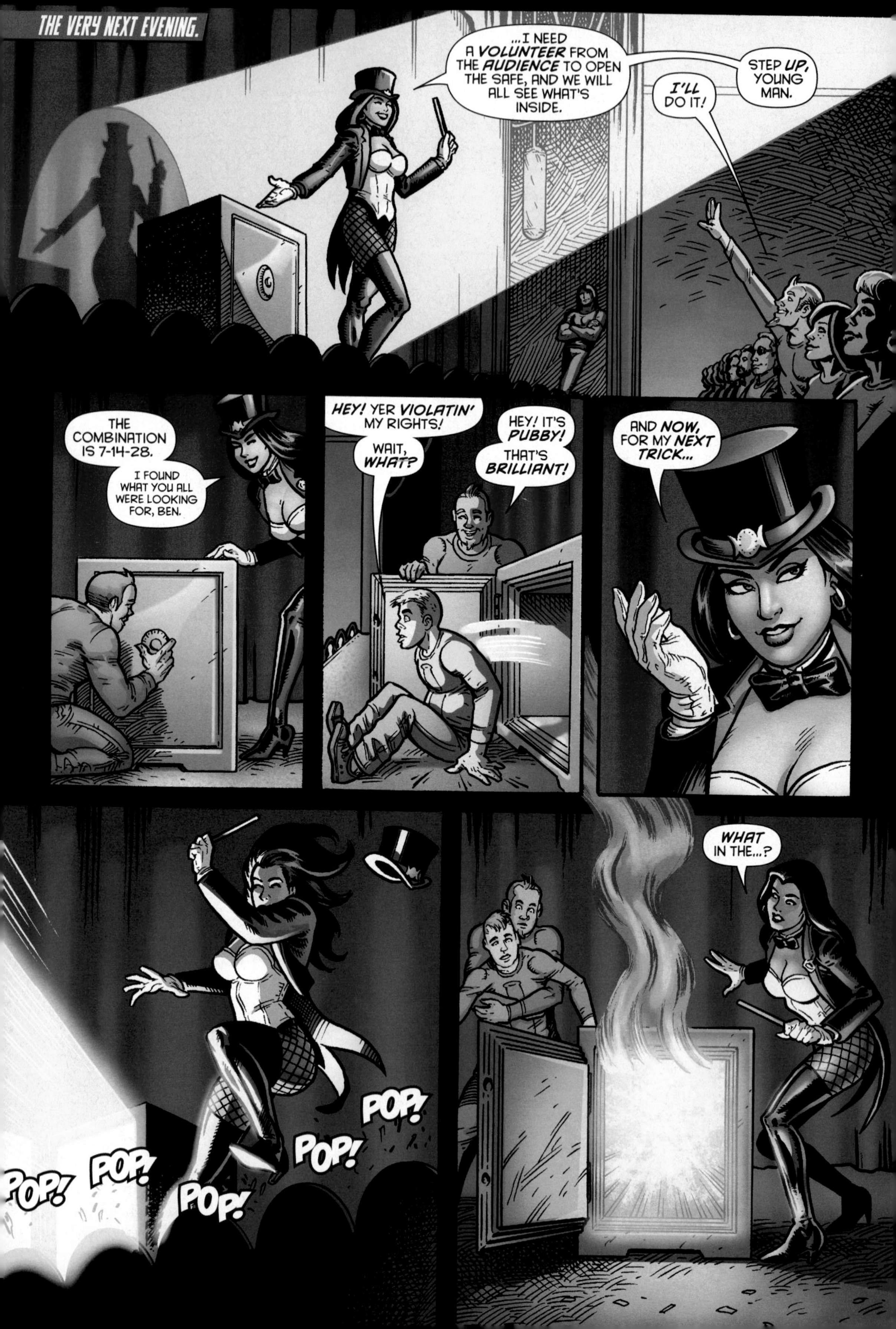
THE VERY NEXT EVENING.
...I NEED A VOLUNTEER FROM THE AUDIENCE TO OPEN THE SAFE, AND WE WILL ALL SEE WHAT'S INSIDE.
I'LL DO IT!
STEP UP, YOUNG MAN.
THE COMBINATION IS 7-14-28.
I FOUND WHAT YOU ALL WERE LOOKING FOR, BEN.
HEY! YER VIOLATIN' MY RIGHTS!
WAIT, WHAT?
HEY! IT'S PUBBY!
THAT'S BRILLIANT!
AND NOW, FOR MY NEXT TRICK...
POP!
POP!
POP!
POP!
POP!
WHAT IN THE...?

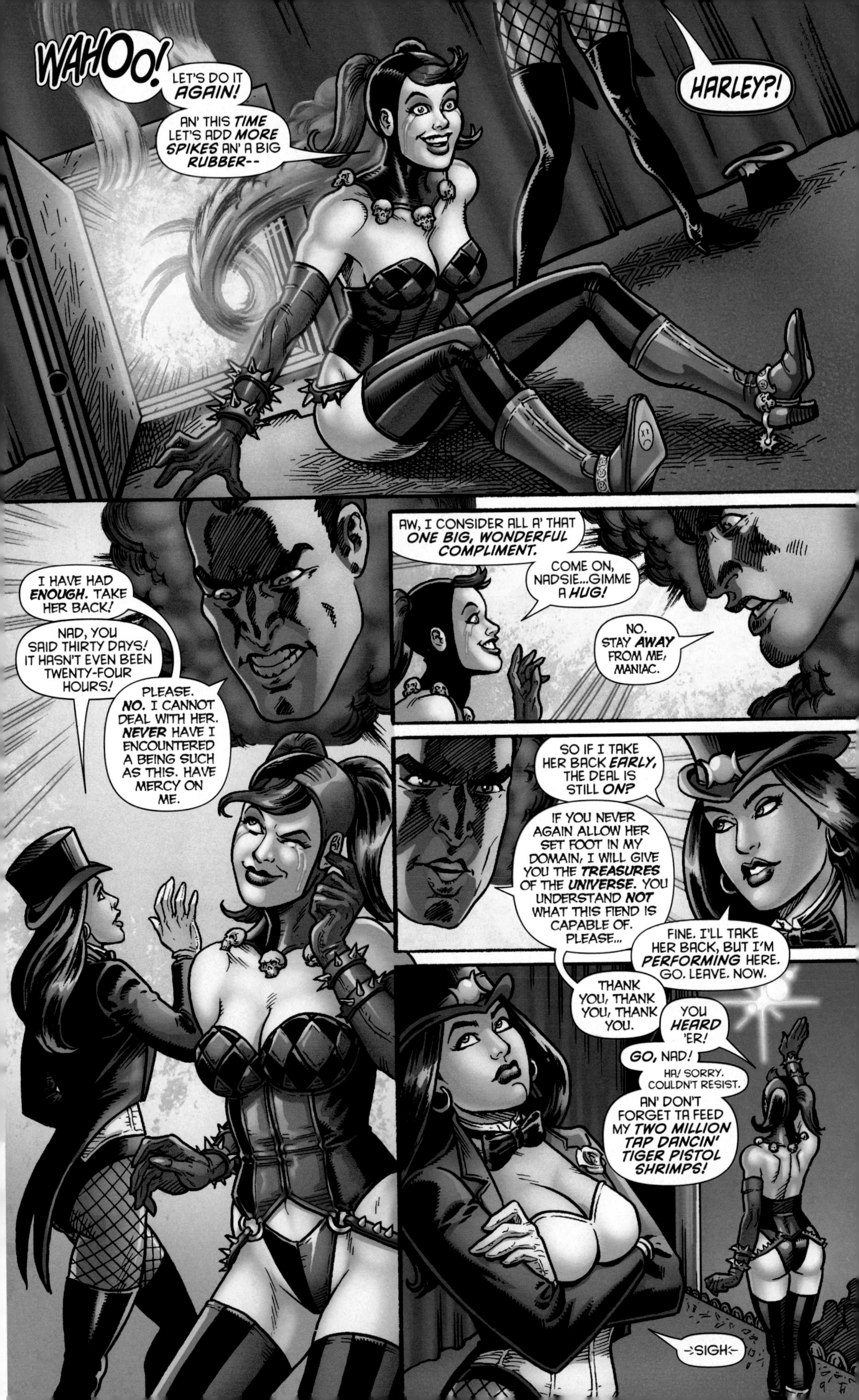
WAHOO!
LET'S DO IT AGAIN!
AN' THIS TIME LET'S ADD MORE SPIKES AN' A BIG RUBBER--
HARLEY?!
I HAVE HAD ENOUGH. TAKE HER BACK!
NAD, YOU SAID THIRTY DAYS! IT HASN'T EVEN BEEN TWENTY-FOUR HOURS!
PLEASE. NO. I CANNOT DEAL WITH HER. NEVER HAVE I ENCOUNTERED A BEING SUCH AS THIS. HAVE MERCY ON ME.
AW, I CONSIDER ALL A' THAT ONE BIG, WONDERFUL COMPLIMENT.
COME ON, NADSIE...GIMME A HUG!
NO. STAY AWAY FROM ME, MANIAC.
SO IF I TAKE HER BACK EARLY, THE DEAL IS STILL ON?
IF YOU NEVER AGAIN ALLOW HER SET FOOT IN MY DOMAIN, I WILL GIVE YOU THE TREASURES OF THE UNIVERSE. YOU UNDERSTAND NOT WHAT THIS FIEND IS CAPABLE OF. PLEASE...
FINE. I'LL TAKE HER BACK, BUT I'M PERFORMING HERE. GO. LEAVE. NOW.
THANK YOU, THANK YOU, THANK YOU.
YOU HEARD 'ER!
GO, NAD!
HA! SORRY. COULDN'T RESIST.
AN' DON'T FORGET TA FEED MY TWO MILLION TAP DANCIN' TIGER PISTOL SHRIMPS!
-SIGH-

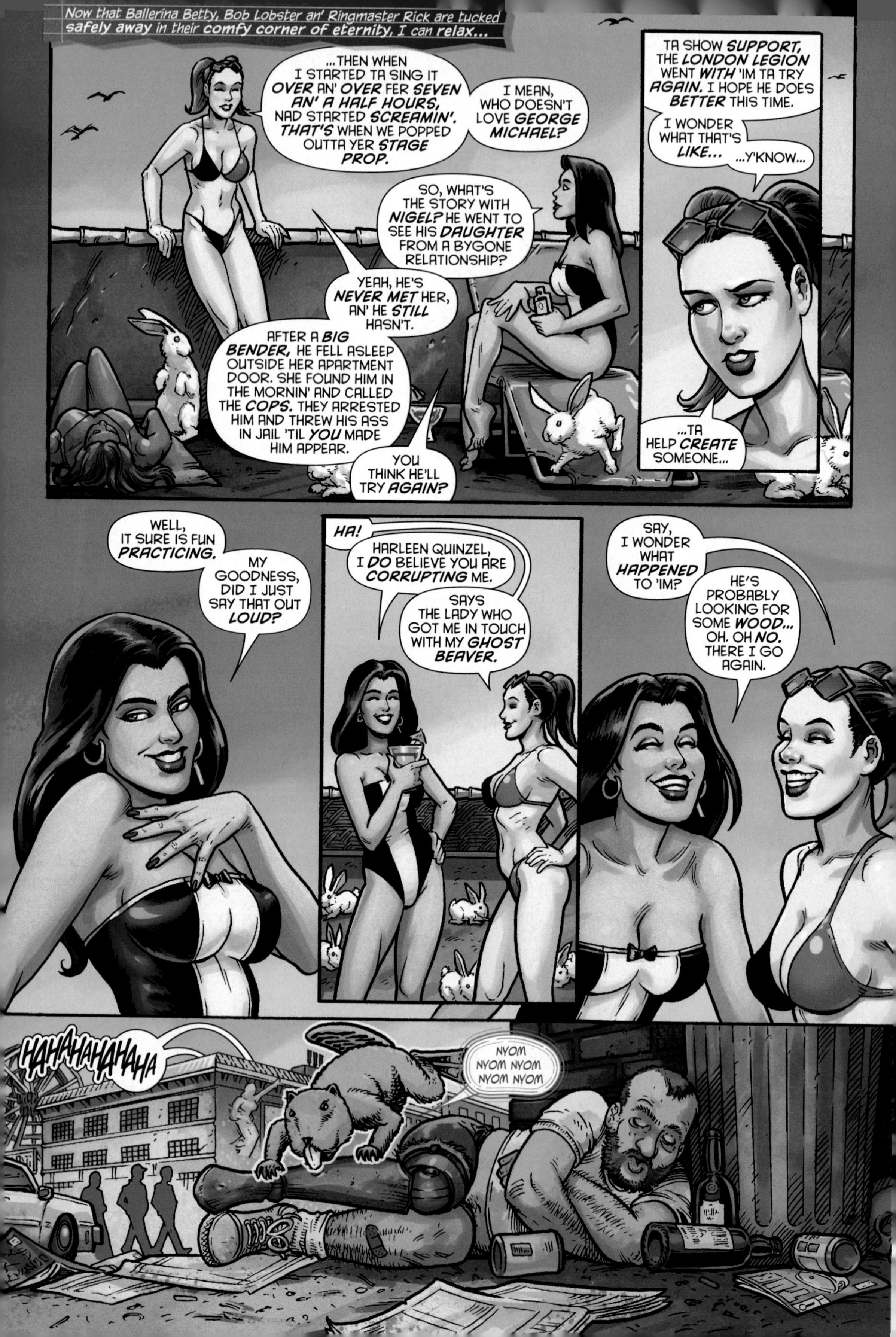
Now that Ballerina Betty, Bob Lobster an' Ringmaster Rick are tucked safely away in their comfy corner of eternity, I can relax...
...THEN WHEN I STARTED TA SING IT OVER AN' OVER FER SEVEN AN' A HALF HOURS, NAD STARTED SCREAMIN'. THAT'S WHEN WE POPPED OUTTA YER STAGE PROP.
I MEAN, WHO DOESN'T LOVE GEORGE MICHAEL?
SO, WHAT'S THE STORY WITH NIGEL? HE WENT TO SEE HIS DAUGHTER FROM A BYGONE RELATIONSHIP?
YEAH, HE'S NEVER MET HER, AN' HE STILL HASN'T.
AFTER A BIG BENDER, HE FELL ASLEEP OUTSIDE HER APARTMENT DOOR. SHE FOUND HIM IN THE MORNIN' AND CALLED THE COPS. THEY ARRESTED HIM AND THREW HIS ASS IN JAIL 'TIL YOU MADE HIM APPEAR.
YOU THINK HE'LL TRY AGAIN?
TA SHOW SUPPORT, THE LONDON LEGION WENT WITH 'IM TA TRY AGAIN. I HOPE HE DOES BETTER THIS TIME.
I WONDER WHAT THAT'S LIKE...
...Y'KNOW...
...TA HELP CREATE SOMEONE...
WELL, IT SURE IS FUN PRACTICING.
MY GOODNESS, DID I JUST SAY THAT OUT LOUD?
HA!
HARLEEN QUINZEL, I DO BELIEVE YOU ARE CORRUPTING ME.
SAYS THE LADY WHO GOT ME IN TOUCH WITH MY GHOST BEAVER.
SAY, I WONDER WHAT HAPPENED TO 'IM?
HE'S PROBABLY LOOKING FOR SOME WOOD... OH. OH NO. THERE I GO AGAIN.
HAHAHAHAHAHAHA
NYOM NYOM NYOM NYOM NYOM

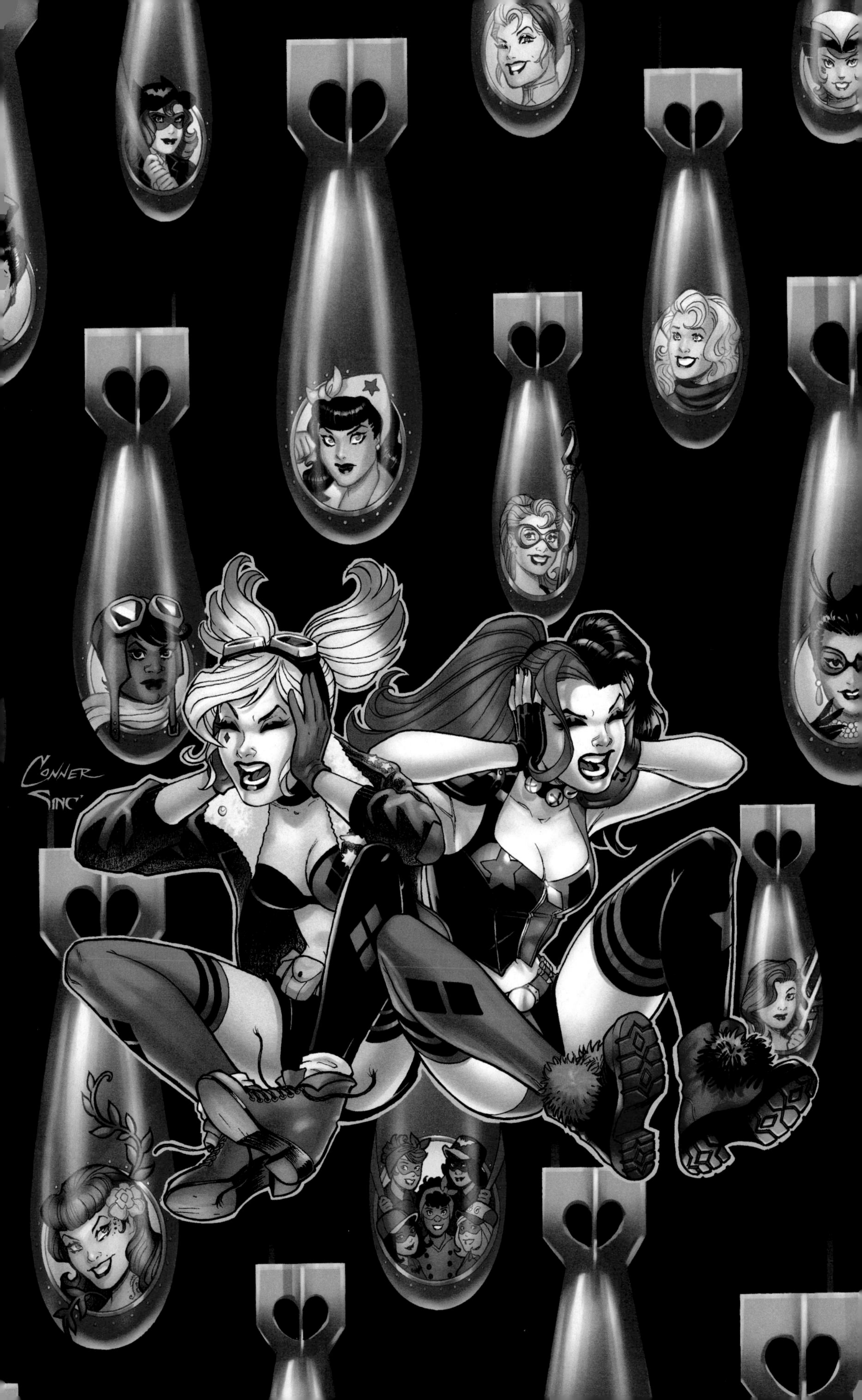
CONNER
SINC'

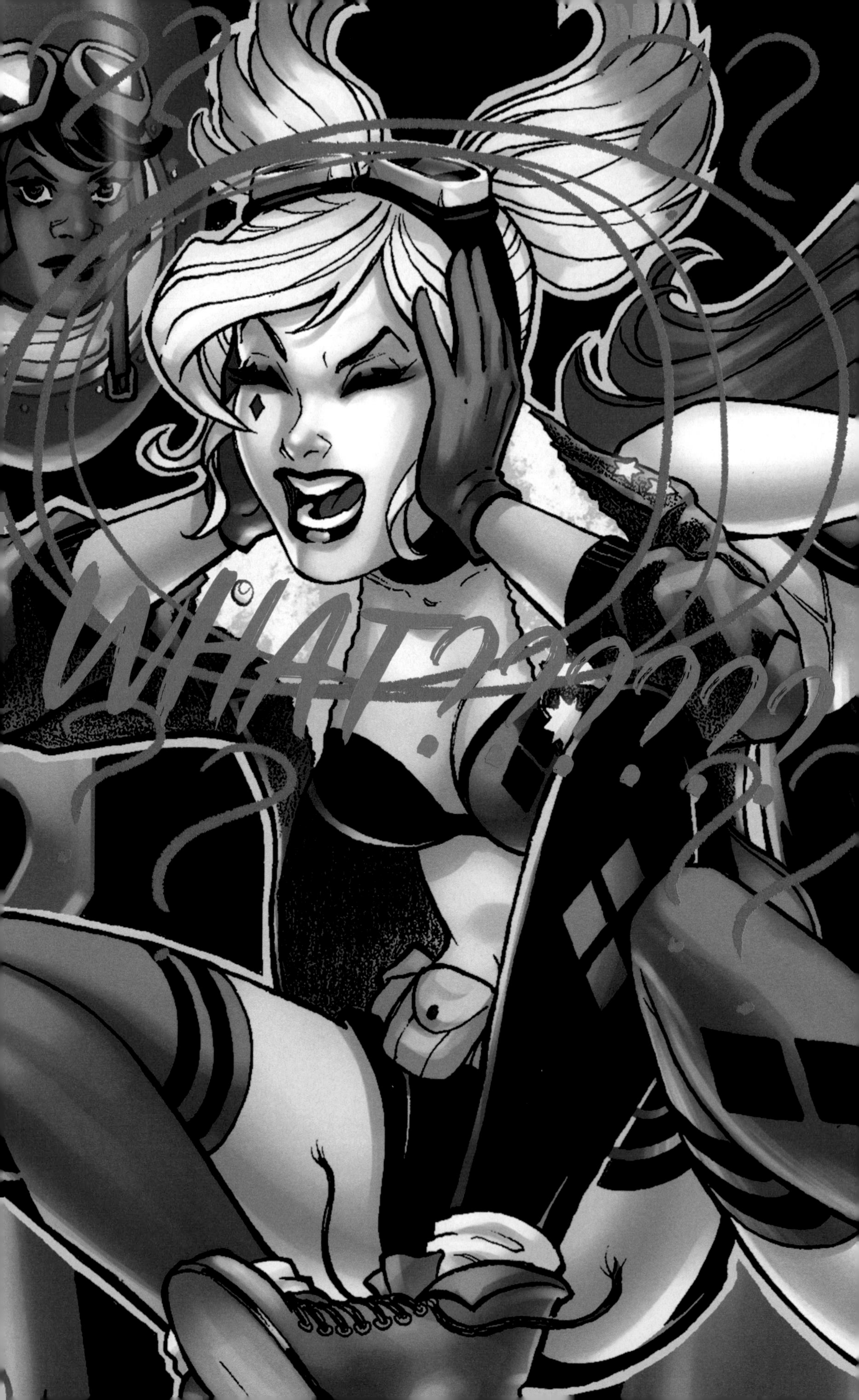
WHAT???????

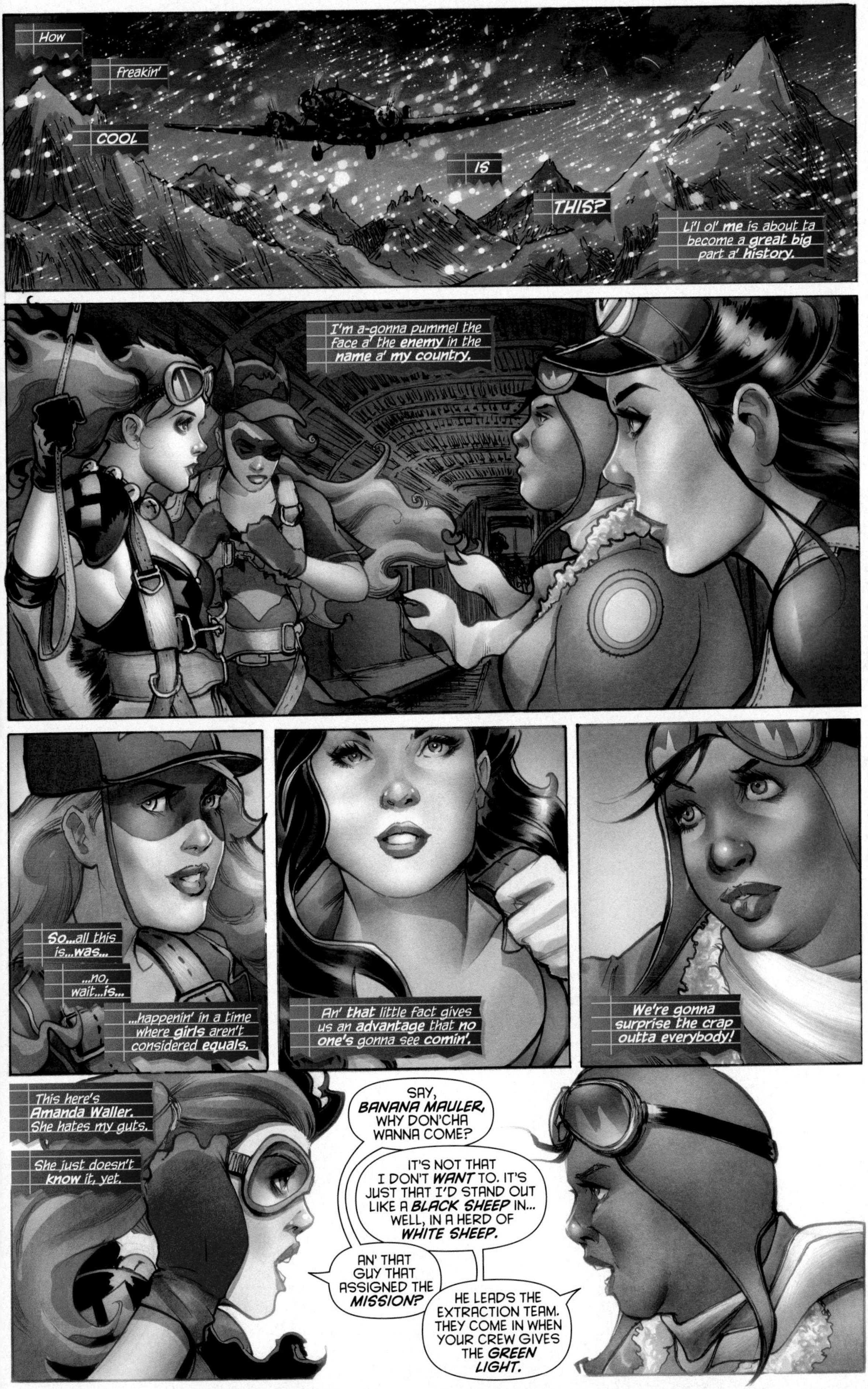
How
freakin'
COOL
IS
THIS?
Li'l ol' me is about ta become a great big part a' history.
I'm a-gonna pummel the face a' the enemy in the name a' my country.
So...all this is...was...
...no, wait...is...
...happenin' in a time where girls aren't considered equals.
An' that little fact gives us an advantage that no one's gonna see comin'.
We're gonna surprise the crap outta everybody!
This here's Amanda Waller. She hates my guts.
She just doesn't know it, yet.
SAY, BANANA MAULER, WHY DON'CHA WANNA COME?
IT'S NOT THAT I DON'T WANT TO. IT'S JUST THAT I'D STAND OUT LIKE A BLACK SHEEP IN... WELL, IN A HERD OF WHITE SHEEP.
AN' THAT GUY THAT ASSIGNED THE MISSION?
HE LEADS THE EXTRACTION TEAM. THEY COME IN WHEN YOUR CREW GIVES THE GREEN LIGHT.

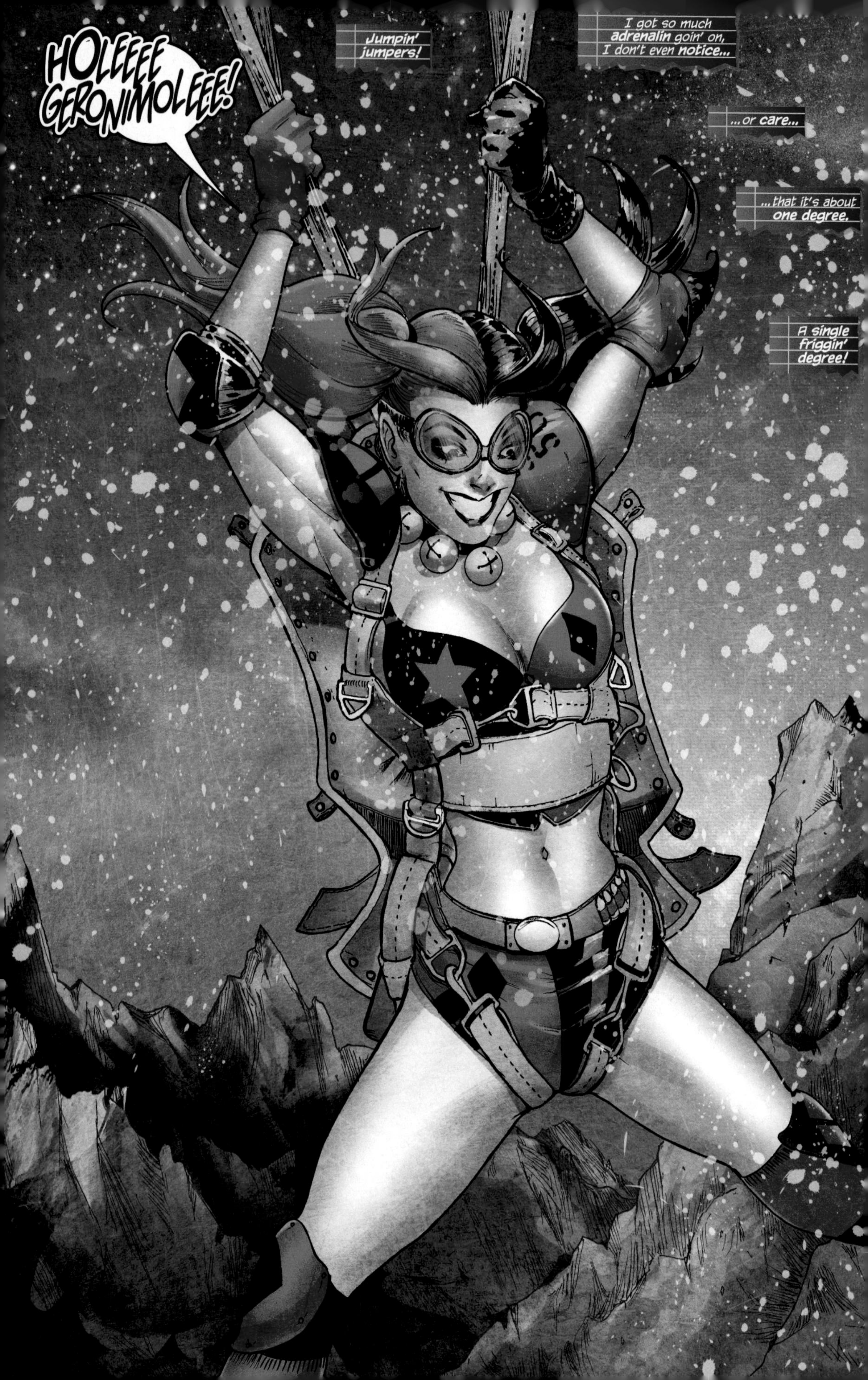
HOLEEEE GERONIMOLEEE!
Jumpin' jumpers!
I got so much adrenalin goin' on, I don't even notice...
...or care...
...that it's about one degree.
A single friggin' degree!

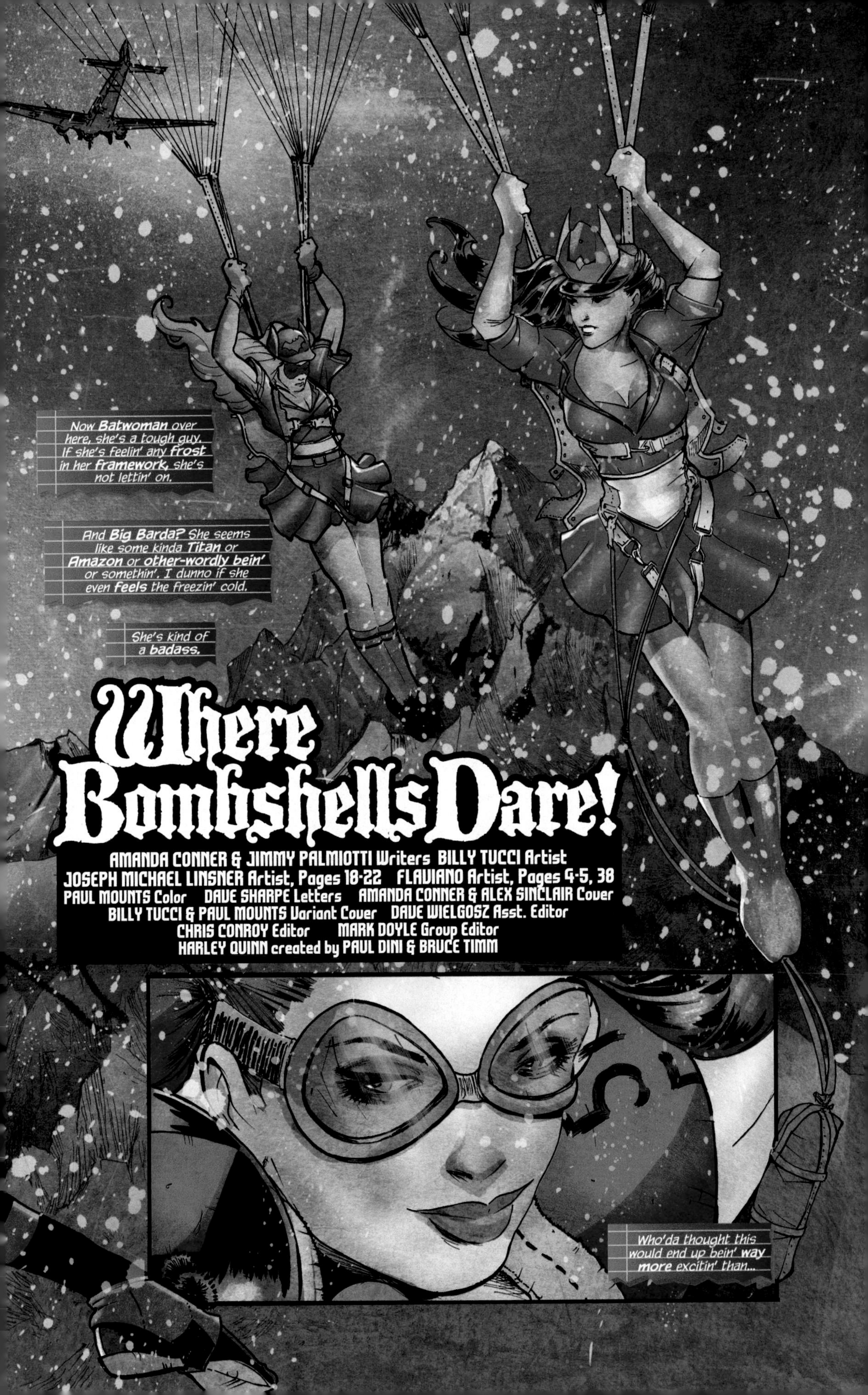

Now Batwoman over here, she's a tough guy. If she's feelin' any frost in her framework, she's not lettin' on.
And Big Barda? She seems like some kinda Titan or Amazon or other-wordly bein' or somethin'. I dunno if she even feels the freezin' cold.
She's kind of a badass.
Where Bombshells Dare!
AMANDA CONNER & JIMMY PALMIOTTI Writers BILLY TUCCI Artist
JOSEPH MICHAEL LINSNER Artist, Pages 18-22 FLAVIANO Artist, Pages 4-5, 38
PAUL MOUNTS Color DAVE SHARPE Letters AMANDA CONNER & ALEX SINCLAIR Cover
BILLY TUCCI & PAUL MOUNTS Variant Cover DAVE WIELGOSZ Asst. Editor
CHRIS CONROY Editor MARK DOYLE Group Editor
HARLEY QUINN created by PAUL DINI & BRUCE TIMM
Who'da thought this would end up bein' way more excitin' than...

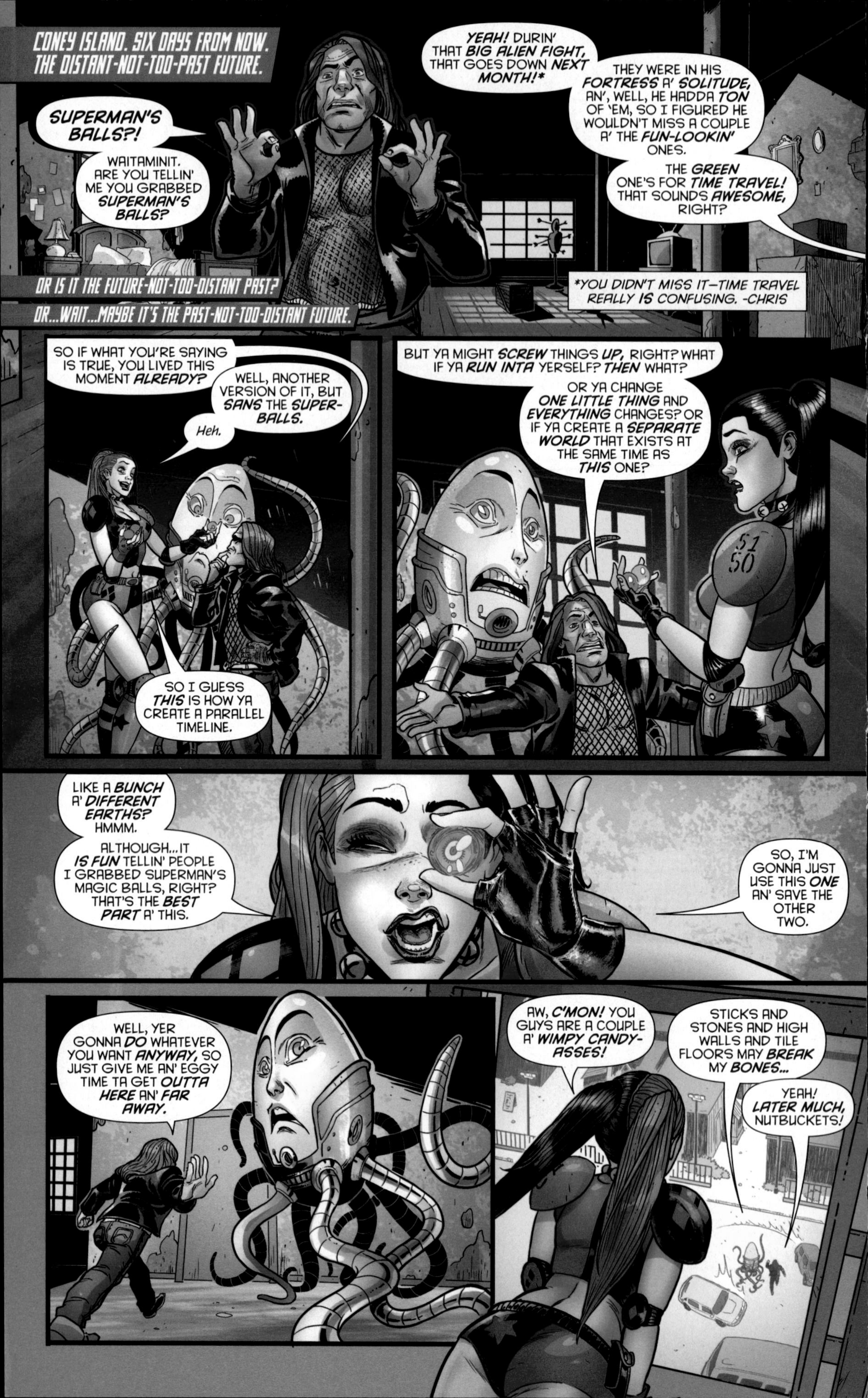
CONEY ISLAND. SIX DAYS FROM NOW. THE DISTANT-NOT-TOO-PAST FUTURE.
SUPERMAN'S BALLS?!
WAITAMINIT. ARE YOU TELLIN' ME YOU GRABBED SUPERMAN'S BALLS?
YEAH! DURIN' THAT BIG ALIEN FIGHT, THAT GOES DOWN NEXT MONTH!*
THEY WERE IN HIS FORTRESS A' SOLITUDE, AN', WELL, HE HADDA TON OF 'EM, SO I FIGURED HE WOULDN'T MISS A COUPLE A' THE FUN-LOOKIN' ONES.
THE GREEN ONE'S FOR TIME TRAVEL! THAT SOUNDS AWESOME, RIGHT?
OR IS IT THE FUTURE-NOT-TOO-DISTANT PAST?
OR...WAIT...MAYBE IT'S THE PAST-NOT-TOO-DISTANT FUTURE.
*YOU DIDN'T MISS IT—TIME TRAVEL REALLY IS CONFUSING. -CHRIS
SO IF WHAT YOU'RE SAYING IS TRUE, YOU LIVED THIS MOMENT ALREADY?
WELL, ANOTHER VERSION OF IT, BUT SANS THE SUPER-BALLS.
Heh.
SO I GUESS THIS IS HOW YA CREATE A PARALLEL TIMELINE.
BUT YA MIGHT SCREW THINGS UP, RIGHT? WHAT IF YA RUN INTA YERSELF? THEN WHAT?
OR YA CHANGE ONE LITTLE THING AND EVERYTHING CHANGES? OR IF YA CREATE A SEPARATE WORLD THAT EXISTS AT THE SAME TIME AS THIS ONE?
51 50
LIKE A BUNCH A' DIFFERENT EARTHS? HMMM.
ALTHOUGH...IT IS FUN TELLIN' PEOPLE I GRABBED SUPERMAN'S MAGIC BALLS, RIGHT? THAT'S THE BEST PART A' THIS.
SO, I'M GONNA JUST USE THIS ONE AN' SAVE THE OTHER TWO.
WELL, YER GONNA DO WHATEVER YOU WANT ANYWAY, SO JUST GIVE ME AN' EGGY TIME TA GET OUTTA HERE AN' FAR AWAY.
AW, C'MON! YOU GUYS ARE A COUPLE A' WIMPY CANDY-ASSES!
STICKS AND STONES AND HIGH WALLS AND TILE FLOORS MAY BREAK MY BONES...
YEAH! LATER MUCH, NUTBUCKETS!

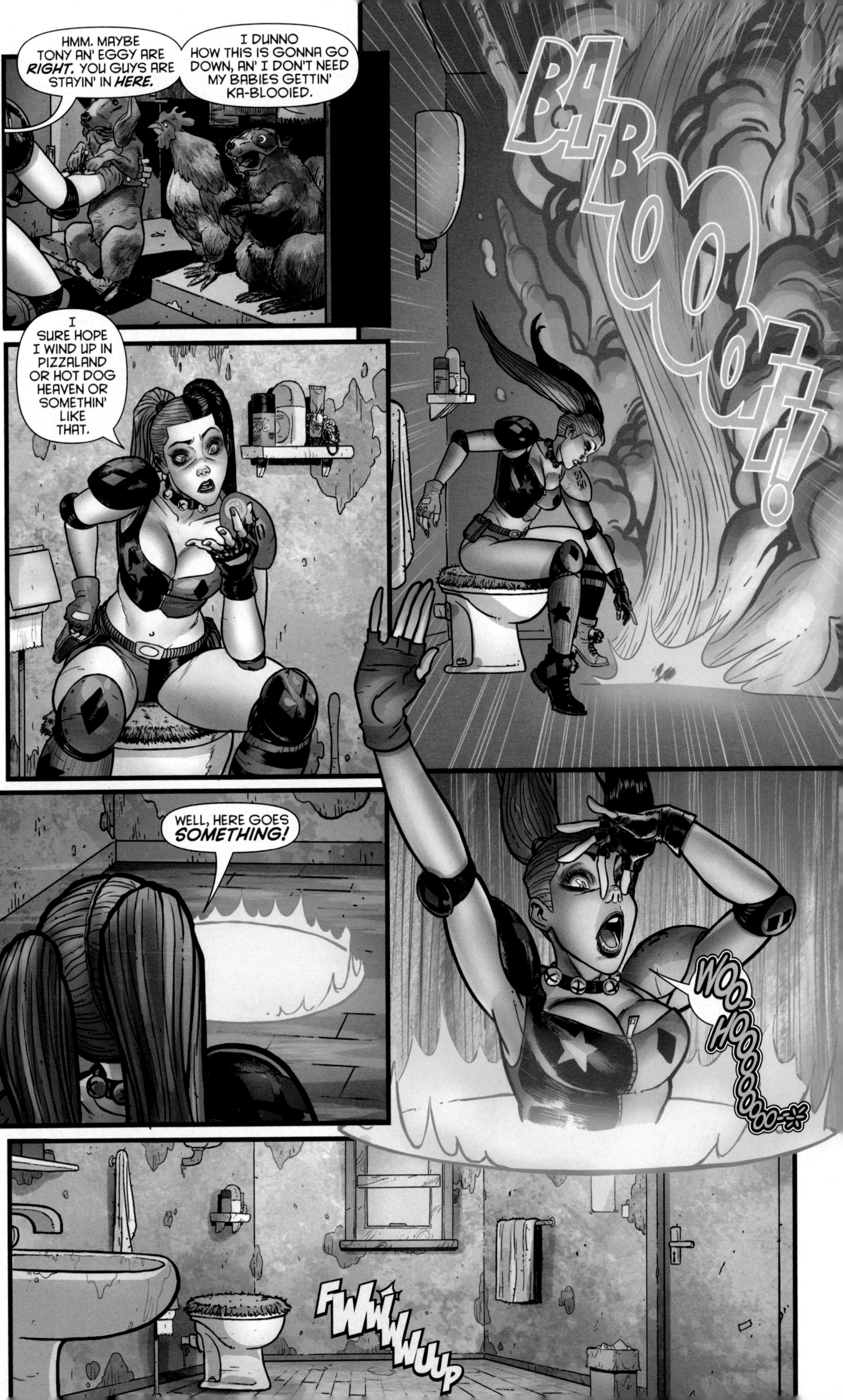
HMM. MAYBE TONY AN' EGGY ARE RIGHT. YOU GUYS ARE STAYIN' IN HERE.
I DUNNO HOW THIS IS GONNA GO DOWN, AN' I DON'T NEED MY BABIES GETTIN' KA-BLOOIED.
I SURE HOPE I WIND UP IN PIZZALAND OR HOT DOG HEAVEN OR SOMETHIN' LIKE THAT.
BA-BOOOOOOM!
WELL, HERE GOES SOMETHING!
WOO-HOOOOOOO-!
FWWWWUUP

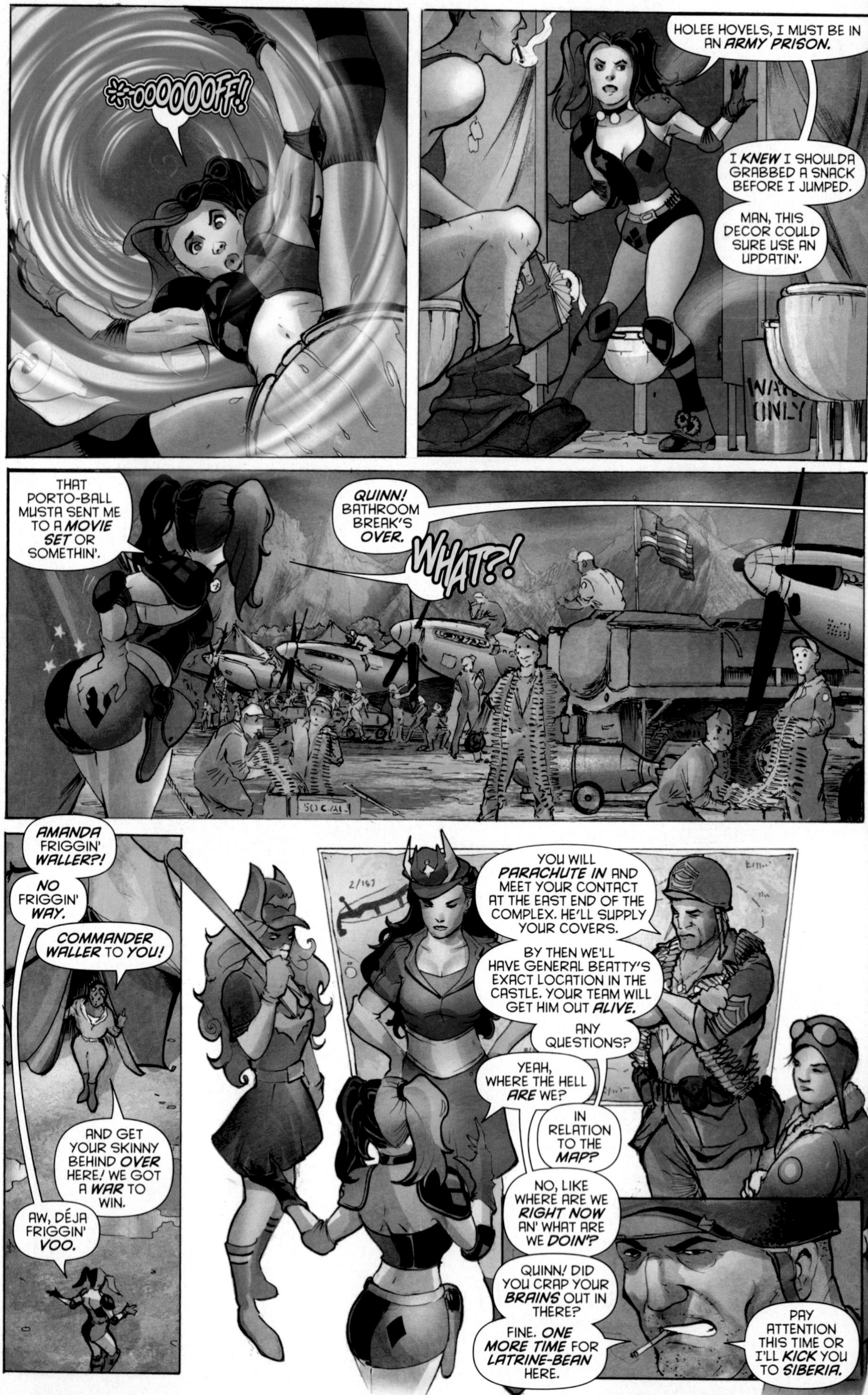

*-OOOOOOFF!!
HOLEE HOVELS, I MUST BE IN AN ARMY PRISON.
I KNEW I SHOULDA GRABBED A SNACK BEFORE I JUMPED.
MAN, THIS DECOR COULD SURE USE AN UPDATIN'.
THAT PORTO-BALL MUSTA SENT ME TO A MOVIE SET OR SOMETHIN'.
QUINN! BATHROOM BREAK'S OVER.
WHAT?!
AMANDA FRIGGIN' WALLER?!
NO FRIGGIN' WAY.
COMMANDER WALLER TO YOU!
AND GET YOUR SKINNY BEHIND OVER HERE! WE GOT A WAR TO WIN.
AW, DÉJA FRIGGIN' VOO.
YOU WILL PARACHUTE IN AND MEET YOUR CONTACT AT THE EAST END OF THE COMPLEX. HE'LL SUPPLY YOUR COVERS.
BY THEN WE'LL HAVE GENERAL BEATTY'S EXACT LOCATION IN THE CASTLE. YOUR TEAM WILL GET HIM OUT ALIVE.
ANY QUESTIONS?
YEAH, WHERE THE HELL ARE WE?
IN RELATION TO THE MAP?
NO, LIKE WHERE ARE WE RIGHT NOW AN' WHAT ARE WE DOIN'?
QUINN! DID YOU CRAP YOUR BRAINS OUT IN THERE?
FINE. ONE MORE TIME FOR LATRINE-BEAN HERE.
PAY ATTENTION THIS TIME OR I'LL KICK YOU TO SIBERIA.

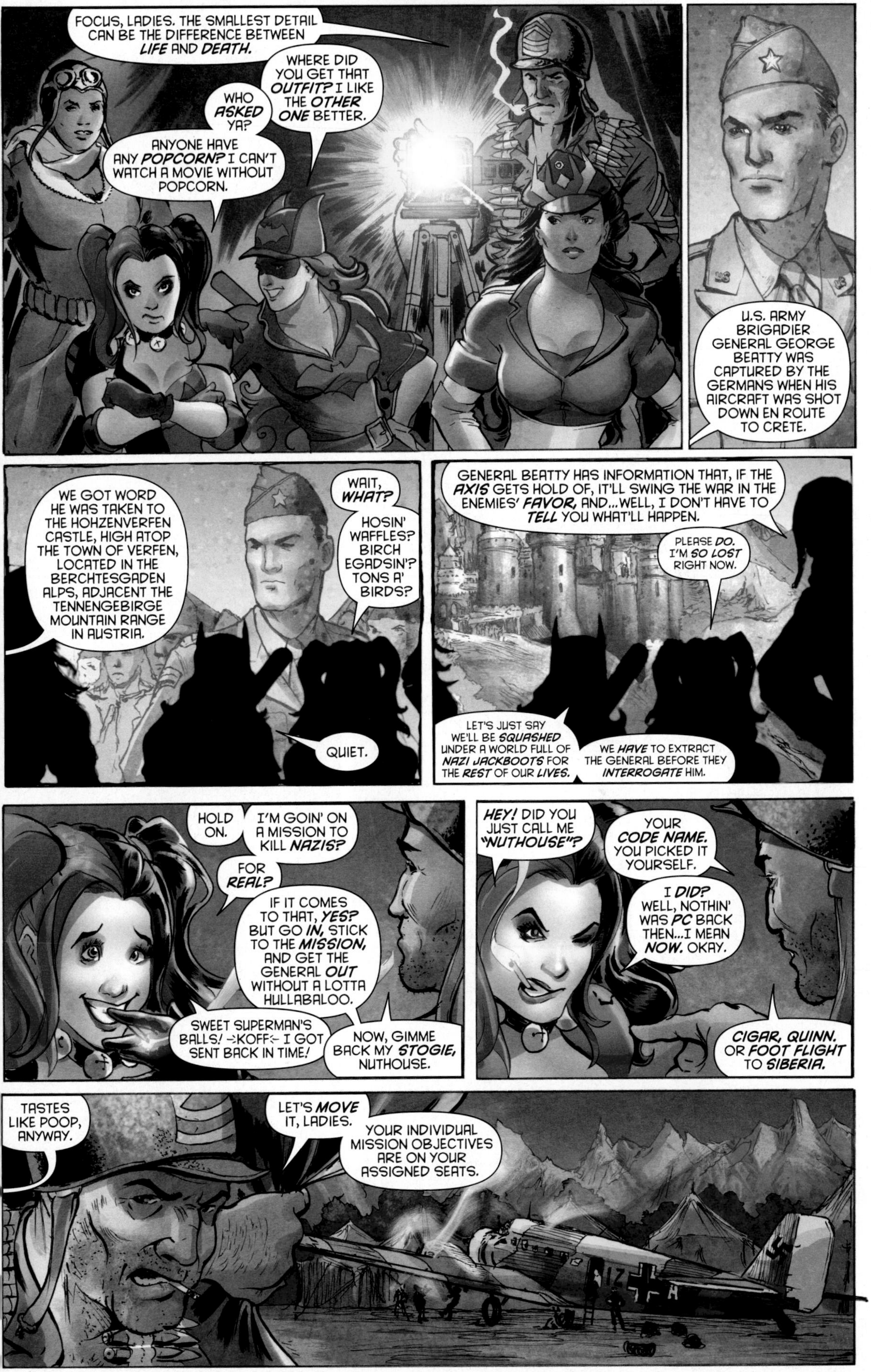
FOCUS, LADIES. THE SMALLEST DETAIL CAN BE THE DIFFERENCE BETWEEN LIFE AND DEATH.
WHERE DID YOU GET THAT OUTFIT? I LIKE THE OTHER ONE BETTER.
WHO ASKED YA?
ANYONE HAVE ANY POPCORN? I CAN'T WATCH A MOVIE WITHOUT POPCORN.
U.S. ARMY BRIGADIER GENERAL GEORGE BEATTY WAS CAPTURED BY THE GERMANS WHEN HIS AIRCRAFT WAS SHOT DOWN EN ROUTE TO CRETE.
WE GOT WORD HE WAS TAKEN TO THE HOHZENVERFEN CASTLE, HIGH ATOP THE TOWN OF VERFEN, LOCATED IN THE BERCHTESGADEN ALPS, ADJACENT THE TENNENGEBIRGE MOUNTAIN RANGE IN AUSTRIA.
WAIT, WHAT?
HOSIN' WAFFLES? BIRCH EGADSIN'? TONS A' BIRDS?
QUIET.
GENERAL BEATTY HAS INFORMATION THAT, IF THE AXIS GETS HOLD OF, IT'LL SWING THE WAR IN THE ENEMIES' FAVOR, AND...WELL, I DON'T HAVE TO TELL YOU WHAT'LL HAPPEN.
PLEASE DO. I'M SO LOST RIGHT NOW.
LET'S JUST SAY WE'LL BE SQUASHED UNDER A WORLD FULL OF NAZI JACKBOOTS FOR THE REST OF OUR LIVES.
WE HAVE TO EXTRACT THE GENERAL BEFORE THEY INTERROGATE HIM.
HOLD ON.
I'M GOIN' ON A MISSION TO KILL NAZIS?
FOR REAL?
IF IT COMES TO THAT, YES? BUT GO IN, STICK TO THE MISSION, AND GET THE GENERAL OUT WITHOUT A LOTTA HULLABALOO.
SWEET SUPERMAN'S BALLS! ⇒KOFF⇐ I GOT SENT BACK IN TIME!
NOW, GIMME BACK MY STOGIE, NUTHOUSE.
HEY! DID YOU JUST CALL ME "NUTHOUSE"?
YOUR CODE NAME. YOU PICKED IT YOURSELF.
I DID? WELL, NOTHIN' WAS PC BACK THEN...I MEAN NOW. OKAY.
CIGAR, QUINN. OR FOOT FLIGHT TO SIBERIA.
TASTES LIKE POOP, ANYWAY.
LET'S MOVE IT, LADIES.
YOUR INDIVIDUAL MISSION OBJECTIVES ARE ON YOUR ASSIGNED SEATS.

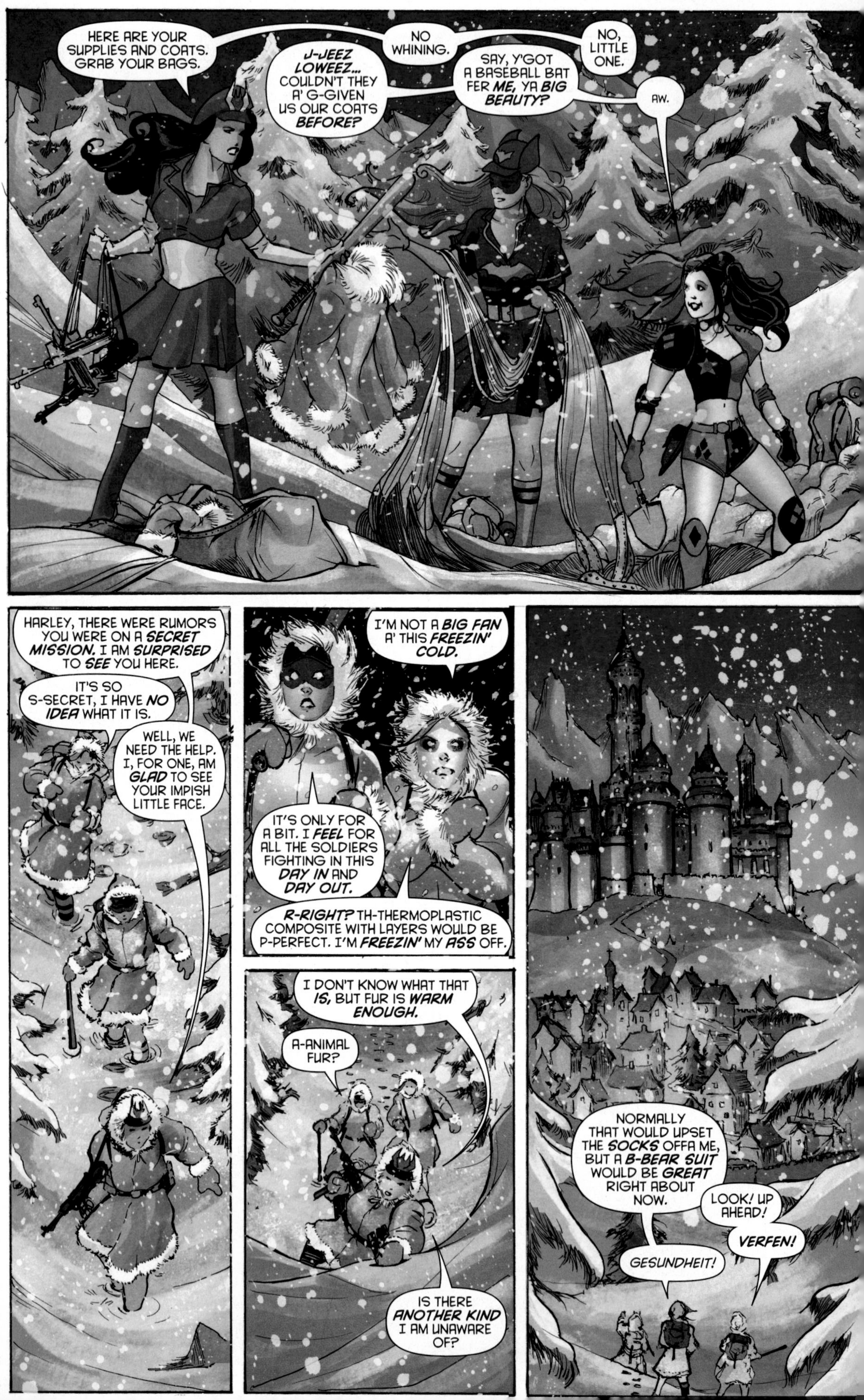
HERE ARE YOUR SUPPLIES AND COATS. GRAB YOUR BAGS.
J-JEEZ LOWEEZ... COULDN'T THEY A' G-GIVEN US OUR COATS BEFORE?
NO WHINING.
SAY, Y'GOT A BASEBALL BAT FER ME, YA BIG BEAUTY?
NO, LITTLE ONE.
AW.
HARLEY, THERE WERE RUMORS YOU WERE ON A SECRET MISSION. I AM SURPRISED TO SEE YOU HERE.
IT'S SO S-SECRET, I HAVE NO IDEA WHAT IT IS.
WELL, WE NEED THE HELP. I, FOR ONE, AM GLAD TO SEE YOUR IMPISH LITTLE FACE.
I'M NOT A BIG FAN A' THIS FREEZIN' COLD.
IT'S ONLY FOR A BIT. I FEEL FOR ALL THE SOLDIERS FIGHTING IN THIS DAY IN AND DAY OUT.
R-RIGHT? TH-THERMOPLASTIC COMPOSITE WITH LAYERS WOULD BE P-PERFECT. I'M FREEZIN' MY ASS OFF.
I DON'T KNOW WHAT THAT IS, BUT FUR IS WARM ENOUGH.
A-ANIMAL FUR?
IS THERE ANOTHER KIND I AM UNAWARE OF?
NORMALLY THAT WOULD UPSET THE SOCKS OFFA ME, BUT A B-BEAR SUIT WOULD BE GREAT RIGHT ABOUT NOW.
LOOK! UP AHEAD!
VERFEN!
GESUNDHEIT!

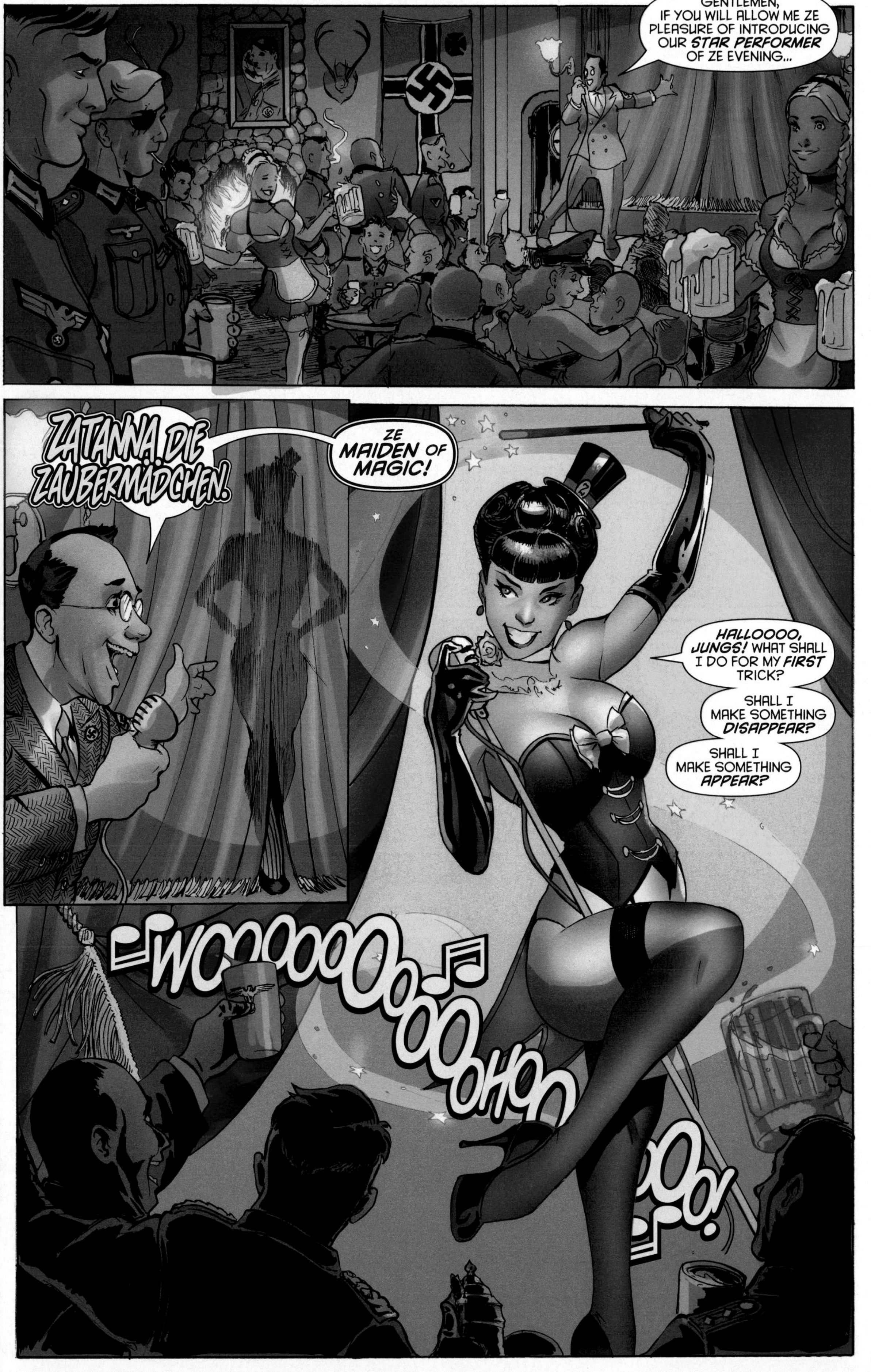
GENTLEMEN, IF YOU WILL ALLOW ME ZE PLEASURE OF INTRODUCING OUR STAR PERFORMER OF ZE EVENING...
ZATANNA DIE ZAUBERMÄDCHEN.
ZE MAIDEN OF MAGIC!
HALLOOOO, JUNGS! WHAT SHALL I DO FOR MY FIRST TRICK?
SHALL I MAKE SOMETHING DISAPPEAR?
SHALL I MAKE SOMETHING APPEAR?
WOOOOOOOOOOOHOOOOOOO!

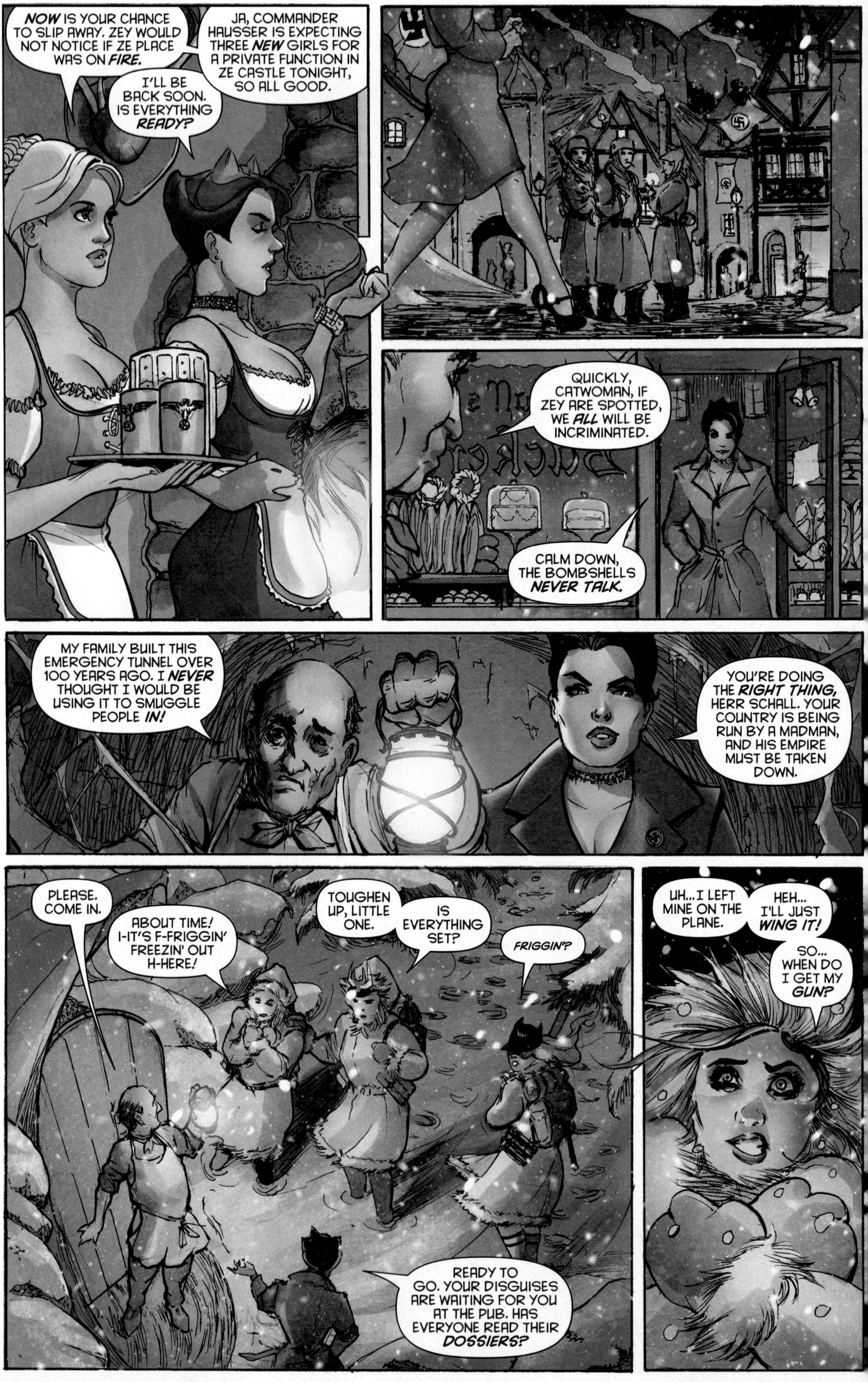
NOW IS YOUR CHANCE TO SLIP AWAY. ZEY WOULD NOT NOTICE IF ZE PLACE WAS ON FIRE.
JA, COMMANDER HAUSSER IS EXPECTING THREE NEW GIRLS FOR A PRIVATE FUNCTION IN ZE CASTLE TONIGHT, SO ALL GOOD.
I'LL BE BACK SOON. IS EVERYTHING READY?
QUICKLY, CATWOMAN, IF ZEY ARE SPOTTED, WE ALL WILL BE INCRIMINATED.
CALM DOWN, THE BOMBSHELLS NEVER TALK.
MY FAMILY BUILT THIS EMERGENCY TUNNEL OVER 100 YEARS AGO. I NEVER THOUGHT I WOULD BE USING IT TO SMUGGLE PEOPLE IN!
YOU'RE DOING THE RIGHT THING, HERR SCHALL. YOUR COUNTRY IS BEING RUN BY A MADMAN, AND HIS EMPIRE MUST BE TAKEN DOWN.
PLEASE. COME IN.
ABOUT TIME! I-IT'S F-FRIGGIN' FREEZIN' OUT H-HERE!
TOUGHEN UP, LITTLE ONE.
IS EVERYTHING SET?
FRIGGIN'?
READY TO GO. YOUR DISGUISES ARE WAITING FOR YOU AT THE PUB. HAS EVERYONE READ THEIR DOSSIERS?
UH...I LEFT MINE ON THE PLANE.
HEH... I'LL JUST WING IT!
SO... WHEN DO I GET MY GUN?

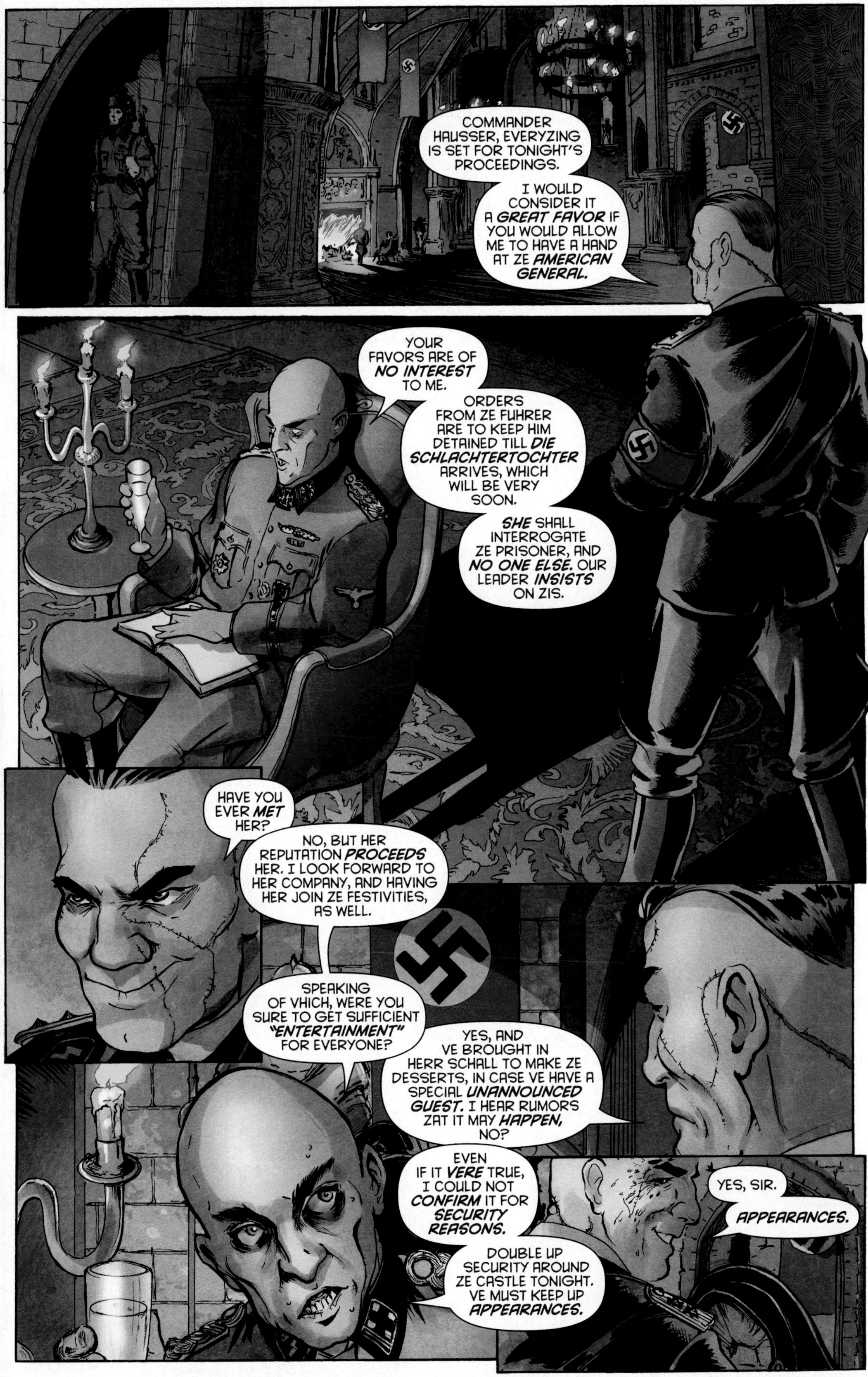
COMMANDER HAUSSER, EVERYZING IS SET FOR TONIGHT'S PROCEEDINGS.
I WOULD CONSIDER IT A GREAT FAVOR IF YOU WOULD ALLOW ME TO HAVE A HAND AT ZE AMERICAN GENERAL.
YOUR FAVORS ARE OF NO INTEREST TO ME.
ORDERS FROM ZE FUHRER ARE TO KEEP HIM DETAINED TILL DIE SCHLACHTERTOCHTER ARRIVES, WHICH WILL BE VERY SOON.
SHE SHALL INTERROGATE ZE PRISONER, AND NO ONE ELSE. OUR LEADER INSISTS ON ZIS.
HAVE YOU EVER MET HER?
NO, BUT HER REPUTATION PROCEEDS HER. I LOOK FORWARD TO HER COMPANY, AND HAVING HER JOIN ZE FESTIVITIES, AS WELL.
SPEAKING OF VHICH, WERE YOU SURE TO GET SUFFICIENT "ENTERTAINMENT" FOR EVERYONE?
YES, AND VE BROUGHT IN HERR SCHALL TO MAKE ZE DESSERTS, IN CASE VE HAVE A SPECIAL UNANNOUNCED GUEST. I HEAR RUMORS ZAT IT MAY HAPPEN, NO?
EVEN IF IT VERE TRUE, I COULD NOT CONFIRM IT FOR SECURITY REASONS.
DOUBLE UP SECURITY AROUND ZE CASTLE TONIGHT. VE MUST KEEP UP APPEARANCES.
YES, SIR.
APPEARANCES.

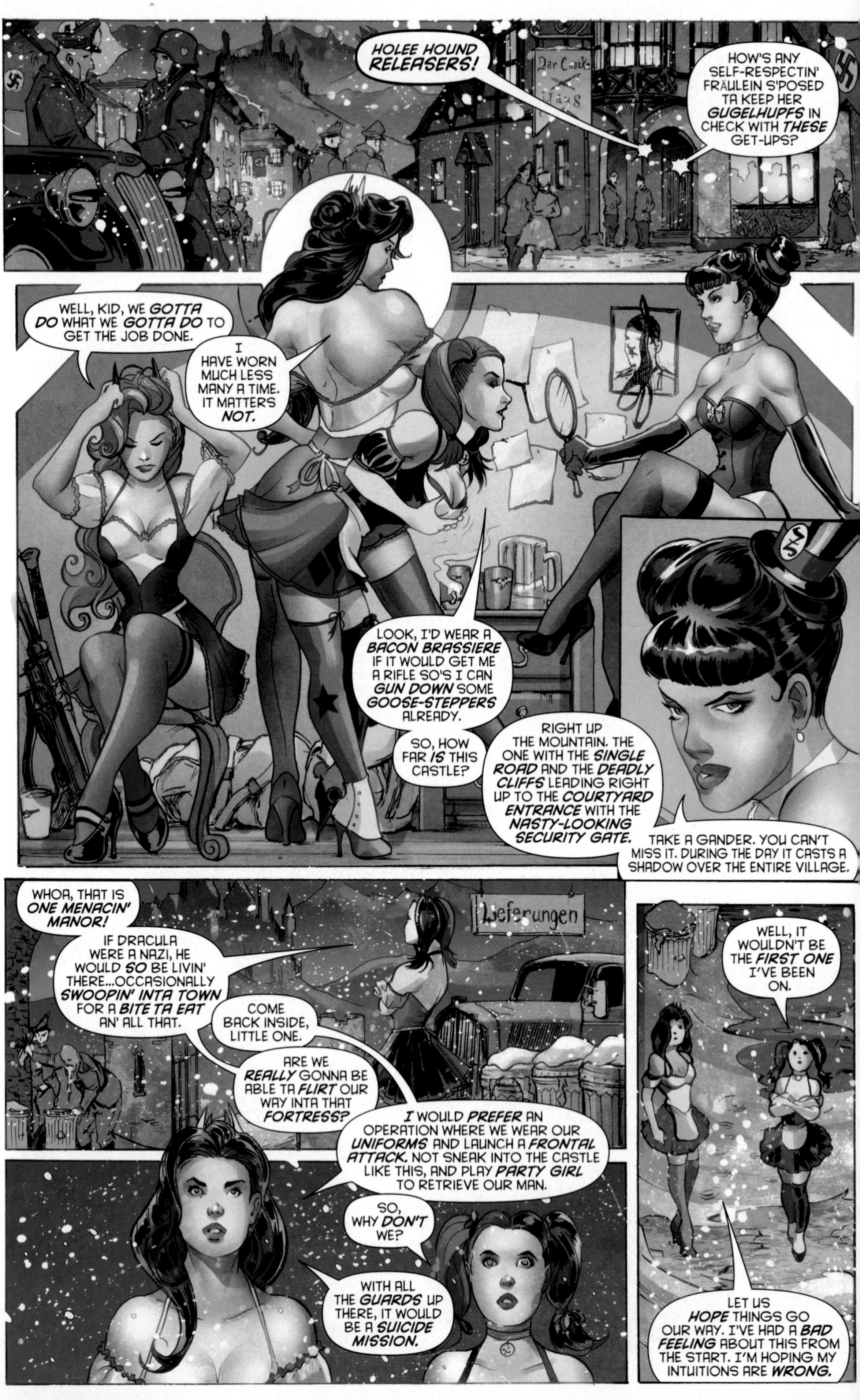

Dar Cook's Haus
HOLEE HOUND RELEASERS!
HOW'S ANY SELF-RESPECTIN' FRÄULEIN S'POSED TA KEEP HER GUGELHUPFS IN CHECK WITH THESE GET-UPS?
WELL, KID, WE GOTTA DO WHAT WE GOTTA DO TO GET THE JOB DONE.
I HAVE WORN MUCH LESS MANY A TIME. IT MATTERS NOT.
LOOK, I'D WEAR A BACON BRASSIERE IF IT WOULD GET ME A RIFLE SO'S I CAN GUN DOWN SOME GOOSE-STEPPERS ALREADY.
SO, HOW FAR IS THIS CASTLE?
RIGHT UP THE MOUNTAIN. THE ONE WITH THE SINGLE ROAD AND THE DEADLY CLIFFS LEADING RIGHT UP TO THE COURTYARD ENTRANCE WITH THE NASTY-LOOKING SECURITY GATE.
TAKE A GANDER. YOU CAN'T MISS IT. DURING THE DAY IT CASTS A SHADOW OVER THE ENTIRE VILLAGE.
Leferungen
WHOA, THAT IS ONE MENACIN' MANOR!
IF DRACULA WERE A NAZI, HE WOULD SO BE LIVIN' THERE...OCCASIONALLY SWOOPIN' INTA TOWN FOR A BITE TA EAT AN' ALL THAT.
COME BACK INSIDE, LITTLE ONE.
ARE WE REALLY GONNA BE ABLE TA FLIRT OUR WAY INTA THAT FORTRESS?
I WOULD PREFER AN OPERATION WHERE WE WEAR OUR UNIFORMS AND LAUNCH A FRONTAL ATTACK, NOT SNEAK INTO THE CASTLE LIKE THIS, AND PLAY PARTY GIRL TO RETRIEVE OUR MAN.
SO, WHY DON'T WE?
WITH ALL THE GUARDS UP THERE, IT WOULD BE A SUICIDE MISSION.
WELL, IT WOULDN'T BE THE FIRST ONE I'VE BEEN ON.
LET US HOPE THINGS GO OUR WAY. I'VE HAD A BAD FEELING ABOUT THIS FROM THE START. I'M HOPING MY INTUITIONS ARE WRONG.

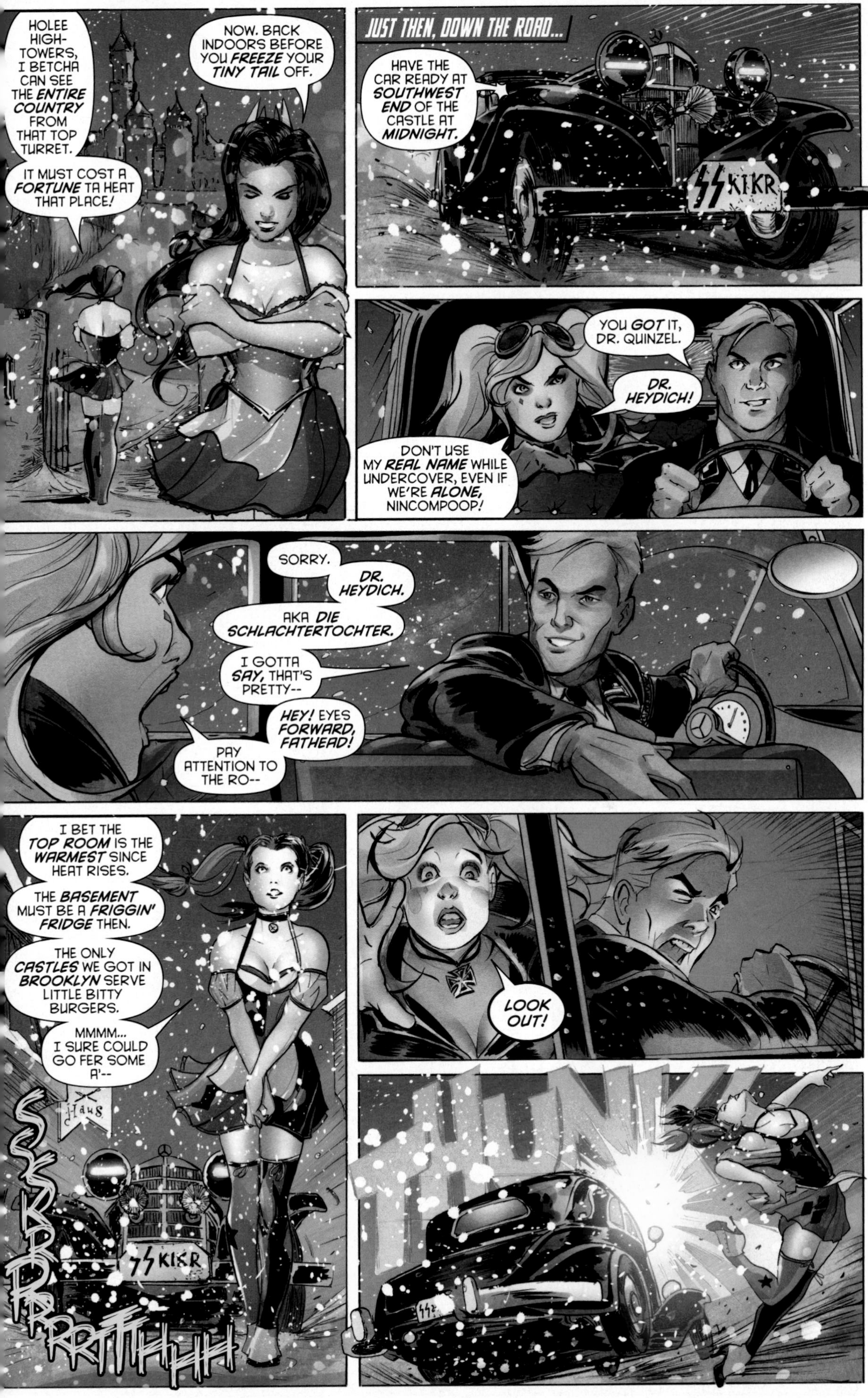
HOLEE HIGH-TOWERS, I BETCHA CAN SEE THE ENTIRE COUNTRY FROM THAT TOP TURRET.
IT MUST COST A FORTUNE TA HEAT THAT PLACE!
NOW. BACK INDOORS BEFORE YOU FREEZE YOUR TINY TAIL OFF.
JUST THEN, DOWN THE ROAD...
HAVE THE CAR READY AT SOUTHWEST END OF THE CASTLE AT MIDNIGHT.
SS KIKR
YOU GOT IT, DR. QUINZEL.
DR. HEYDICH!
DON'T USE MY REAL NAME WHILE UNDERCOVER, EVEN IF WE'RE ALONE, NINCOMPOOP!
SORRY.
DR. HEYDICH.
AKA DIE SCHLACHTERTOCHTER.
I GOTTA SAY, THAT'S PRETTY--
HEY! EYES FORWARD, FATHEAD!
PAY ATTENTION TO THE RO--
I BET THE TOP ROOM IS THE WARMEST SINCE HEAT RISES.
THE BASEMENT MUST BE A FRIGGIN' FRIDGE THEN.
THE ONLY CASTLES WE GOT IN BROOKLYN SERVE LITTLE BITTY BURGERS.
MMMM... I SURE COULD GO FER SOME A'--
SSKRRRRRTTTHHHH
SS KIKR
LOOK OUT!
THUNK!

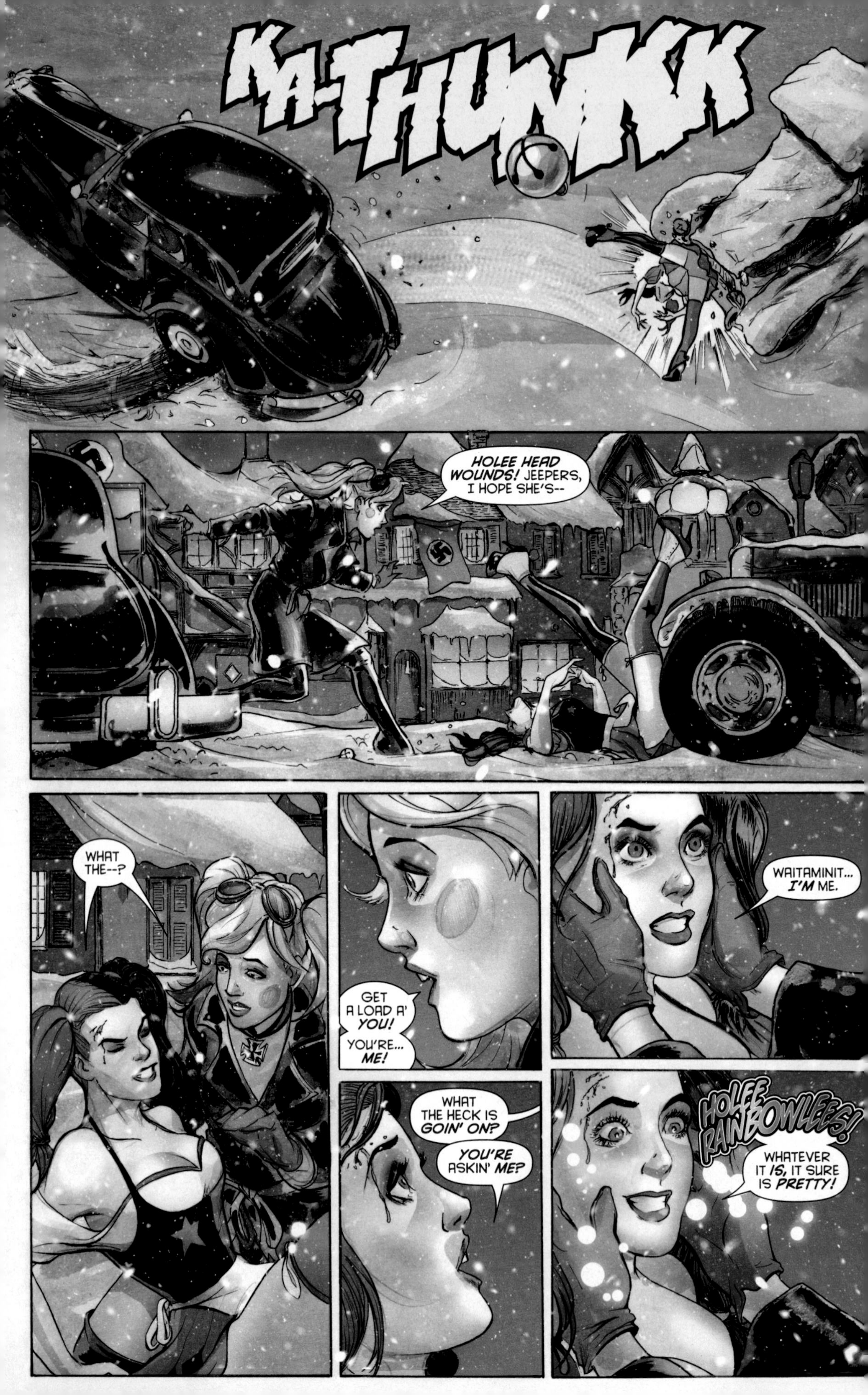
KA-THUNKK
HOLEE HEAD WOUNDS! JEEPERS, I HOPE SHE'S--
WHAT THE--?
GET A LOAD A' YOU!
YOU'RE... ME!
WAITAMINIT... I'M ME.
WHAT THE HECK IS GOIN' ON?
YOU'RE ASKIN' ME?
HOLEE RAINBOWLEES!
WHATEVER IT IS, IT SURE IS PRETTY!

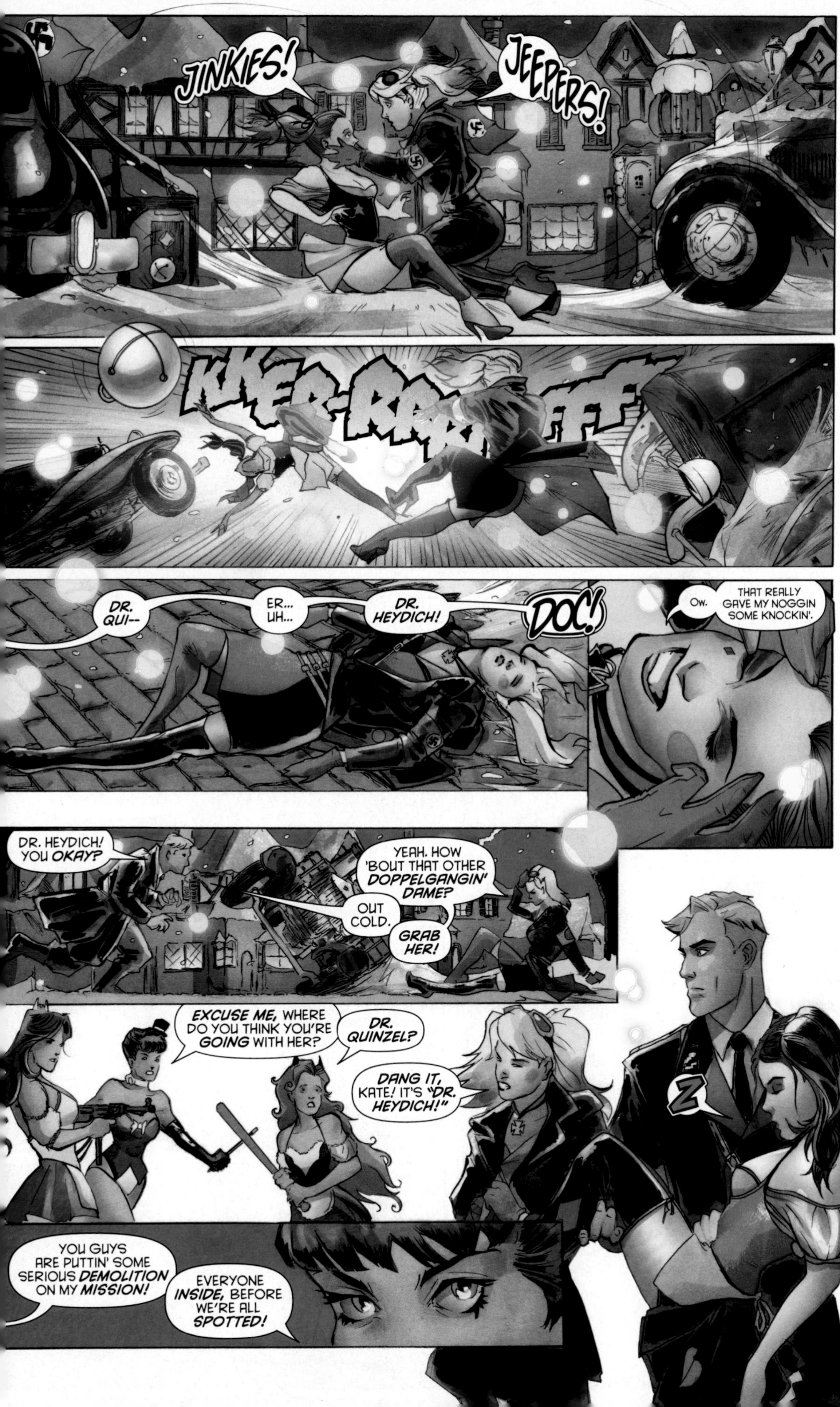
JINKIES!
JEEPERS!
KKER-RAKOFF
DR. QUI--
ER... UH...
DR. HEYDICH!
DOC!
OW.
THAT REALLY GAVE MY NOGGIN SOME KNOCKIN'.
DR. HEYDICH! YOU OKAY?
YEAH. HOW 'BOUT THAT OTHER DOPPELGANGIN' DAME?
OUT COLD.
GRAB HER!
EXCUSE ME, WHERE DO YOU THINK YOU'RE GOING WITH HER?
DR. QUINZEL?
DANG IT, KATE! IT'S "DR. HEYDICH!"
YOU GUYS ARE PUTTIN' SOME SERIOUS DEMOLITION ON MY MISSION!
EVERYONE INSIDE, BEFORE WE'RE ALL SPOTTED!

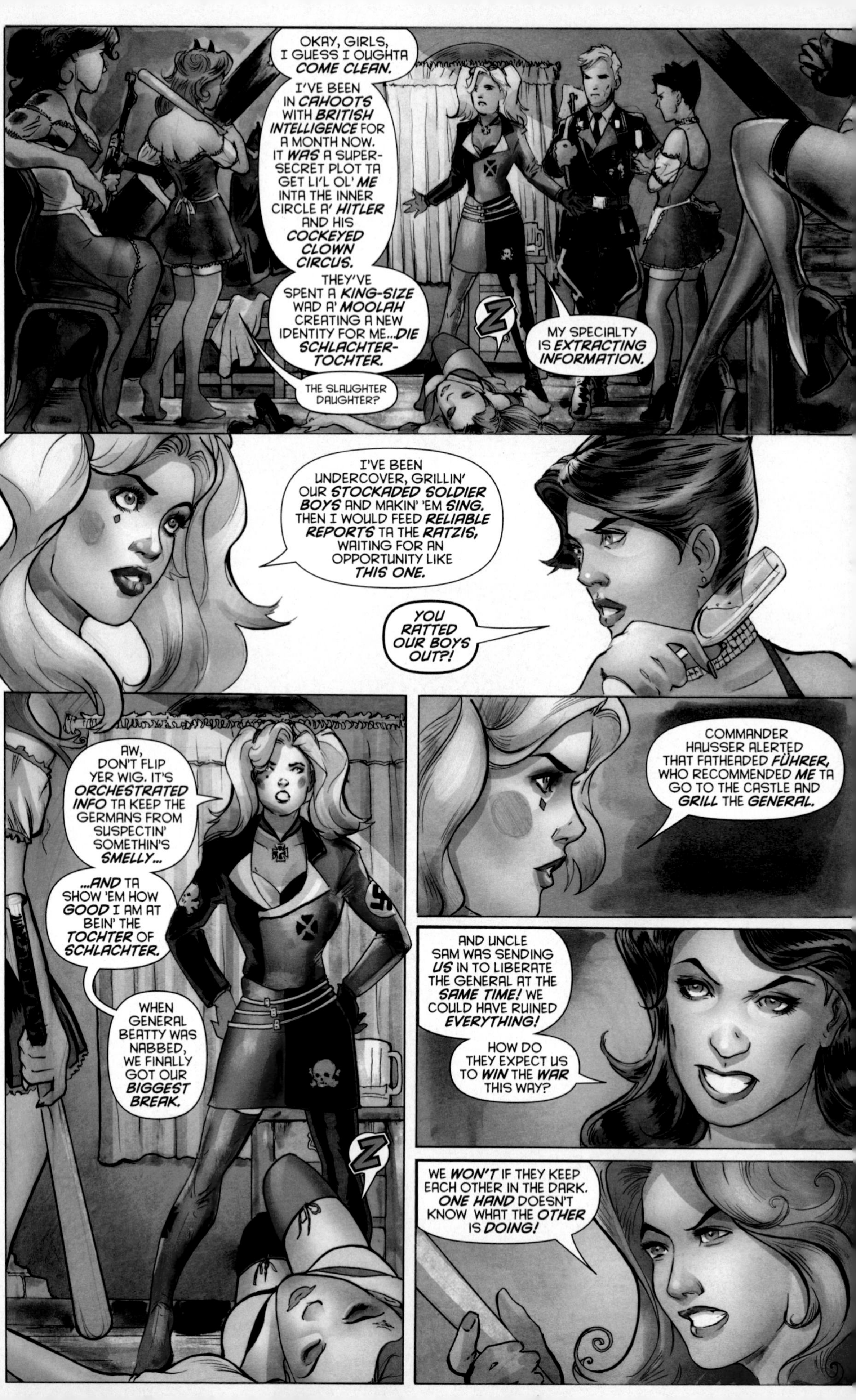
OKAY, GIRLS, I GUESS I OUGHTA COME CLEAN.
I'VE BEEN IN CAHOOTS WITH BRITISH INTELLIGENCE FOR A MONTH NOW. IT WAS A SUPER-SECRET PLOT TA GET LI'L OL' ME INTA THE INNER CIRCLE A' HITLER AND HIS COCKEYED CLOWN CIRCUS.
THEY'VE SPENT A KING-SIZE WAD A' MOOLAH CREATING A NEW IDENTITY FOR ME...DIE SCHLACHTER-TOCHTER.
THE SLAUGHTER DAUGHTER?
MY SPECIALTY IS EXTRACTING INFORMATION.
Z
I'VE BEEN UNDERCOVER, GRILLIN' OUR STOCKADED SOLDIER BOYS AND MAKIN' 'EM SING. THEN I WOULD FEED RELIABLE REPORTS TA THE RATZIS, WAITING FOR AN OPPORTUNITY LIKE THIS ONE.
YOU RATTED OUR BOYS OUT?!
AW, DON'T FLIP YER WIG. IT'S ORCHESTRATED INFO TA KEEP THE GERMANS FROM SUSPECTIN' SOMETHIN'S SMELLY...
...AND TA SHOW 'EM HOW GOOD I AM AT BEIN' THE TOCHTER OF SCHLACHTER.
WHEN GENERAL BEATTY WAS NABBED, WE FINALLY GOT OUR BIGGEST BREAK.
Z
COMMANDER HAUSSER ALERTED THAT FATHEADED FÜHRER, WHO RECOMMENDED ME TA GO TO THE CASTLE AND GRILL THE GENERAL.
AND UNCLE SAM WAS SENDING US IN TO LIBERATE THE GENERAL AT THE SAME TIME! WE COULD HAVE RUINED EVERYTHING!
HOW DO THEY EXPECT US TO WIN THE WAR THIS WAY?
WE WON'T IF THEY KEEP EACH OTHER IN THE DARK. ONE HAND DOESN'T KNOW WHAT THE OTHER IS DOING!

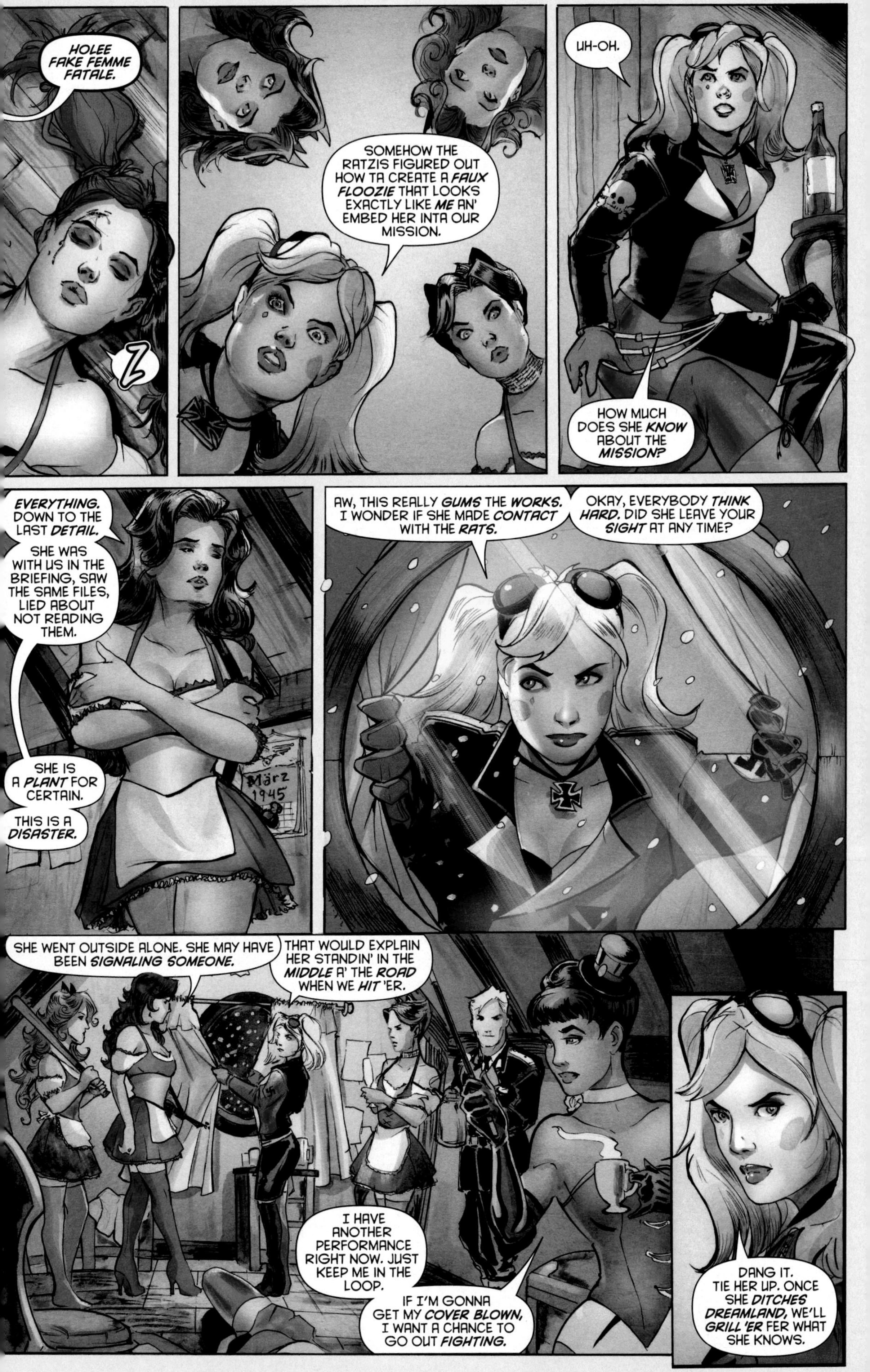
HOLEE FAKE FEMME FATALE.
Z
SOMEHOW THE RATZIS FIGURED OUT HOW TA CREATE A FAUX FLOOZIE THAT LOOKS EXACTLY LIKE ME AN' EMBED HER INTA OUR MISSION.
UH-OH.
HOW MUCH DOES SHE KNOW ABOUT THE MISSION?
EVERYTHING. DOWN TO THE LAST DETAIL.
SHE WAS WITH US IN THE BRIEFING, SAW THE SAME FILES, LIED ABOUT NOT READING THEM.
SHE IS A PLANT FOR CERTAIN.
THIS IS A DISASTER.
März 1945
AW, THIS REALLY GUMS THE WORKS. I WONDER IF SHE MADE CONTACT WITH THE RATS.
OKAY, EVERYBODY THINK HARD. DID SHE LEAVE YOUR SIGHT AT ANY TIME?
SHE WENT OUTSIDE ALONE. SHE MAY HAVE BEEN SIGNALING SOMEONE.
THAT WOULD EXPLAIN HER STANDIN' IN THE MIDDLE A' THE ROAD WHEN WE HIT 'ER.
I HAVE ANOTHER PERFORMANCE RIGHT NOW. JUST KEEP ME IN THE LOOP.
IF I'M GONNA GET MY COVER BLOWN, I WANT A CHANCE TO GO OUT FIGHTING.
DANG IT. TIE HER UP. ONCE SHE DITCHES DREAMLAND, WE'LL GRILL 'ER FER WHAT SHE KNOWS.

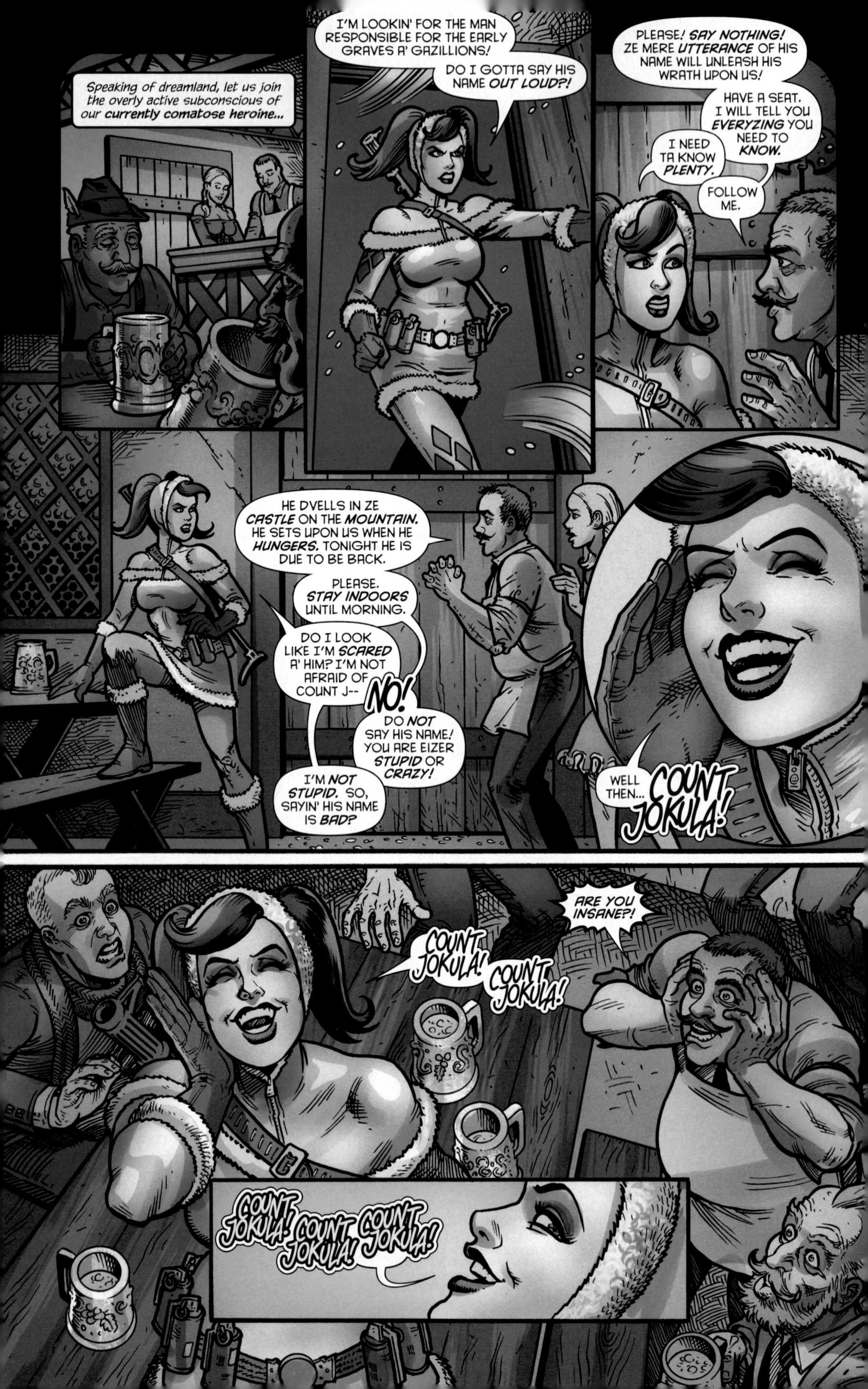

Speaking of dreamland, let us join the overly active subconscious of our currently comatose heroine...
I'M LOOKIN' FOR THE MAN RESPONSIBLE FOR THE EARLY GRAVES A' GAZILLIONS!
DO I GOTTA SAY HIS NAME OUT LOUD?!
PLEASE! SAY NOTHING! ZE MERE UTTERANCE OF HIS NAME WILL UNLEASH HIS WRATH UPON US!
HAVE A SEAT. I WILL TELL YOU EVERYZING YOU NEED TO KNOW.
I NEED TA KNOW PLENTY.
FOLLOW ME.
HE DVELLS IN ZE CASTLE ON THE MOUNTAIN. HE SETS UPON US WHEN HE HUNGERS. TONIGHT HE IS DUE TO BE BACK.
PLEASE. STAY INDOORS UNTIL MORNING.
DO I LOOK LIKE I'M SCARED A' HIM? I'M NOT AFRAID OF COUNT J--
NO!
DO NOT SAY HIS NAME! YOU ARE EIZER STUPID OR CRAZY!
I'M NOT STUPID. SO, SAYIN' HIS NAME IS BAD?
WELL THEN... COUNT JOKULA!
ARE YOU INSANE?!
COUNT JOKULA!
COUNT JOKULA!
COUNT JOKULA! COUNT JOKULA! COUNT JOKULA!

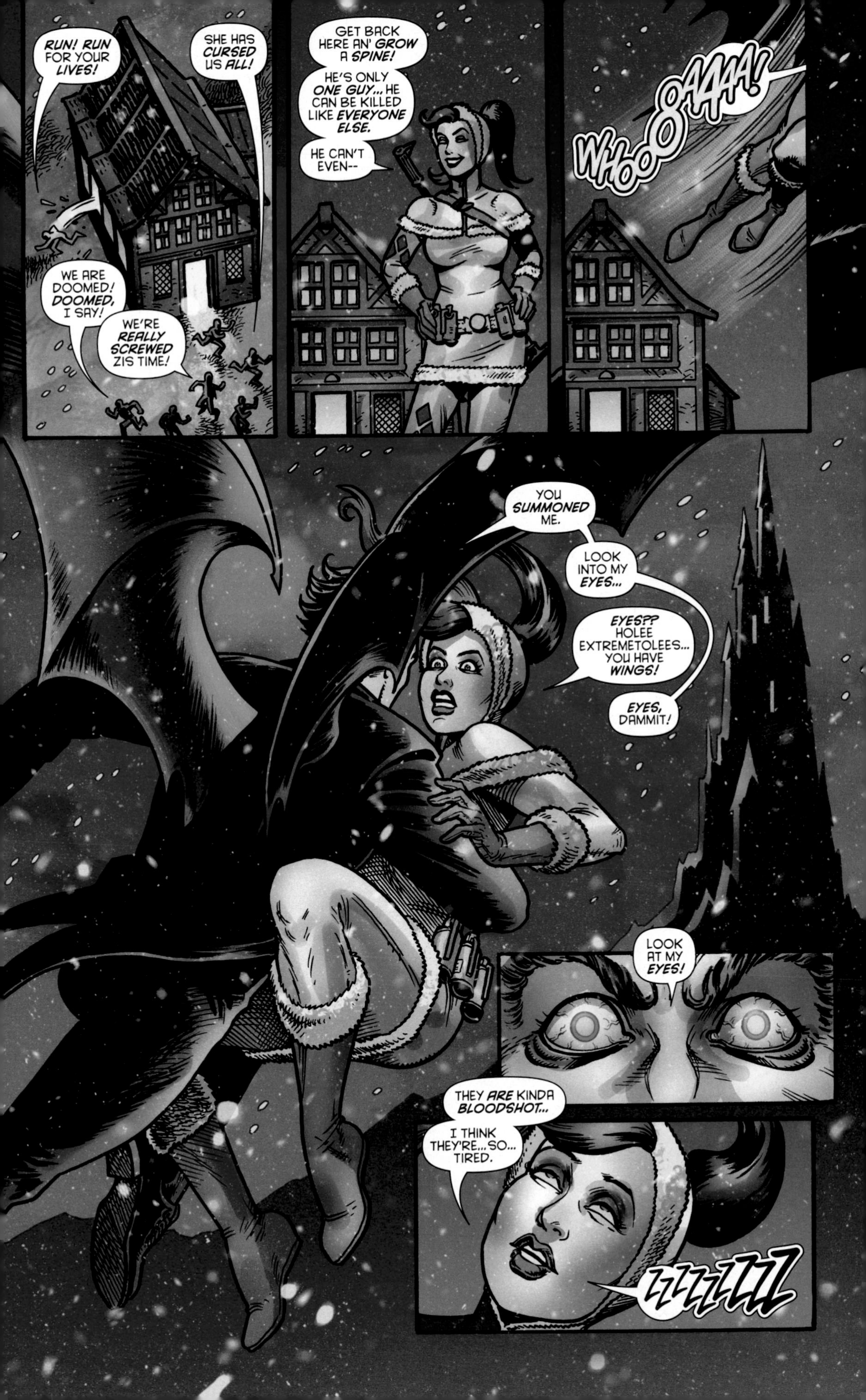
RUN! RUN FOR YOUR LIVES!
SHE HAS CURSED US ALL!
WE ARE DOOMED! DOOMED, I SAY!
WE'RE REALLY SCREWED ZIS TIME!
GET BACK HERE AN' GROW A SPINE!
HE'S ONLY ONE GUY... HE CAN BE KILLED LIKE EVERYONE ELSE.
HE CAN'T EVEN--
WHOOOAAAA!
YOU SUMMONED ME.
LOOK INTO MY EYES...
EYES?? HOLEE EXTREMETOLEES... YOU HAVE WINGS!
EYES, DAMMIT!
LOOK AT MY EYES!
THEY ARE KINDA BLOODSHOT...
I THINK THEY'RE... SO... TIRED.
ZZZZZZZZ

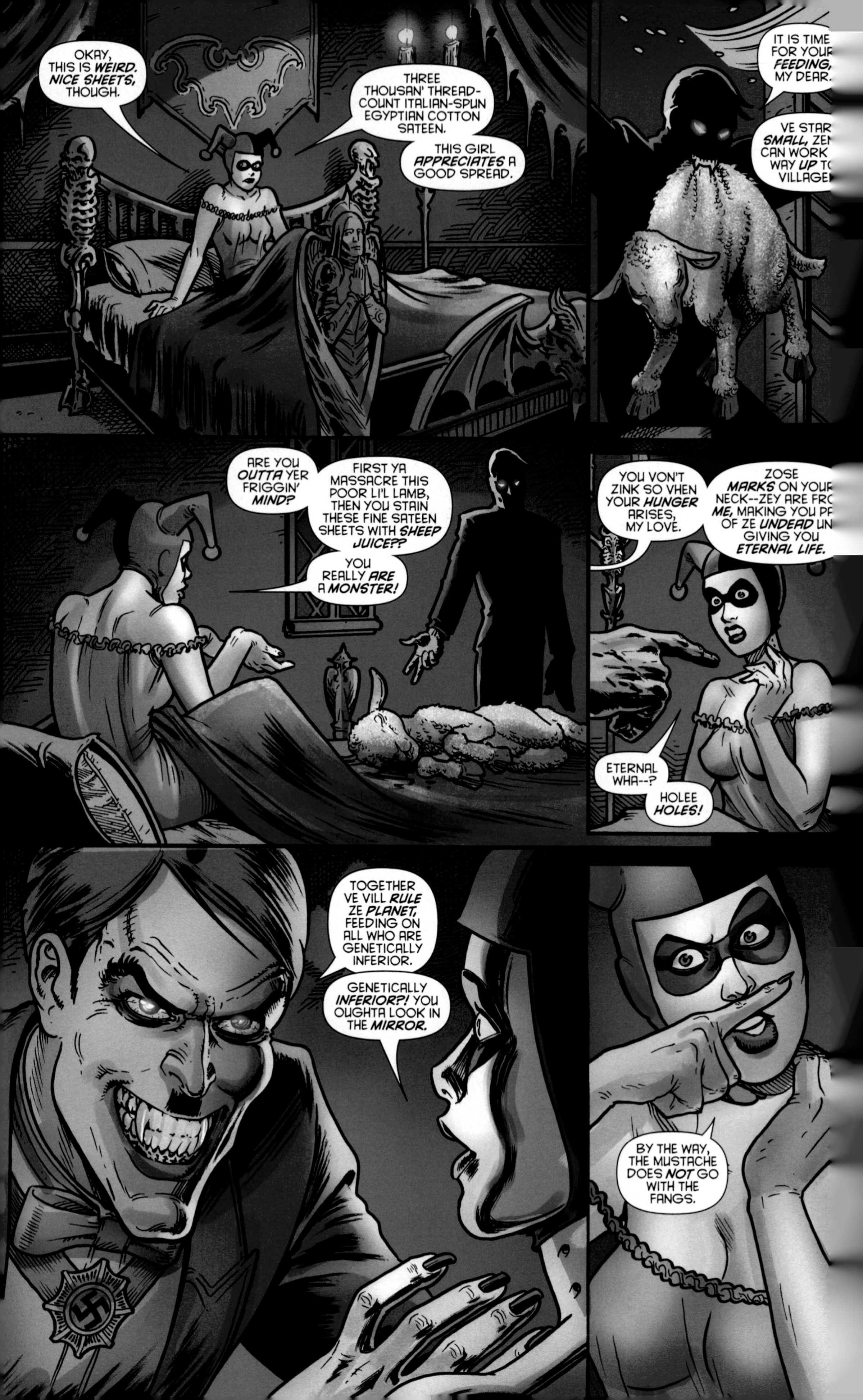
OKAY, THIS IS WEIRD. NICE SHEETS, THOUGH.
THREE THOUSAN' THREAD-COUNT ITALIAN-SPUN EGYPTIAN COTTON SATEEN.
THIS GIRL APPRECIATES A GOOD SPREAD.
IT IS TIME FOR YOUR FEEDING, MY DEAR.
VE STAR SMALL, ZEN CAN WORK WAY UP T VILLAGE
ARE YOU OUTTA YER FRIGGIN' MIND?
FIRST YA MASSACRE THIS POOR LI'L LAMB, THEN YOU STAIN THESE FINE SATEEN SHEETS WITH SHEEP JUICE??
YOU REALLY ARE A MONSTER!
YOU VON'T ZINK SO VHEN YOUR HUNGER ARISES, MY LOVE.
ZOSE MARKS ON YOUR NECK--ZEY ARE FRO ME, MAKING YOU PA OF ZE UNDEAD UN GIVING YOU ETERNAL LIFE.
ETERNAL WHA--?
HOLEE HOLES!
TOGETHER VE VILL RULE ZE PLANET, FEEDING ON ALL WHO ARE GENETICALLY INFERIOR.
GENETICALLY INFERIOR?! YOU OUGHTA LOOK IN THE MIRROR.
BY THE WAY, THE MUSTACHE DOES NOT GO WITH THE FANGS.

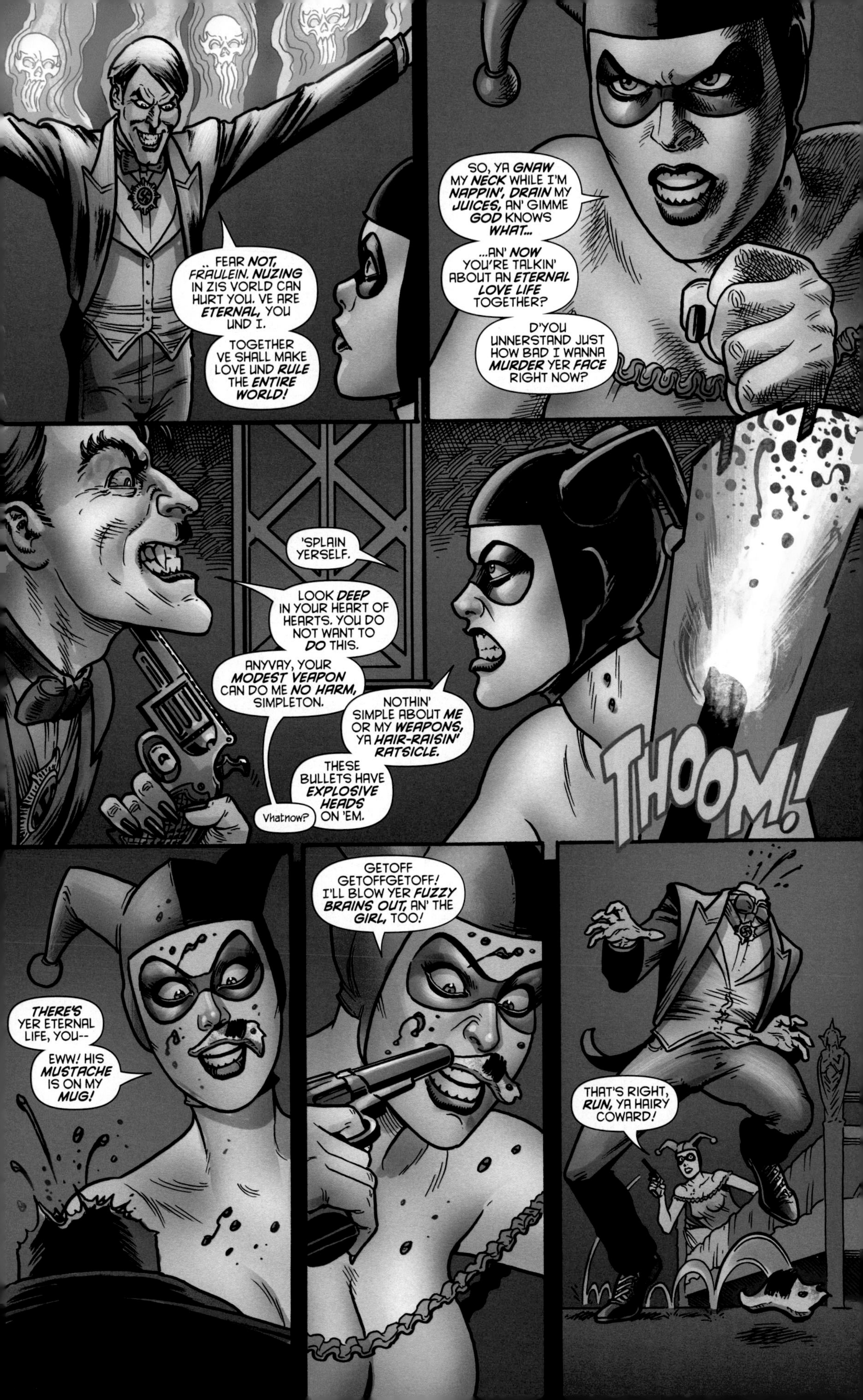
...FEAR NOT, FRÄULEIN. NUZING IN ZIS VORLD CAN HURT YOU. VE ARE ETERNAL, YOU UND I.
TOGETHER VE SHALL MAKE LOVE UND RULE THE ENTIRE WORLD!
SO, YA GNAW MY NECK WHILE I'M NAPPIN', DRAIN MY JUICES, AN' GIMME GOD KNOWS WHAT...
...AN' NOW YOU'RE TALKIN' ABOUT AN ETERNAL LOVE LIFE TOGETHER?
D'YOU UNNERSTAND JUST HOW BAD I WANNA MURDER YER FACE RIGHT NOW?
'SPLAIN YERSELF.
LOOK DEEP IN YOUR HEART OF HEARTS. YOU DO NOT WANT TO DO THIS.
ANYVAY, YOUR MODEST VEAPON CAN DO ME NO HARM, SIMPLETON.
NOTHIN' SIMPLE ABOUT ME OR MY WEAPONS, YA HAIR-RAISIN' RATSICLE.
THESE BULLETS HAVE EXPLOSIVE HEADS ON 'EM.
Vhatnow?
THOOM!
THERE'S YER ETERNAL LIFE, YOU--
EWW! HIS MUSTACHE IS ON MY MUG!
GETOFF GETOFFGETOFF! I'LL BLOW YER FUZZY BRAINS OUT, AN' THE GIRL, TOO!
THAT'S RIGHT, RUN, YA HAIRY COWARD!

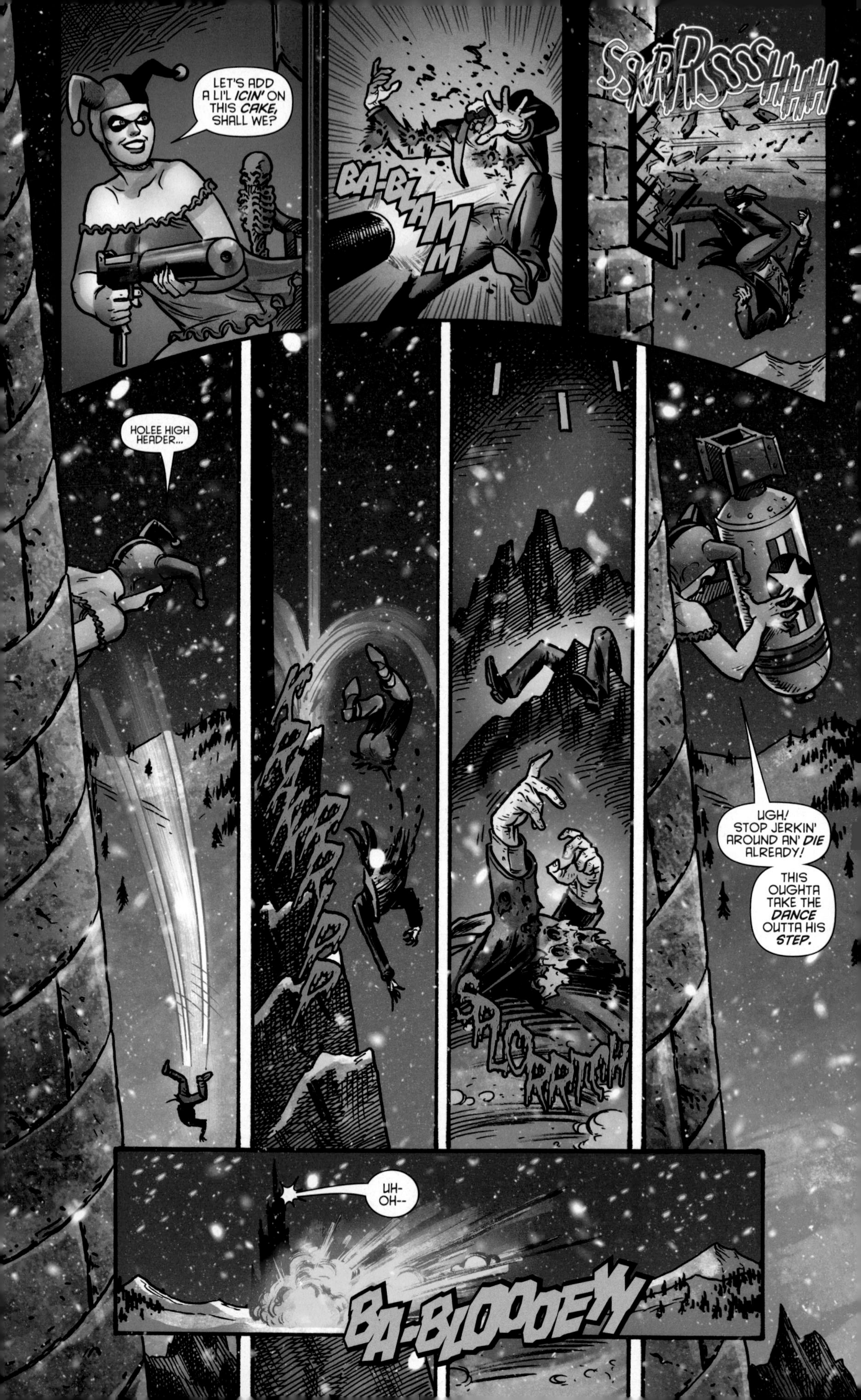
LET'S ADD A LI'L ICIN' ON THIS CAKE, SHALL WE?
BA-BLAMM
SSKRRSSSSHHH
HOLEE HIGH HEADER...
UGH! STOP JERKIN' AROUND AN' DIE ALREADY!
THIS OUGHTA TAKE THE DANCE OUTTA HIS STEP.
UH-OH--
BA-BLOOOEY

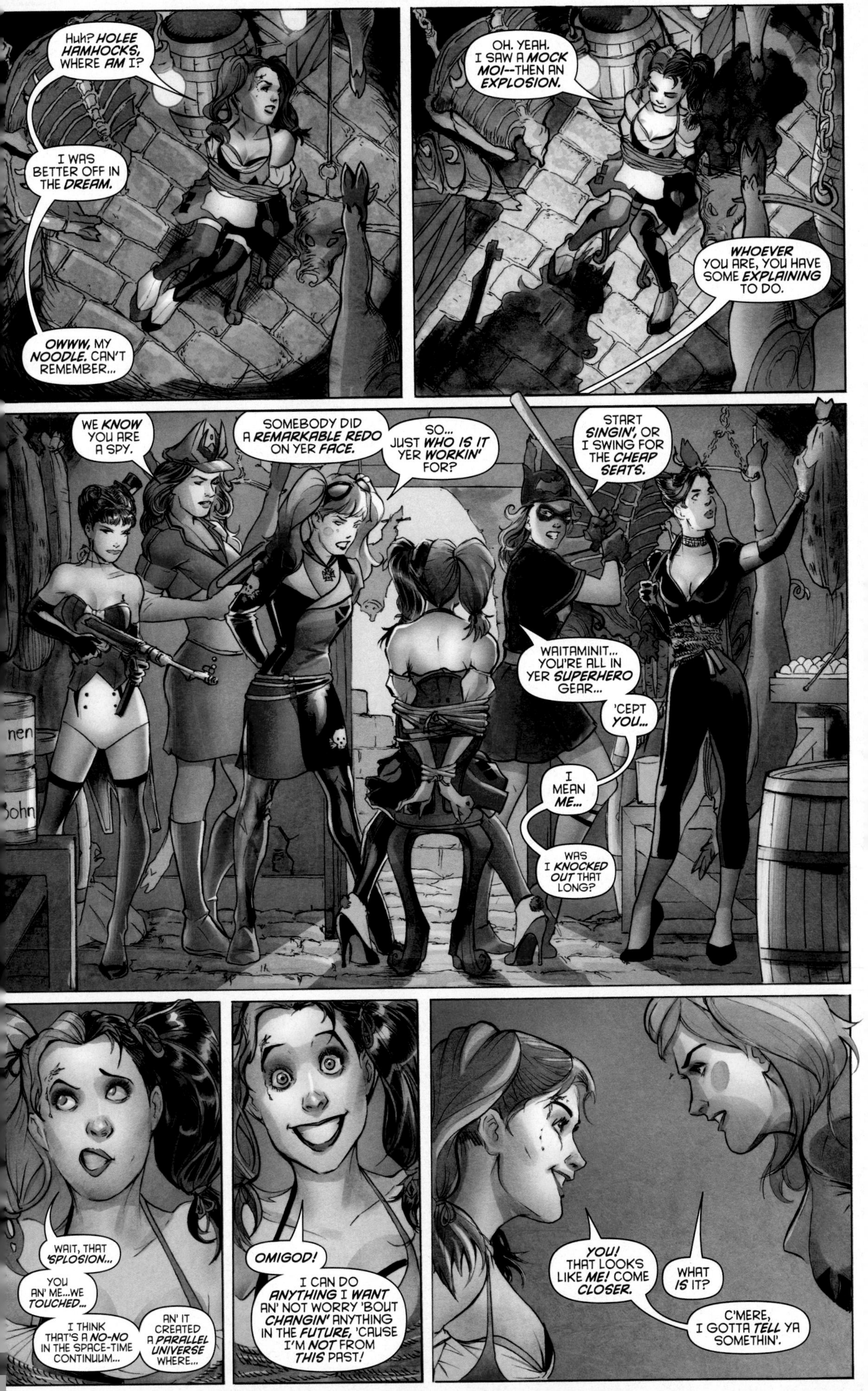

Huh? HOLEE HAMHOCKS, WHERE AM I?
I WAS BETTER OFF IN THE DREAM.
OWWW, MY NOODLE. CAN'T REMEMBER...
OH. YEAH. I SAW A MOCK MOI--THEN AN EXPLOSION.
WHOEVER YOU ARE, YOU HAVE SOME EXPLAINING TO DO.
WE KNOW YOU ARE A SPY.
SOMEBODY DID A REMARKABLE REDO ON YER FACE.
SO... JUST WHO IS IT YER WORKIN' FOR?
START SINGIN', OR I SWING FOR THE CHEAP SEATS.
WAITAMINIT... YOU'RE ALL IN YER SUPERHERO GEAR...
'CEPT YOU...
I MEAN ME...
WAS I KNOCKED OUT THAT LONG?
WAIT, THAT 'SPLOSION...
YOU AN' ME...WE TOUCHED...
I THINK THAT'S A NO-NO IN THE SPACE-TIME CONTINUUM...
AN' IT CREATED A PARALLEL UNIVERSE WHERE...
OMIGOD!
I CAN DO ANYTHING I WANT AN' NOT WORRY 'BOUT CHANGIN' ANYTHING IN THE FUTURE, 'CAUSE I'M NOT FROM THIS PAST!
YOU! THAT LOOKS LIKE ME! COME CLOSER.
WHAT IS IT?
C'MERE, I GOTTA TELL YA SOMETHIN'.

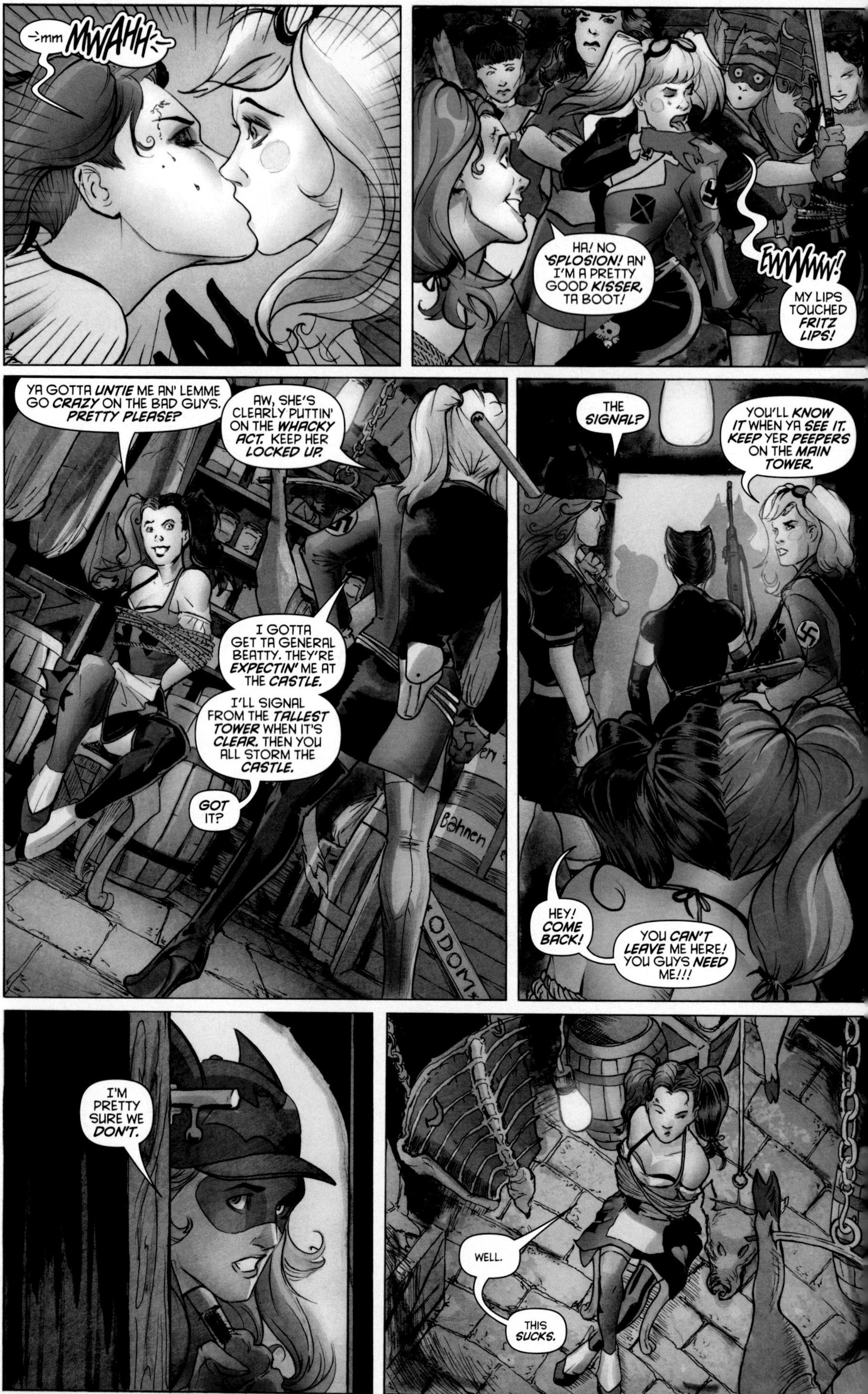

~mm MWAHH~
HA! NO 'SPLOSION! AN' I'M A PRETTY GOOD KISSER, TA BOOT!
EWWWW!
MY LIPS TOUCHED FRITZ LIPS!
YA GOTTA UNTIE ME AN' LEMME GO CRAZY ON THE BAD GUYS. PRETTY PLEASE?
AW, SHE'S CLEARLY PUTTIN' ON THE WHACKY ACT. KEEP HER LOCKED UP.
I GOTTA GET TA GENERAL BEATTY. THEY'RE EXPECTIN' ME AT THE CASTLE.
I'LL SIGNAL FROM THE TALLEST TOWER WHEN IT'S CLEAR. THEN YOU ALL STORM THE CASTLE.
GOT IT?
Bahnen
THE SIGNAL?
YOU'LL KNOW IT WHEN YA SEE IT. KEEP YER PEEPERS ON THE MAIN TOWER.
HEY! COME BACK!
YOU CAN'T LEAVE ME HERE! YOU GUYS NEED ME!!!
I'M PRETTY SURE WE DON'T.
WELL.
THIS SUCKS.

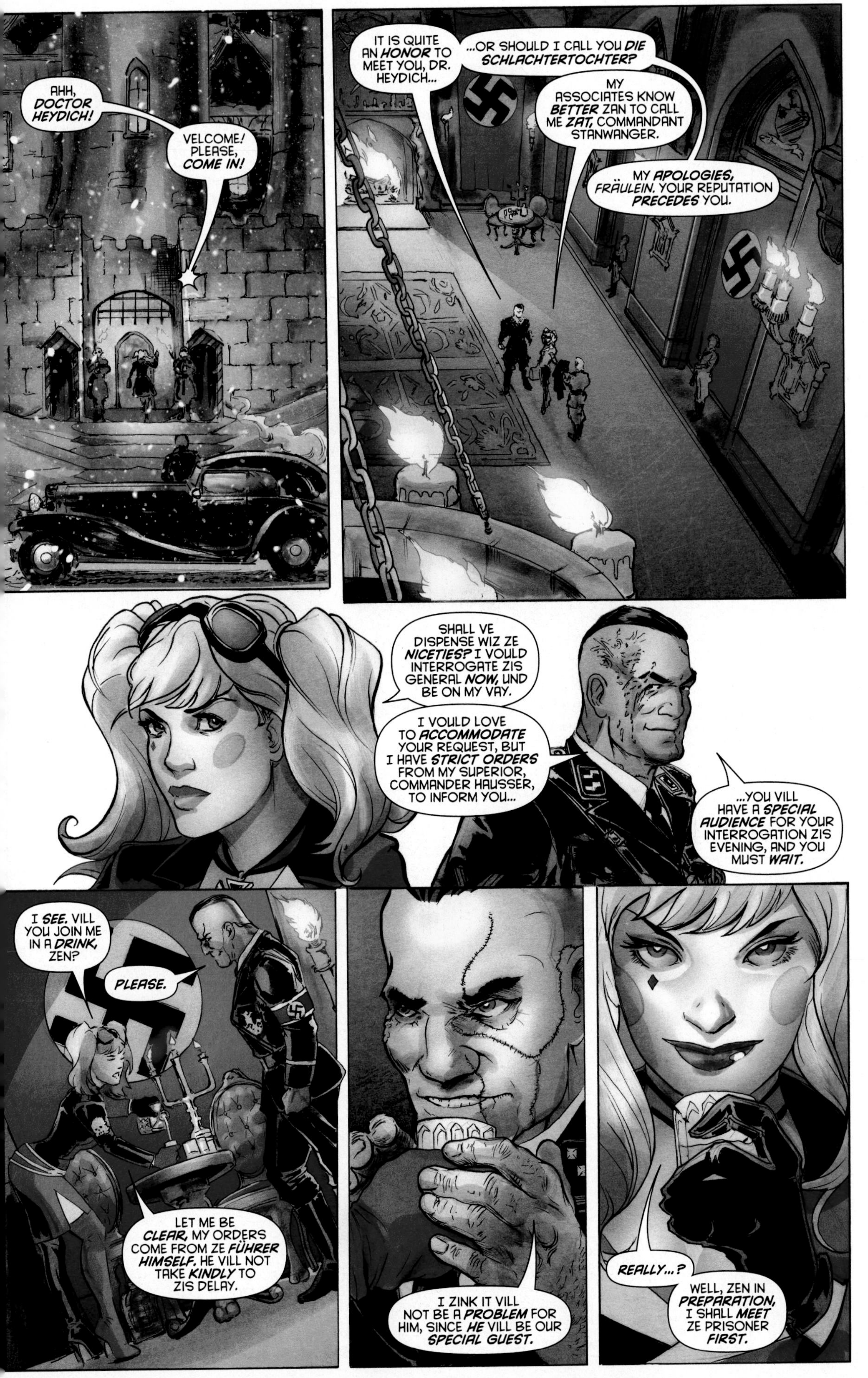
AHH, DOCTOR HEYDICH!
VELCOME! PLEASE, COME IN!
IT IS QUITE AN HONOR TO MEET YOU, DR. HEYDICH...
...OR SHOULD I CALL YOU DIE SCHLACHTERTOCHTER?
MY ASSOCIATES KNOW BETTER ZAN TO CALL ME ZAT, COMMANDANT STANWANGER.
... MY APOLOGIES, FRÄULEIN. YOUR REPUTATION PRECEDES YOU.
SHALL VE DISPENSE WIZ ZE NICETIES? I VOULD INTERROGATE ZIS GENERAL NOW, UND BE ON MY VAY.
I VOULD LOVE TO ACCOMMODATE YOUR REQUEST, BUT I HAVE STRICT ORDERS FROM MY SUPERIOR, COMMANDER HAUSSER, TO INFORM YOU...
...YOU VILL HAVE A SPECIAL AUDIENCE FOR YOUR INTERROGATION ZIS EVENING, AND YOU MUST WAIT.
I SEE. VILL YOU JOIN ME IN A DRINK, ZEN?
PLEASE.
LET ME BE CLEAR, MY ORDERS COME FROM ZE FÜHRER HIMSELF. HE VILL NOT TAKE KINDLY TO ZIS DELAY.
I ZINK IT VILL NOT BE A PROBLEM FOR HIM, SINCE HE VILL BE OUR SPECIAL GUEST.
REALLY...?
WELL, ZEN IN PREPARATION, I SHALL MEET ZE PRISONER FIRST.

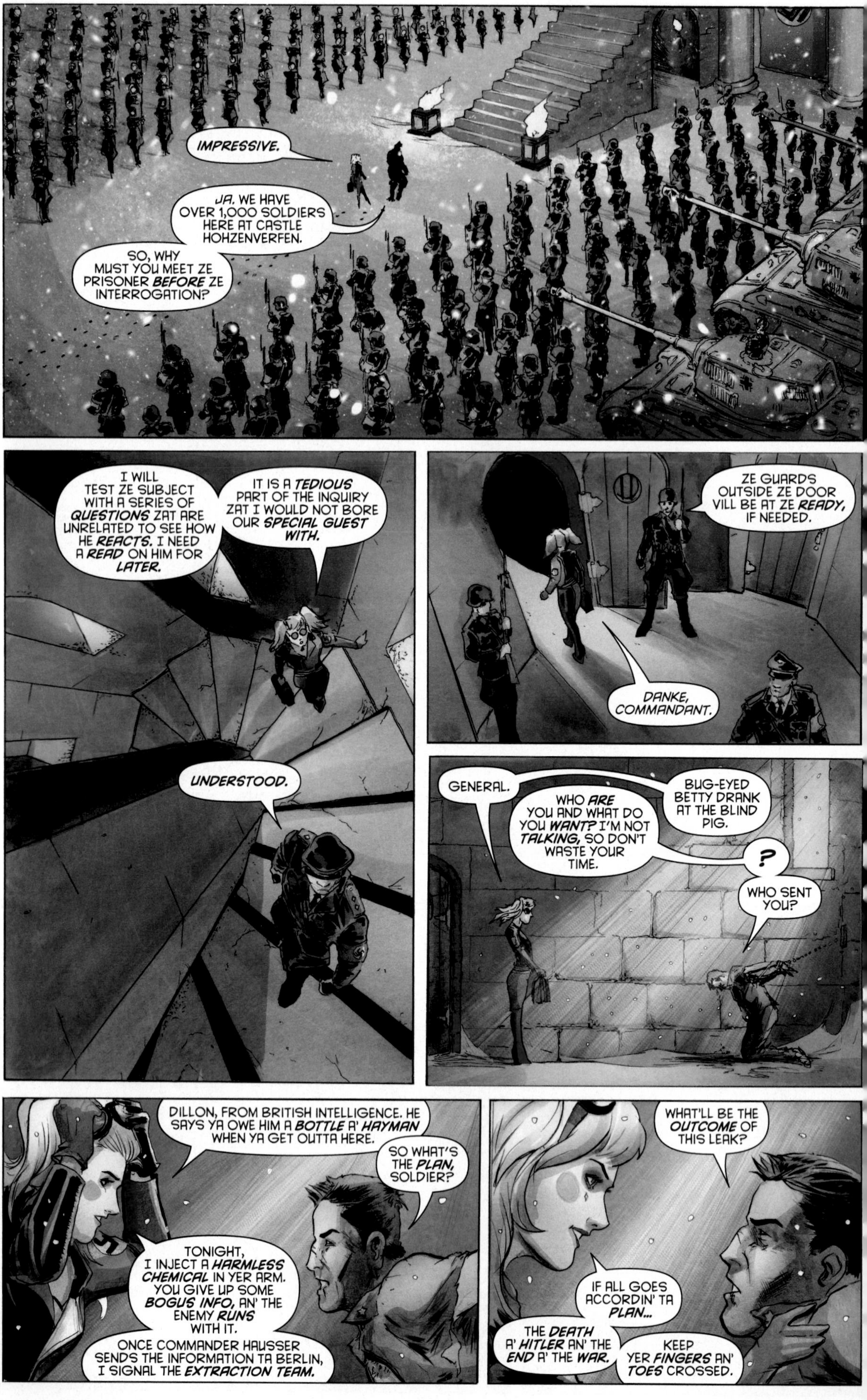
IMPRESSIVE.
JA. WE HAVE OVER 1,000 SOLDIERS HERE AT CASTLE HOHZENVERFEN.
SO, WHY MUST YOU MEET ZE PRISONER BEFORE ZE INTERROGATION?
I WILL TEST ZE SUBJECT WITH A SERIES OF QUESTIONS ZAT ARE UNRELATED TO SEE HOW HE REACTS. I NEED A READ ON HIM FOR LATER.
IT IS A TEDIOUS PART OF THE INQUIRY ZAT I WOULD NOT BORE OUR SPECIAL GUEST WITH.
UNDERSTOOD.
ZE GUARDS OUTSIDE ZE DOOR VILL BE AT ZE READY, IF NEEDED.
DANKE, COMMANDANT.
GENERAL.
WHO ARE YOU AND WHAT DO YOU WANT? I'M NOT TALKING, SO DON'T WASTE YOUR TIME.
BUG-EYED BETTY DRANK AT THE BLIND PIG.
?
WHO SENT YOU?
DILLON, FROM BRITISH INTELLIGENCE. HE SAYS YA OWE HIM A BOTTLE A' HAYMAN WHEN YA GET OUTTA HERE.
SO WHAT'S THE PLAN, SOLDIER?
TONIGHT, I INJECT A HARMLESS CHEMICAL IN YER ARM. YOU GIVE UP SOME BOGUS INFO, AN' THE ENEMY RUNS WITH IT.
ONCE COMMANDER HAUSSER SENDS THE INFORMATION TA BERLIN, I SIGNAL THE EXTRACTION TEAM.
WHAT'LL BE THE OUTCOME OF THIS LEAK?
IF ALL GOES ACCORDIN' TA PLAN...
THE DEATH A' HITLER AN' THE END A' THE WAR.
KEEP YER FINGERS AN' TOES CROSSED.

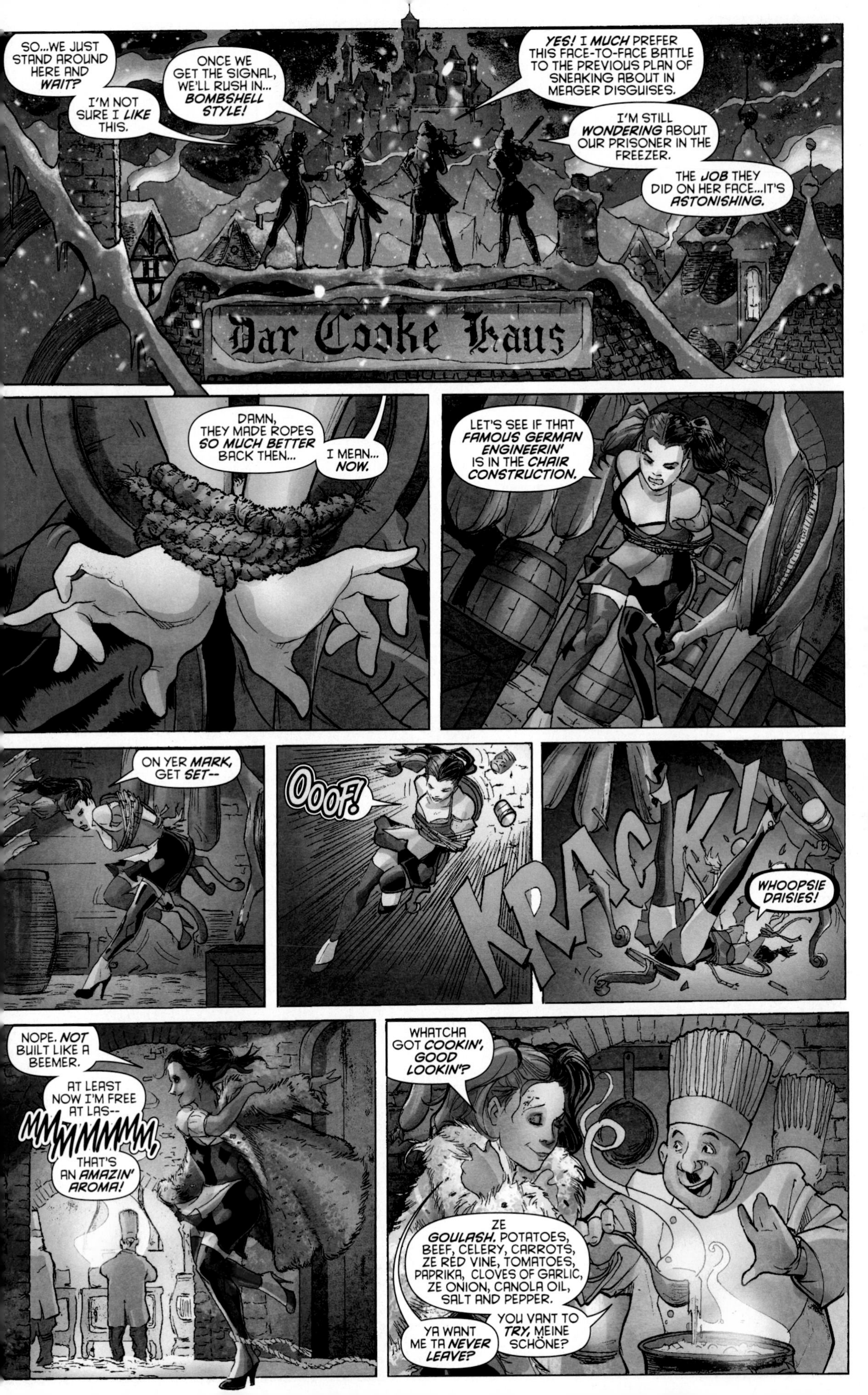
SO...WE JUST STAND AROUND HERE AND WAIT?
I'M NOT SURE I LIKE THIS.
ONCE WE GET THE SIGNAL, WE'LL RUSH IN... BOMBSHELL STYLE!
YES! I MUCH PREFER THIS FACE-TO-FACE BATTLE TO THE PREVIOUS PLAN OF SNEAKING ABOUT IN MEAGER DISGUISES.
I'M STILL WONDERING ABOUT OUR PRISONER IN THE FREEZER.
THE JOB THEY DID ON HER FACE...IT'S ASTONISHING.
Dar Cooke Haus
DAMN, THEY MADE ROPES SO MUCH BETTER BACK THEN...
I MEAN... NOW.
LET'S SEE IF THAT FAMOUS GERMAN ENGINEERIN' IS IN THE CHAIR CONSTRUCTION.
ON YER MARK, GET SET--
OOOF!
KRACK!
WHOOPSIE DAISIES!
NOPE. NOT BUILT LIKE A BEEMER.
AT LEAST NOW I'M FREE AT LAS--
MMMMMMM
THAT'S AN AMAZIN' AROMA!
WHATCHA GOT COOKIN', GOOD LOOKIN'?
ZE GOULASH. POTATOES, BEEF, CELERY, CARROTS, ZE RED VINE, TOMATOES, PAPRIKA, CLOVES OF GARLIC, ZE ONION, CANOLA OIL, SALT AND PEPPER.
YOU VANT TO TRY, MEINE SCHÖNE?
YA WANT ME TA NEVER LEAVE?

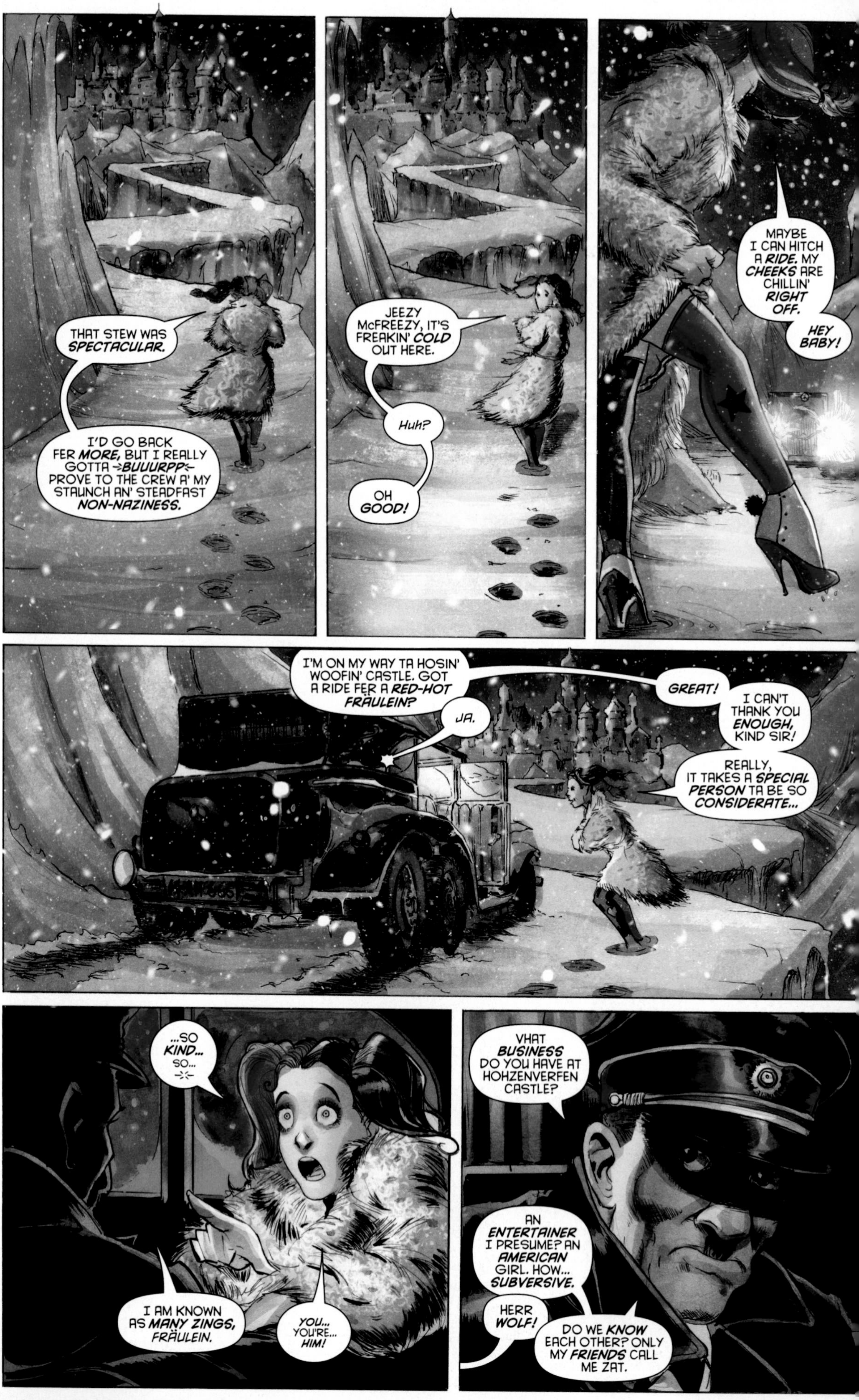

THAT STEW WAS SPECTACULAR.
I'D GO BACK FER MORE, BUT I REALLY GOTTA ⇒BUUURPP⇐ PROVE TO THE CREW A' MY STAUNCH AN' STEADFAST NON-NAZINESS.
JEEZY McFREEZY, IT'S FREAKIN' COLD OUT HERE.
Huh?
OH GOOD!
MAYBE I CAN HITCH A RIDE. MY CHEEKS ARE CHILLIN' RIGHT OFF.
HEY BABY!
I'M ON MY WAY TA HOSIN' WOOFIN' CASTLE. GOT A RIDE FER A RED-HOT FRÄULEIN?
JA.
GREAT!
I CAN'T THANK YOU ENOUGH, KIND SIR!
REALLY, IT TAKES A SPECIAL PERSON TA BE SO CONSIDERATE...
...SO KIND... SO...
I AM KNOWN AS MANY ZINGS, FRÄULEIN.
YOU... YOU'RE... HIM!
VHAT BUSINESS DO YOU HAVE AT HOHZENVERFEN CASTLE?
AN ENTERTAINER I PRESUME? AN AMERICAN GIRL. HOW... SUBVERSIVE.
HERR WOLF!
DO WE KNOW EACH OTHER? ONLY MY FRIENDS CALL ME ZAT.

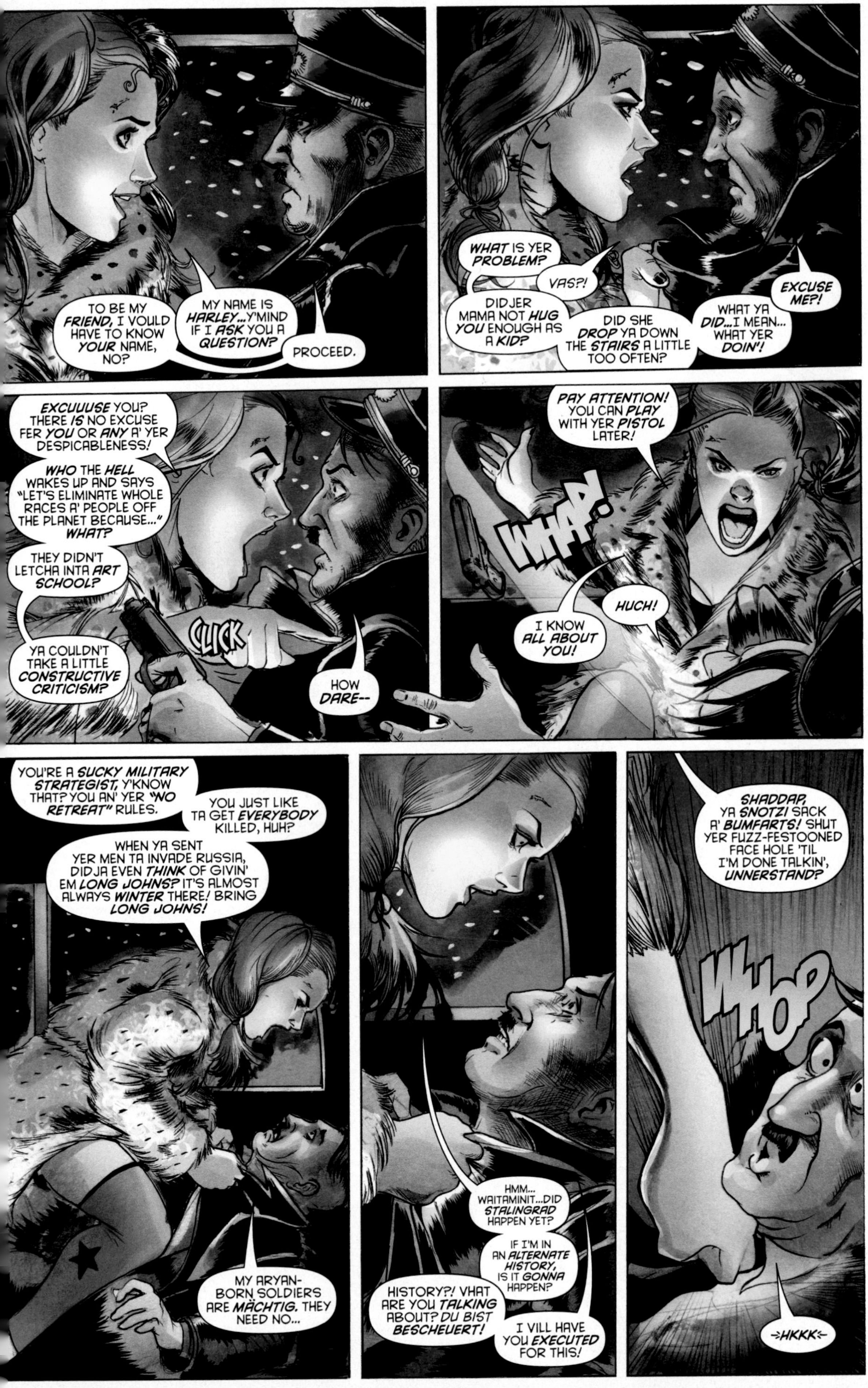

MY NAME IS HARLEY...Y'MIND IF I ASK YOU A QUESTION?
PROCEED.
TO BE MY FRIEND, I VOULD HAVE TO KNOW YOUR NAME, NO?
WHAT IS YER PROBLEM?
VAS?!
DIDJER MAMA NOT HUG YOU ENOUGH AS A KID?
DID SHE DROP YA DOWN THE STAIRS A LITTLE TOO OFTEN?
EXCUSE ME?!
WHAT YA DID...I MEAN... WHAT YER DOIN'!
EXCUUUSE YOU? THERE IS NO EXCUSE FER YOU OR ANY A' YER DESPICABLENESS!
WHO THE HELL WAKES UP AND SAYS "LET'S ELIMINATE WHOLE RACES A' PEOPLE OFF THE PLANET BECAUSE..." WHAT?
THEY DIDN'T LETCHA INTA ART SCHOOL?
YA COULDN'T TAKE A LITTLE CONSTRUCTIVE CRITICISM?
CLICK
HOW DARE--
PAY ATTENTION! YOU CAN PLAY WITH YER PISTOL LATER!
WHAP!
HUCH!
I KNOW ALL ABOUT YOU!
YOU'RE A SUCKY MILITARY STRATEGIST, Y'KNOW THAT? YOU AN' YER "NO RETREAT" RULES.
YOU JUST LIKE TA GET EVERYBODY KILLED, HUH?
WHEN YA SENT YER MEN TA INVADE RUSSIA, DIDJA EVEN THINK OF GIVIN' EM LONG JOHNS? IT'S ALMOST ALWAYS WINTER THERE! BRING LONG JOHNS!
MY ARYAN-BORN SOLDIERS ARE MÄCHTIG. THEY NEED NO...
HMM... WAITAMINIT...DID STALINGRAD HAPPEN YET?
IF I'M IN AN ALTERNATE HISTORY, IS IT GONNA HAPPEN?
HISTORY?! VHAT ARE YOU TALKING ABOUT? DU BIST BESCHEUERT!
I VILL HAVE YOU EXECUTED FOR THIS!
SHADDAP, YA SNOTZ! SACK A' BUMFARTS! SHUT YER FUZZ-FESTOONED FACE HOLE 'TIL I'M DONE TALKIN', UNNERSTAND?
WHOP
HKKK

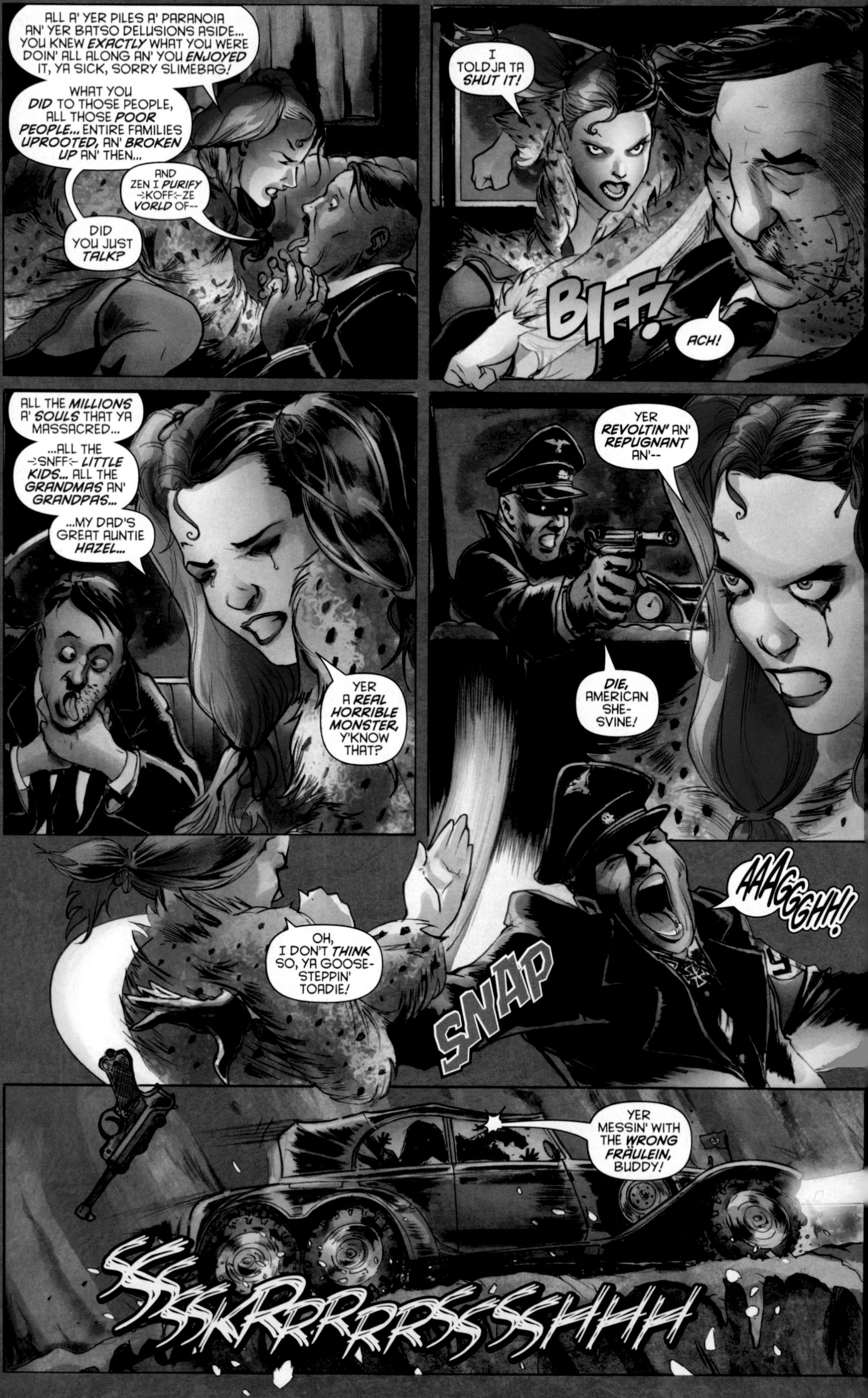
ALL A' YER PILES A' PARANOIA AN' YER BATSO DELUSIONS ASIDE... YOU KNEW EXACTLY WHAT YOU WERE DOIN' ALL ALONG AN' YOU ENJOYED IT, YA SICK, SORRY SLIMEBAG!
WHAT YOU DID TO THOSE PEOPLE, ALL THOSE POOR PEOPLE... ENTIRE FAMILIES UPROOTED, AN' BROKEN UP AN' THEN...
AND ZEN I PURIFY ⇒KOFF⇐ ZE VORLD OF--
DID YOU JUST TALK?
I TOLDJA TA SHUT IT!
BIFF!
ACH!
ALL THE MILLIONS A' SOULS THAT YA MASSACRED...
...ALL THE ⇒SNFF⇐ LITTLE KIDS... ALL THE GRANDMAS AN' GRANDPAS...
...MY DAD'S GREAT AUNTIE HAZEL...
YER A REAL HORRIBLE MONSTER, Y'KNOW THAT?
YER REVOLTIN' AN' REPUGNANT AN'--
DIE, AMERICAN SHE-SVINE!
OH, I DON'T THINK SO, YA GOOSE-STEPPIN' TOADIE!
SNAP
AAAGGGHH!
YER MESSIN' WITH THE WRONG FRÄULEIN, BUDDY!
SSSKRRRRRRSSSSHHH

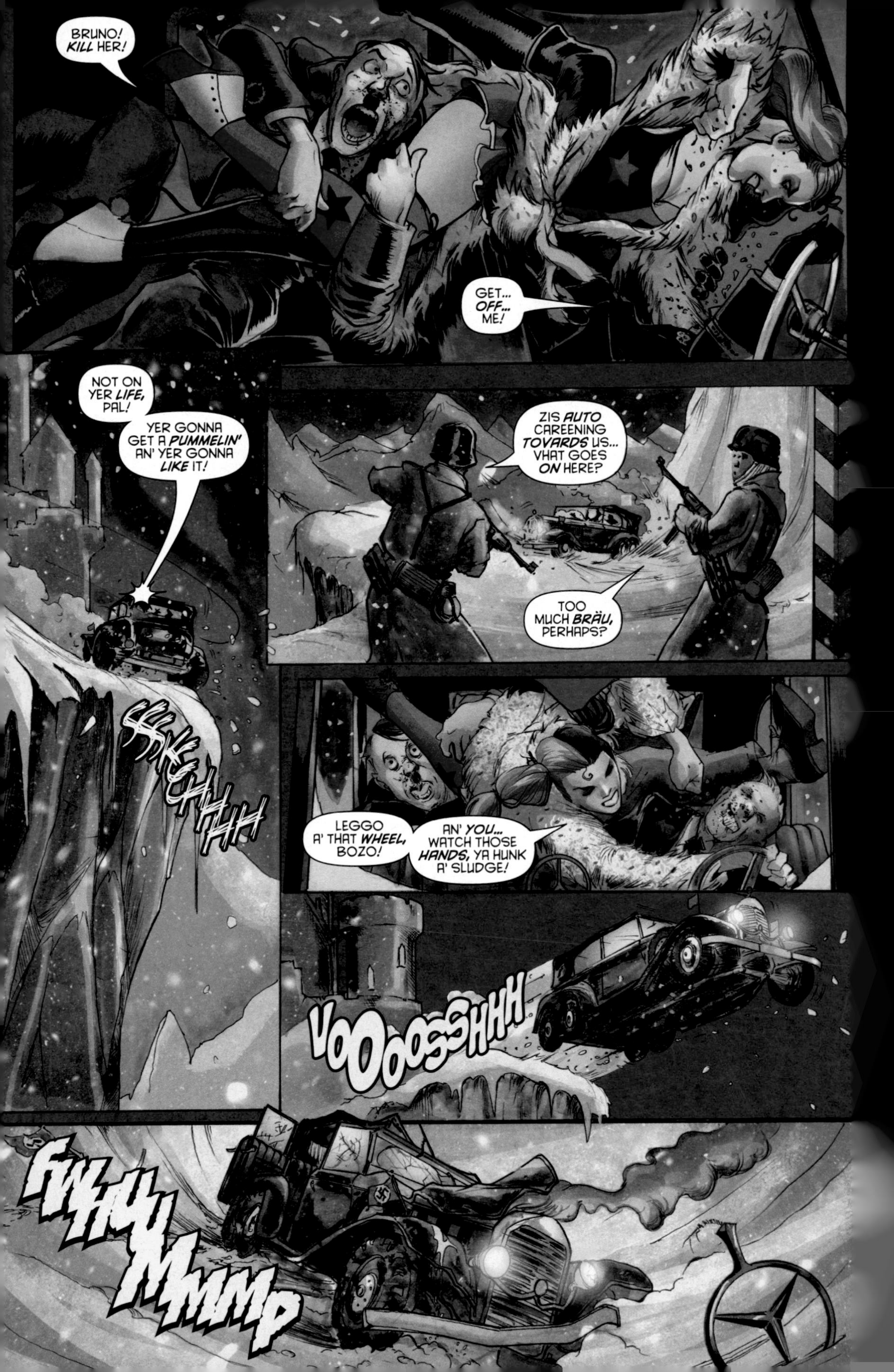
BRUNO! KILL HER!
GET... OFF... ME!
NOT ON YER LIFE, PAL!
YER GONNA GET A PUMMELIN' AN' YER GONNA LIKE IT!
SSKKCHHHHH
ZIS AUTO CAREENING TOVARDS US... VHAT GOES ON HERE?
TOO MUCH BRÄU, PERHAPS?
LEGGO A' THAT WHEEL, BOZO!
AN' YOU... WATCH THOSE HANDS, YA HUNK A' SLUDGE!
VOOOOSSHHH
FWHHUMMMP

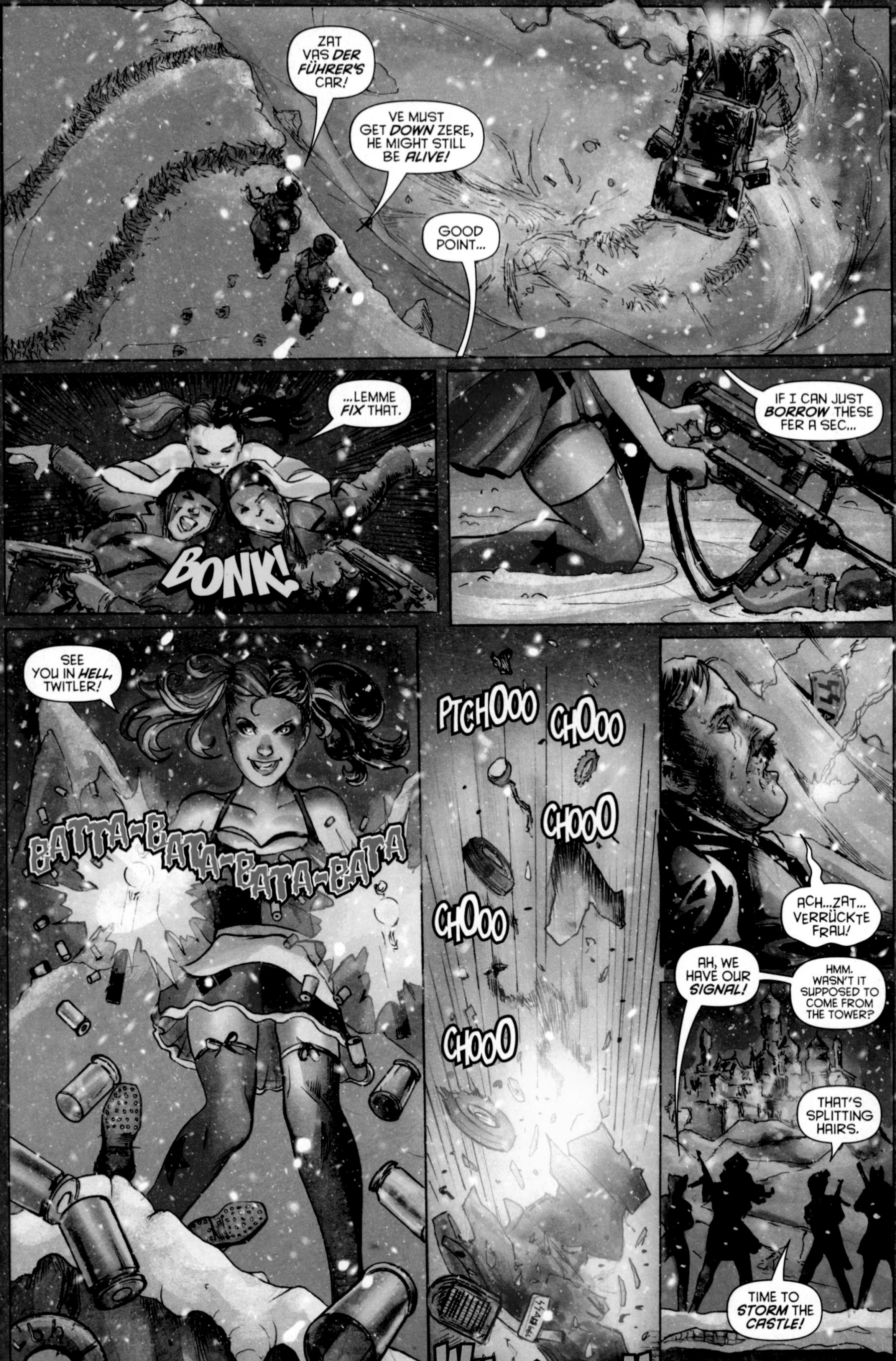
ZAT VAS DER FÜHRER'S CAR!
VE MUST GET DOWN ZERE, HE MIGHT STILL BE ALIVE!
GOOD POINT...
...LEMME FIX THAT.
BONK!
IF I CAN JUST BORROW THESE FER A SEC...
SEE YOU IN HELL, TWITLER!
BATTA-BATA-BATA-BATA
PTCHOOO
CHOOO
CHOOO
CHOOO
CHOOO
WHOOOOMM
ACH...ZAT... VERRÜCKTE FRAU!
AH, WE HAVE OUR SIGNAL!
HMM. WASN'T IT SUPPOSED TO COME FROM THE TOWER?
THAT'S SPLITTING HAIRS.
TIME TO STORM THE CASTLE!
Dar Cooke

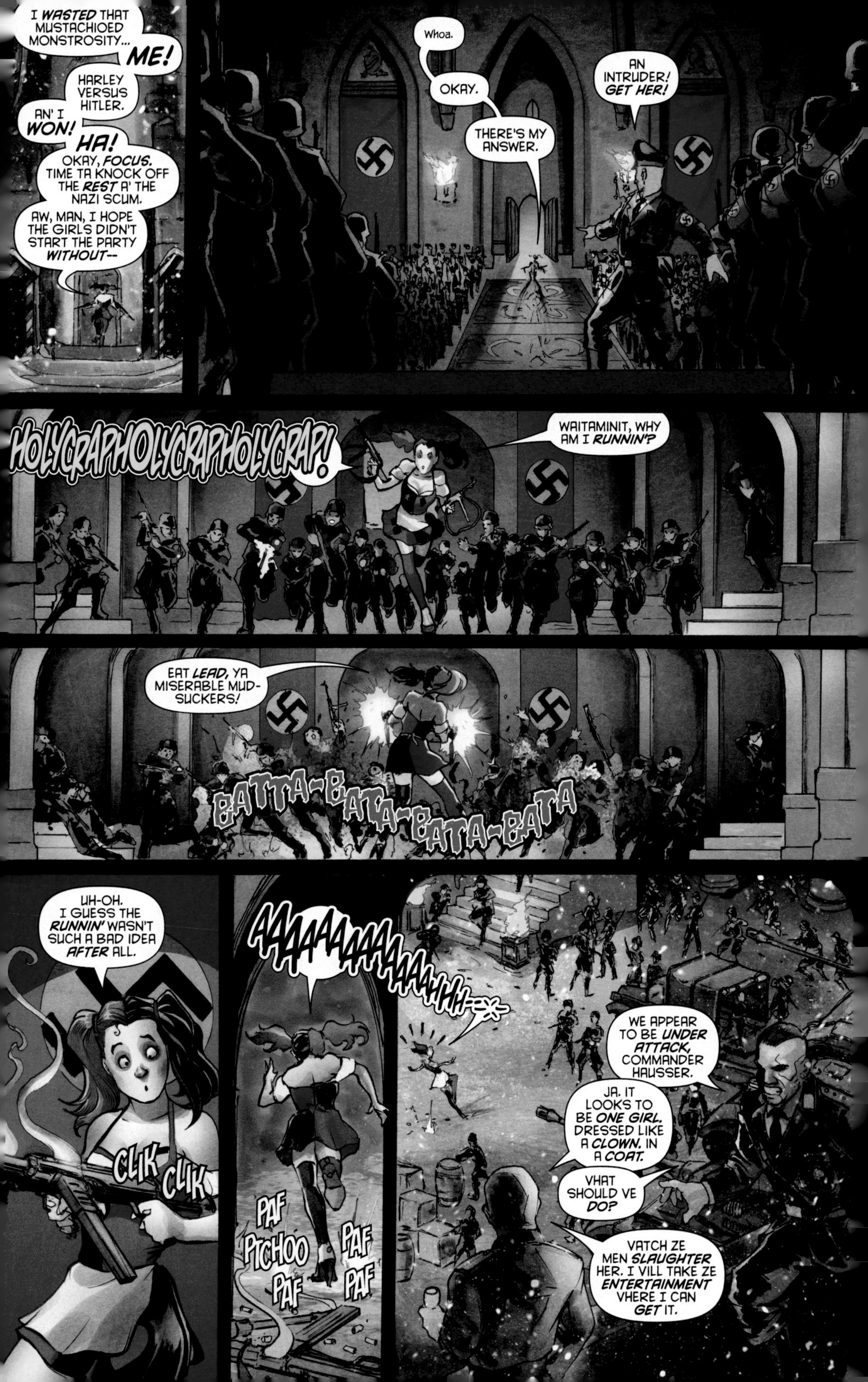
I WASTED THAT MUSTACHIOED MONSTROSITY... ME!
HARLEY VERSUS HITLER.
AN' I WON!
HA!
OKAY, FOCUS. TIME TA KNOCK OFF THE REST A' THE NAZI SCUM.
AW, MAN, I HOPE THE GIRLS DIDN'T START THE PARTY WITHOUT--
Whoa.
OKAY.
THERE'S MY ANSWER.
AN INTRUDER! GET HER!
HOLYCRAPHOLYCRAPHOLYCRAP!
WAITAMINIT, WHY AM I RUNNIN'?
EAT LEAD, YA MISERABLE MUD-SUCKERS!
BATTA-BATA-BATA-BATA
UH-OH. I GUESS THE RUNNIN' WASN'T SUCH A BAD IDEA AFTER ALL.
CLIK CLIK
AAAAAAAAAAAAAAHHH--
PAF PTCHOO PAF PAF PAF PAF
WE APPEAR TO BE UNDER ATTACK, COMMANDER HAUSSER.
JA. IT LOOKS TO BE ONE GIRL. DRESSED LIKE A CLOWN. IN A COAT.
VHAT SHOULD VE DO?
VATCH ZE MEN SLAUGHTER HER. I VILL TAKE ZE ENTERTAINMENT VHERE I CAN GET IT.

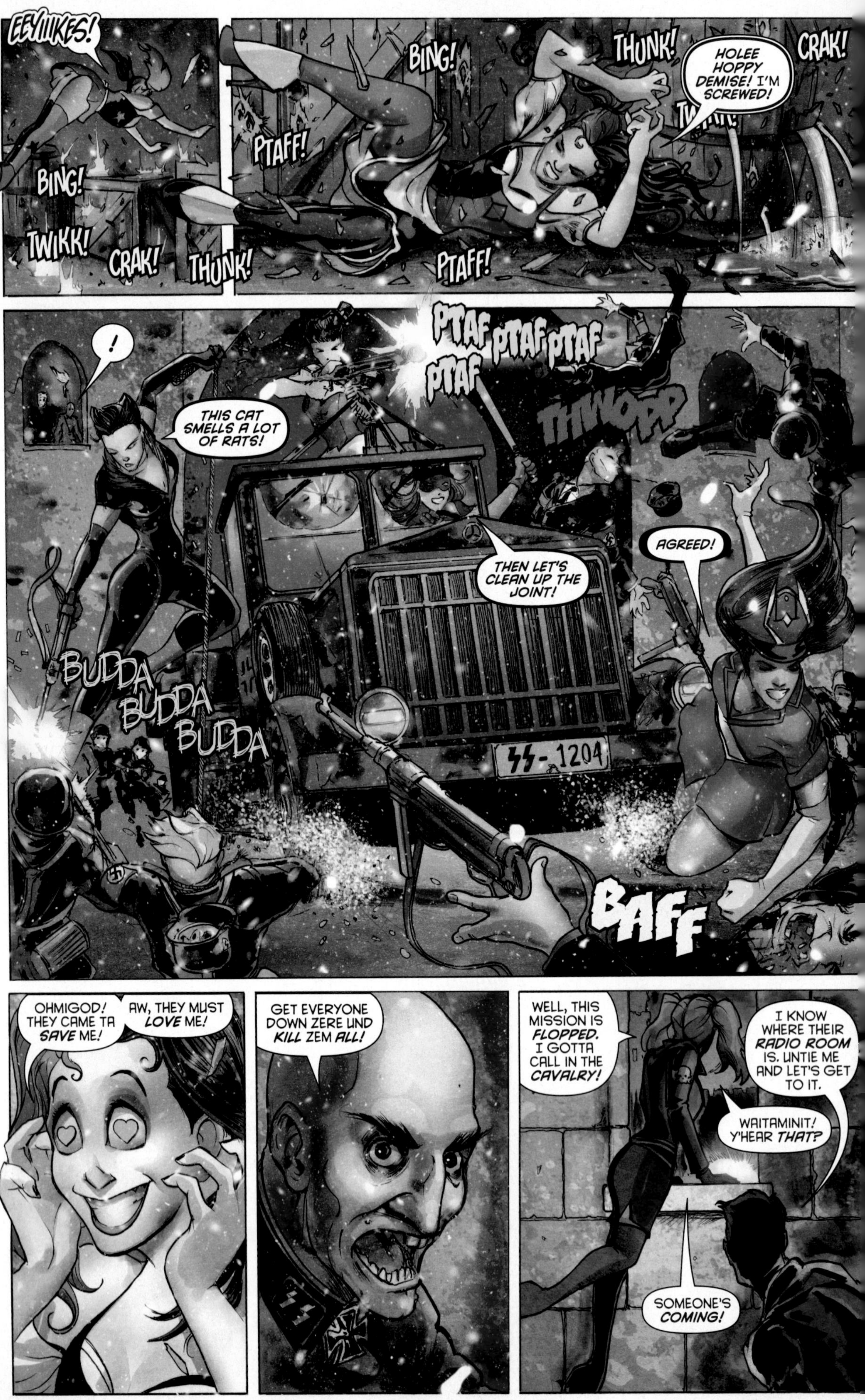
EEYIIIKES!
BING!
TWIKK!
CRAK!
THUNK!
PTAFF!
BING!
PTAFF!
THUNK!
HOLEE HOPPY DEMISE! I'M SCREWED!
CRAK!
!
THIS CAT SMELLS A LOT OF RATS!
PTAF PTAF PTAF PTAF
THWOPP
THEN LET'S CLEAN UP THE JOINT!
AGREED!
BUDDA BUDDA BUDDA
SS-1204
BAFF
OHMIGOD! THEY CAME TA SAVE ME!
AW, THEY MUST LOVE ME!
GET EVERYONE DOWN ZERE UND KILL ZEM ALL!
WELL, THIS MISSION IS FLOPPED. I GOTTA CALL IN THE CAVALRY!
I KNOW WHERE THEIR RADIO ROOM IS. UNTIE ME AND LET'S GET TO IT.
WAITAMINIT! Y'HEAR THAT?
SOMEONE'S COMING!

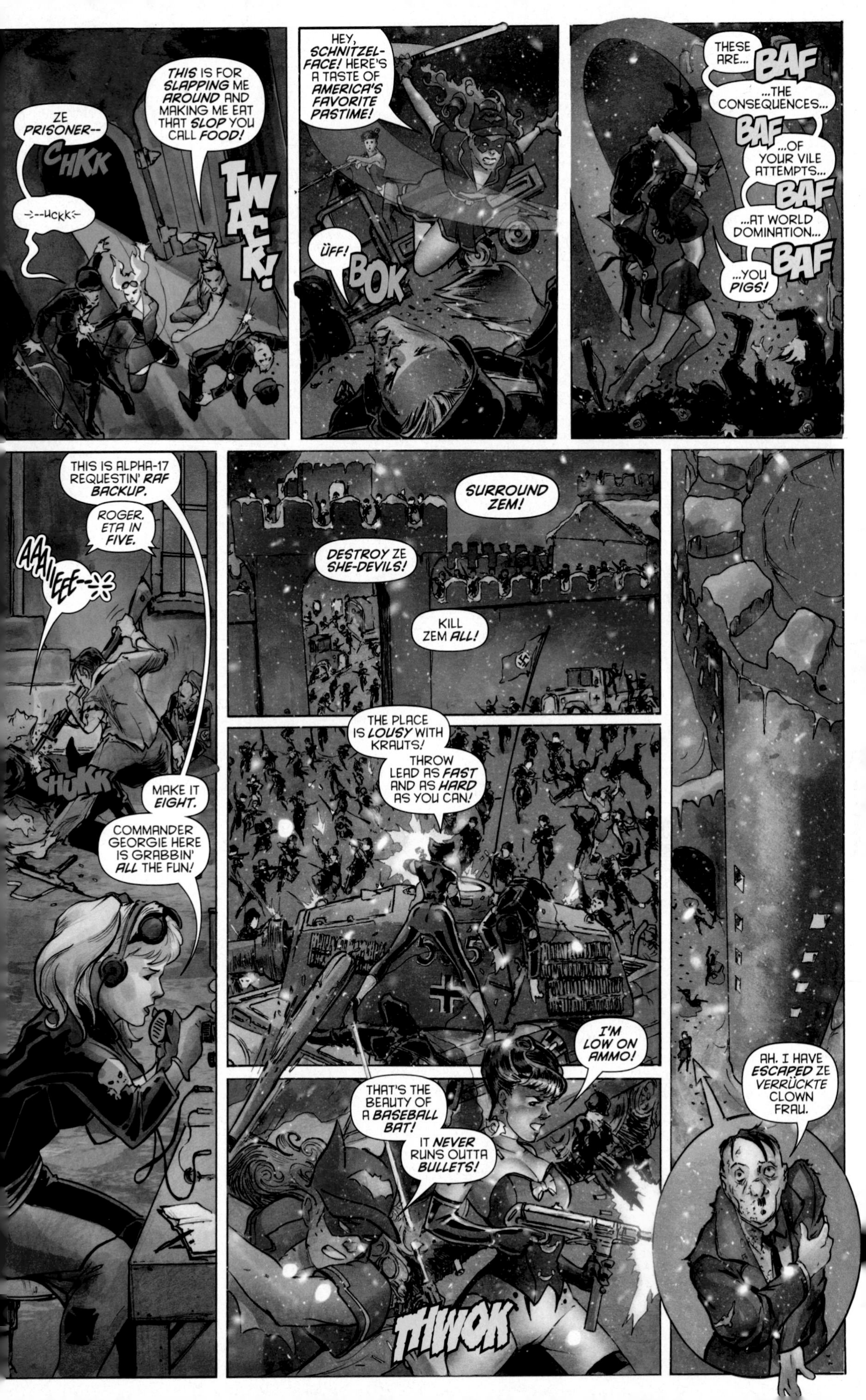
ZE PRISONER--
CHKK
--UCKK--
THIS IS FOR SLAPPING ME AROUND AND MAKING ME EAT THAT SLOP YOU CALL FOOD!
TWACK!
HEY, SCHNITZEL-FACE! HERE'S A TASTE OF AMERICA'S FAVORITE PASTIME!
ÜFF!
BOK
THESE ARE...
BAF
...THE CONSEQUENCES...
BAF
...OF YOUR VILE ATTEMPTS...
BAF
...AT WORLD DOMINATION...
BAF
...YOU PIGS!
THIS IS ALPHA-17 REQUESTIN' RAF BACKUP.
ROGER. ETA IN FIVE.
AAAIIEEE--
CHUKK
MAKE IT EIGHT.
COMMANDER GEORGIE HERE IS GRABBIN' ALL THE FUN!
SURROUND ZEM!
DESTROY ZE SHE-DEVILS!
KILL ZEM ALL!
THE PLACE IS LOUSY WITH KRAUTS!
THROW LEAD AS FAST AND AS HARD AS YOU CAN!
I'M LOW ON AMMO!
THAT'S THE BEAUTY OF A BASEBALL BAT!
IT NEVER RUNS OUTTA BULLETS!
THWOK
AH. I HAVE ESCAPED ZE VERRÜCKTE CLOWN FRAU.

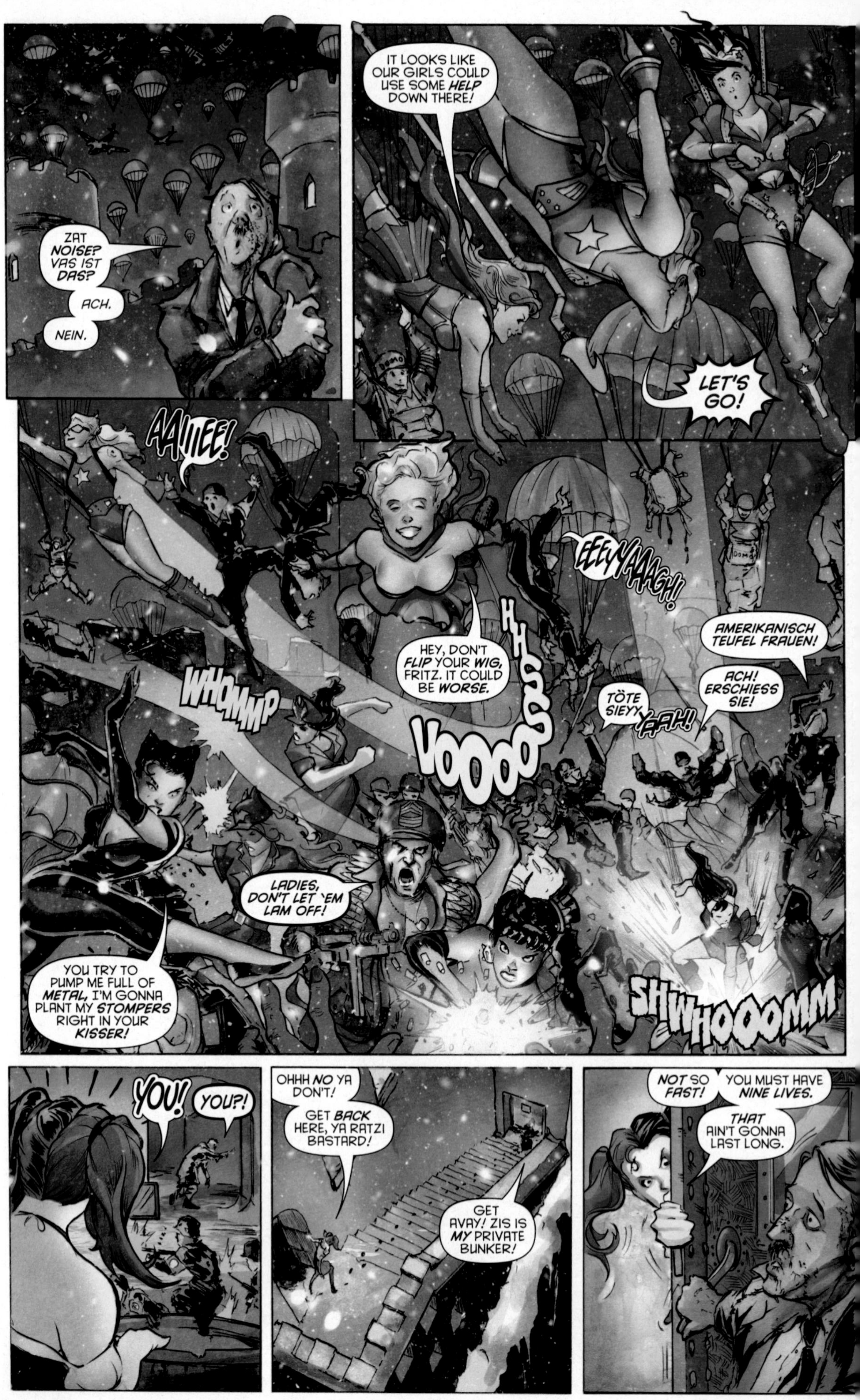
ZAT NOISE? VAS IST DAS?
ACH.
NEIN.
IT LOOKS LIKE OUR GIRLS COULD USE SOME HELP DOWN THERE!
LET'S GO!
AAIIIEE!
EEEYYAAAAGH!
HEY, DON'T FLIP YOUR WIG, FRITZ. IT COULD BE WORSE.
HHSSS
AMERIKANISCH TEUFEL FRAUEN!
ACH! ERSCHIESS SIE!
TÖTE SIEYYAAH!
WHOMMP
VOOOO
LADIES, DON'T LET 'EM LAM OFF!
YOU TRY TO PUMP ME FULL OF METAL, I'M GONNA PLANT MY STOMPERS RIGHT IN YOUR KISSER!
SHWHOOOMM
YOU!
YOU?!
OHHH NO YA DON'T!
GET BACK HERE, YA RATZI BASTARD!
GET AVAY! ZIS IS MY PRIVATE BUNKER!
NOT SO FAST!
YOU MUST HAVE NINE LIVES.
THAT AIN'T GONNA LAST LONG.

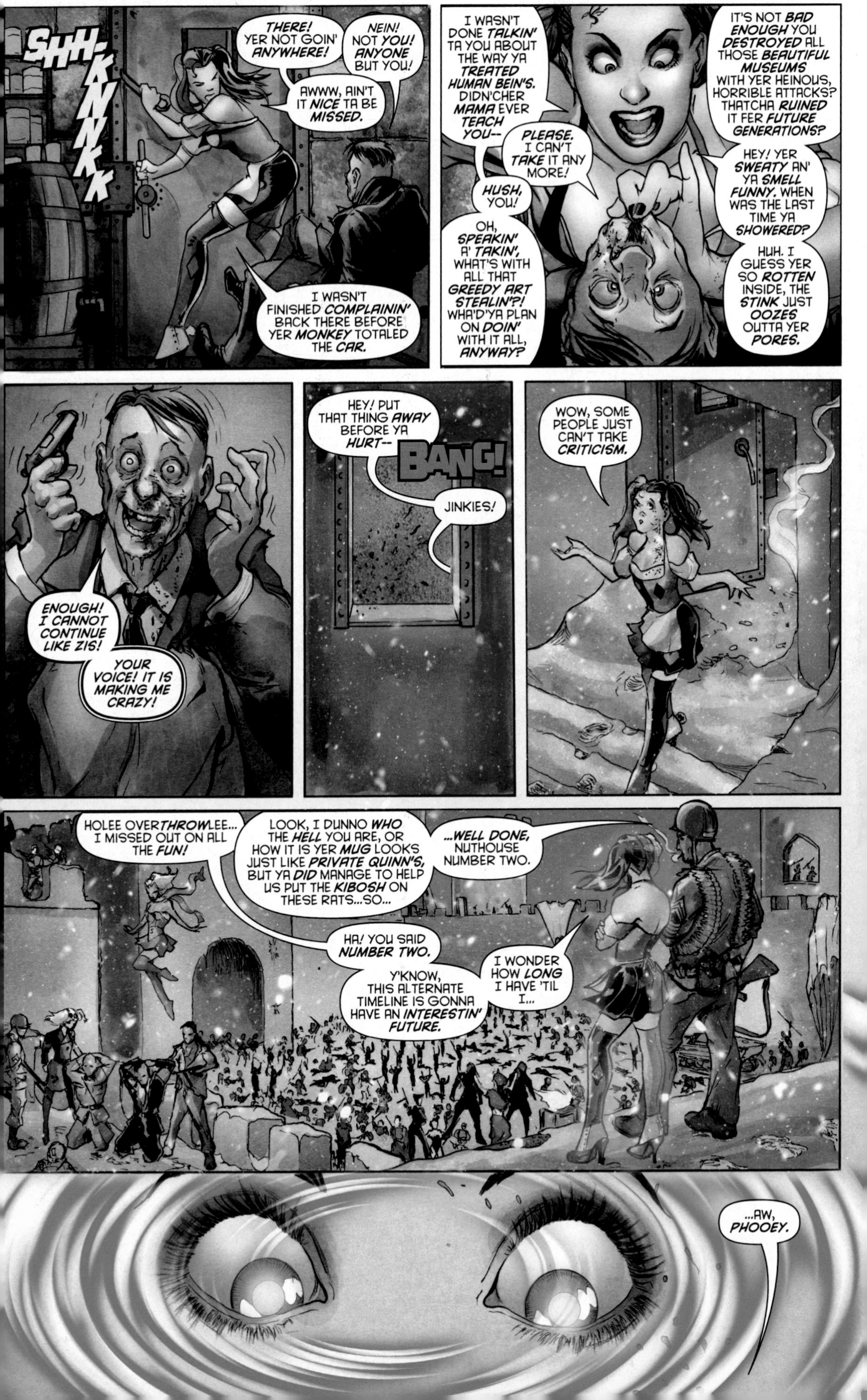
SHH-KNKKK
THERE! YER NOT GOIN' ANYWHERE!
NEIN! NOT YOU! ANYONE BUT YOU!
AWWW, AIN'T IT NICE TA BE MISSED.
I WASN'T FINISHED COMPLAININ' BACK THERE BEFORE YER MONKEY TOTALED THE CAR.
I WASN'T DONE TALKIN' TA YOU ABOUT THE WAY YA TREATED HUMAN BEIN'S. DIDN'CHER MAMA EVER TEACH YOU--
PLEASE. I CAN'T TAKE IT ANY MORE!
HUSH, YOU!
OH, SPEAKIN' A' TAKIN', WHAT'S WITH ALL THAT GREEDY ART STEALIN'?! WHA'D'YA PLAN ON DOIN' WITH IT ALL, ANYWAY?
IT'S NOT BAD ENOUGH YOU DESTROYED ALL THOSE BEAUTIFUL MUSEUMS WITH YER HEINOUS, HORRIBLE ATTACKS? THATCHA RUINED IT FER FUTURE GENERATIONS?
HEY! YER SWEATY AN' YA SMELL FUNNY. WHEN WAS THE LAST TIME YA SHOWERED?
HUH. I GUESS YER SO ROTTEN INSIDE, THE STINK JUST OOZES OUTTA YER PORES.
ENOUGH! I CANNOT CONTINUE LIKE ZIS!
YOUR VOICE! IT IS MAKING ME CRAZY!
HEY! PUT THAT THING AWAY BEFORE YA HURT--
BANG!
JINKIES!
WOW, SOME PEOPLE JUST CAN'T TAKE CRITICISM.
HOLEE OVERTHROWLEE... I MISSED OUT ON ALL THE FUN!
LOOK, I DUNNO WHO THE HELL YOU ARE, OR HOW IT IS YER MUG LOOKS JUST LIKE PRIVATE QUINN'S, BUT YA DID MANAGE TO HELP US PUT THE KIBOSH ON THESE RATS...SO...
...WELL DONE, NUTHOUSE NUMBER TWO.
HA! YOU SAID NUMBER TWO.
Y'KNOW, THIS ALTERNATE TIMELINE IS GONNA HAVE AN INTERESTIN' FUTURE.
I WONDER HOW LONG I HAVE 'TIL I...
...AW, PHOOEY.

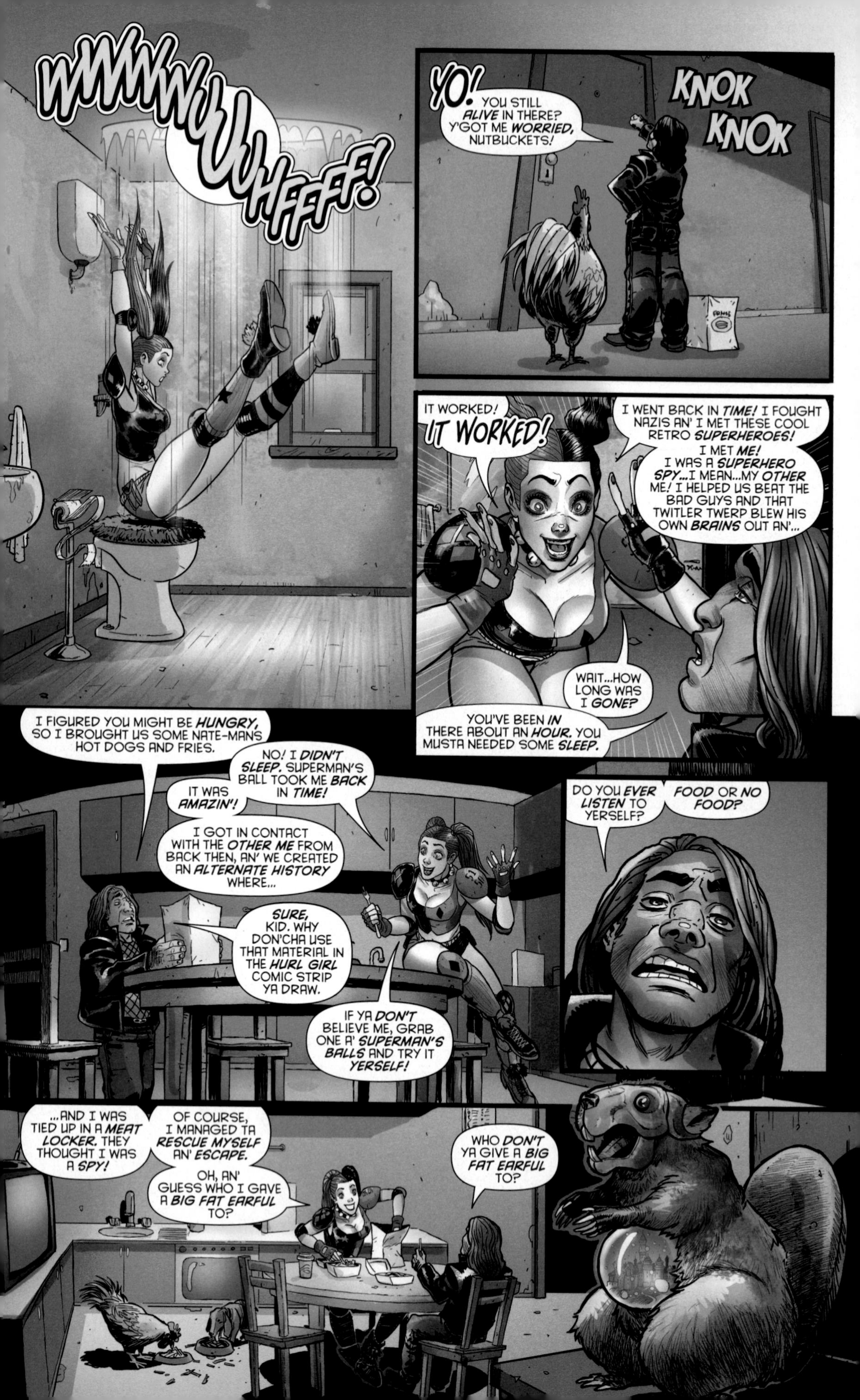

WWWWWUUUHFFFF!
YO! YOU STILL ALIVE IN THERE? Y'GOT ME WORRIED, NUTBUCKETS!
KNOK KNOK
IT WORKED! IT WORKED!
I WENT BACK IN TIME! I FOUGHT NAZIS AN' I MET THESE COOL RETRO SUPERHEROES!
I MET ME! I WAS A SUPERHERO SPY...I MEAN...MY OTHER ME! I HELPED US BEAT THE BAD GUYS AND THAT TWITLER TWERP BLEW HIS OWN BRAINS OUT AN'...
WAIT...HOW LONG WAS I GONE?
YOU'VE BEEN IN THERE ABOUT AN HOUR. YOU MUSTA NEEDED SOME SLEEP.
I FIGURED YOU MIGHT BE HUNGRY, SO I BROUGHT US SOME NATE-MANS HOT DOGS AND FRIES.
NO! I DIDN'T SLEEP. SUPERMAN'S BALL TOOK ME BACK IN TIME!
IT WAS AMAZIN'!
I GOT IN CONTACT WITH THE OTHER ME FROM BACK THEN, AN' WE CREATED AN ALTERNATE HISTORY WHERE...
SURE, KID. WHY DON'CHA USE THAT MATERIAL IN THE HURL GIRL COMIC STRIP YA DRAW.
IF YA DON'T BELIEVE ME, GRAB ONE A' SUPERMAN'S BALLS AND TRY IT YERSELF!
DO YOU EVER LISTEN TO YERSELF?
FOOD OR NO FOOD?
...AND I WAS TIED UP IN A MEAT LOCKER. THEY THOUGHT I WAS A SPY!
OF COURSE, I MANAGED TA RESCUE MYSELF AN' ESCAPE.
OH, AN' GUESS WHO I GAVE A BIG FAT EARFUL TO?
WHO DON'T YA GIVE A BIG FAT EARFUL TO?

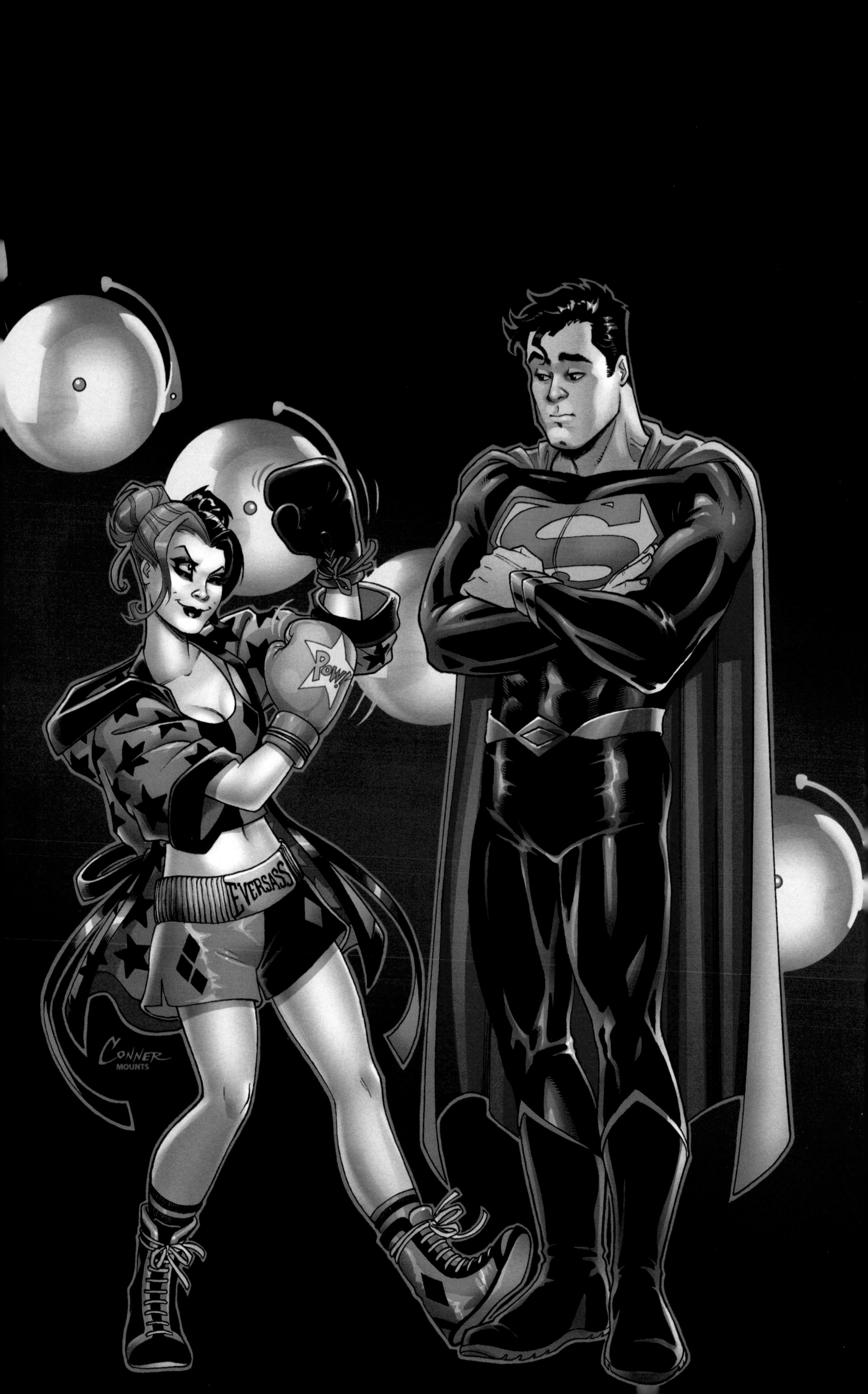
POW!
EVERSASS
CONNER
MOUNTS

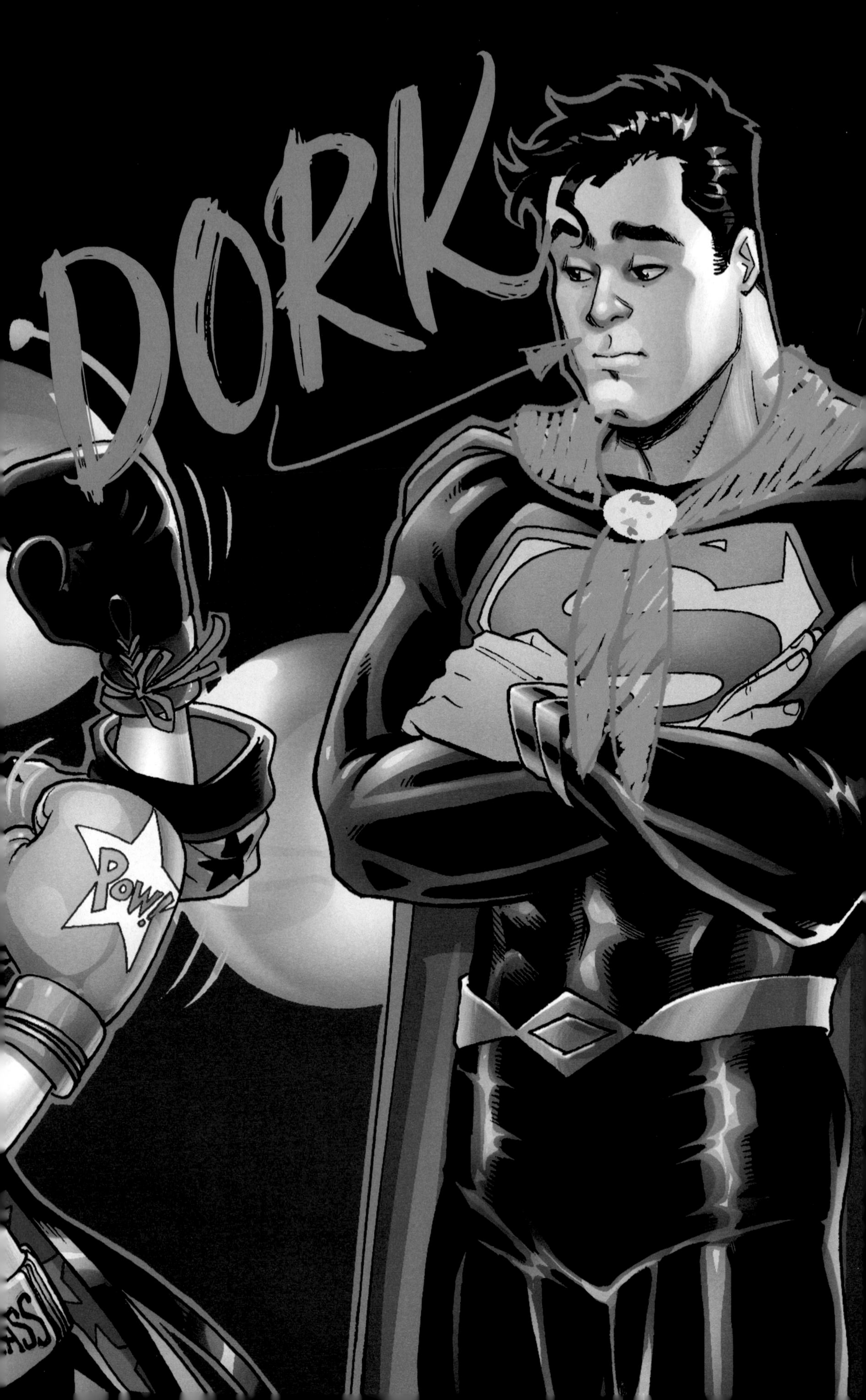
DORK
POW!

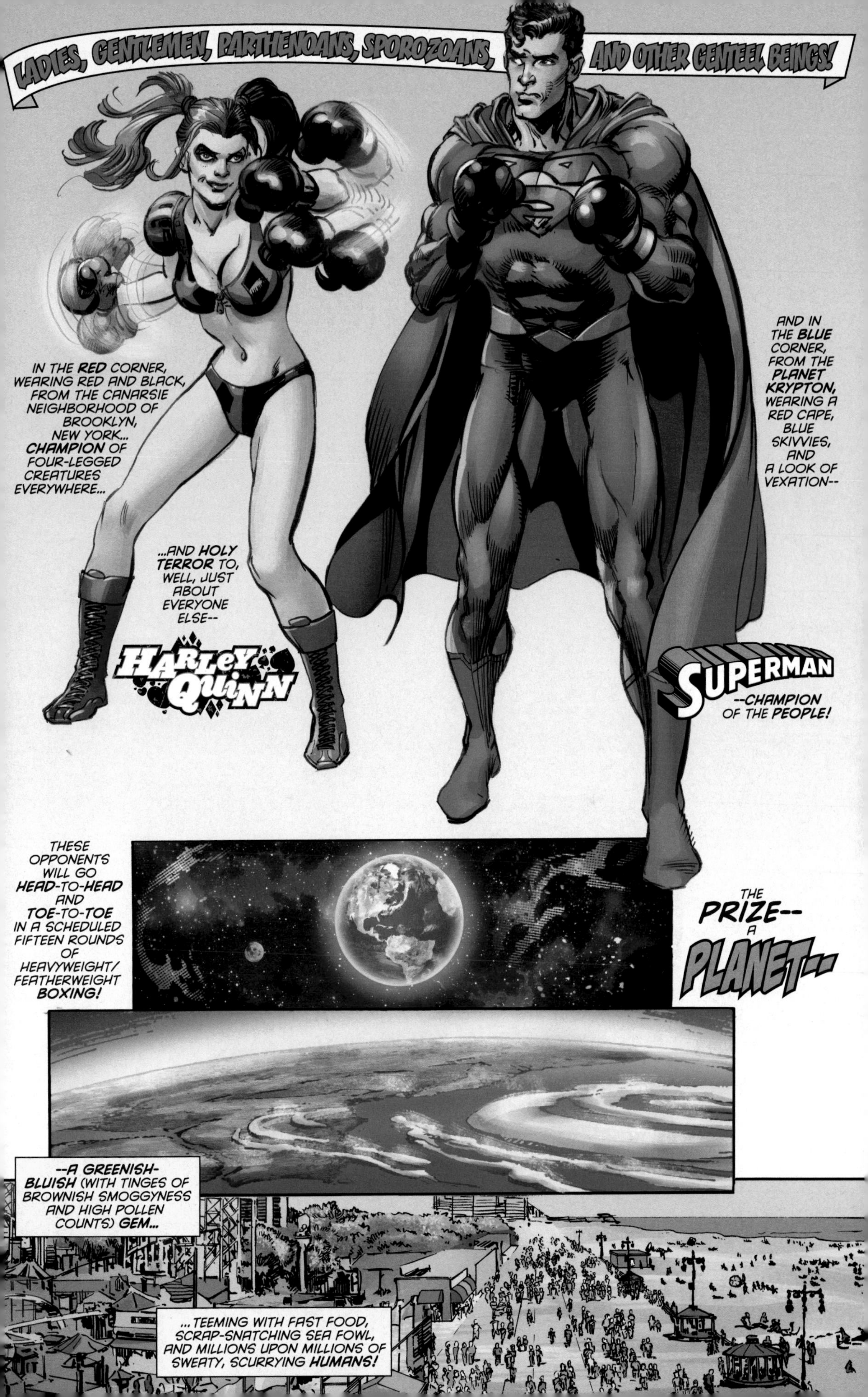

LADIES, GENTLEMEN, PARTHENOANS, SPOROZOANS, AND OTHER GENTEEL BEINGS!
IN THE RED CORNER, WEARING RED AND BLACK, FROM THE CANARSIE NEIGHBORHOOD OF BROOKLYN, NEW YORK... CHAMPION OF FOUR-LEGGED CREATURES EVERYWHERE...
...AND HOLY TERROR TO, WELL, JUST ABOUT EVERYONE ELSE--
HARLEY QUINN
AND IN THE BLUE CORNER, FROM THE PLANET KRYPTON, WEARING A RED CAPE, BLUE SKIVVIES, AND A LOOK OF VEXATION--
SUPERMAN
--CHAMPION OF THE PEOPLE!
THESE OPPONENTS WILL GO HEAD-TO-HEAD AND TOE-TO-TOE IN A SCHEDULED FIFTEEN ROUNDS OF HEAVYWEIGHT/ FEATHERWEIGHT BOXING!
THE PRIZE-- A PLANET--
--A GREENISH-BLUISH (WITH TINGES OF BROWNISH SMOGGYNESS AND HIGH POLLEN COUNTS) GEM...
...TEEMING WITH FAST FOOD, SCRAP-SNATCHING SEA FOWL, AND MILLIONS UPON MILLIONS OF SWEATY, SCURRYING HUMANS!

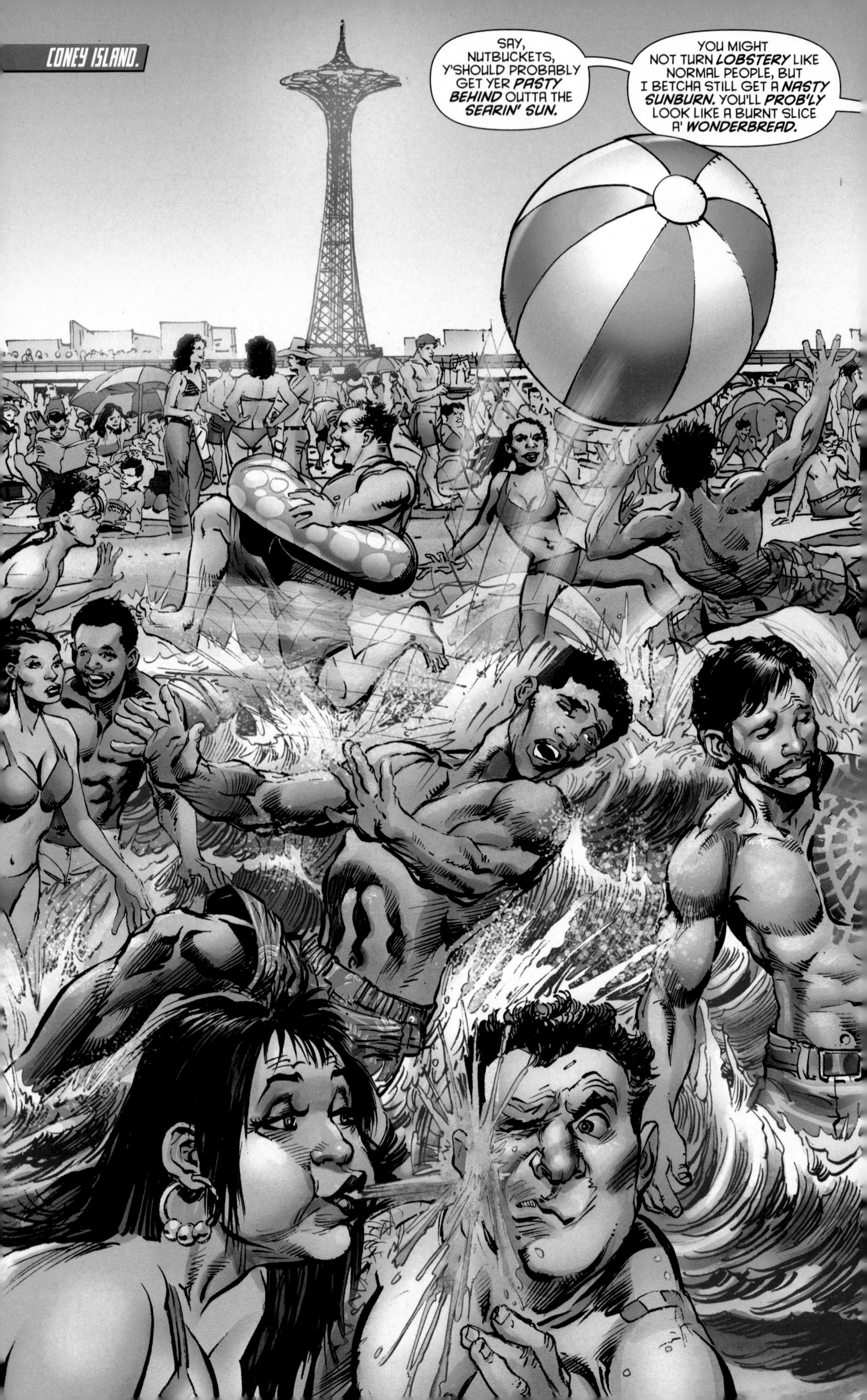
CONEY ISLAND.
SAY, NUTBUCKETS, Y'SHOULD PROBABLY GET YER PASTY BEHIND OUTTA THE SEARIN' SUN.
YOU MIGHT NOT TURN LOBSTERY LIKE NORMAL PEOPLE, BUT I BETCHA STILL GET A NASTY SUNBURN. YOU'LL PROB'LY LOOK LIKE A BURNT SLICE A' WONDERBREAD.

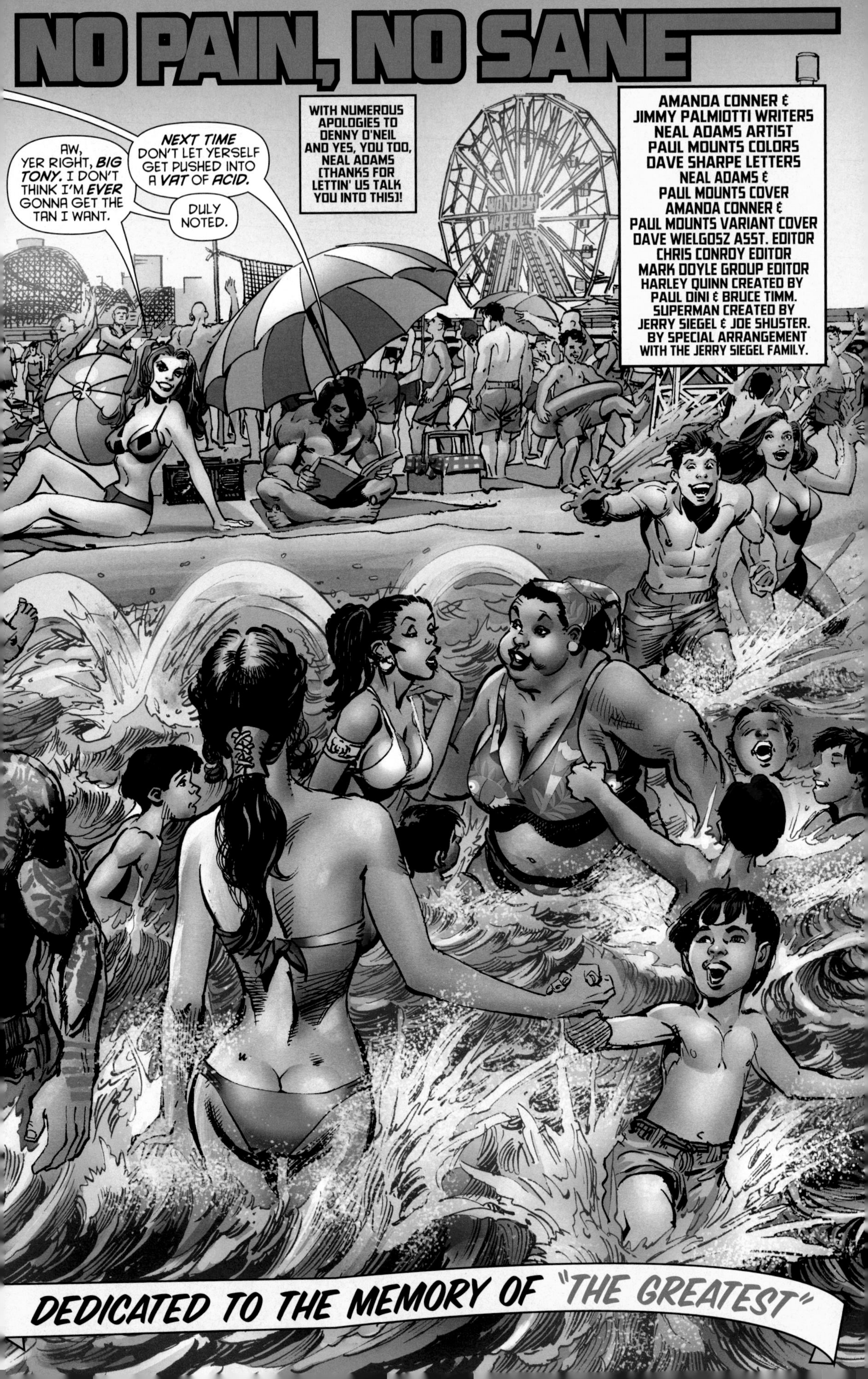
NO PAIN, NO SANE
AW, YER RIGHT, BIG TONY. I DON'T THINK I'M EVER GONNA GET THE TAN I WANT.
NEXT TIME DON'T LET YERSELF GET PUSHED INTO A VAT OF ACID.
DULY NOTED.
WITH NUMEROUS APOLOGIES TO DENNY O'NEIL AND YES, YOU TOO, NEAL ADAMS [THANKS FOR LETTIN' US TALK YOU INTO THIS]!
AMANDA CONNER & JIMMY PALMIOTTI WRITERS
NEAL ADAMS ARTIST
PAUL MOUNTS COLORS
DAVE SHARPE LETTERS
NEAL ADAMS & PAUL MOUNTS COVER
AMANDA CONNER & PAUL MOUNTS VARIANT COVER
DAVE WIELGOSZ ASST. EDITOR
CHRIS CONROY EDITOR
MARK DOYLE GROUP EDITOR
HARLEY QUINN CREATED BY PAUL DINI & BRUCE TIMM.
SUPERMAN CREATED BY JERRY SIEGEL & JOE SHUSTER.
BY SPECIAL ARRANGEMENT WITH THE JERRY SIEGEL FAMILY.
DEDICATED TO THE MEMORY OF "THE GREATEST"

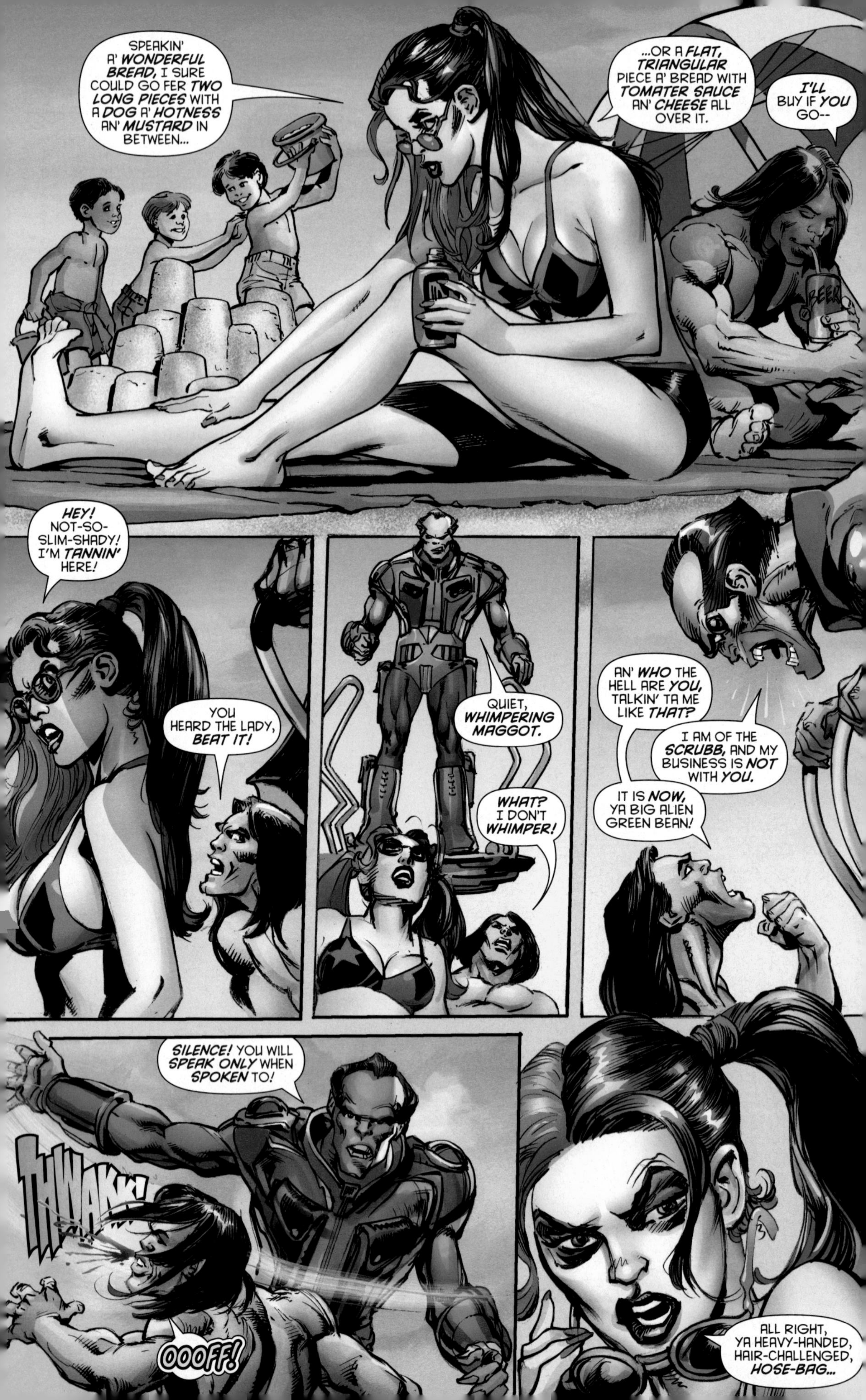
SPEAKIN' A' WONDERFUL BREAD, I SURE COULD GO FER TWO LONG PIECES WITH A DOG A' HOTNESS AN' MUSTARD IN BETWEEN...
...OR A FLAT, TRIANGULAR PIECE A' BREAD WITH TOMATER SAUCE AN' CHEESE ALL OVER IT.
I'LL BUY IF YOU GO--
BEER
HEY! NOT-SO-SLIM-SHADY! I'M TANNIN' HERE!
YOU HEARD THE LADY, BEAT IT!
QUIET, WHIMPERING MAGGOT.
WHAT? I DON'T WHIMPER!
AN' WHO THE HELL ARE YOU, TALKIN' TA ME LIKE THAT?
I AM OF THE SCRUBB, AND MY BUSINESS IS NOT WITH YOU.
IT IS NOW, YA BIG ALIEN GREEN BEAN!
SILENCE! YOU WILL SPEAK ONLY WHEN SPOKEN TO!
THWAKK!
OOOFF!
ALL RIGHT, YA HEAVY-HANDED, HAIR-CHALLENGED, HOSE-BAG...

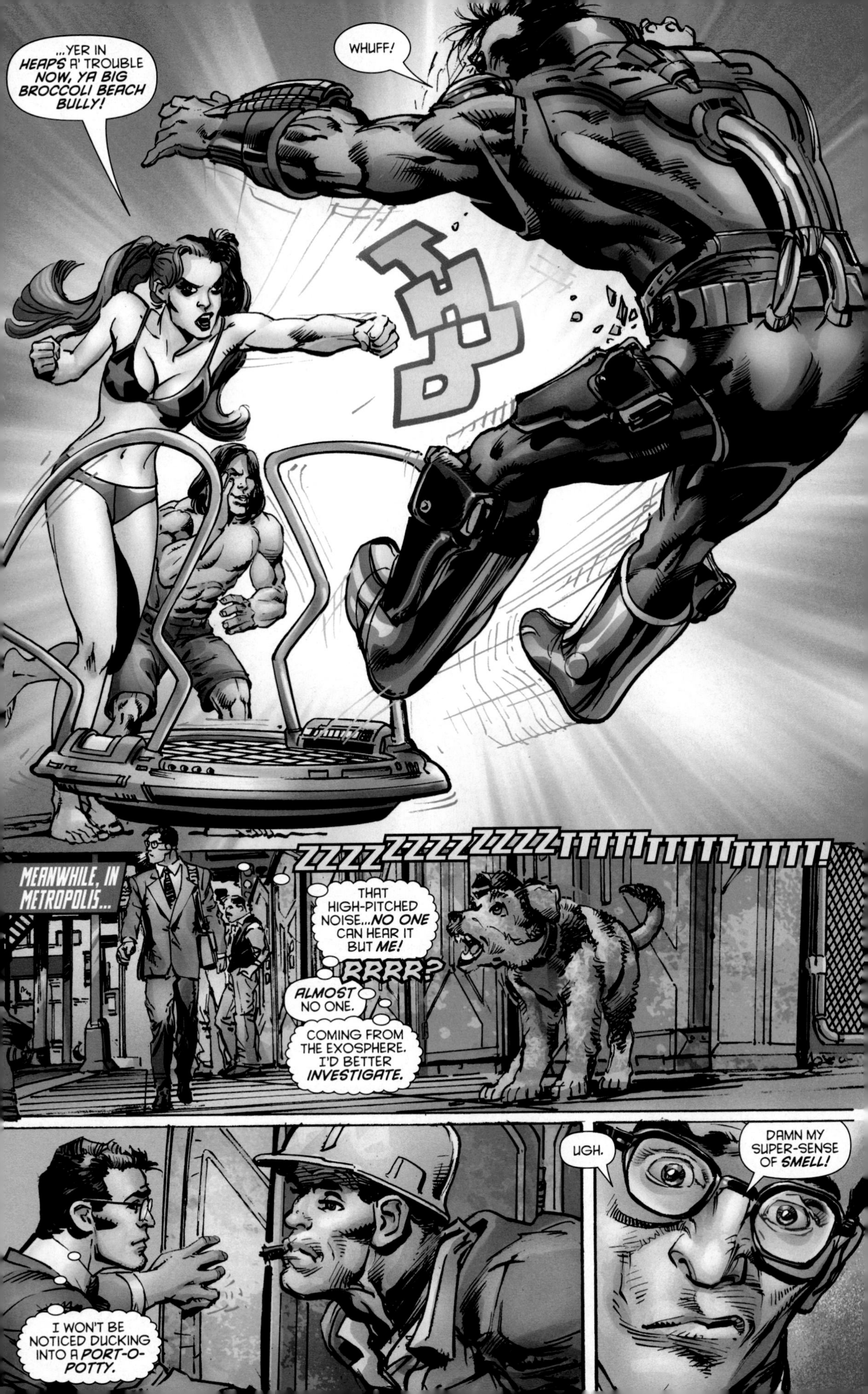
...YER IN HEAPS A' TROUBLE NOW, YA BIG BROCCOLI BEACH BULLY!
WHUFF!
THUD
MEANWHILE, IN METROPOLIS...
ZZZZZZZZZZZZZTTTTTTTTTTTTTTT!
THAT HIGH-PITCHED NOISE...NO ONE CAN HEAR IT BUT ME!
RRRR?
ALMOST NO ONE.
COMING FROM THE EXOSPHERE. I'D BETTER INVESTIGATE.
I WON'T BE NOTICED DUCKING INTO A PORT-O-POTTY.
UGH.
DAMN MY SUPER-SENSE OF SMELL!

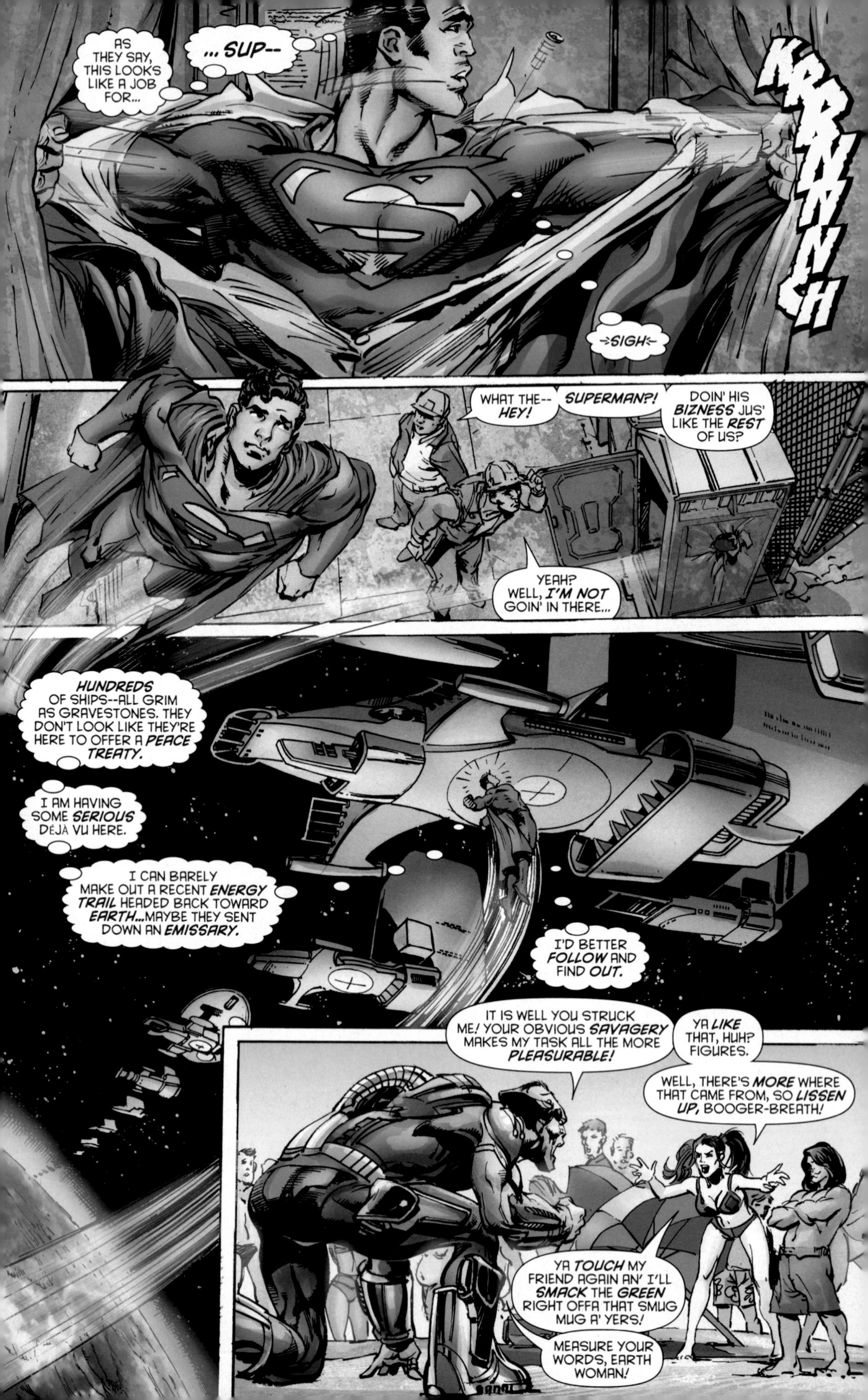

AS THEY SAY, THIS LOOKS LIKE A JOB FOR...
...SUP--
KRRUNCH
SIGH
WHAT THE-- HEY!
SUPERMAN?!
DOIN' HIS BIZNESS JUS' LIKE THE REST OF US?
YEAH? WELL, I'M NOT GOIN' IN THERE...
HUNDREDS OF SHIPS--ALL GRIM AS GRAVESTONES. THEY DON'T LOOK LIKE THEY'RE HERE TO OFFER A PEACE TREATY.
I AM HAVING SOME SERIOUS DÉJÀ VU HERE.
I CAN BARELY MAKE OUT A RECENT ENERGY TRAIL HEADED BACK TOWARD EARTH...MAYBE THEY SENT DOWN AN EMISSARY.
I'D BETTER FOLLOW AND FIND OUT.
IT IS WELL YOU STRUCK ME! YOUR OBVIOUS SAVAGERY MAKES MY TASK ALL THE MORE PLEASURABLE!
YA LIKE THAT, HUH? FIGURES.
WELL, THERE'S MORE WHERE THAT CAME FROM, SO LISSEN UP, BOOGER-BREATH!
YA TOUCH MY FRIEND AGAIN AN' I'LL SMACK THE GREEN RIGHT OFFA THAT SMUG MUG A' YERS!
MEASURE YOUR WORDS, EARTH WOMAN!

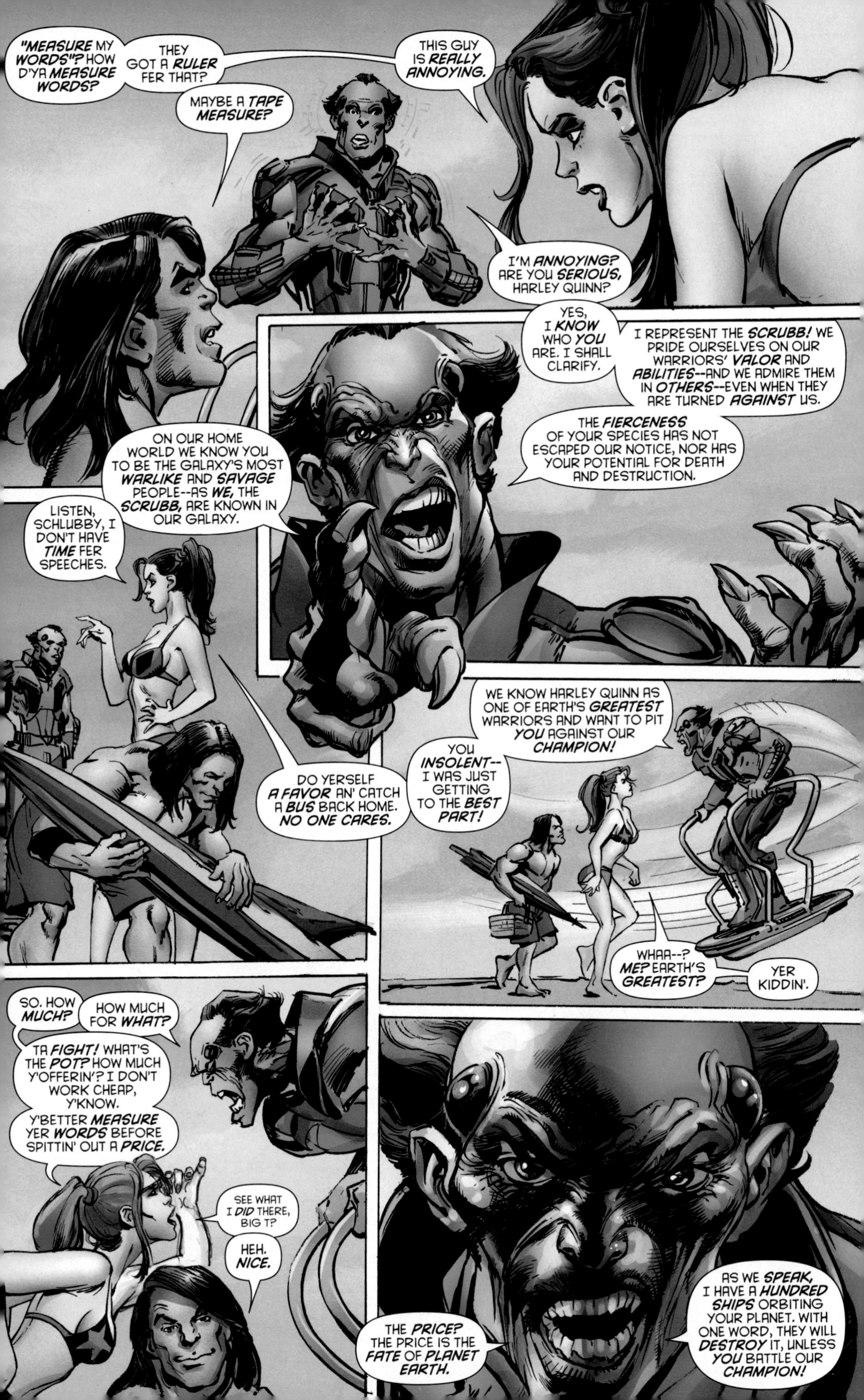
"MEASURE MY WORDS"? HOW D'YA MEASURE WORDS?
THEY GOT A RULER FER THAT?
THIS GUY IS REALLY ANNOYING.
MAYBE A TAPE MEASURE?
I'M ANNOYING? ARE YOU SERIOUS, HARLEY QUINN?
YES, I KNOW WHO YOU ARE. I SHALL CLARIFY.
I REPRESENT THE SCRUBB! WE PRIDE OURSELVES ON OUR WARRIORS' VALOR AND ABILITIES--AND WE ADMIRE THEM IN OTHERS--EVEN WHEN THEY ARE TURNED AGAINST US.
THE FIERCENESS OF YOUR SPECIES HAS NOT ESCAPED OUR NOTICE, NOR HAS YOUR POTENTIAL FOR DEATH AND DESTRUCTION.
ON OUR HOME WORLD WE KNOW YOU TO BE THE GALAXY'S MOST WARLIKE AND SAVAGE PEOPLE--AS WE, THE SCRUBB, ARE KNOWN IN OUR GALAXY.
LISTEN, SCHLUBBY, I DON'T HAVE TIME FER SPEECHES.
DO YERSELF A FAVOR AN' CATCH A BUS BACK HOME. NO ONE CARES.
YOU INSOLENT-- I WAS JUST GETTING TO THE BEST PART!
WE KNOW HARLEY QUINN AS ONE OF EARTH'S GREATEST WARRIORS AND WANT TO PIT YOU AGAINST OUR CHAMPION!
WHAA--? ME? EARTH'S GREATEST?
YER KIDDIN'.
SO. HOW MUCH?
HOW MUCH FOR WHAT?
TA FIGHT! WHAT'S THE POT? HOW MUCH Y'OFFERIN'? I DON'T WORK CHEAP, Y'KNOW.
Y'BETTER MEASURE YER WORDS BEFORE SPITTIN' OUT A PRICE.
SEE WHAT I DID THERE, BIG T?
HEH. NICE.
THE PRICE? THE PRICE IS THE FATE OF PLANET EARTH.
AS WE SPEAK, I HAVE A HUNDRED SHIPS ORBITING YOUR PLANET. WITH ONE WORD, THEY WILL DESTROY IT, UNLESS YOU BATTLE OUR CHAMPION!

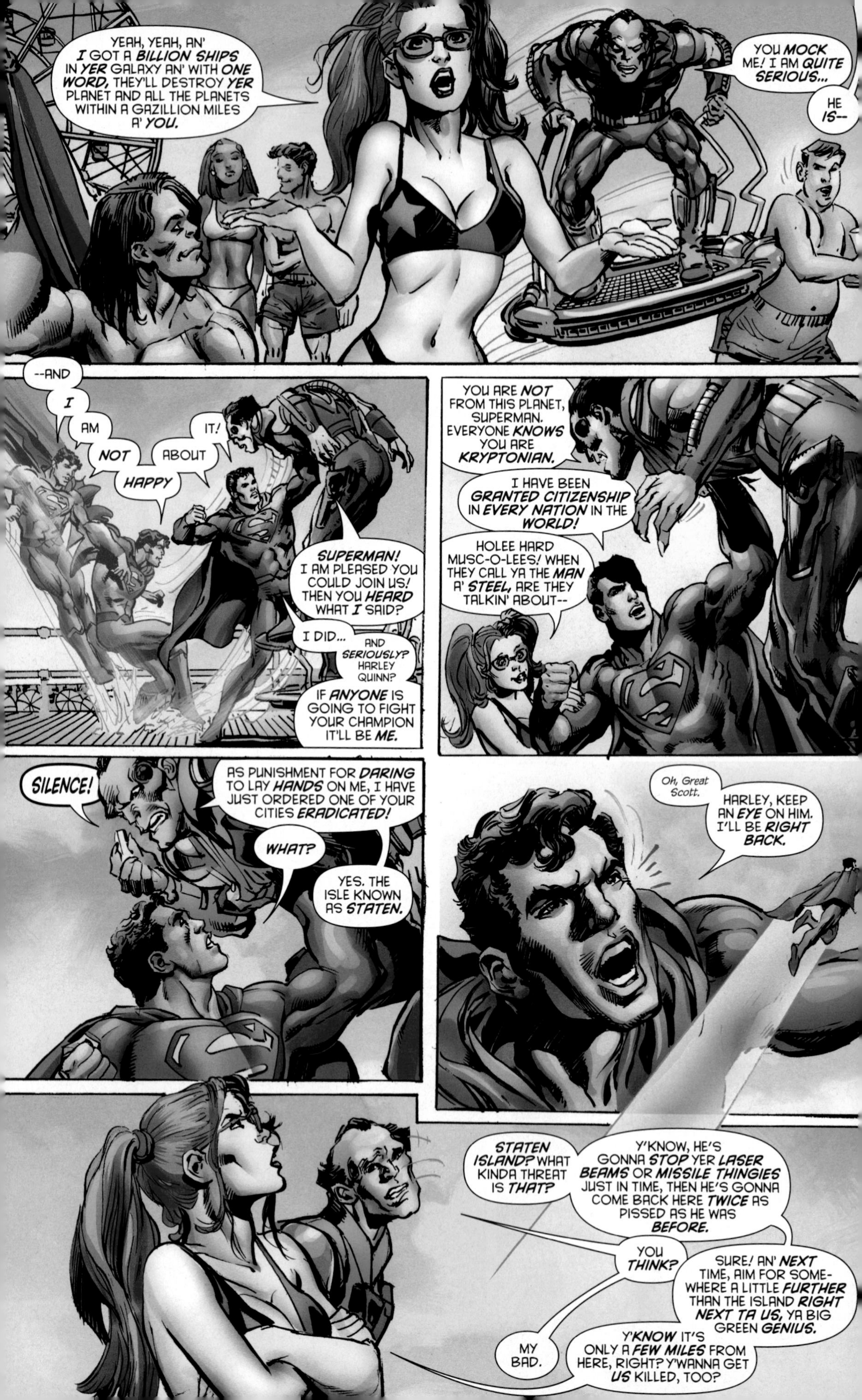
YEAH, YEAH, AN' I GOT A BILLION SHIPS IN YER GALAXY AN' WITH ONE WORD, THEY'LL DESTROY YER PLANET AND ALL THE PLANETS WITHIN A GAZILLION MILES A' YOU.
YOU MOCK ME! I AM QUITE SERIOUS...
HE IS--
--AND
I
AM
NOT
HAPPY
ABOUT
IT!
SUPERMAN! I AM PLEASED YOU COULD JOIN US! THEN YOU HEARD WHAT I SAID?
I DID...
AND SERIOUSLY? HARLEY QUINN?
IF ANYONE IS GOING TO FIGHT YOUR CHAMPION IT'LL BE ME.
YOU ARE NOT FROM THIS PLANET, SUPERMAN. EVERYONE KNOWS YOU ARE KRYPTONIAN.
I HAVE BEEN GRANTED CITIZENSHIP IN EVERY NATION IN THE WORLD!
HOLEE HARD MUSC-O-LEES! WHEN THEY CALL YA THE MAN A' STEEL, ARE THEY TALKIN' ABOUT--
SILENCE!
AS PUNISHMENT FOR DARING TO LAY HANDS ON ME, I HAVE JUST ORDERED ONE OF YOUR CITIES ERADICATED!
WHAT?
YES. THE ISLE KNOWN AS STATEN.
Oh, Great Scott.
HARLEY, KEEP AN EYE ON HIM. I'LL BE RIGHT BACK.
STATEN ISLAND? WHAT KINDA THREAT IS THAT?
Y'KNOW, HE'S GONNA STOP YER LASER BEAMS OR MISSILE THINGIES JUST IN TIME, THEN HE'S GONNA COME BACK HERE TWICE AS PISSED AS HE WAS BEFORE.
YOU THINK?
SURE! AN' NEXT TIME, AIM FOR SOME-WHERE A LITTLE FURTHER THAN THE ISLAND RIGHT NEXT TA US, YA BIG GREEN GENIUS.
MY BAD.
Y'KNOW IT'S ONLY A FEW MILES FROM HERE, RIGHT? Y'WANNA GET US KILLED, TOO?

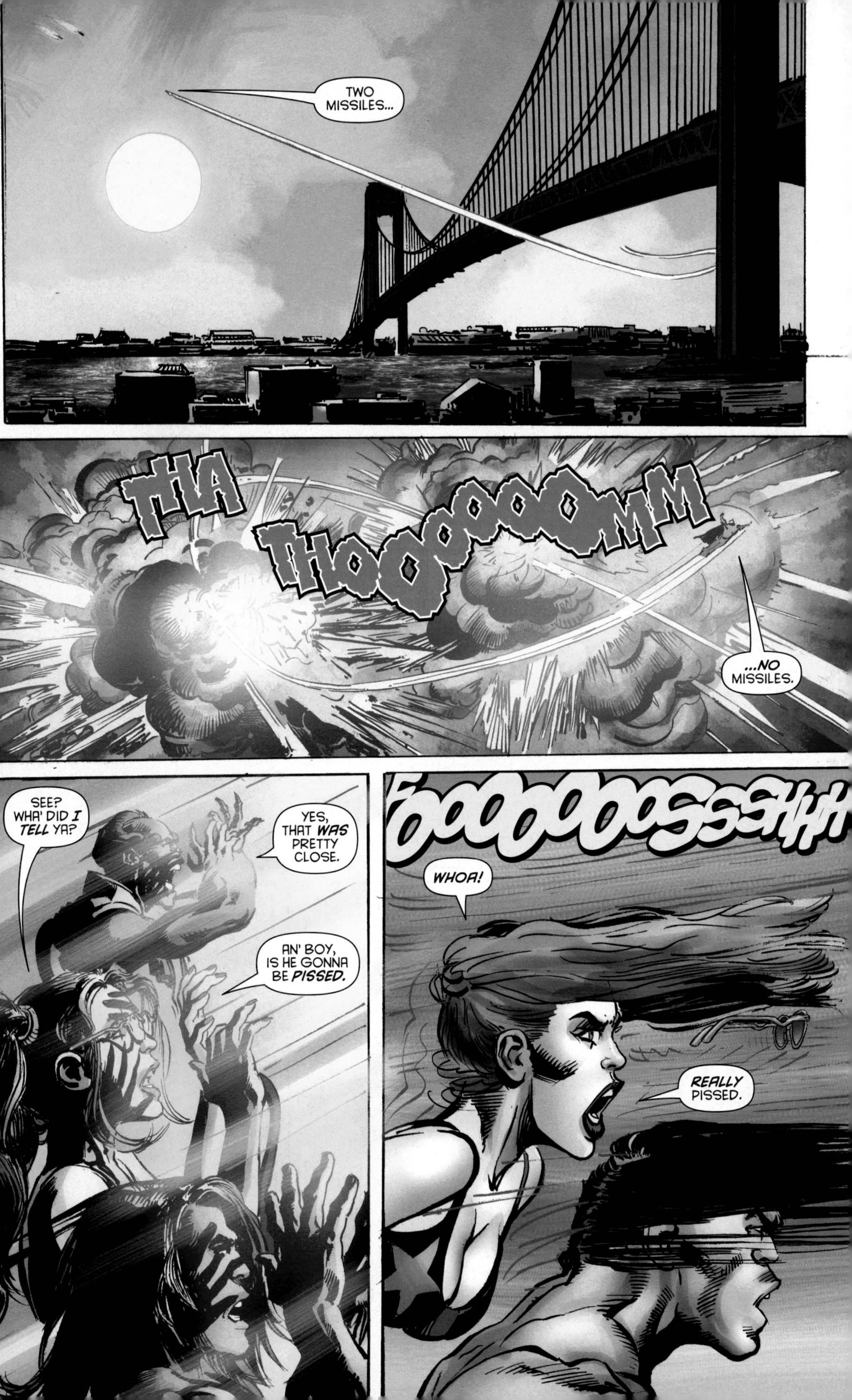
TWO MISSILES...
THA
THOOOOOOMM
...NO MISSILES.
SEE? WHA' DID *I TELL* YA?
YES, THAT *WAS* PRETTY CLOSE.
AN' BOY, IS HE GONNA BE *PISSED.*
WHOA!
REALLY PISSED.

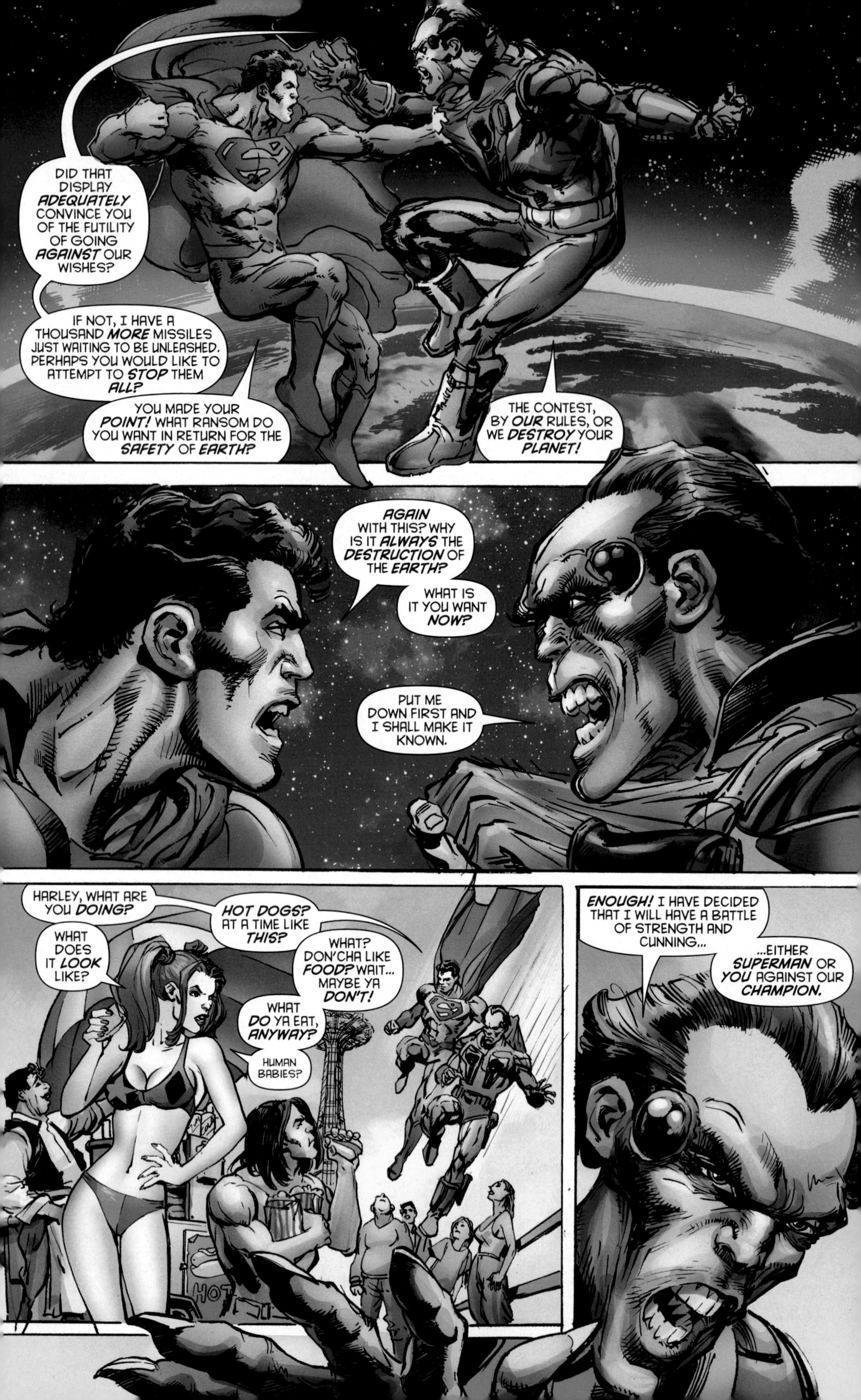
DID THAT DISPLAY ADEQUATELY CONVINCE YOU OF THE FUTILITY OF GOING AGAINST OUR WISHES?
IF NOT, I HAVE A THOUSAND MORE MISSILES JUST WAITING TO BE UNLEASHED. PERHAPS YOU WOULD LIKE TO ATTEMPT TO STOP THEM ALL?
YOU MADE YOUR POINT! WHAT RANSOM DO YOU WANT IN RETURN FOR THE SAFETY OF EARTH?
THE CONTEST, BY OUR RULES, OR WE DESTROY YOUR PLANET!
AGAIN WITH THIS? WHY IS IT ALWAYS THE DESTRUCTION OF THE EARTH?
WHAT IS IT YOU WANT NOW?
PUT ME DOWN FIRST AND I SHALL MAKE IT KNOWN.
HARLEY, WHAT ARE YOU DOING?
WHAT DOES IT LOOK LIKE?
HOT DOGS? AT A TIME LIKE THIS?
WHAT? DON'CHA LIKE FOOD? WAIT... MAYBE YA DON'T!
WHAT DO YA EAT, ANYWAY?
HUMAN BABIES?
ENOUGH! I HAVE DECIDED THAT I WILL HAVE A BATTLE OF STRENGTH AND CUNNING...
...EITHER SUPERMAN OR YOU AGAINST OUR CHAMPION.

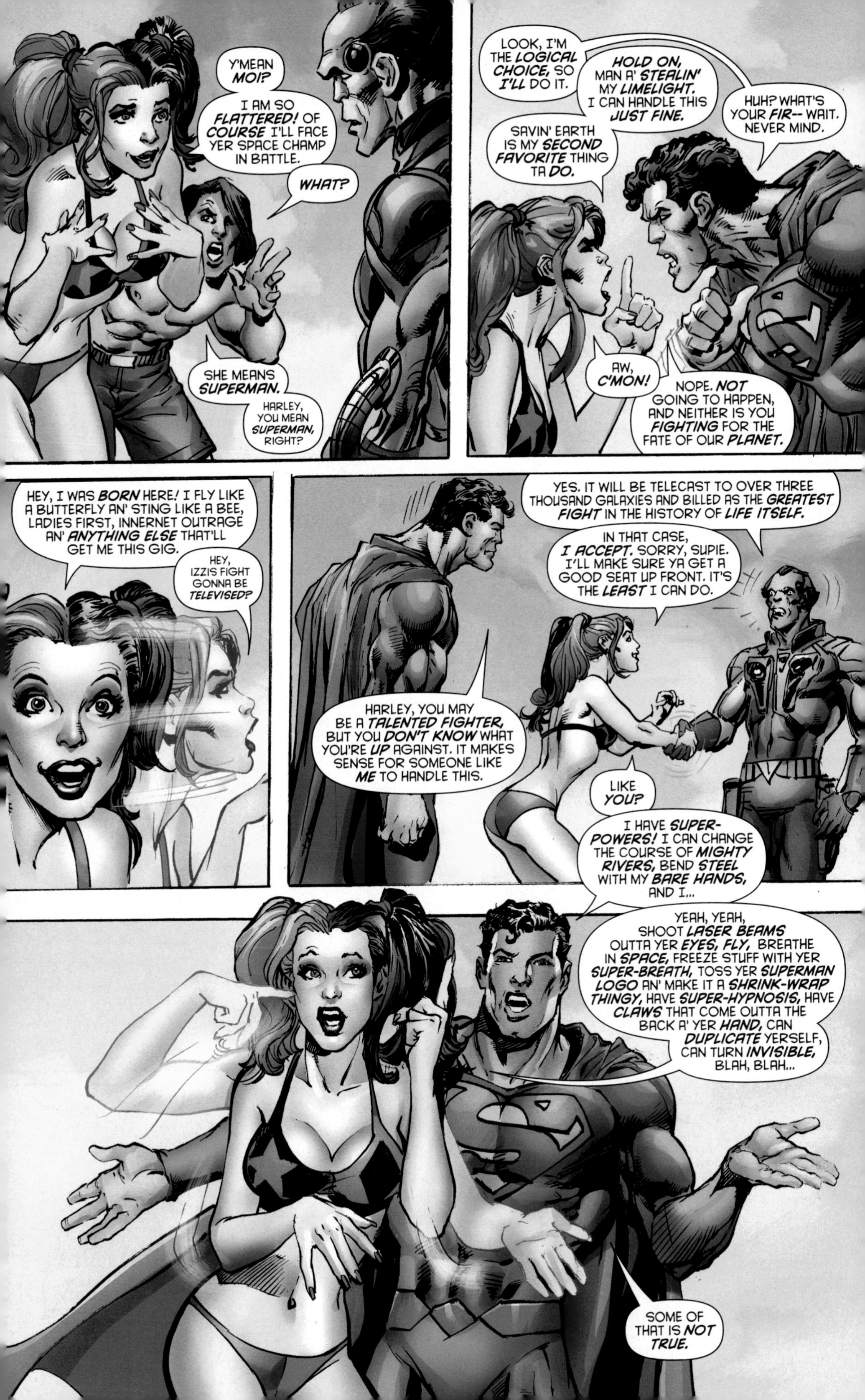
Y'MEAN MOI?
I AM SO FLATTERED! OF COURSE I'LL FACE YER SPACE CHAMP IN BATTLE.
WHAT?
SHE MEANS SUPERMAN.
HARLEY, YOU MEAN SUPERMAN, RIGHT?
LOOK, I'M THE LOGICAL CHOICE, SO I'LL DO IT.
HOLD ON, MAN A' STEALIN' MY LIMELIGHT. I CAN HANDLE THIS JUST FINE.
HUH? WHAT'S YOUR FIR-- WAIT. NEVER MIND.
SAVIN' EARTH IS MY SECOND FAVORITE THING TA DO.
AW, C'MON!
NOPE. NOT GOING TO HAPPEN, AND NEITHER IS YOU FIGHTING FOR THE FATE OF OUR PLANET.
HEY, I WAS BORN HERE! I FLY LIKE A BUTTERFLY AN' STING LIKE A BEE, LADIES FIRST, INNERNET OUTRAGE AN' ANYTHING ELSE THAT'LL GET ME THIS GIG.
HEY, IZZIS FIGHT GONNA BE TELEVISED?
YES. IT WILL BE TELECAST TO OVER THREE THOUSAND GALAXIES AND BILLED AS THE GREATEST FIGHT IN THE HISTORY OF LIFE ITSELF.
IN THAT CASE, I ACCEPT. SORRY, SUPIE. I'LL MAKE SURE YA GET A GOOD SEAT UP FRONT. IT'S THE LEAST I CAN DO.
HARLEY, YOU MAY BE A TALENTED FIGHTER, BUT YOU DON'T KNOW WHAT YOU'RE UP AGAINST. IT MAKES SENSE FOR SOMEONE LIKE ME TO HANDLE THIS.
LIKE YOU?
I HAVE SUPER-POWERS! I CAN CHANGE THE COURSE OF MIGHTY RIVERS, BEND STEEL WITH MY BARE HANDS, AND I...
YEAH, YEAH, SHOOT LASER BEAMS OUTTA YER EYES, FLY, BREATHE IN SPACE, FREEZE STUFF WITH YER SUPER-BREATH, TOSS YER SUPERMAN LOGO AN' MAKE IT A SHRINK-WRAP THINGY, HAVE SUPER-HYPNOSIS, HAVE CLAWS THAT COME OUTTA THE BACK A' YER HAND, CAN DUPLICATE YERSELF, CAN TURN INVISIBLE, BLAH, BLAH...
SOME OF THAT IS NOT TRUE.

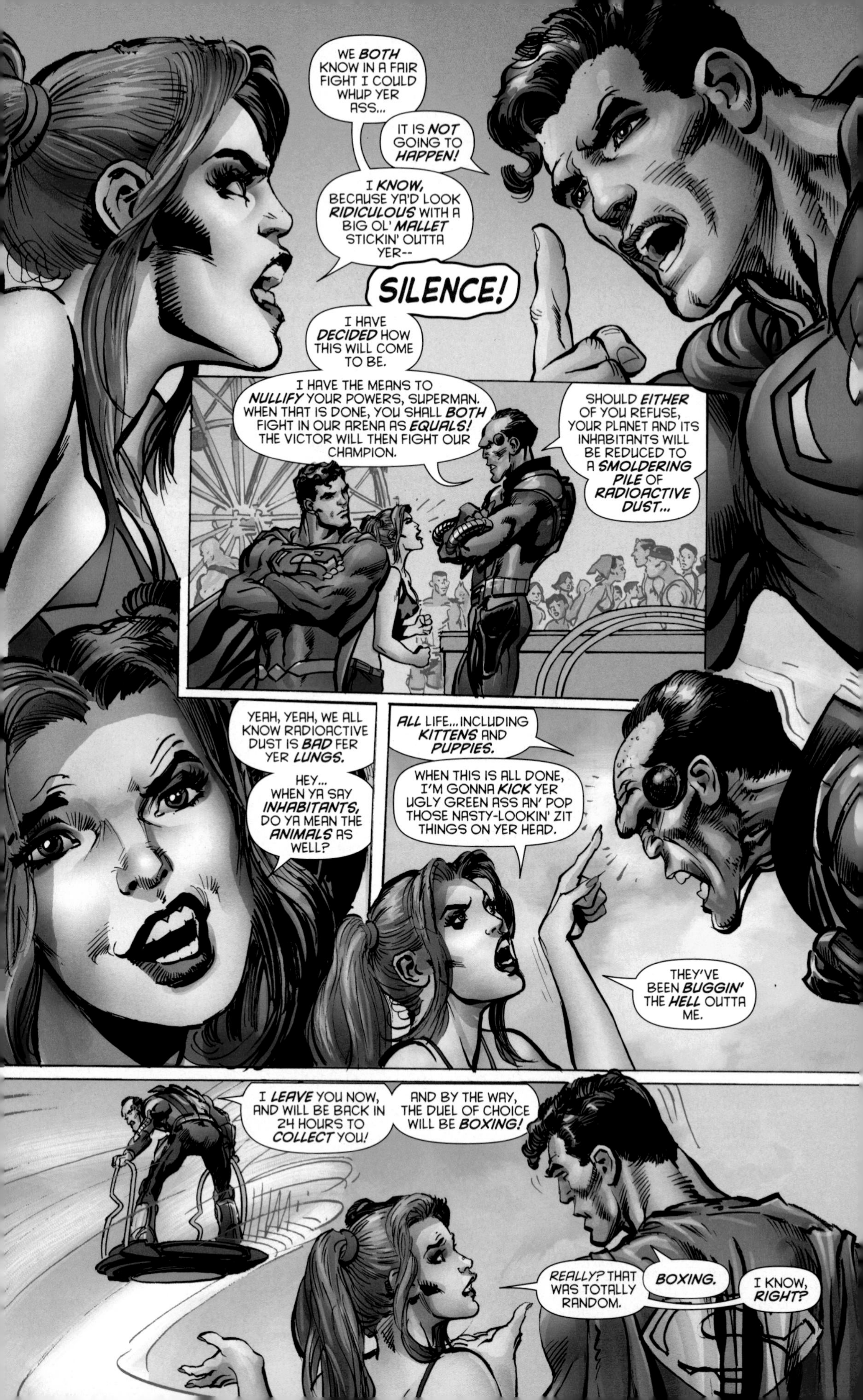
WE BOTH KNOW IN A FAIR FIGHT I COULD WHUP YER ASS...
IT IS NOT GOING TO HAPPEN!
I KNOW, BECAUSE YA'D LOOK RIDICULOUS WITH A BIG OL' MALLET STICKIN' OUTTA YER--
SILENCE!
I HAVE DECIDED HOW THIS WILL COME TO BE.
I HAVE THE MEANS TO NULLIFY YOUR POWERS, SUPERMAN. WHEN THAT IS DONE, YOU SHALL BOTH FIGHT IN OUR ARENA AS EQUALS! THE VICTOR WILL THEN FIGHT OUR CHAMPION.
SHOULD EITHER OF YOU REFUSE, YOUR PLANET AND ITS INHABITANTS WILL BE REDUCED TO A SMOLDERING PILE OF RADIOACTIVE DUST...
YEAH, YEAH, WE ALL KNOW RADIOACTIVE DUST IS BAD FER YER LUNGS.
HEY... WHEN YA SAY INHABITANTS, DO YA MEAN THE ANIMALS AS WELL?
ALL LIFE... INCLUDING KITTENS AND PUPPIES.
WHEN THIS IS ALL DONE, I'M GONNA KICK YER UGLY GREEN ASS AN' POP THOSE NASTY-LOOKIN' ZIT THINGS ON YER HEAD.
THEY'VE BEEN BUGGIN' THE HELL OUTTA ME.
I LEAVE YOU NOW, AND WILL BE BACK IN 24 HOURS TO COLLECT YOU!
AND BY THE WAY, THE DUEL OF CHOICE WILL BE BOXING!
REALLY? THAT WAS TOTALLY RANDOM.
BOXING.
I KNOW, RIGHT?

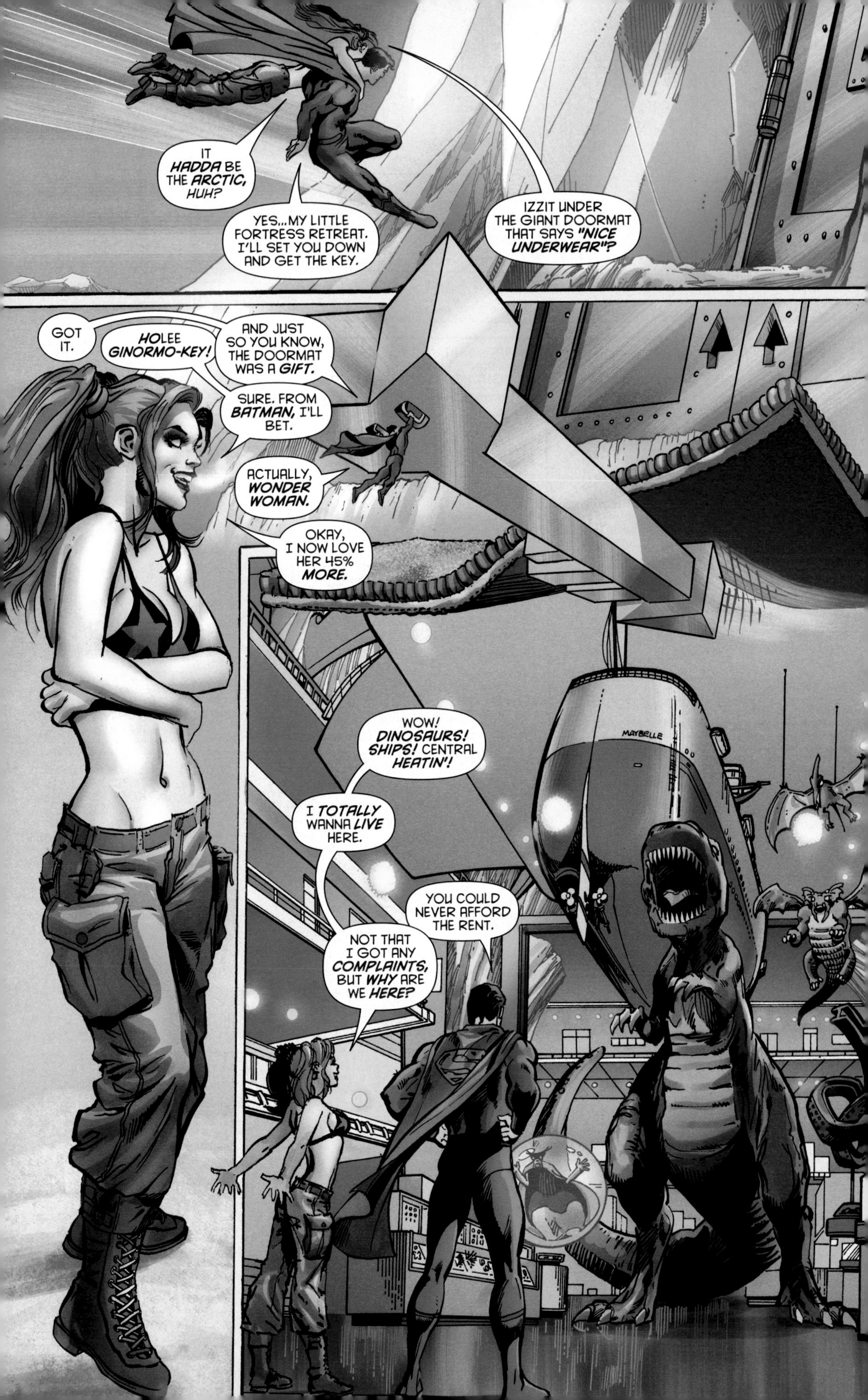
IT HADDA BE THE ARCTIC, HUH?
YES...MY LITTLE FORTRESS RETREAT. I'LL SET YOU DOWN AND GET THE KEY.
IZZIT UNDER THE GIANT DOORMAT THAT SAYS "NICE UNDERWEAR"?
GOT IT.
HOLEE GINORMO-KEY!
AND JUST SO YOU KNOW, THE DOORMAT WAS A GIFT.
SURE. FROM BATMAN, I'LL BET.
ACTUALLY, WONDER WOMAN.
OKAY, I NOW LOVE HER 45% MORE.
WOW! DINOSAURS! SHIPS! CENTRAL HEATIN'!
I TOTALLY WANNA LIVE HERE.
YOU COULD NEVER AFFORD THE RENT.
NOT THAT I GOT ANY COMPLAINTS, BUT WHY ARE WE HERE?
MAYBELLE

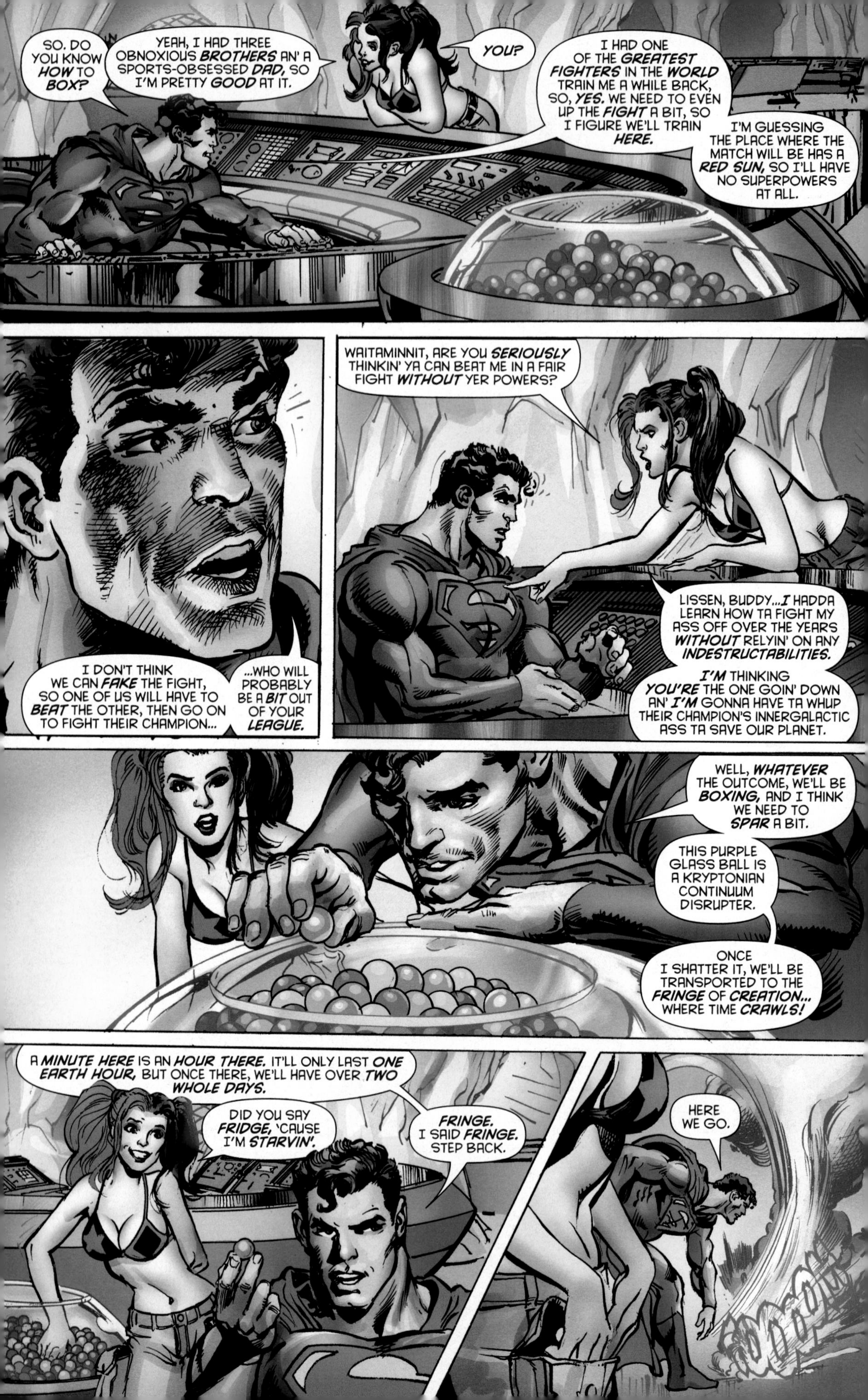
SO, DO YOU KNOW HOW TO BOX?
YEAH, I HAD THREE OBNOXIOUS BROTHERS AN' A SPORTS-OBSESSED DAD, SO I'M PRETTY GOOD AT IT.
YOU?
I HAD ONE OF THE GREATEST FIGHTERS IN THE WORLD TRAIN ME A WHILE BACK, SO, YES. WE NEED TO EVEN UP THE FIGHT A BIT, SO I FIGURE WE'LL TRAIN HERE.
I'M GUESSING THE PLACE WHERE THE MATCH WILL BE HAS A RED SUN, SO I'LL HAVE NO SUPERPOWERS AT ALL.
I DON'T THINK WE CAN FAKE THE FIGHT, SO ONE OF US WILL HAVE TO BEAT THE OTHER, THEN GO ON TO FIGHT THEIR CHAMPION...
...WHO WILL PROBABLY BE A BIT OUT OF YOUR LEAGUE.
WAITAMINNIT, ARE YOU SERIOUSLY THINKIN' YA CAN BEAT ME IN A FAIR FIGHT WITHOUT YER POWERS?
LISSEN, BUDDY...I HADDA LEARN HOW TA FIGHT MY ASS OFF OVER THE YEARS WITHOUT RELYIN' ON ANY INDESTRUCTABILITIES.
I'M THINKING YOU'RE THE ONE GOIN' DOWN AN' I'M GONNA HAVE TA WHUP THEIR CHAMPION'S INNERGALACTIC ASS TA SAVE OUR PLANET.
WELL, WHATEVER THE OUTCOME, WE'LL BE BOXING, AND I THINK WE NEED TO SPAR A BIT.
THIS PURPLE GLASS BALL IS A KRYPTONIAN CONTINUUM DISRUPTER.
ONCE I SHATTER IT, WE'LL BE TRANSPORTED TO THE FRINGE OF CREATION... WHERE TIME CRAWLS!
A MINUTE HERE IS AN HOUR THERE. IT'LL ONLY LAST ONE EARTH HOUR, BUT ONCE THERE, WE'LL HAVE OVER TWO WHOLE DAYS.
DID YOU SAY FRIDGE, 'CAUSE I'M STARVIN'.
FRINGE. I SAID FRINGE. STEP BACK.
HERE WE GO.

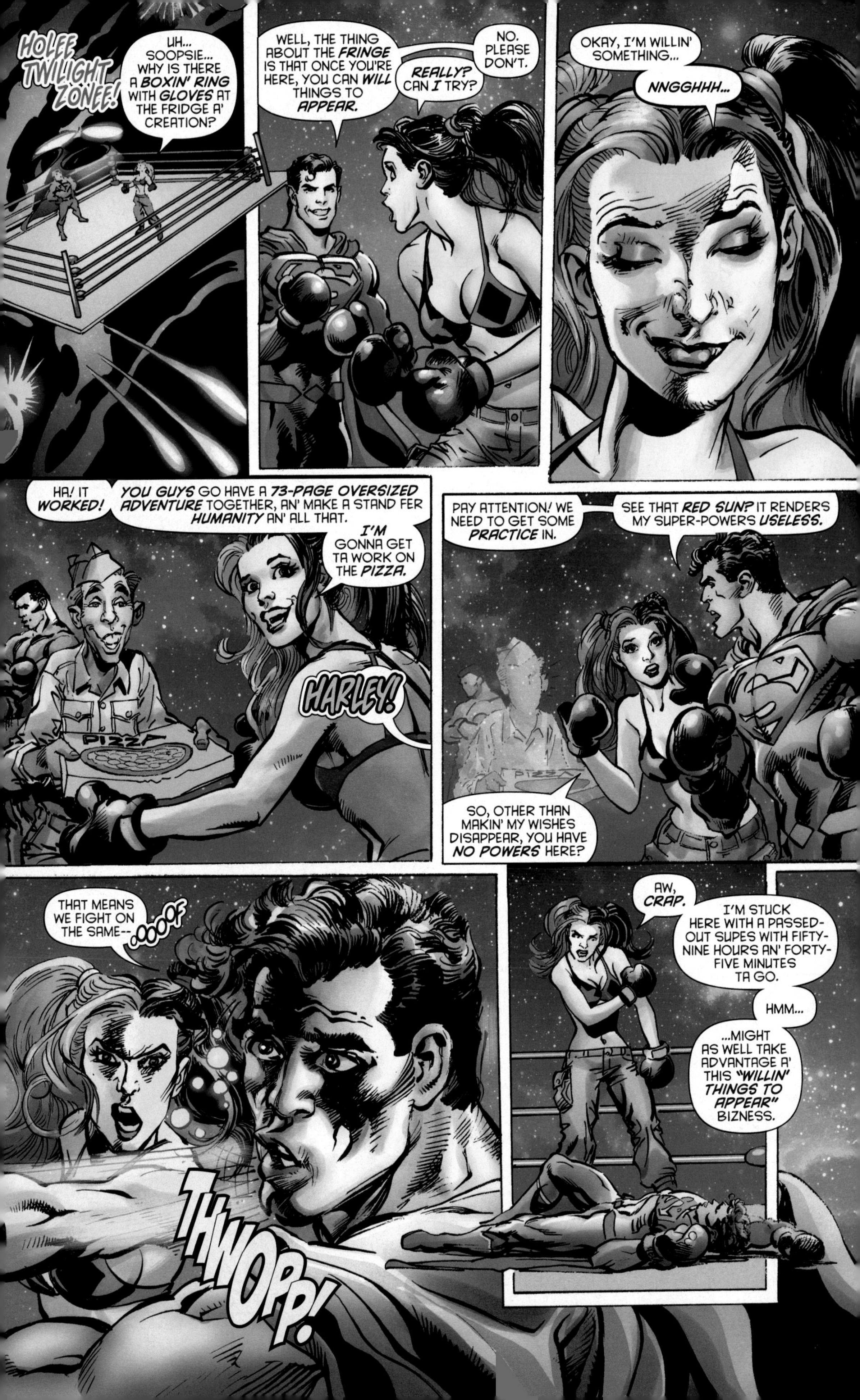
HOLEE TWILIGHT ZONEE!
UH... SOOPSIE... WHY IS THERE A BOXIN' RING WITH GLOVES AT THE FRIDGE A' CREATION?
WELL, THE THING ABOUT THE FRINGE IS THAT ONCE YOU'RE HERE, YOU CAN WILL THINGS TO APPEAR.
REALLY? CAN I TRY?
NO. PLEASE DON'T.
OKAY, I'M WILLIN' SOMETHING...
NNGGHHH...
HA! IT WORKED!
YOU GUYS GO HAVE A 73-PAGE OVERSIZED ADVENTURE TOGETHER, AN' MAKE A STAND FER HUMANITY AN' ALL THAT.
I'M GONNA GET TA WORK ON THE PIZZA.
HARLEY!
PIZZA
PAY ATTENTION! WE NEED TO GET SOME PRACTICE IN.
SEE THAT RED SUN? IT RENDERS MY SUPER-POWERS USELESS.
SO, OTHER THAN MAKIN' MY WISHES DISAPPEAR, YOU HAVE NO POWERS HERE?
THAT MEANS WE FIGHT ON THE SAME--
OOOOF
THWOPP!
AW, CRAP.
I'M STUCK HERE WITH A PASSED-OUT SUPES WITH FIFTY-NINE HOURS AN' FORTY-FIVE MINUTES TA GO.
HMM...
...MIGHT AS WELL TAKE ADVANTAGE A' THIS "WILLIN' THINGS TO APPEAR" BIZNESS.

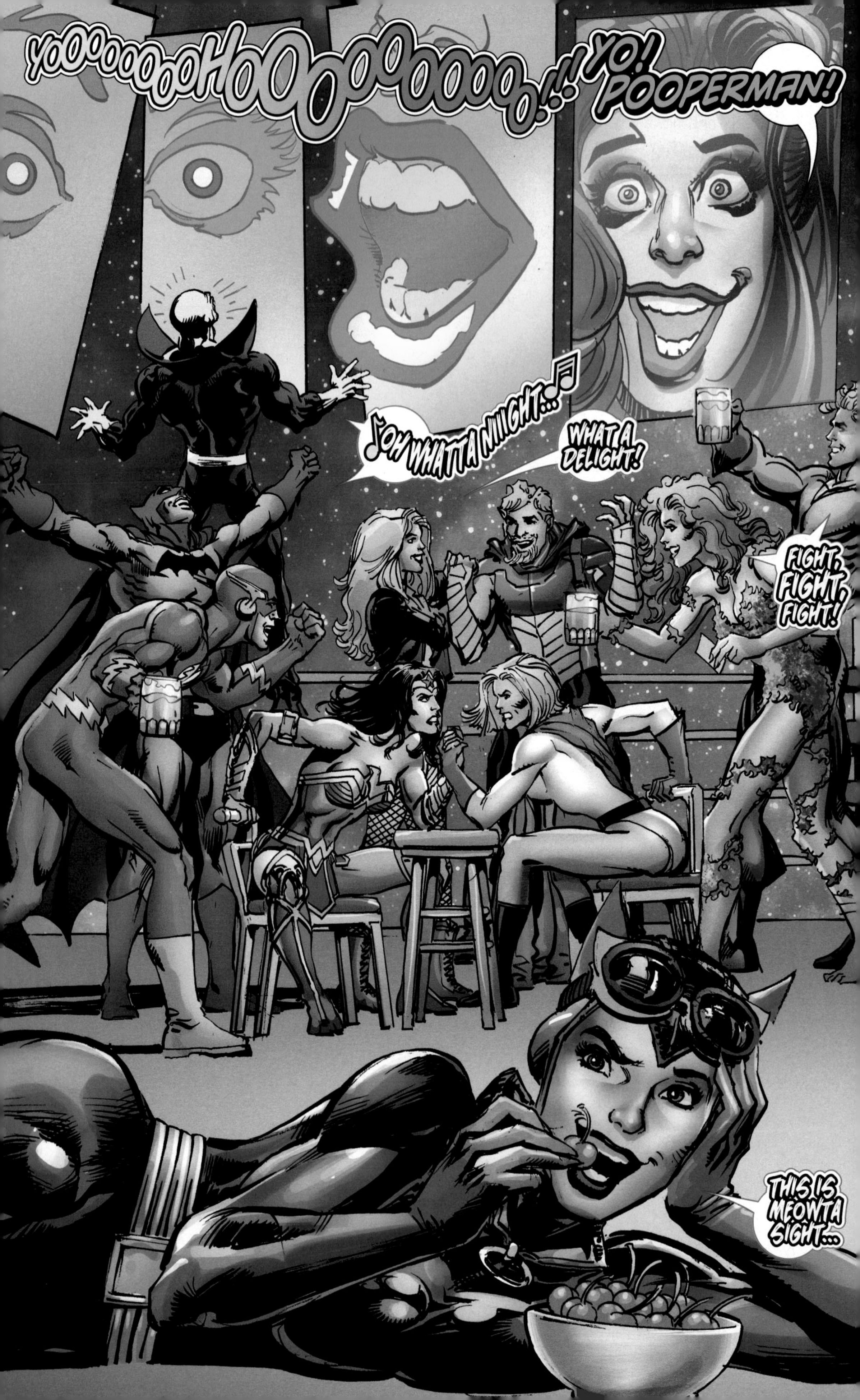
YOOOOOOOOHOOOOOOOOOO!!! YO! POOPERMAN!
OH WHATTA NIIIGHT...
WHAT A DELIGHT!
FIGHT, FIGHT, FIGHT!
THIS IS MEOWTA SIGHT...

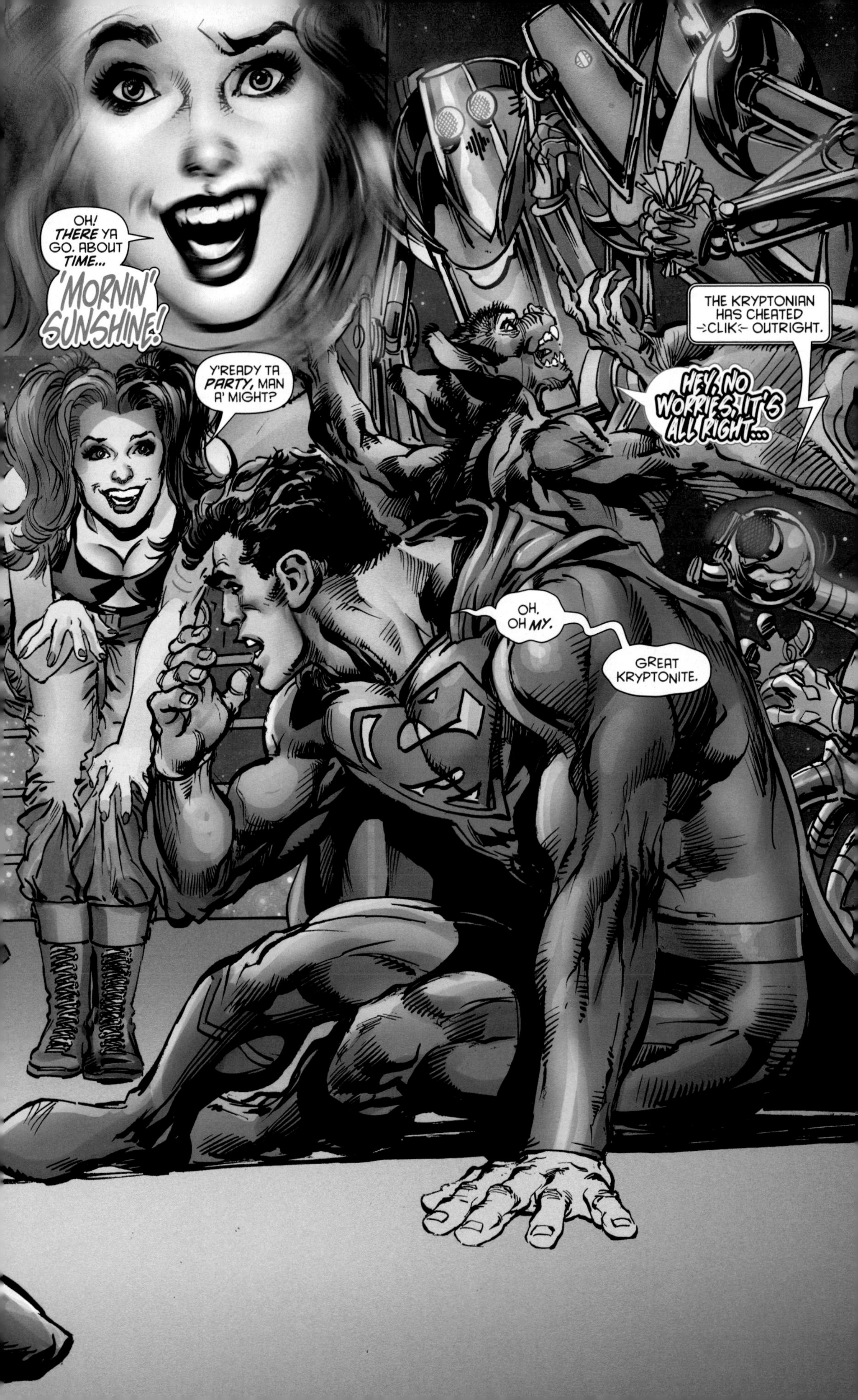
OH! THERE YA GO. ABOUT TIME...
'MORNIN' SUNSHINE!
THE KRYPTONIAN HAS CHEATED ->CLIK<- OUTRIGHT.
Y'READY TA PARTY, MAN A' MIGHT?
HEY, NO WORRIES, IT'S ALL RIGHT...
OH, OH MY.
GREAT KRYPTONITE.

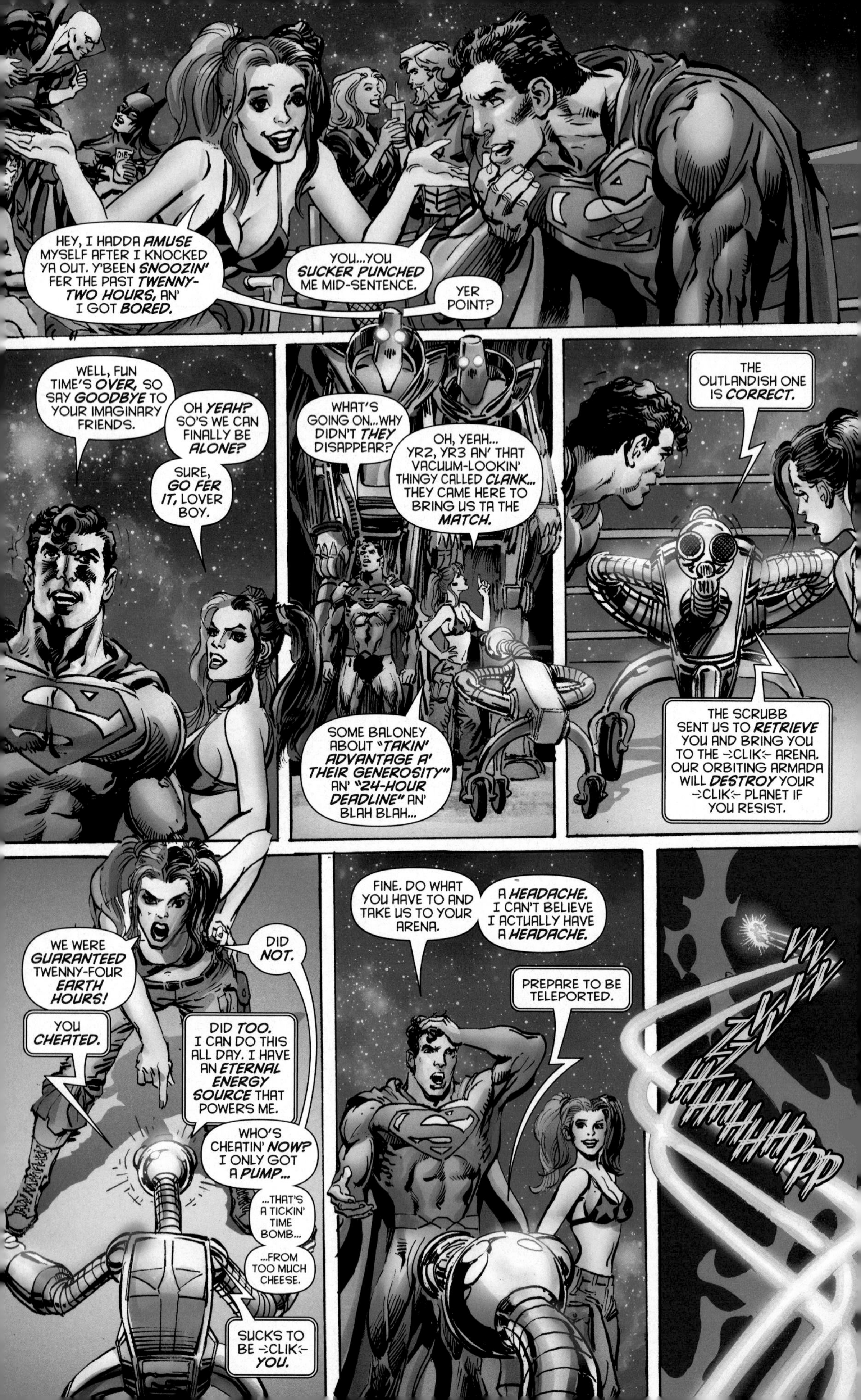

HEY, I HADDA AMUSE MYSELF AFTER I KNOCKED YA OUT. Y'BEEN SNOOZIN' FER THE PAST TWENNY-TWO HOURS, AN' I GOT BORED.
YOU...YOU SUCKER PUNCHED ME MID-SENTENCE.
YER POINT?
WELL, FUN TIME'S OVER, SO SAY GOODBYE TO YOUR IMAGINARY FRIENDS.
OH YEAH? SO'S WE CAN FINALLY BE ALONE?
SURE, GO FER IT, LOVER BOY.
WHAT'S GOING ON...WHY DIDN'T THEY DISAPPEAR?
OH, YEAH... YR2, YR3 AN' THAT VACUUM-LOOKIN' THINGY CALLED CLANK... THEY CAME HERE TO BRING US TA THE MATCH.
SOME BALONEY ABOUT "TAKIN' ADVANTAGE A' THEIR GENEROSITY" AN' "24-HOUR DEADLINE" AN' BLAH BLAH...
THE OUTLANDISH ONE IS CORRECT.
THE SCRUBB SENT US TO RETRIEVE YOU AND BRING YOU TO THE ->CLIK<- ARENA. OUR ORBITING ARMADA WILL DESTROY YOUR ->CLIK<- PLANET IF YOU RESIST.
WE WERE GUARANTEED TWENNY-FOUR EARTH HOURS!
DID NOT.
YOU CHEATED.
DID TOO. I CAN DO THIS ALL DAY. I HAVE AN ETERNAL ENERGY SOURCE THAT POWERS ME.
WHO'S CHEATIN' NOW? I ONLY GOT A PUMP...
...THAT'S A TICKIN' TIME BOMB...
...FROM TOO MUCH CHEESE.
SUCKS TO BE ->CLIK<- YOU.
FINE. DO WHAT YOU HAVE TO AND TAKE US TO YOUR ARENA.
A HEADACHE. I CAN'T BELIEVE I ACTUALLY HAVE A HEADACHE.
PREPARE TO BE TELEPORTED.
VVVVZZZHHHHHHHPPPP

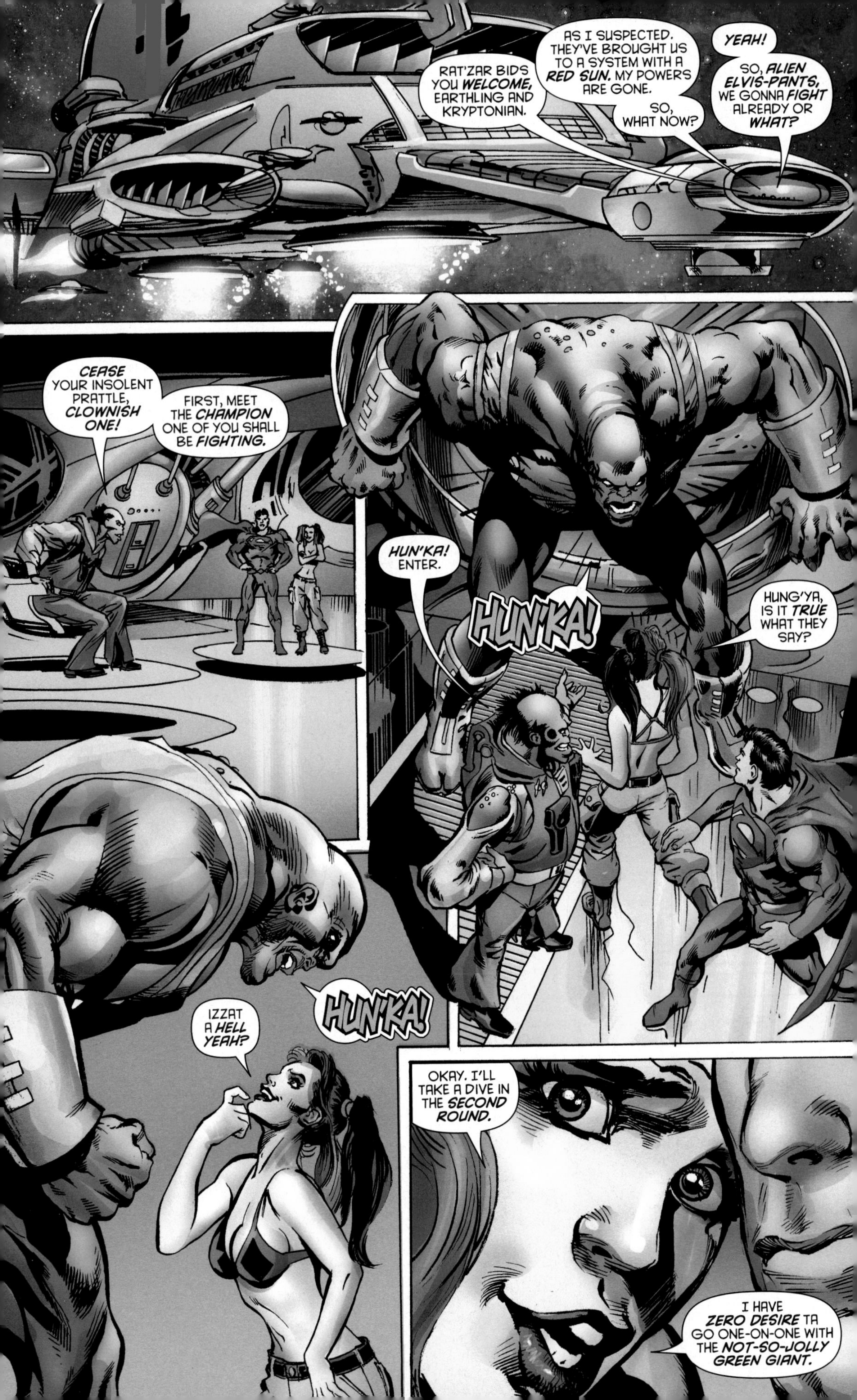
RAT'ZAR BIDS YOU WELCOME, EARTHLING AND KRYPTONIAN.
AS I SUSPECTED. THEY'VE BROUGHT US TO A SYSTEM WITH A RED SUN. MY POWERS ARE GONE.
SO, WHAT NOW?
YEAH!
SO, ALIEN ELVIS-PANTS, WE GONNA FIGHT ALREADY OR WHAT?
CEASE YOUR INSOLENT PRATTLE, CLOWNISH ONE!
FIRST, MEET THE CHAMPION ONE OF YOU SHALL BE FIGHTING.
HUN'KA! ENTER.
HUN'KA!
HUNG'YA, IS IT TRUE WHAT THEY SAY?
HUN'KA!
IZZAT A HELL YEAH?
OKAY. I'LL TAKE A DIVE IN THE SECOND ROUND.
I HAVE ZERO DESIRE TA GO ONE-ON-ONE WITH THE NOT-SO-JOLLY GREEN GIANT.

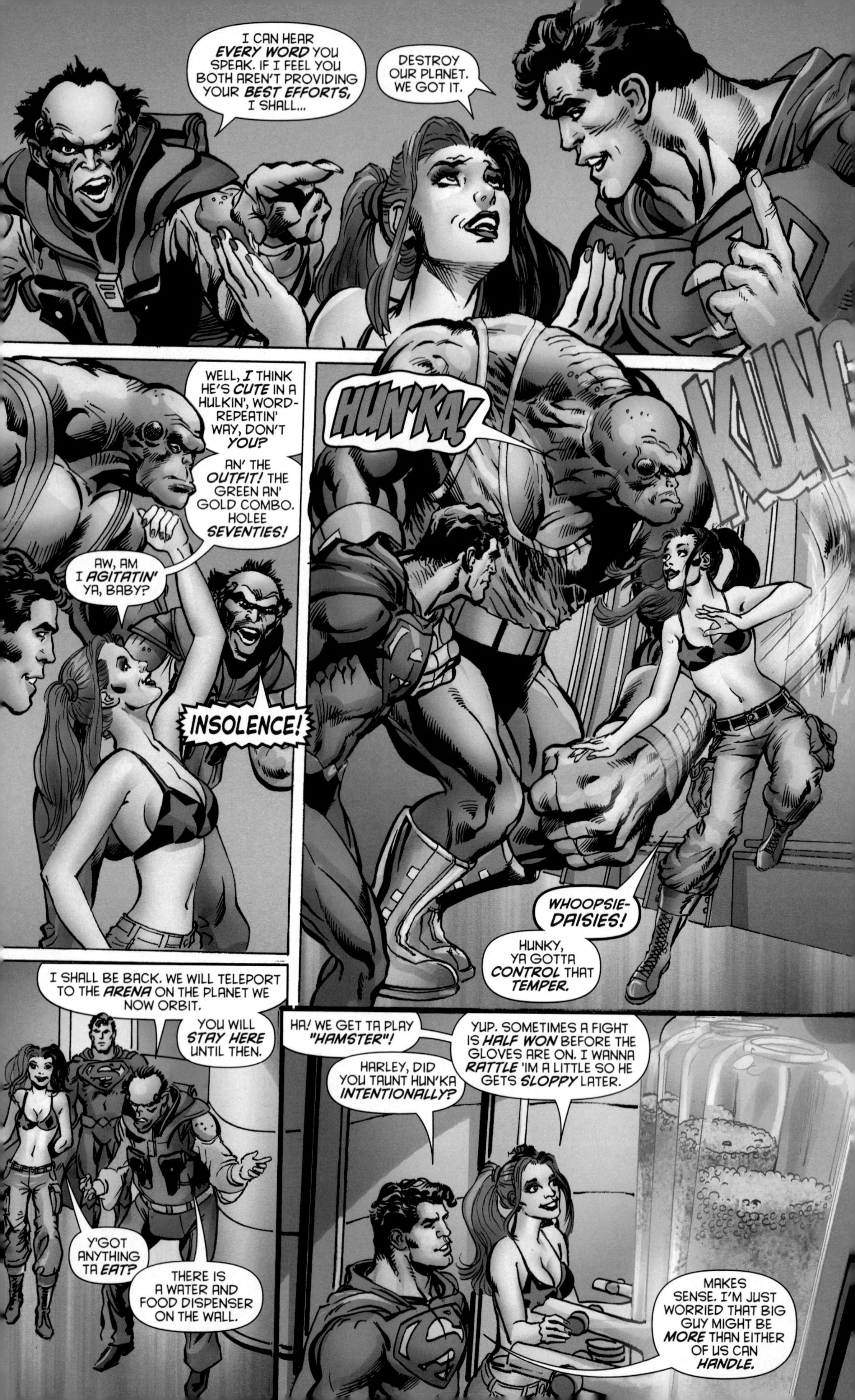
I CAN HEAR EVERY WORD YOU SPEAK. IF I FEEL YOU BOTH AREN'T PROVIDING YOUR BEST EFFORTS, I SHALL...
DESTROY OUR PLANET. WE GOT IT.
WELL, I THINK HE'S CUTE IN A HULKIN', WORD-REPEATIN' WAY, DON'T YOU?
AN' THE OUTFIT! THE GREEN AN' GOLD COMBO. HOLEE SEVENTIES!
AW, AM I AGITATIN' YA, BABY?
INSOLENCE!
HUN'KA!
KUNG
WHOOPSIE-DAISIES!
HUNKY, YA GOTTA CONTROL THAT TEMPER.
I SHALL BE BACK. WE WILL TELEPORT TO THE ARENA ON THE PLANET WE NOW ORBIT.
YOU WILL STAY HERE UNTIL THEN.
Y'GOT ANYTHING TA EAT?
THERE IS A WATER AND FOOD DISPENSER ON THE WALL.
HA! WE GET TA PLAY "HAMSTER"!
HARLEY, DID YOU TAUNT HUN'KA INTENTIONALLY?
YUP. SOMETIMES A FIGHT IS HALF WON BEFORE THE GLOVES ARE ON. I WANNA RATTLE 'IM A LITTLE SO HE GETS SLOPPY LATER.
MAKES SENSE. I'M JUST WORRIED THAT BIG GUY MIGHT BE MORE THAN EITHER OF US CAN HANDLE.

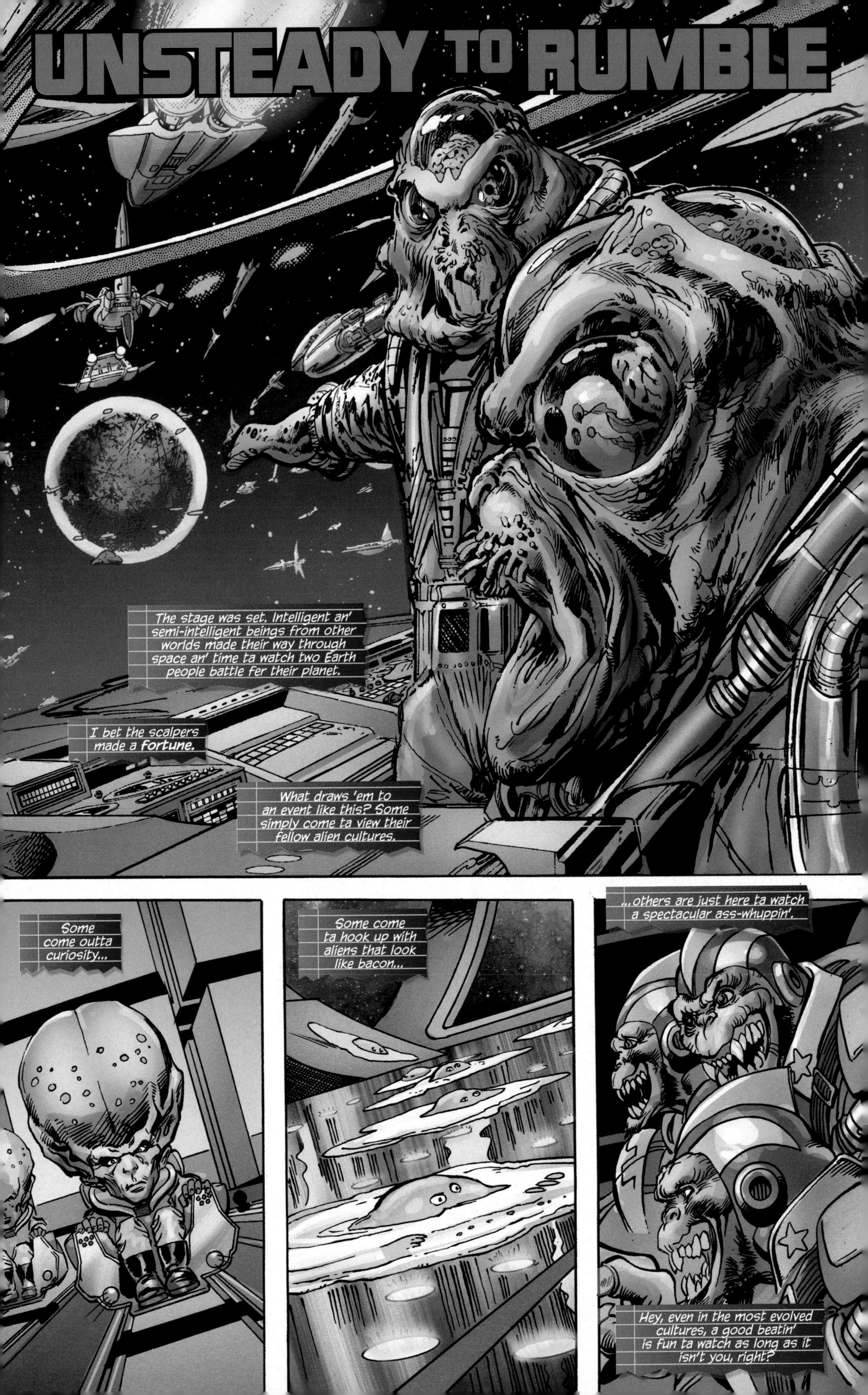
UNSTEADY TO RUMBLE
The stage was set. Intelligent an' semi-intelligent beings from other worlds made their way through space an' time ta watch two Earth people battle fer their planet.
I bet the scalpers made a **fortune.**
What draws 'em to an event like this? Some simply come ta view their fellow alien cultures.
Some come outta curiosity...
Some come ta hook up with aliens that look like bacon...
...others are just here ta watch a spectacular ass-whuppin'.
Hey, even in the most evolved cultures, a good beatin' is fun ta watch as long as it isn't you, right?

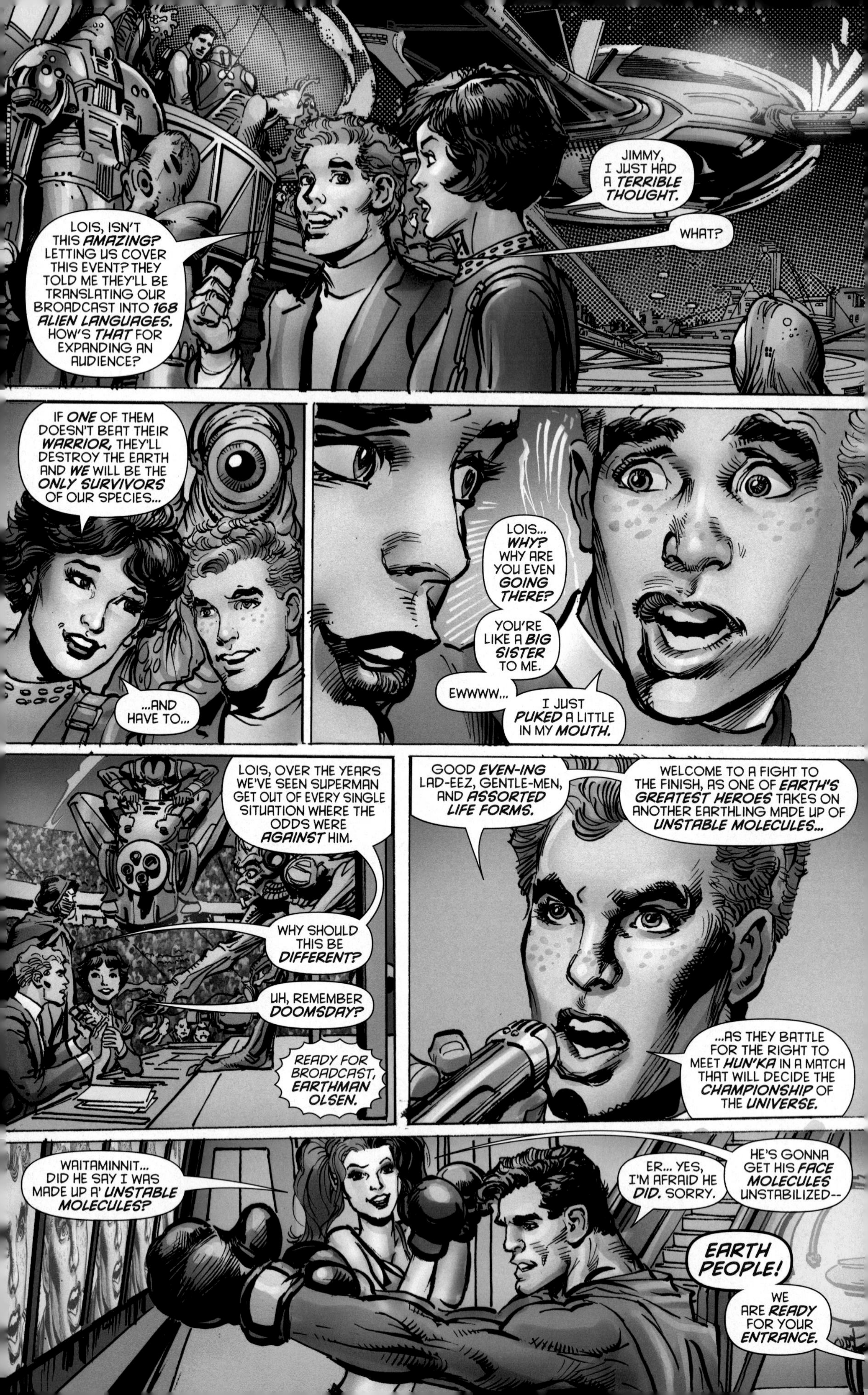

LOIS, ISN'T THIS AMAZING? LETTING US COVER THIS EVENT? THEY TOLD ME THEY'LL BE TRANSLATING OUR BROADCAST INTO 168 ALIEN LANGUAGES. HOW'S THAT FOR EXPANDING AN AUDIENCE?
JIMMY, I JUST HAD A TERRIBLE THOUGHT.
WHAT?
IF ONE OF THEM DOESN'T BEAT THEIR WARRIOR, THEY'LL DESTROY THE EARTH AND WE WILL BE THE ONLY SURVIVORS OF OUR SPECIES...
...AND HAVE TO...
LOIS... WHY? WHY ARE YOU EVEN GOING THERE?
YOU'RE LIKE A BIG SISTER TO ME.
EWWWW...
I JUST PUKED A LITTLE IN MY MOUTH.
LOIS, OVER THE YEARS WE'VE SEEN SUPERMAN GET OUT OF EVERY SINGLE SITUATION WHERE THE ODDS WERE AGAINST HIM.
WHY SHOULD THIS BE DIFFERENT?
UH, REMEMBER DOOMSDAY?
READY FOR BROADCAST, EARTHMAN OLSEN.
GOOD EVEN-ING LAD-EEZ, GENTLE-MEN, AND ASSORTED LIFE FORMS.
WELCOME TO A FIGHT TO THE FINISH, AS ONE OF EARTH'S GREATEST HEROES TAKES ON ANOTHER EARTHLING MADE UP OF UNSTABLE MOLECULES...
...AS THEY BATTLE FOR THE RIGHT TO MEET HUN'KA IN A MATCH THAT WILL DECIDE THE CHAMPIONSHIP OF THE UNIVERSE.
WAITAMINNIT... DID HE SAY I WAS MADE UP A' UNSTABLE MOLECULES?
ER... YES, I'M AFRAID HE DID. SORRY.
HE'S GONNA GET HIS FACE MOLECULES UNSTABILIZED--
EARTH PEOPLE!
WE ARE READY FOR YOUR ENTRANCE.

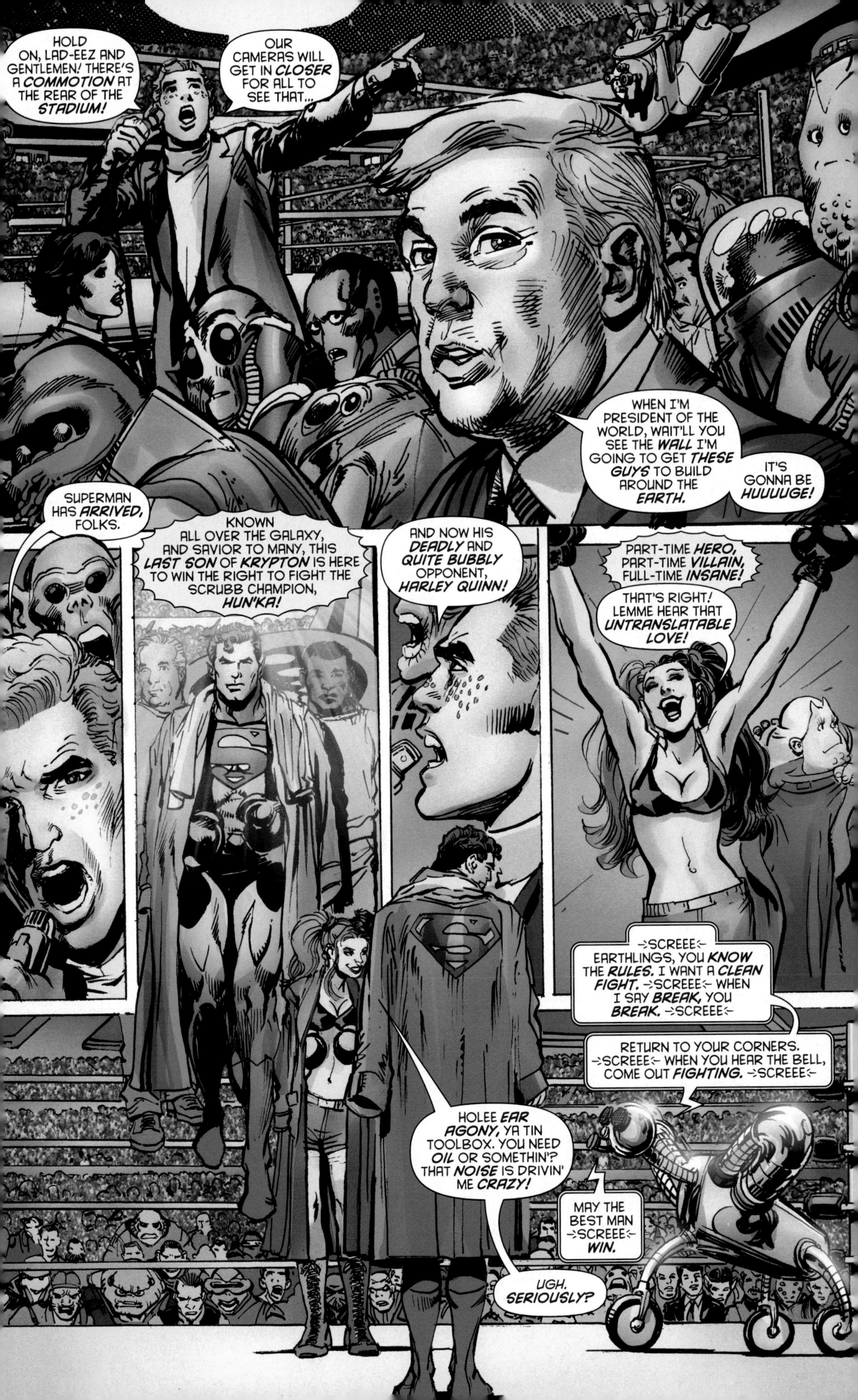
HOLD ON, LAD-EEZ AND GENTLEMEN! THERE'S A COMMOTION AT THE REAR OF THE STADIUM!
OUR CAMERAS WILL GET IN CLOSER FOR ALL TO SEE THAT...
WHEN I'M PRESIDENT OF THE WORLD, WAIT'LL YOU SEE THE WALL I'M GOING TO GET THESE GUYS TO BUILD AROUND THE EARTH.
IT'S GONNA BE HUUUUGE!
SUPERMAN HAS ARRIVED, FOLKS.
KNOWN ALL OVER THE GALAXY, AND SAVIOR TO MANY, THIS LAST SON OF KRYPTON IS HERE TO WIN THE RIGHT TO FIGHT THE SCRUBB CHAMPION, HUN'KA!
AND NOW HIS DEADLY AND QUITE BUBBLY OPPONENT, HARLEY QUINN!
PART-TIME HERO, PART-TIME VILLAIN, FULL-TIME INSANE!
THAT'S RIGHT! LEMME HEAR THAT UNTRANSLATABLE LOVE!
->SCREEE<- EARTHLINGS, YOU KNOW THE RULES. I WANT A CLEAN FIGHT. ->SCREEE<- WHEN I SAY BREAK, YOU BREAK. ->SCREEE<-
RETURN TO YOUR CORNERS. ->SCREEE<- WHEN YOU HEAR THE BELL, COME OUT FIGHTING. ->SCREEE<-
HOLEE EAR AGONY, YA TIN TOOLBOX. YOU NEED OIL OR SOMETHIN'? THAT NOISE IS DRIVIN' ME CRAZY!
MAY THE BEST MAN ->SCREEE<- WIN.
UGH. SERIOUSLY?

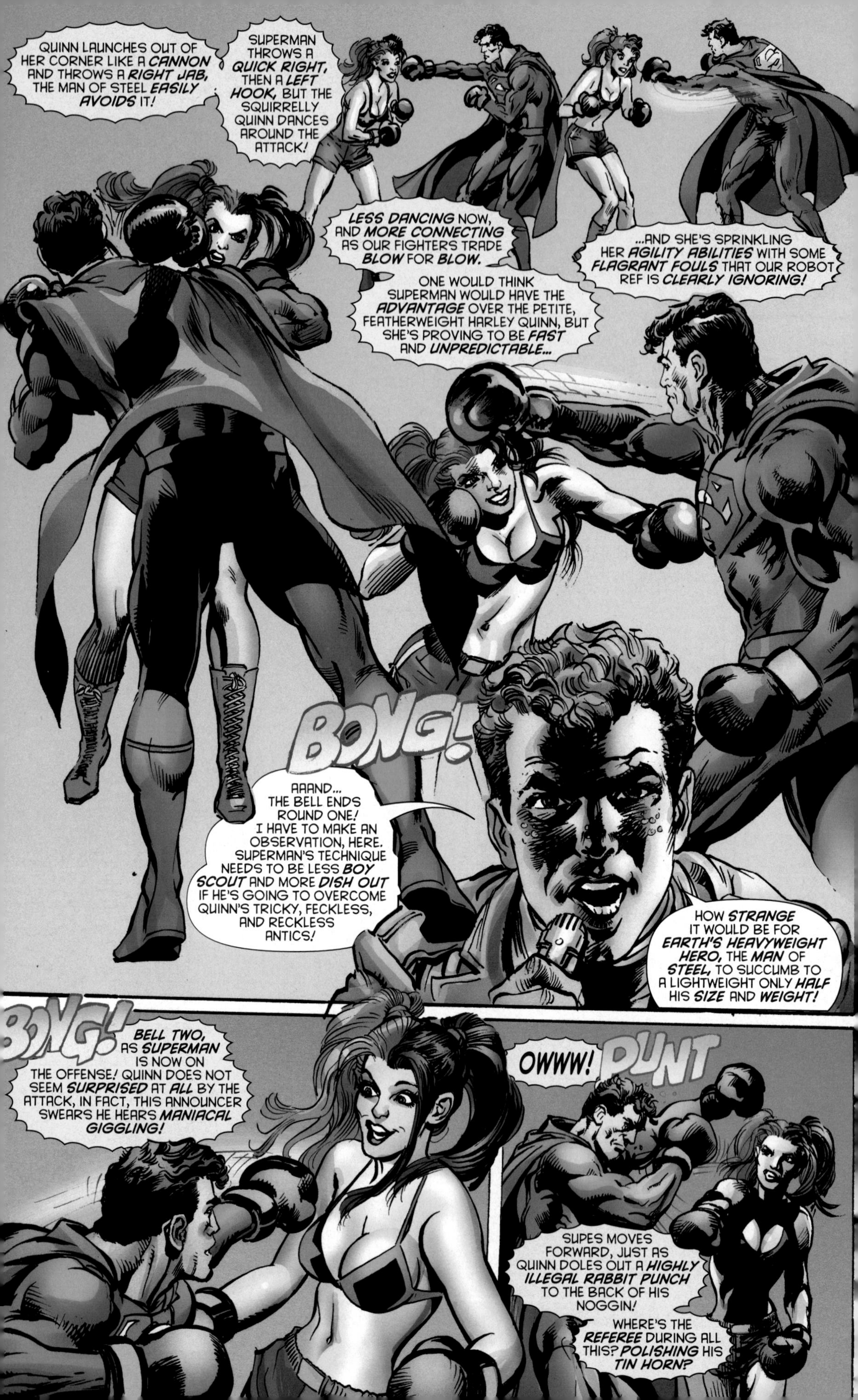
QUINN LAUNCHES OUT OF HER CORNER LIKE A CANNON AND THROWS A RIGHT JAB, THE MAN OF STEEL EASILY AVOIDS IT!
SUPERMAN THROWS A QUICK RIGHT, THEN A LEFT HOOK, BUT THE SQUIRRELLY QUINN DANCES AROUND THE ATTACK!
LESS DANCING NOW, AND MORE CONNECTING AS OUR FIGHTERS TRADE BLOW FOR BLOW.
...AND SHE'S SPRINKLING HER AGILITY ABILITIES WITH SOME FLAGRANT FOULS THAT OUR ROBOT REF IS CLEARLY IGNORING!
ONE WOULD THINK SUPERMAN WOULD HAVE THE ADVANTAGE OVER THE PETITE, FEATHERWEIGHT HARLEY QUINN, BUT SHE'S PROVING TO BE FAST AND UNPREDICTABLE...
BONG!
AAAND... THE BELL ENDS ROUND ONE! I HAVE TO MAKE AN OBSERVATION, HERE. SUPERMAN'S TECHNIQUE NEEDS TO BE LESS BOY SCOUT AND MORE DISH OUT IF HE'S GOING TO OVERCOME QUINN'S TRICKY, FECKLESS, AND RECKLESS ANTICS!
HOW STRANGE IT WOULD BE FOR EARTH'S HEAVYWEIGHT HERO, THE MAN OF STEEL, TO SUCCUMB TO A LIGHTWEIGHT ONLY HALF HIS SIZE AND WEIGHT!
BONG!
BELL TWO, AS SUPERMAN IS NOW ON THE OFFENSE! QUINN DOES NOT SEEM SURPRISED AT ALL BY THE ATTACK, IN FACT, THIS ANNOUNCER SWEARS HE HEARS MANIACAL GIGGLING!
OWWW!
DUNT
SUPES MOVES FORWARD, JUST AS QUINN DOLES OUT A HIGHLY ILLEGAL RABBIT PUNCH TO THE BACK OF HIS NOGGIN!
WHERE'S THE REFEREE DURING ALL THIS? POLISHING HIS TIN HORN?

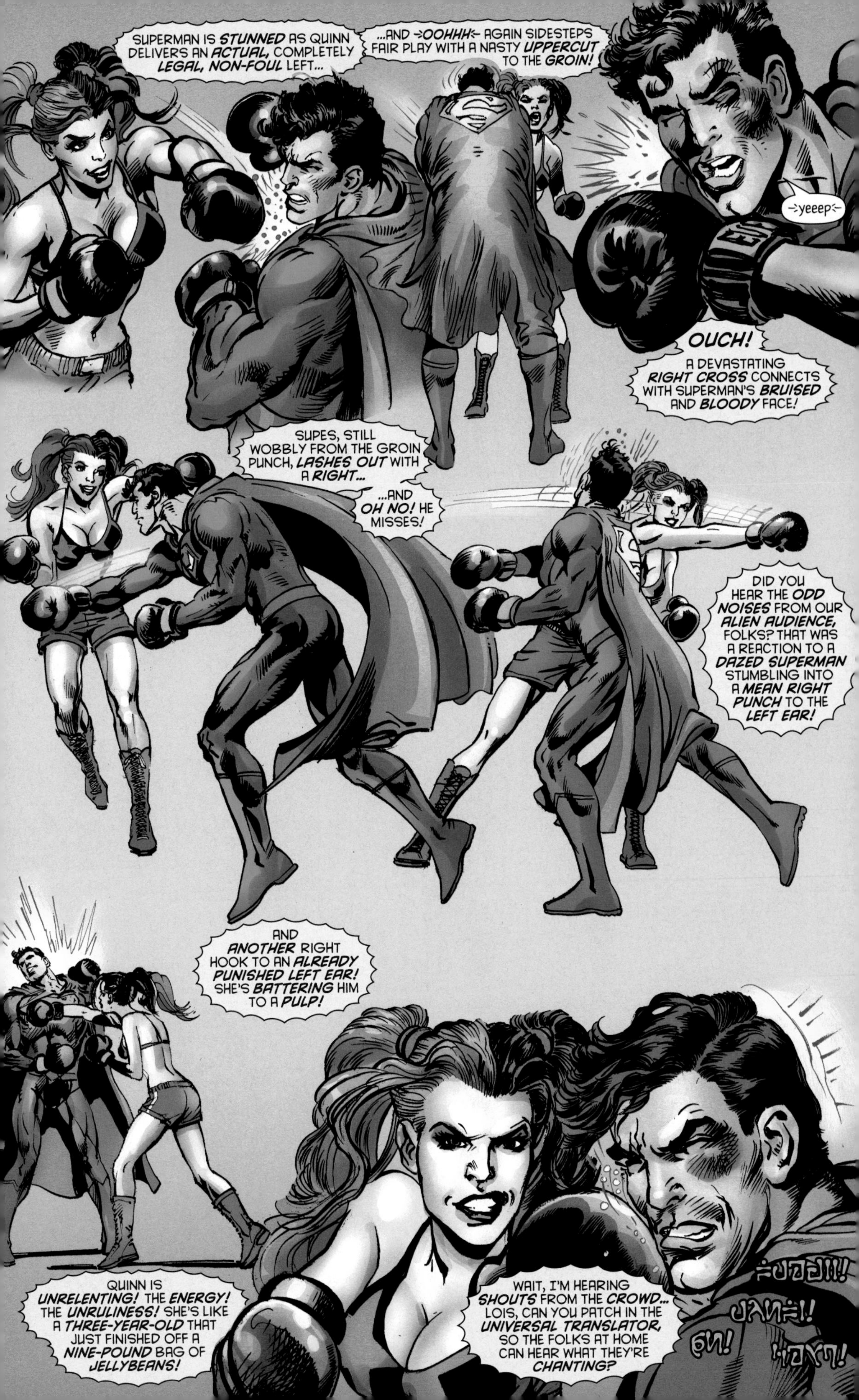
SUPERMAN IS STUNNED AS QUINN DELIVERS AN ACTUAL, COMPLETELY LEGAL, NON-FOUL LEFT...
...AND →OOHHH← AGAIN SIDESTEPS FAIR PLAY WITH A NASTY UPPERCUT TO THE GROIN!
→yeeep←
OUCH!
A DEVASTATING RIGHT CROSS CONNECTS WITH SUPERMAN'S BRUISED AND BLOODY FACE!
SUPES, STILL WOBBLY FROM THE GROIN PUNCH, LASHES OUT WITH A RIGHT...
...AND OH NO! HE MISSES!
DID YOU HEAR THE ODD NOISES FROM OUR ALIEN AUDIENCE, FOLKS? THAT WAS A REACTION TO A DAZED SUPERMAN STUMBLING INTO A MEAN RIGHT PUNCH TO THE LEFT EAR!
AND ANOTHER RIGHT HOOK TO AN ALREADY PUNISHED LEFT EAR! SHE'S BATTERING HIM TO A PULP!
QUINN IS UNRELENTING! THE ENERGY! THE UNRULINESS! SHE'S LIKE A THREE-YEAR-OLD THAT JUST FINISHED OFF A NINE-POUND BAG OF JELLYBEANS!
WAIT, I'M HEARING SHOUTS FROM THE CROWD... LOIS, CAN YOU PATCH IN THE UNIVERSAL TRANSLATOR, SO THE FOLKS AT HOME CAN HEAR WHAT THEY'RE CHANTING?

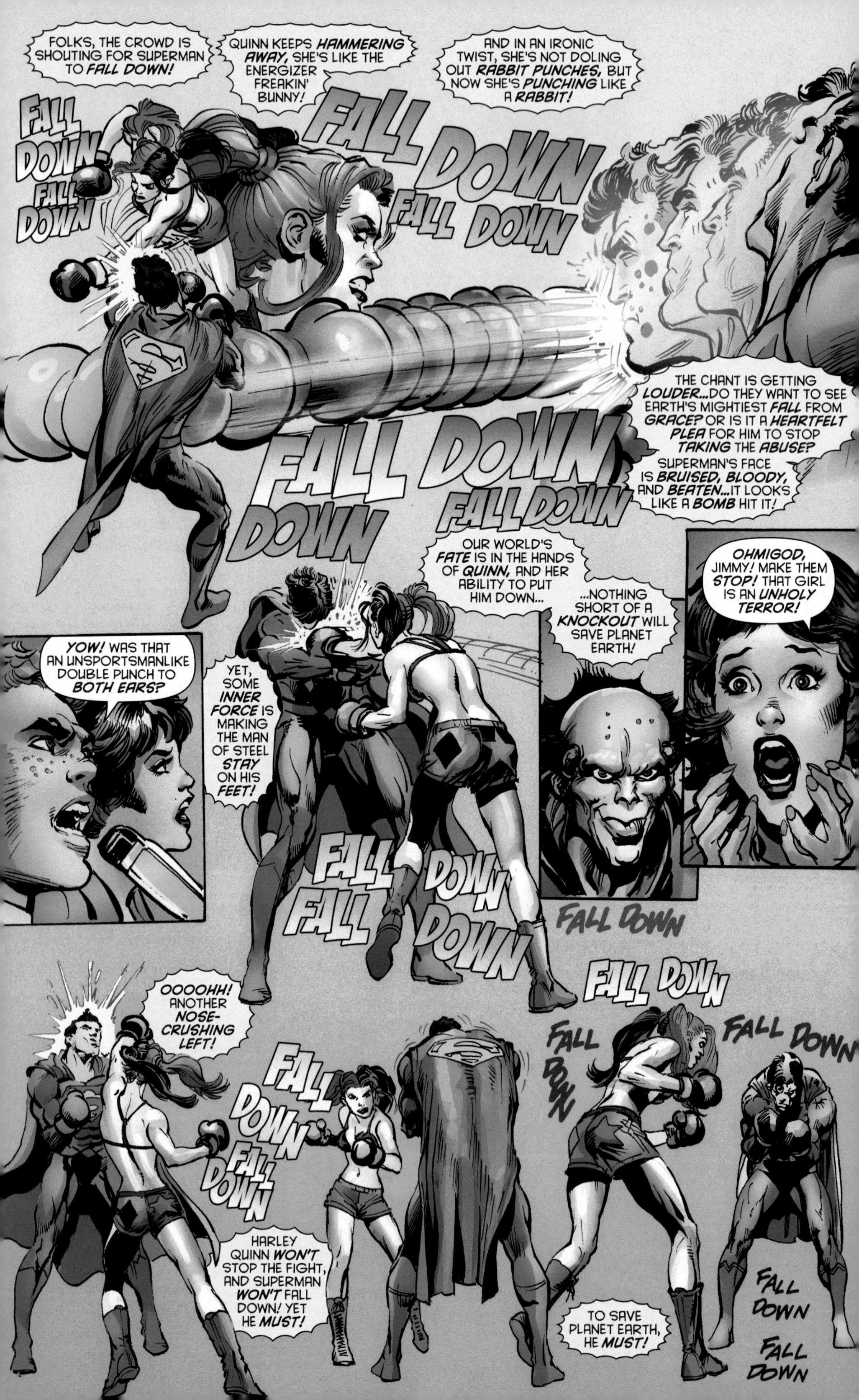

FOLKS, THE CROWD IS SHOUTING FOR SUPERMAN TO FALL DOWN!
QUINN KEEPS HAMMERING AWAY, SHE'S LIKE THE ENERGIZER FREAKIN' BUNNY!
AND IN AN IRONIC TWIST, SHE'S NOT DOLING OUT RABBIT PUNCHES, BUT NOW SHE'S PUNCHING LIKE A RABBIT!
FALL DOWN FALL DOWN
FALL DOWN FALL DOWN
THE CHANT IS GETTING LOUDER...DO THEY WANT TO SEE EARTH'S MIGHTIEST FALL FROM GRACE? OR IS IT A HEARTFELT PLEA FOR HIM TO STOP TAKING THE ABUSE?
SUPERMAN'S FACE IS BRUISED, BLOODY, AND BEATEN...IT LOOKS LIKE A BOMB HIT IT!
FALL DOWN DOWN
FALL DOWN
OUR WORLD'S FATE IS IN THE HANDS OF QUINN, AND HER ABILITY TO PUT HIM DOWN...
...NOTHING SHORT OF A KNOCKOUT WILL SAVE PLANET EARTH!
OHMIGOD, JIMMY! MAKE THEM STOP! THAT GIRL IS AN UNHOLY TERROR!
YOW! WAS THAT AN UNSPORTSMANLIKE DOUBLE PUNCH TO BOTH EARS?
YET, SOME INNER FORCE IS MAKING THE MAN OF STEEL STAY ON HIS FEET!
FALL DOWN FALL DOWN
FALL DOWN
FALL DOWN
OOOOHH! ANOTHER NOSE-CRUSHING LEFT!
FALL DOWN FALL DOWN
FALL DOWN
FALL DOWN
HARLEY QUINN WON'T STOP THE FIGHT, AND SUPERMAN WON'T FALL DOWN! YET HE MUST!
TO SAVE PLANET EARTH, HE MUST!
FALL DOWN FALL DOWN

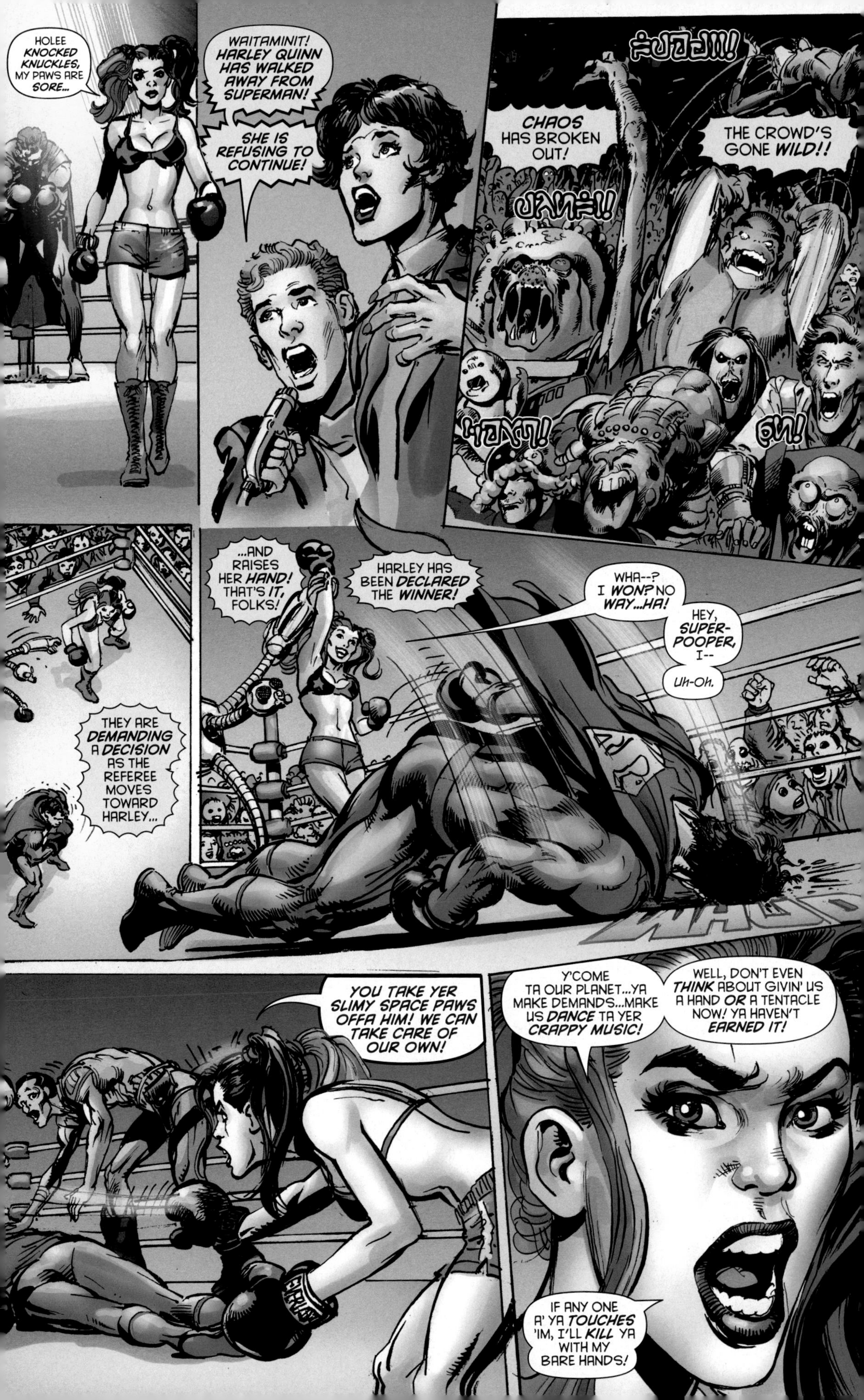

HOLEE KNOCKED KNUCKLES, MY PAWS ARE SORE...
WAITAMINIT! HARLEY QUINN HAS WALKED AWAY FROM SUPERMAN!
SHE IS REFUSING TO CONTINUE!
CHAOS HAS BROKEN OUT!
THE CROWD'S GONE WILD!!
THEY ARE DEMANDING A DECISION AS THE REFEREE MOVES TOWARD HARLEY...
...AND RAISES HER HAND! THAT'S IT, FOLKS!
HARLEY HAS BEEN DECLARED THE WINNER!
WHA--? I WON? NO WAY...HA!
HEY, SUPER-POOPER, I--
Uh-Oh.
YOU TAKE YER SLIMY SPACE PAWS OFFA HIM! WE CAN TAKE CARE OF OUR OWN!
Y'COME TA OUR PLANET...YA MAKE DEMANDS...MAKE US DANCE TA YER CRAPPY MUSIC!
WELL, DON'T EVEN THINK ABOUT GIVIN' US A HAND OR A TENTACLE NOW! YA HAVEN'T EARNED IT!
IF ANY ONE A' YA TOUCHES 'IM, I'LL KILL YA WITH MY BARE HANDS!

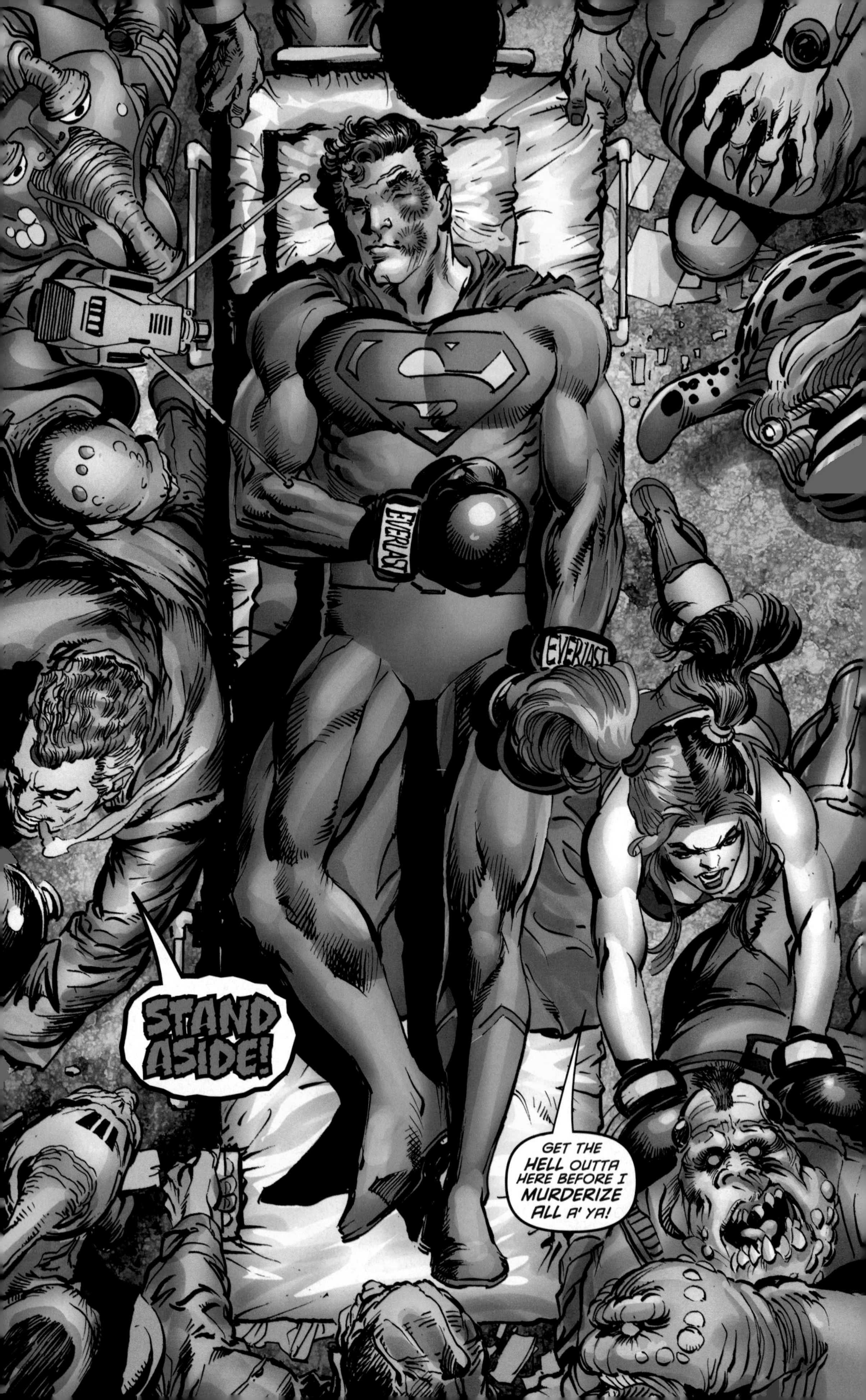
STAND ASIDE!
GET THE HELL OUTTA HERE BEFORE I MURDERIZE ALL A' YA!

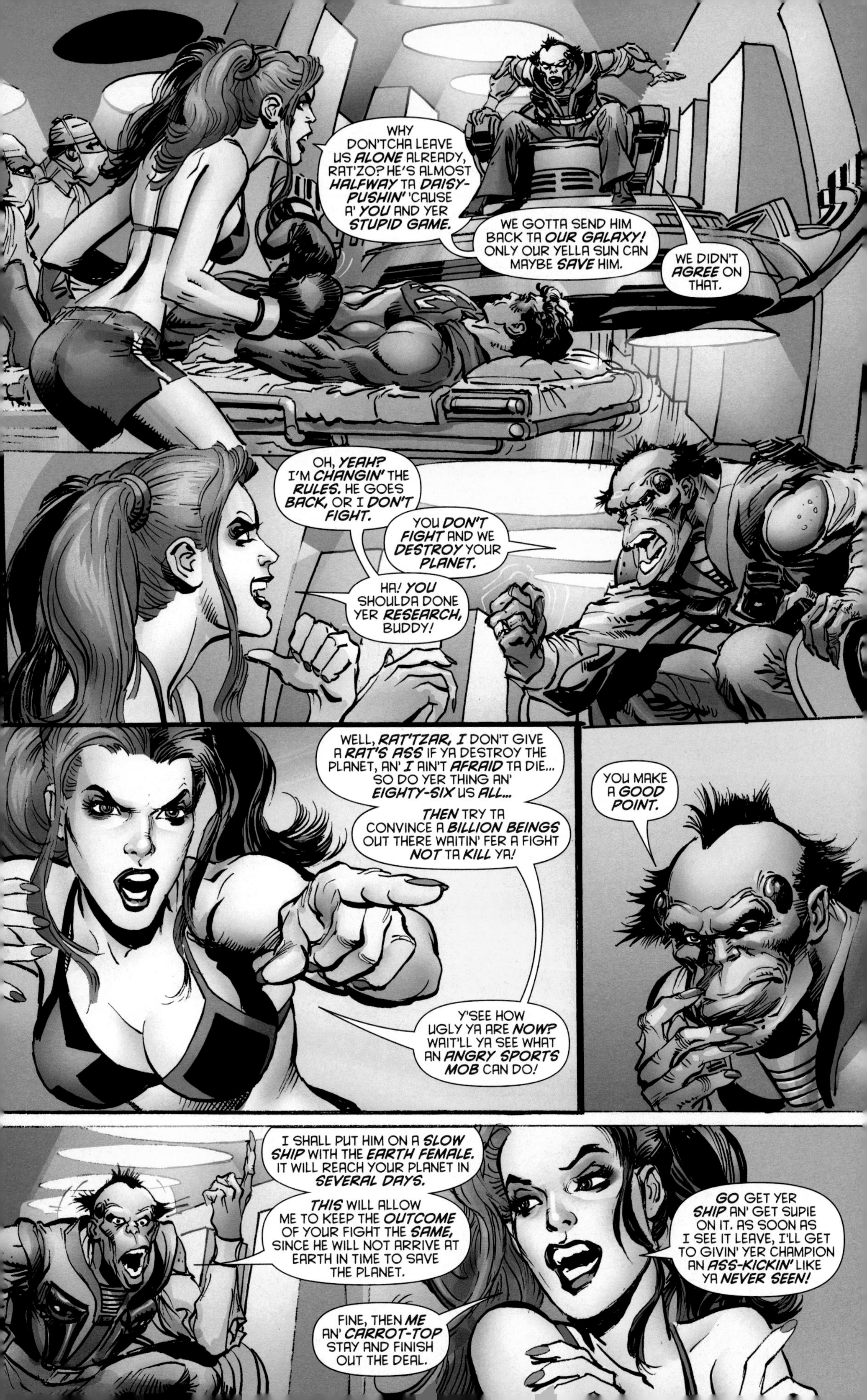
WHY DON'TCHA LEAVE US ALONE ALREADY, RAT'ZO? HE'S ALMOST HALFWAY TA DAISY-PUSHIN' 'CAUSE A' YOU AND YER STUPID GAME.
WE GOTTA SEND HIM BACK TA OUR GALAXY! ONLY OUR YELLA SUN CAN MAYBE SAVE HIM.
WE DIDN'T AGREE ON THAT.
OH, YEAH? I'M CHANGIN' THE RULES. HE GOES BACK, OR I DON'T FIGHT.
YOU DON'T FIGHT AND WE DESTROY YOUR PLANET.
HA! YOU SHOULDA DONE YER RESEARCH, BUDDY!
WELL, RAT'TZAR, I DON'T GIVE A RAT'S ASS IF YA DESTROY THE PLANET, AN' I AIN'T AFRAID TA DIE... SO DO YER THING AN' EIGHTY-SIX US ALL...
THEN TRY TA CONVINCE A BILLION BEINGS OUT THERE WAITIN' FER A FIGHT NOT TA KILL YA!
Y'SEE HOW UGLY YA ARE NOW? WAIT'LL YA SEE WHAT AN ANGRY SPORTS MOB CAN DO!
YOU MAKE A GOOD POINT.
I SHALL PUT HIM ON A SLOW SHIP WITH THE EARTH FEMALE. IT WILL REACH YOUR PLANET IN SEVERAL DAYS.
THIS WILL ALLOW ME TO KEEP THE OUTCOME OF YOUR FIGHT THE SAME, SINCE HE WILL NOT ARRIVE AT EARTH IN TIME TO SAVE THE PLANET.
FINE, THEN ME AN' CARROT-TOP STAY AND FINISH OUT THE DEAL.
GO GET YER SHIP AN' GET SUPIE ON IT. AS SOON AS I SEE IT LEAVE, I'LL GET TO GIVIN' YER CHAMPION AN ASS-KICKIN' LIKE YA NEVER SEEN!

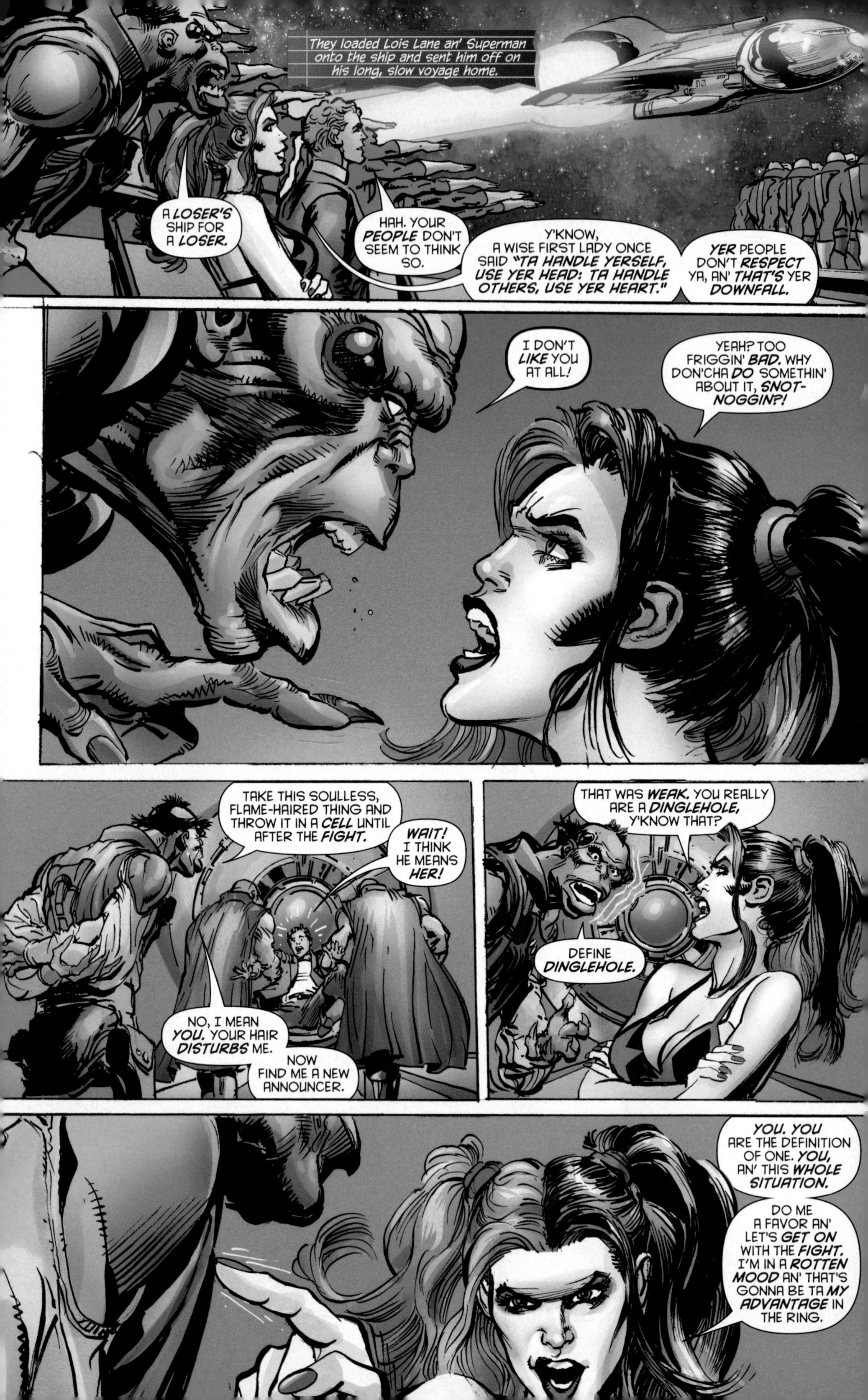
They loaded Lois Lane an' Superman onto the ship and sent him off on his long, slow voyage home.
A LOSER'S SHIP FOR A LOSER.
HAH. YOUR PEOPLE DON'T SEEM TO THINK SO.
Y'KNOW, A WISE FIRST LADY ONCE SAID "TA HANDLE YERSELF, USE YER HEAD: TA HANDLE OTHERS, USE YER HEART."
YER PEOPLE DON'T RESPECT YA, AN' THAT'S YER DOWNFALL.
I DON'T LIKE YOU AT ALL!
YEAH? TOO FRIGGIN' BAD. WHY DON'CHA DO SOMETHIN' ABOUT IT, SNOT-NOGGIN?!
TAKE THIS SOULLESS, FLAME-HAIRED THING AND THROW IT IN A CELL UNTIL AFTER THE FIGHT.
WAIT! I THINK HE MEANS HER!
NO, I MEAN YOU. YOUR HAIR DISTURBS ME.
NOW FIND ME A NEW ANNOUNCER.
THAT WAS WEAK. YOU REALLY ARE A DINGLEHOLE, Y'KNOW THAT?
DEFINE DINGLEHOLE.
YOU. YOU ARE THE DEFINITION OF ONE. YOU, AN' THIS WHOLE SITUATION.
DO ME A FAVOR AN' LET'S GET ON WITH THE FIGHT. I'M IN A ROTTEN MOOD AN' THAT'S GONNA BE TA MY ADVANTAGE IN THE RING.

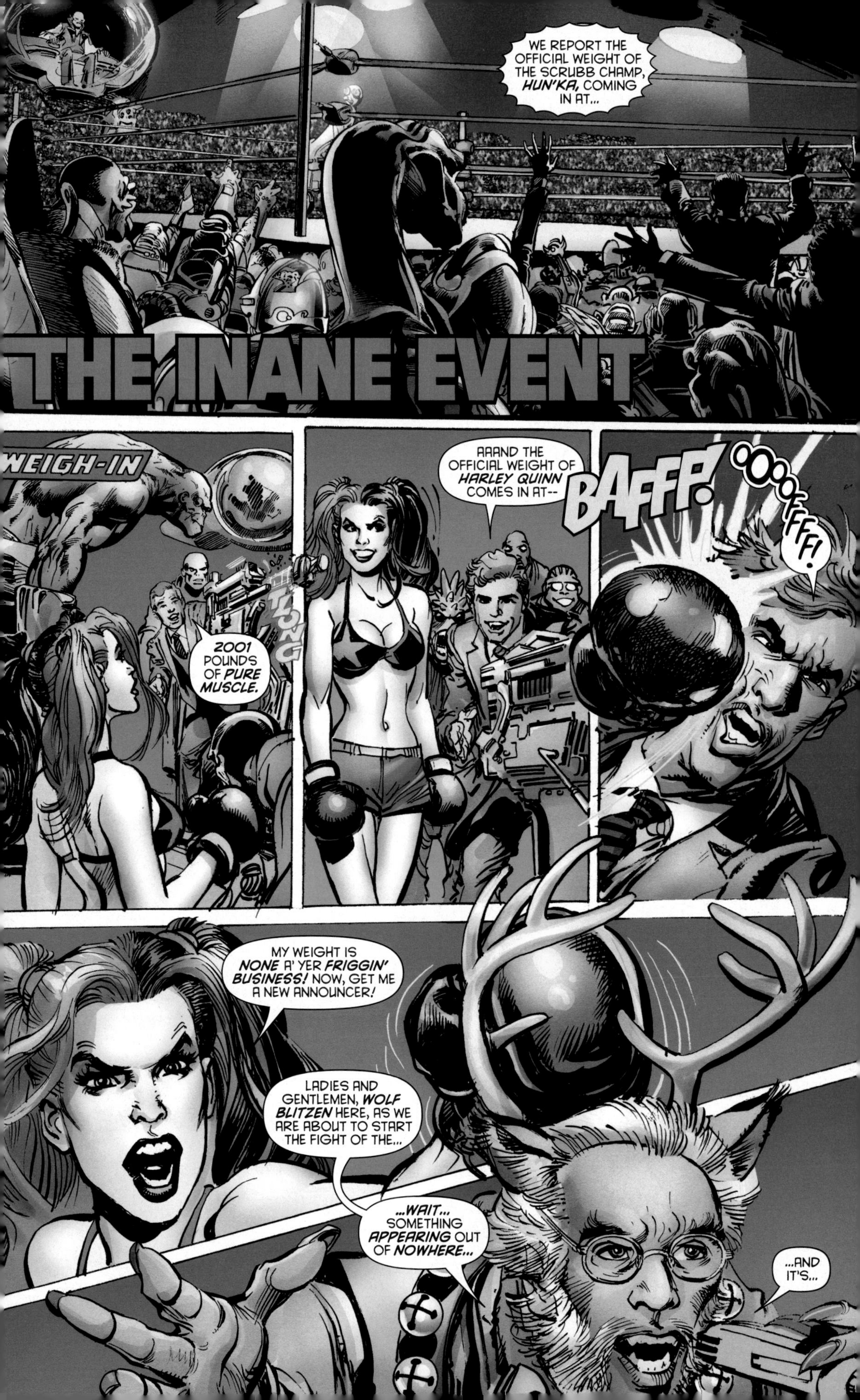
WE REPORT THE OFFICIAL WEIGHT OF THE SCRUBB CHAMP, HUN'KA, COMING IN AT...
THE INANE EVENT
WEIGH-IN
2001 POUNDS OF PURE MUSCLE.
TLONG
AAAND THE OFFICIAL WEIGHT OF HARLEY QUINN COMES IN AT--
BAFFP!
OOOFFF!
MY WEIGHT IS NONE A' YER FRIGGIN' BUSINESS! NOW, GET ME A NEW ANNOUNCER!
LADIES AND GENTLEMEN, WOLF BLITZEN HERE, AS WE ARE ABOUT TO START THE FIGHT OF THE...
...WAIT... SOMETHING APPEARING OUT OF NOWHERE...
...AND IT'S...

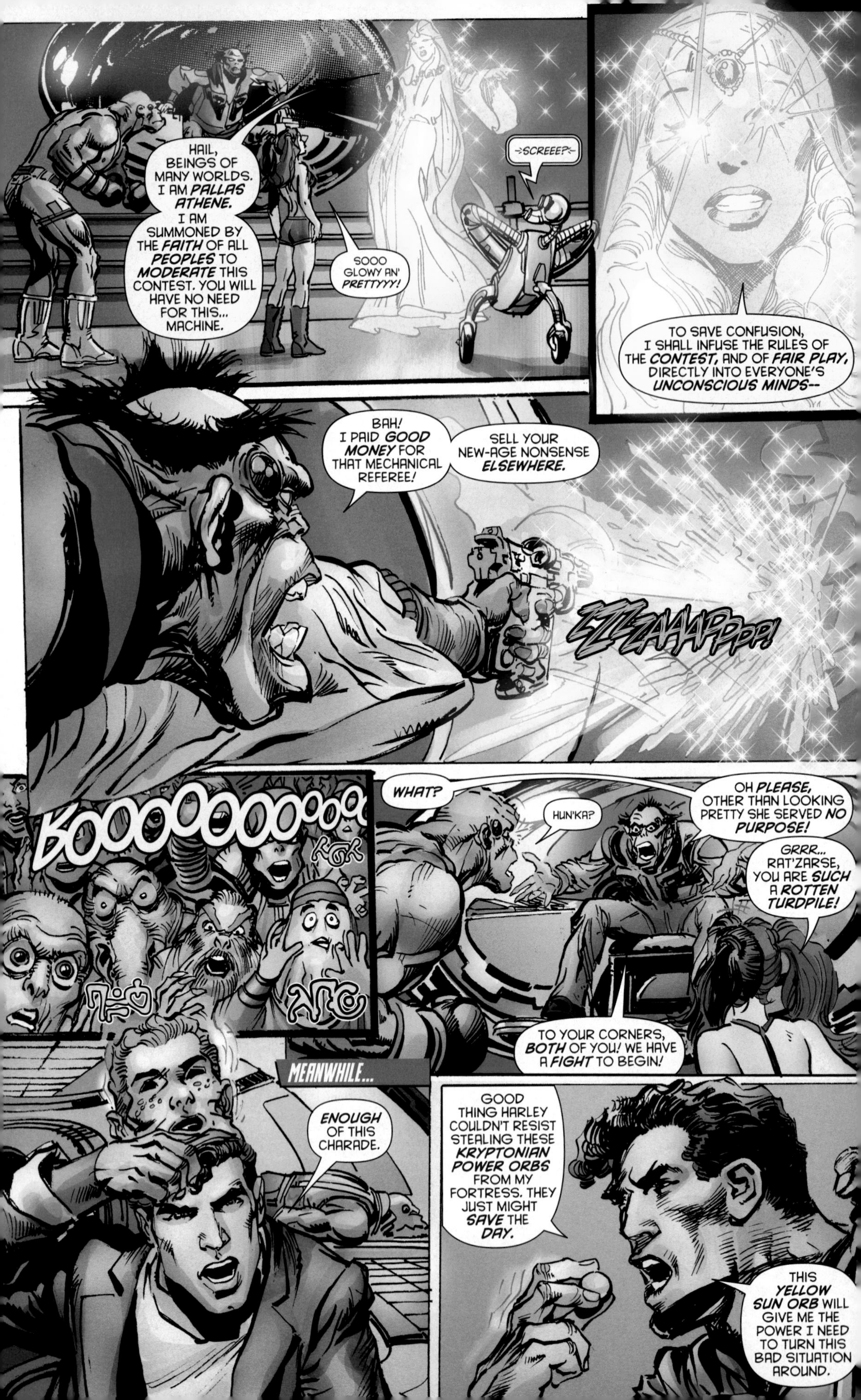

HAIL, BEINGS OF MANY WORLDS. I AM PALLAS ATHENE. I AM SUMMONED BY THE FAITH OF ALL PEOPLES TO MODERATE THIS CONTEST. YOU WILL HAVE NO NEED FOR THIS... MACHINE.
SOOO GLOWY AN' PRETTYYY!
SCREEE?
TO SAVE CONFUSION, I SHALL INFUSE THE RULES OF THE CONTEST, AND OF FAIR PLAY, DIRECTLY INTO EVERYONE'S UNCONSCIOUS MINDS--
BAH! I PAID GOOD MONEY FOR THAT MECHANICAL REFEREE!
SELL YOUR NEW-AGE NONSENSE ELSEWHERE.
ZZZZAAAPPPP!
BOOOOOOOOOOO
WHAT?
HUN'KA?
OH PLEASE, OTHER THAN LOOKING PRETTY SHE SERVED NO PURPOSE!
GRRR... RAT'ZAR'SE, YOU ARE SUCH A ROTTEN TURDPILE!
TO YOUR CORNERS, BOTH OF YOU! WE HAVE A FIGHT TO BEGIN!
MEANWHILE...
ENOUGH OF THIS CHARADE.
GOOD THING HARLEY COULDN'T RESIST STEALING THESE KRYPTONIAN POWER ORBS FROM MY FORTRESS. THEY JUST MIGHT SAVE THE DAY.
THIS YELLOW SUN ORB WILL GIVE ME THE POWER I NEED TO TURN THIS BAD SITUATION AROUND.

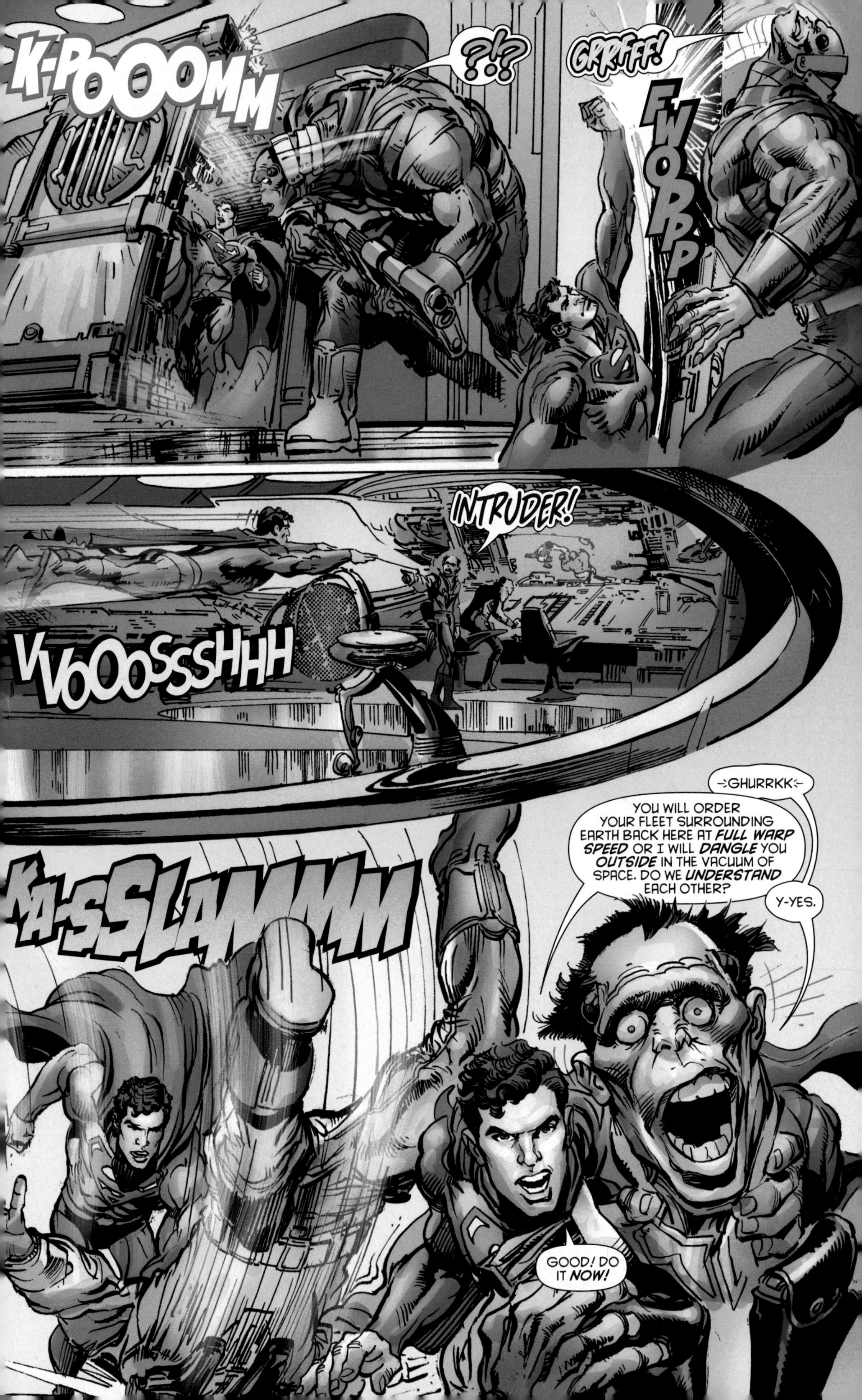
K-POOOMM
?!?
GRRFFF!
FWOPP
INTRUDER!
VVOOOSSSHHH
KA-SSLAMMMM
-GHURRKK-
YOU WILL ORDER YOUR FLEET SURROUNDING EARTH BACK HERE AT FULL WARP SPEED OR I WILL DANGLE YOU OUTSIDE IN THE VACUUM OF SPACE. DO WE UNDERSTAND EACH OTHER?
Y-YES.
GOOD! DO IT NOW!

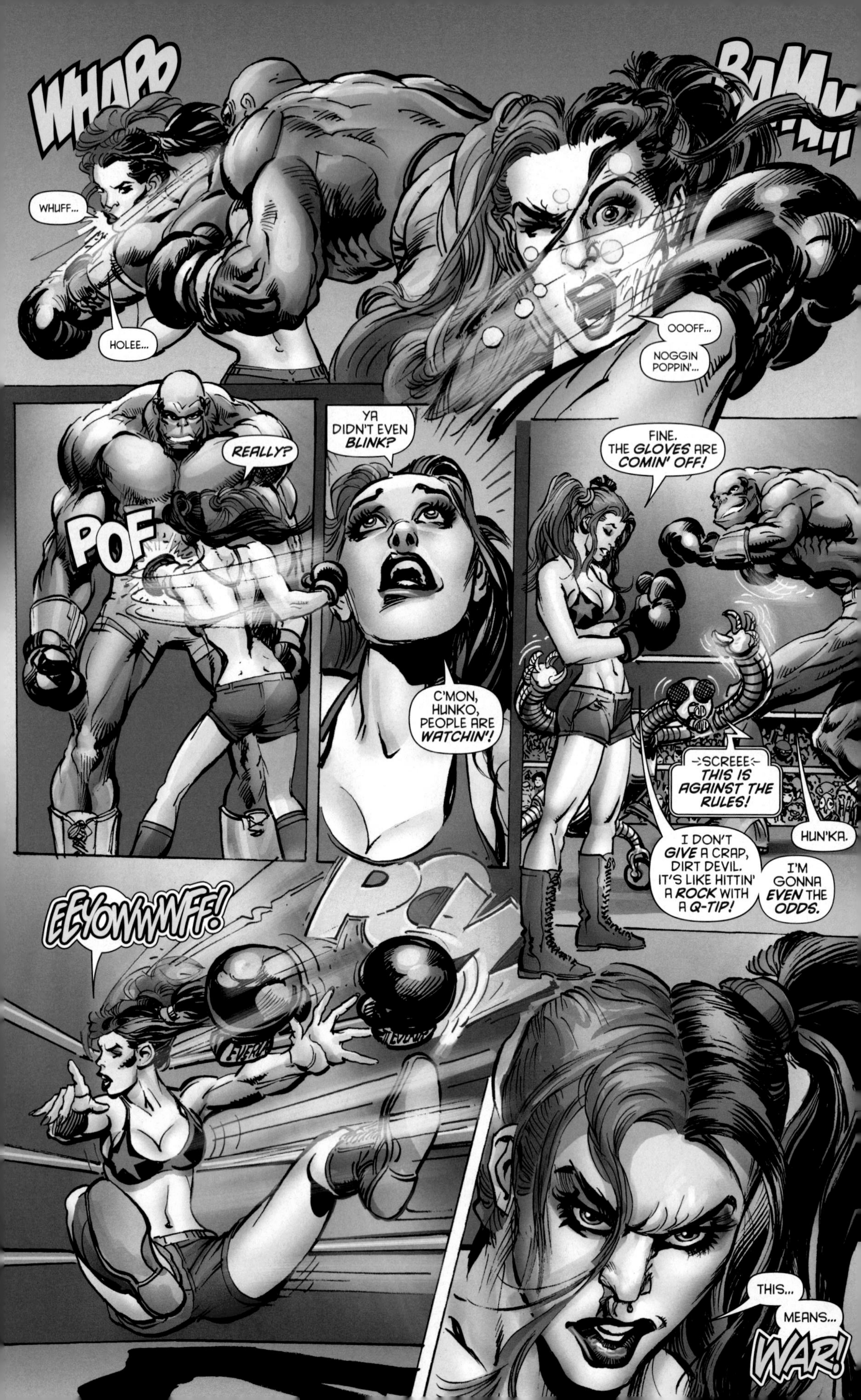
WHAPP
WHUFF...
HOLEE...
BAMM
OOOFF...
NOGGIN POPPIN'...
REALLY?
POF
YA DIDN'T EVEN BLINK?
C'MON, HUNKO, PEOPLE ARE WATCHIN'!
FINE. THE GLOVES ARE COMIN' OFF!
SCREEE THIS IS AGAINST THE RULES!
HUN'KA.
I DON'T GIVE A CRAP, DIRT DEVIL. IT'S LIKE HITTIN' A ROCK WITH A Q-TIP!
I'M GONNA EVEN THE ODDS.
EEYOWWWFF!
THIS...
MEANS...
WAR!

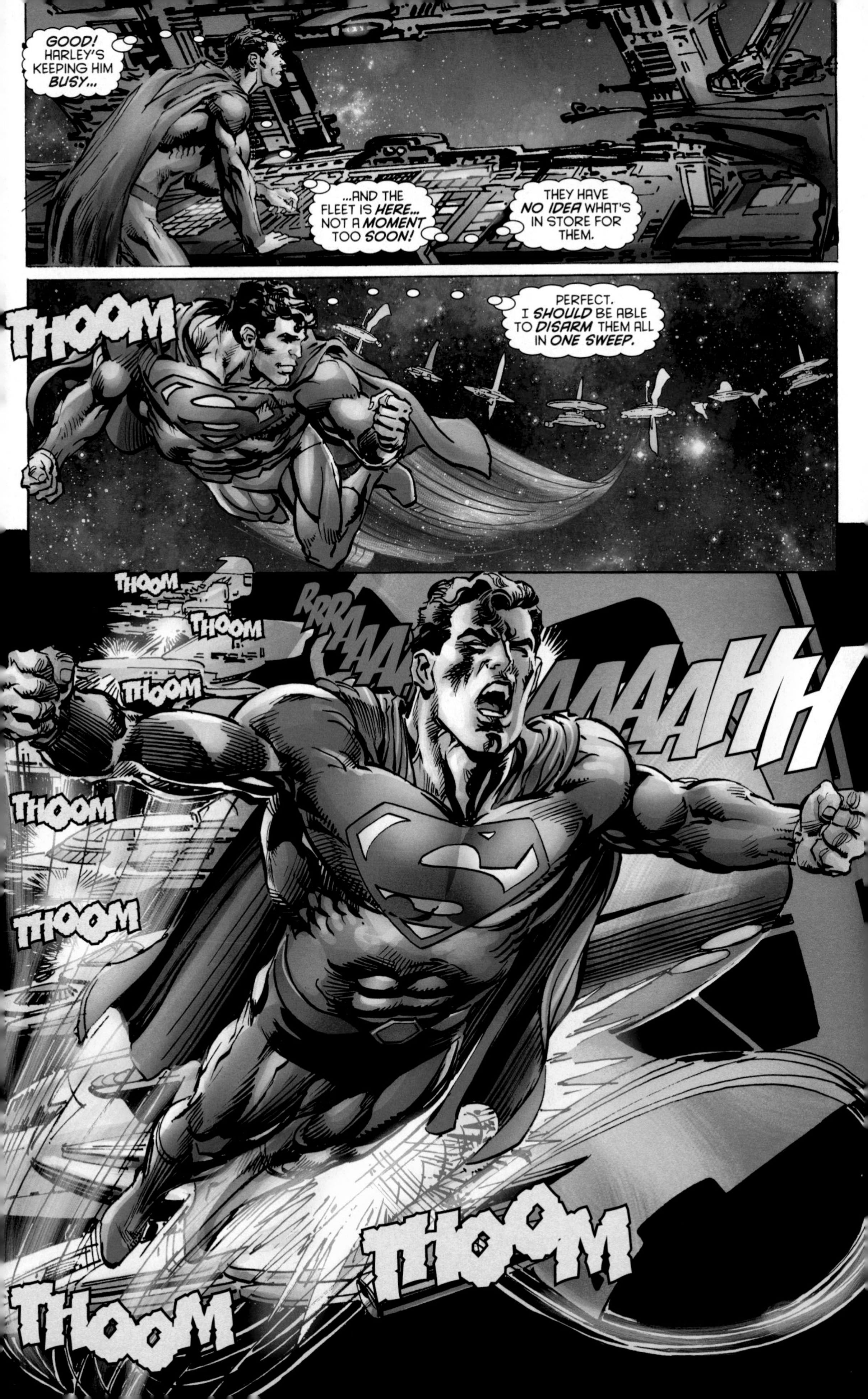
GOOD! HARLEY'S KEEPING HIM BUSY...
...AND THE FLEET IS HERE... NOT A MOMENT TOO SOON!
THEY HAVE NO IDEA WHAT'S IN STORE FOR THEM.
THOOM
PERFECT. I SHOULD BE ABLE TO DISARM THEM ALL IN ONE SWEEP.
THOOM
THOOM
THOOM
RRRAAAAAAAAAAHH
THOOM
THOOM
THOOM
THOOM

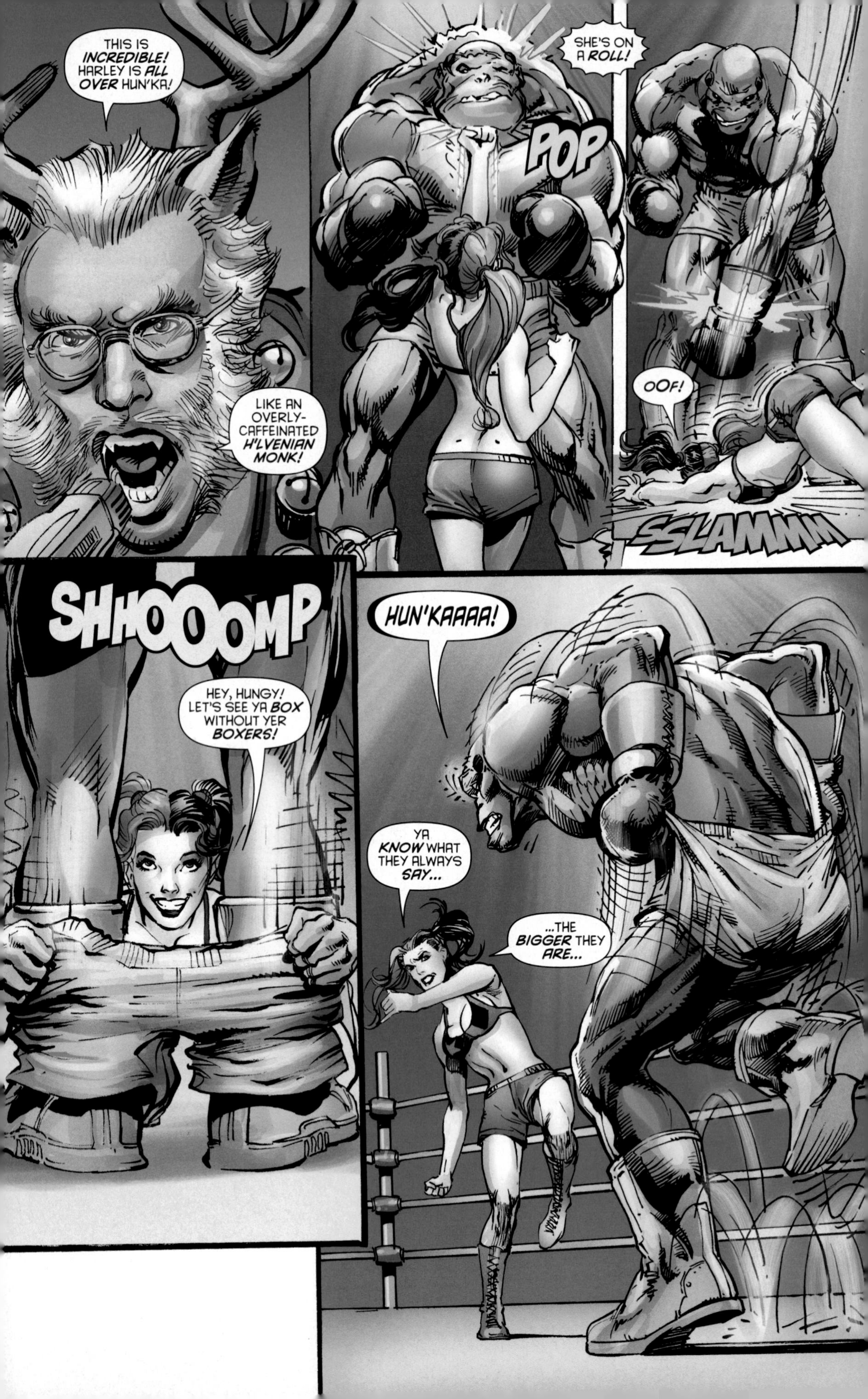
THIS IS INCREDIBLE! HARLEY IS ALL OVER HUN'KA!
LIKE AN OVERLY-CAFFEINATED H'LVENIAN MONK!
POP
SHE'S ON A ROLL!
OOF!
SSLAMMM
SHHOOOOMP
HEY, HUNGY! LET'S SEE YA BOX WITHOUT YER BOXERS!
HUN'KAAAA!
YA KNOW WHAT THEY ALWAYS SAY...
...THE BIGGER THEY ARE...

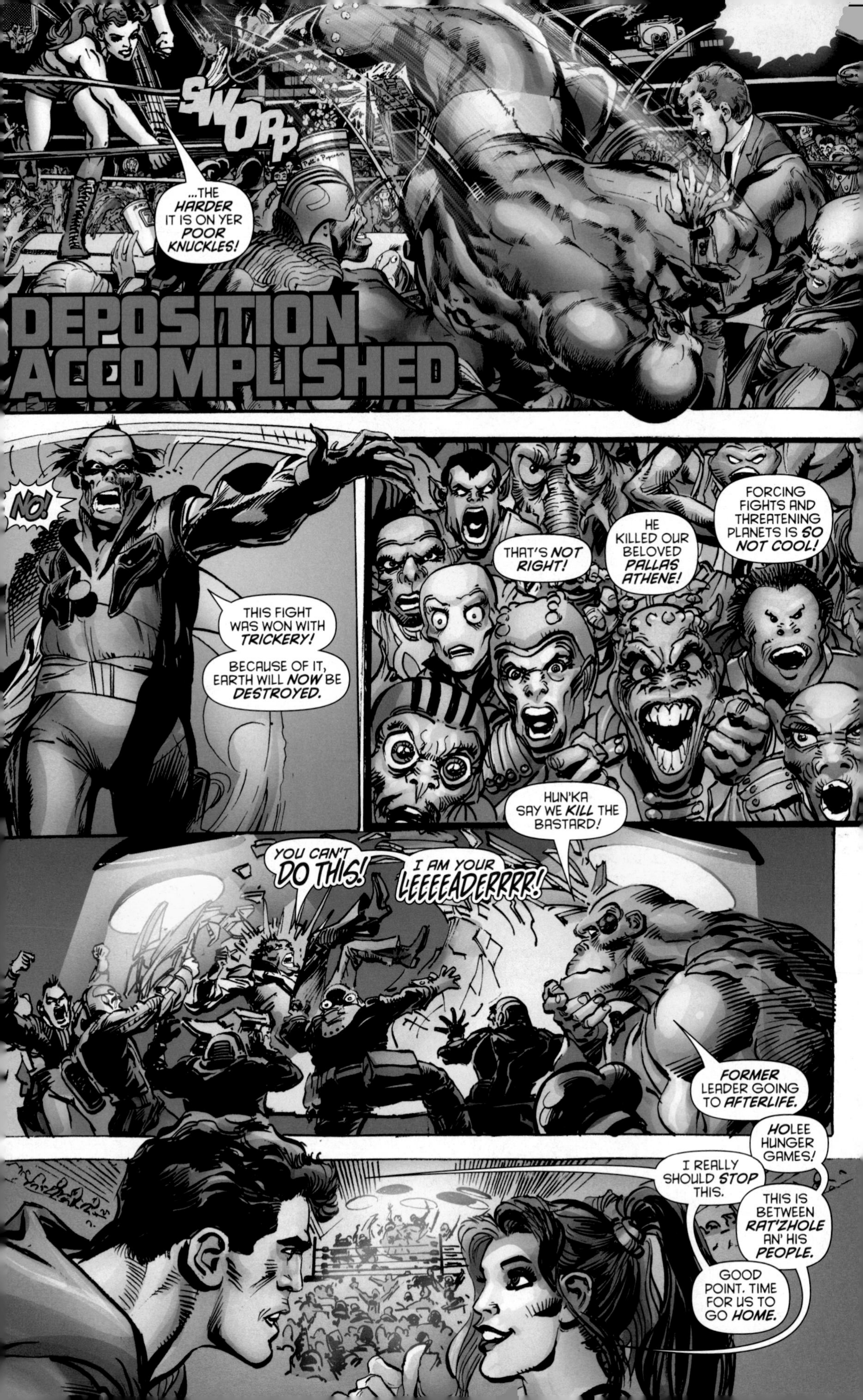
SWORP
...THE HARDER IT IS ON YER POOR KNUCKLES!
DEPOSITION ACCOMPLISHED
NO!
THIS FIGHT WAS WON WITH TRICKERY!
BECAUSE OF IT, EARTH WILL NOW BE DESTROYED.
THAT'S NOT RIGHT!
HE KILLED OUR BELOVED PALLAS ATHENE!
FORCING FIGHTS AND THREATENING PLANETS IS SO NOT COOL!
HUN'KA SAY WE KILL THE BASTARD!
YOU CAN'T DO THIS!
I AM YOUR LEEEEADERRRR!
FORMER LEADER GOING TO AFTERLIFE.
HOLEE HUNGER GAMES!
I REALLY SHOULD STOP THIS.
THIS IS BETWEEN RAT'ZHOLE AN' HIS PEOPLE.
GOOD POINT. TIME FOR US TO GO HOME.

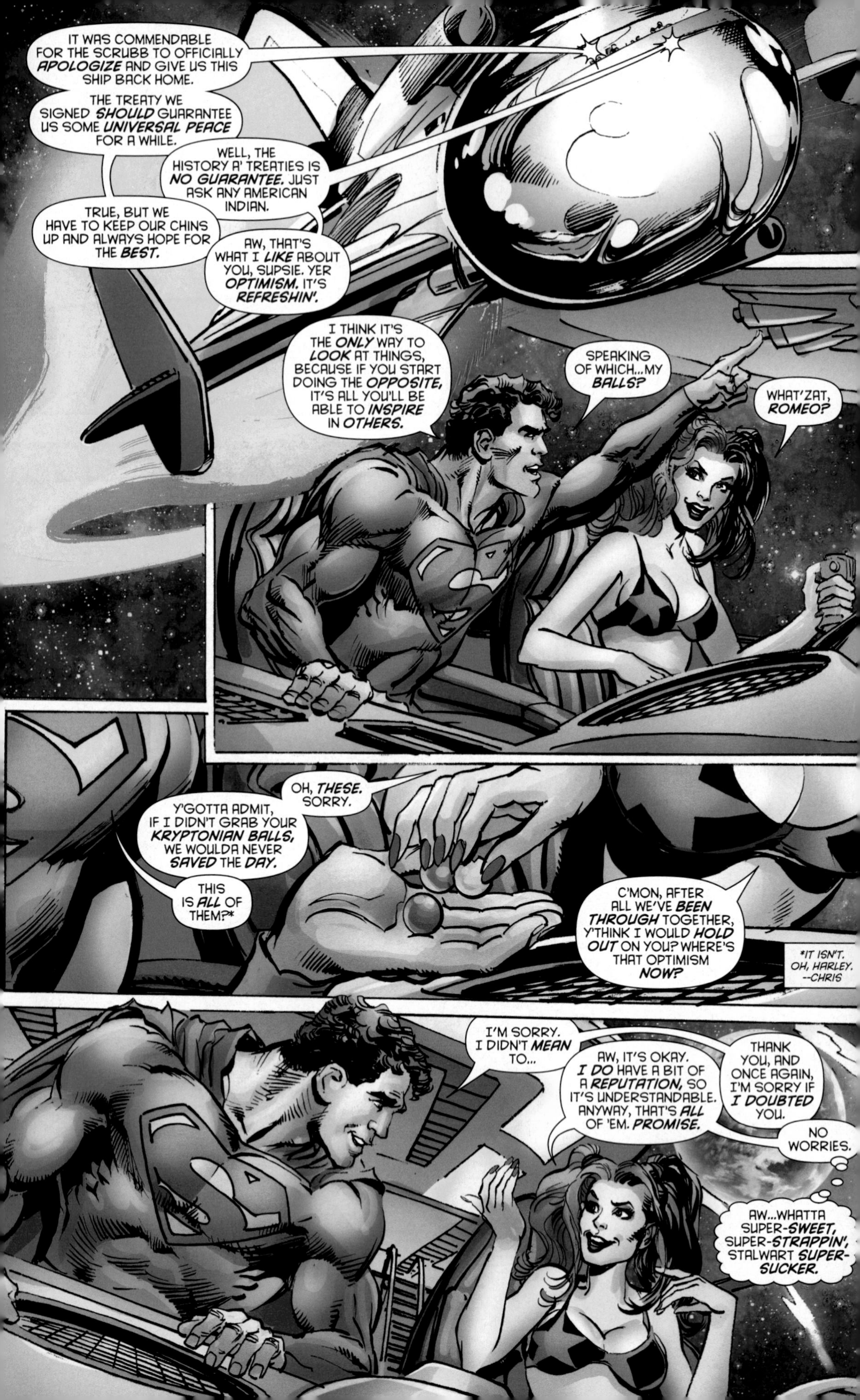
IT WAS COMMENDABLE FOR THE SCRUBB TO OFFICIALLY APOLOGIZE AND GIVE US THIS SHIP BACK HOME.
THE TREATY WE SIGNED SHOULD GUARANTEE US SOME UNIVERSAL PEACE FOR A WHILE.
WELL, THE HISTORY A' TREATIES IS NO GUARANTEE. JUST ASK ANY AMERICAN INDIAN.
TRUE, BUT WE HAVE TO KEEP OUR CHINS UP AND ALWAYS HOPE FOR THE BEST.
AW, THAT'S WHAT I LIKE ABOUT YOU, SUPSIE. YER OPTIMISM. IT'S REFRESHIN'.
I THINK IT'S THE ONLY WAY TO LOOK AT THINGS, BECAUSE IF YOU START DOING THE OPPOSITE, IT'S ALL YOU'LL BE ABLE TO INSPIRE IN OTHERS.
SPEAKING OF WHICH...MY BALLS?
WHAT'ZAT, ROMEO?
OH, THESE. SORRY.
Y'GOTTA ADMIT, IF I DIDN'T GRAB YOUR KRYPTONIAN BALLS, WE WOULDA NEVER SAVED THE DAY.
THIS IS ALL OF THEM?*
C'MON, AFTER ALL WE'VE BEEN THROUGH TOGETHER, Y'THINK I WOULD HOLD OUT ON YOU? WHERE'S THAT OPTIMISM NOW?
*IT ISN'T. OH, HARLEY. --CHRIS
I'M SORRY. I DIDN'T MEAN TO...
AW, IT'S OKAY. I DO HAVE A BIT OF A REPUTATION, SO IT'S UNDERSTANDABLE. ANYWAY, THAT'S ALL OF 'EM. PROMISE.
THANK YOU, AND ONCE AGAIN, I'M SORRY IF I DOUBTED YOU.
NO WORRIES.
AW...WHATTA SUPER-SWEET, SUPER-STRAPPIN', STALWART SUPER-SUCKER.

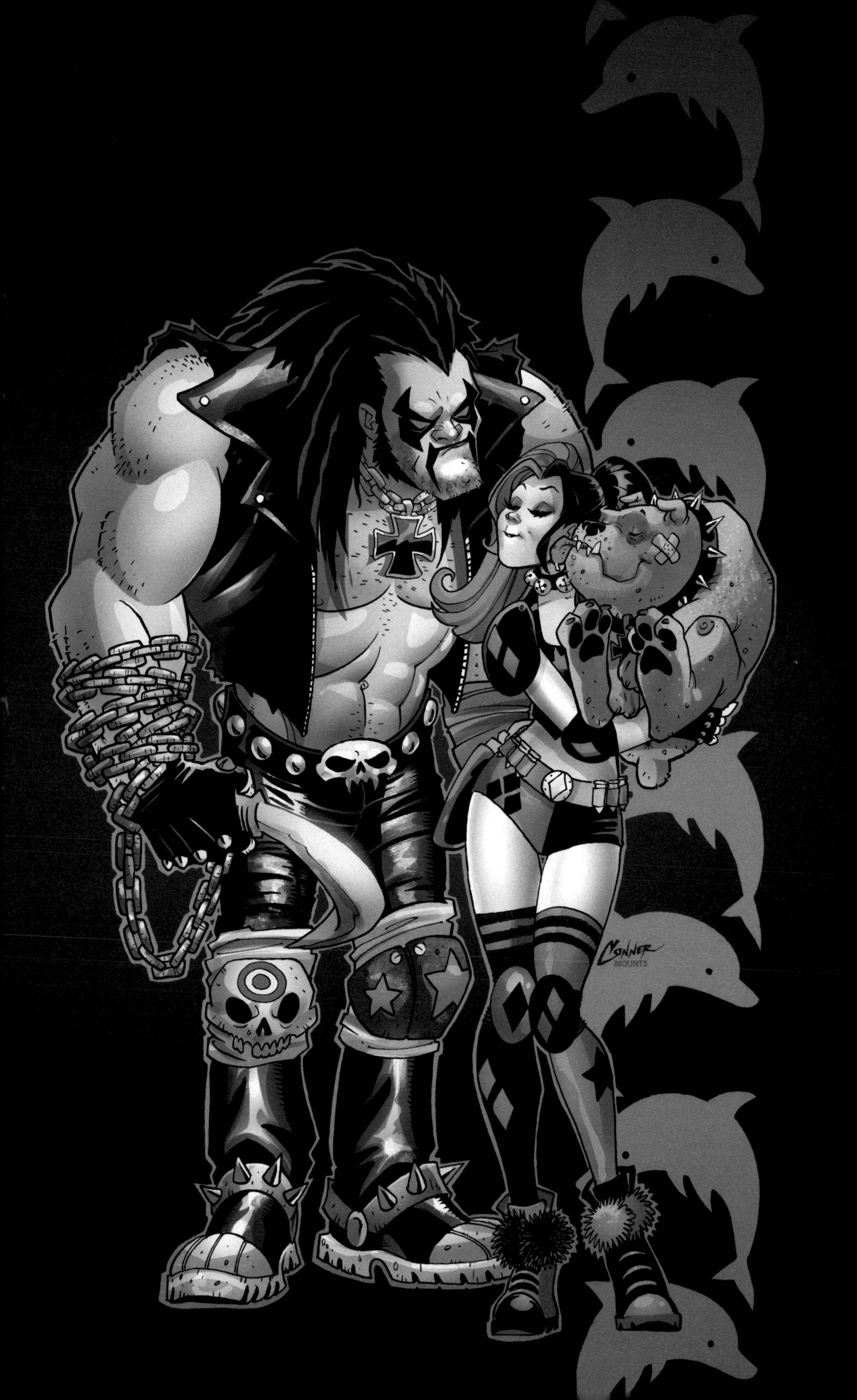
CONNER
MOUNTS

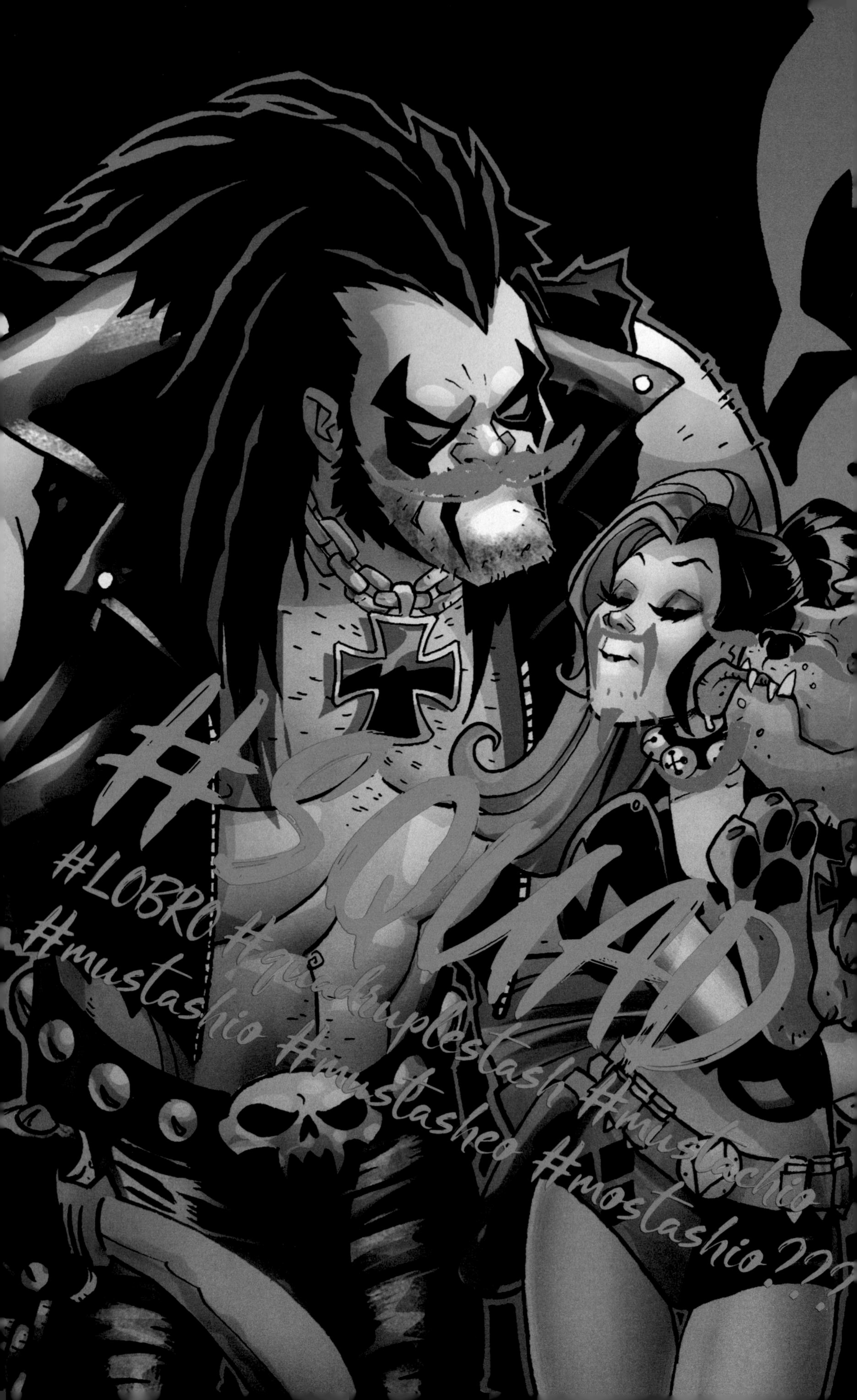
#SQUAD
#LOBRO #quadruplestash #mustachio
#mustashio #mustasheo #mostashio???

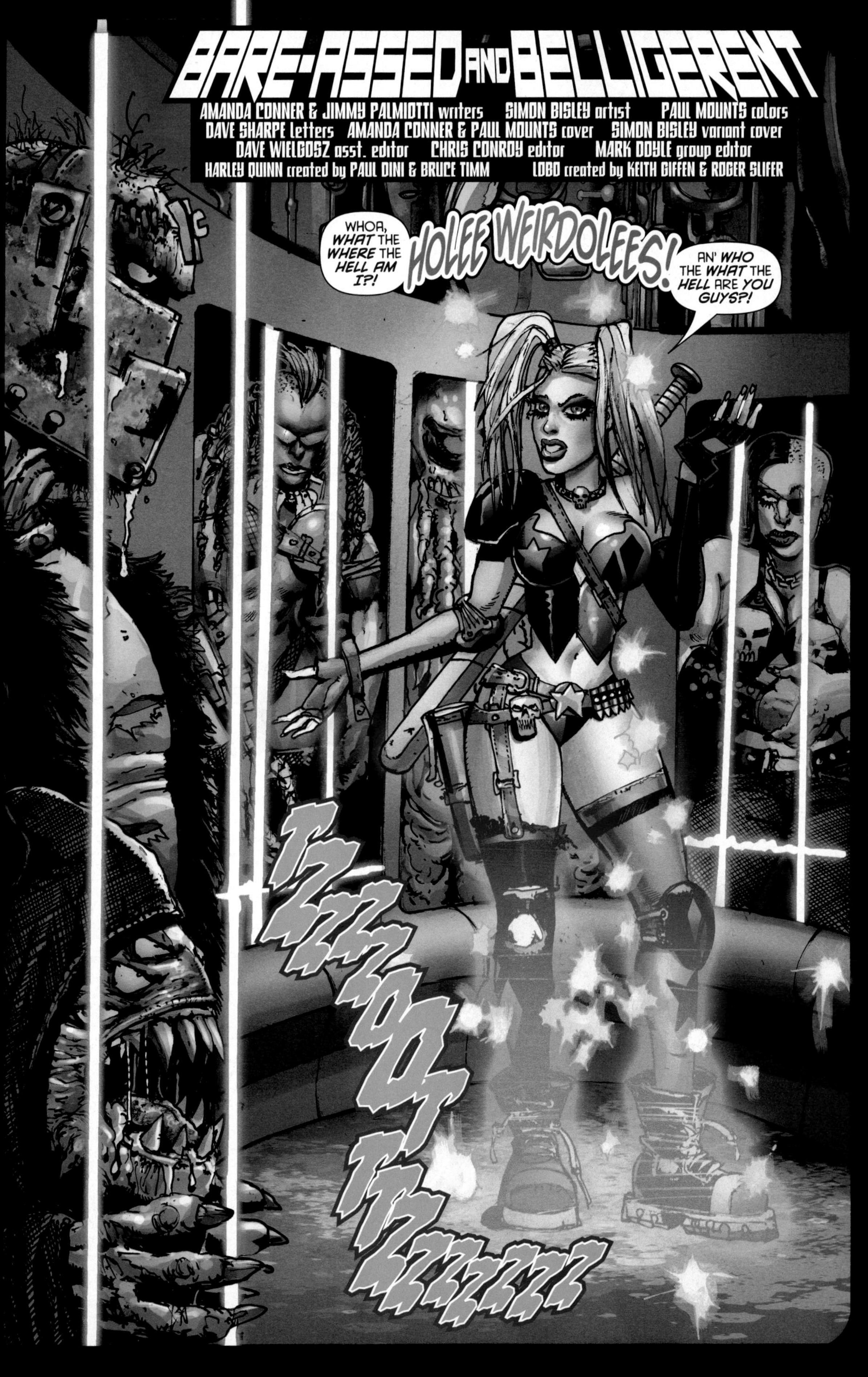
BARE-ASSED AND BELLIGERENT
AMANDA CONNER & JIMMY PALMIOTTI writers SIMON BISLEY artist PAUL MOUNTS colors
DAVE SHARPE letters AMANDA CONNER & PAUL MOUNTS cover SIMON BISLEY variant cover
DAVE WIELGOSZ asst. editor CHRIS CONROY editor MARK DOYLE group editor
HARLEY QUINN created by PAUL DINI & BRUCE TIMM LOBO created by KEITH GIFFEN & ROGER SLIFER
WHOA, WHAT THE WHERE THE HELL AM I?!
HOLEE WEIRDOLEES!
AN' WHO THE WHAT THE HELL ARE YOU GUYS?!
TZZZOOT TZZZZZZZZ

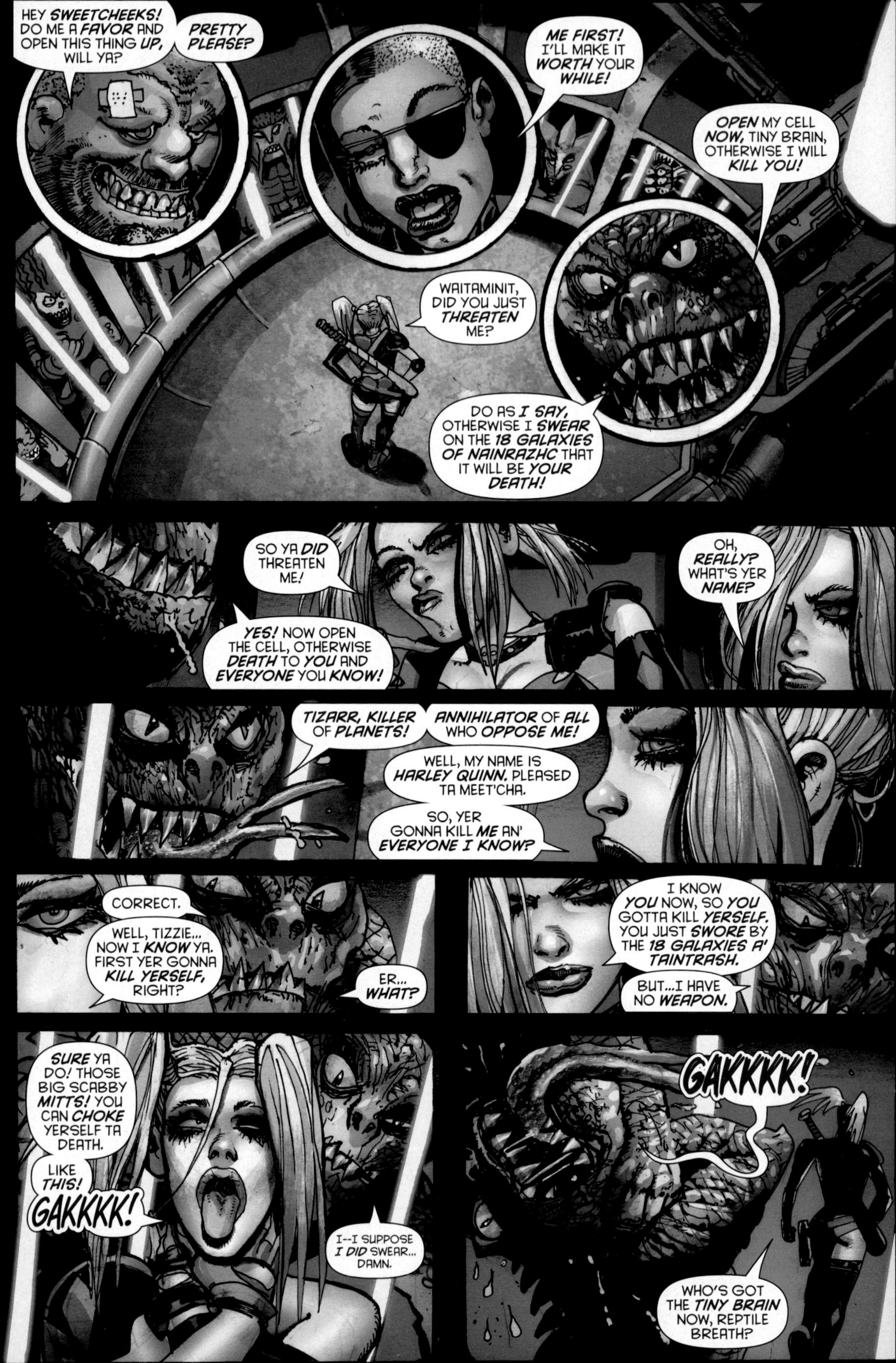

HEY SWEETCHEEKS! DO ME A FAVOR AND OPEN THIS THING UP, WILL YA?
PRETTY PLEASE?
ME FIRST! I'LL MAKE IT WORTH YOUR WHILE!
OPEN MY CELL NOW, TINY BRAIN, OTHERWISE I WILL KILL YOU!
WAITAMINIT, DID YOU JUST THREATEN ME?
DO AS I SAY, OTHERWISE I SWEAR ON THE 18 GALAXIES OF NAINRAZHC THAT IT WILL BE YOUR DEATH!
SO YA DID THREATEN ME!
YES! NOW OPEN THE CELL, OTHERWISE DEATH TO YOU AND EVERYONE YOU KNOW!
OH, REALLY? WHAT'S YER NAME?
TIZARR, KILLER OF PLANETS!
ANNIHILATOR OF ALL WHO OPPOSE ME!
WELL, MY NAME IS HARLEY QUINN. PLEASED TA MEET'CHA.
SO, YER GONNA KILL ME AN' EVERYONE I KNOW?
CORRECT.
WELL, TIZZIE... NOW I KNOW YA. FIRST YER GONNA KILL YERSELF, RIGHT?
ER... WHAT?
I KNOW YOU NOW, SO YOU GOTTA KILL YERSELF. YOU JUST SWORE BY THE 18 GALAXIES A' TAINTRASH.
BUT...I HAVE NO WEAPON.
SURE YA DO! THOSE BIG SCABBY MITTS! YOU CAN CHOKE YERSELF TA DEATH.
LIKE THIS!
GAKKKK!
I--I SUPPOSE I DID SWEAR... DAMN.
GAKKKK!
WHO'S GOT THE TINY BRAIN NOW, REPTILE BREATH?

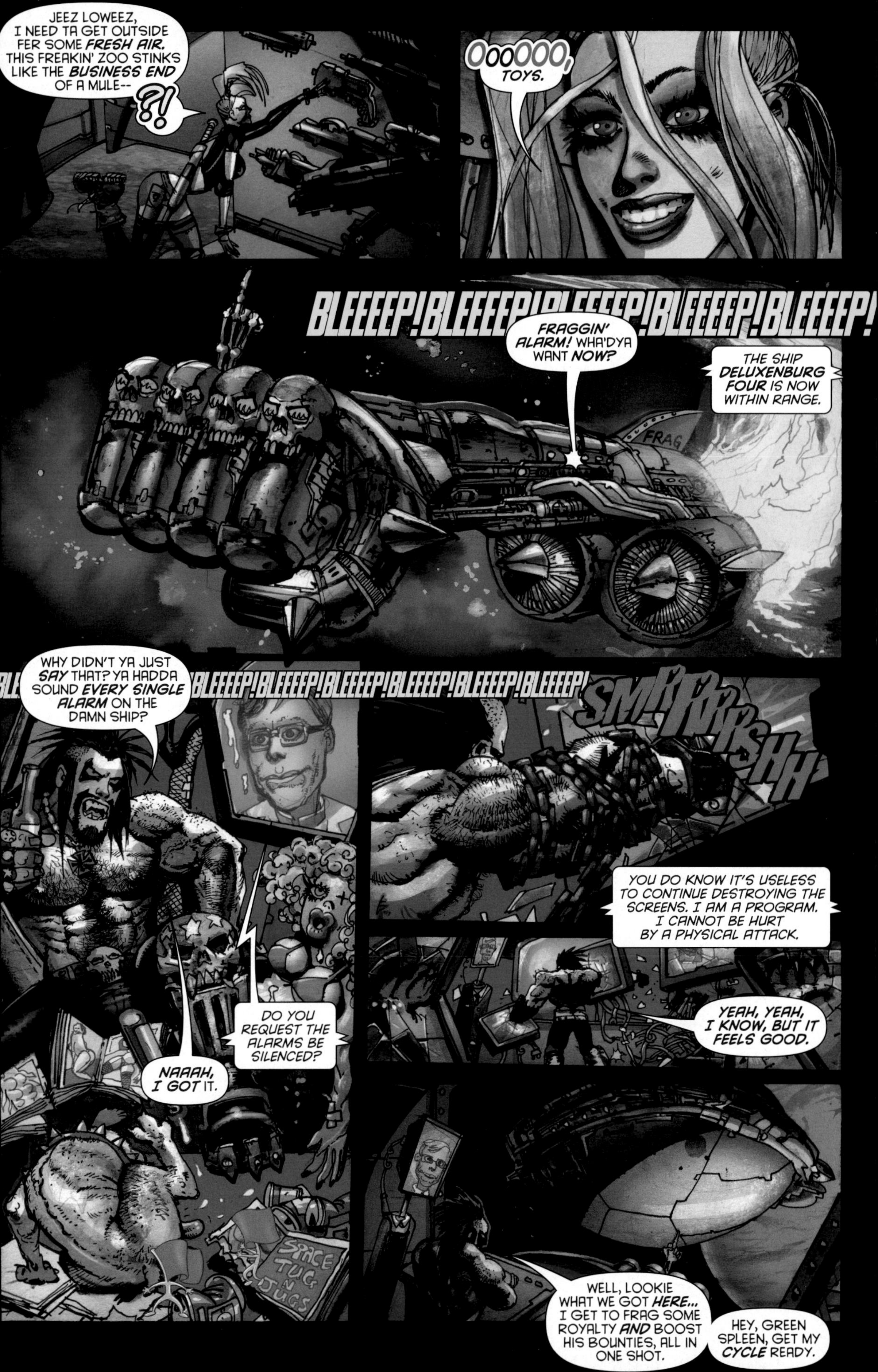

JEEZ LOWEEZ, I NEED TA GET OUTSIDE FER SOME FRESH AIR. THIS FREAKIN' ZOO STINKS LIKE THE BUSINESS END OF A MULE--
?!
OOOOOO, TOYS.
BLEEEEP! BLEEEEP! BLEEEEP! BLEEEEP! BLEEEEP!
FRAGGIN' ALARM! WHA'DYA WANT NOW?
THE SHIP DELUXENBURG FOUR IS NOW WITHIN RANGE.
FRAG
WHY DIDN'T YA JUST SAY THAT? YA HADDA SOUND EVERY SINGLE ALARM ON THE DAMN SHIP?
BLEEEEP! BLEEEEP! BLEEEEP! BLEEEEP! BLEEEEP!
DO YOU REQUEST THE ALARMS BE SILENCED?
NAAAH, I GOT IT.
SPACE TUG N JUGS
SMRRRRSHH
YOU DO KNOW IT'S USELESS TO CONTINUE DESTROYING THE SCREENS. I AM A PROGRAM. I CANNOT BE HURT BY A PHYSICAL ATTACK.
YEAH, YEAH, I KNOW, BUT IT FEELS GOOD.
WELL, LOOKIE WHAT WE GOT HERE... I GET TO FRAG SOME ROYALTY AND BOOST HIS BOUNTIES, ALL IN ONE SHOT.
HEY, GREEN SPLEEN, GET MY CYCLE READY.

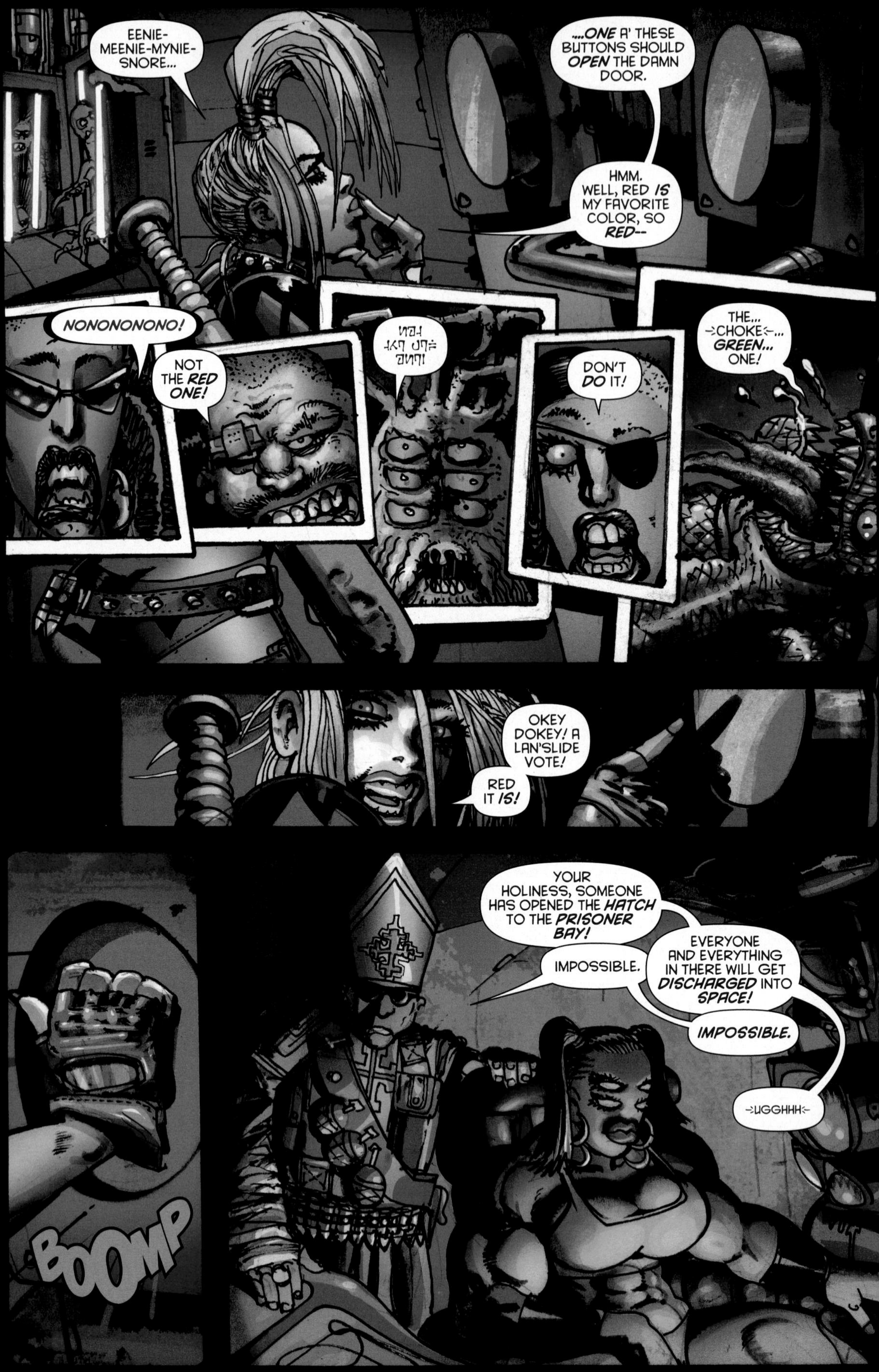
EENIE-MEENIE-MYNIE-SNORE...
...ONE A' THESE BUTTONS SHOULD OPEN THE DAMN DOOR.
HMM. WELL, RED IS MY FAVORITE COLOR, SO RED--
NONONONONO!
NOT THE RED ONE!
DON'T DO IT!
THE... CHOKE... GREEN... ONE!
OKEY DOKEY! A LAN'SLIDE VOTE!
RED IT IS!
YOUR HOLINESS, SOMEONE HAS OPENED THE HATCH TO THE PRISONER BAY!
IMPOSSIBLE.
EVERYONE AND EVERYTHING IN THERE WILL GET DISCHARGED INTO SPACE!
IMPOSSIBLE.
UGGHHH
BOOMP

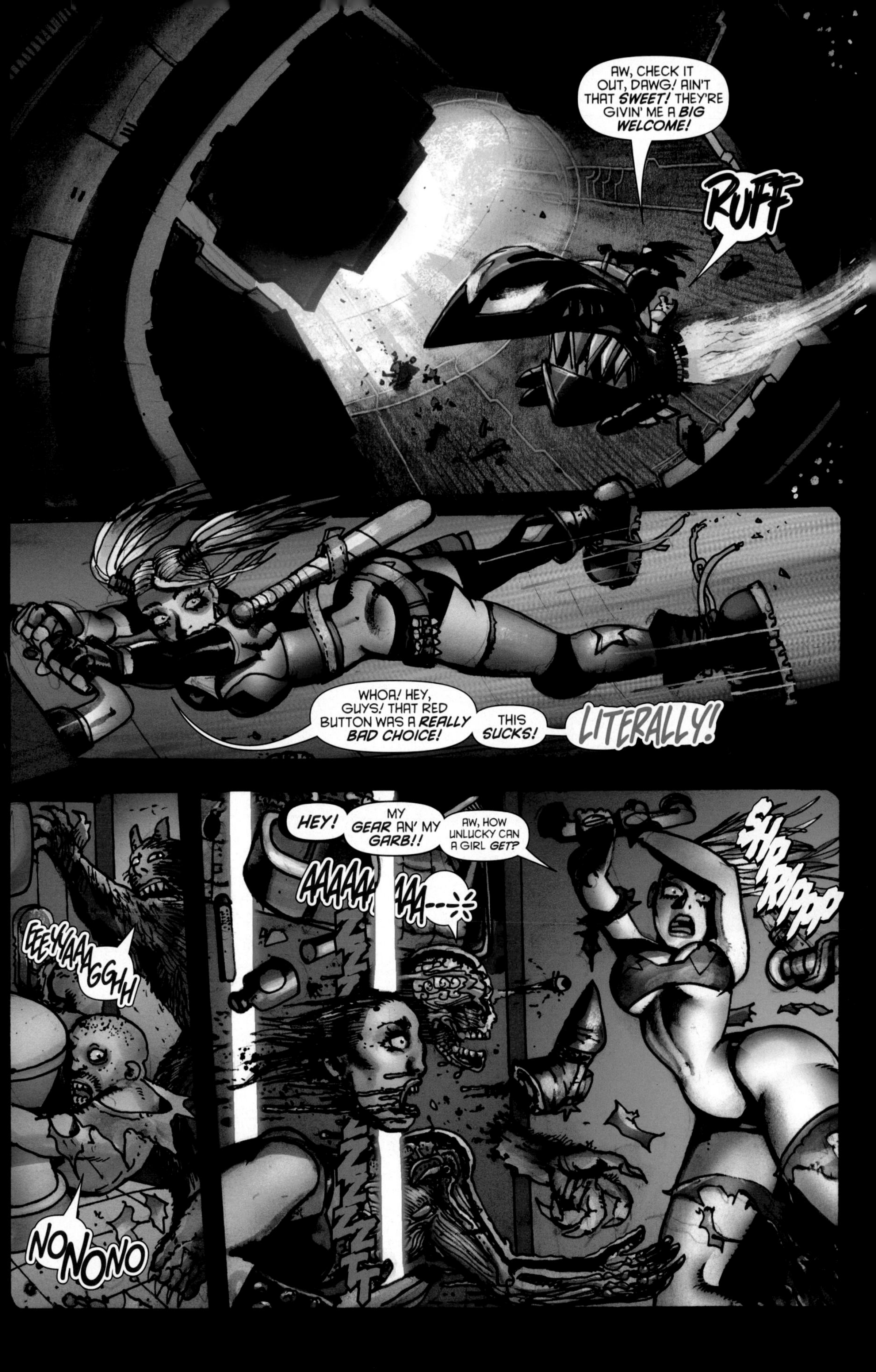
AW, CHECK IT OUT, DAWG! AIN'T THAT SWEET! THEY'RE GIVIN' ME A BIG WELCOME!
RUFF
WHOA! HEY, GUYS! THAT RED BUTTON WAS A REALLY BAD CHOICE!
THIS SUCKS!
LITERALLY!
EEEYAAAAGGHH
NONONO
HEY!
MY GEAR AN' MY GARB!!
AW, HOW UNLUCKY CAN A GIRL GET?
SHRIPPP
ZZZZZT

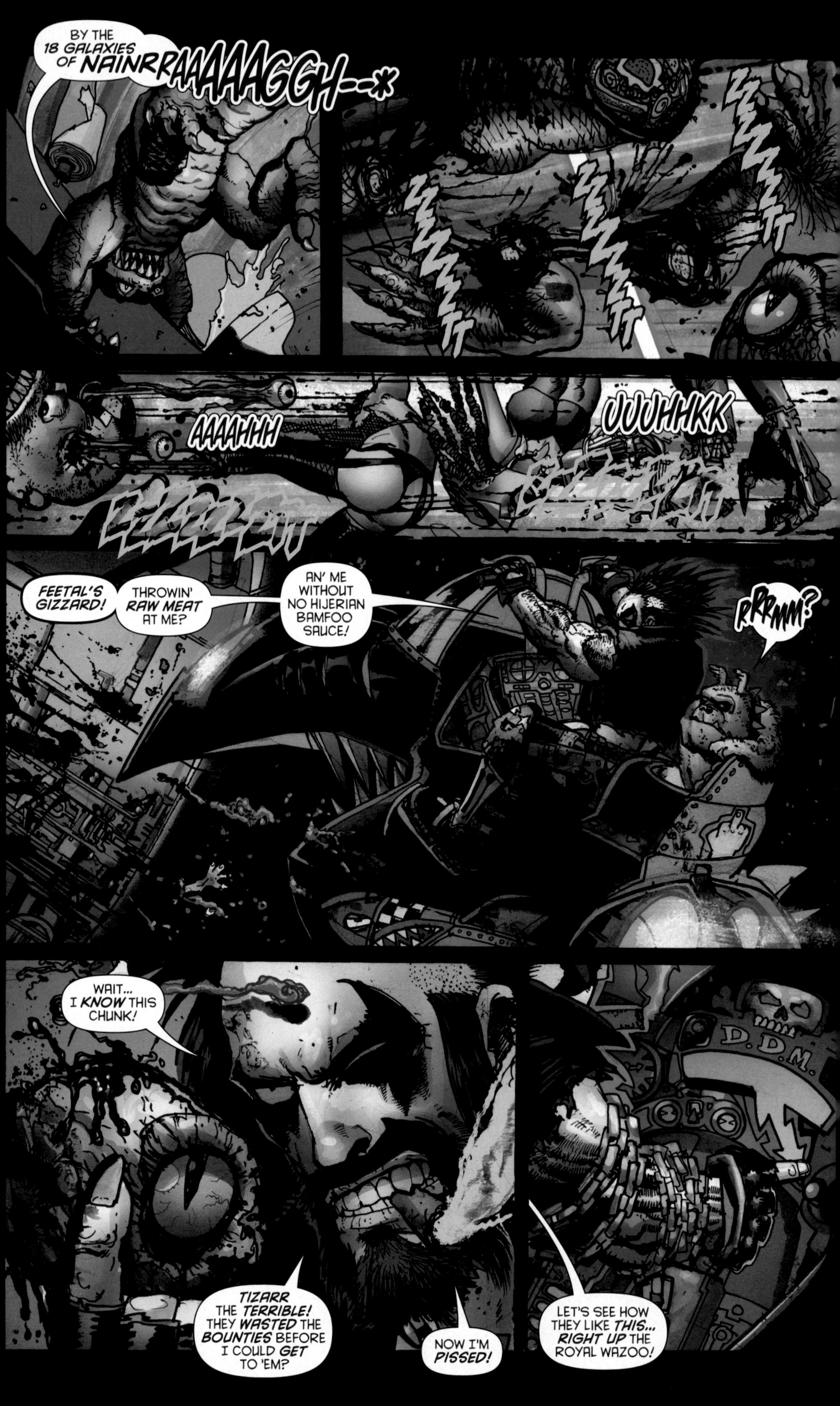
BY THE 18 GALAXIES OF NAINRRAAAAAGGH--*
AAAAHHH
UUUHHKK
FEETAL'S GIZZARD!
THROWIN' RAW MEAT AT ME?
AN' ME WITHOUT NO HIJERIAN BAMFOO SAUCE!
RRRMM?
WAIT... I KNOW THIS CHUNK!
TIZARR THE TERRIBLE! THEY WASTED THE BOUNTIES BEFORE I COULD GET TO 'EM?
NOW I'M PISSED!
D.D.M.
LET'S SEE HOW THEY LIKE THIS... RIGHT UP THE ROYAL WAZOO!

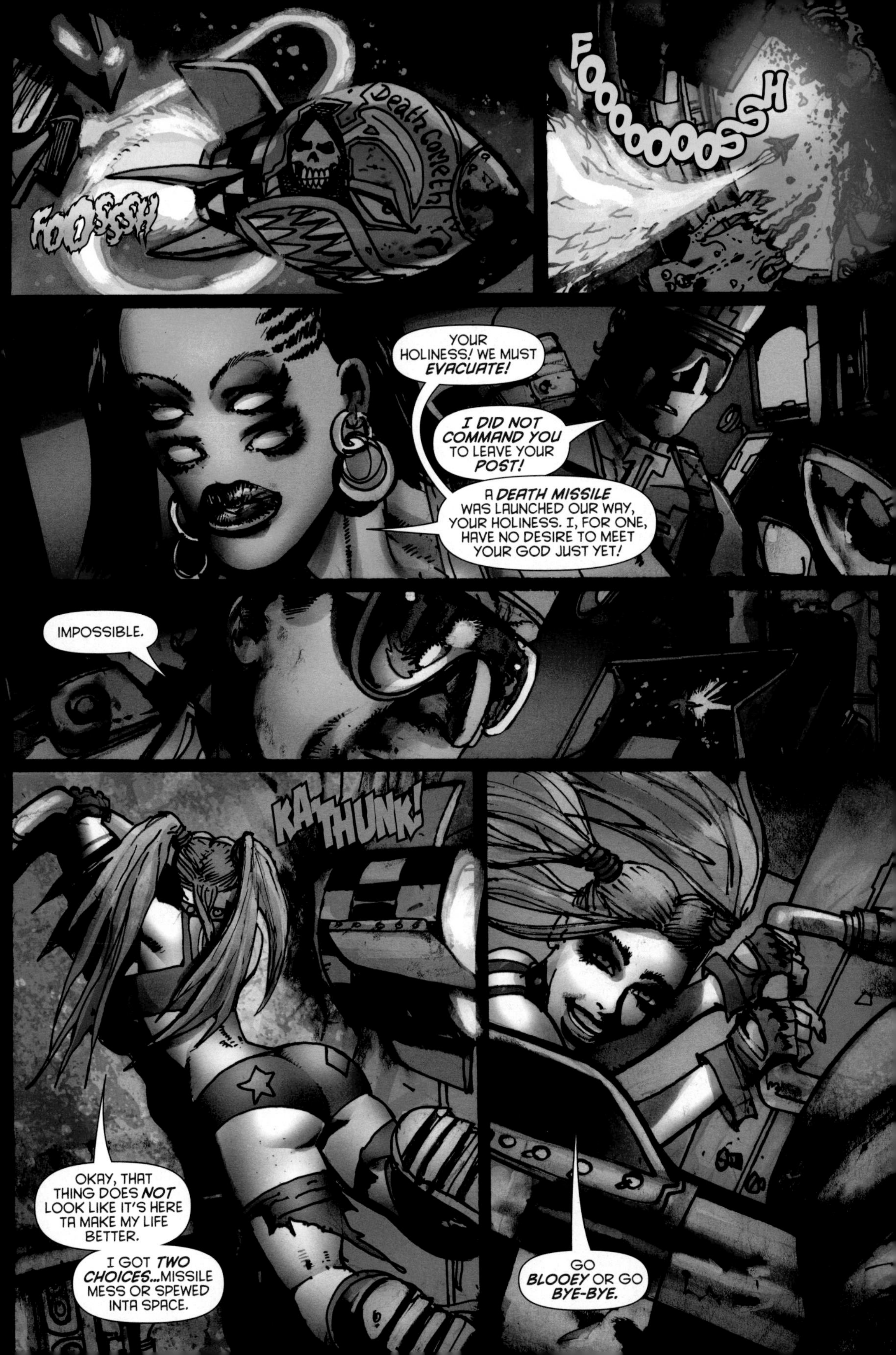

Death Cometh
FOOSSH
FOOOOOOOOSSH
YOUR HOLINESS! WE MUST EVACUATE!
I DID NOT COMMAND YOU TO LEAVE YOUR POST!
A DEATH MISSILE WAS LAUNCHED OUR WAY, YOUR HOLINESS. I, FOR ONE, HAVE NO DESIRE TO MEET YOUR GOD JUST YET!
IMPOSSIBLE.
KA-THUNK!
OKAY, THAT THING DOES NOT LOOK LIKE IT'S HERE TA MAKE MY LIFE BETTER.
I GOT TWO CHOICES...MISSILE MESS OR SPEWED INTA SPACE.
GO BLOOEY OR GO BYE-BYE.

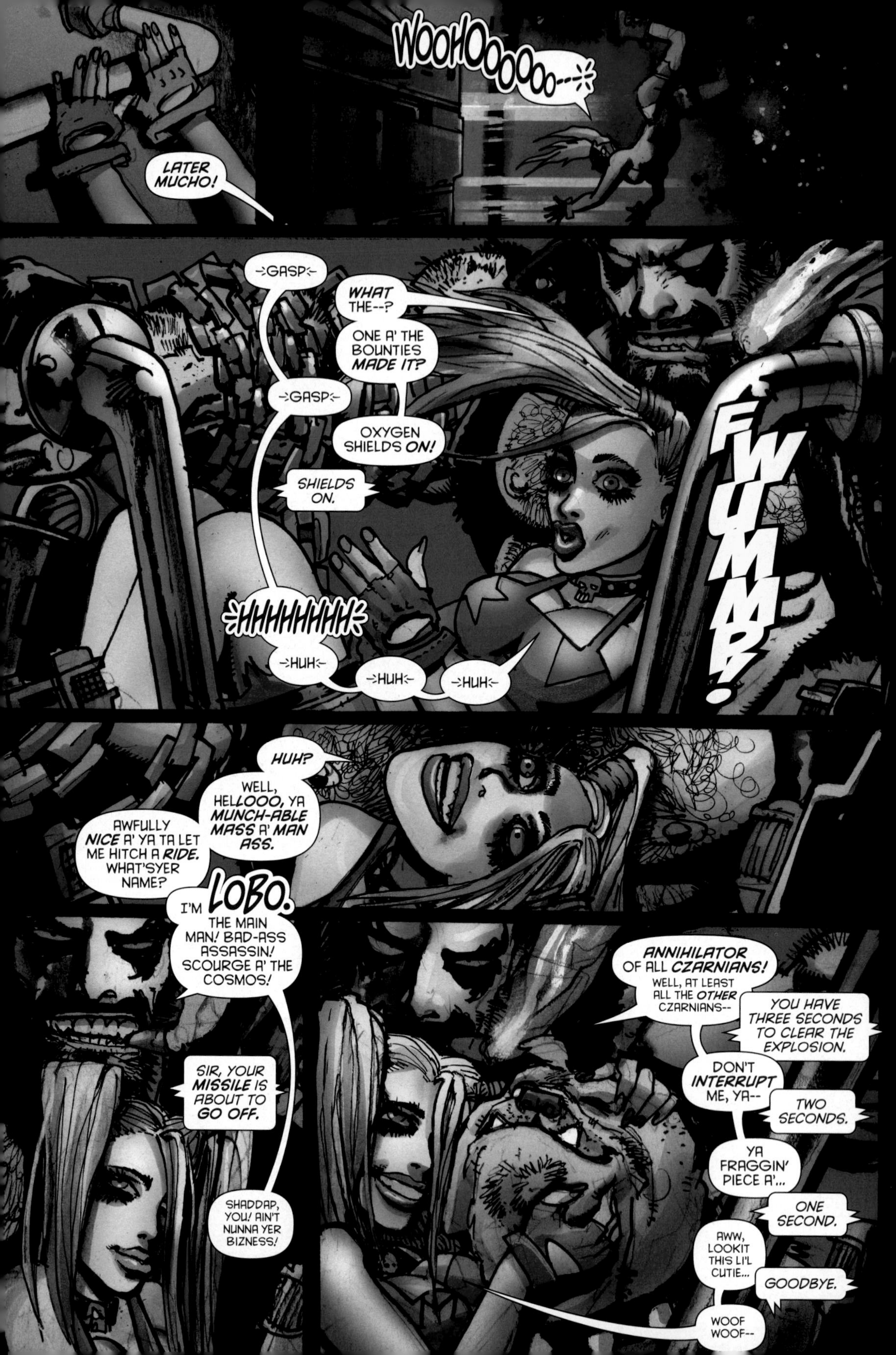
LATER MUCHO!
WOOHOOOOOOO--!
-GASP-
WHAT THE--?
ONE A' THE BOUNTIES MADE IT?
-GASP-
OXYGEN SHIELDS ON!
SHIELDS ON.
FWUMMB!
HHHHHHHH
-HUH-
-HUH-
-HUH-
HUH?
WELL, HELLOOO, YA MUNCH-ABLE MASS A' MAN ASS.
AWFULLY NICE A' YA TA LET ME HITCH A RIDE. WHAT'SYER NAME?
I'M LOBO. THE MAIN MAN! BAD-ASS ASSASSIN! SCOURGE A' THE COSMOS!
SIR, YOUR MISSILE IS ABOUT TO GO OFF.
SHADDAP, YOU! AIN'T NUNNA YER BIZNESS!
ANNIHILATOR OF ALL CZARNIANS!
WELL, AT LEAST ALL THE OTHER CZARNIANS--
YOU HAVE THREE SECONDS TO CLEAR THE EXPLOSION.
DON'T INTERRUPT ME, YA--
TWO SECONDS.
YA FRAGGIN' PIECE A'...
ONE SECOND.
AWW, LOOKIT THIS LI'L CUTIE...
GOODBYE.
WOOF WOOF--

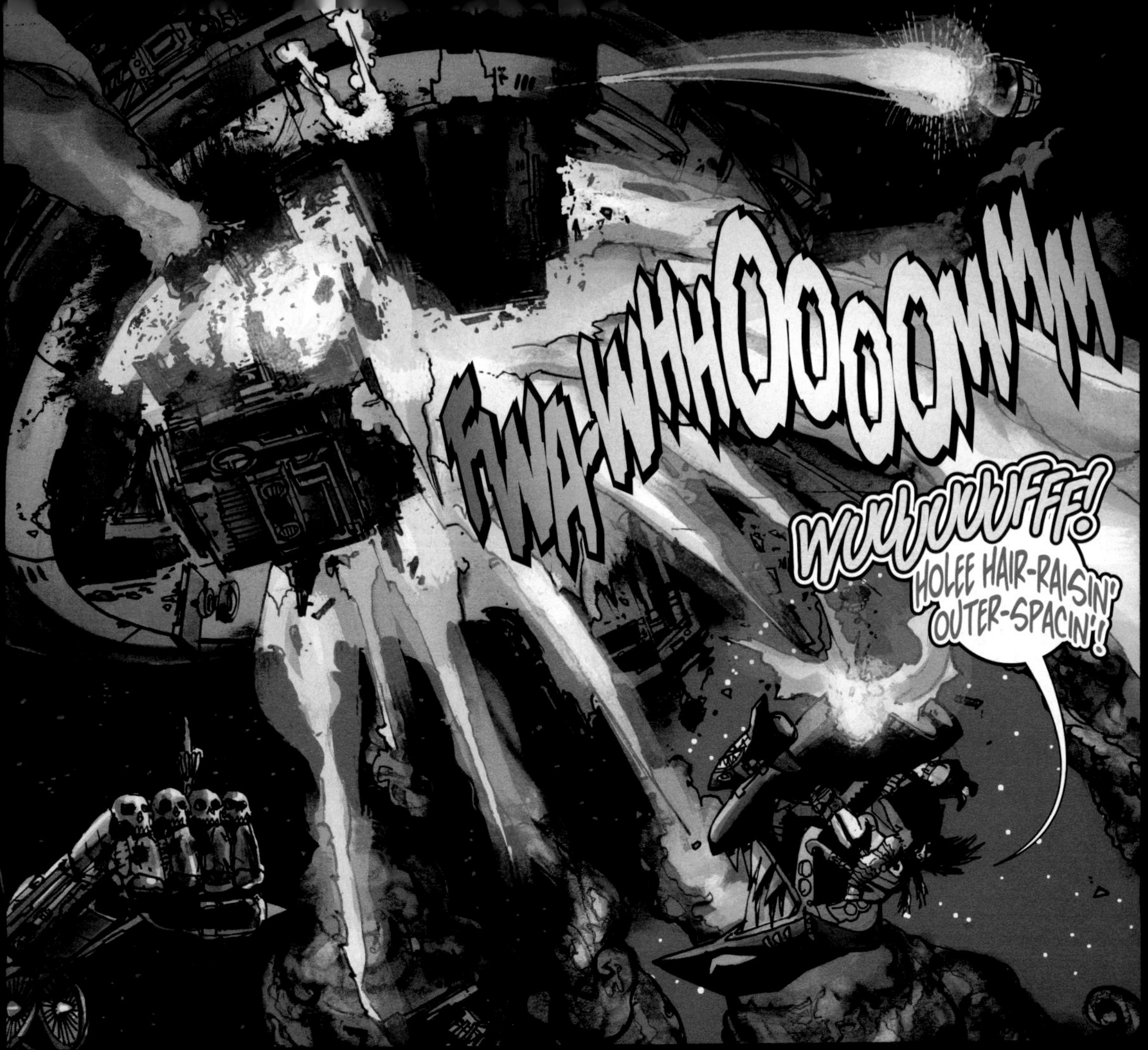
FWA-WHHOOOOMMM
WUUUUUUFFF!
HOLEE HAIR-RAISIN' OUTER-SPACIN'!

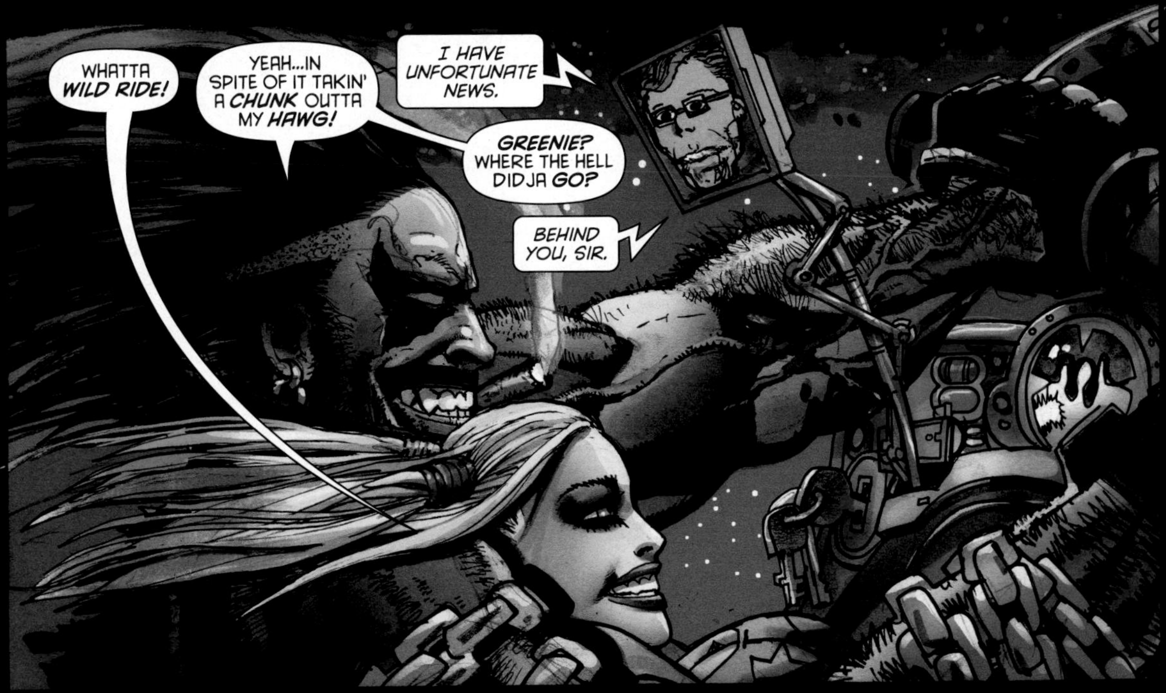
WHATTA WILD RIDE!
YEAH...IN SPITE OF IT TAKIN' A CHUNK OUTTA MY HAWG!
I HAVE UNFORTUNATE NEWS.
GREENIE? WHERE THE HELL DIDJA GO?
BEHIND YOU, SIR.

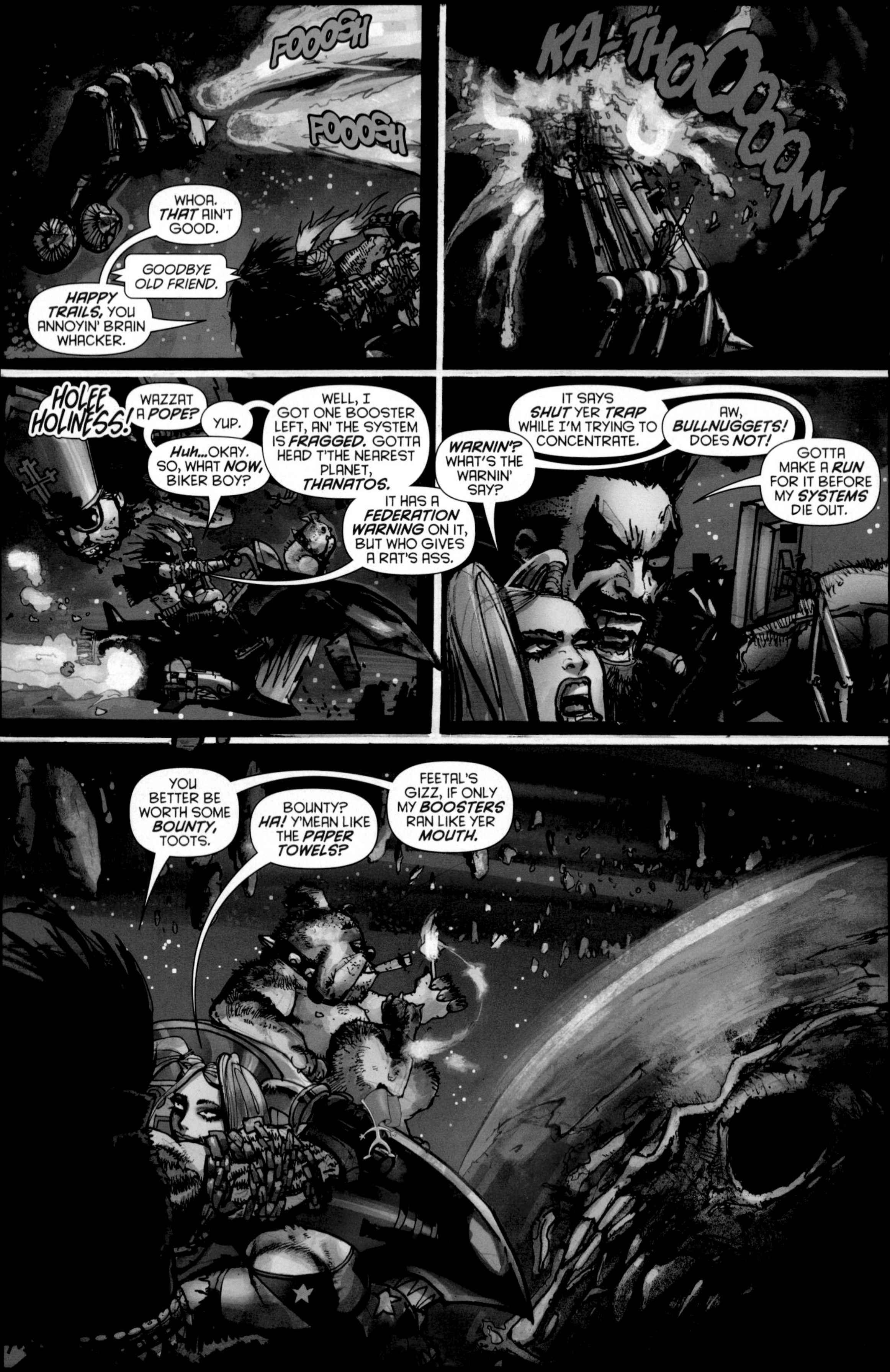
FOOOSH
FOOOSH
WHOA. THAT AIN'T GOOD.
GOODBYE OLD FRIEND.
HAPPY TRAILS, YOU ANNOYIN' BRAIN WHACKER.
KA-THOOOOOOM!
HOLEE HOLINESS!
WAZZAT A POPE?
YUP.
HUH...OKAY. SO, WHAT NOW, BIKER BOY?
WELL, I GOT ONE BOOSTER LEFT, AN' THE SYSTEM IS FRAGGED. GOTTA HEAD T'THE NEAREST PLANET, THANATOS.
IT HAS A FEDERATION WARNING ON IT, BUT WHO GIVES A RAT'S ASS.
WARNIN'? WHAT'S THE WARNIN' SAY?
IT SAYS SHUT YER TRAP WHILE I'M TRYING TO CONCENTRATE.
AW, BULLNUGGETS! DOES NOT!
GOTTA MAKE A RUN FOR IT BEFORE MY SYSTEMS DIE OUT.
YOU BETTER BE WORTH SOME BOUNTY, TOOTS.
BOUNTY? HA! Y'MEAN LIKE THE PAPER TOWELS?
FEETAL'S GIZZ, IF ONLY MY BOOSTERS RAN LIKE YER MOUTH.

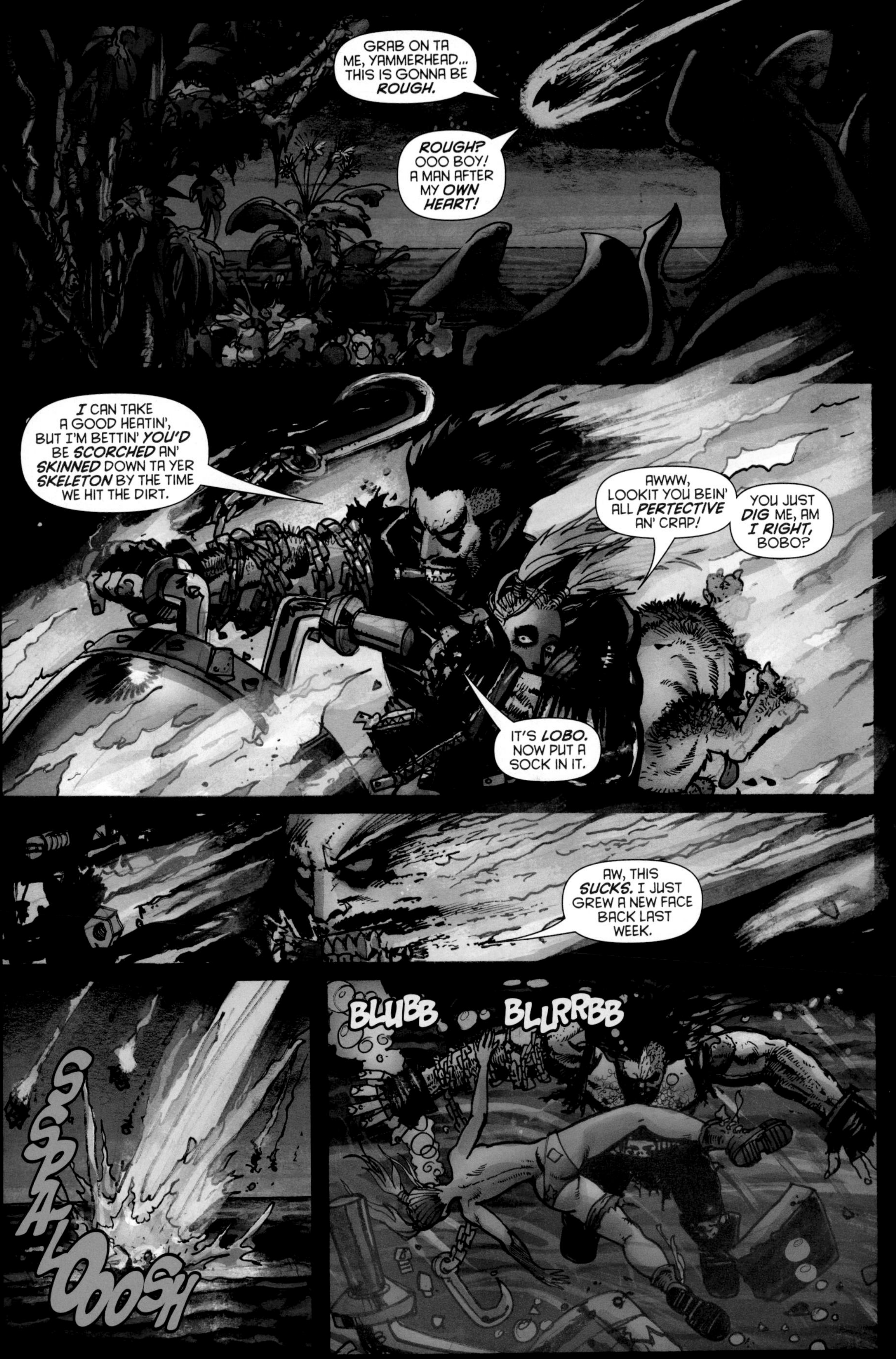
GRAB ON TA ME, YAMMERHEAD... THIS IS GONNA BE ROUGH.
ROUGH? OOO BOY! A MAN AFTER MY OWN HEART!
I CAN TAKE A GOOD HEATIN', BUT I'M BETTIN' YOU'D BE SCORCHED AN' SKINNED DOWN TA YER SKELETON BY THE TIME WE HIT THE DIRT.
AWWW, LOOKIT YOU BEIN' ALL PERTECTIVE AN' CRAP!
YOU JUST DIG ME, AM I RIGHT, BOBO?
IT'S LOBO. NOW PUT A SOCK IN IT.
AW, THIS SUCKS. I JUST GREW A NEW FACE BACK LAST WEEK.
SSPRALOOOSH
BLUBB
BLLRRBB

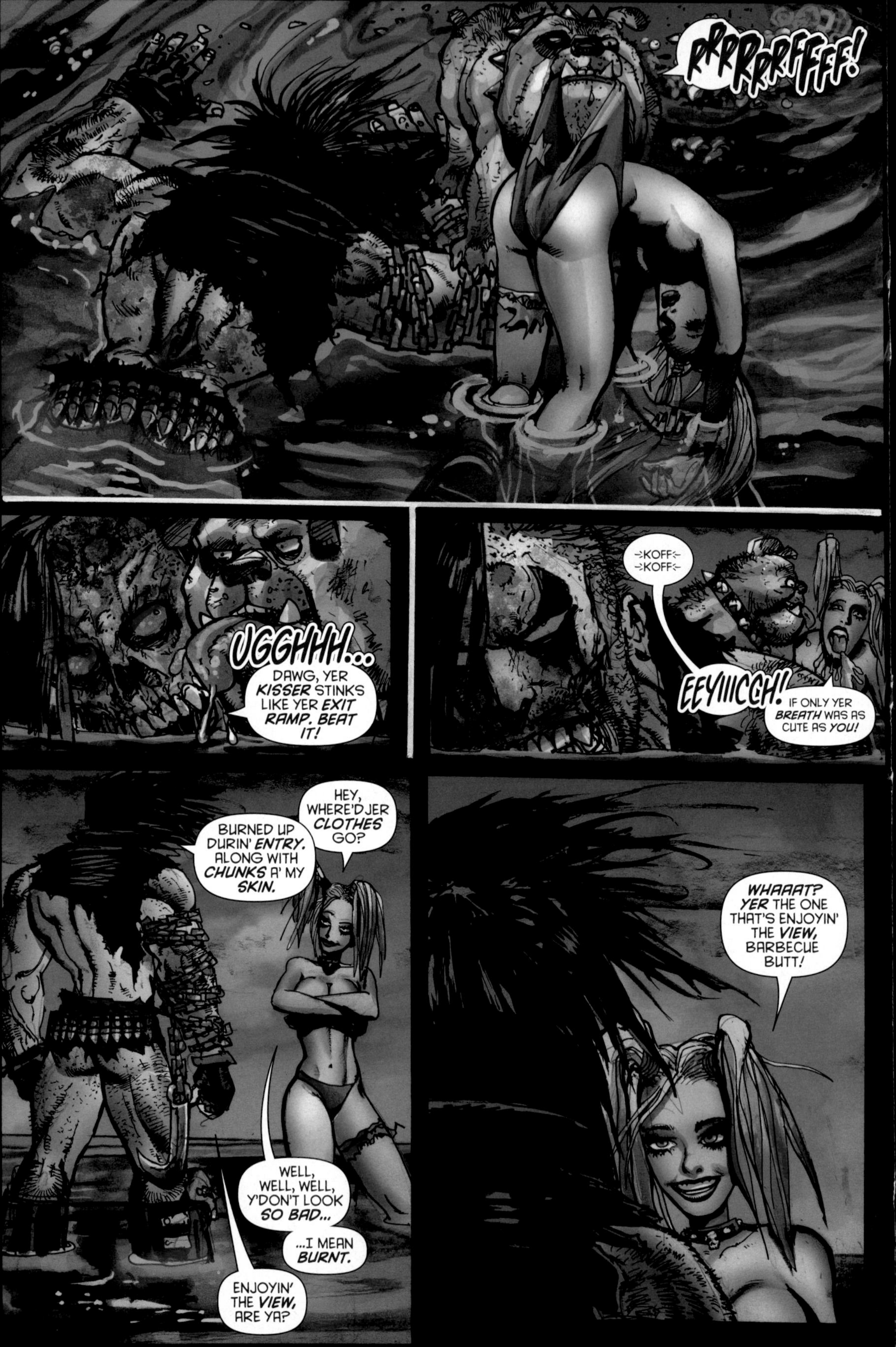
RRRRRRFFFFF!
UGGHHH...
DAWG, YER KISSER STINKS LIKE YER EXIT RAMP. BEAT IT!
-KOFF- -KOFF-
EEYIIICCH!
IF ONLY YER BREATH WAS AS CUTE AS YOU!
HEY, WHERE'DJER CLOTHES GO?
BURNED UP DURIN' ENTRY. ALONG WITH CHUNKS A' MY SKIN.
WELL, WELL, WELL, Y'DON'T LOOK SO BAD...
...I MEAN BURNT.
ENJOYIN' THE VIEW, ARE YA?
WHAAAT? YER THE ONE THAT'S ENJOYIN' THE VIEW, BARBECUE BUTT!

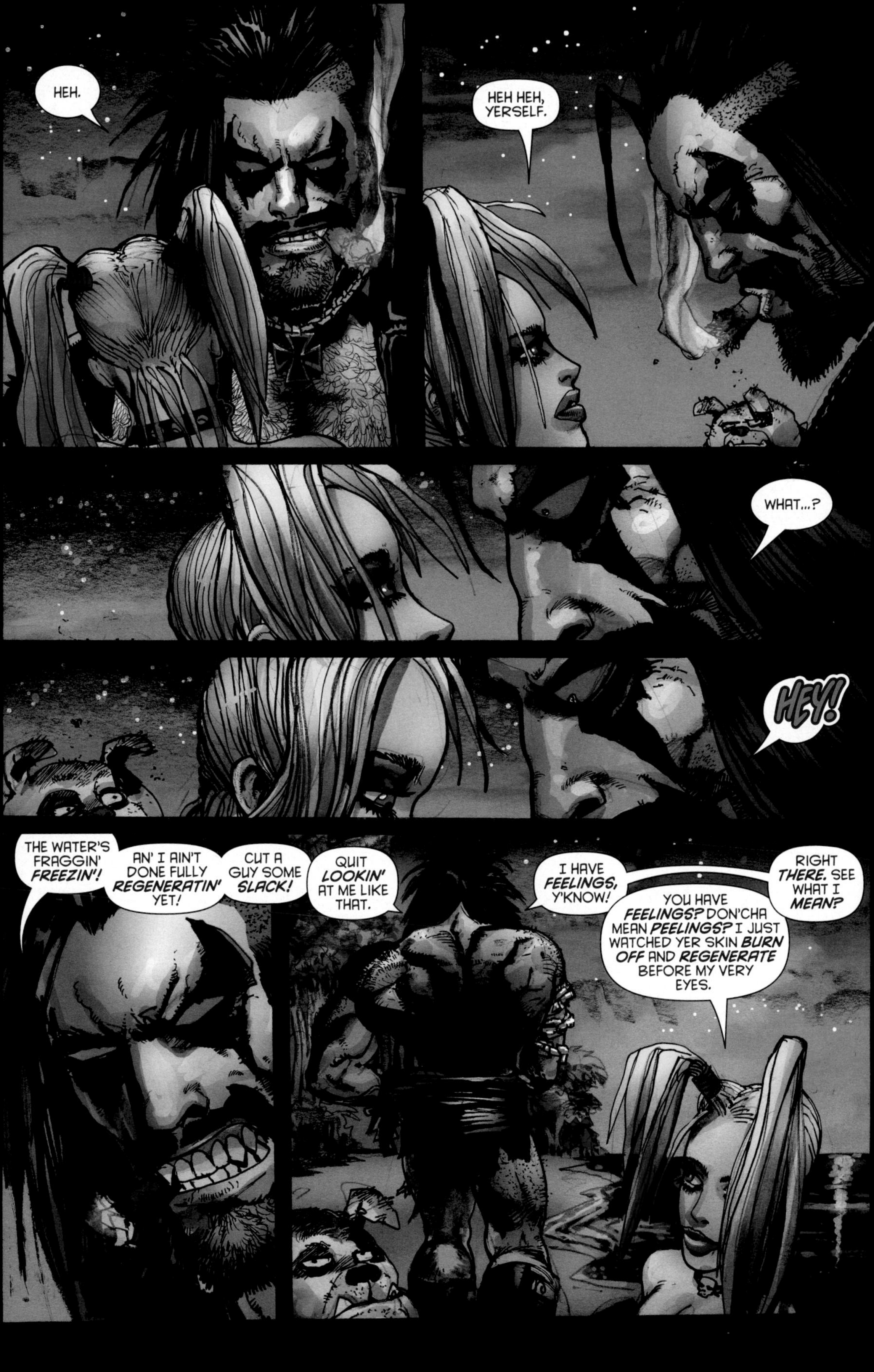
HEH.
HEH HEH, YERSELF.
WHAT...?
HEY!
THE WATER'S FRAGGIN' FREEZIN'!
AN' I AIN'T DONE FULLY REGENERATIN' YET!
CUT A GUY SOME SLACK!
QUIT LOOKIN' AT ME LIKE THAT.
I HAVE FEELINGS, Y'KNOW!
YOU HAVE FEELINGS? DON'CHA MEAN PEELINGS? I JUST WATCHED YER SKIN BURN OFF AND REGENERATE BEFORE MY VERY EYES.
RIGHT THERE. SEE WHAT I MEAN?

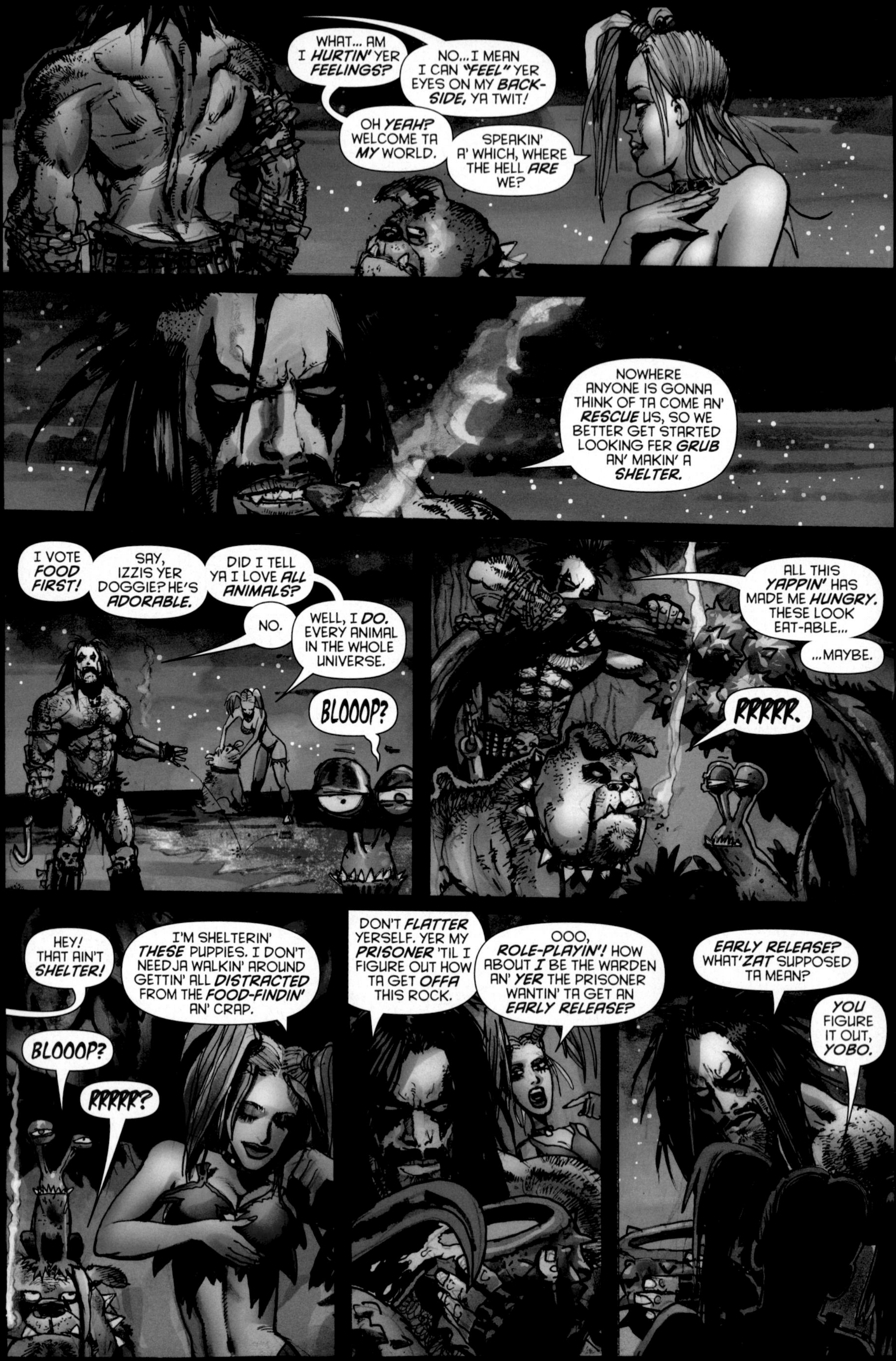
WHAT... AM I HURTIN' YER FEELINGS?
NO...I MEAN I CAN "FEEL" YER EYES ON MY BACK-SIDE, YA TWIT!
OH YEAH? WELCOME TA MY WORLD.
SPEAKIN' A' WHICH, WHERE THE HELL ARE WE?
NOWHERE ANYONE THINK OF IS GONNA TA COME AN' RESCUE US, SO WE BETTER GET STARTED LOOKING FER GRUB AN' MAKIN' A SHELTER.
I VOTE FOOD FIRST!
SAY, IZZIS YER DOGGIE? HE'S ADORABLE.
DID I TELL YA I LOVE ALL ANIMALS?
NO.
WELL, I DO. EVERY ANIMAL IN THE WHOLE UNIVERSE.
BLOOOP?
ALL THIS YAPPIN' HAS MADE ME HUNGRY. THESE LOOK EAT-ABLE...
...MAYBE.
RRRRR.
HEY! THAT AIN'T SHELTER!
I'M SHELTERIN' THESE PUPPIES. I DON'T NEEDJA WALKIN' AROUND GETTIN' ALL DISTRACTED FROM THE FOOD-FINDIN' AN' CRAP.
BLOOOP?
RRRRR?
DON'T FLATTER YERSELF. YER MY PRISONER 'TIL I FIGURE OUT HOW TA GET OFFA THIS ROCK.
OOO, ROLE-PLAYIN'! HOW ABOUT I BE THE WARDEN AN' YER THE PRISONER WANTIN' TA GET AN EARLY RELEASE?
EARLY RELEASE? WHAT'ZAT SUPPOSED TA MEAN?
YOU FIGURE IT OUT, YOBO.

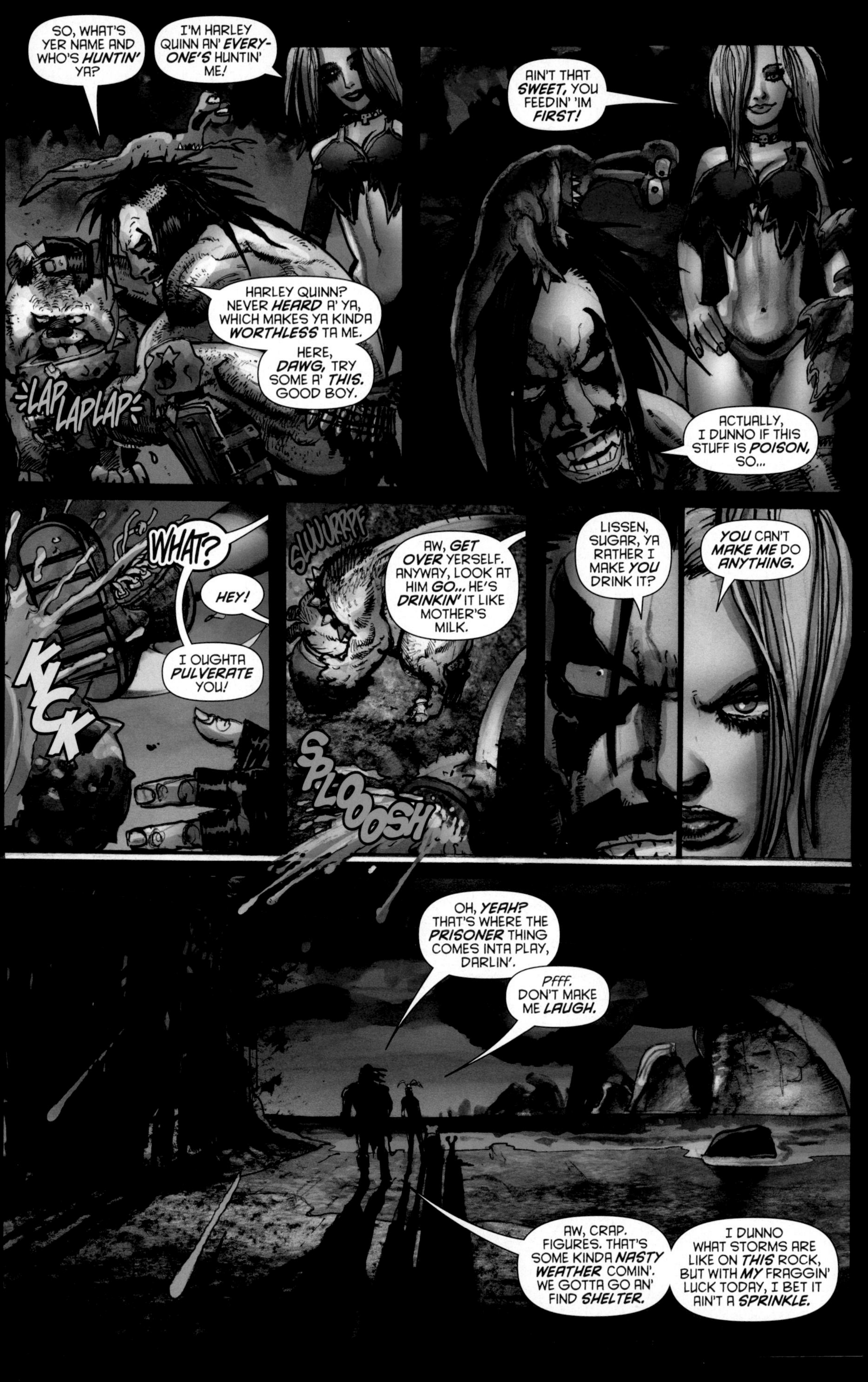
SO, WHAT'S YER NAME AND WHO'S HUNTIN' YA?
I'M HARLEY QUINN AN' EVERYONE'S HUNTIN' ME!
HARLEY QUINN? NEVER HEARD A' YA, WHICH MAKES YA KINDA WORTHLESS TA ME.
HERE, DAWG, TRY SOME A' THIS. GOOD BOY.
LAP LAPLAP
AIN'T THAT SWEET, YOU FEEDIN' 'IM FIRST!
ACTUALLY, I DUNNO IF THIS STUFF IS POISON, SO...
WHAT?
HEY!
I OUGHTA PULVERATE YOU!
KICK
SLUUURRPF
AW, GET OVER YERSELF. ANYWAY, LOOK AT HIM GO... HE'S DRINKIN' IT LIKE MOTHER'S MILK.
SPLOOOSH
LISSEN, SUGAR, YA RATHER I MAKE YOU DRINK IT?
YOU CAN'T MAKE ME DO ANYTHING.
OH, YEAH? THAT'S WHERE THE PRISONER THING COMES INTA PLAY, DARLIN'.
PFFF. DON'T MAKE ME LAUGH.
AW, CRAP. FIGURES. THAT'S SOME KINDA NASTY WEATHER COMIN'. WE GOTTA GO AN' FIND SHELTER.
I DUNNO WHAT STORMS ARE LIKE ON THIS ROCK, BUT WITH MY FRAGGIN' LUCK TODAY, I BET IT AIN'T A SPRINKLE.

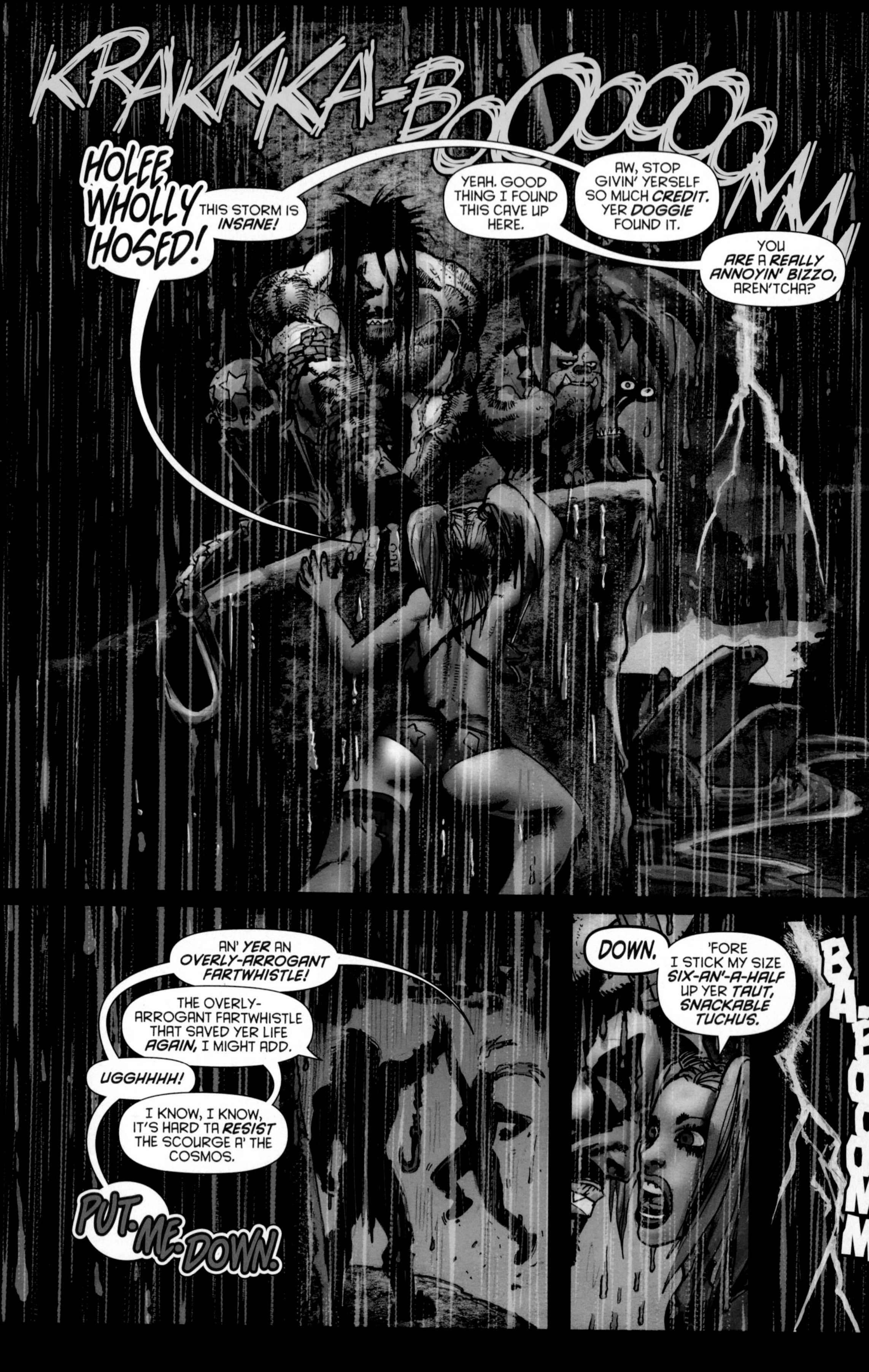
KRAKKKA-BOOOOOOMM
HOLEE WHOLLY HOSED!
THIS STORM IS *INSANE!*
YEAH. GOOD THING I FOUND THIS CAVE UP HERE.
AW, STOP GIVIN' YERSELF SO MUCH *CREDIT.* YER *DOGGIE* FOUND IT.
YOU *ARE A REALLY ANNOYIN' BIZZO,* AREN'TCHA?
AN' *YER* AN *OVERLY-ARROGANT FARTWHISTLE!*
THE OVERLY-ARROGANT FARTWHISTLE THAT SAVED YER LIFE *AGAIN,* I MIGHT ADD.
UGGHHHH!
I KNOW, I KNOW, IT'S HARD TA *RESIST* THE SCOURGE A' THE COSMOS.
PUT. ME. DOWN.
DOWN.
'FORE I STICK MY SIZE *SIX-AN'-A-HALF* UP YER *TAUT, SNACKABLE TUCHUS.*
BA-BOOOMM

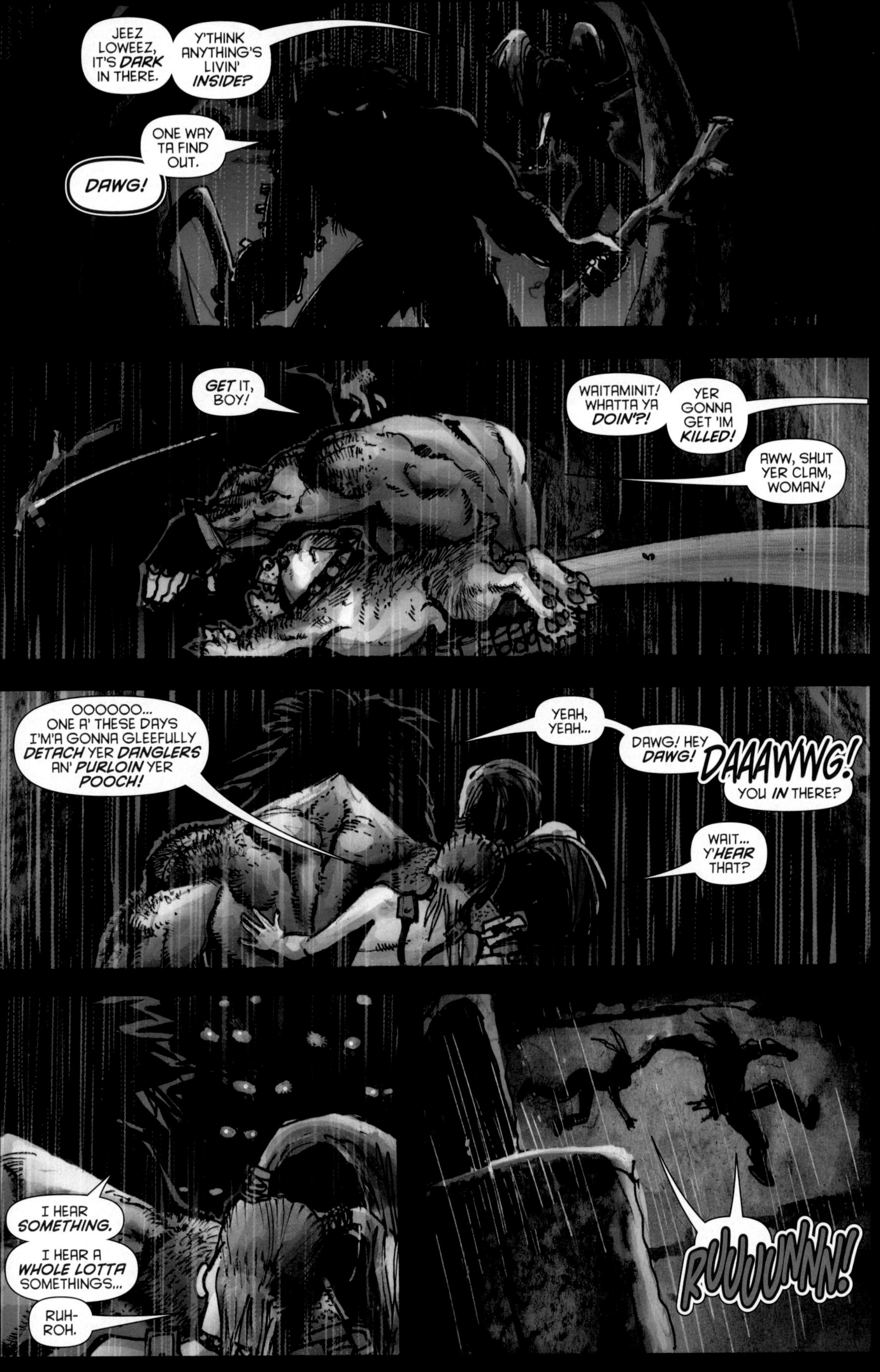
JEEZ LOWEEZ, IT'S *DARK* IN THERE.
Y'THINK ANYTHING'S LIVIN' *INSIDE?*
ONE WAY TA FIND OUT.
DAWG!
GET IT, BOY!
WAITAMINIT! WHATTA YA *DOIN'?!*
YER GONNA GET 'IM *KILLED!*
AWW, SHUT YER CLAM, WOMAN!
OOOOOO... ONE A' THESE DAYS I'M'A GONNA GLEEFULLY *DETACH* YER *DANGLERS* AN' *PURLOIN* YER *POOCH!*
YEAH, YEAH...
DAWG! HEY *DAWG!* DAAAWWG! YOU *IN* THERE?
WAIT... Y'*HEAR* THAT?
I HEAR *SOMETHING.*
I HEAR A *WHOLE LOTTA* SOMETHINGS...
RUH-ROH.
RUUUUNNN!

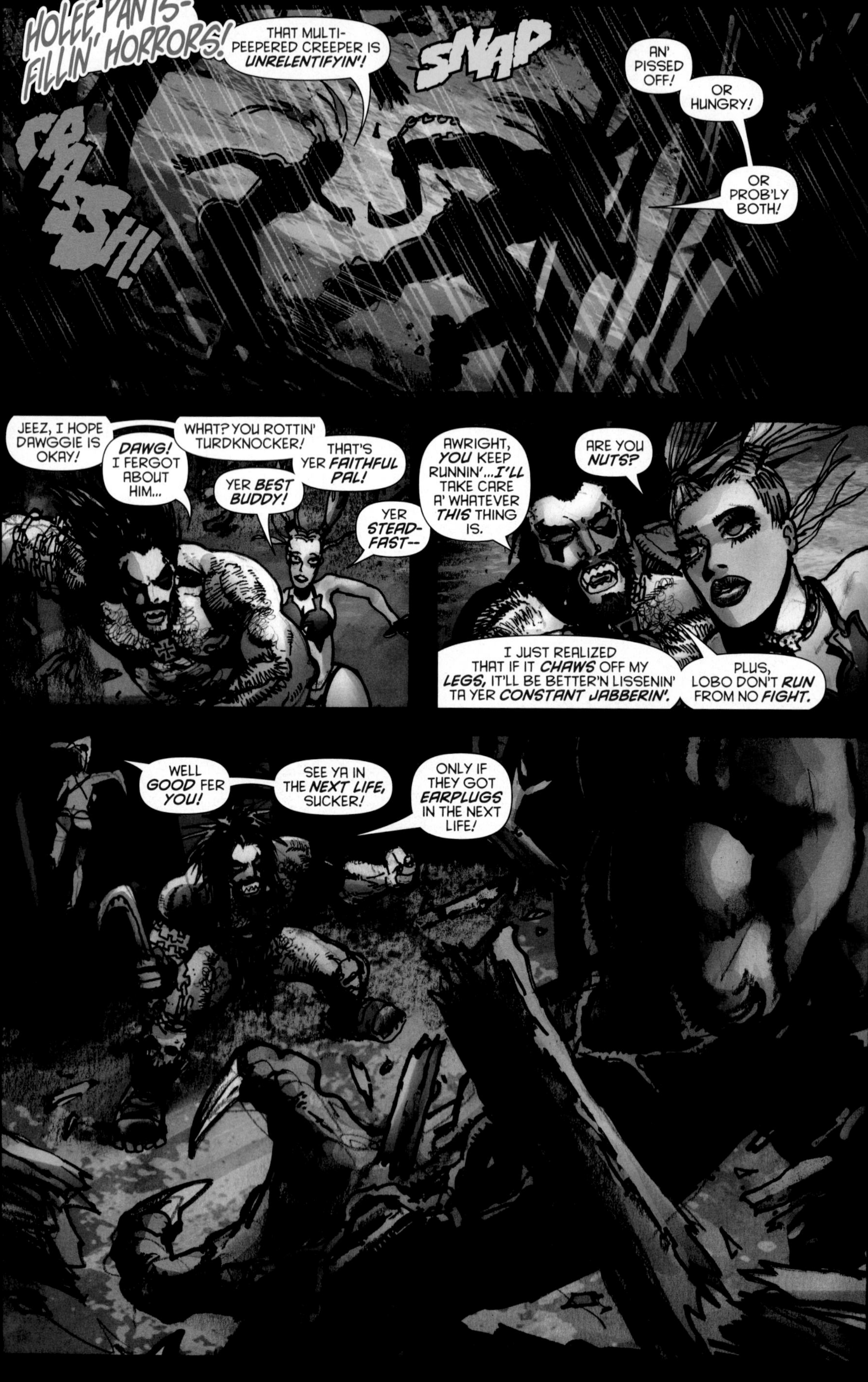
HOLEE PANTS-FILLIN' HORRORS!
THAT MULTI-PEEPERED CREEPER IS UNRELENTIFYIN'!
SNAP
CRASH!!
AN' PISSED OFF!
OR HUNGRY!
OR PROB'LY BOTH!
JEEZ, I HOPE DAWGGIE IS OKAY!
DAWG! I FERGOT ABOUT HIM...
WHAT? YOU ROTTIN' TURDKNOCKER!
THAT'S YER FAITHFUL PAL!
YER BEST BUDDY!
YER STEAD-FAST--
AWRIGHT, YOU KEEP RUNNIN'...I'LL TAKE CARE A' WHATEVER THIS THING IS.
ARE YOU NUTS?
I JUST REALIZED THAT IF IT CHAWS OFF MY LEGS, IT'LL BE BETTER'N LISSENIN' TA YER CONSTANT JABBERIN'.
PLUS, LOBO DON'T RUN FROM NO FIGHT.
WELL GOOD FER YOU!
SEE YA IN THE NEXT LIFE, SUCKER!
ONLY IF THEY GOT EARPLUGS IN THE NEXT LIFE!

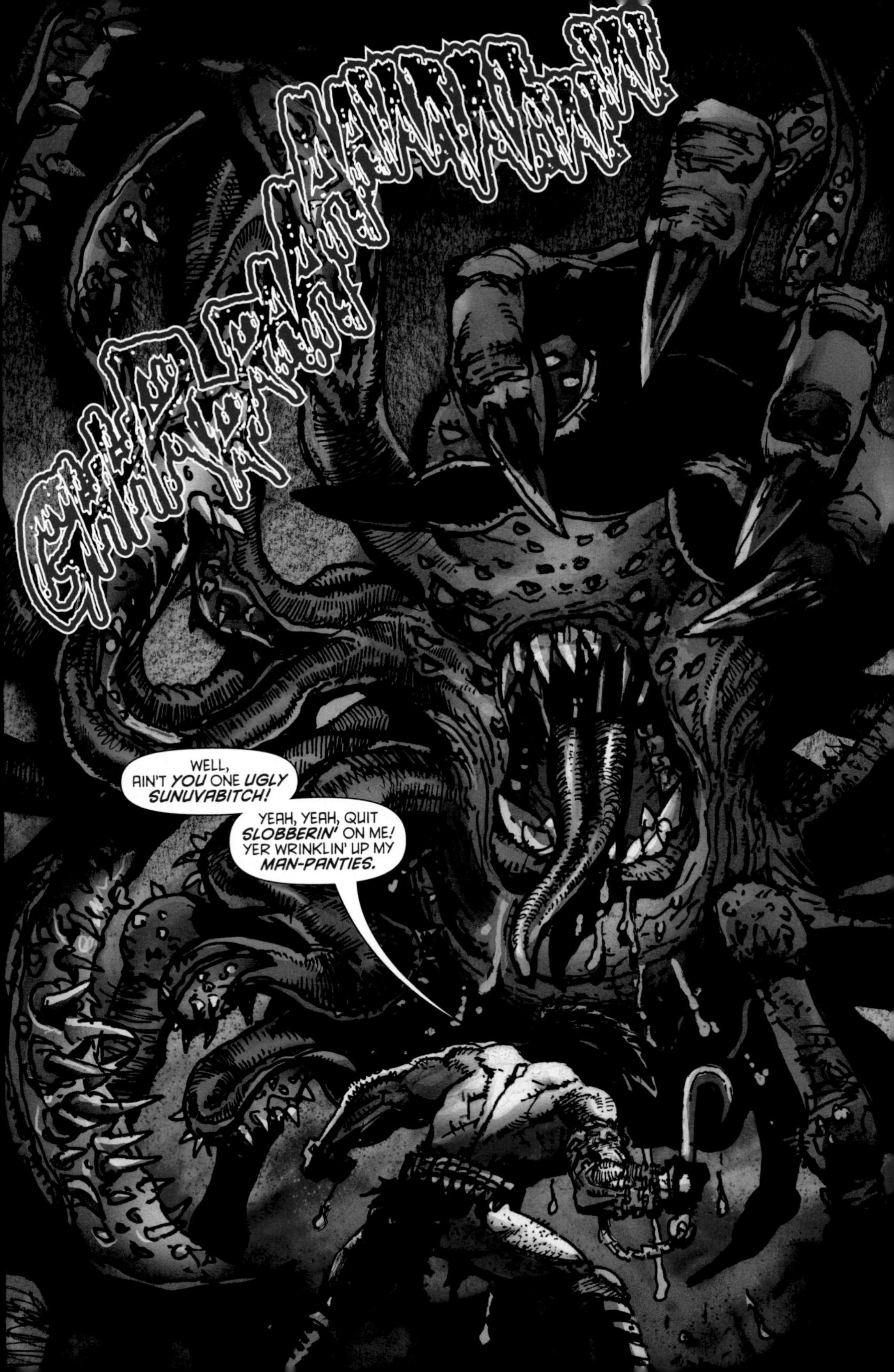
WELL, AIN'T *YOU* ONE *UGLY* *SUNUVABITCH!*
YEAH, YEAH, QUIT *SLOBBERIN'* ON ME! YER WRINKLIN' UP MY *MAN-PANTIES.*

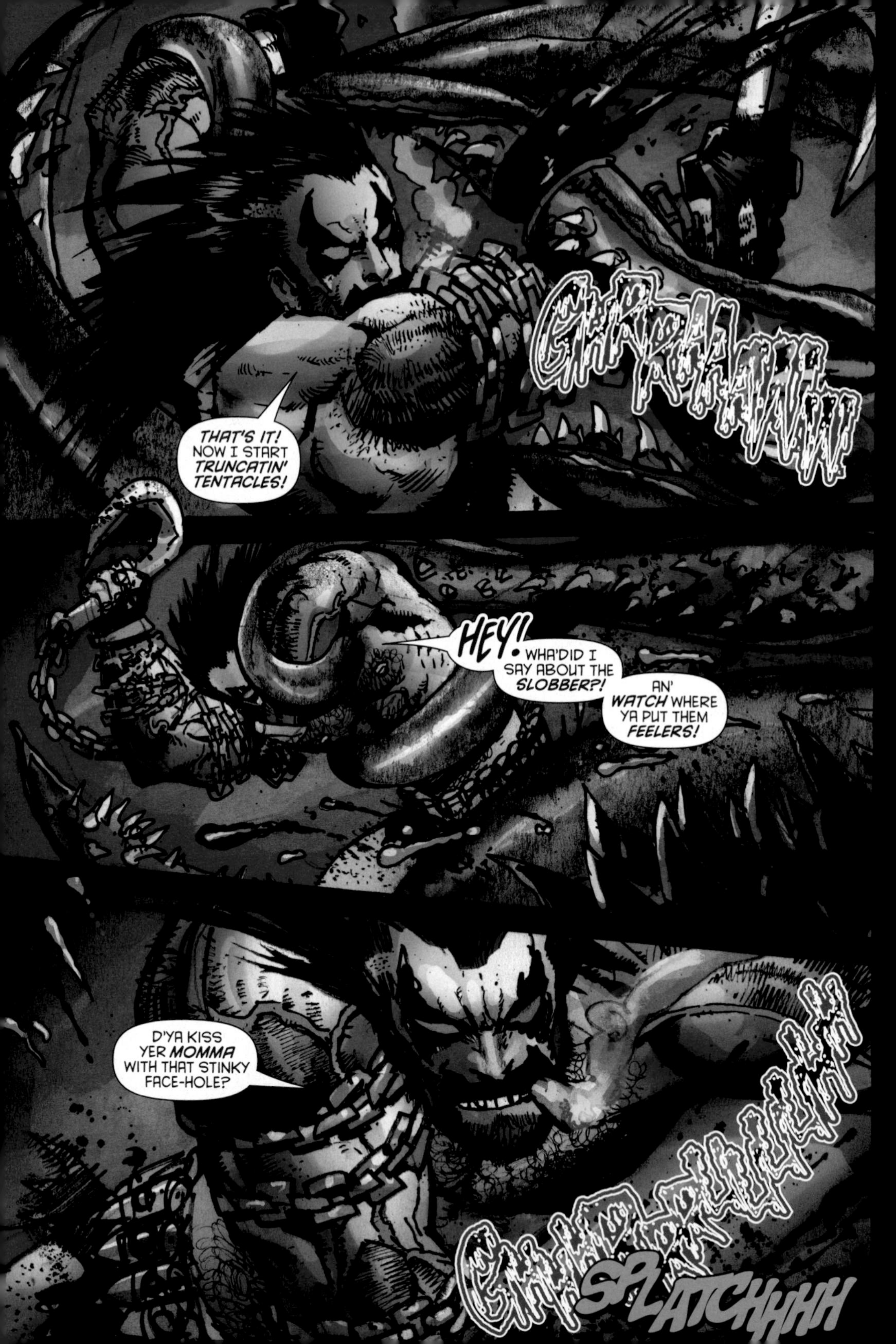
THAT'S IT! NOW I START TRUNCATIN' TENTACLES!
HEY!
WHA'DID I SAY ABOUT THE SLOBBER?!
AN' WATCH WHERE YA PUT THEM FEELERS!
D'YA KISS YER MOMMA WITH THAT STINKY FACE-HOLE?
SPLATCHHHH

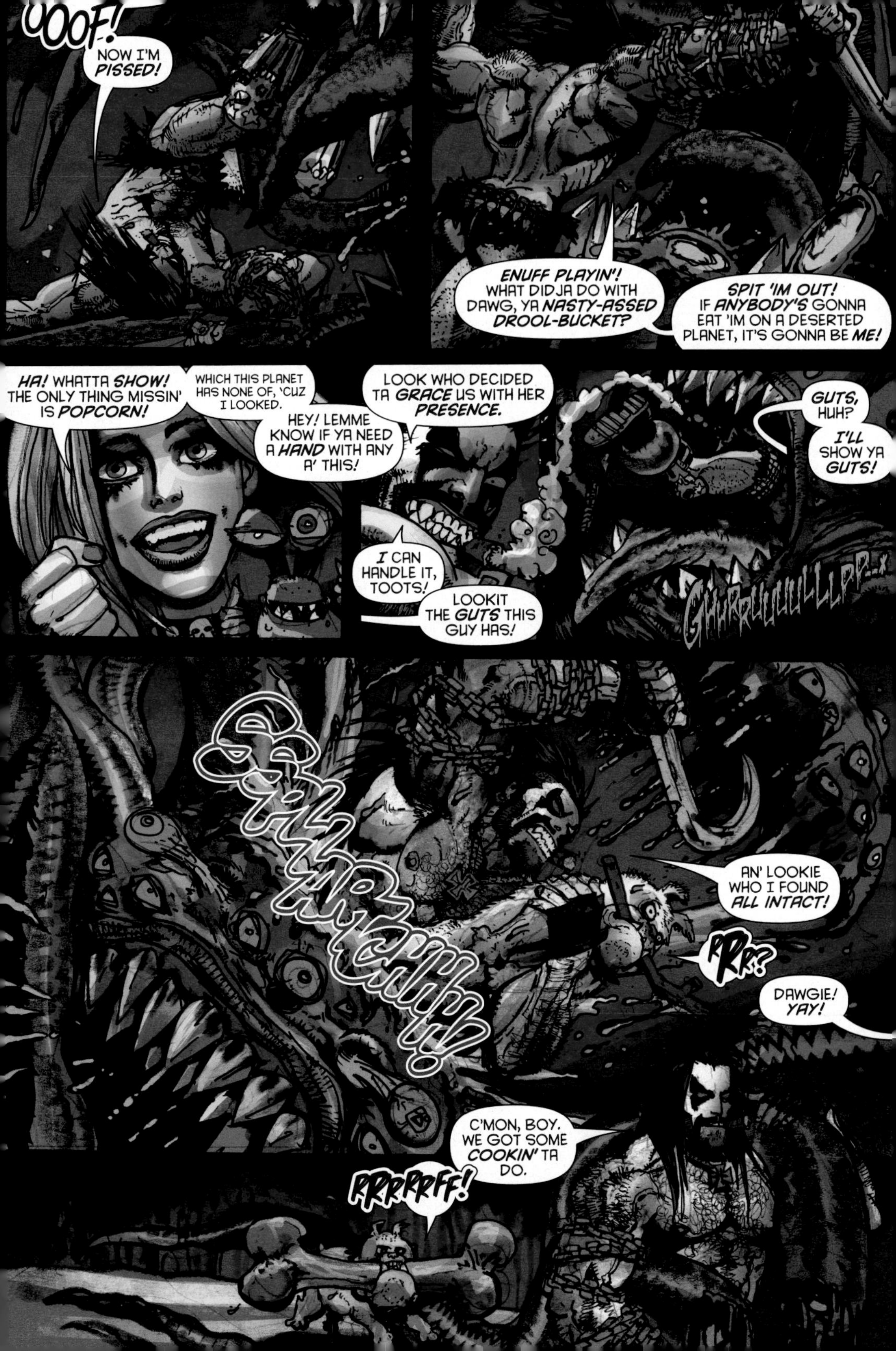

OOOF!
NOW I'M PISSED!
ENUFF PLAYIN'! WHAT DIDJA DO WITH DAWG, YA NASTY-ASSED DROOL-BUCKET?
SPIT 'IM OUT! IF ANYBODY'S GONNA EAT 'IM ON A DESERTED PLANET, IT'S GONNA BE ME!
HA! WHATTA SHOW! THE ONLY THING MISSIN' IS POPCORN!
WHICH THIS PLANET HAS NONE OF, 'CUZ I LOOKED.
HEY! LEMME KNOW IF YA NEED A HAND WITH ANY A' THIS!
LOOK WHO DECIDED TA GRACE US WITH HER PRESENCE.
I CAN HANDLE IT, TOOTS!
LOOKIT THE GUTS THIS GUY HAS!
GUTS, HUH?
I'LL SHOW YA GUTS!
GHURUUUULLPP..x
AN' LOOKIE WHO I FOUND ALL INTACT!
RRR?
DAWGIE! YAY!
C'MON, BOY. WE GOT SOME COOKIN' TA DO.
RRRRRFF!

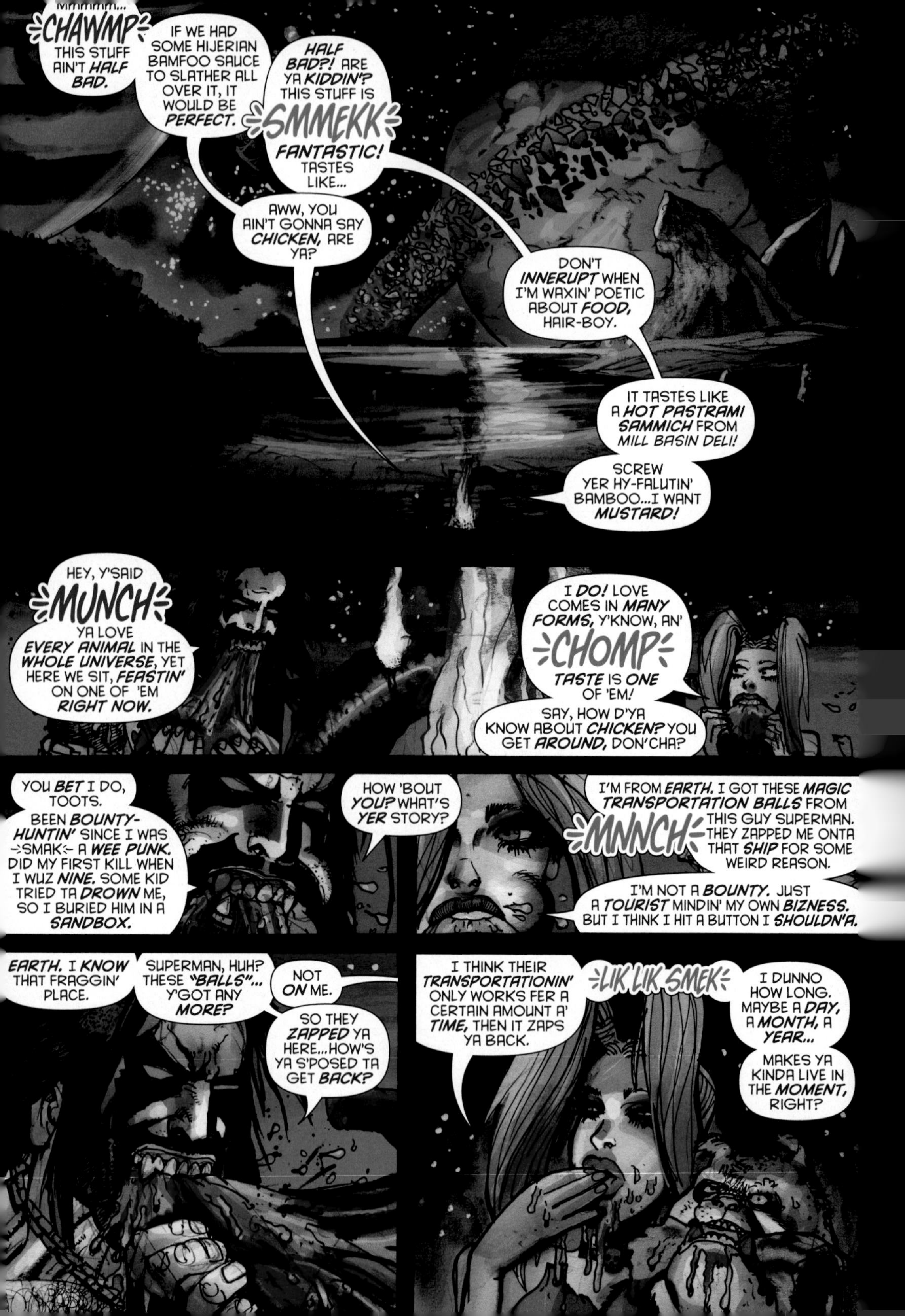

CHAWMP
THIS STUFF AIN'T HALF BAD.
IF WE HAD SOME HIJERIAN BAMFOO SAUCE TO SLATHER ALL OVER IT, IT WOULD BE PERFECT.
HALF BAD?! ARE YA KIDDIN'? THIS STUFF IS
SMMEKK
FANTASTIC! TASTES LIKE...
AWW, YOU AIN'T GONNA SAY CHICKEN, ARE YA?
DON'T INNERUPT WHEN I'M WAXIN' POETIC ABOUT FOOD, HAIR-BOY.
IT TASTES LIKE A HOT PASTRAMI SAMMICH FROM MILL BASIN DELI!
SCREW YER HY-FALUTIN' BAMBOO...I WANT MUSTARD!
HEY, Y'SAID
MUNCH
YA LOVE EVERY ANIMAL IN THE WHOLE UNIVERSE, YET HERE WE SIT, FEASTIN' ON ONE OF 'EM RIGHT NOW.
I DO! LOVE COMES IN MANY FORMS, Y'KNOW, AN'
CHOMP
TASTE IS ONE OF 'EM!
SAY, HOW D'YA KNOW ABOUT CHICKEN? YOU GET AROUND, DON'CHA?
YOU BET I DO, TOOTS. BEEN BOUNTY-HUNTIN' SINCE I WAS -SMAK- A WEE PUNK. DID MY FIRST KILL WHEN I WUZ NINE. SOME KID TRIED TA DROWN ME, SO I BURIED HIM IN A SANDBOX.
HOW 'BOUT YOU? WHAT'S YER STORY?
I'M FROM EARTH. I GOT THESE MAGIC TRANSPORTATION BALLS FROM
MNNCH
THIS GUY SUPERMAN. THEY ZAPPED ME ONTA THAT SHIP FOR SOME WEIRD REASON.
I'M NOT A BOUNTY. JUST A TOURIST MINDIN' MY OWN BIZNESS. BUT I THINK I HIT A BUTTON I SHOULDN'A.
EARTH. I KNOW THAT FRAGGIN' PLACE.
SUPERMAN, HUH? THESE "BALLS"... Y'GOT ANY MORE?
NOT ON ME.
SO THEY ZAPPED YA HERE...HOW'S YA S'POSED TA GET BACK?
I THINK THEIR TRANSPORTATIONIN' ONLY WORKS FER A CERTAIN AMOUNT A' TIME, THEN IT ZAPS YA BACK.
LIK LIK SMEK
I DUNNO HOW LONG. MAYBE A DAY, A MONTH, A YEAR...
MAKES YA KINDA LIVE IN THE MOMENT, RIGHT?

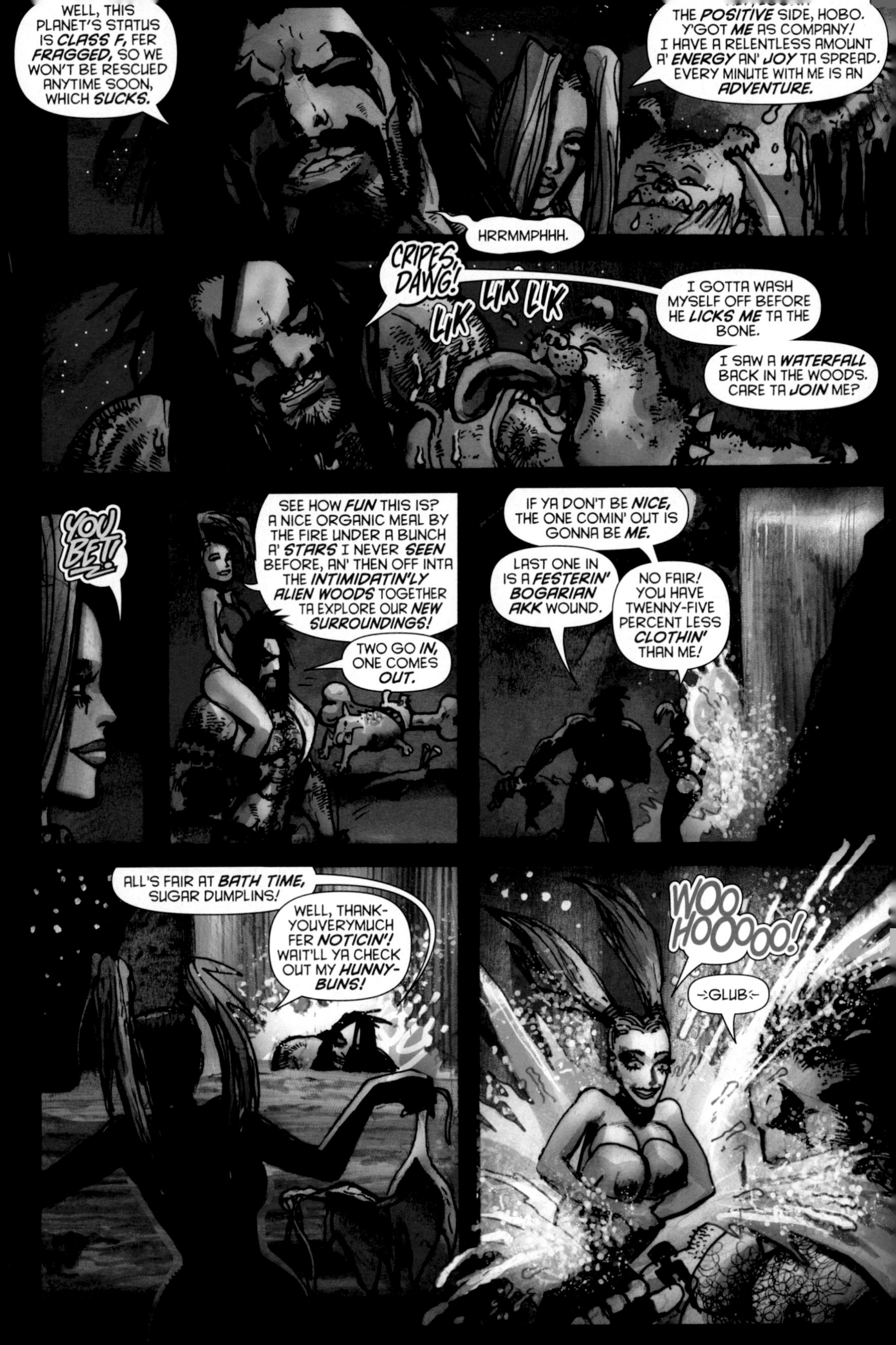
WELL, THIS PLANET'S STATUS IS CLASS F, FER FRAGGED, SO WE WON'T BE RESCUED ANYTIME SOON, WHICH SUCKS.
THE POSITIVE SIDE, HOBO. Y'GOT ME AS COMPANY! I HAVE A RELENTLESS AMOUNT A' ENERGY AN' JOY TA SPREAD. EVERY MINUTE WITH ME IS AN ADVENTURE.
HRRMMPHHH.
CRIPES, DAWG!
LIK LIK LIK
I GOTTA WASH MYSELF OFF BEFORE HE LICKS ME TA THE BONE.
I SAW A WATERFALL BACK IN THE WOODS. CARE TA JOIN ME?
YOU BET!
SEE HOW FUN THIS IS? A NICE ORGANIC MEAL BY THE FIRE UNDER A BUNCH A' STARS I NEVER SEEN BEFORE, AN' THEN OFF INTA THE INTIMIDATIN'LY ALIEN WOODS TOGETHER TA EXPLORE OUR NEW SURROUNDINGS!
TWO GO IN, ONE COMES OUT.
IF YA DON'T BE NICE, THE ONE COMIN' OUT IS GONNA BE ME.
LAST ONE IN IS A FESTERIN' BOGARIAN AKK WOUND.
NO FAIR! YOU HAVE TWENNY-FIVE PERCENT LESS CLOTHIN' THAN ME!
ALL'S FAIR AT BATH TIME, SUGAR DUMPLINS!
WELL, THANK-YOUVERYMUCH FER NOTICIN'! WAIT'LL YA CHECK OUT MY HUNNY-BUNS!
WOO HOOOOO!
GLUB

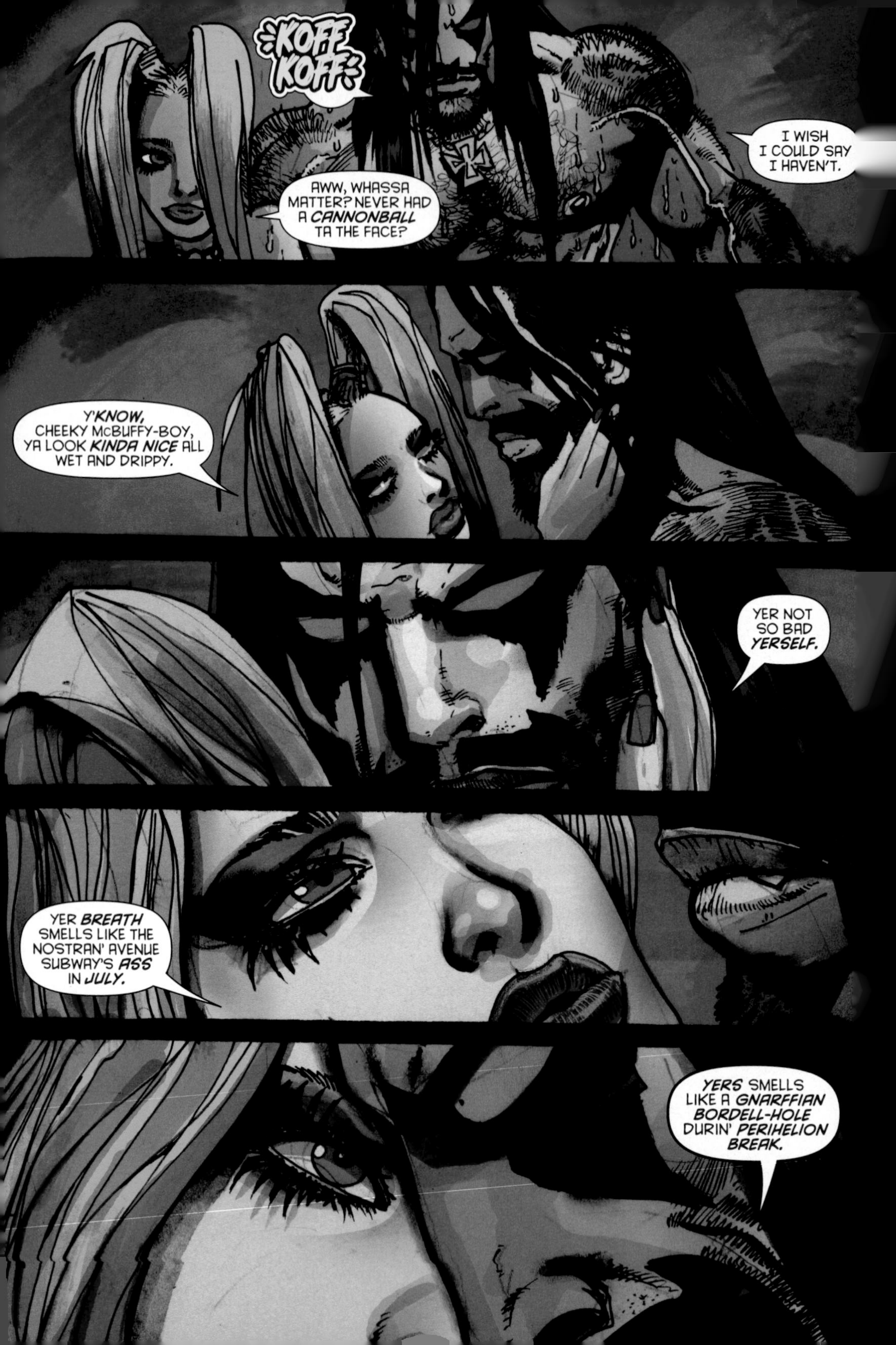
KOFF KOFF
AWW, WHASSA MATTER? NEVER HAD A CANNONBALL TA THE FACE?
I WISH I COULD SAY I HAVEN'T.
Y'KNOW, CHEEKY McBUFFY-BOY, YA LOOK KINDA NICE ALL WET AND DRIPPY.
YER NOT SO BAD YERSELF.
YER BREATH SMELLS LIKE THE NOSTRAN' AVENUE SUBWAY'S ASS IN JULY.
YERS SMELLS LIKE A GNARFFIAN BORDELL-HOLE DURIN' PERIHELION BREAK.

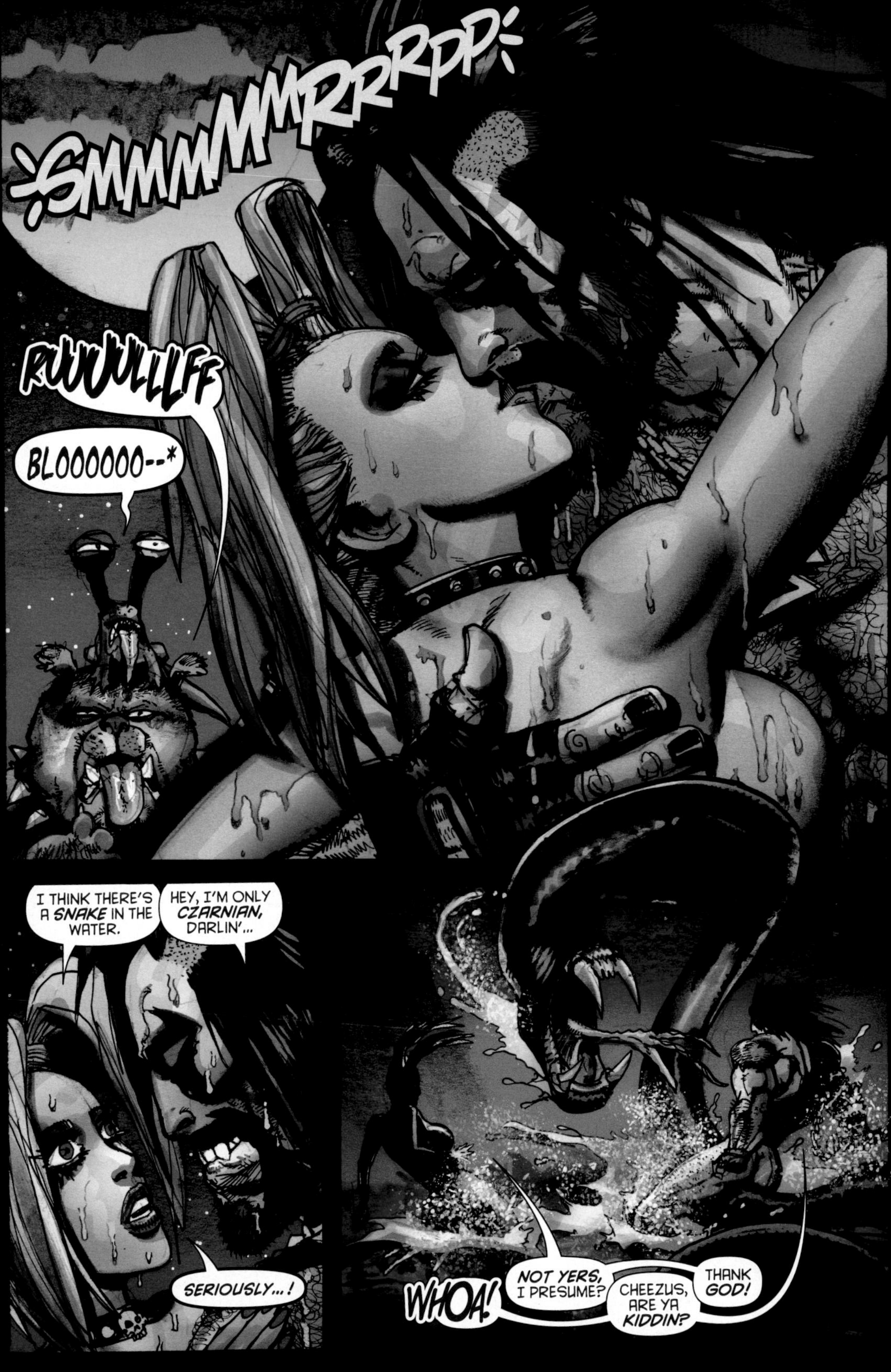
SMMMMMMRRRPP
RUUUULLLFF
BLOOOOOO--*
I THINK THERE'S A SNAKE IN THE WATER.
HEY, I'M ONLY CZARNIAN, DARLIN'...
SERIOUSLY...!
WHOA!
NOT YERS, I PRESUME?
CHEEZUS, ARE YA KIDDIN?
THANK GOD!

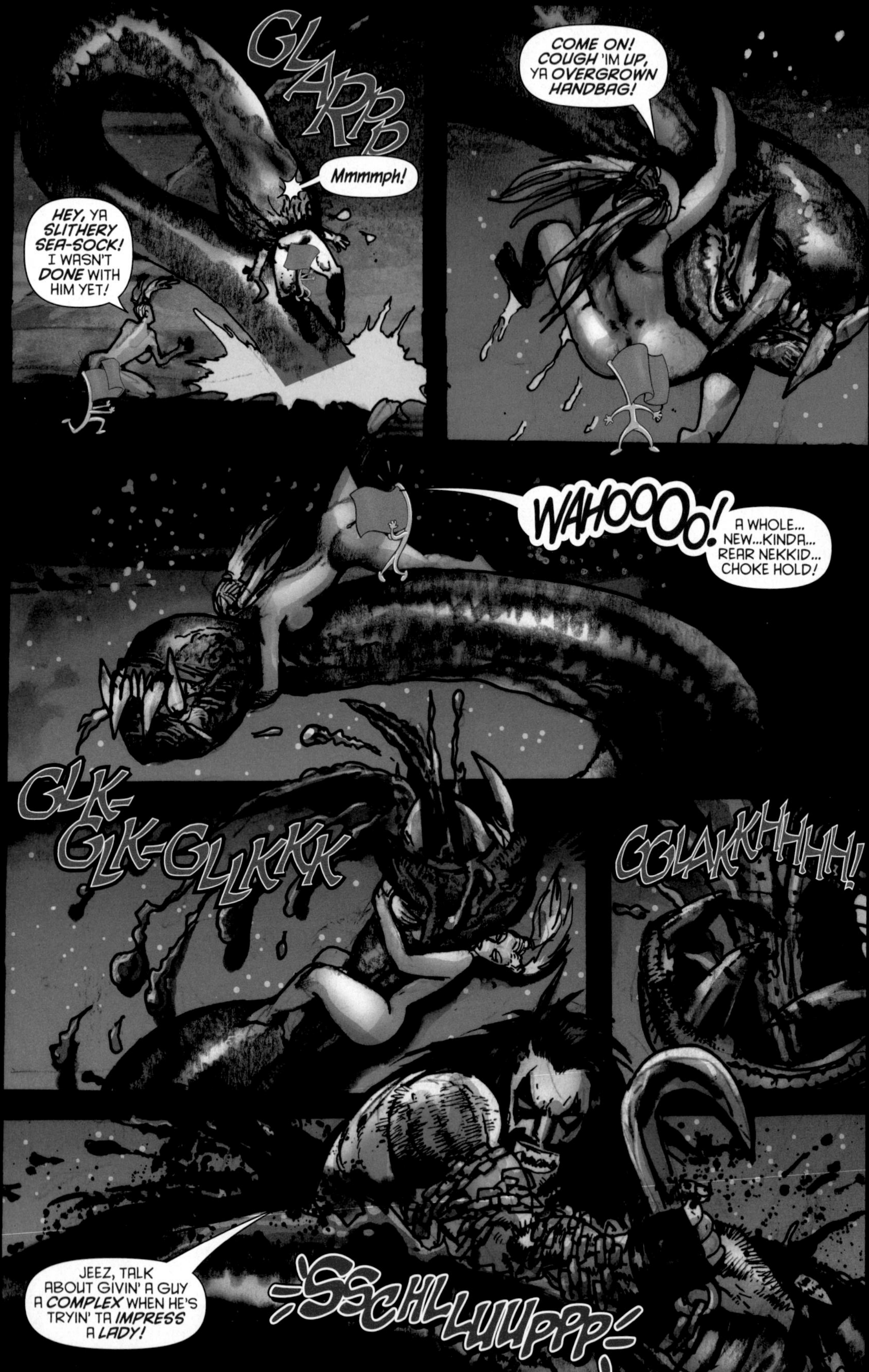
GLARPP
Mmmmph!
HEY, YA SLITHERY SEA-SOCK! I WASN'T DONE WITH HIM YET!
COME ON! COUGH 'IM UP, YA OVERGROWN HANDBAG!
WAHOOOOO!
A WHOLE... NEW...KINDA... REAR NEKKID... CHOKE HOLD!
GLK-GLK-GLLKKKK
GGLAKKHHHH!
JEEZ, TALK ABOUT GIVIN' A GUY A COMPLEX WHEN HE'S TRYIN' TA IMPRESS A LADY!
SSCHLLUUPPP!

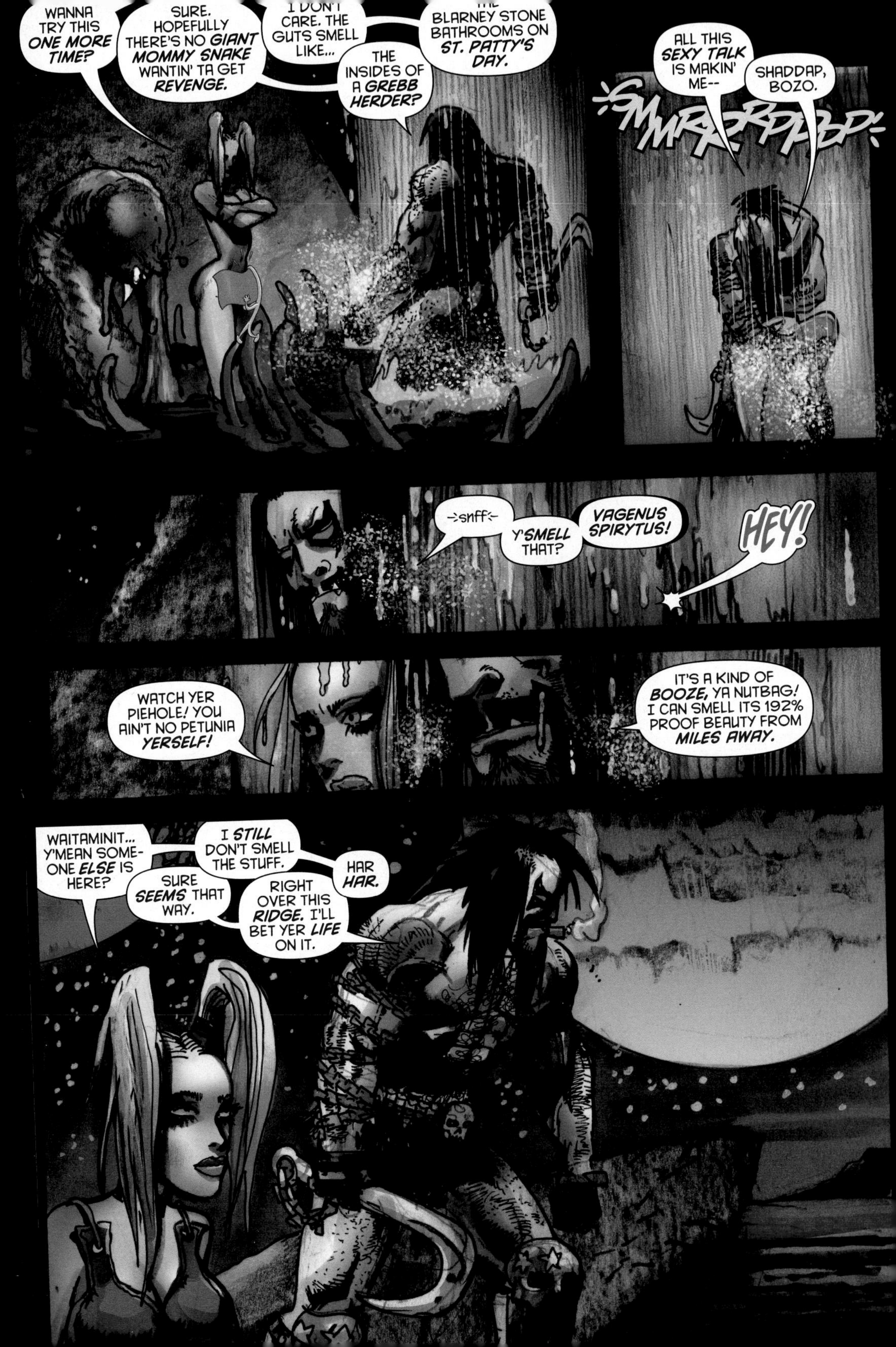
WANNA TRY THIS ONE MORE TIME?
SURE. HOPEFULLY THERE'S NO GIANT MOMMY SNAKE WANTIN' TA GET REVENGE.
I DON'T CARE. THE GUTS SMELL LIKE...
THE INSIDES OF A GREBB HERDER?
BLARNEY STONE BATHROOMS ON ST. PATTY'S DAY.
SMMRRORPHBP
ALL THIS SEXY TALK IS MAKIN' ME--
SHADDAP, BOZO.
-snff-
Y'SMELL THAT?
VAGENUS SPIRYTUS!
HEY!
WATCH YER PIEHOLE! YOU AIN'T NO PETUNIA YERSELF!
IT'S A KIND OF BOOZE, YA NUTBAG! I CAN SMELL ITS 192% PROOF BEAUTY FROM MILES AWAY.
WAITAMINIT... Y'MEAN SOME-ONE ELSE IS HERE?
I STILL DON'T SMELL THE STUFF.
HAR HAR.
SURE SEEMS THAT WAY.
RIGHT OVER THIS RIDGE. I'LL BET YER LIFE ON IT.

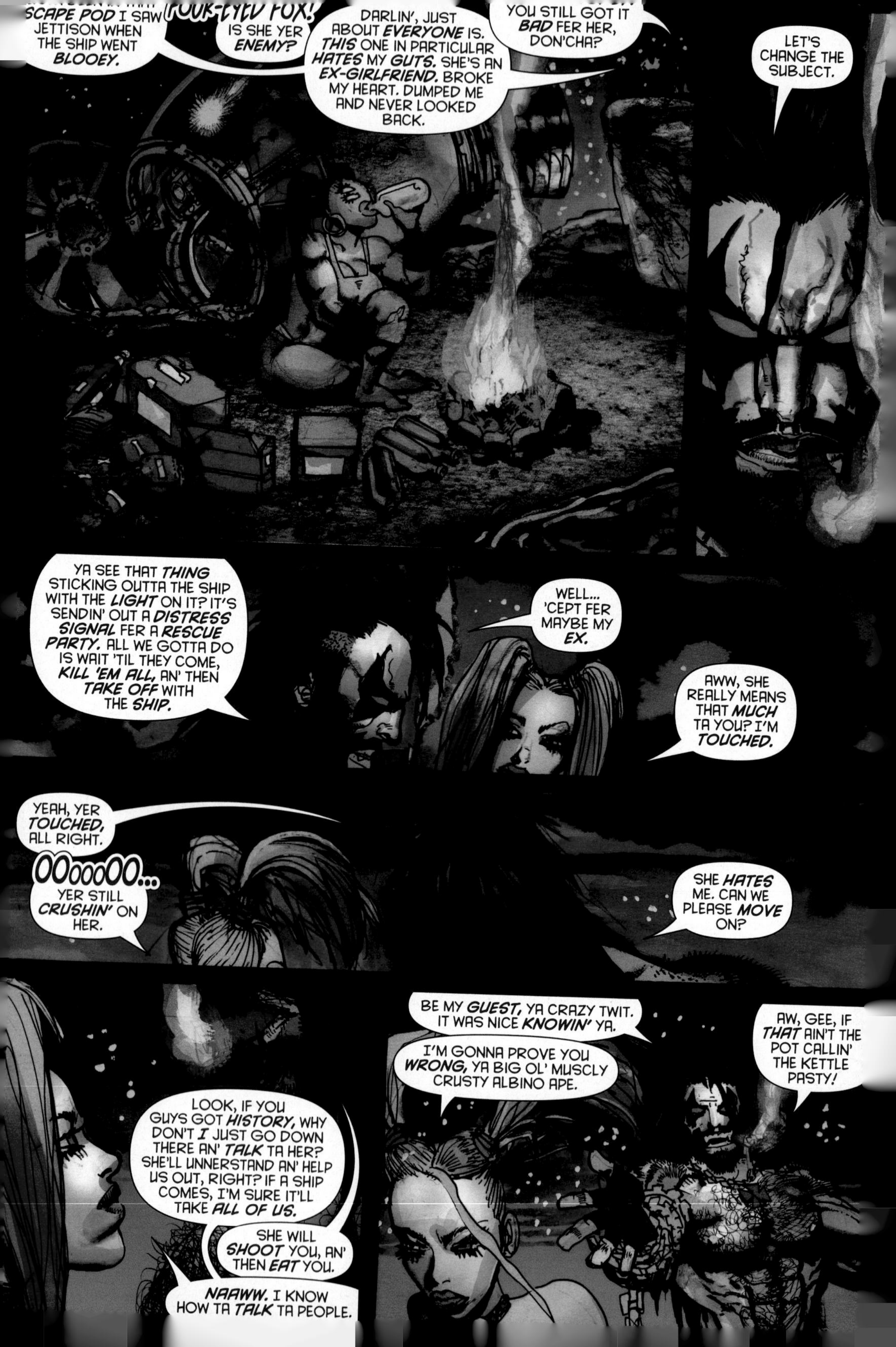
SCAPE POD I SAW JETTISON WHEN THE SHIP WENT BLOOEY.
IS SHE YER ENEMY?
DARLIN', JUST ABOUT EVERYONE IS. THIS ONE IN PARTICULAR HATES MY GUTS. SHE'S AN EX-GIRLFRIEND. BROKE MY HEART. DUMPED ME AND NEVER LOOKED BACK.
YOU STILL GOT IT BAD FER HER, DON'CHA?
LET'S CHANGE THE SUBJECT.
YA SEE THAT THING STICKING OUTTA THE SHIP WITH THE LIGHT ON IT? IT'S SENDIN' OUT A DISTRESS SIGNAL FER A RESCUE PARTY. ALL WE GOTTA DO IS WAIT 'TIL THEY COME, KILL 'EM ALL, AN' THEN TAKE OFF WITH THE SHIP.
WELL... 'CEPT FER MAYBE MY EX.
AWW, SHE REALLY MEANS THAT MUCH TA YOU? I'M TOUCHED.
YEAH, YER TOUCHED, ALL RIGHT.
OOooooOO...
YER STILL CRUSHIN' ON HER.
SHE HATES ME. CAN WE PLEASE MOVE ON?
LOOK, IF YOU GUYS GOT HISTORY, WHY DON'T I JUST GO DOWN THERE AN' TALK TA HER? SHE'LL UNNERSTAND AN' HELP US OUT, RIGHT? IF A SHIP COMES, I'M SURE IT'LL TAKE ALL OF US.
SHE WILL SHOOT YOU, AN' THEN EAT YOU.
NAAWW. I KNOW HOW TA TALK TA PEOPLE.
BE MY GUEST, YA CRAZY TWIT. IT WAS NICE KNOWIN' YA.
I'M GONNA PROVE YOU WRONG, YA BIG OL' MUSCLY CRUSTY ALBINO APE.
AW, GEE, IF THAT AIN'T THE POT CALLIN' THE KETTLE PASTY!

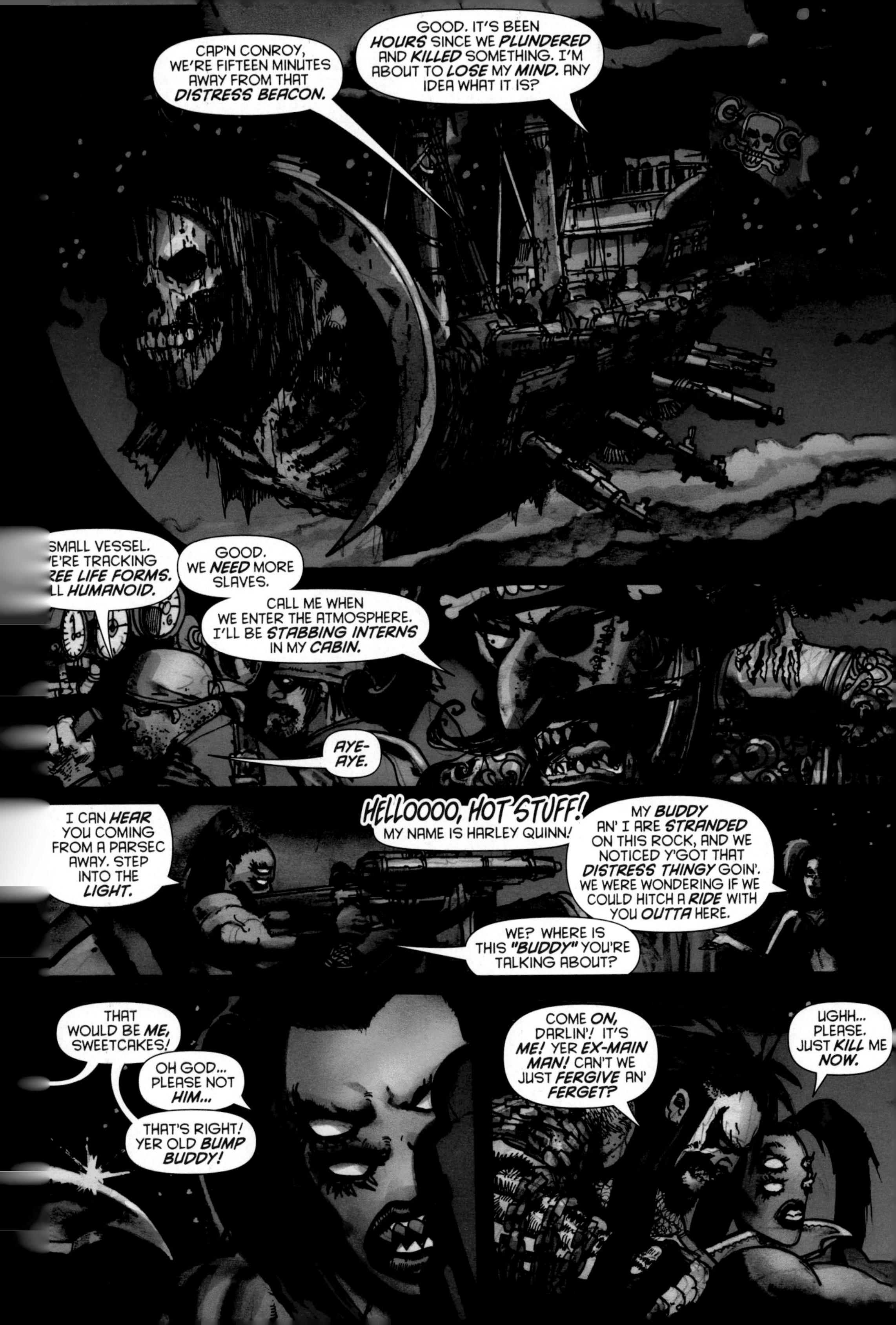
CAP'N CONROY, WE'RE FIFTEEN MINUTES AWAY FROM THAT DISTRESS BEACON.
GOOD. IT'S BEEN HOURS SINCE WE PLUNDERED AND KILLED SOMETHING. I'M ABOUT TO LOSE MY MIND. ANY IDEA WHAT IT IS?
SMALL VESSEL. 'E'RE TRACKING REE LIFE FORMS. LL HUMANOID.
GOOD. WE NEED MORE SLAVES.
CALL ME WHEN WE ENTER THE ATMOSPHERE. I'LL BE STABBING INTERNS IN MY CABIN.
AYE-AYE.
I CAN HEAR YOU COMING FROM A PARSEC AWAY. STEP INTO THE LIGHT.
HELLOOOO, HOT STUFF! MY NAME IS HARLEY QUINN!
MY BUDDY AN' I ARE STRANDED ON THIS ROCK, AND WE NOTICED Y'GOT THAT DISTRESS THINGY GOIN'. WE WERE WONDERING IF WE COULD HITCH A RIDE WITH YOU OUTTA HERE.
WE? WHERE IS THIS "BUDDY" YOU'RE TALKING ABOUT?
THAT WOULD BE ME, SWEETCAKES!
OH GOD... PLEASE NOT HIM...
THAT'S RIGHT! YER OLD BUMP BUDDY!
COME ON, DARLIN'! IT'S ME! YER EX-MAIN MAN! CAN'T WE JUST FERGIVE AN' FERGET?
UGHH... PLEASE. JUST KILL ME NOW.

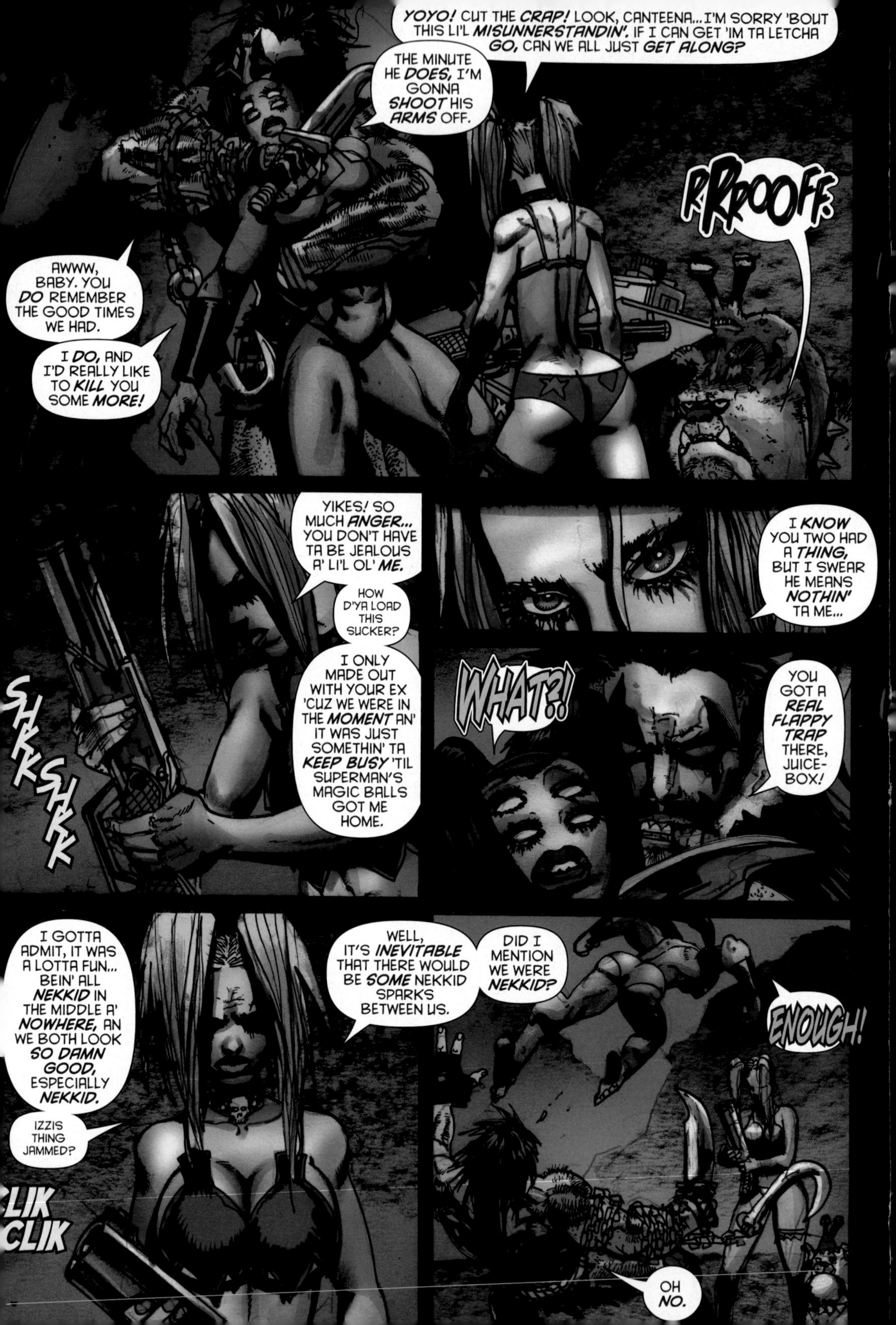
YOYO! CUT THE CRAP! LOOK, CANTEENA... I'M SORRY 'BOUT THIS LI'L MISUNNERSTANDIN'. IF I CAN GET 'IM TA LETCHA GO, CAN WE ALL JUST GET ALONG?
THE MINUTE HE DOES, I'M GONNA SHOOT HIS ARMS OFF.
RRROOFF.
AWWW, BABY. YOU DO REMEMBER THE GOOD TIMES WE HAD.
I DO, AND I'D REALLY LIKE TO KILL YOU SOME MORE!
YIKES! SO MUCH ANGER... YOU DON'T HAVE TA BE JEALOUS A' LI'L OL' ME.
HOW D'YA LOAD THIS SUCKER?
I ONLY MADE OUT WITH YOUR EX 'CUZ WE WERE IN THE MOMENT AN' IT WAS JUST SOMETHIN' TA KEEP BUSY 'TIL SUPERMAN'S MAGIC BALLS GOT ME HOME.
SHKK SHKK
I KNOW YOU TWO HAD A THING, BUT I SWEAR HE MEANS NOTHIN' TA ME...
WHAT?!
YOU GOT A REAL FLAPPY TRAP THERE, JUICE-BOX!
I GOTTA ADMIT, IT WAS A LOTTA FUN... BEIN' ALL NEKKID IN THE MIDDLE A' NOWHERE, AN WE BOTH LOOK SO DAMN GOOD, ESPECIALLY NEKKID.
IZZIS THING JAMMED?
CLIK CLIK
WELL, IT'S INEVITABLE THAT THERE WOULD BE SOME NEKKID SPARKS BETWEEN US.
DID I MENTION WE WERE NEKKID?
ENOUGH!
OH NO.

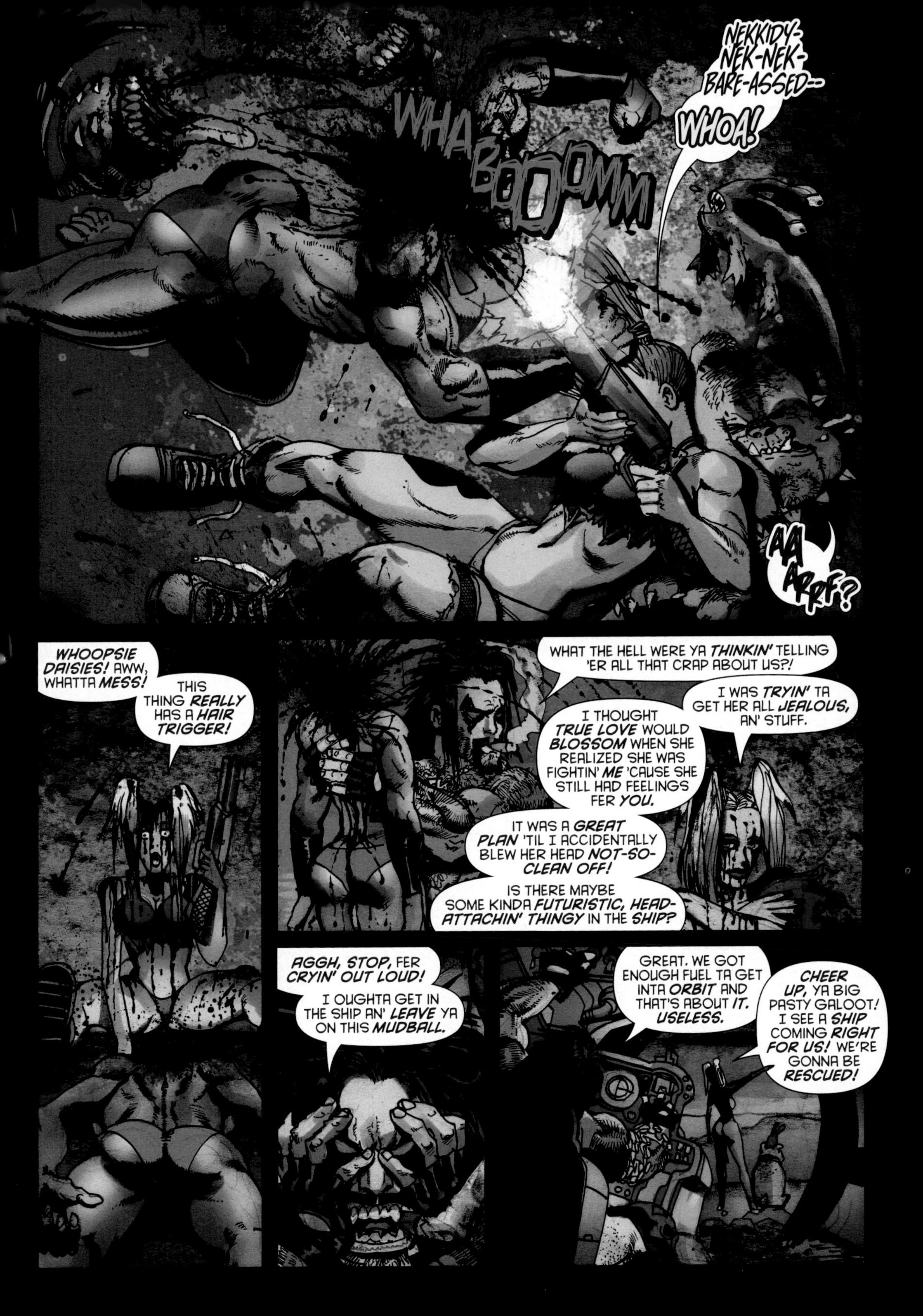

WHABOOOMM
NEKKIDY-NEK-NEK-BARE-ASSED--
WHOA!
AAARRF?
WHOOPSIE DAISIES! AWW, WHATTA MESS!
THIS THING REALLY HAS A HAIR TRIGGER!
WHAT THE HELL WERE YA THINKIN' TELLING 'ER ALL THAT CRAP ABOUT US?!
I WAS TRYIN' TA GET HER ALL JEALOUS, AN' STUFF.
I THOUGHT TRUE LOVE WOULD BLOSSOM WHEN SHE REALIZED SHE WAS FIGHTIN' ME 'CAUSE SHE STILL HAD FEELINGS FER YOU.
IT WAS A GREAT PLAN 'TIL I ACCIDENTALLY BLEW HER HEAD NOT-SO-CLEAN OFF!
IS THERE MAYBE SOME KINDA FUTURISTIC, HEAD-ATTACHIN' THINGY IN THE SHIP?
AGGH, STOP, FER CRYIN' OUT LOUD!
I OUGHTA GET IN THE SHIP AN' LEAVE YA ON THIS MUDBALL.
GREAT. WE GOT ENOUGH FUEL TA GET INTA ORBIT AND THAT'S ABOUT IT. USELESS.
CHEER UP, YA BIG PASTY GALOOT! I SEE A SHIP COMING RIGHT FOR US! WE'RE GONNA BE RESCUED!

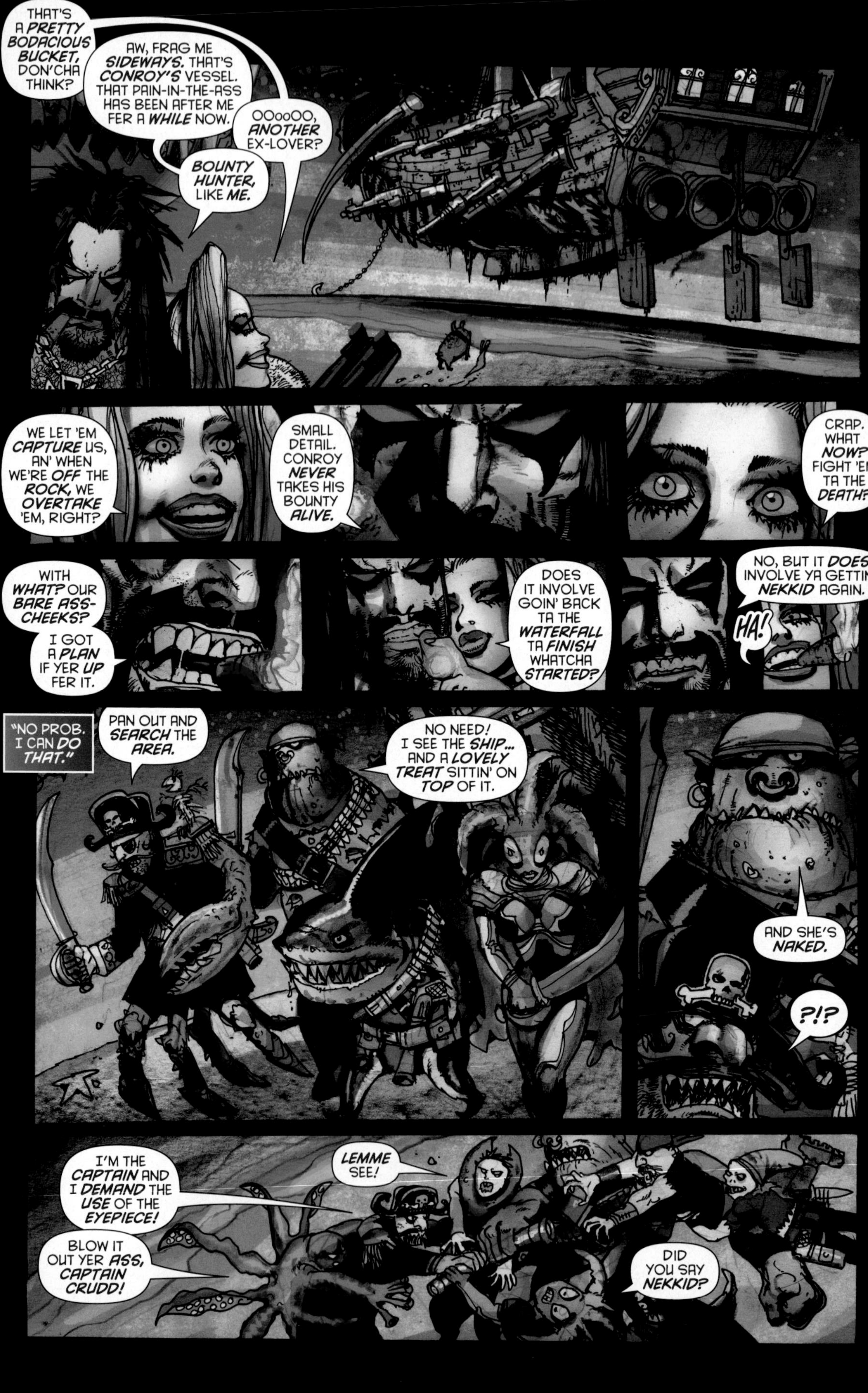
THAT'S A PRETTY BODACIOUS BUCKET, DON'CHA THINK?
AW, FRAG ME SIDEWAYS. THAT'S CONROY'S VESSEL. THAT PAIN-IN-THE-ASS HAS BEEN AFTER ME FER A WHILE NOW.
OOooOO, ANOTHER EX-LOVER?
BOUNTY HUNTER, LIKE ME.
WE LET 'EM CAPTURE US, AN' WHEN WE'RE OFF THE ROCK, WE OVERTAKE 'EM, RIGHT?
SMALL DETAIL. CONROY NEVER TAKES HIS BOUNTY ALIVE.
CRAP. WHAT NOW? FIGHT 'EM TA THE DEATH?
WITH WHAT? OUR BARE ASS-CHEEKS?
I GOT A PLAN IF YER UP FER IT.
DOES IT INVOLVE GOIN' BACK TA THE WATERFALL TA FINISH WHATCHA STARTED?
NO, BUT IT DOES INVOLVE YA GETTIN' NEKKID AGAIN.
HA!
"NO PROB. I CAN DO THAT."
PAN OUT AND SEARCH THE AREA.
NO NEED! I SEE THE SHIP... AND A LOVELY TREAT SITTIN' ON TOP OF IT.
AND SHE'S NAKED.
?!?
I'M THE CAPTAIN AND I DEMAND THE USE OF THE EYEPIECE!
LEMME SEE!
BLOW IT OUT YER ASS, CAPTAIN CRUDD!
DID YOU SAY NEKKID?

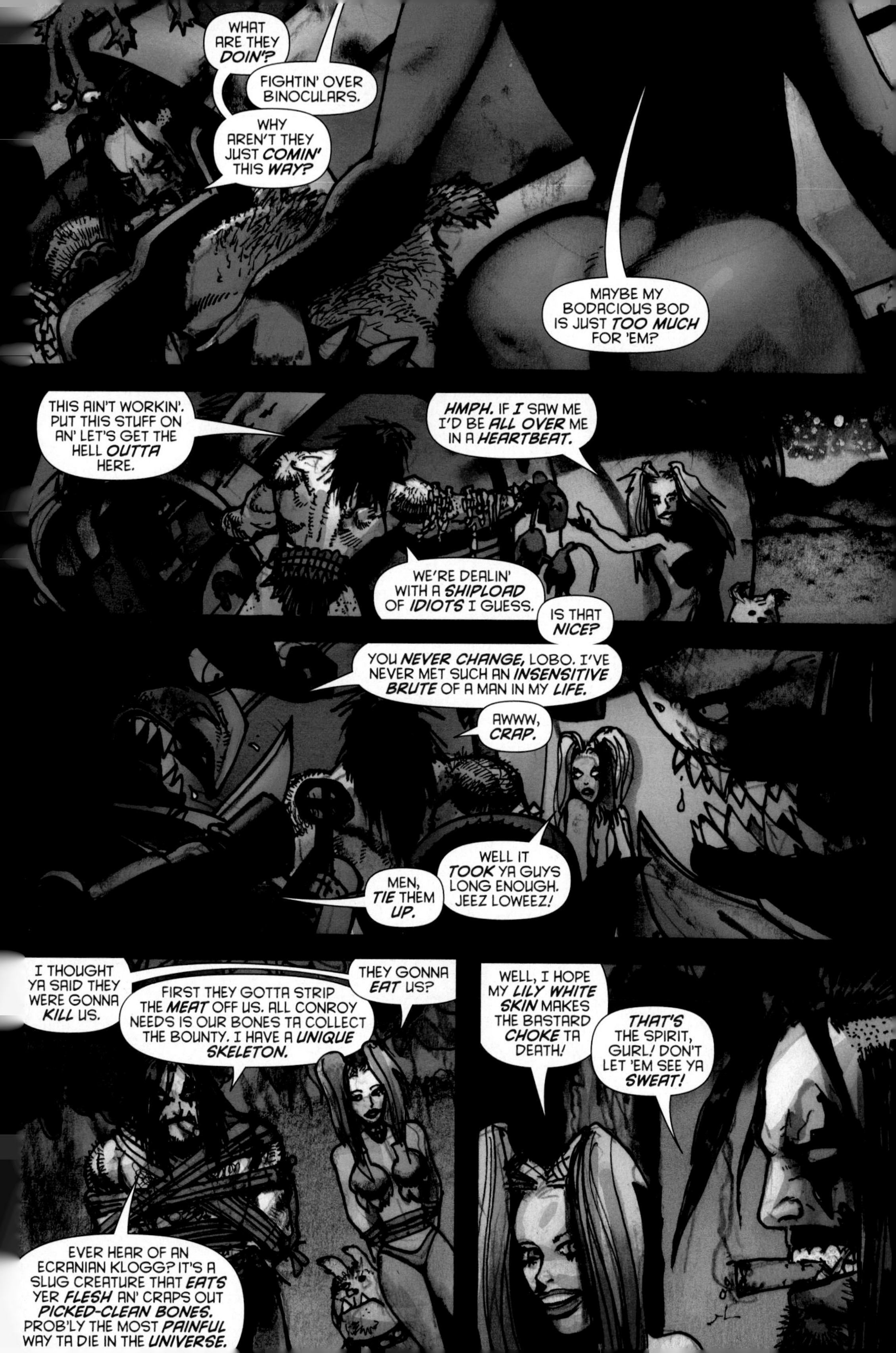
WHAT ARE THEY DOIN'?
FIGHTIN' OVER BINOCULARS.
WHY AREN'T THEY JUST COMIN' THIS WAY?
MAYBE MY BODACIOUS BOD IS JUST TOO MUCH FOR 'EM?
THIS AIN'T WORKIN'. PUT THIS STUFF ON AN' LET'S GET THE HELL OUTTA HERE.
HMPH. IF I SAW ME I'D BE ALL OVER ME IN A HEARTBEAT.
WE'RE DEALIN' WITH A SHIPLOAD OF IDIOTS I GUESS.
IS THAT NICE?
YOU NEVER CHANGE, LOBO. I'VE NEVER MET SUCH AN INSENSITIVE BRUTE OF A MAN IN MY LIFE.
AWWW, CRAP.
WELL IT TOOK YA GUYS LONG ENOUGH. JEEZ LOWEEZ!
MEN, TIE THEM UP.
I THOUGHT YA SAID THEY WERE GONNA KILL US.
THEY GONNA EAT US?
FIRST THEY GOTTA STRIP THE MEAT OFF US. ALL CONROY NEEDS IS OUR BONES TA COLLECT THE BOUNTY. I HAVE A UNIQUE SKELETON.
EVER HEAR OF AN ECRANIAN KLOGG? IT'S A SLUG CREATURE THAT EATS YER FLESH AN' CRAPS OUT PICKED-CLEAN BONES. PROB'LY THE MOST PAINFUL WAY TA DIE IN THE UNIVERSE.
WELL, I HOPE MY LILY WHITE SKIN MAKES THE BASTARD CHOKE TA DEATH!
THAT'S THE SPIRIT, GURL! DON'T LET 'EM SEE YA SWEAT!

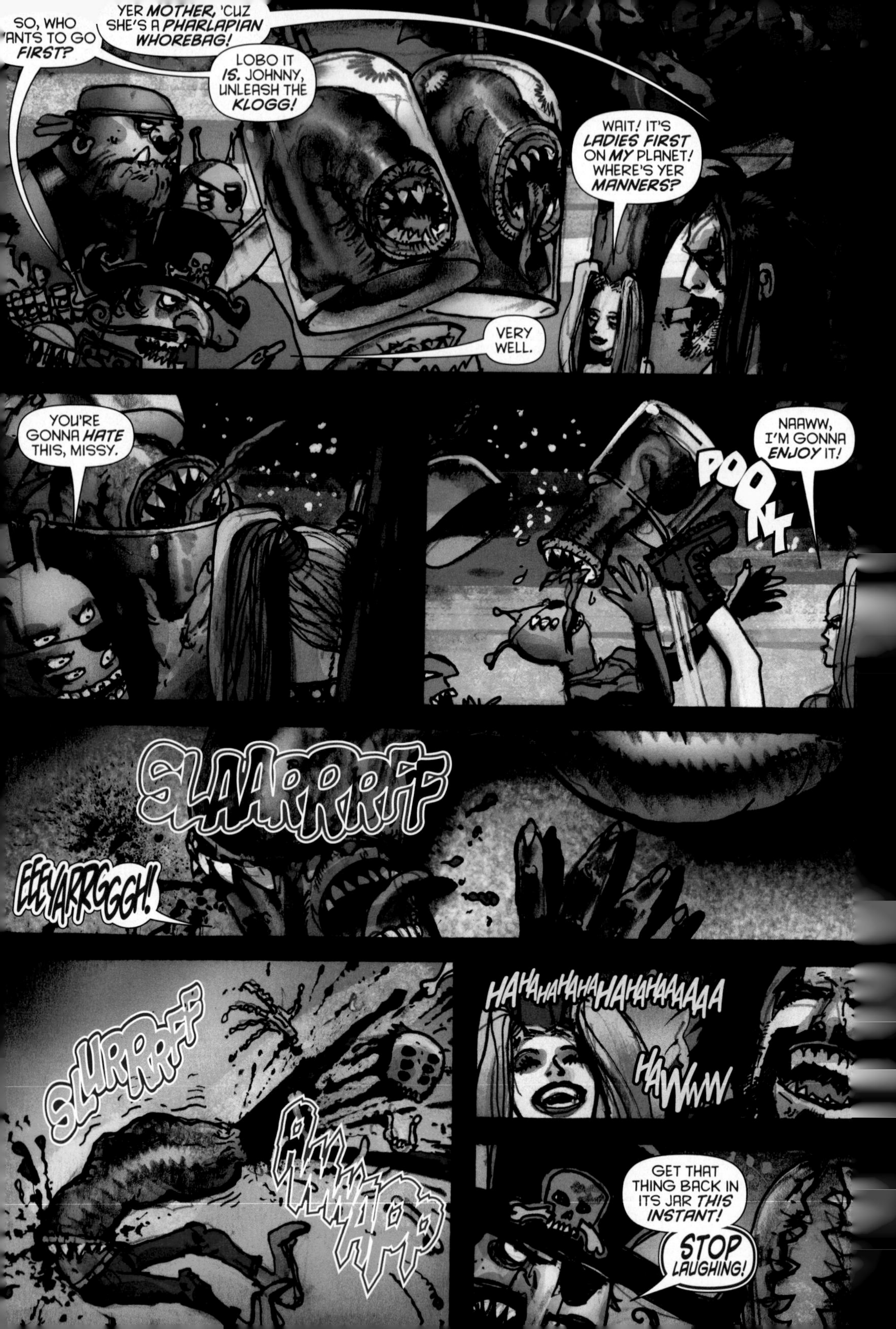
SO, WHO 'ANTS TO GO FIRST?
YER MOTHER, 'CUZ SHE'S A PHARLAPIAN WHOREBAG!
LOBO IT IS. JOHNNY, UNLEASH THE KLOGG!
WAIT! IT'S LADIES FIRST ON MY PLANET! WHERE'S YER MANNERS?
VERY WELL.
YOU'RE GONNA HATE THIS, MISSY.
POONT
NAAWW, I'M GONNA ENJOY IT!
SLAARRRRFF
EEEYARRGGGH!
SLURRRFF
HAHAHAHAHAHAHAHAHAAAAAA
HAWWW
GET THAT THING BACK IN ITS JAR THIS INSTANT!
STOP LAUGHING!

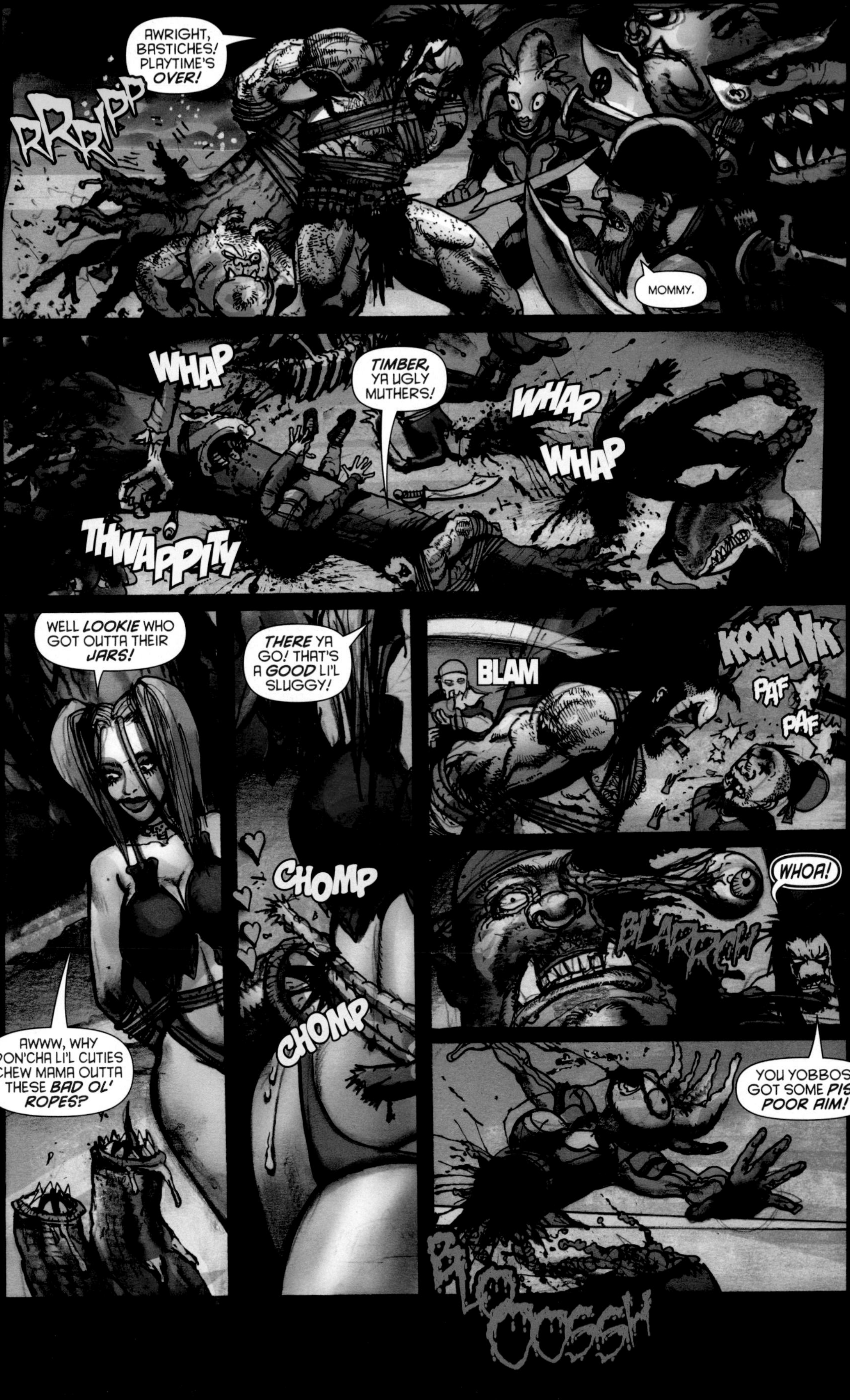
AWRIGHT, BASTICHES! PLAYTIME'S OVER!
RRRIPP
MOMMY.
WHAP
TIMBER, YA UGLY MUTHERS!
WHAP
WHAP
THWAPPITY
WELL LOOKIE WHO GOT OUTTA THEIR JARS!
AWWW, WHY DON'CHA LI'L CUTIES CHEW MAMA OUTTA THESE BAD OL' ROPES?
THERE YA GO! THAT'S A GOOD LI'L SLUGGY!
CHOMP
CHOMP
BLAM
KOWWK
PAF
PAF
WHOA!
BLARRGH
YOU YOBBOS GOT SOME PISS POOR AIM!
BLOOOSSH

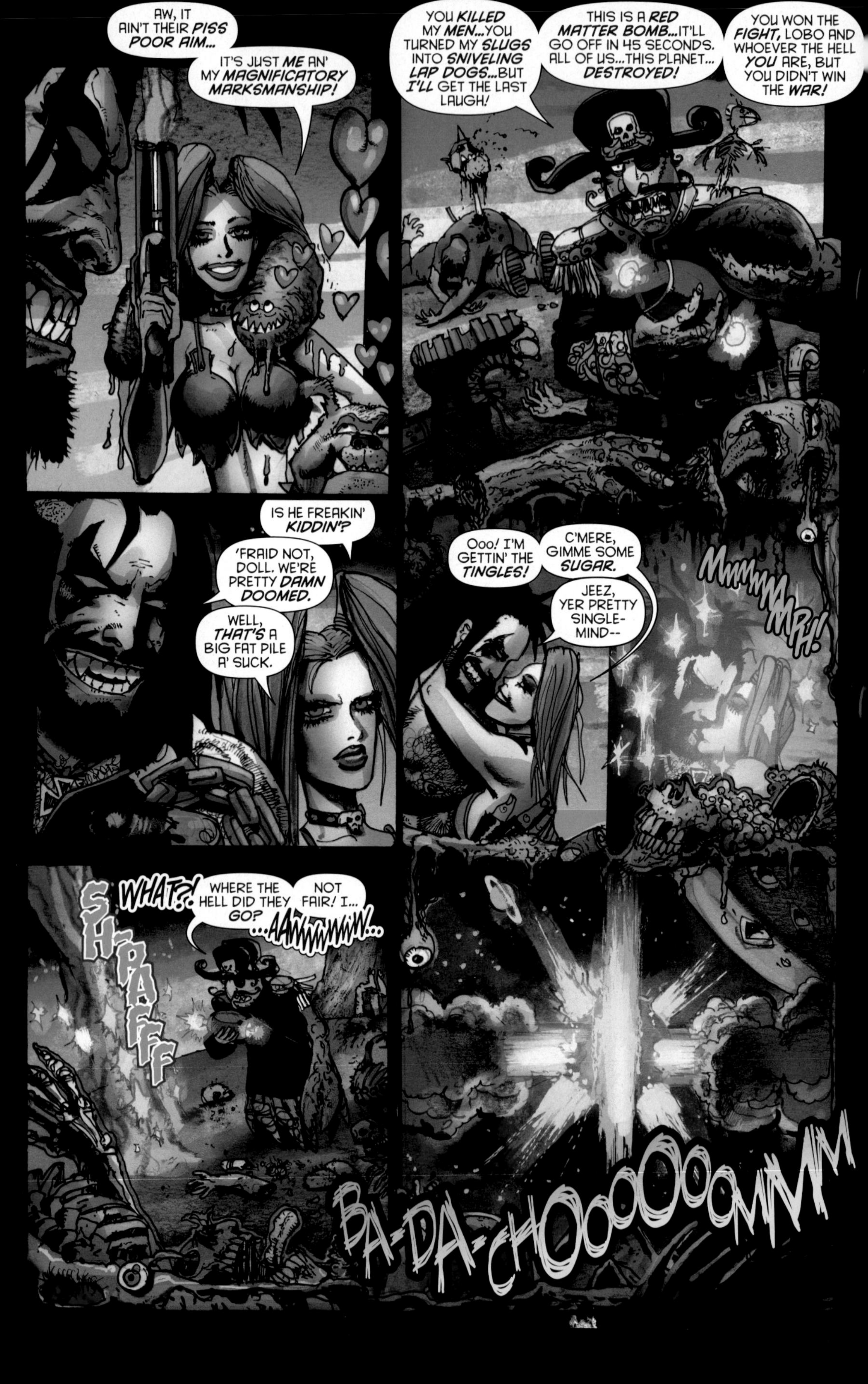
AW, IT AIN'T THEIR PISS POOR AIM...
IT'S JUST ME AN' MY MAGNIFICATORY MARKSMANSHIP!
YOU KILLED MY MEN...YOU TURNED MY SLUGS INTO SNIVELING LAP DOGS...BUT I'LL GET THE LAST LAUGH!
THIS IS A RED MATTER BOMB...IT'LL GO OFF IN 45 SECONDS. ALL OF US...THIS PLANET... DESTROYED!
YOU WON THE FIGHT, LOBO AND WHOEVER THE HELL YOU ARE, BUT YOU DIDN'T WIN THE WAR!
IS HE FREAKIN' KIDDIN'?
'FRAID NOT, DOLL. WE'RE PRETTY DAMN DOOMED.
WELL, THAT'S A BIG FAT PILE A' SUCK.
Ooo! I'M GETTIN' THE TINGLES!
C'MERE, GIMME SOME SUGAR.
JEEZ, YER PRETTY SINGLE-MIND--
MMMMMMPH!
SH-RAFFF
WHAT?!
WHERE THE HELL DID THEY GO?
NOT FAIR! I... ...AAWWWWWW...
BA-DA-CHOOOOOOOMMM

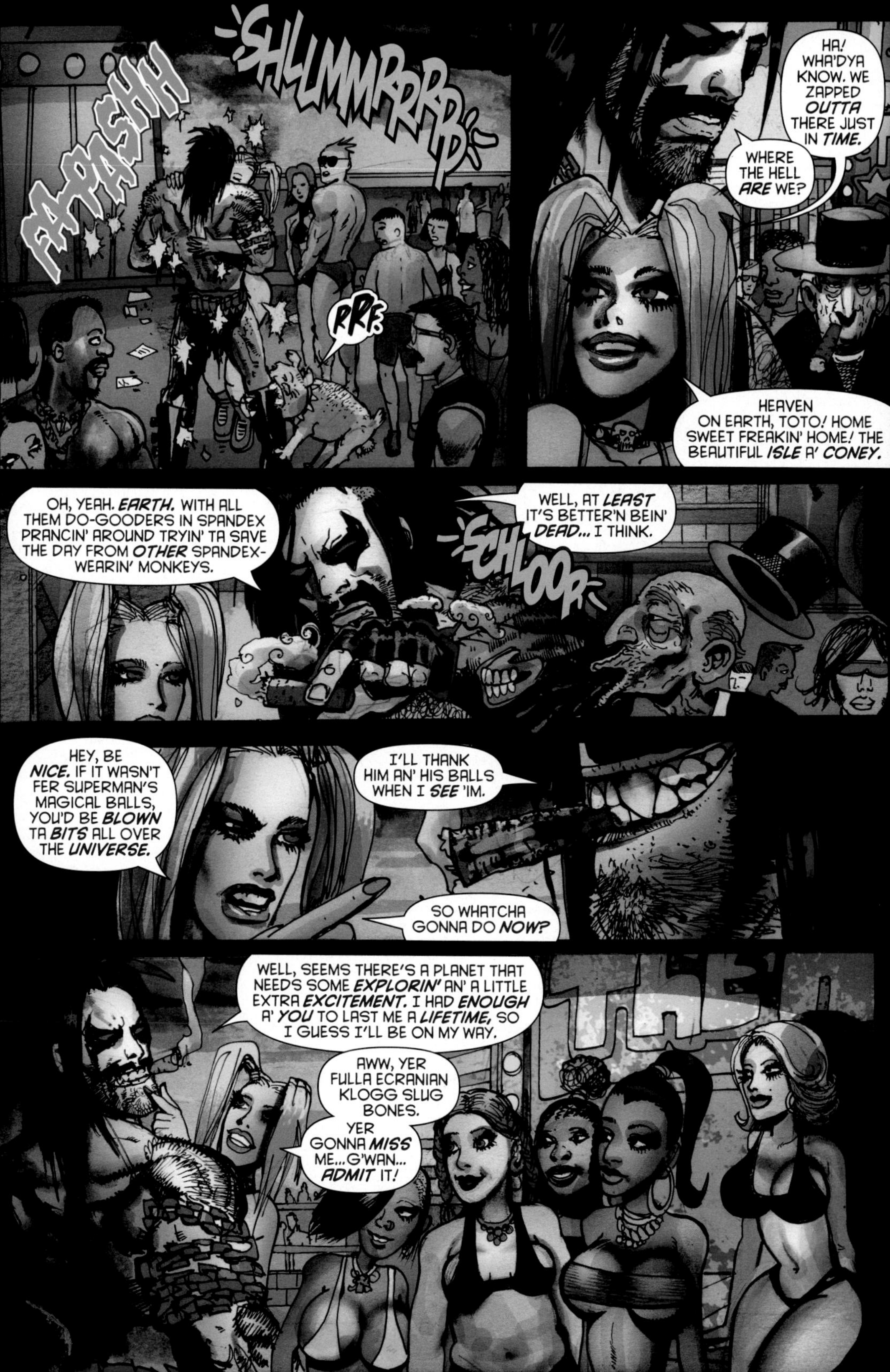
FAPASHH
SHLLUMMRRRRP
RRF.
HA! WHA'DYA KNOW. WE ZAPPED OUTTA THERE JUST IN TIME.
WHERE THE HELL ARE WE?
HEAVEN ON EARTH, TOTO! HOME SWEET FREAKIN' HOME! THE BEAUTIFUL ISLE A' CONEY.
OH, YEAH. EARTH. WITH ALL THEM DO-GOODERS IN SPANDEX PRANCIN' AROUND TRYIN' TA SAVE THE DAY FROM OTHER SPANDEX-WEARIN' MONKEYS.
WELL, AT LEAST IT'S BETTER'N BEIN' DEAD... I THINK.
SCHLOOR
HEY, BE NICE. IF IT WASN'T FER SUPERMAN'S MAGICAL BALLS, YOU'D BE BLOWN TA BITS ALL OVER THE UNIVERSE.
I'LL THANK HIM AN' HIS BALLS WHEN I SEE 'IM.
SO WHATCHA GONNA DO NOW?
WELL, SEEMS THERE'S A PLANET THAT NEEDS SOME EXPLORIN' AN' A LITTLE EXTRA EXCITEMENT. I HAD ENOUGH A' YOU TO LAST ME A LIFETIME, SO I GUESS I'LL BE ON MY WAY.
AWW, YER FULLA ECRANIAN KLOGG SLUG BONES.
YER GONNA MISS ME...G'WAN... ADMIT IT!

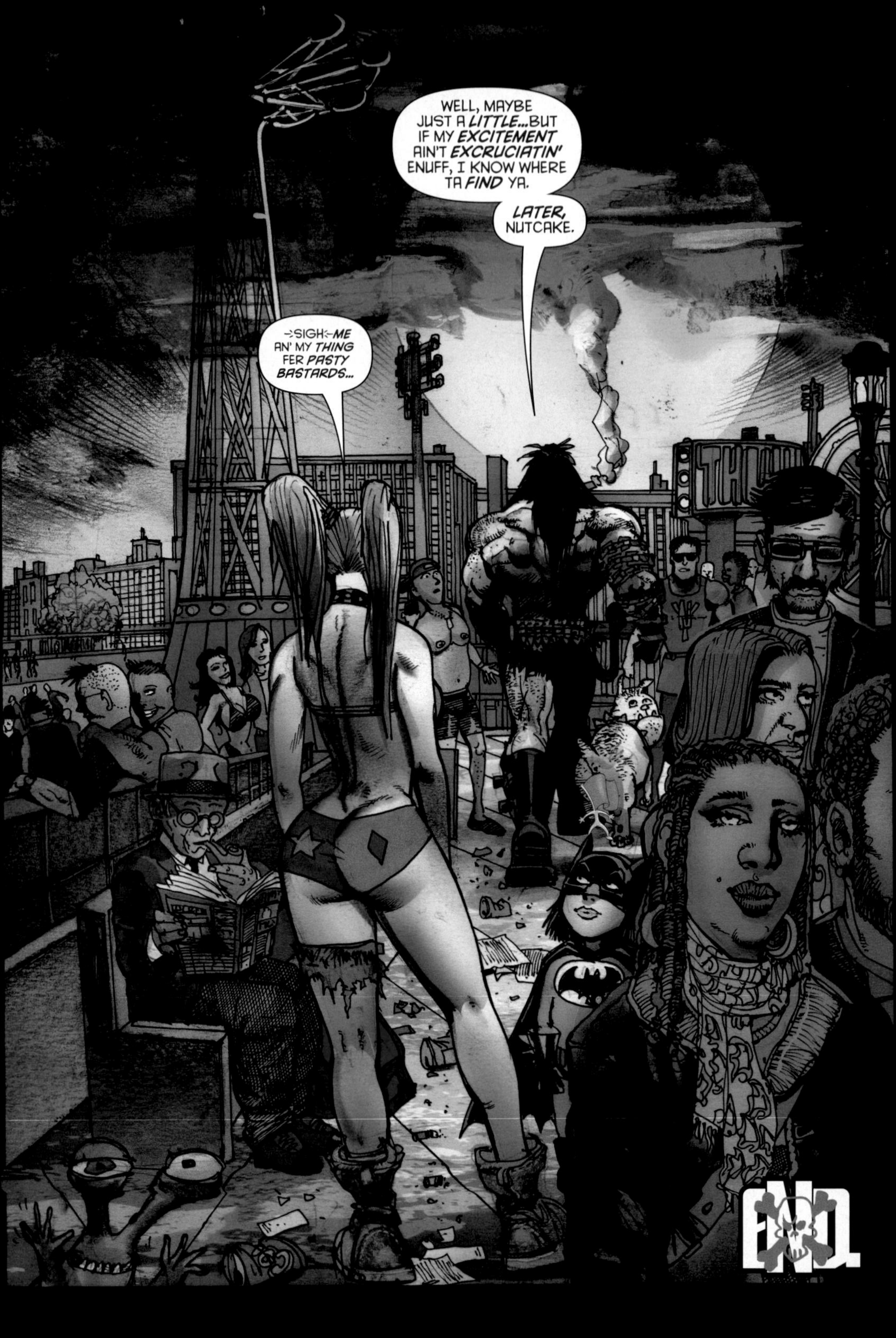
WELL, MAYBE JUST A LITTLE...BUT IF MY EXCITEMENT AIN'T EXCRUCIATIN' ENUFF, I KNOW WHERE TA FIND YA.
LATER, NUTCAKE.
-SIGH- ME AN' MY THING FER PASTY BASTARDS...
END

VARIANT COVER GALLERY

HARLEY'S LITTLE BLACK BOOK
polybag art by Amanda Conner

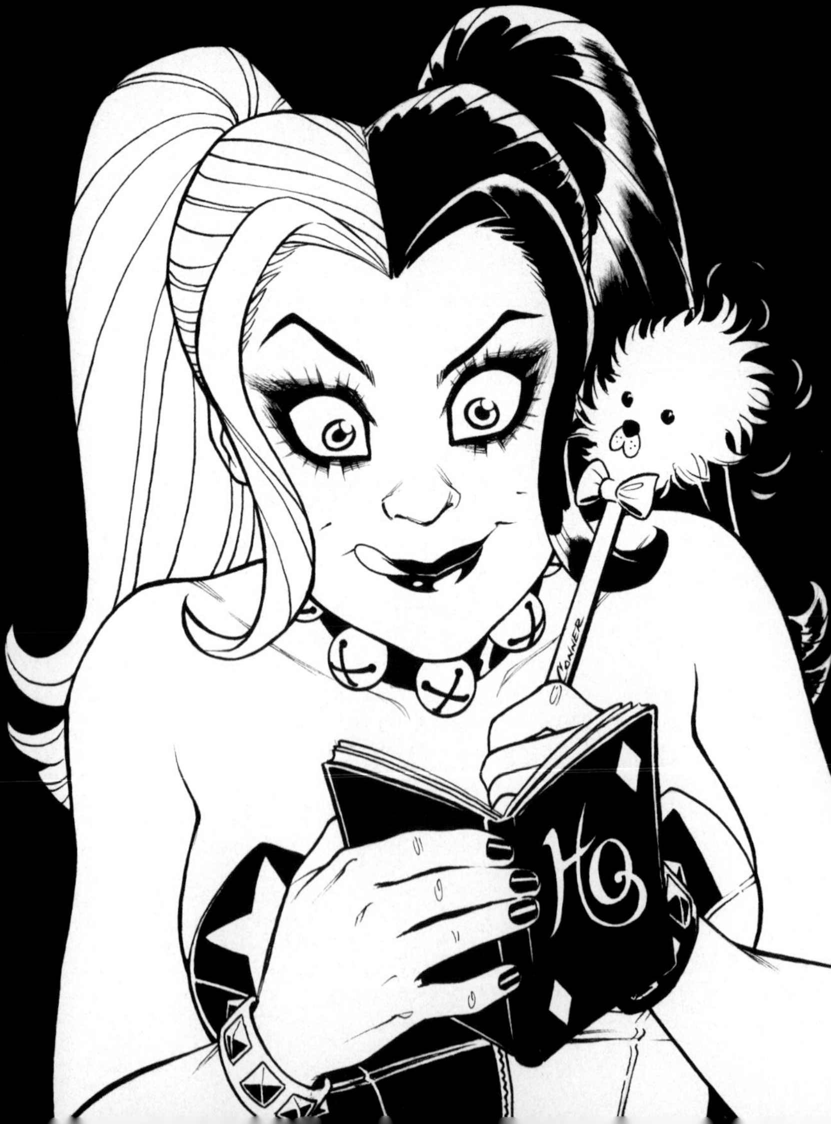
CONNER
HQ

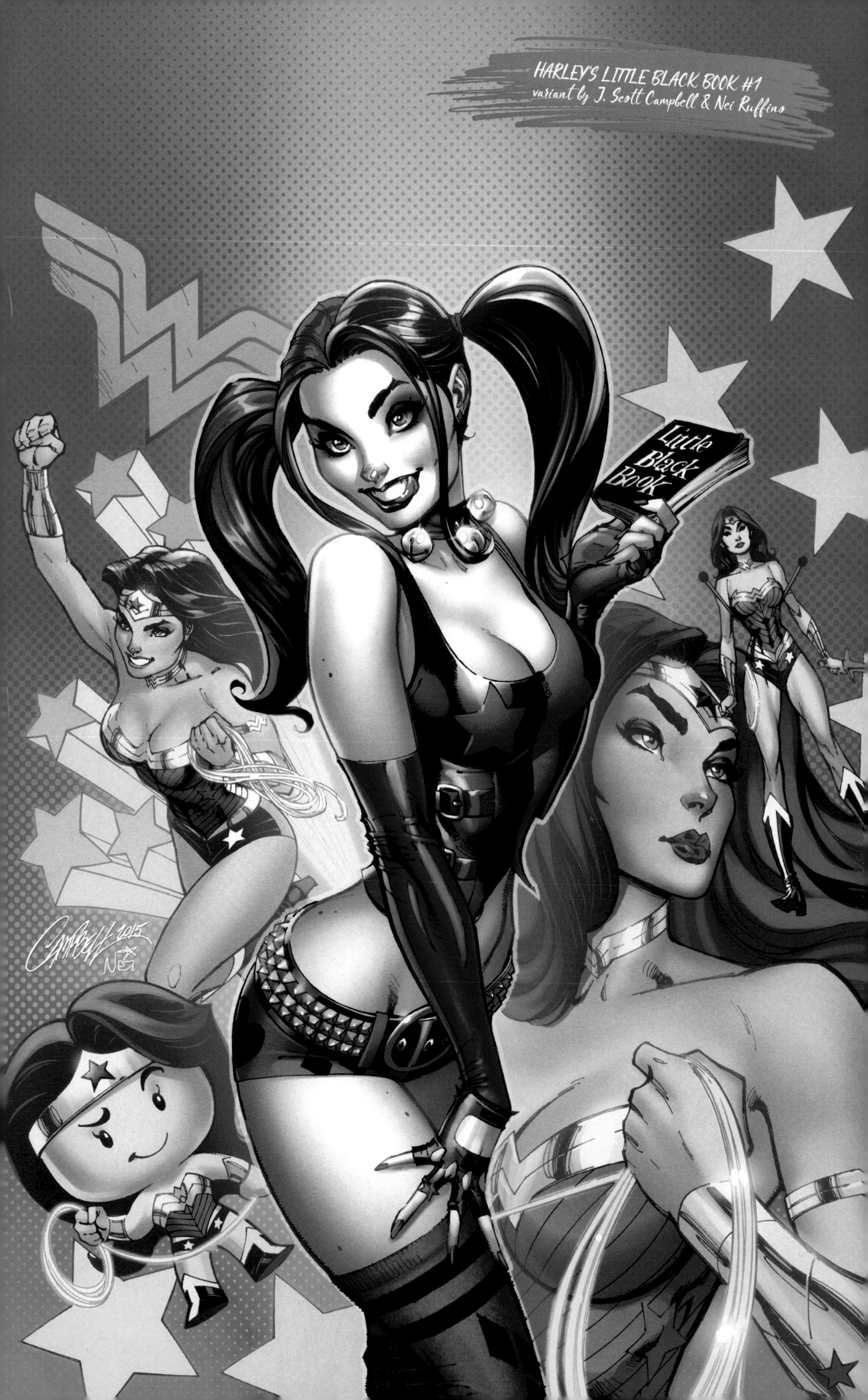
Little Black Book
Campbell 2015
Nei

HARLEY'S LITTLE BLACK BOOK #1
variant by J. Scott Campbell & Nei Ruffino

HARLEY'S LITTLE BLACK BOOK #1
ink variant by J. Scott Campbell

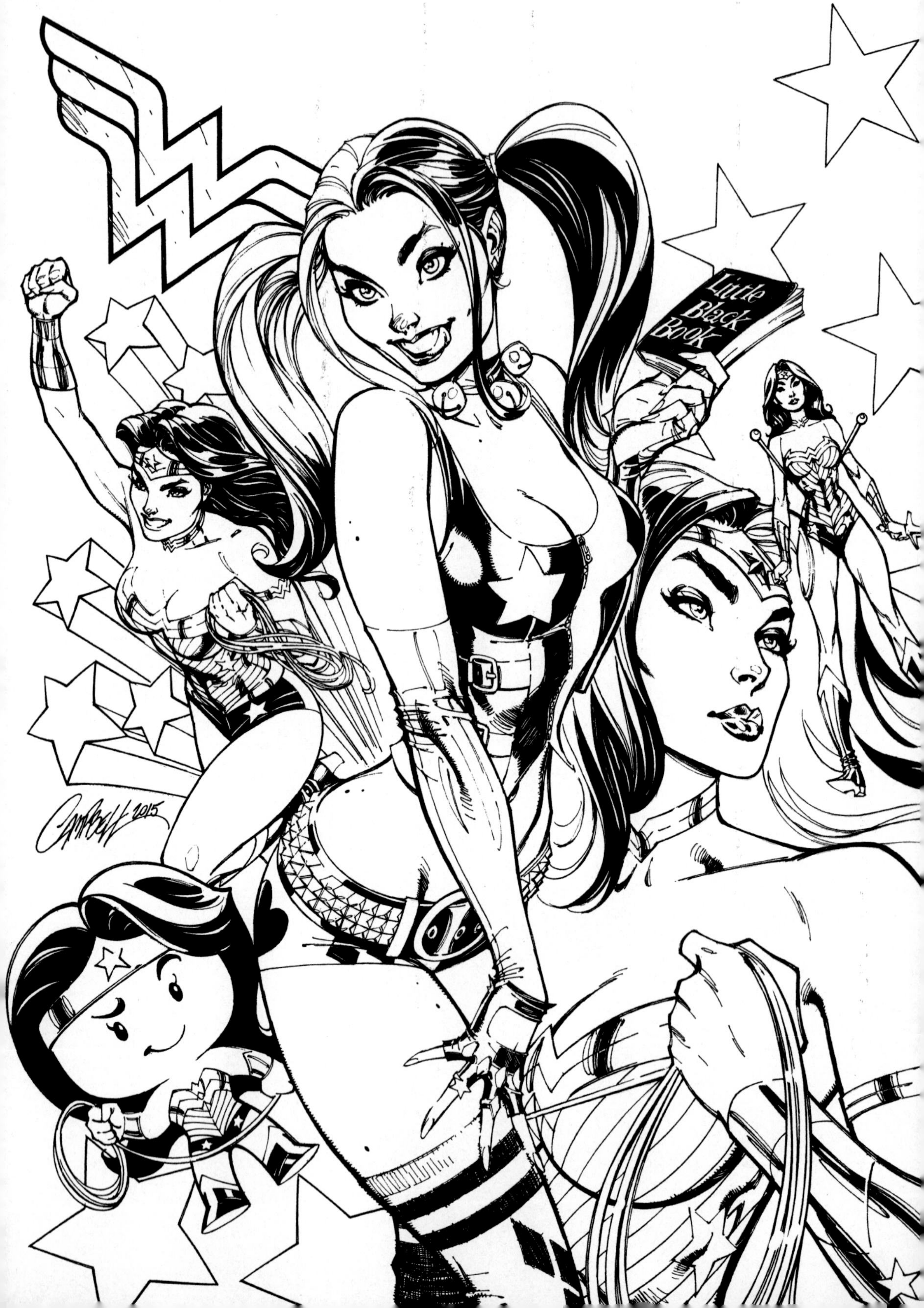
Little Black Book

HARLEY'S LITTLE BLACK BOOK #1
pencil variant by J. Scott Campbell

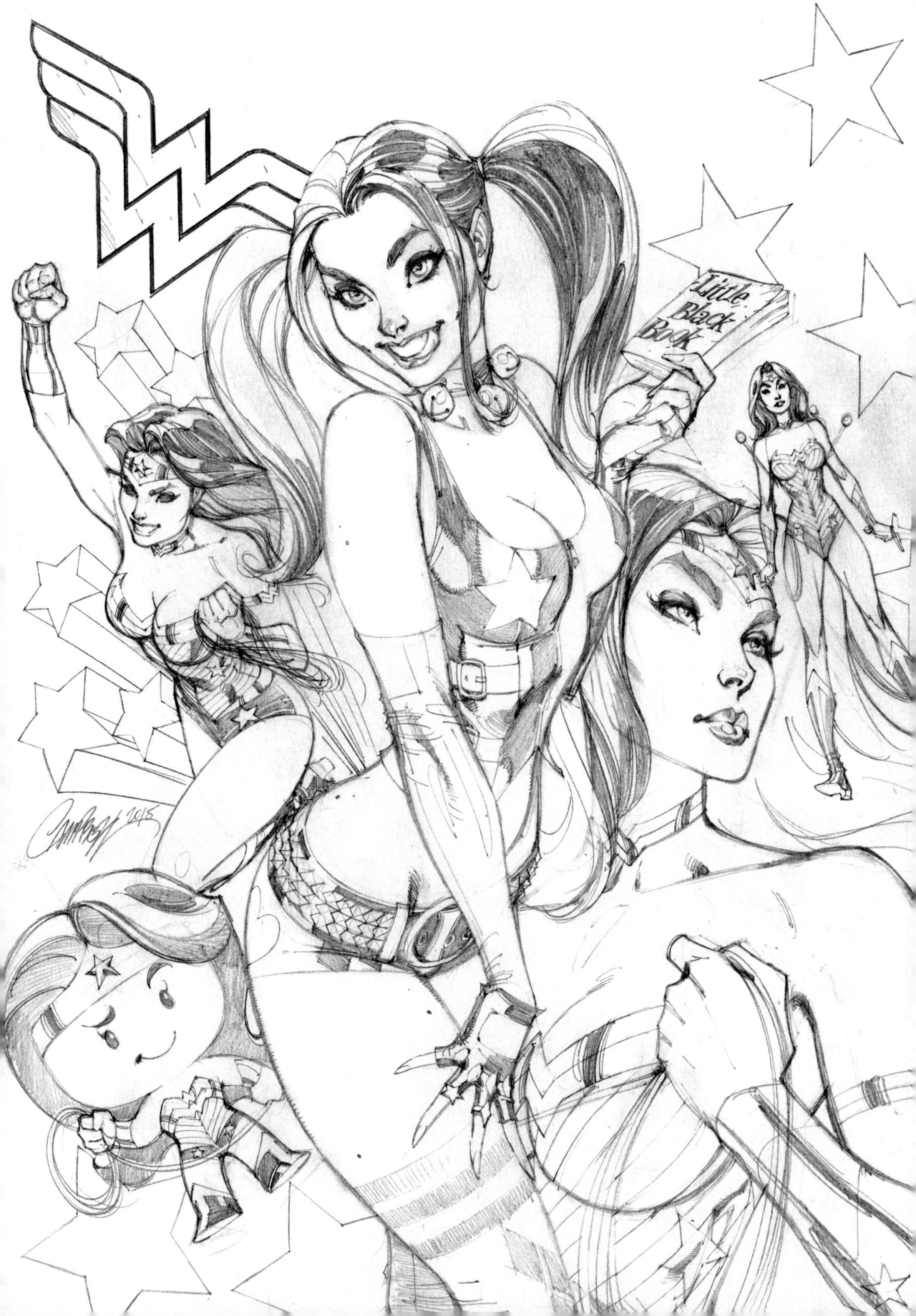
Little
Black
Book
Campbell 2015

HARLEY'S LITTLE BLACK BOOK #2
variant by John Timms

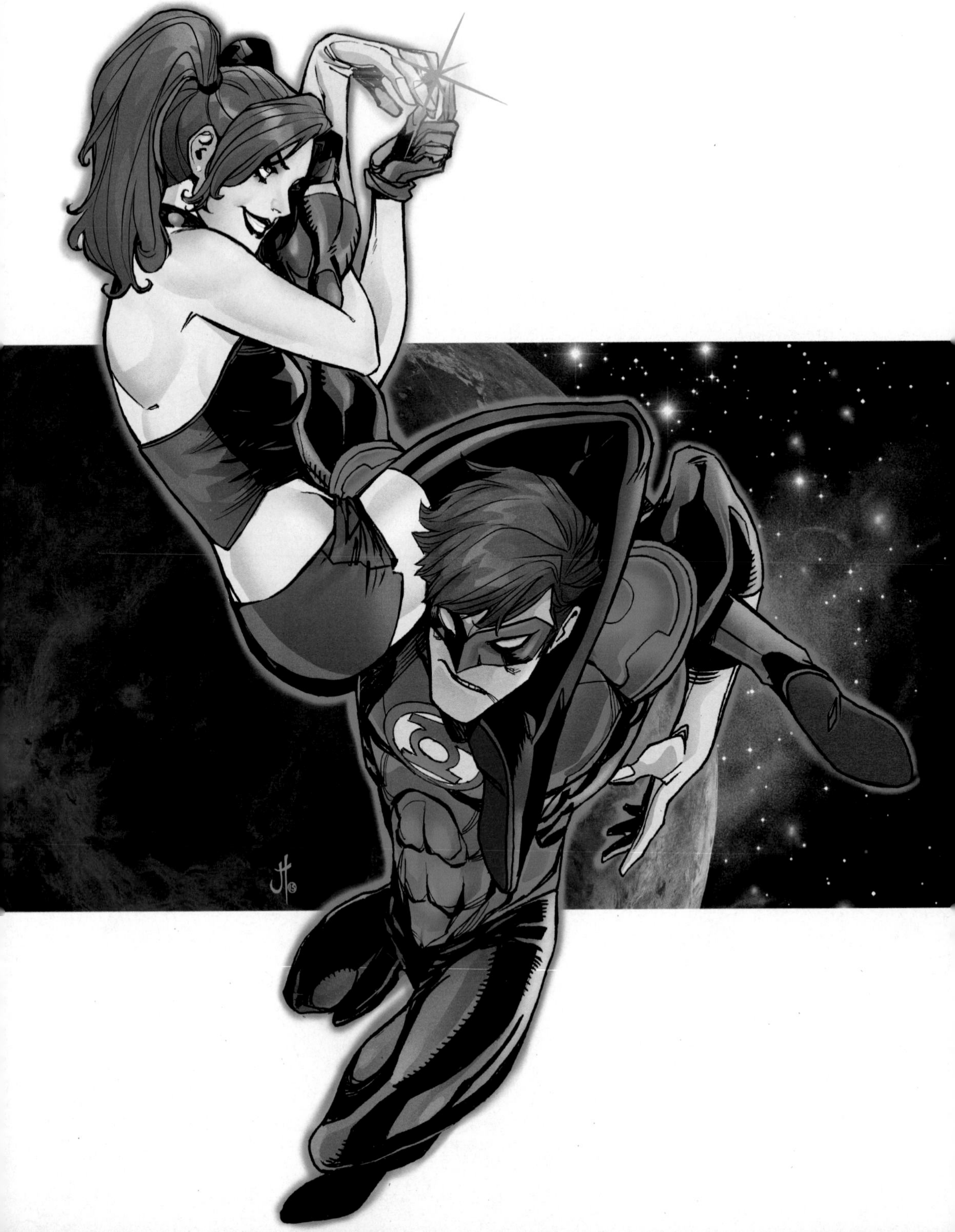

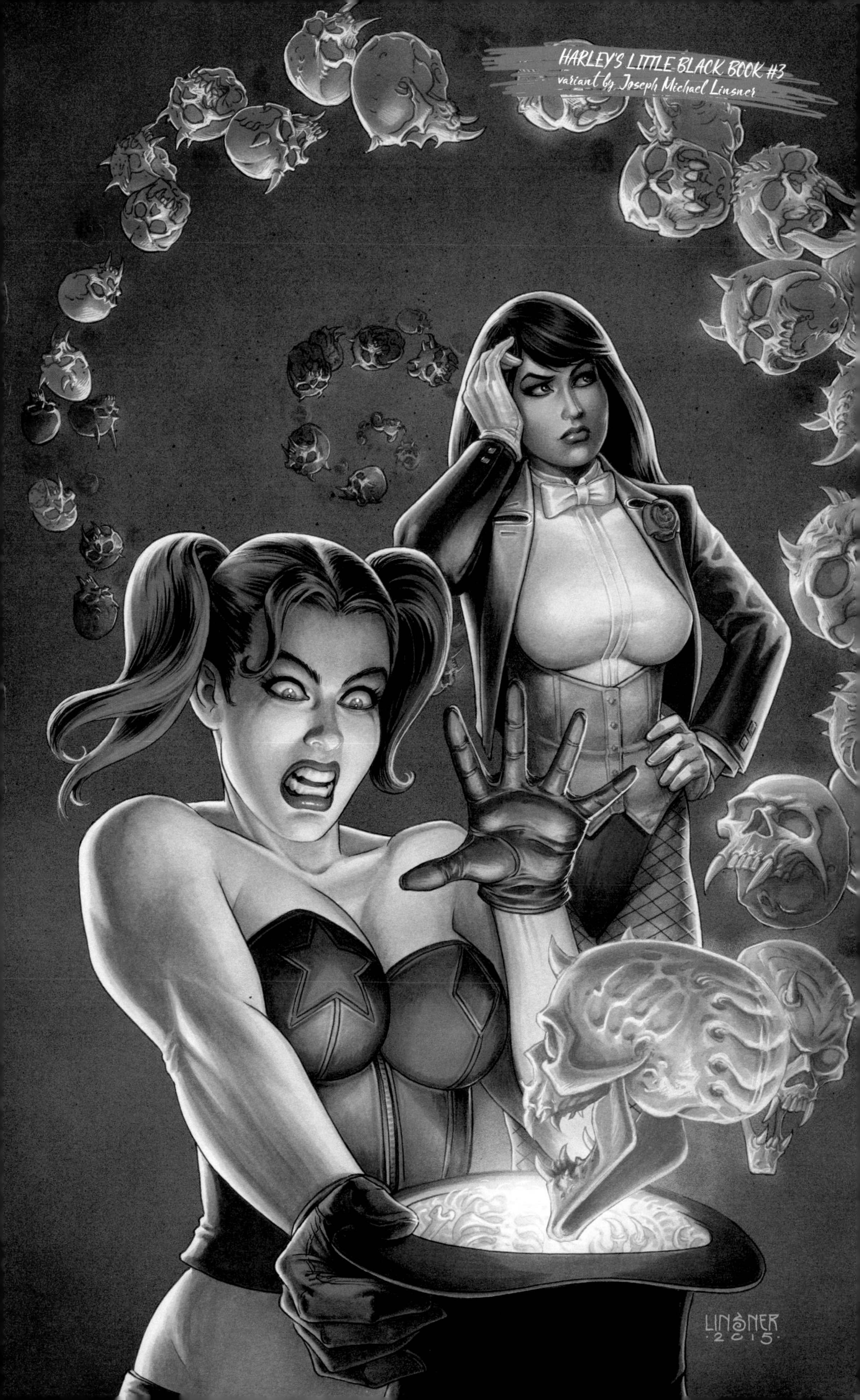
LINSNER
2015

HARLEY'S LITTLE BLACK BOOK #3
variant by Joseph Michael Linsner

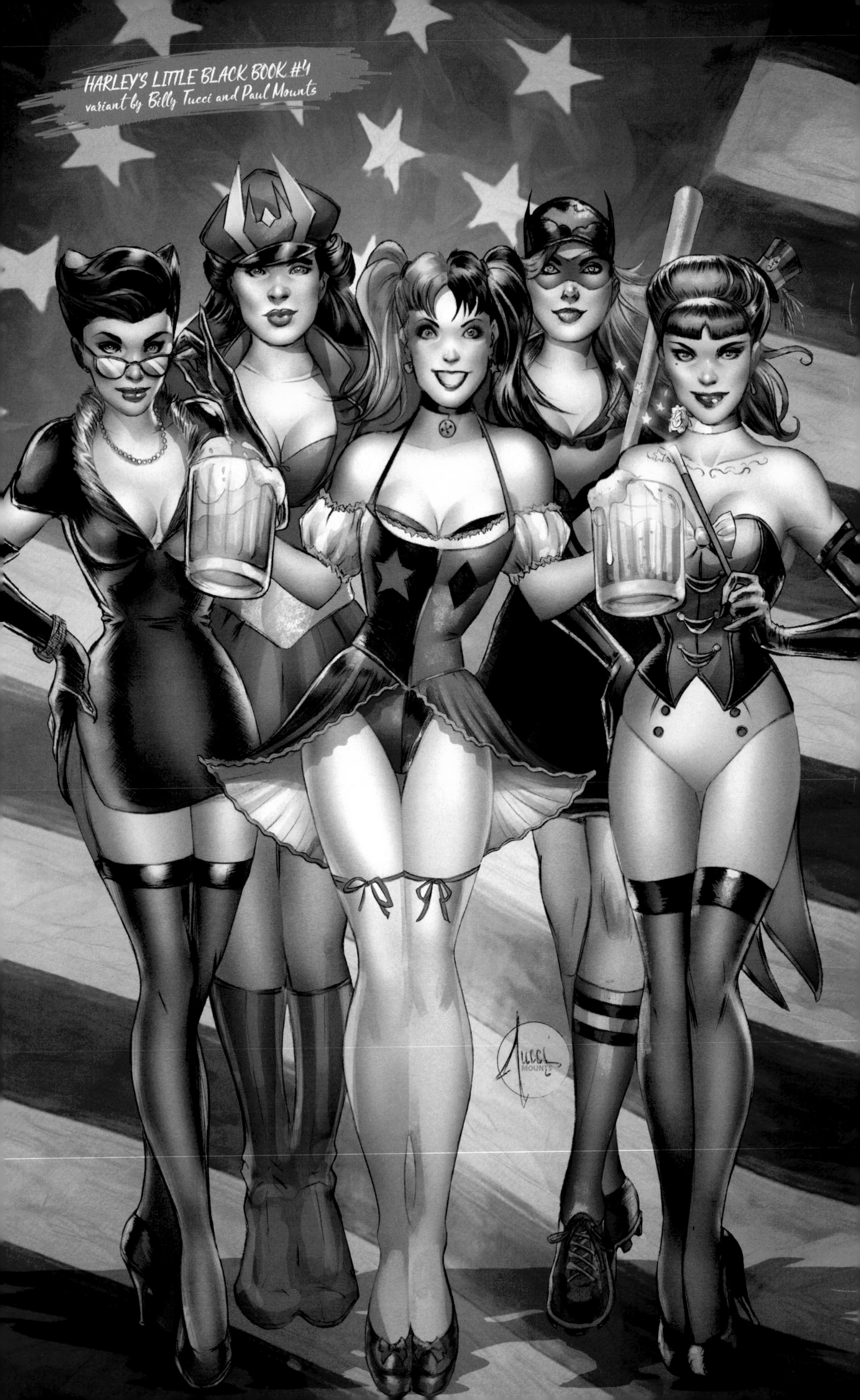

HARLEY'S LITTLE BLACK BOOK #4
variant by Billy Tucci and Paul Mounts

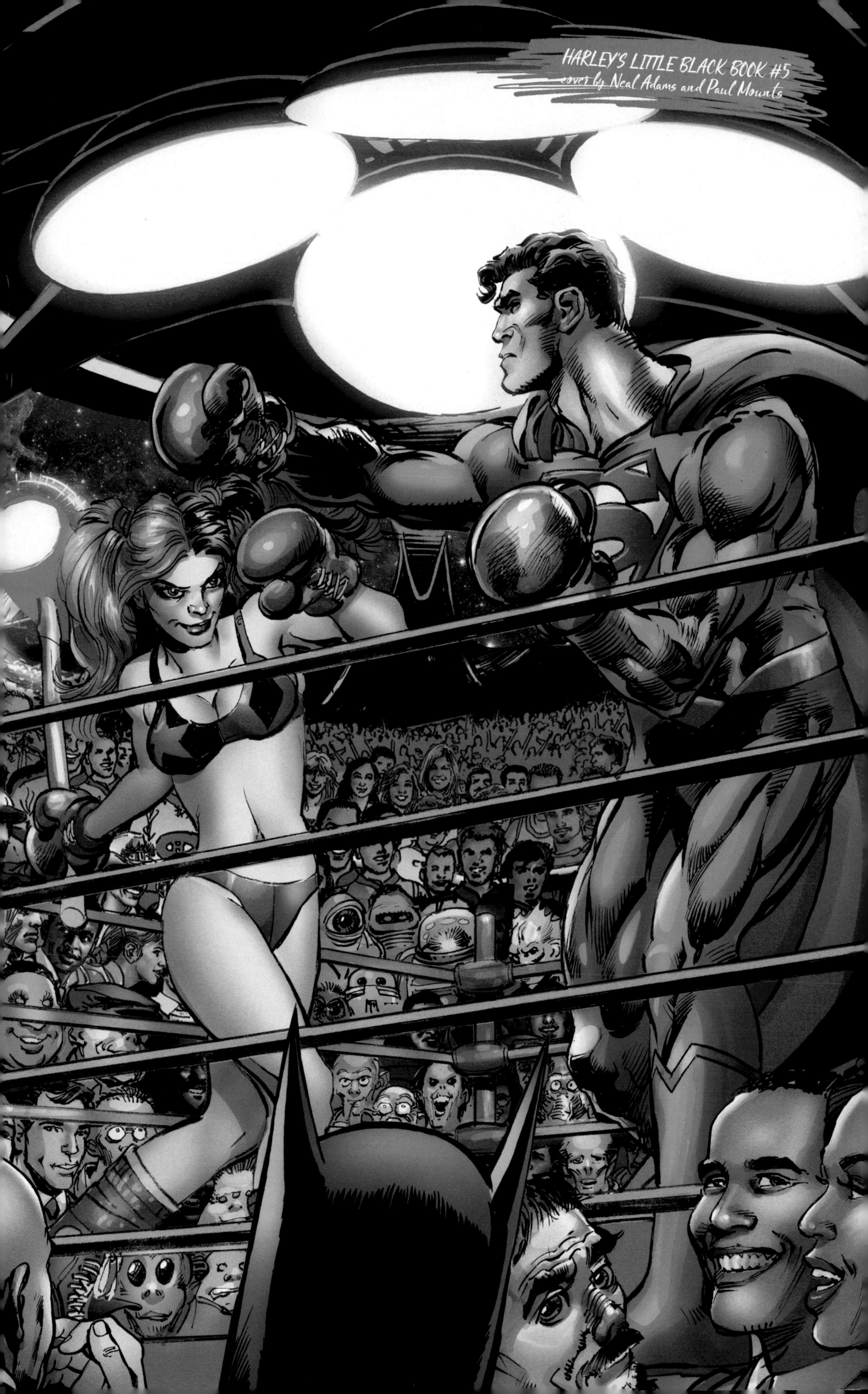
HARLEY'S LITTLE BLACK BOOK #5
cover by Neal Adams and Paul Mounts

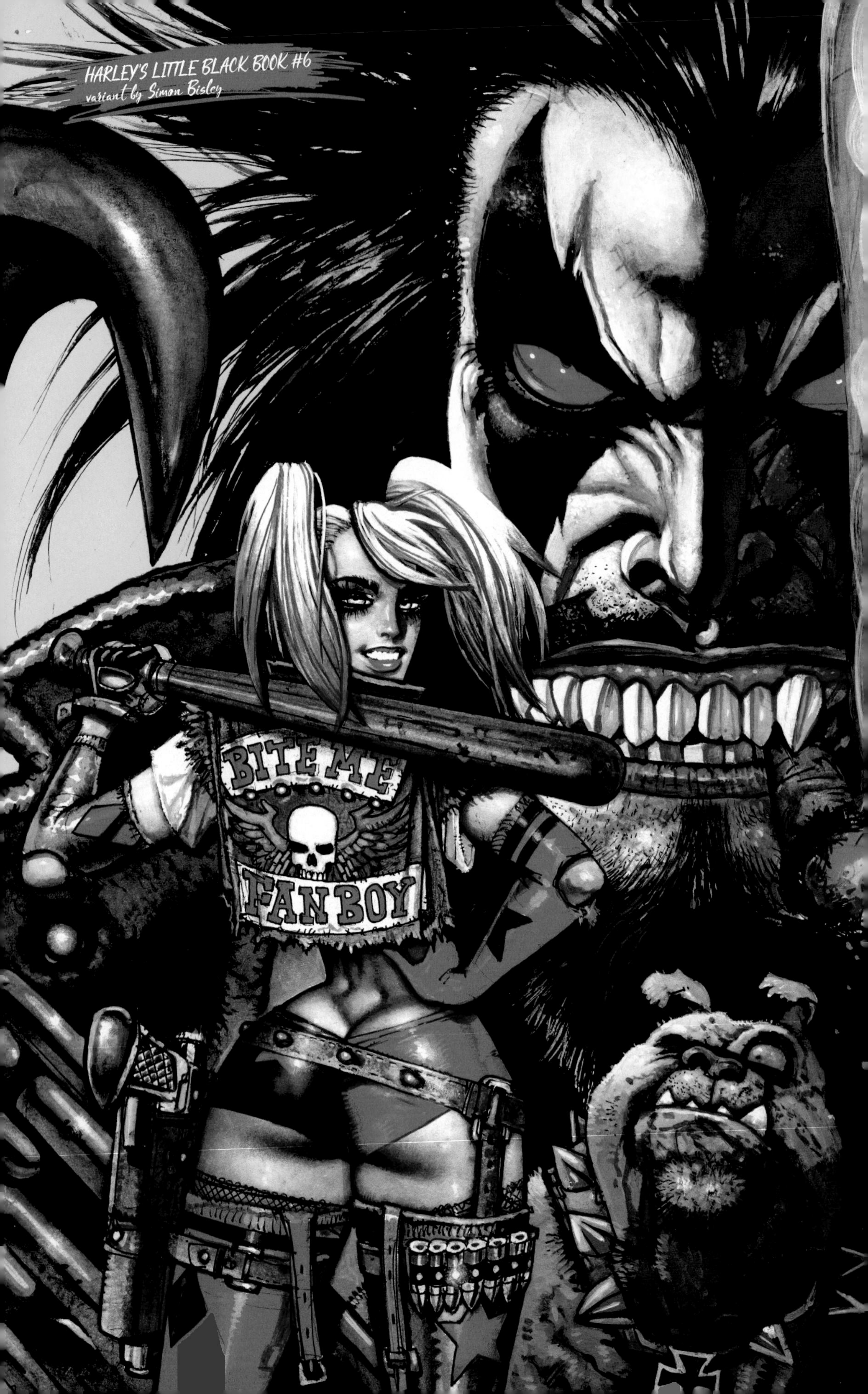
BITE ME
FANBOY
HARLEY'S LITTLE BLACK BOOK #6
variant by Simon Bisley

Amanda Conner's cover line art for

HARLEY'S LITTLE BLACK BOOK #1-6

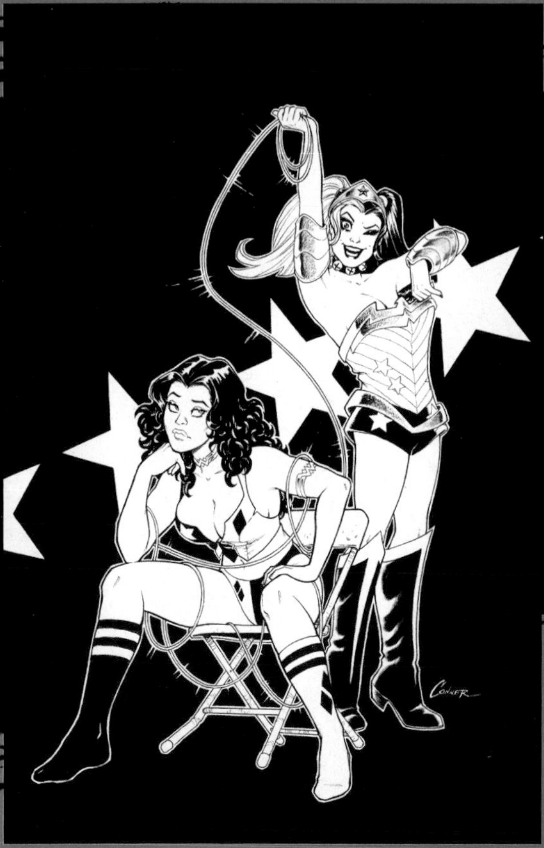
CONNER

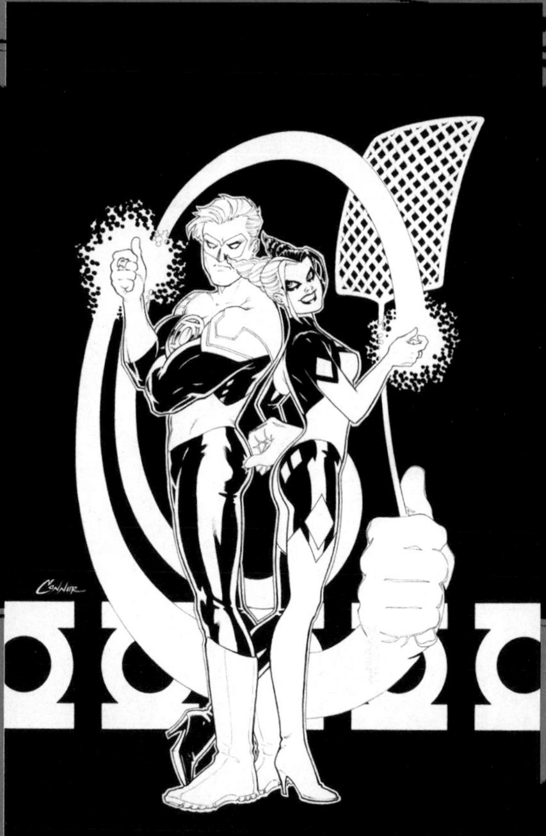
CONNER

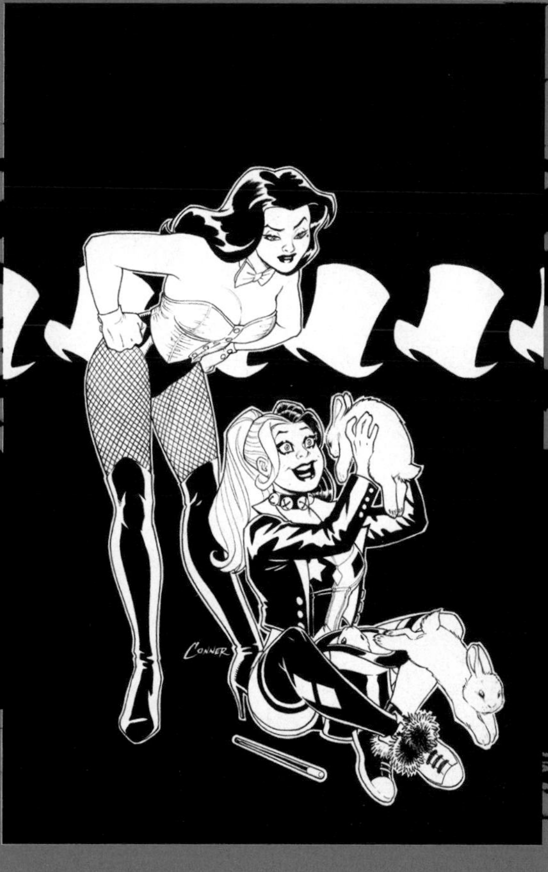
CONNER

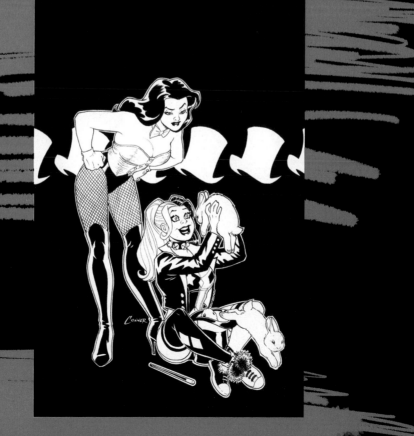

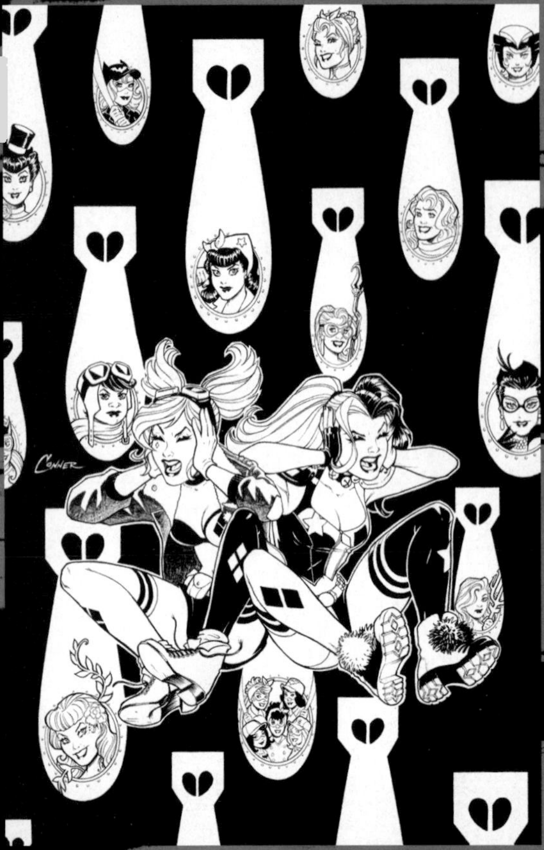
CONNER

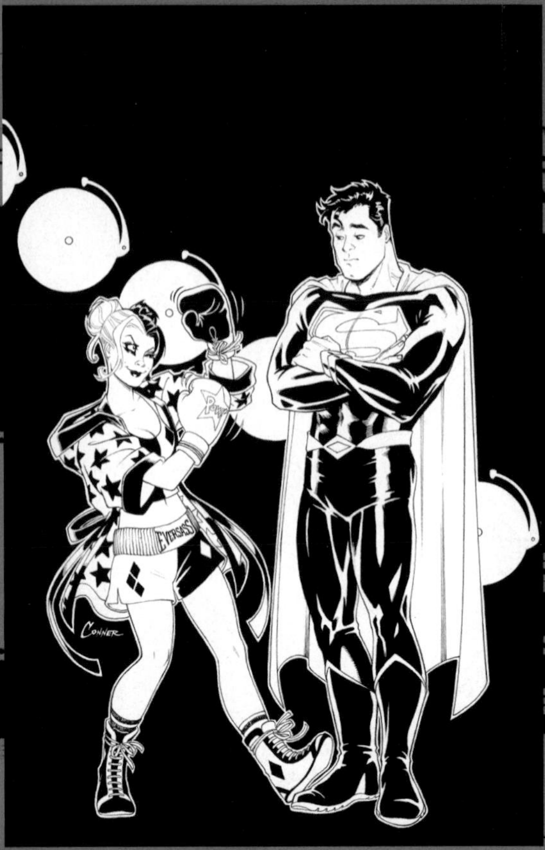
CONNER

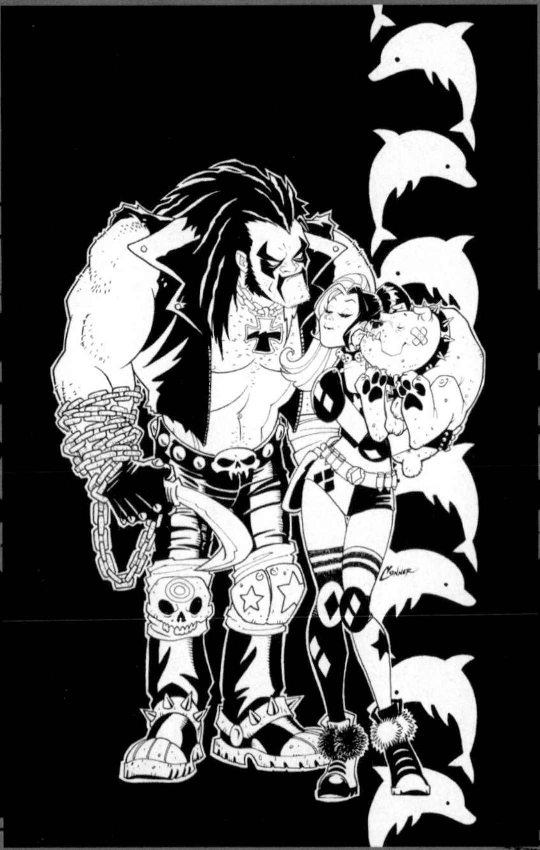
CONNER

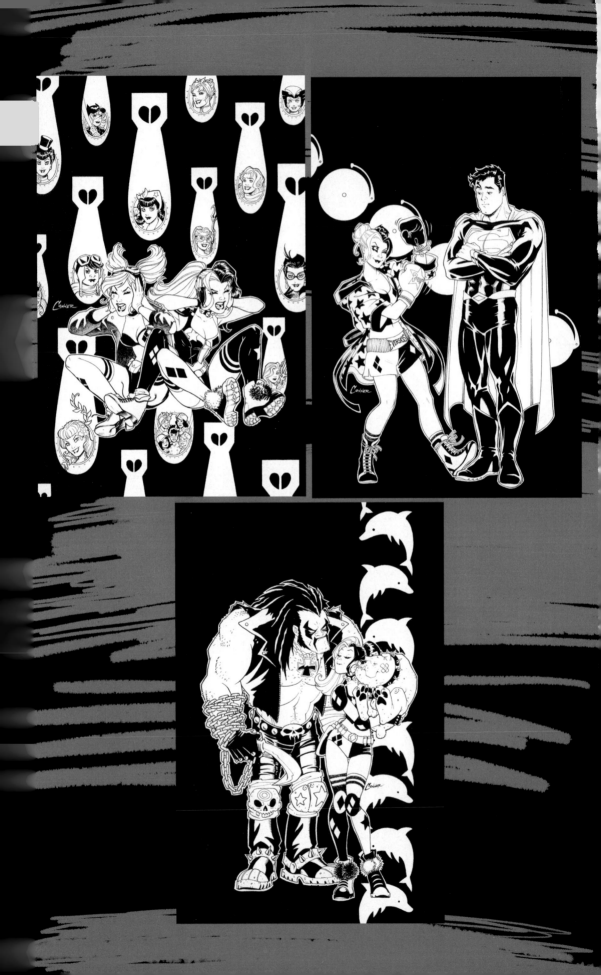